An Introduction to Marital and Family Therapy
Counseling Toward Healthier Family Systems Across the Lifespan

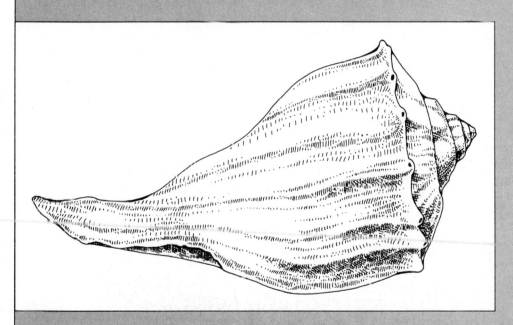

Michele Burhard Thomas
Tennessee State University

MERRILL, an imprint of
MACMILLAN PUBLISHING COMPANY
New York
MAXWELL MACMILLAN CANADA
Toronto
MAXWELL MACMILLAN INTERNATIONAL
New York • Oxford • Singapore • Sydney

Cover art: Leslie L. Beaber
Editor: Linda A. Sullivan
Production Editor: Regina Sanford
Art Coordinator: Lorraine Woost
Text Designer: Connie Young
Cover Designer: Russ Maselli
Production Buyer: Pamela D. Bennett
Electronic Publishing Coordinator: Tonia Kinniard

This book was set in Garamond by The Clarinda Company and was printed and bound by R. R. Donnelley & Sons Company. The cover was printed by Lehigh Press, Inc.

Macmillan Publishing Company
866 Third Avenue
New York, NY 10022

Macmillan Publishing Company is part of the
Maxwell Communication Group of Companies.

Maxwell Macmillan Canada, Inc.
1200 Eglington Avenue East, Suite 200
Don Mills, Ontario M3C 3N1

Library of Congress Cataloging-in-Publication Data

    Thomas, Michele Burhard.
    An introduction to marital and family therapy: counseling toward healthier family systems across the lifespan/Michele Burhard Thomas.
        p. cm.
    Includes bibliographical references and index.
    ISBN 0-675-21128-X
    1. Marital psychotherapy. 2. Family psychotherapy. I. Title.
    [DNLM: 1. Family Health. 2. Family Therapy. 3. Marital Therapy.
WM 55 T459i]
RC488.5.T495   1992
616.89′156 — dc20
DNLM/DLC   91-11091
for Library of Congress   CIP

Printing: 1 2 3 4 5 6 7 8 9   Year: 2 3 4 5

Quotation credits: p. 170, Extract taken from *TA TE CHING* by Lao-tzu, translated by Chu Ta-kao, reproduced by kind permission of Unwin Hyman Ltd. Copyright © 1937 by Unwin Hyman Ltd.; p. 315, From "Among School Children" in *The Tower* by W. B. Yeats, p. 60. Reprinted with permission of Macmillan Publishing. Copyright © 1928 by Macmillan Publishing.

To all of the McGonagle clan in the big white
house on Ninth Street with their sounds of laughter and singing

To my grandmother, Gertrude Schorr McGonagle,
who lived to be 101 and taught me what family can mean

To my mother, Mary McGonagle Burhard,
who counseled her many friends and loved to cook
and to dance—who valued the role of motherhood so
highly that she risked her life to bring me and Therese into the
world and struggled with chronic illness daily to be there to guide us

The strutting of the sea birds represents the dance of
interactions in human relationships, especially the couple dyad.

To my father, Carl Leo Burhard, who loves to
collect books and to sing in the choir—whose challenges at the
dinner table cultivated my intellectual skills and who supported my education
where and when it was not popular to encourage women to pursue higher education

Most of all, to Jack Anthony Thomas, Ed.D., with love
on our silver anniversary in gratitude, trust, and deep respect for
supporting, sharing, and challenging my dreams for self, family, and career.

And to the future of our daughters, Maria Theresia, Jacqueline Ann, and Renate Margareta

Foreword

How we wish we had had this book 50 years ago when we began our graduate work in the helping field! How glad we are to have it today!

Michele Thomas has given us a book that we believe will be invaluable for both students and veteran therapists. We are intrigued by her use of the Lightning Whelk as a symbol around which students can organize their understanding of the multidimensional dynamic family system as well as the complex field of family therapy. This symbol also gives professional clinicians and researchers a manageable framework for their efforts to help families move toward health and wholeness.

In this book Michele Thomas demonstrates her competence as a person and as a professional. She openly shares herself with the reader by beginning with a statement of her philosophy, her faith, and her belief in persons and families. The book is evidence of her thoroughness as a teacher, as a researcher, and as a clinician. More importantly, we experience her exemplifying in her personal life what she professes for her students, clients, and other therapists.

She emphasizes the value of developing marriage and family therapy based on strengths, wellness, and growth. This emphasis encourages us to see the possibilities and rewarding experiences of *becoming* across the life span. At the same time this wholeness approach helps us to see persons as interacting members of families and to see families in the total context of their lives.

This introduction to the theory and practice of marriage and family therapy goes beyond an overview of the various approaches to family systems work. Because of the author's emphasis on values and openness to the future we are challenged to move ahead with further growth and development in the family field.

The growth model stimulates marriage and family therapists to cooperate with other professionals in the helping field in developing more effective methods in prevention and maintenance of healthy marriages. In the area of prevention this includes our searching for better ways of helping couples prepare for marriage. As marriage and family therapists we have the opportunity to join with educators and other professionals in finding more effective methods of maintaining healthy marriages. We have unique contributions to make to the marriage and family enrichment movement. For example, couples may need our help in deciding whether they can benefit best from therapy or enrichment at a particular time in their growth. Also we have found that in some of the best marriage enrichment leader couples one (or both) is a therapist.

This holistic growth model of therapy reminds us that a healthy family system is one which functions well within itself and at the same time has a positive effect on society. This model challenges marriage and family therapists to work with other professionals in helping families be aware of their responsibilities and opportunities to contribute to the general welfare.

We hope each reader will be as excited as we are about this exceptional text. As you work through these pages we hope you will enjoy the journey and at the same time be stimulated to go far beyond this introduction to a fascinating field.

Antoinette and Leon Smith

Preface

This is a book conceived at mid life! One of the key tasks of development in the middle years is the reconciliation of opposites. Traits, events, ideologies, feelings, even people that at earlier stages of life seemed unrelated and incapable of co-existing together have become friends, not only tolerating each other but learning from the contrasting lights and shadows.

Focus

Thus, it is with health and illness. Through exposure to illness, perspectives toward health change as individuals take responsibility for holistic regimens of diet, exercise, plans for self-improvement, and consultation with medical experts to maintain and improve their health. The context of health and of the marital and family therapist as a health-care provider are overarching themes which spiral throughout the book as opposing forces of health/illness, prevention/intervention, differentiation/integration, centripetal/centrifugal, separation/belongingness, love/work, and life/death reconcile at higher levels of maturity and development.

Therefore, the focus of this text is the reconciliation of health and illness within marital and family therapy approaches. Health is the map or prototype toward which each family moves, with techniques of marital and family therapy designed to aid families in their journey from illness toward greater health. Throughout the text, models of healthy family functioning are highlighted with a special shell symbol. Specific techniques from each theoretical framework are included to enable the practitioner of marital and family therapy to assist the family to move toward this prototype of health.

Systems theory is stressed throughout the book. The text moves from the *macro-system* or *context* in which marital and family therapy is practiced (the health-care system in the United States and the historical framework from which marital and family therapy grew) to an elaboration of *healthy family systems over time,* and then to the *subsystem* of the individual self. The *process* of marital and family therapy, according to different broad theoretical approaches to treatment, is emphasized, and then the specific details of *practice* as a health-care professional are discussed. Recognizing that all of these systems and sub-systems are impacting each other simultaneously in any given moment, the marital and family therapist facilitates progress or growth on the part of individual family members and the family as a whole.

There are a number of different definitions of the term "system" as it is used in marital and family therapy approaches. One definition is biological, emanating from the work of von Bertanlanffy, a biologist who emphasized the processes of anamorphosis and homeostasis. Another comes from Capra's work on physics which presents a co-evolutionary model of a system in which the therapist is not only an observer but is also part of the system, being changed by it as it is being changed by the therapist. Yet a third model emphasizes the culture, ethnic group, and gender socialization patterns which the therapist brings to the therapy and those that family members share. The context affects the system and its sub-systems within such a definition of system. This latter definition is broader and encompasses the other definitions of system. Therefore, it provides the systemic frame for this book within which the other definitions of systems are at points emphasized.

In particular, the cultural, ethnic, and gender contexts have been elaborated as they affect the world views of both the therapist and the family. Efforts were made to weave the research related to culture, ethnicity, and gender throughout the chapters of the book in an integrated manner.

Since marital and family therapists are being held liable for practicing as health-care professionals, two chapters have been devoted to the role of a professional, the importance of belonging to professional associations, assessment of suicidal and homicidal risk, duty to warn, the establishment of practice policies, and ethics. My experience serving as a member and chair of a state licensing board influenced me to emphasize the process of working through ethical dilemmas and preventing them by appropriate problem solving before beginning a practice.

The text is designed for introductory graduate courses in marital and family therapy in which the graduate student may take only one or two courses as electives or as required courses within a broader graduate program in counseling, psychology, social work, home economics/family living, nursing, pastoral counseling, marital or family therapy, or psychiatry. Having taught such a course in marital and family therapy for more than 10 years, material was selected carefully for the text to encompass everything a beginning graduate student needs to know in order to practice marital and family therapy in the future. The text can be used for a family therapy course, a marital therapy class, a course in family development, or for a class in theories of counseling. The entire text can be used or chapters can be selected to meet the needs of a particular instructor, curriculum, course, or group of students.

Organization

The book has been divided into three parts. Part One emphasizes healthy family systems over time. The theme of the reconciliation of health and illness is elaborated. The role of the marital and family therapist, historically and presently, as a health-care provider is emphasized. The research on healthy families is combined with a detailed explanation of family systems. The family life cycle and the development of individuals are represented symbolically by the lightning whelk. Over time the family grows and develops through a spiralling process as does the individual. The marital and family therapist should take care to recognize the interaction of family life cycle transitions with the transitions of individuals.

Part Two focuses on the process of marital and family therapy. An overview of ways of integrating theories of family therapy is presented so that graduate students can develop their own personal theories of marital and family therapy. Then each major theory of marital and family therapy is presented: the experiential/humanistic therapies, the psychoanalytically oriented approaches, the intergenerational theories, the behavioral and cognitive behavioral systems, the structural school, brief therapy, the strategic approach, and the systemic school from Milan.

Part Three stresses the practice of marital and family therapy in the health-care setting of private practice. The stages of treatment from the initial session to termination are discussed. Most importantly, what it means to be a professional, a member of the health-care team in the United States in the decade of the 1990s, is elaborated from the priority of client welfare to concerns over malpractice. The "nuts and bolts" of setting up a practice are detailed, including examples of practice policies, an intake protocol, a systems assessment checklist, and forms for family treatment plans.

Features

The outstanding features of this text include the following:

- *The marriage and family therapist as a health-care provider* is modeled for students.
- *Historical tables* document the contributions of key proponents of marital and family therapy and major present as well as future trends.
- *Family Health Wheel* is used to assist families to move toward health in spiritual, intellectual, behavioral, emotional, imaginal, sensual, sexual, physical, interpersonal, social, and financial/career domains.
- *Systems theory* is stressed throughout the book, together with a systems assessment checklist.
- *Recent major contributions to theories of family development and individual development* are included with implications for the practice of marital and family therapy.
- *Research on adult transitions* has been integrated, with applications for marital therapy.
- *Cases* from actual practice are used as examples and as exercises.

- *Comprehensive comparison tables* contrast 8 approaches to marital and family therapy on 12 variables including view of healthy functioning, history and key proponents, major theoretical concepts, major techniques, goals of treatment, role of the therapist, use of assessment, nature of initial session, stages of therapy, therapeutic outcomes, dysfunction, and contributions/limitations.
- *Therapeutic outcomes* of diverse models of marital and family therapy focus on what techniques have been found to work with which target populations and are included in each of the chapters on approaches to marital and family therapy.
- *Practical techniques* for working with couples and families are emphasized.
- *Substance-abuse research and examples* are woven throughout the text.
- *Class-tested experiential exercises* at the end of each chapter start at a basic level and increase in challenge as the course unfolds.
- *A cross-cultural perspective* is achieved through integration of examples and research on the effects of culture, ethnicity, and gender upon family systems.
- *Interdisciplinary approach* is used with research studies from journals in medicine, psychiatry, psychology, counseling, social work, pastoral counseling, psychiatric nursing, home economics, family living, and marriage and family therapy.
- *Helpful summaries, diagrams, tables, pictures and cartoons* present material in a user-friendly format to motivate students and to facilitate learning.
- *The instructor's manual* contains test items, sample tests, and tips for teaching each chapter.

Acknowledgments

Special gratitude is extended to Maria Thomas, my oldest daughter, without whose editorial assistance, this manuscript would not have been completed. I also want to thank Renate Thomas, my youngest daughter, for many of the photographs in the book. Her creative and artistic talents are greatly appreciated. I am thankful to my husband, Jack Thomas, who also furnished a number of photographs from his private collection. Thanks are extended to Lisa Davies for her library and technical assistance early in the book's development. Additional important editorial assistance was furnished by Katie Meehan who helped to condense the manuscript. I appreciate the thorough and professional work of Effie Aman Cherry in compiling the indexes and Anne Lawrence for her computer work on both the indexes and the instructor's manual.

I wish to thank the staff of the Libraries/Media Center at Tennessee State University including Georgianna Cumberbatch-Lavender, Murle Kenerson, and Fletcher Moon for their help and support throughout the study. The assistance of the librarians at the Education Library and the Medical Center Library of Vanderbilt University, the University of Nebraska-Lincoln, the Alcohol Studies Library of Rutgers University, and several of the libraries at Harvard University is gratefully acknowledged. I am also indebted to Father James McQuade of John XXIII Center at the University of Tennessee-Knoxville and the librarians at UT-Knoxville for their support in the final revisions of the manuscript.

Special thanks is extended to Linda Sullivan, the Senior Administrative Editor at Macmillan, who believed in my dream and was willing to take a chance on me. I value her expertise, intuition, and judgment implicitly. Without her support in birthing this text, it would not have come into being. David Faherty, Marketing Manager, gave helpful feedback in the process. As Production Editor, Regina Sanford, supervised the culmination of the project and added to the enjoyment of working with the professional team at Macmillan.

In particular, I would like to acknowledge the assistance of reviewers from colleges and universities across the country who provided valuable feedback that was used to refine the manuscript and help me to reach my goal of producing the finest text possible. Thank you to Reece Chaney, Indiana State University; Sam Gladding, Wake Forest University; Larry Golden, University of Texas, San Antonio; Richard Langford, California State University, Humboldt; Lawrence Winkler, George Washington University; Robert Stahman, Brigham Young University; and Thomas Russo, University of Wisconsin-River Falls.

The dream of writing a book on marital and family therapy began more than 10 years ago. I wish to acknowledge the mentorship of Tom Elmore of Wake Forest University, past president of the Association for Counselor Education and Supervision, and the members of the ACES Marriage and Family Counseling Interest Network whom he appointed (Sam Gladding, Barbara Okun, Alan Hovestadt, Jim Hansen, Margaret Burgraff, Fred Piercy, Charlie Huber, Barbara Cooney and Stan Chernowsky) for nurturing that dream through the years. I owe a special debt of gratitude to Elizabeth Burgess of Denver, a special author/mentor, whose encouragement and knowledge of publishing inspired me to persevere. To Leon and Antoinette Smith, pioneers in the field and authors of *Preparing for Christian Marriage,* who have served as role models of what a marital relationship can be, thank you for your vote of confidence in writing the foreword and for your support. Thank you to Pat Nourse and Betty Salzman for being family polestars for us. The motivation for this text emanated from the energy and intellectual stimulation found in the national Building Family Strengths Network of the Center for Family Strengths of the University of Nebraska, Lincoln — my appreciation to the staff and to the professionals that I have had the pleasure to train from 10 states in the Building Strengths Model and from whom I have learned much. The support of the Prudential Insurance Company of America that funded a fellowship for the Rutgers University Summer School of Alcohol Studies is especially acknowledged.

My special mentors, David McMillan, Randy Mack, Melbourne Williams, Vernon Sharp, Esco McBay, Jim Nash, William McConnville, and Katherine Rea challenged me to grow and develop. The inspiration and personal encouragement of Senator Avon Williams, Jr., will long be cherished. To fellow practitioners— Elliott Ward, Judith Weiss, Richard Call, John Griffin, Tom Pettigrew, Dwight Steiner, and Peggy Bancroft—I appreciate the opportunities you have given me to evolve as a professional. I am grateful to my colleagues during my term on the state licensing board, whose interaction I value, especially Eric Theiner and Jim Paavola. To the professional colleagues who mean so much to me, I say a special thank you: Anne Durrant, Irene Ratner, Linda Rudolph, Jeannette Heritage, Maryruth Nivens, Larry DeRidder, Bob Davis, Don C. Locke, Burl Gilliland, Sherwell Tolleson, Corrine Bell, Bill Floyd, Janet Birch, Keith Carlson, Beryl West, Bernard Crowell, Ruby Martin, Paul Caraher, Kitty Myatt, Helen Moore, Jean Cecil, Vernon Sheeley, Ted Remley, Sunny Hansen, Larry Brammer, Bob Nejedlo, Nancy Scott, Mary Maples, George Gazda, Tom Hosie, Marianne Mitchell, Donald Freedheim, Hans Strupp, Mary Frances Hall, Frank Jones, Murphy Thomas, Jeannie Williams, Esco McBay, Jeff Binder, Jill Haydel, Bernie Lyons, Bob Niemi, Stephen Puckett, Jim Buechele, Larry Blanz, Michelle Coop, Dan Murphy, Steve McCallum, Jerry Morton, Ed Smith, Harvey Kaufman, Michael Buckner, Phil Barkley, Larry Lyda and names too numerous to mention in the Association for Counselor Education and Supervision and the Southern and Tennessee Associations for Counselor Education and Supervision; Divisions 17, 29, 35, 42 and 43 of the American Psychological Association; the Tennessee and Nashville Area Psychological Associations; the Tennessee Association of School Psychologists; the American and Tennessee Associations for Marriage and Family Therapy; the American and Tennessee Associations for Counseling and Development; the National Career Development Association; the American Association of State Psychology Boards; the International Association of Marriage and Family Counselors; and, the International Round Table for the Advancement of Counselling.

My colleagues in the Department of Psychology at Tennessee State University listened to my woes, tolerated my time constraints, and supported me throughout the process: Andrew Adler, Helen Barrett, James Chatman, Roosevelt Faulkner, Sue Fuller, Dorothy Granberry, Bruce Hancock, Alberta Herron, Roger Jones, John Joyner, Gloria Lewis, David Martin, Barbara Murrell, Harold Phelps, Jim Stewart, David Terrell, and Jim Threalkill. In particular, Pearl Gore Dansby has expected excellence in research from all of us throughout the years—never less than our best efforts. Tennessee State University has been an exciting and intellectually stimulating place to work.

I especially appreciate my students at Tennessee State University who have co-evolved with me over the past 17 years. Special gratitude is expressed to the students in PSY 678 Class of Fall, 1989, with whom I first piloted the text and who gave very helpful feedback and suggestions. In particular, David Weatherford, LuAnnette Butler, and Linda Scariot spent many hours giving me their written comments about what they did and did not like about the text.

In closing, writing this book has been a challenge and an adventure! To see a dream of 10 years become a reality has special meaning for me. Your feedback and comments on this text would be greatly appreciated and can be sent to me at P. O. Box 644, Tennessee State University, 3500 John Merritt Boulevard, Nashville, TN 37209-1561 (Phone 615-269-4990). My wish for you is that whatever your dreams are, they, too, will be achieved. May you be able to create and love your own family as well as help other families to create themselves!

The ocean is an analogy for the ebb and flow of human and family life.

Prologue
Toward Health

What is it about the ocean that is healing? Perhaps it has to do with letting go. Dads in their forties are out riding the waves on rubber floats, enjoying themselves openly in front of the disbelieving eyes of their 10-year-olds. Grandmas, with delight on their faces, are walking their grandbabies through the gentle waves that wash against the shore. Age seems to make no difference. We are all children at heart, and the ocean allows us all to play, bringing us together despite our hard-won differences.

Life is a journey. Its direction is more important than its destination. Whether you try surfing at 30 or 80, the fact that you reached out to experience it is the key. I'm always leery when I think "I have arrived," for then the creative process in me erupts to jolt me to the realization that the journey is never-ending and the essence of being human.

Which wave to ride? Which to pass up? The ocean mirrors the decisions of life. One hefty wave spills me mercilessly to the shore shattering my illusion of its glory, while another less infamous, carries me, gently planting me on the welcome beach, giving me much more than I had expected.

Expectations are the problem—those thoughts and predictions that the right brain churns out as though from an actuarial table. How many experiences are ruined because they do not meet our preconceived notions of what they "should" be. Lord, take away my "pile of shoulds" and replace it with an increased capacity to laugh at myself and my shortcomings!

There is something about the ocean that heals. Even the sound of the waves roaring into the shore relaxes me. It's like life—always struggling against some obstacle only to win and then begin again with a new goal.

There are two sea birds walking side by side, squawking to the heavens, not at each other, as though to protest their plight, joined in closeness by squawking beside each other. Then begins their dance, first one leading in a strut with the other waddling behind; then they reverse with the follower becoming the leader to boast and strut in another direction. "Ah! Ah! To experience pain! To die! Why? What is the meaning of it all?" Is this what the sea birds are saying?

Could it be that by feeling the pain, the joy is felt more fully? The sky darkens as the storm clouds roll in and the ocean turns gloomy and gray, making the joy of the sun on the morning tide more vibrant.

Can I thank my Creator for this day—its pain, its joy, its routine, quiet calm? My tears mingle with the sea water, healing my soul.

Life is a spiral. At each stage issues repeat themselves like challenging circles defying being broken. Again I deal with loss and separation, with committing myself to risk both pain and joy, each time confronting the paradox at a deeper level with fledgling skills newly acquired at this particular life stage. I can choose. It is my lot as a human being to choose growth.

Contents

Chapter 9
Intergenerational Theorists   258

Chapter 10
Behavioral and Cognitive Approaches to Marital and Family Therapy   285

Chapter 11
The Structural School   315

PART ONE
THE MAP OF MARITAL
AND FAMILY THERAPY
Healthy Family Systems Over Time

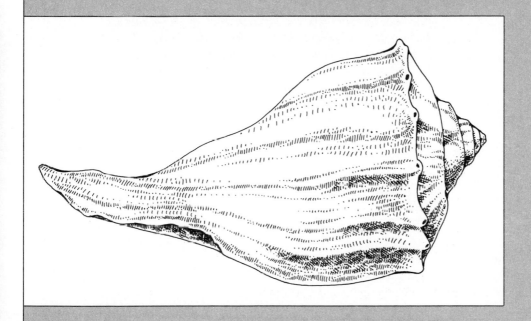

Chapter 1
Setting the Context
Toward Health

The ocean roars. The life force in each of us bellows for expression. "Spunky" people get well. They take charge of their own healing process and heal themselves. In family therapy, don't be afraid of the anger which often surfaces. Instead, reframe it as the spirit of growth and change making itself known.

Michele Thomas, Cherry Grove Beach, South Carolina

INTRODUCTION

Marital and family therapy is a challenging and meaningful endeavor—its purpose is to make a significant difference in people's lives and to help them move toward health and healthier family systems. It demands the best that professionals can give and is rarely mundane or routine. Surprises and puzzling events often occur in work with families.

It is an exciting time in the history of marital and family therapy because it is now being accepted as the key approach to effecting change in families. Just as a family may have a family lawyer, a family physician, and an accountant to help with income taxes, a typical family in America may have a marital and family therapist that they consult on a regular basis or at crisis points in their relationships.

Marital and family therapy is the treatment of choice for the acute care of problems such as marital conflict, the conduct disorders of children, anorexia nervosa, and other illnesses. In addition, marital and family therapy is often part of a multimethod treatment plan to increase the family support and compliance with treatment regimens of patients with such chronic illnesses as cardiovascular disease and cancer. As the health-care system shifts toward an emphasis on bio-behavioral mechanisms, marital and family therapy will increase in popularity.

A couple exercises together at the Baptist Health & Fitness Center in Nashville, Tennessee—working toward a healthier lifestyle. (Photo courtesy of Baptist Health & Fitness Center)

Also, the current generation is interested in self-growth and wants to participate in preventive programs and support groups to enhance their relationships. Marital enrichment and family support groups are being organized across the country, often sponsored by churches, synagogues, and other religious groups. Marital and family therapists were and will continue to be leaders in such preventive efforts.

Marital and family therapists are involved in both treatment and prevention—the reconciliation of health and dysfunction. The literature presented in this chapter clearly demonstrates that marital and family therapy does make a significant difference. Research studies have documented positive therapeutic outcomes of marital and family treatment for marital distress, divorce adjustment, conduct disorders, anorexia nervosa and bulimia, drug addiction, depression, schizophrenia, and many other dysfunctions. Now that studies have been amassed over more than 30 years that provide evidence of the effectiveness of marital and family therapy, additional research studies are needed to explore the mechanisms in the therapeutic process that bring about such positive changes (Gurman, Kniskern, & Pinsof, 1986). The question is no longer "Is marital and family therapy effective?" but rather "How is it effective?"

There is no doubt that marital and family therapy has evolved a long way from its early beginnings, but it still has far to go. In fact, the 1990s have been termed "The Age of Accountability" for marital and family therapy. More and better-designed research studies are needed to identify specific therapeutic techniques that are linked to effective outcomes with families experiencing various problems and illnesses. Such process research can shed light on what specific techniques to use with what particular family at a certain stage of family development. The future of family therapy points to increased research as a foundation for increased practice. As practitioners receive third-party payments from insurance companies and governmental agencies, they will be held accountable for results in the health-care arena.

After defining what is meant by marital and family therapy, this chapter focuses on the contexts in which marital and family therapists function—both the health-care delivery system and the historical framework. From a systems point of view, this book begins with the macrosystems and moves toward the consideration of the family system and then the individual subsystem—from largest to smallest. First, the macrosystem of health-care delivery is explored to orient the potential marital and family therapist to the setting of the main system in which the professional works. Knowledge of the trends in the broader health-care context builds confidence in the future of practice in marital and family therapy. Likewise, knowledge of how marital and family therapy developed and of the key factors that presently influence its practice is essential for effective professional functioning. But what is marital and family therapy? What types of professionals conduct such therapy?

WHAT IS MARITAL AND FAMILY THERAPY?

As a starting point, therapy is any treatment intended to remedy or alleviate a disorder. In marital and family therapy, the subject of that treatment is a married couple, a family, or even an individual. Contrary to what one might believe, marital and family therapy can encompass individual therapy from a family point of view. Treatment differs from more traditional individual-directed approaches, however, because it focuses on the individual as part of an interactional network, that is, part of a couple or a family.

Thus, marital and family therapy encompasses services provided to individuals, couples, and families and focuses on improvement or enhancement of interpersonal relationships. Such therapy functions from a broader point of view, in terms of individuals and how they interact or relate within a system, namely, as part of a marriage, a family, a community, and a society. This approach makes marital and family therapy much more effective for problems of marital or family conflict than other treatments, such as individual psychotherapy, and it is often more beneficial than individual treatment for problems that people present as being intrapsychic (Gurman & Kniskern, 1981; Gurman et al. 1986).

Given the broad definition of marital and family therapy, many different professionals from varying educational and experiential backgrounds must be involved in marital and family therapy—psychologists, psychiatrists, counselors, social workers, nurses, and pastors, to name a few. Educational preparation for professionals conducting such therapy ranges from the minimum of an associate degree to at most a

medical or doctoral degree. Regardless of the length or nature of professional training, the practitioner of marital and family therapy will be held accountable for the
provision of health-care services.

THE MARITAL AND FAMILY THERAPIST AS HEALTH-CARE PROVIDER

As part of the health-care delivery system, the marital and family therapist must understand models of health. Knowledge of the mechanisms leading to health and
illness is crucial to effective marital and family therapy, especially since mental health
practitioners are now held liable for failure to refer clients for treatment of their
medical problems (Woody, 1989).

What Is Health?

What distinguishes health from illness? Traditionally, health has often meant the absence of disease or defects. More recent definitions have included a condition of
mental, social, and physical well-being coupled with freedom from disease and ab-
normality (*Mosby's Medical and Nursing Dictionary,* 1986). Health is not viewed as a
static condition but rather as a constant state of change and adaptation to stress,
resulting in an equilibrium or homeostatic balance. In this text, health in human
beings is defined as dynamic progress toward optimal levels of functioning and well-
being, achieved through balance between external and internal environments. In
contrast, illness is the presence of symptoms to such a degree that they interrupt the
functioning of individuals in their social roles.

The predominant model of health and illness has been the biomedical model, with
roots going back to the 17th century and emphasized in the Flexner report of 1910,
which provided direction for medical education (Woody & Springer, 1985). In this
model, every disease can be reduced to a biological cause. The physician is the key
specialist with specific knowledge related to diverse diseases who can diagnose using
the most up-to-date technology available. Interventions are often pharmacological in
nature and designed to eradicate microbes or to change the biophysical chemistry
creating the problem. Health constitutes the absence of disease.

Such a model of health and illness has served our society well. No longer do
parents fear that their children will contract poliomyelitis and become crippled.
Whooping cough, diphtheria, and other devastating infections have become foreign to
the vocabularies of this generation.

Today the illnesses that remain as the national killers are, for the most part, degenerative diseases—heart disease, arteriosclerosis, stroke, cancer, diabetes mellitus,
cirrhosis of the liver, and emphysema (Anderson, 1988). Smoking cessation, weight
loss, a regular exercise program, and reduction in alcohol consumption are some
lifestyle factors that have been linked to the reduced incidence of degenerative illnesses. The higher the educational level of individuals, the less likely they are to
engage in high-risk behaviors.

In particular, the appearance and proliferation of acquired immune deficiency
syndrome (AIDS) have taxed the biomedical model of health and illness. If our society
waits until a vaccine is discovered for this complex virus, millions of people may die

unnecessarily. Therefore, a model of health and illness that encourages behavioral changes in lifestyle is needed. Ostrow (1987), in *Biobehavioral Control of AIDS*, clearly states:

> [I]n order to control a disease with the complex medical, psychological, social and political characteristics of AIDS, effective control programs would have to be informed from both a behavioral and a biological perspective. . . . By this I mean we have found ourselves nearly helpless in preventing the rapid growth of this disease not only because of the early lack of information about its biology but because of the difficulty in dealing with a disease which is sexually transmitted and whose controls must involve the modification of sexual and other basic human behaviors. (p. 2)

In the last decade of this century, American society finds itself in the midst of redefining health and illness as formerly delineated by the biomedical model; at the same time, this society is experiencing a revolution in the health-care delivery system that is unknown to earlier generations. John Freymann (1987) elaborates on the changes occurring while the paradigm shifts in medicine. As the population in the United States has become better educated, people have become more knowledgeable about risk factors and health care. They question health-care providers and take responsibility for health-oriented regimens to improve their health and increase their quality of life. To meet this consumer revolution and to increase the quality of life, broader definitions of health and illness that encompass and extend the biomedical model are being developed and debated (Table 1–1).

All recent models of health and illness expand the biomedical model to include certain psychological and social factors that influence health and illness. The link between the mind and the body is emphasized, as well as the effects of social support on health and illness. Human beings are seen as holistic organisms operating within social contexts. The culture and environment of the patient should be taken into consideration in treatment planning.

In addition, the most recent models of health and illness highlight the patient's phenomenological perceptions of the illness (or how the patient sees the sickness). By using the patient's explanation of the reasons for the illness and what the patient knows about that illness, the health-care provider can recommend and negotiate treatment with the patient, thereby increasing compliance with the health-care regimen (Kleinman, 1980).

How Are Health and Illness Related?
What is the relationship between health and pathology? What are the characteristics of healthy families and those families who are labeled dysfunctional? These are complex questions with no simple answers. The human condition is such that people are simultaneously well and sick. They love and hate those close to them, containing within themselves strong opposing emotions. For example, Henry weighs 235 pounds, stands 5 feet, 6 inches tall, has a job with which he is satisfied, and has a tendency toward high blood pressure. Henry has a wife and two children whom he physically abuses. Is Henry healthy or sick?

TABLE 1–1 Models of health and illness

Biomedical Model. Health is the absence of disease. Disease can be reduced to its biological cause, which can be diagnosed with technology and treated with pharmacological agents.

Holistic Health Model. Patients take responsibility for their health and growth toward higher levels of wellness in which there is a harmony among spirit, mind, and body. Illness can be an opportunity to grow. Alternative therapeutic modalities may be utilized such as rolfing, acupuncture, therapeutic massage, yoga, chiropractic, visualizing, and diet (Grossman, 1985).

Biopsychosocial Model. Three concentric and overlapping circles compose the biological, psychological, and social domains of health. The individual is a hierarchical system from atom to organ to person to family to universe (Engel, 1977). A biopsychosocial assessment is conducted, leading to a list of illnesses and a plan identifying the problems, sources of stress, and social support.

Ethnomedical-Cultural Model. Health care professionals emphasize the meaning of the illness in the culture by eliciting the health beliefs and expectations that individuals bring to treatment (Kleinman, 1980). In particular, the reasons that patients give for their illnesses (explanatory model—EM) and their illness prototype (IP) should be obtained by listening to the patient.

Illness Behavior Model. Six components comprise this model: (1) the measurement of physiological symptoms including arousal of the autonomic system; (2) affective integration; (3) the cognitions whereby symptoms are explained using external sources such as social support or internal sources such as memory; (4) the process by which meaning is attached to the symptoms to produce a sense of distress or well-being; (5) the coping responses, including self-care or seeking help from a physician or other source; and (6) the ethnocultural factors that influence human behavior and the entire model (McHugh & Vallis, 1986).

Ecological-Transactional Model. The transactions between the physician and the patient (routines, rituals, and dramas) are based on the characteristics of the individual (a holistic union of biological and psychocultural factors), the environment (microsystem, exosystem, and macrosystem), and the health-seeking process (defining the symptom, shifting roles, seeking consultation, the action of healing, and adapting to the illness) (Miller, 1988).

One professional might talk with Henry and decide that he is well because he lacks identifiable symptoms: there are no microbes invading his physical systems. Another professional might focus on Henry's areas of health. He has a job with which he is satisfied, a major accomplishment for a man in American society. Still another professional might label Henry ill because of his obesity and encourage diet and exercise to prevent high blood pressure. Yet another professional might label Henry mentally ill because he physically abuses his wife and children. Which professional is correct? They all are. Each one views Henry from a different perspective. Indeed, Henry is both healthy and ill at the same time. Even as a person is being treated for a life-threatening illness, parts of the total organism are healthy.

On a Changing Continuum.   It is more useful to view health and illness as two poles of a continuum between which a human being fluctuates over time (McHugh & Vallis, 1986; Meeks & Heit, 1988; Ryan & Travis, 1981). Individuals can take responsibility for actions that help them move closer to the health end of the continuum (Figure 1–1). Illness represents a perceived sense of distress and lack of functioning in social role(s), whereas health is a perceived sense of well-being and optimal functioning in social role(s). Individuals can choose behaviors leading to health and a better quality lifestyle. Individuals can make decisions to reduce risk behaviors by refusing to participate (Meeks & Heit, 1988). For example, adolescents and adults can decide to abstain from sexual intercourse because of the risk of AIDS. Each decision affects a person's total lifestyle and quality of life.

Health-illness continuums can be constructed for all major facets of human development: spiritual, intellectual, behavioral, emotional, imaginal, sensual, sexual, physical, and interpersonal. Individuals can compare their current degrees of health in each area of development with those of the past. Profiles of health-illness change over time. For example, people may diet and improve their physical health and self-images, but at the same time tax their interpersonal relationships because of increased irritability.

The different types of development can be defined (Figure 1–2). When any one area of development changes and grows, other areas of development are affected, which reflects the concept of interaction or synergy.

In Figure 1–2, the individual has charted personal perceptions of degrees of health and illness on the Health-Illness Wheel. The person perceives not only a high sense of well-being and functioning in the area of intellectual development, as the shaded area clearly shows, but also a low sense of well-being and poor functioning in the area of physical development. The person can then use intellectual skills to plan a physical fitness program of diet and exercise to choose to move toward the health sector in the area of physical development. In addition, the person could choose to join an interest

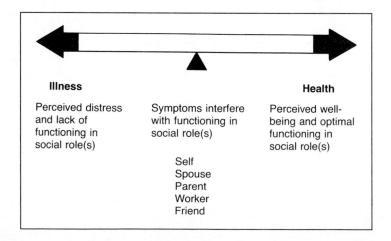

FIGURE 1–1   The health-illness continuum

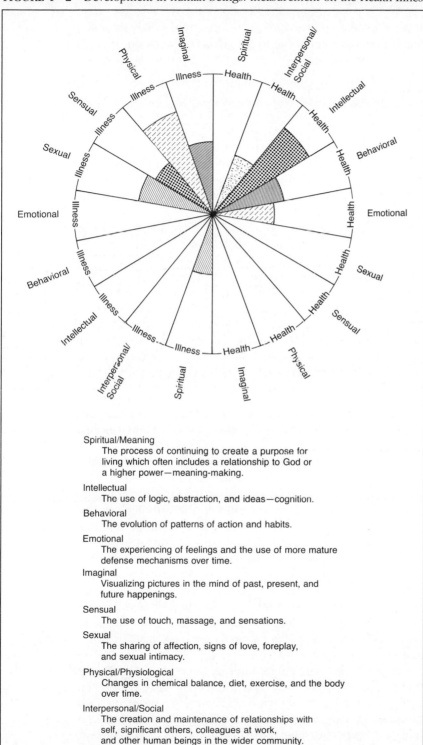

Spiritual/Meaning
      The process of continuing to create a purpose for
      living which often includes a relationship to God or
      a higher power—meaning-making.

Intellectual
      The use of logic, abstraction, and ideas—cognition.

Behavioral
      The evolution of patterns of action and habits.

Emotional
      The experiencing of feelings and the use of more mature
      defense mechanisms over time.

Imaginal
      Visualizing pictures in the mind of past, present, and
      future happenings.

Sensual
      The use of touch, massage, and sensations.

Sexual
      The sharing of affection, signs of love, foreplay,
      and sexual intimacy.

Physical/Physiological
      Changes in chemical balance, diet, exercise, and the body
      over time.

Interpersonal/Social
      The creation and maintenance of relationships with
      self, significant others, colleagues at work,
      and other human beings in the wider community.

group to improve social development. After mapping all nine areas of development on the Health-Illness Wheel, a person can choose to set goals and work on selected areas of development.

With Circularity.   Energy flows synergistically in human beings—that is, one area affects another. For example, feelings of hope and peace influence physical development. Likewise, increased thoughts of positive expectancies affect moods. Positive interpersonal interactions with a spouse may lead to peak sexual experiences with that mate. Feelings of self-worth lead to behavioral patterns of discipline and active participation. Long hot baths may stimulate feelings of contentment. An image of confidently succeeding may influence the demonstration of behaviors that lead to success. The circularity and interrelatedness of the processes of human development and human systems are evident.

In human beings, these areas of development are constantly changing, interacting, and affecting each other in circular chains that can be traced. Steps toward growth in one area of development will influence other areas of development. Counselors and therapists intervene to stimulate movement in one area of development, which then impacts other areas. Clients are no longer "stuck," but moving forward for themselves.

Sometimes people repeat what brings them success to the detriment of other areas of development. For example, an accountant may use her intellectual skills daily, increasing her logical and analytical abilities by working overtime and never taking vacations. When this happens, her interpersonal development suffers as well as other areas of development. Feelings of resentment toward her job may begin to build up, triggering consideration of a job change at mid-life.

Through Balance.   Paradoxically, any action leading to health can become entrenched with repetition, causing illness. The jogger who runs too often and too long may eventually require foot surgery. Parents who order their children to finish everything on their plates may set up processes leading to anorexia nervosa—a life-threatening loss of weight—in their offspring. What is directed toward health may lead to illness. Like army ants who rigidly march forward using the same direct tactics, unable to change direction, only to march to their deaths in the turbulent stream (Watzlawick, 1955), human actions aimed toward health may lead to self-destruction. Contradictions and the resolution of opposites are integral parts of human existence.

For example, Siegel (1986, 1989) discusses the characteristics of his patients who recover from cancer. They tend to exhibit the survivor personality, that is, be a combination of many opposites. They are serious-minded and love to have fun. They assert themselves and are gentle. They work hard and are lazy. They are intuitive and logical, aggressive and shy, extroverted and introspective. In particular, they want things to work well for themselves and others. They want to leave the world a better place than when they found it.

Exceptional patients are more likely to exhibit an internal locus of control, taking responsibility for the self and being guided by their own internal standards rather than by what other people think. Developing one's own individuality is one of the best protections of health and longevity. They analyze what needs the illness met and set goals in the various areas of development to meet those needs in other healthier ways.

Reconciliation of Illness and Health:
A Model for Coping with Chronic Illness

Programs for treating chronic illness often lead their initiators to better health than those who have no chronic illnesses. Anderson (1987), who created the Hazelden Foundation which has provided national leadership in services to alcoholics and their families over the years, is now concerned about other chronic illnesses. At the present time, more than 10% of the gross national product, or over $425 billion yearly, is being spent on health-care costs in the United States. Only 5% of these health-care dollars are used for prevention. Of the more than $170 billion dollars spent for alcoholism, less than 1% goes for preventive programs.

How does one deal with a chronic illness? A model for the treatment of chronic illness consisting of acute care, self-care, marital and family therapy, and mutual help support groups is proposed. Rather than ignoring symptoms and delaying diagnosis, it is important to obtain appropriate professional treatment as quickly as possible. For some illnesses, marital and family therapy would be the treatment of choice. A program of after-care—or strategies that the individual uses on a regular basis to prevent further deterioration—is an integral component of this model. Compliance with the self-care regimen, which may consist of physical exercise, special diet, vitamins, relaxation techniques, visualization, counseling, or other modes, may be difficult to sustain. Family support gained through improvement in relationships via marital and family therapy can help to increase compliance, bolster the immune system, and decrease the rate of the degenerative disease processes. The support of a mutual help support group encourages the individual to continue self-management of the illness.

Particularly paradoxical are the data which demonstrate that people with chronic illnesses take better care of themselves than those who are not ill. In so doing, the chronically ill often live longer lives of better quality. As Anderson (1987) states, "The cracked vases last longer." Since 70% to 80% of all illnesses in the United States are chronic, in comparison to 20% categorized as acute, the challenge of the health-care system of the 1990s and beyond will be the prevention and treatment of degenerative diseases. Marital and family therapy can be a major means of treating and coping with these chronic illnesses.

THE ROLES OF THE MARITAL AND FAMILY THERAPIST IN THE HEALTH-CARE SYSTEM

Marital and family therapists serve four primary roles in America's health-care system: (1) delivering acute-care services; (2) increasing family support for those patients suffering from acute, chronic or terminal illnesses; (3) identifying the views of illness of patients and their support systems and thereby altering misconceptions and improving support; and (4) health promotion. These four functions are discussed in the following sections.

Acute Care

Research indicates that marital and family therapy does make a significant difference for those individuals, couples, and families undergoing acute-care treatment. With regard to relief or cessation of interactional problems, participating in any style of family therapy was more effective than no formal treatment. Exhaustive and highly regarded, authoritative reviews of the outcome literature on marital and family therapy emphasize the effectiveness of both therapeutic modalities (Gurman et al., 1986; Hazelrigg, Cooper, & Borduin, 1987; Russell, Olson, & Sprenkle, 1983). According to Gurman and Kniskern (1978, 1981), with conjoint marital therapy (in which the couple is seen together either in a session devoted just to them or in a group of other couples), 65% of presenting couples improved. With family therapy, 73% of the families improved.

Hazelrigg et al. (1987) reviewed the various studies of family therapy outcomes using integrated statistical analysis. Family therapy had positive effects, as measured by behavior ratings and family interactions, when compared with alternative treatment groups and control groups receiving no treatment. Russell et al. (1983) reviewed the outcome literature on family therapy. They concluded that when the symptom was linked to its function in the family system, there were positive changes in family process and therapeutic outcome.

By contacting participants 5 years after marital treatment, Cookerly (1980) compared six types of marital therapy: (1) conjoint therapy with both spouses seen in the same session, (2) conjoint group therapy in which both spouses were treated in a session with other couples, (3) concurrent therapy in which each spouse was seen separately in individual sessions, (4) concurrent group therapy in which both spouses were treated in separate groups, (5) individual psychotherapy in which only one spouse was seen, and (6) individual group therapy in which only one spouse was seen in a group. Participants reported a significantly higher percentage of good marital relationship outcomes (as measured by the self-reports of married couples who said growth had occurred accompanied by a mature relationship of love) and fewer divorces with conjoint therapy. In fact, 56.4% of the couples who had received such treatment as a couple or in a group remained married, compared to only 29.8% of those who did not receive conjoint marital treatment. Regardless of theoretical stance, conjoint marital therapy where both spouses are involved in the same treatment process leads to the best outcome 5 years later. When clients present with marital problems, conjoint marital therapy is the treatment modality of choice.

Jacobson et al. (1984), reanalyzing data from a number of published studies, found that more than half of the couples who participated in behavioral marital therapy (BMT) improved and that deterioration was rare. He and his associates examined the success rates of components of behavioral marital therapy in another study (Jacobson, Schmaling, & Holtzworth-Munroe, 1987). There were no significant differences among a complete BMT treatment package, the component of behavior exchange, or the communication/problem-solving training component. All three groups of couples had higher levels of marital satisfaction and fewer marital problems when followed up 2 years after BMT. Jacobson (1989) conducted further research in a laboratory setting at the University of Washington and found that almost one half of the couples treated with BMT improved and maintained their gains at follow-up 2 years later. Another one third who improved initially returned to baseline distress within 2 years. Hahlweg, Revenstorf, and Schindler (1984) in Germany found that BMT improved the problem-solving and communication skills of the couples studied. In addition, Hahlweg and his associates used meta-analysis in reviewing American and European studies of BMT. Hahlweg and Markman (1988) found that BMT was effective and that gains were typically maintained and equal in both American and European couples. Therefore, BMT is effective in treating marital distress. Furthermore, techniques that improve the communication skills of couples regardless of the theoretical orientation of the therapy are an essential part of effective marital therapy (Birchler, 1979; Gottman, 1982; Jacobson, 1979).

Additional outcome studies linked to particular theoretical approaches will be discussed as each theory is elaborated in the following chapters. A brief summary of research studies that show the effectiveness of particular marital or family therapy approaches in the acute care of various clinical diagnoses or illnesses is provided in Table 1–2. Of course, marital and family therapy is the treatment of choice for marital distress, divorce, and family conflict. Various approaches to marital and family therapy also have been effective in treating children with conduct disorders; tics; psychosomatic illnesses, including diabetes and asthma; anorexia nervosa; and emotional, behavioral, and school problems. Adolescents have benefited from marital and family therapy to treat bulimia and anorexia nervosa, schizophrenia, juvenile delinquency, and drug addiction. With adults, diverse approaches to marital and family therapy have been used to treat alcoholism of one or both spouses, drug addiction, depression, multiple personality disorder, agoraphobia and other anxiety disorders, closed head injury, sexual problems, and schizophrenia. As these outcome studies point out, marital and/or family therapy serves as an effective treatment modality for many illnesses and conditions for which individuals seek health care. Thus, marital and family therapists are health-care providers and are an integral part of the country's health-care system.

As previously mentioned, outcome studies are needed linking specific therapeutic techniques to the treatment of the specific problems of families at particular stages of the family life cycle. Wynne (1988) edited a volume of readings on suggested strategies for improving family therapy research, which is recommended for anyone who is taking courses in marital and family therapy. In addition, several techniques are suggested for studying outcomes in marital and family therapy: meta-analysis (Shapiro & Shapiro, 1983; Wampler, 1982) repeated-measure designs (Schumm, Bugaighis, & Jurich, 1985), and single-case designs (Rabin, 1981). Despite the need for additional process research linked to effective outcomes at diverse stages of family development, the evidence is overwhelmingly clear that marital and family therapy produces improvement in interpersonal relationships and a variety of dysfunctions.

Increasing Family Support

In one of their roles as health-care professionals, marital and family therapists often provide services to increase family support during times of acute, terminal, or chronic illness. Research has indicated that family support makes a significant difference in the course of illnesses and affects their severity. For example, Kushi (1981) found that recovery rates increased for cancer patients whose family members were physically and emotionally supportive, while those whose families were not supportive did not recover.

TABLE 1-2 Studies of the effectiveness of marital and family therapy

Problem or Illness	Effective Treatment	Source
Improvement of healthy functioning	Premarital, marital, and family enrichment	Doherty et al., 1986 Giblin, 1986 Zimpfer, 1988
Marital distress	Behavioral marital therapy	Hahlweg et al., 1984 Hahlweg & Markham, 1988 Jacobson, 1978, 1989 Jacobson et al., 1984, 1987
	Cognitive marital therapy	Emmelkamp et al., 1988
	Relationship enhancement therapy	Ross et al., 1985
	Emotionally-focused marital therapy	Johnson & Greenberg, 1985, 1988
Divorce	Mediation	Sprenkle & Storm, 1983
Childhood antisocial behaviors and conduct disorders	Behavioral parent training	Patterson, 1974, 1989 Patterson et al., 1982
	Behavioral family therapy	Patterson, 1971 Gordon & Davidson, 1981
	Behavioral marital therapy	Patterson et al., 1976
Childhood emotional and behavioral problems	Structural family therapy and behavioral family therapy	Szykula et al., 1987
Childhood tics	Structural family therapy	Teichman & Eliahu, 1986
Anorexia and bulimia	Structural family therapy	Minuchin et al., 1975 Russell et al., 1987
	Systemic family therapy	Selvini et al., 1978, 1989 Stierlin & Weber, 1989
Psychosomatic illnesses of children and adolescents (including asthma and diabetes)	Structural family therapy	Minuchin et al., 1975 Minuchin et al., 1978

One of the most famous studies documenting the importance of family and social support is *The Roseto Story,* an 18-year follow-up study of several small towns in Pennsylvania (Bruhn & Wolf, 1979). Roseto, a town composed of close-knit Italian immigrants, had less than half of the mortality rate of the surrounding villages and the nation. The key difference among the towns was the strength of the social relationships in Roseto. Strong family and social networks helped to protect the citizens of Roseto from sudden cardiac death and heart attacks.

In a study of Alameda County in California, nearly 7,000 people were studied over a 9-year period to check mortality rates and the level of social ties such as marital status, membership in a church, visits with friends, belonging to organizations, and visits with relatives (Berkman & Syme, 1979). The more social support people had, the

TABLE 1–2 *continued*

Problem or Illness	Effective Treatment	Source
School problems	Family therapy	Bernal et al., 1987
Juvenile delinquency	Behavioral-systems family therapy	Barton & Alexander, 1981
	Functional family therapy	Gordon et al., 1988
	Structural family therapy	Minuchin et al., 1967
Drug addiction	Structural family therapy	Kosten et al., 1983
		Stanton et al., 1979
		Todd, 1984
Alcoholism of spouse	Marital and family therapy	O'Farrell, 1989
Depression	Strategic marital therapy	Coyne, 1987, 1984
	In-patient family intervention	Glick et al., 1985
		Haas et al., 1988
	Family therapy	Bernal et al., 1987
Schizophrenia	Psychoeducational family groups	Anderson & Reiss, 1982
	Family-based management	Falloon et al., 1985
	Inpatient family intervention	Glick et al., 1985
		Haas et al., 1988
	Couple therapy	Bowen, 1978
	Strategic family therapy	Haley, 1980
Multiple personality disorder	Marital and/or family therapy	Sachs et al., 1985
Closed head injury	Family therapy	Zarski et al., 1987
Sexual problems	Behavioral sex therapy	Libman et al., 1985
		Morokoff & LoPiccolo, 1986
		Schover & LoPiccolo, 1982
Family conflict	Brief family therapy	de Shazer, 1985
		Weakland et al., 1974

lower their mortality rates at all ages. House, Robbins, and Metzner (1982) replicated the study and found that increased social networks were linked with lower rates of mortality for males. In particular, church attendance was the single variable that predicted reduced mortality rates.

In reviewing the literature on the impact of the family on health, Campbell (1986) concluded that social support was a major influence on mortality and that the most important part of this effect was due to family support. Social support includes affective support (feeling loved and cared for as a person), self-esteem support (valuing and respecting a person), and network support (having a role with duties and expectations) (Cobb, 1982). In particular, the support of a spouse was crucial to younger people, while the support of a child was essential to the longevity of the elderly.

Caplan (1982) stated that the family support system also fulfills the following functions: (1) disseminator of information about the external world, (2) unit of guidance giving feedback about a family member's behavior, (3) source of belief system, (4) model for problem solving, (5) resource for help and services, (6) place to recuperate, (7) source of control, (8) affirmer of identity, and (9) facilitator in talking through feelings in transitions rather than forming premature judgments.

Since the amount of family support affects the patient's compliance with requested attitudinal changes, exercise, and imagery programs, Matthews-Simonton, Simonton, and Creighton (1978) involve the closest family member in the cancer treatment process. Their book, *Getting Well Again: A Step-by-Step, Self-Help Guide to Overcoming Cancer for Patients and Their Families*, includes a dialogue demonstrating healthy family functioning—encouraging family members to meet their own needs, emphasizing open expression of feelings and supportive communication, and rewarding the patient's initiative and responsibility for self. The potential impact of family support on many other types of illnesses and conditions is shown in Table 1–3.

A national task force (Blackburn et al., 1987) that focused on primary prevention of coronary heart disease concluded that increased family, community, and workplace support was the strategy that demonstrated the most promise for health promotion and maintenance of healthier lifestyles. Hartley et al. (1987) recommend that health-care professionals suggest to their patients that they widen and deepen their social networks of marriage, family, friends, and social groups and maintain high levels of involvement in these networks, especially during stressful life events. Such social support should constitute an integral part of a comprehensive program of diet, exercise, weight control, medication, cessation of smoking, and psychological counseling to prevent cardiovascular diseases (Blumenthal & Levenson, 1987).

Influencing the Family's Perceptions of Illness

Due to the significance of family support, it is important for the marital and family therapist as a health-care provider to ask questions about how the family sees the etiology of the illness and mastery of the outcome. Family beliefs are often based on religious views, ethnic background, and, most importantly, past experiences with the mastery of similar or different illnesses in the family of origin. A family's sense of mastery over illness can become more fatalistic as a result of their interactions with health-care professionals, which in turn affects their reactions to future illnesses and those of their children. Marital and family therapists must be sensitive to subtle cues and language that indicate a shift to a less productive family-illness paradigm, and they must confront such shifts. Of course, how a family functions during an illness of a family member depends on various characteristics of the illness and the family's sense of mastery over the illness.

Rolland (1984, 1987, 1988) created a three-dimensional psychosocial typology of illness. Illnesses can be classified by onset (gradual or acute), course (constant, deteriorating, or relapsing), outcome (no effect on the length of life, shortened life or a sudden death, or terminal), and degree of disablement (none to partial to total). The time phases of an illness include terminal, chronic, and first crisis, with transitions experienced between phases.

TABLE 1–3 The impact of family support

Type of Illness or Condition	Effects of Family Support
Compliance with medical treatment	Attitude of family can lead to better or worse compliance. When family supports compliance, it increases significantly.
Bereavement	Can prevent premature death of widowers within 6 months after bereavement.
Terminal illness	Reduce probability of spouse becoming ill.
Overall mortality	Support of spouse for younger group and support of children for elderly reduces overall mortality.
Diabetes	When marital distress is reduced, diabetic and nondiabetic children are helped.
Failure to thrive	Lack of family support.
Asthma	Family therapy focusing on increasing the family's coping skills to deal with attacks decreased daily wheezing and thoracic gas volumes.
Hypertension and myocardial infarctions (heart attacks)	Family support, especially the support of the spouse, reduces mortality and increases compliance with weight reduction, medication, and lifestyle changes.
Coronary heart disease, coronary artery disease, and bypass surgery	Reducing occupational stress of wife and increasing social support reduces incidence and mortality, and improves outcomes.
Obesity	Simultaneous participation of the spouse in a weight-loss program improves outcome but not of the parent with an adolescent who wants to lose weight. Asking family not to interfere can also help, as does training family members to reinforce.
Chronic illness	Another family member may be a hidden patient.
Behavior problems of preschool or school-age children	If marital strain is decreased, problems improve.
Problems of adolescents	Clear boundaries between generations and effective coalition of parents or care givers aids the growth of adolescents.
Pregnancy	Support tends to reduce complications.
Depression	Critical comments by family members increase probability of relapse. Parental affectionless control is linked to depression when the client becomes an adult. Therapy is effective in treating marital conflicts that can trigger depressive episodes.
Schizophrenia	Reduction in contact with overinvolved relative who makes critical comments (expressed emotion), or changed behavior on the part of this relative through family education or family therapy, and compliance with medication are linked to a decrease in rehospitalization.
Alcoholism	Low conflict in the marital relationship with high cohesion linked to best response to treatment.
Drug abuse	Family therapy to reduce enmeshed cross-generational parent-child involvement is effective.
Anorexia nervosa	Family therapy is found to be effective.

From "When Is It Helpful to Convene the Family?" by D. D. Schmidt in *The Journal of Family Practice,* *16,* 5, (967–973) 1983. Adapted by permission of Appleton & Lange, Inc. and David D. Schmidt. Also adapted by permission of Family Process, Inc. from Campbell (1986).

Components of family functioning include the family's belief about mastery over the illness in relation to outcome. For example, family members may believe that the control of the illness is out of their hands and up to fate. Therefore, they may not establish strong relationships with doctors and other health-care professionals because they believe there is nothing anyone can do about the illness—an external locus of control. If a family member improves, it is attributed to good luck; if she dies, it is attributed to fate.

Other families may believe that external, powerful others, such as doctors, hold mastery over the illness. In this case they believe the health-care professionals and do whatever they ask. If they believe in flexible participation with health-care professionals, they will develop relationships with them and participate in treatment, attributing a positive outcome to their successful participation. If the family member becomes worse, they will become sad without blame. However, if the family is rigid, they will attribute a positive outcome to successful control and a negative outcome to powerful others, blaming health providers, other family members, and God for what has happened.

In a third scenario, family members may believe that they have control over the outcome of the illness—an internal locus of control. If they believe in flexible participation, they will cooperate fully with health-care professionals and attribute a positive outcome to their successful participation or feel sad without blame if the family member becomes worse. If family members are rigid, however, they attribute a positive outcome to successful control on their parts and a negative outcome to themselves, with self-blame, guilt, and even shame resulting. These family members may experience physical health problems themselves, as well as depression and other psychiatric symptoms. It is important for a marital and family therapist to recognize the family's perception of illness and inappropriate attributions that may create problems.

Health Promotion

Marital and family therapists not only have a role in diagnosis and treatment, but they also play an important part in health promotion and disease prevention (J. D. Woody, 1985; R. H. Woody, 1985). Woody and Springer (1985) make the following recommendations of specific family therapy techniques to promote health in families: (1) structure family therapy sessions to encourage each family member to attain needs and goals; (2) assist each family member to increase self-esteem and develop a healthy self-concept; (3) encourage healthy communication in the family; (4) be a model of healthy stress management, which should include proper breathing, diet, weight control, and fitness; (5) confront, persuade, and influence family members to give up unhealthy habits such as smoking or substance abuse, and substitute healthy alternatives; (6) guide family members toward increased intimacy, including emotional sharing as well physical touch and interaction; (7) encourage family members to talk about sex and its healthy expression; (8) disseminate brochures and handouts to educate the family about health matters; (9) learn about referral sources in the community; and (10) support the efforts of family members to become more spiritual.

The role of the marital and family therapist in assisting families to move toward health is not a new one. Marital and family therapy began as family life education in the early 1900s. Courses on parenting, the family, and marriage became electives in many college curricula when professors of disciplines such as home economics, sociology, psychology, and theology became concerned about the growth and development of their students as human beings and as future parents. They designed courses to meet the requests and needs of their students for information and help concerning family life. Thus, marital and family therapy began as prevention.

It is very appropriate as the profession of marital and family therapy moves toward the next century that efforts be made to study the roots or historical beginnings of the field because they emanate from a healthy preventive base which became intertwined with therapeutic intervention. In the early years of this century, there was close interaction and overlap between prevention and intervention—a perspective that our society needs now.

THE FORCES INFLUENCING THE DEVELOPMENT OF MARITAL AND FAMILY THERAPY

In detailing the history of marital and family therapy, an emphasis is placed first on the forces influencing the development of the specialization or field without regard to a time chronology (Table 1–4). Many of these forces continue to have significant impact on the practice of marriage and family therapy today. Therefore, it is important to emphasize these more global factors because they create recurrent, cyclical, or continuous influences on marital and family therapy. A selection of the most significant factors has been made based on a review of the following sources on the history of the field: Broderick and Schrader, 1981; Guerin, 1976; Kaslow, 1977, 1982, 1987; Liddle, 1987; Olson, 1970; Olson, Russell, and Sprenkle, 1980. After the major forces have been discussed, a chronological history of events will be presented.

1. The family life education movement
2. Federal and state legislation
3. Meeting the societal needs of children
4. The leadership of professionals
5. The beginning and continued growth of marriage counseling
6. Sex therapy and the contributions of sexologists
7. The psychoanalytic movement and reactions to it
8. The contributions of communication theorists
9. Research on schizophrenia
10. Research on healthy families

TABLE 1–4 Forces influencing the development of marital and family therapy

Adapted from Broderick and Schrader (1981), Guerin (1976), and Kaslow (1982).

Family-Life Education Movement

As with medicine and law, marital and family therapy developed to meet societal needs, in this case, the needs expressed by people who wanted to know more about marriage, parenting, and family life. They looked to experts such as college professors and clergy for this information. The family life education movement was born. It is important to remember that the field of marital and family therapy emanated from a preventive, information-oriented growth model—what every person needed to know to move through the normal stages and transitions of adult life.

The National Council of Family Relations (NCFR) was founded in 1938 to promote parenting (Broderick & Schrader, 1981). At the present time, the NCFR has created a new credential, Family Life Educator, as a way of recognizing those individuals who have expertise in family life education in addition to or separate from expertise in treatment of marital/family dysfunctions. Composed of home economists, ministers, teachers, psychologists, agricultural home extension agents, psychiatrists, social workers, counselors, and others who provide preventive and therapeutic information to families, the National Council of Family Relations is an interdisciplinary group of professionals dedicated to the improvement of family life in the United States.

Federal and State Legislation

There have been many federal laws that have directly or indirectly affected families in the United States. In fact, it is difficult to find a bill that does not affect the family in some way (Schroeder, 1989). For example, the Smith-Lever and Smith-Hughes acts created the position of agricultural home extension agent to promote family life. Federal statutes established community mental health centers to help individuals, married couples, and families. Of particular interest now are those bills that also affect the profession, such as legislation to permit marital and family therapists and other providers of marital and family services such as psychologists, social workers, and counselors, to be reimbursed by Medicare.

The broader role of the federal government in the development of the specialization and the profession of marital and family therapy has been a supportive one. For example, CHAMPUS, the insurance provider for the military, has reimbursed practitioners for marital and family services. This practice can serve as a model for the United States. In addition, state legislatures have passed licensure and/or certification bills for marriage and family therapy. Legislation at the state level has particularly influenced the practice of marriage and family therapy within a given state.

The Needs of Children

The first juvenile court was established in 1909 to provide rehabilitative services to young offenders, who were viewed as having different needs and potentials than adult criminals (Kaslow, 1982). Juveniles were required to attend treatment sessions in child guidance clinics, where a psychiatrist or psychologist saw the child, with a social worker talking with the mother—a forerunner of family treatment.

Many of the charitable groups that were founded in the early 1900s to provide financial assistance to the poor began to offer other types of services, usually provided by social workers. In the 1950s a child psychiatrist and analyst named Nathan W.

Ackerman was hired by the Jewish Family Service in New York City to provide the first official family therapy (Guerin, 1976). With the current divorce rate and its accompanying effects on children, judges and courts continue to be concerned about custody agreements and the treatment of children, often requiring evaluations or treatments at such family service agencies.

The Leadership of Professionals

From its very beginning, marital and family therapy has been a multidisciplinary field, often consisting of professionals whose primary affiliation and identification has been with another profession, such as medicine, psychiatry, psychology, social work, home economics, pastoral counseling, psychiatric nursing, or mental health counseling. Such dual allegiances have had a double-edged effect. Cross-disciplinary perspectives and resources have been strengths, but the inconsistency of the knowledge base, due to the publication by many of their work in the journals of their primary fields, has been a source of weakness (Olson, 1970).

Historically, pioneers in the social work profession were first to emphasize the family (Broderick & Schrader, 1981). In particular, Mary Richmond wrote *A Real Story of a Real Family* in 1908, focusing on the treatment and importance of the total family. Social workers have consistently conducted more marital and family therapy over the years than any other group. From the early 1900s they have involved the members of the family in treatment, often seeing a mother or a father of a disturbed child.

Social workers participated in the presentations of papers on family treatment, but they often were not heard or went unrecognized for their efforts. They were working with the families, producing results, without recognition. Some say that the employment hierarchy of psychiatry, psychology, and social work prevalent in previous decades influenced the impact of what early social work pioneers said and did. Others say that the gender differences (psychiatrists and psychologists tended to be male, while most social workers were female) subtly affected professional decisions.

Others document that social workers veered away from their original emphasis on the family to follow the medical profession's emphasis on psychoanalytic approaches, which focused on the individual (Broderick & Schrader, 1981). When noted psychiatrists bucked the medical establishment to found family therapy in the late 1950s and early 1960s, social workers followed. Virginia Satir, a social worker who is often called "The Columbus of Family Therapy," was consistent in her emphasis on marital and family therapy, initiating the first training program for family therapy at the Mental Research Institute in Palo Alto, California, from 1959–1964. The long and consistent contributions of social workers to marital and family therapy should be highlighted rather than minimized.

The American Home Economics Association was formed. Home economists often taught courses at the high school level in sewing, cooking, money management, and the responsibilities of married life (Broderick & Schrader, 1981). Students taking such courses often sought additional help from their teachers about impending marriages or family problems, which led to informal marital counseling.

The American Association of Marriage Counselors (AAMC) was founded in 1942. With the growth of family therapy in the 1950s and 1960s, the name of the association was changed to the American Association of Marriage and Family Counselors (AAMFC) in 1970, and then to the American Association for Marriage and Family Therapy (AAMFT) in 1978 (Broderick & Schrader, 1981; Olson, 1970). The AAMFT continues to be interdisciplinary in composition, but with a majority of members now identifying primarily with the profession of marital and family therapy. The AAMFT provides leadership to the movement of marital and family therapy to assume its place as a separate field of health-care provision—marital and family therapists as health-care providers.

The movement of psychiatry toward a psychosocial orientation also influenced the development of marital and family therapy (Kaslow, 1982). The end of World War II and the Korean War heralded the return of many veterans who needed services. There were not enough psychiatrists to provide traditional one-on-one analytic psychotherapy to these returning veterans. A pragmatic, innovative spirit of designing alternative treatments that were cost effective yet provided positive outcomes prevailed. Psychiatrists developed marital and family therapy to treat people effectively in the shortest amount of time.

John Elderkin Bell was the first psychologist to treat families as a group (Broderick & Shrader, 1981). He presented his work at meetings of the psychological associations and wrote one of the first monographs in the field.

In 1977, the American Family Therapy Association was formed, with Murray Bowen as president (Kaslow, 1982). This association functions as a scientific society and is composed mainly of psychiatrists and other researchers in the field of family therapy.

The Division of Family Psychology (Division 43) of the American Psychological Association was established in 1984 (Kaslow, 1987). The *Journal of Family Psychology* was inaugurated in 1987 to provide a scholarly mechanism for representing and promoting the systems perspective within mainstream psychology. Psychologists by training whose research interests or practices were devoted to family treatment now had a home base within the American Psychological Association within which they could relate.

As interest in marital and family therapy continued to increase within the counseling profession, the International Association of Marriage and Family Counselors became an organizational affiliate of the American Association for Counseling and Development in 1989. Mental health counselors and school counselors who worked with married couples and families could share their knowledge and expertise.

The leadership of professional associations will continue to exert one of the most powerful influences on marital and family therapy. It is important for a student to become involved in professional associations in the field while in training. Most of these professional groups have student discount membership rates that include one or more journals or newsletters.

The Growth of Marriage Counseling

Marriage counseling centers began in New York City, Los Angeles, and Philadelphia around 1930. In all these centers, the emphasis was on marriage counseling, even though only one individual typically was seen.

Those who identify themselves as marital therapists have routinely been the largest group of the AAMFT. Marriage counseling will continue to have a major impact on the development of marital and family therapy because of the number of practitioners who conduct marital therapy exclusively.

Sex Therapy and the Contributions of Sexologists
Many of the problems that people bring to marriage counseling are sexual in nature. Not all marital therapists have training in sex therapy because sex therapy developed as a separate area of expertise, although Lester Dearborn, a sex therapist, was one of the founders of the AAMC (Broderick & Schrader, 1981).

The American Association of Sex Educators and Counselors has formulated criteria for the certification of sex therapists on a national basis. Since most marital and family therapists who remain in the field over a period of time take additional courses or attend workshops about sex therapy in order to be able to treat distressed couples, sex therapy will continue to influence the field of marital and family therapy.

The Psychoanalytic Movement and Reactions to It
A major force affecting marital and family therapy was and is the psychoanalytic movement and reactions to it (Kaslow, 1982). Many of the founders of family therapy were trained as psychoanalysts (medical doctors who undergo a four-year intensive psychoanalysis four to five times a week) or had extensive psychoanalytically oriented training.

Most recently, interest has heightened concerning the application of the theories of the British object relations school to family therapy (Nichols, 1987; Scharff & Scharff, 1987). Those marital and family therapists who do long-term intensive work will continue to use and learn more about psychoanalytically oriented therapy. Marital and family therapy over years typically requires an understanding of psychoanalytic theory and practice which will continue to influence marital and family therapy in future decades.

The Contributions of Communication Theorists
The science of cybernetics influenced the development of marital and family therapy. Norbert Wiener (1948) was a mathematician who coined the term *cybernetics* to include the field of communication and control theory. Ashby wrote *An Introduction to Cybernetics* in 1956. Gregory Bateson (1972) applied their theories of cybernetics to human beings and families. Today, communication theorists continue to make discoveries in the cognitive sciences. Using complex computers to simulate communication between human beings, such neuroscientists are making basic discoveries with profound influences on marital and family therapy.

Research on Schizophrenia
One of the most important forces influencing the development of marital and family therapy has been and continues to be the research conducted on the families of schizophrenics. Key pioneers include Don Jackson, Jay Haley, Murray Bowen, Theodore Lidz, Lyman Wynne, and Ivan Boszormenyi-Nagy. Most of their research identified types of communication problems within the families of schizophrenics and developed family therapy techniques to change the family process, in order to cure the schizophrenia.

In contrast, the research of Anderson, Reiss, and Hogarty (1986) at the Department of Psychiatry at the University of Pittsburgh focuses on the design and evaluation of a family education and support program that reduces the rehospitalization rates of schizophrenics. Falloon and colleagues (1984) in England have also created a behavioral program for families to educate them about schizophrenia and provide support. These programs are based on the assumption that schizophrenia is a chronic illness that cannot be cured, but the frequency and severity of the acute crises can be reduced through family support and medication.

Both approaches to the treatment of schizophrenics impact the development of family therapy and will continue to do so into future decades. The debate as to whether both perspectives can be utilized simultaneously or if a choice should be made based on the history of a given family is still raging.

Research on Healthy Families

The body of research on healthy family functioning provides a map or optimal prototype toward which therapists may aim. Zimmerman and Cervantes (1960) wrote the first book on successful families. The most influential studies on healthy family functioning are those completed at the Timberlawn Psychiatric Research Foundation, where the interactions of families were videotaped while they were performing assigned tasks. The only interactional study of healthy black working-class families ever conducted in the United States was completed by Lewis and Looney (1983) at Timberlawn and is called *The Long Struggle: Well Functioning Working-Class Black Families*.

From 1977 to 1987, Stinnett and his associates published eight edited volumes of research on strong families (see Chapter 3 bibliography) and sponsored a yearly National Symposium on Building Family Strengths. They conducted cross-cultural research on family strengths and sponsored an international symposium on the subject. Such cross-cultural research supported certain basic strengths found in families from all cultures, although additional strengths varied from culture to culture.

The research of David Olson and colleagues focused on the characteristics of healthy family functioning at different stages of the family life cycle using the Circumplex Model of Marital and Family Systems (Olson, Sprenkle, & Russell, 1979). They found that the optimal levels of family cohesion and adaptability varied at different stages of the family life cycle.

Such research on healthy family functioning continues to influence practitioners in the field. They may wish to tailor their interventions to the various stages of the family life cycle of the presenting family and to take the family's culture into consideration. Further research on the strengths of diverse types of families will impact on the maps or models that all therapists carry of what they would like presenting families to become.

THE HISTORY OF MARITAL AND FAMILY THERAPY

Important, historic names and dates are contained in Table 1–5. A narrative chronology of important events follows.

Before 1930: Focus on Prevention—The Beginning of Marriage and Family-Life Education

Marital and family therapy began as preventive classes and courses to meet the normal needs of people, especially women, who wanted to know more about marriage, parenting, and family life. As colleges and universities began to admit their first female students, these students requested courses on the family. In 1908, 20 colleges were offering such courses (Broderick & Schrader, 1981). Before 1930, the focus was on prevention and the delivery of family life education through courses and workshops.

Often, students or homemakers attending such courses sought specific advice or information about their own marital and family questions. The college professors in sociology, home economics, religion, and psychology began to answer such questions and to do informal counseling of their students upon request, as did the agricultural extension agents involved in home demonstration.

The 1930s: The Strengthening of Family-Life Education and the Beginning of Marriage Counseling

From these early attempts at informal counseling, the need for more formal marital counseling evolved, with centers established in Los Angeles, New York City, and Philadelphia around 1930. Typically counselors at these centers saw individuals, usually women, who presented with marital problems.

At the same time, the family life education movement grew. Professionals taking leadership roles in family life education courses and workshops were also prominent practitioners of marriage counseling. For example, Paul Popenoe presented more than 100 workshops in churches and on college campuses across California during the 1930s, while his private practice, the American Institute of Family Relations, grew and prospered. Prevention, family life education, and the provision of marriage counseling and other treatment services have always been tied together throughout the history of marital and family therapy. As family life education flourished, marriage counseling was born. Both continue to complement each other.

The 1940s: The Professionalization of Marriage Counseling

In the 1940s, marriage counselors pressed for the formation of a professional association, the American Association of Marriage Counselors (AAMC). The association was composed mainly of practitioners with widely diverse backgrounds and family-life educators. In England, David Mace helped to initiate over 200 centers for marriage counseling, which later joined the National Marriage Council where he served as executive director.

World War II created intense strain on individuals and married couples. Husbands and wives were separated by distance because of military assignments. Wives were often left alone to raise the children or went back to live with parents or other relatives who helped them. Soldiers were shipped abroad and participated in brutal battles, which left emotional scars that affected many marriages. Sometimes individuals married in haste because they were drafted, or they met a war bride or groom abroad who had difficulties adjusting when leaving relatives to relocate permanently

TABLE 1–5 A history of marital and family therapy (pp. 26–28)

Before 1930: Focus on Prevention—The Beginning of Marriage and Family-Life Education

1. In 1883, groups of mothers came together to apply pedagogy to parenting.
2. Charles R. Henderson taught first college "family as an institution" course at the University of Chicago in 1893.
3. Home economics courses proliferated after the founding of the American Home Economics Association in 1908.
4. County agricultural home extension agents funded through Smith-Lever Act (1914) and Smith Hughes Act (1917).
5. First preparatory parenthood course taught at the college level at Vassar College in 1923.
6. In 1924, Ernest Groves taught first parenthood course for credit at Boston University and non-credit course on marriage

The 1930s: The Strengthening of Family-Life Education and the Beginning of Marriage Counseling

1. Abraham and Hannah Stone started marriage counseling before 1929 in New York City.
2. Paul Popenoe formed the American Institute of Family Relations in 1930 in Los Angeles and coined the term *marriage counseling.*
3. In 1932, Emily Mudd began the Marriage Council of Philadelphia.
4. Ernest R. Groves taught the first "functional" family course in 1936 at the University of North Carolina.
5. The National Council of Family Relations founded in 1938; *Marriage and Family Living,* the first professional journal of the NCFR, founded in 1939.

The 1940s: The Professionalization of Marriage Counseling

1. The American Association of Marriage Counselors (AAMC) founded in 1942.
2. In 1945, Ernest Groves, first President of AAMC.
3. In 1943, the first Marriage Guidance Center in England founded by David Mace.
4. Unique characteristics of marriage counseling began to develop—an emphasis on the marital relationship and the use of conjoint marital therapy.

The 1950s: The Era of Research Undergirding Family Therapy

1. In 1953, John Elderkin Bell, a psychologist, saw family members together in treatment—family group therapy.
2. "Toward a Theory of Schizophrenia," first article linking certain communication patterns to the families of schizophrenics, published by Bateson, Jackson, Haley, and Weakland in 1956.
3. Jackson organized the Mental Research Institute in Palo Alto, hiring Satir and Riskin to study schizophrenics and their families.
4. Theodore Lidz studied schizophrenics and their families in Baltimore and then at Yale.
5. In 1954, Murray Bowen hospitalized schizophrenics and their families at NIMH in Washington, testing family therapy techniques in the treatment of schizophrenia.
6. At NIMH, Lyman Wynne studied the communication deviances of the families of schizophrenics.

TABLE 1-5 *continued*

7. In 1957, Boszormenyi-Nagy at Eastern Pennsylvania Psychiatric Institute near Philadelphia used psychoanalytically oriented therapy with schizophrenics and their families.

8. Christian F. Midelfort—first book on family therapy, *The Family and Psychotherapy,* 1957.

9. Carl Whitaker hosted the first informal meeting of researchers on schizophrenia at Sea Island, Georgia.

10. John Speigel was chairperson of the first panel presenting research on the families of schizophrenics at the American Orthopsychiatric Association in 1957.

The 1960s: Training Family Therapists

1. As "The Columbus of Family Therapy," Virginia Satir began the first family therapy training program at the Mental Research Institute in Palo Alto.

2. Nathan Ackerman trained family therapists at the New York Family Institute and was founder of the first journal in family therapy, *Family Process,* in 1962.

3. Murray Bowen trained family therapists at Georgetown University in Washington to work with couples.

4. Israel Zwerling is noted for training at Albert Einstein College of Medicine in New York City.

5. Salvador Minuchin conducted research on family therapy with the families of delinquents and trained therapists at the Child Guidance Center in Philadelphia.

The 1970s: Certification and Licensure of Marital and Family Therapists

1. The expansion of the AAMC to AAMFT.

2. Convergence of family life education, marriage counseling, and family therapy to form a separate field of marital and family therapy with emphasis on the relationship context.

3. Licensure/certification bills passed in a number of state legislatures.

4. Various classifications of marital and family theories were proposed.

5. The development of schools of family therapy.

6. Outcome studies improved in quality and quantity.

7. Interactional research studies conducted on healthy families at Timberlawn Psychiatric Research Foundation.

8. Formation of the American Family Therapy Association with Bowen as president in 1977.

9. In 1978, AAMFT was recognized as the official accrediting agency for marital and family therapy programs by HEW.

The 1980s: Toward Integration of Theoretical Models, Specialization, and Self-Help

1. Search for integrative models accelerated.

2. Assessment tools and outcome studies were refined.

3. Increased collaboration between researchers, academic theoreticians, and clinical practitioners.

4. Additional specialties developed for which credentials were created, such as Family Life Educator, Divorce Mediator.

5. The number of accredited programs was increased.

TABLE 1—5 *continued*

6. The number of states with licensing/certification bills increased.

7. Interest groups and divisions formed within already existing professional organizations.

8. Additional research centers, such as the Center for Family Strengths at the University of Nebraska-Lincoln, developed to study healthy families.

9. Self-help marital enrichment groups grew in strength.

1990s and Beyond: Reconciliation of Opposites

1. Divorce rates will increase, yet the meaning of the family will become more important, intensifying demands for marital and family therapy.

2. Professional standards in marital and family therapy will increase, while married couples and families will also take responsibility for their own health, seeking out enrichment programs and self-help support groups led by lay leaders.

3. Programs will increase in medical settings to involve families in the treatment and compliance of patients. Likewise, families will be included in research on the prevention of disabling conditions.

4. Marital and family therapy will be more widely accepted as a treatment modality reimbursed by insurance companies as health care. At the same time, churches and other community agencies will offer more free or low-cost family enhancement preventive programs.

5. Research will focus on specific techniques for treating families with specific problems at different stages of the family life cycle. In contrast, healthy families of diverse structures and cultures will also be studied.

6. Diverse techniques will be reconciled in eclectic systemic models which can be used effectively in private-practice settings by single practitioners.

Adapted from Broderick & Schrader (1981), Guerin (1976), and Kaslow (1982).

in the United States. Death claimed the lives of many servicemen and severed marriages. The 1940s were turbulent times for families.

In response to the great need, marriage counseling grew and developed, providing the impetus for the establishment of a professional association of practitioners dedicated to improving the quality of the services that they provided. From the beginning, the AAMC emphasized the marital relationship and the value of conjoint marital therapy (seeing both spouses together in the treatment room), although the most frequent type of marital treatment actually practiced until the 1970s was seeing one individual, usually the wife (Olson, 1970).

The 1950s: The Era of Research Undergirding Family Therapy

Some early research on effective outcomes had been conducted by Emily Mudd, who had evaluated the process of marriage counseling at her center. Since every profession by definition requires a distinctive body of knowledge, research base, scope of practice, and ethical code, the field was strengthened by the research undertaken by psychiatrists, psychologists, social workers, and communication theorists in the 1950s. Most of this research was conducted with the families of schizophrenics and undergirded the development of family therapy as a separate therapeutic modality in contrast to marital therapy, although marital treatment might be a part of ongoing family therapy. Much of this research was conducted in medical settings. The idea of the family therapist as a member of the health-care treatment team was born.

The 1960s: Training Family Therapists

Family therapy developed differently from marriage counseling. Techniques of family therapy emanated from research on families, whereas marriage counseling arose as a practical response to a societal need. Much of the research on schizophrenics and their families highlighted inappropriate communication patterns, but researchers had different ideas of how to correct the problems. Therefore, family therapy techniques varied from one project or center to another. Training centers flourished in Palo Alto, New York City, Philadelphia, and Washington, with the evolution of other centers in neighboring locations and states. Some researchers were better than others in translating research findings into effective family therapy techniques.

Perhaps the most famous for the creation of family therapy techniques, that is, the art of family therapy, is Virginia Satir. A social worker, Satir began the first family therapy training program at the Mental Research Institute (MRI) in Palo Alto, California, in 1959 and wrote *Conjoint Family Therapy* in 1964. More clinicians are aware of her techniques than those of any other family therapist, as evidenced by recent surveys of practitioners (Kolevzon & Green, 1985), probably because of her emphasis on training and her practical, highly readable books.

Professionals from many disciplines and from all over the United States and the world made the pilgrimage to the MRI or attended one of Satir's numerous workshops and demonstrations or those of the members of her Avanta Training Network. Her personal charisma and dogged persistence made an enormous impact on the field, popularizing family therapy among a wide cross-section of service providers. One can only conjecture what might have happened to the family therapy movement without Satir. Perhaps the family therapy modality would have remained within research hospital settings, somewhat of a mystery to the average therapist in the field. The Avanta Network in Palo Alto, California, continues to disseminate the training and techniques developed by Satir.

Although Nathan Ackerman did not have a federal grant for research on schizophrenics, he was a leader in the training of family therapists. Trained as a child analyst, Ackerman accepted the position as director of the first, newly formed family mental health unit at the Jewish Family Service. He founded the New York Family Institute, where he began to train family therapists. Since his death, the NYFI has been called the Ackerman Institute; it is a major training center in family therapy.

Another researcher who focused intensively on training was Murray Bowen. Basing his family therapy style on the results of his research and personal experience, he developed a training center at Georgetown University in Washington, D.C. He worked almost exclusively with couples and wrote *Family Therapy in Clinical Practice*, published in 1978. Externships and internships were available at the center, which continues to be one of the main training sites in family therapy.

Another noted training site was the Bronx State Family Studies Section of the Albert Einstein College of Medicine in New York City where many hopefuls came to learn from Israel Zwerling (Guerin, 1976). This section became the Family Institute, with

Andrew Ferber as director in 1964. Later, Beels, Scheflen, and Fogarty, under the direction of Guerin, strengthened the internship program and created externships. Nearly 150 trainees stayed in-house or were trained externally each year. Eventually, a center was set up in Westchester, New York, to offer preventive education programs for families and an externship program for students. By 1973, Guerin had established the Center for Family Learning, located in New Rochelle, New York, where Peggy Papp, Betty Carter, and Tom Fogarty joined him.

Salvador Minuchin received federal funding to focus on the treatment of the families of delinquents. His first book, *Families of the Slums,* explains his techniques and methods of assessing effective outcomes in family treatment. He developed action-oriented techniques, which were particularly helpful to these families, and trained therapists at the Child Guidance Center in Philadelphia. Although Minuchin has retired, professionals can receive excellent training in family therapy at the Child Guidance Center.

Through the continuous and persistent work of faculty and practitioners at these and other training centers, family therapy became known to the clinical community. Even though social workers had often seen members of the same family separately or sometimes together in the early 1900s, this family therapy training movement emanated from medical centers backed by the results of substantial and costly research. The entrepreneurs of family therapy had a significant and widespread effect on the adoption of family therapy by the treatment community.

The 1970s: Certification and Licensure of Marital and Family Therapists as Health-Care Professionals

There was no separate professional association for family therapists. Family therapists belonged to the professional association of their specialty, for example, psychiatry, psychology, social work, counseling, ministry, or nursing. They requested that AAMC change its name to the American Association of Marriage and Family Counselors (AAMFC) and that they be allowed to join. AAMC did change its name to AAMFC and eventually voted to change it again to the American Association for Marriage and Family Therapy (AAMFT).

Such changes are significant because they are symbols of the evolution of the image of the membership to an identity as health care providers. A convergence of family-life education, marriage counseling, and family therapy had occurred to form a separate field of marital and family therapy with emphasis on the relationship context.

With many members already employed in medical and health-care settings, the association began to lobby for certification or licensure bills to recognize independent practice as health-care providers. Many state legislatures passed such bills. Licensed marital and family therapists began to receive third-party payments from insurance companies as approved health-care providers.

During the 1970s, research on family therapy continued. A research base had been built. In particular, research studies on healthy family interactions began. Lewis, Beavers, Gossett, and Phillips (1976) wrote *No Single Thread: Psychological Health in Family Systems,* based on 7 years of research at the Timberlawn Psychiatric Research Foundation in Dallas, Texas. In this study, family interaction was videotaped and analyzed to identify the characteristics that distinguished the optimally healthy from the adequate, the mid-range, and the severely dysfunctional families.

The 1980s: Toward Integration of Theoretical Models, Specialization, and Self-Help

With the proliferation of diverse theories of marital and family therapy during the 1970s, a search for integrative models accelerated. More than 50 journal articles alone were published in a 5-year span to attempt to reconcile the complexity of techniques being used in the field and to provide a unifying theoretical framework that would give direction for their appropriate implementation. In these efforts, there was increased collaboration among researchers, academic theoreticians, and clinical practitioners, many of whom played more than one role.

Efforts toward professionalization intensified. The number of accredited programs increased, as did the number of states with certification or licensing bills. Additional specializations within the field of marital and family therapy developed for which credentials were created, such as Family Life Educator and Divorce Mediator.

Additional research centers were developed to study healthy families such as the Center for Family Strengths at the University of Nebraska-Lincoln, directed by Nick Stinnett. The 10th anniversary celebration of the center was held in May 1987 at the Tenth Annual Symposium on Building Family Strengths. David Olson and associates (1979) developed the Circumplex Model of healthy family functioning and studied a cross-section of families at different stages in the family life cycle. David Reiss and colleagues (1981) identified the characteristics of the family paradigm in healthy families.

Such research paralleled and undergirded the emerging emphasis on family members and families taking responsibility for the quality of their lives and their health, with preventive and therapeutic programs increasing in marital enrichment and family enhancement. David and Vera Mace founded the Association of Couples for Marriage Enrichment in July of 1973 on their 40th wedding anniversary. They have trained lay leaders to run self-help support groups for marital enrichment and to train others to continue the work.

The Marriage Encounter movement begun by Father Calvo in the Catholic church flourished, as did marriage enrichment efforts in other churches such as those of Leon and Antoinette Smith in the United Methodist church. Family support activities, similar to the programs in place in the Mormon church where one night a week is family night, were beginning to be encouraged by diverse churches and agencies.

While efforts to professionalize increased in the 1980s, theoreticians grappled with models to integrate the diverse approaches in the field into one all-encompassing theoretical frame. Special credentials to recognize high levels of skill in particular specializations within marital and family therapy were developed. Research on healthy families buttressed the increased growth of marital and family enrichment. Similar to the early beginnings of the field, family life education and therapeutic treatment were intertwined, often being delivered by the same professionals. The marital and family therapist had become a fully functioning and recognized member of the health-care team.

THE 1990s AND BEYOND: THE FUTURE
OF MARITAL AND FAMILY THERAPY

There will be increased need and consumer demand for marital and family therapy. With the high divorce rate, a concomitant increase in blended families, and the acceptance of professional helpers, especially as they are popularized on television, more married couples and families will seek help to make their lives better.

Therapists will be more highly trained in a multitude of techniques within a systems perspective and a theoretical framework, which integrates seemingly diverse approaches. Often they will specialize in a particular area of treatment, such as divorce mediation or sex therapy. These therapists will continue to learn new techniques by attending workshops and participating in externships. Typically, they will also deliver classes to the community in marital and family enrichment.

As the family's role in social support is highlighted and better utilized to confront chronic illnesses, programs will be increased in medical settings to involve families in the compliance and treatment of patients with diverse illnesses. Family therapy, marital therapy, family support groups, and marital support groups will flourish within in-patient and out-patient programs.

Research on family therapy will continue to increase. Particular approaches to treating specific family problems at various stages of the family life cycle will be tested. Research studies on healthy single-parent families, healthy stepfamilies, and healthy military families will be funded to identify coping skills and to design programs based on knowledge of healthy prototypes.

Most importantly, the number of married couples and families who take responsibility for their health and quality of life will increase dramatically. They will seek out enrichment programs and family enhancement activities. In particular, marital support groups such as those sponsored by the Association of Couples for Marriage Enrichment, as well as those initiated by local and national churches, will increase.

As the link between relationships and emotional as well as physical illnesses is better documented, marital and family therapy will be even more widely recognized as a treatment modality and reimbursed as health care by insurance companies. Marital and family therapists will be increasingly viewed as full members of the health-care delivery team across the country. The field will become more professionalized, and special interest groups will increase in strength within the diverse professional associations in the helping fields.

In summary, the reconciliation of seeming opposites will occur as there will be increasing professionalization of marital and family therapy and at the same time a proliferation of self-help and growth groups with lay leadership; research on specific techniques for specific problems of families at different stages of the family life cycle and research on healthy families of diverse structures and cultures; and, finally the involvement of spouses and families in the treatment of individuals with chronic illnesses and research on family support to prevent disabling illnesses.

SUMMARY

Marital and family therapy can be defined as services provided to individuals, couples, and families that focus on the improvement of their relationships. A marital and family therapist views client(s) from a broad perspective, basing interventions on how clients interact within their social systems—their marriages, families, communities, and societies.

Research studies of therapeutic outcome document the effectiveness of marital and family therapy. For example, conjoint marital treatment—seeing the couple together in the same session—leads to improvement and stability in the marriage.

The macrosystems in which the marital and family therapist functions—the health-care delivery system and the history of marriage and family therapy as a profession—were emphasized in this chapter. These broad contextual factors influence the practice of marital and family therapy today.

Models of health versus illness are expanding to include psychological and social factors, which influence health and illness. *Health* is defined as dynamic progress toward optimal levels of functioning and well-being achieved through balance between external and internal environments. To combat such degenerative illnesses as heart disease and AIDS, people need to change their lifestyles to reduce risk factors and to increase the social support found in their marital and family relationships.

Human beings can move toward health in the developmental domains of the Health-Illness Wheel: spiritual, intellectual, behavioral, emotional, imaginal, sensual, sexual, physical, and interpersonal/social.

Marital and family therapists assist people in moving toward health as they serve these primary roles in the health-care system: (1) delivery of acute-care services; (2) enhancement of the family support of patients suffering from acute, chronic, or terminal diseases; (3) alteration of the perceptions that family members have of illnesses; and (4) health promotion.

Historically, prevention and treatment have been intertwined in the practice of marriage and family therapy. The ten main forces influencing the development of marital and family therapy include (1) the family life education movement, (2) federal and state legislation, (3) meeting the societal needs of children, (4) the leadership of professionals, (5) the beginning and continued growth of marriage counseling, (6) the contributions of sexologists and sex therapy, (7) the psychoanalytic movement and reactions to it, (8) the contributions of communication theorists, (9) research on schizophrenia, and (10) healthy family research.

The history of marital and family therapy can be divided into eight periods: (1) a focus on prevention before 1930 with the beginning of family life education; (2) the strengthening of family life education in the 1930s; (3) the professionalization of marriage counseling in the 1940s; (4) the pioneer family therapy research of the 1950s; (5) the training of family therapists in the 1960s; (6) professionalization of marital and family therapists as health-care providers in the 1970s; (7) trends toward integration of theoretical models in the 1980s, with the opposing forces of specialization and self-help activities proliferating; and (8) the reconciliation of opposites in the future of marital and family therapy.

The following exercises are optional. Your instructor may assign some to be done in class or at home, or you may be free to explore them on your own. People have diverse learning styles. The exercises at the end of this and each chapter are aids to accessing the material, in order to understand it. One person may learn the material better through completing a given exercise while another person may be turned off by or detest that exercise. People are different; this is what makes the world such an exciting and interesting place.

1. On one side of a sheet of paper, write down your expectations for this course. Turn the paper over and write down what you think might block or impede you in the course. Break up into small groups, and appoint a group leader, who will report to the class. Share your expectations with the group. The group leaders will report on the groups' observations as your instructor asks them. Share the impeding factors with your group. The group leaders will report as your instructor asks them.

2. Close your eyes. Imagine a marital and family therapist at work. When your instructor directs, turn to the person next to you and talk about your mental picture of a marital and family therapist. How would you define marital and family therapy?

3. What is the role of a marital and family therapist in health care? Share your ideas with your partner in the dyads formed according to your instructor's directions.

4. Using the Health-Illness Wheel in Figure 1–2, plot your present status in each of the areas of development by marking the spokes of the wheel. At the end of the course, where would you like to be in each area? Devise a plan to reach your health goals. Choose a partner and share your assessments. Encourage each other in your plans, providing social support.

5. Take out a piece of paper and draw a time line representing the history of marital and family therapy, including various prevention and intervention events. How do prevention and intervention relate throughout the history of marital and family therapy?

Chapter 2
What Is a Family System?

Family systems are like quiet streams. Looking the same to observers, they are continuously changing as fresh water energetically flows into their stagnant pools, recreating them from within.

Michele Thomas, 1989

A definition of marital and family therapy is incomplete without examining the subject of treatment, namely, the family. The importance of such an examination is obvious given the central role the family has played in all societies. The family system continues to have a vital role in America today; however, its traditional existence has been altered in such a way that society must begin to redefine what is meant by *family*. This is particularly significant for marital and family therapists, who must assimilate a broadened, worldwide view of the family system.

THE EVOLVING FAMILY

Before the turn of the century in the United States, defining the word *family* would have been fairly straightforward. After all, a family was a group connected by blood or legal bonds who usually, but not always, lived within the same physical residence. For example, Aunt Henrietta who retired to Florida was part of the family by blood, even though she lived many miles from her children in Pennsylvania. Children who had been legally adopted were (and still are) considered members of the nuclear family. The cultural image of the family consisted of the father as breadwinner, the mother in the kitchen as homemaker, and the children around the hearth.

Some scholars today (Gutman, 1976) question this idyllic picture of the family, saying that it represented a stereotype or myth even in those days. During pioneer times, for example, life was physically strenuous and many adults died of tuberculosis, pneumonia, yellow fever, typhoid, and smallpox. Hence, there must have been single-parent families on the frontier, as well as stepfamilies, extended families, and orphans. Working women were also part of the homesteading efforts on the prairie lands, where wives often helped their husbands with the enormous amount of labor required to homestead. In the years before the Emancipation Act, it was often the custom to separate black families by sending the father to another plantation while the mother and children remained. This fear of being divided as a family was a constant, living terror for black families, as Haley (1976) so aptly portrayed in *Roots*.

This traditional view of the nuclear family—husband as provider, wife as homemaker, and children under 18 living at home—continues to remain the predominant view of the "ideal" family. In fact, when people of diverse backgrounds are asked to draw a picture of their ideal family, most invariably produce the nuclear family. Very few people, if any, in the context of a group setting draw variations on the nuclear family. Jung (1959) might say that the collective unconscious is at work here by eliciting the faint impressions from the unconscious of what past generations considered the ideal family and thereby stimulating the blueprint for family life today. This is evident when people are asked why their family should be organized as a nuclear family, and they can respond only that a deep, emotional gut reaction prompted their responses. Jung's collective unconscious—of which there has been no scientific proof—is only one possible theory for this phenomenon. After all, the concept of family is culturally defined at an early age, when children begin to observe their own families as well as others they may visit or see in the media.

Yet the nuclear family is not the only structure that rears healthy children and meets the emotional needs of its members. Due to an increased number of divorces; the importance of mobility in a person's career; a decrease in the annual, per capita median national disposable income; and the aging of a majority of America's population, the traditional nuclear family has been altered to produce myriad examples of family structures: cohabiting couples, communes, commuter marriages, extended families, single-parent families, stepfamilies, and therapeutic communities are among the present-day options.

A phenomenological definition of *family* may be more inclusive than what the term *family* means in 20th century America. If a person perceives other individuals as family, such as in the case of a therapeutic community like Alcoholics Anonymous, then those individuals are in fact the person's family. Therefore, *family* may be defined as any group of people who are related legally or by blood, or who are perceived to be family by an individual. Such a definition includes those who are united by ties of marriage, blood, adoption, common-law marriage, support groups, communes, or religious communities such as monasteries or convents. Thus, a person's family fold would consist of all those to whom that person feels close and with whom the person feels comfortable, even if they are not necessarily living in the same residence. For example, the black community has one of the lowest rates of runaways because black families have traditionally taken in children who are having problems and have allowed them to become part of their families (Weber, 1977; Wolf, 1983).

Thus, many people must be living in alternative family structures. According to the United States Bureau of the Census (1982), only 18% of all American households were composed of a nuclear family in which the father worked and the mother stayed home with the children. Most Americans are presently living in what would have been called nontraditional families in earlier historical periods, and diversity in family structure is the norm today. Thus, therapists cannot assume that their patients are members of traditional, nuclear families, but rather that they are probably part of other types of family structures.

With this assumption, therapists should exert special care when using language during their sessions with clients. For example, a therapist should rarely use the words *father* and *mother* to describe a family, especially in group settings. The use of such words may be damaging to someone who does not come from a home with a mother or father. For example, suppose a therapist asks a group of clients to draw a picture of the family dinner table; to place circles for mother, father, and children at the table; and to color each circle to represent the feelings experienced toward that person. (This is a popular family exercise.) Even before the therapist finishes explaining the directions, one of the women begins sobbing and runs out of the room. Upon further discovery, the therapist finds that she felt alienated and hurt because she had been raised by her cousin, and they did not own a dinner table. To avoid this kind of misunderstanding, directions might be rephrased as "Draw the people who were important to you when you were growing up." These instructions do not presuppose any particular family pattern or structure, but rather leave the choice of whom to include up to each individual.

For the marital and family therapist, the variations on family structure must be seen as positive and necessary. The therapist places importance on identifying the strengths of a family's structure and what that structure contributes to the overall healthy functioning of its members. After all, there is no one way of being a family, but rather many different ways of creating strong families.

Often, people have mental images of what they think a normal family is. From television shows like "Leave It to Beaver" and interactions with teachers and other professionals, children may think that a nuclear family is typical when this is no longer even the norm (Figure 2–1). Alternative structures that might be seen as negative or abnormal (but are actually frequent occurrences today) by therapists and/or their patients include commuter marriages, single-parent families, blended families or stepfamilies, single adults, emotional families of adults and children, cohabiting couples, and extended families. As an example, a commuter marriage might pose a problem for a therapist who saw the couple as divided over commitment to family or career. Studies indicate, however, that partners in such marriages are highly committed to both career and family (Winfield, 1985).

The concept of family continues to include the idea of a mutual exchange in which needs are met, and it is still the social milieu in which the developmental tasks of socialization and individuation occur. In addition, most would agree that the family provides for the major emotional needs of its members. As the structure of the family changes and diversifies, so does its functions.

However, many other types of needs, formerly provided for in the context of a nuclear family, are being satisfied in other ways and by other means. For example, a

FIGURE 2–1   All family structures have strengths

"We never had a chance, coming from a single-parent family."

Courtesy of *The Spectator,* London.

wife may have a job and not need her husband to support her financially, or a teenage child may take a part-time job to pay for clothes, entertainment, and transportation. Also, a wife or husband may spend time with a same-sex best friend while the other spouse works extra hours. In general, the traditional family of the past had to place more importance on providing for the physical survival of its members, but today the bottom line for American families is satisfying the emotional needs of its members. Often divorce occurs because these emotional needs are not being met, even though financial, physical, social, and intellectual needs are being satisfied.

GENERAL SYSTEMS THEORY

The family is still the major network in which human beings find satisfaction for many of their needs. That network functions as a system and as such has special characteristics. Examining these characteristics is vital to understanding the nature of families and how they operate. The first question one might ask is simply, "What is a system?" So it is here that a discussion of family systems begins.

The basis for the development of systems concepts is biology and in the helping professions originates from Ludwig von Bertalanffy's book, *Problems of Life: An Evaluation of Modern Biological Thought* (1949). He postulated several laws of life. Like the Heraclitean metaphor of a river in which fresh, new water is ever-flowing, life is never the same and a person cannot experience the exact same stream twice. Living organisms are happening, a continuous flow of energy and matter passing through and constituting these life forms.

One characteristic of living organisms is continuous change. On the surface they appear to be relatively constant, but this is due to the dynamic birth, growth, repair, and death of their subsystems. Individual cells may grow and die, only to be replaced by new cells within the organism.

Living organisms are open systems, continuously taking in and giving off matter and maintaining a steady state. The organism is equifinal; that is, the state that is reached is dependent only on the ratio between outflow and inflow, between growth and decay, and not on the initial conditions of the system. A balance between the inflow and outflow is called the steady state, a characteristic of an open system. Self-regulation is a key property of living organisms.

Chemical and other non-living systems exhibit entropy (a decrease of energy over time), leading to more chaotic organization and deterioration—closed systems. In contrast, living organisms take in energy from the environment over time, leading to higher levels of organization—open systems. In *General System Theory: Foundations, Development, Applications,* von Bertalanffy (1986) defines a system as "a set of elements standing in interrelations" (p. 55)—a complex of interacting parts.

HUMAN SYSTEMS

In *A Systems View of Man,* von Bertalanffy (1981) points to the human being's use of symbols as distinguishing the species from animals. Symbols permit the development of a history, the ability to think about actions in advance, and true purposiveness. A person can choose an act or thing which is desirable within a particular frame of reference—a value.

Human beings are also active systems. They create disequilibrium, influencing a higher level of the *steady state,* advancing toward greater levels of organization and functioning. Human beings as open systems exhibit *anamorphosis,* or movement toward higher forms of order. In addition to gratifying one's needs and adapting to the environment, people create their lives obtaining "function pleasure" from the nature of the activities themselves that they choose to perform.

Paradoxically, a human system seeks change and stability at the same time. Anamorphosis is the inclination of a system to grow and change becoming innovative and creative. Homeostasis is the tendency of the system to maintain stability. Each human being develops a balance between anamorphosis (change) and homeostasis (stability), which is called the steady state.

An active human organism seeks out change while at the same time attempting to remain stable. At particular times of the life cycle, a person may look for more change than at other times. For example, at mid-life individuals often make significant changes in their lifestyles because they realize that life is finite and time is running out. Even as they make these changes, they attempt to keep some aspects of their daily routines the same, providing stability.

The steady state or balance between change and stability evolves to higher levels throughout the life cycle as individuals tolerate increasing stress and changes, while endeavoring to become more stable, organized, and routine. The steady state of a healthy, functioning adult at 60 will be greater than the steady state of that adult at 20. In contrast, the steady state of severely dysfunctional individuals may decrease with age as they become more chaotic and disorganized.

As is the case with individuals, anamorphosis must occur over the family life cycle. Families seek long-term goals for change: to send their children to college, develop a family business, or build a new home. Parents should not treat functioning teenagers the same way that they treat 3-year-olds. The rules should be different. At each developmental stage, these changes will be made to accommodate the needs of growing children, while the stability (homeostasis) of certain family routines continues. The garbage will be taken out. The clothes will be washed. Meals will be prepared. The house notes and utility bills will be paid. Certain repetitive, emotional patterns that reduce tension in the system will be followed, such as father always shouting at the dog. The balance between change and stability represents the steady state. The level of the steady state will increase over the life cycle of the family as greater levels of change are combined with increased levels of routine.

Subsystems

The family can be viewed as a living organism composed of interdependent subsystems, or smaller complexes of interacting parts within a larger system. The subsystems include the parental coalition, the sibling subsystem, the parent-child dyads, and the individual subsystems represented by each family member (Figure 2–2).

In addition, the family is one subsystem of the ethnic, cultural group to which the family belongs, which in turn is a subsystem of the neighborhood, which is a subsystem of the community, which is a subsystem of the state, which is a subsystem of

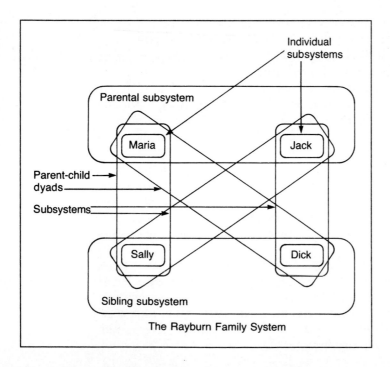

FIGURE 2–2 Subsystems of the Rayburn family system

The sibling subsystem. An older sister helps her younger sister, even though she may not want help!

the nation, which is but another subsystem of the world. Becvar and Becvar (1982) indicate that any subsystem is ultimately part of a cosmic suprasystem. An example is the Strobel family who represents a subsystem of the German Catholic ethnic cultural group of the German Village neighborhood of the city of Columbus in the state of Ohio, part of the United States, the world, and the universe.

But subsystems have boundaries that separate them from other subsystems and the larger system as a whole. Schultz (1984) indicates that elements of a subsystem resemble each other in certain boundary-defining behaviors. Such behaviors are usually relative rather than absolute. For example, teachers typically talk and students ask questions, but in a healthy classroom students also make presentations, thereby talking to the rest of the class, but even then they usually don't talk as much as the teachers. Clarifying boundaries is helpful because if they become too rigid (not allowing communication with the larger system, which can lead to disengagement) or too diffuse (communicating so much with other subsystems or the system as a whole that the subsystem becomes enmeshed with the larger system and it is difficult to distinguish the two), problems in conducting external or internal affairs can arise.

Another way of looking at boundaries is simply by asking who talks to whom about what. There are certain secrets that each subsystem has that they will not share with the other subsystems or the larger system as a whole. For example, in a healthy family, the mother and father typically do not discuss their sex life with the children. When the marriage is conflicted and on the verge of divorce, a spouse may confide in a child about the affairs of the other spouse, thereby diffusing the boundary of the parental subsystem and enmeshing the child in the conflicted marital relationship. Likewise, children often will not discuss the pranks they have played or their indiscretions with their parents, reserving these for long talks with their brothers or sisters. The subject of surprise teenage parties that may have occurred while parents were out of town will not be volunteered to parents, but rather earmarked for discussions only within the sibling subsystem.

It is important for the marital and family therapist to observe very carefully the boundaries of the subsystems of a presenting family. Do the parents talk to each other, or does one of the children interrupt, talking in between parents on a consistent basis? This may indicate a diffuse boundary of the parental subsystem, with an enmeshed symptomatic child whose energy toward differentiation of the self has been dissipated in attempting to reduce the tension within the marital coalition. Do the parents sit together on the couch, or does one parent sit with a child on the couch, leaving the other parent to sit in a chair alone? This could exemplify a parentified child enmeshed in the diffuse boundary of the parental coalition. Are the parents concentrating so much on each other that they do not notice the child in the treatment room (which can occur in the honeymoon stage of a remarriage)? Here, a rigid parental boundary permitting little communication with the stepchildren may exist. The concept of "boundary" is, indeed, a fruitful one for the clinician.

Organization and Structure

According to Nichols and Everett (1986), organization implies the consistent way in which the people in the family system are related. For example, a family could be organized around a matriarch and her compliant husband, or around a dominant male patriarch and his submissive spouse. One technique of identifying the organization of a family system is the family drawing. Even young children often indicate in a poignant way the organization of their own families (see Figure 2–3). The proximity of the family members and their sizes, detail, and other physical characteristics can imply a certain organization within the family. Such information is helpful to the therapist in developing directions for treatment.

Such family pictures also point to the structure or arrangement of both the components and subsystems of the family. *Structure* has many meanings. It can refer to the various family arrangements, such as a nuclear family, a single-parent family, or an extended family. For example, when asked to draw their family, children being brought up in extended families usually include an elderly grandmother or grandfather who currently lives with them.

FIGURE 2–3 Jake's drawings of himself with his father and stepmother (A) and with his mother and stepfather (B). The organization of both families is evident, as is the increased amount of interaction for Jake when he is with his mother.

In contrast, in structural approaches to family therapy, *structure* typically means the way in which the components and subsystems of the family are arranged. For example, Minuchin (1974) diagrams the structure of three families (Figure 2–4). In the family diagrammed on the left, there is a healthy parental coalition with a permeable boundary between the parents and the child. Mom and dad share thoughts and feelings about their sex life only between themselves (a parental boundary) but listen to the thoughts and feelings of their child, supporting the child's growth and differentiation. In the middle diagram, the boundary between the mother and the child is diffuse. The mother talks about the father to the child. The mother feels closer to the child than to the father—an example of a parentified child taking the place of the father. This structure can easily occur if the father is alcoholic or absent from the home. In the diagram on the right, the boundary between mother, father, and child is diffuse. When the mother talks to the father, the child interrupts. When the parents argue the child is caught in the middle—a triangulated structure. In both the parentified and triangulated structures the child's energy is drained and not available for growth and differentiation. Minuchin calls these diagrams "structural analyses." One of the main tasks of the therapist in an initial session of family therapy is to observe the family interaction in order to create a structural map of the family.

Culture has a definite impact on the structure and boundaries within families. According to Casas (1979), South American families are patriarchal. The father plays a dominant role in family decision-making and relates with other male friends at a deep level over the long term. In a number of African cultures, the role of mother is held in greater esteem than that of wife (Thomas & Dansby, 1984). Children are often closer to their mothers than their mothers are to their husbands—a normal, socially exemplary structure in these cultures. Thus, a therapist in analyzing the structure of the family should be careful not to judge certain family structures as better than others, but rather should honor the cultural traditions of the presenting family, working within the parameters of the given culture.

FIGURE 2–4   Structural analyses of families

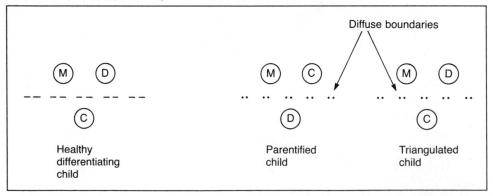

Reprinted by permission of the publishers from *Families and Family Therapy* by Salvador Minuchin, Cambridge, MA: Harvard Univ. Press, Copyright © 1974 by the President and Fellows of Harvard College.

The Ainu chieftain represents an anthropological mystery. The Ainu are a Caucasian race found on the northernmost island of Japan—Hokkaido. No one knows how Caucasians found their way there, although there are many theories. Each culture has its own set of rules that set expectations for behaviors.

Structure also carries the connotation of chain of command. Within a business, the structure determines to whom memoranda should be sent and to whom an employee reports. Although information may flow informally outside the structure of the institution, the formal mechanism of information distribution is the structure. The military establishment is an example of a hierarchical structure in which members of each level of the organization report to the next higher level. In the family system, a structural analysis tells the family therapist who gives orders to whom and under what conditions. To uncover the structure of the family in the initial session, some therapists ask the children who gives them orders and who punishes them if they disobey. The structure of the family is thus revealed.

Rules

All family systems have rules or ways of operating. Some rules are unspoken and others are negotiated. Since human beings use symbols, they can perceive future goals and tell others what behaviors are expected within a human system. Family rules are expectations for certain types of behavior that are set by the parent(s) in the family system.

Too many rules and too few rules can create problems—a balance is optimal (Patterson & Stouthamer-Loeber, 1984). In healthy families, parents make rules together, discussing them to reach consensus before implementing the rules with the children. Some suggestions for sticking together include expecting each parent (even divorced or separated parents) to work as a teammate when making rules, making rules that both parents believe in, meeting regularly for a short time to go over any needs regarding rule making or enforcement, negotiating rules together before bringing them up with children, and supporting both joint decisions and the other parent who is enforcing the rule (Doub & Scott, 1987). Children often try to divide and conquer, playing one parent against another, so negotiating differences on the part of the parents is particularly important.

Regardless of the type of family structure, consistency in the process of making rules and enforcing them is crucial to the psychological health of the children. A single parent whose mother babysits the children should discuss and decide upon the rules with his mother, with the dyad acting as a parental coalition. Having someone with whom to discuss the rules and who consistently enforces them gives the parent confidence and engenders respect for the parent from the children. This person may be a babysitter, an ex-spouse, a mother, a stepparent, or a professional. For example, home visitation programs have significant positive outcomes because it does help a parent to have someone to talk with and listen to parenting problems on a consistent basis (Gray & Ruttle, 1980; Greenspan & Wieder, 1984; Thomas & Dansby, 1985).

Rules should state clearly what behaviors are expected. Parents should also be ready to enforce the rules if they are not obeyed. Often, setting rules so that natural consequences result from breaking the rules is most helpful in teaching children responsibility for their own behavior. Doub and Scott (1987) present the following tips and traps concerning rules. Rules must be necessary (or wanted by the parents or children), measurable, enforceable, changeable (if no longer effective), and stated in sentence form. Consider the comfort of both the parents and the children when setting rules, and try to anticipate where and when a child will need a rule. Although parents should expect resistance, they should try to hear their children's views before making final decisions.

Roles

Each member of the family system plays a role exhibiting a set of predictable behaviors. Often role behavior is strongly influenced by the family of origin. When people marry, they often begin the marriage by playing the role that was played in the family of origin, or the opposite of it. For example, Juanita came from a family where her mother did not work. Her mother cooked all the meals and did the household cleaning. Her father sat in his easy chair, where Juanita's mother would bring him a cup of coffee or a snack. Before her marriage, Juanita had been independent with a responsible job. After the wedding, she noticed that she felt guilty when the dishes were not done and the meals were not cooked for her new husband. She found herself doing more and more for her husband even though he never asked her for anything. She began to play the role of the wife based on the predictable pattern of behaviors from her family of origin.

As another example, Jennifer grew up in an abusive home where both her parents were alcoholics. She could hardly wait to leave when she graduated from high school, and she married one month after graduation. Jake, her new husband, was quiet. She perceived him as the strong, silent type, the opposite from her loud, angry father. She knew that she could make things better, and her marriage would be different from that of her parents. She worked harder and harder to please Jake, keeping her feelings inside and never asking for anything. The pressure built up inside her, especially when Jake bought a new car without even talking to her about it and charged purchases at several stores. She could not understand why she was beginning to feel so anxious, even angry. When Jake and she went to the local dance hall, where they would have a few drinks, she would feel much better, sometimes letting Jake have it. Jennifer had begun to abuse Jake, adopting the abusive role from her family of origin. Pressman (1987) uses family-of-origin therapy in the treatment of abusive clients to help them confront the roles learned from parents.

In families, the roles of husband and wife are continuously renegotiated through short verbal and nonverbal interactions in each relationship. These roles need to change with time and the developmental stages of the participants (Becvar & Becvar, 1982). Learning to talk openly about expectations and negotiating acceptable expectations for each partner at a given time are major tasks for a family. In addition, each person brings a different perception of what it means to be a parent to the family system. Negotiating expected role behaviors without seeing one way as the only way is a continuous process within the family system.

Besides the spouse and parental roles, family members may play other roles such as victim, persecutor, and rescuer, shifting from one role to another in a given situation (Nichols and Everett, 1986). There are many role games that people play in relationships (Berne, 1964). "Poor me" is one of the most common to elicit the help of someone else, thereby limiting responsibility for the self. A family therapist must be observant in order to identify and to understand what role each family member may be playing in a given family—the martyr role, the scapegoat, the hero. In playing such roles, people dissipate their energy from further differentiation and growth of a healthy self. There is only a finite amount of time. No one can give us more than 24 hours in one day. If most of this time is spent on game playing, there is no room for healthy self-exploration and pursuing activities based on interest.

The World View

Constantine (1986) indicates that families are makers of meaning. They provide individuals with a sense of identity and belonging. Most importantly, they encourage the production of shared constructs and ways of viewing the world. One of the most unsettling aspects of divorce is the destruction of meaning for the individuals involved and the challenge of the constructs by which the world is viewed and lives are lived.

According to von Bertalanffy (1981), human beings can contemplate their own deaths and use intellectual constructs as windows through which to view the world.

As a human system, each family has a *weltanschauung*, a way of perceiving the world or a world view. Some families see the world outside the family as a nurturing, positive place with caring people ready to help if asked. Other families view the world outside their home as a threatening place, where people cannot be trusted because they are against the family. Still other families not only see the world outside the family as a threatening place, they do not trust the motives of their own immediate family members, seeing them as malicious and focused on hurting them. (Domestic violence has a higher incidence in families with this view of the world.)

Families can be placed on a continuum from illness to health based on their *weltanschauung,* or world view (Figure 2–5). The healthiest families have the most optimistic view of the world and their place in it, while the most dysfunctional families mistrust their own family members and see the world as a threatening place where people cannot be trusted.

These basic expectations of the world color all the activities and human interactions in which family members engage. From expectancy theory (Phares, 1976; Rotter, 1966), it follows that these expectations become self-fulfilling prophecies. For example, if a family believes that the world is a positive place and that people will help if asked, a family member will have a higher probability of asking others for help when it is needed and will continue to ask others, even when rejected several times, not taking the rejections personally. Because of the law of probability, the more people a family member asks, the more likely that person is to find an individual who will help, fulfilling the expectation that indeed the world has helpful, caring people. It is as though members of these families were wearing "rose-colored glasses" through which they view human interactions. Such a perspective tends to prevent depression and to be linked to health (Abramson & Alloy, 1981; Alloy & Abramson, 1979).

Likewise, if a family sees the world outside the family as a threatening, dangerous place with people who cannot be trusted, a family member may approach a person for help and, if rejected the first time, think "See, I told you, nobody can be trusted." In

FIGURE 2–5   Family *weltanschauung* (world view) and health

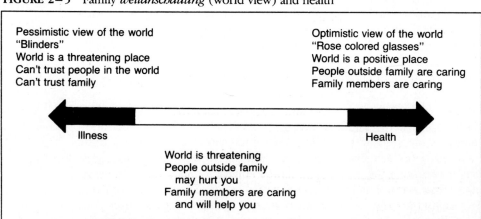

Pessimistic view of the world
"Blinders"
World is a threatening place
Can't trust people in the world
Can't trust family

Optimistic view of the world
"Rose colored glasses"
World is a positive place
People outside family are caring
Family members are caring

Illness

Health

World is threatening
People outside family
   may hurt you
Family members are caring
   and will help you

some cases, such a family member may expect a negative reply and thus may procrastinate in asking until the last minute, which increases the probability of a negative reply. After the first rejection, the family member will have a higher probability of giving up because the initial rejection has matched the family's expectation of the world.

Finally, in the family that views both family members and the outside world as people and places not to be trusted, a family member will probably not even ask people outside the family. Such a person will begin with the family only to be rejected, thereby saying, "Even my mother won't help because she doesn't love me, so how could anyone out there help?"

These examples of three families demonstrate how expectations affect behavior and reinforce themselves in self-fulfilling prophecies. Of course, there are many families at different points across the continuum of illness to health. Expectations have a definite effect on behavior, feelings, and outcomes of family life. It is crucial for marital and family therapists to become aware of the family's *weltanschauung* during the initial session and to tailor treatment plans, taking this all-encompassing factor into consideration.

The world view that each family brings to therapy determines to a great degree how the work will proceed. Extremely dysfunctional families may never trust the therapist enough to form a therapeutic alliance because their world view predisposes them to look for behaviors on the part of the therapist that render him untrustworthy. For example, Scheinfeld (1983) found that statements by the mothers supporting increased involvement by pre-adolescent black males in the world were linked to their future achievement, whereas defensive isolation on the part of the mothers—seeing the environment as threatening and controlling the pre-adolescent's every move—was related to low achievement.

Family therapists are attempting to influence the values, sentences, constructs, and meaning that the family brings to therapy, because these symbols of reality in the presenting family function in such a way that they produce symptoms in one or more of the family members. Psychopathology in our times is not based on lack of economic survival in the most basic sense, but rather on the lack of meaning or adoption of inappropriate symbolic needs for status, comfort, and position. True systems therapy addresses these expectancies of the world that families bring to the treatment room.

SPECIFIC CHARACTERISTICS OF THE FAMILY SYSTEM

The family system has certain characteristics typical of any other system: (1) the family is dynamic and changing constantly; (2) the family regulates itself to maintain homeostasis (providing for routine functions like preparation of meals, cleaning of clothes, and the provision of shelter); (3) the family operates according to the principle of equifinality—regardless of the initial source of the problem, the same patterns are used in the family to maintain balance; (4) all family behavior, including symptoms, serve positive functions for the entire family system; (5) every member of the family plays a part in the working of the whole—a holistic approach; and (6) every action in the family influences a reaction or feedback, although it is not a causal relationship.

The Family Is a Dynamic System

Each human being in the family is biologically changing, growing, developing, and aging, and each seeks out ways of meeting needs and actualizing to a more differentiated self. Each member of the family is changing, often at a different rate.

For example, the Gordon family is composed of Mary and John (the parental coalition), their teenage children (John Jr., aged 18, and Sally, aged 11), Grandpa Carl, and a cat named Duffy. John is questioning his career commitments at mid-life and is thinking about changing jobs. There has been a merger at the company where he has worked and a change of supervisors which have intensified John's feelings of dissatisfaction with what he is doing. Mary feels unloved and wonders what will happen to the family when John Jr. goes off to college. John Jr. is struggling with the task of deciding what college to attend. Each day he thinks he has found the perfect one to meet his needs, only to be enticed by a new catalog or the comments of a friend. Grandpa is concerned about his health and is reading about vitamins and diet which might eliminate some of the symptoms of his arthritis. Sally is experiencing the hormone changes associated with becoming a woman, expecting her first menstrual period at any moment. She often fluctuates between crying over a statement someone has made and wanting to be treated as an independent adult. Duffy the cat has experienced a loss of attention since Sally has been spending more time with her friends. He mopes and will not let anyone hold him.

Each member of this family system is changing, and the interactions between the members are changing. Even the composition and structure of this family are poised for change as the family moves along the developmental continuum from birth to death. Yet to look at this family from the outside, an astute observer would have to study the family carefully, as the routines of the family seem ritualized and constant.

Homeostasis

As a system, the family tends to return to a steady state. When there is an action, a reaction occurs in the family to balance the system. This system-adjusting mechanism was emphasized by Bateson (1972) in *Steps to an Ecology of Mind*. Similar to a chemical reaction, the system functions to restore equilibrium. However, homeostasis refers to the balance in metabolic functioning, whereby food is eaten and digested, keeping a chemical equilibrium in the body. By contrast, in a healthy family there is a disequilibrium leading to growth (anamorphosis) coupled with a homeostatic mechanism which determines routines, keeping the household going. The balance of anamorphosis and homeostasis represents the steady state of the open system. Often in families presenting for treatment, there is an emphasis on tension-reducing homeostatic process to the detriment of the creative growth producing disequilibrium. Families sometimes try hard to remain "stuck," repeating the same interactional patterns and maintaining the same routines. For example, the family who presents for treatment with teenagers who are required to go to bed at 8:00 P.M. like the younger children (simply because it is the routine of the family) is adhering rigidly to homeostasis. A disequilibrium could be introduced by encouraging the parents to listen to the teenage children. The hope is that the parents will initiate some changes while maintaining the continuity of certain routines (homeostasis) to achieve a higher functioning steady state.

Root, Fallon, and Friedrich (1986) in discussing the problems of bulimic families indicate that the homeostasis of the family system is maintained when parents who have a conflicted and distressful marital relationship focus on the bulimic behavior of the daughter. For example, Mark is a well-to-do dermatologist known for his innovative approaches in grafting hair. His wife Sharon is a first-born daughter in a family of girls who likes to manage and control the activities of the family. Mark and Sharon have difficulty resolving conflicts. Neither one wishes to give in, to compromise, or to find a new alternative solution. They argue constantly but never resolve any specific conflict. Lately the bickering has increased to the point that it is no longer pleasant to be at home when they are both there. Their 18-year-old daughter Alice, who is an active cheerleader, begins to overeat in a binge cycle, only to purge herself later. Her bulimic behavior concerns her parents, who unite to focus on ways of helping her. As they spend time talking about what to do about Alice, they stop their bickering. Alice has succeeded in keeping her parents together and in maintaining homeostasis in the family.

The action of the parents in arguing and escalating their conflicts but never resolving them influenced a reaction on the part of Alice, who developed symptoms of bulimia. This in turn influenced the parents to focus on her, thereby reducing the tension between them. The individual development of Alice as a person is delayed because her energy is dissipated in frightening symptoms that threaten her health and well-being. Just as in a chemical experiment, where the action of the chemicals influenced a reaction in the system until an equilibrium was achieved, the system has returned to the status quo. In contrast, a steady state would include encouragement of Alice's college plans (individuation) and weekend trips together for the parents (a disequilibrium) coupled with the continuance of routines such as meals (homeostasis).

Equifinality

The family system is equifinal; that is, the steady state that is reached is dependent only on the ratio between outflow and inflow, between growth and decay, and not on the initial conditions of the system. Okun and Rappaport (1980) give the example of the family that is scapegoating one of its members. Even though the oldest child ate the pie in the refrigerator, the family blames the middle child for not making popcorn, which would have saved the pie. The results are the same no matter where they begin: The middle child is blamed even if another child started the problem.

These ingrained interactional patterns in the family are repeated and reach the same result, bringing the system to equilibrium and homeostasis. It is the principle of equifinality that most often creates the difficulties that bring families to treatment. The identified patient who is the scapegoat of the family is the reason for which the family presents for treatment. This child feels the pain of the family in a special way and is always blamed for the tension of the family.

Another example of equifinality is the situation in which a grandmother raised five grandchildren together. The mother of three of the children had died of tuberculosis, so the grandmother was helping her son raise them. Two of the children had parents who were stage performers and always on the road, so the grandmother agreed to raise them for her daughter, for which the daughter sent sizable cash each month. When the grandmother attempted to discipline the children, she used the same interactional pattern, regardless of what occurred or which child acted up. In an unconscious effort to ensure that the children of her wealthy daughter were happy and never complained, she was gentle with their discipline but harsh with the oldest grandson, Fred, the child of her son. If Dorothy and Harvey climbed into a tree, she would say, "If you don't come down from that tree, I'll spank Fred." Fred was the scapegoat of the system that operated according to the principle of equifinality. Although Dorothy and Harvey were the source of the initial problem, the results were the same: Fred was the child who was always punished. Fred's self-esteem suffered, and he grew up with intense feelings of inadequacy. Regardless of how well he performed, the results were always the same.

All Behavior Is Functional

In a family system every behavior serves a function. Treadway (1985) indicates that a symptom may be a family's way of reaching out to the world outside the family. The behavior serves the function of engaging concerned helpers. In some cases, a behavior may serve a protective function for the system. If a father is alcoholic and a mother is stuck in an entrenched pattern of trying to convince him to quit drinking, a child may manifest a symptom such as drug abuse, which helps stabilize the system. Thus, family therapists or counselors should continually ask themselves, "What positive function does this behavior serve for the total family system?" One family therapist usually thanks the identified patient for having the symptom that brought the family into treatment.

Another example illustrating the function of behavior in systems is proposed by Root, Fallon, and Friedrich in *Bulimia: A Systems Approach to Treatment*. In an overprotective family, the bulimia allows the identified patient to remain dependent and young. The symptom justifies the worries of the parents that their daughter does, in fact, need to be protected and is not ready for launching. The bulimia permits the daughter to shut her feelings down when they might be unacceptable to the family if expressed. The symptoms provide a method of creating a boundary or personal space, especially between the enmeshed mother and daughter. The bulimic can express anger in a passive way without direct rebellion. In bulimic families, the father is often the scapegoat and the child experiences guilt at the thought of leaving the mother alone with the father. The parents may unite to convey a familiar message that leaving home is premature. The system returns to homeostasis at the expense of the child's development to adulthood.

Wholeness

The property of a family system that delineates the relationship between the system and its components is called wholeness. The whole is greater than the sum of its parts. For example, as Okun and Rappaport (1980) explain, if you are going to visit Harold and Rebecca Simons and their children Peter and Michele, you are visiting the Simons family. If Peter is away at college, you are still visiting the Simons family. Likewise if one member of a family comes for treatment, the whole system will be affected to a greater degree than the sum of the changes within each individual in the system. Therefore, it is better for a member of a family or the total family to be involved in treatment than not to experience any mode of treatment at all. The system will be affected by the individual therapy of one parent.

Circularity

One of the most useful concepts emanating from systems approaches to the family is the concept of circularity. When an action occurs in the family, predictable reactions will occur (Figure 2–6). Questions of what, when, how, and with whom lead to factual data from which the sequence of interactions can be mapped. Rather than linear thinking, in which x causes y, there is no cause-and-effect relationship; therefore, blaming is diffused. In linear thinking, a person causes something, which means the person can be blamed, thereby allowing the blamer not to take responsibility for his actions.

Dulfano (1982) sees this wider focus as an advantage of the systems model. A family member is seen as acting and reacting in a chain. A therapist can trace the sequence of interaction. For example, Mel had a stressful interaction with his boss at work and came home to drink two stingers. Seeing his behavior, his wife Ora reacted with a question about how he was feeling, to which he angrily replied. He was tired and angry with his boss. He drank to numb the pain. Ora was concerned but it sounded like nagging to Mel. He became angry with her. She was hurt. He felt guilty and

---

Linear causality

A influences B, but B does not influence A.

"I treat you like a child because you behave like a child."

"I behave like a child because you treat me like a child."

A ⟶ B

Circularity

A and B are in dynamic interaction.

"When I treat you like a child, you behave like a child, and then I treat you like a child even more and you behave even more like a child. We sure have a vicious cycle going, don't we."

"When I behave like a child, you treat me like a child, and then I behave like a child even more. We are sure caught up with each other, aren't we."

FIGURE 2–6 Linear and circular causality

From *System Theory and Family Therapy: A Primer* (pp. 6–7) by R. J. Becvar and D. S. Becvar, 1982, Lanham, MD: University Press of America. Reprinted by permission.

ashamed. He drank to numb the pain, and so on. Thus, certain behaviors form a circular chain of actions and reactions. The therapist can work with this circular sequence in the therapy session without blaming either partner.

Huberty and Huberty (1986) point out that causality is circular in systems theory. When one family member does or says something, it is a stimulus to which another family member responds, and this stimulus evokes additional responses in another family member (see Figure 2–7). This pattern of circular causality is more complex than a simple stimulus-response, cause-effect linear paradigm. Bowen (1978) contrasts systems thinking with conventional thinking by emphasizing that systems approaches focus on what human beings do and not on why they do it. What happened (the facts of what, how, when, and where) is the key, rather than worrying about why. The Milan style of family therapy actually utilizes circular questioning to maximize and make use of the property of circularity of the family system in a special way.

Feedback and Cybernetics   —thermostat

Feedback is the property of the system that represents this interaction between the parts of the system whereby information about performance influences future responses in a closed loop (Keeney, 1983). For example, a heating system has a computer control. When the temperature drops below a certain point, the computer is activated and turns on the furnace. After the furnace is on for an allotted period of

FIGURE 2–7   Circularity in the family

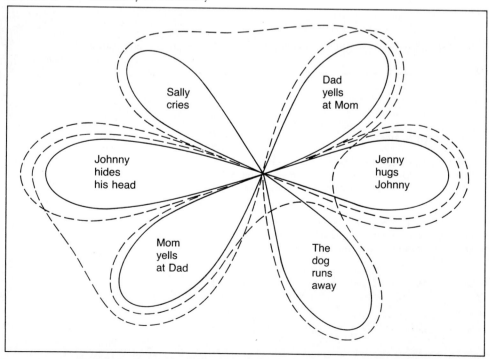

time, the computer is activated and the furnace is turned off, but a blower fan continues until the temperature drops again, which again activates the computer, which turns on the furnace.

Schultz (1984) explains the example of a furnace as a cybernetic prototype (see Figure 2–8). The receptor is the thermometer that senses the temperature. The analyzer is the computer control that processes the input from the receptor and makes a decision. The furnace is the effector that implements the decision of the analyzer. Deviation-reducing and deviation-amplifying mechanisms are aspects of a cybernetic system. According to Becvar and Becvar (1982), positive feedback is deviation-amplifying (the initial response to new behavior), whereas negative feedback is deviation-reducing (guards the status quo).

Feedforward—a redirection of new behavior to match family values—is one of the most effective ways of obtaining desired positive changes. Rather than criticizing new behavior that might increase the undesirable change, feedforward tends to stimulate new, desirable behaviors. For example, when a child has not put away the dishes, a parent might say, "I expect you to put away the dishes. I know it is difficult when you're talking on the phone to tell your friends that you have to put away the dishes, but we expect you to tell them that you'll call them back after you've put away the dishes."

The feedback loop occurs in family systems. For example, a mother tells Rosita, her daughter, to wash the dishes. Rosita complains to her father, who tells the mother that the dishes are her job and not Rosita's. Then the mother feels hurt and withdraws to the bedroom, where she goes to sleep and ignores the father's sexual overtures. The mother is resentful of Rosita and makes a similar request the next day. The father is angry because of his rejection the night before and again supports Rosita instead of his wife. This feedback loop repeats itself over and over again in a predictable sequence.

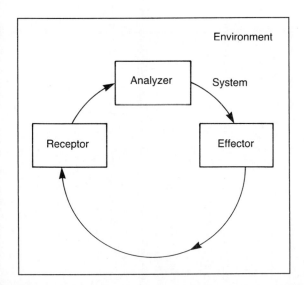

FIGURE 2–8 A cybernetic prototype. Here the system consists of three subsystems (receptor, analyzer, and effector) connected by a closed-information loop.

From *Family Systems Therapy: An Integration* (p. 65) by S. J. Schultz, 1984, Northvale, NJ: Jason Aronson Inc. Adapted by permission.

TABLE 2–1 Comparisons of open and closed systems

	Open System	Closed System
Boundary	Movement of social transaction is bidirectional, balanced, sought.	Impermeable or selectively permeable to conform to the state of equilibrium within. Becomes more closed by change within and/or without.
Relatedness	Organized, integrated, interdependent accepting.	Disorganized, disintegrated, dependency phobic or obsessed.
Response to change	Energizes, sustains vitality.	Favors degradation, further boundary closure and isolation from greater system(s).
Dynamic	Synergistically competitive reciprocity between selves.	Oscillation between feeling antithesis. (good-bad, closeness-distance, peaceful-conflictual, agreeable-disagreeable, one-up-one-down) within and between selves (or pseudo-selves).
Dynamic function	Re-energizing, growing, difference seeking, new paradigm receptive.	Monosthetic consensuality (sameness seeking).
Cognitive state	(Feeling) thinking-action objectifying.	(Thinking) feeling-reaction subjectifying.
Neuro-Anatomic predisposition	Cortical and limbic system synergistic. Neocortex predominant.	Limbic system hypersensitive. Asthenic or circularly engaged neo-cortex.
Causality	Cybernetic with working self and system feedback sustaining goal directedness.	Circular without awareness. Paradigm of awareness is linear. No feedback corrective circuit, but waywardness. Goal-less except to feelings.
Language	Expressing for objectifying and clarification.	Expressing for emotional release—reengagement cycling.
End point state	Differentiated uniqueness, entelechy, emergence.	Anomie, death.
Philosophic compatibility	Vitalism.	Mechanicism.

From *Systems Therapy—Selected Papers* (p. 4), Jack O. Bradt, M.D., and Carolyn J. Moynihan, ACSW (Eds.) 1971. Available through the Family Place, 300 W. Main St., Mt. Horeb, WI 53572. Reprinted by permission.

A family therapist can intervene to encourage one member of the system to choose another behavior, thereby interrupting the feedback loop. Known as negentropy, this process occurs when new information enters a cybernetic system. According to Nichols and Everett (1986), uncertainty is reduced and the system can operate at a higher level of organization.

Open and Closed Systems

An open family system permits exchange with the community outside the family through permeable family boundaries. Bradt and Moynihan (1971) emphasize that differentiation of family members and uniqueness of the family organization occur as part of an open system. In an open system, family members are free to say, to feel, and to think. An "I" position is honored, and individuation is tolerated, if not encouraged. The member of an open system has a sense of being an individual self; of being able to reflect on the relationship between the self and the family; and of perceiving self as part of the local community, the nation, and even the world. Awareness of the boundaries of self and others in the family system means that differentiation of self does not occur at the expense of others.

In an open system, the organization of the family is characterized by goal orientation and directiveness. In an open system, feedback maintains the directionality of the family. Functional capacities of individuals and the family system in light of the larger social systems are fulfilled.

According to Bradt and Moynihan (1971), a closed system does not permit nurturing from the outside. It has impervious boundaries. Family members lean on other family members for fulfillment of all their emotional needs, which is impossible for such human resources to deliver. A sense of "we-ness" is maintained at all costs. Members of a closed system seek stable relationships within the family, avoid change, and conserve their emotional energy. Eventually members become more like others in the family than unique persons in their own right.

All families can be placed on a continuum between an open and closed system. Under stress and over time, families can move closer to one pole of the continuum or the other, becoming more or less open or closed. Table 2–1 compares some of the characteristics of open and closed systems.

It is important for a therapist to facilitate movement of the family toward a more open system. By being alert to the ways in which a family reacts to stressors, a therapist can plan more effective interventions. The following are some questions that a therapist might think about answering during the first few sessions: (1) How open is this system? (2) Prior to this current stressor, how closed was the family system? (3) What effect is the present crisis having on the family? Is it becoming more open or more closed? (4) Has some particular event in the past, such as death, illness, divorce, or other loss, caused the system to become more open or more closed?

SUMMARY

The family is evolving in America today. The nuclear family—father as breadwinner, mother as homemaker, and children at home—represented only 18% of the families in the 1980 census. Alternative family structures are increasing, such as single-parent families, stepfamilies, extended families, commuter marriages, and therapeutic communities. *Family* can be defined as any group of people who are related legally or by blood or are perceived to be family by an individual.

Ludwig von Bertalanffy studied biological organisms and defined a system as a group of elements interacting with each other. Living organisms are continually changing, taking in and giving off matter. Self-regulation is a key property of living systems.

Likewise, human beings are active systems. They create disequilibrium, advancing toward greater levels of organization and functioning (anamorphosis), while paradoxically seeking stability at the same time (homeostasis). The steady state or balance between change and stability evolves to higher levels throughout the life cycle.

Family systems exhibit anamorphosis by seeking long-term goals such as building a home or sending children to college while maintaining stability or homeostasis through daily family routines and holiday rituals. Each family system is composed of subsystems that have boundaries. Families have structures which can mean different ways of being organized, such as single-parent or nuclear families. Structure also includes the chain of command, which could be matriarchal or patriarchal.

All family systems have rules that are renegotiated as the needs of the individuals in the family change. Each family member plays a role, exhibiting a set of predictable behaviors in the family system. Each family has a *weltanschauung* or way of viewing the world, which influences the way family members interact with others.

There are specific characteristics of family systems: (1) constant change, (2) self-regulation to maintain homeostasis, (3) equifinality, (4) all symptoms serving positive functions, (5) wholeness, (6) circularity, and (7) cybernetic properties, where the family is influenced through feedback loops consisting of interactions between the parts of the systems. Positive feedback is deviation amplifying, and negative feedback is deviation reducing.

An open family system permits exchange with the community outside the family through permeable family boundaries. In contrast, a closed system has impervious boundaries that do not permit nurturing from the outside. It is important for a therapist to facilitate movement of the family toward a more open system.

EXERCISES

1. Count off in small groups according to your instructor's directions. Appoint a group leader who will write down the ideas of group members and report them to the class. Share your ideas of what a family is. How would you define *family*?

2. Turn to the student sitting next to you. Taking turns in dyads, share what you think is meant by the following terms: the dynamic organism, human beings as active organisms, system, subsystem, boundary, organization, structure, rule, role, *weltanschauung,* homeostasis, anamorphosis, steady state, equifinality, wholeness, circular-

ity, open system, closed system, cybernetics, and feedback.

3. You as the therapist obtain the following information in the initial session with a family who has come to you for treatment. Diagram a structural analysis of the family (see Figure 2–3). Present your diagram to the class if your instructor requests it.

The Hawthorne family, consisting of Elise (the mother), Richard (the father), Jonathon (the oldest child), Rita (the oldest daughter), and Ruth (the adopted youngest daughter), requested family treatment because Ruth had lied to everyone at school, stating that her female physical education teacher had made homosexual advances toward her when the teacher had not. In the treatment room, Elise and Rita sat together on one couch holding hands. Richard sat alone at first, until Jonathon and Ruth joined him. Richard began talking and answered all of the questions for everyone else, even though you addressed the questions to other members of the family. You interrupted him, stating that one rule of the therapy would be that people should speak for themselves using "I" statements. Elise began to answer some questions, then Rita, and finally Jonathon,

who subsequently began to argue with his father. Ruth never said anything.

4. Count off in dyads according to the directions of your instructor. Reflect for a moment or two on the implicit, unspoken, and explicitly stated rules of your family of origin. Taking turns, partners should share one rule that they would like to keep for themselves and one rule that they would like to change. As "active organisms," human beings can take the initiative to negotiate or change rules or to keep them as they are.

Chapter 3
Toward Healthier Family Systems

*The great thing in this world is not so much where we stand, as in
what direction we are moving.*

Oliver Wendell Holmes, 1889

Many, if not most, adults in the United States, through no fault of their own,
have never experienced a healthy family. Alcoholism, chronic illness, mental problems, overwork, or other difficulties of one or both parents left them with few or no
models of the healthy interactional patterns that undergird normal functional families.
This is often especially true of professional helpers, such as marital and family therapists. Dedicated to helping those less fortunate—whether in mental health facilities,
clinics, social agencies, or schools—they themselves have often experienced the pain
of living within dysfunctional families and only guess at what "normal" functioning is.
Therefore, it is important that helping professionals learn as much as possible about
healthy family functioning.

For example, Sally's mother was chronically ill when Sally was growing up and had
little time or energy to share feelings with Sally or to teach Sally how to share her
feelings with others. Her father, John, made all the decisions for his wife which made
him feel powerful and masked the inadequacy he felt inside because his own mother
had died of tuberculosis before he was 2 years old. He felt strong, even god-like, as
his wife became more and more incapacitated by her illness. Sally and her sister,
Madge, felt intimidated by their domineering father, who was never to be questioned.

When Sally begins to raise her own family, she will probably feel insecure, noting a feeling of discomfort when her children ask questions and show spirit. She'll wonder if this is normal. Likewise, when Sally becomes a family counselor, she may experience doubts about what a healthy family is. In her family of origin, strong feelings were not directly expressed because they might "kill" or hurt her chronically ill mother. An unrealistic picture of an idyllic family that does not express anger may limit her capacity to help the families who see her.

Sally and other marital and family therapy professionals need to know the characteristics of strong families and what various types of healthy family functioning are, so that they will have maps by which to guide their clients toward more effective family life. In addition, therapists must continue to work on family-of-origin issues as they arise in therapeutic relationships with clients as a crucial part of their professional, personal, and interactional growth.

But what makes a client's family system healthy? Such a question is complex and not easily answered. Most of the early research on families and family therapy, especially that written in the fifties, focused on pathology. In the sixties, however, more attention began to be directed toward the strengths of families. Later, in the mid- and late seventies, the examination and importance of healthy families finally became the focus of research. That research serves as a basis for models and theories developed in the early and mid-eighties. These distinctive models are based on surveys of family strengths, observational studies of healthy family functioning and other research on the classifications, perceptions, and expectations of families. After discussing these models, an integrative delineation of healthy family functioning will be presented

FAMILY STRENGTHS

Much of the leadership in the research and application of family strengths—defined as those factors in the relationships of the family that foster the personal development of the family members and that bring satisfaction to family life (Otto, 1962)—can be attributed to the Center for Family Strengths at the University of Nebraska-Lincoln. Its first National Symposium on Building Family Strengths was held in 1978 and brought together those interested in improving the quality of family life and preventing family dysfunction. By 1987, eight volumes of research on building family strengths had been published through the Center for Family Strengths of the Department of Human Development and the Family of the College of Home Economics of the University of Nebraska-Lincoln (Lingren et al., 1987; Rowe et al., 1984; Stinnett, Chesser, & DeFrain, 1979; Stinnett, Chesser, DeFrain, & Knaub, 1980; Stinnett, DeFrain, King, Knaub, & Rowe, 1981; Stinnett et al., 1982; Van Zandt et al., 1986; Williams et al., 1985).

The decade of their research, as well as other studies conducted on family strengths, has been summarized in *Secrets of Strong Families,* by Stinnett and DeFrain (1985). The authors concluded that strong families share the qualities of commitment, mutual appreciation, communication, time, spirituality, and coping ability.

Stinnett and Sauer (1977) had also identified most of these strengths when they surveyed 99 "healthy" families in Oklahoma. However, their research failed to call attention to the importance of coping with crisis and stress (Table 3–1). In a study of 400 families who responded to a newspaper advertisement nationwide, Sanders

TABLE 3–1 A chronological summary of research on family strengths

Study	Number of strengths	Strengths cited
Otto, 1962, 1963, 1964 1967, 1975, 1976	6	1. Shared religious, moral values. 2. Love coupled with caring. 3. Common interests/goals. 4. Happy children. 5. Playing and working together. 6. Sharing leisure-time activities.
Gabler and Otto, 1964	15	1. Family strong within itself. 2. Sound marital relationship. 3. Parenting strength. 4. Parents assist children to grow and develop. 5. Family relationships. 6. Doing things together as a family. 7. A satisfactory financial and social status. 8. Religious values. 9. Positive environment in the home. 10. Participation in community affairs. 11. Level of education. 12. Ability to change and adapt. 13. Maintenance of relationships with in-laws. 14. Positive attitudes toward sex. 15. Seeking and accepting help when needed.

(1979) cited five of the six strengths identified by Stinnett and DeFrain. Like the Stinnett and Sauer study, Sanders omitted coping ability. He also included the following strengths: love, understanding, ego support, trust, and individuality. Many of these characteristics can be considered results of the six strengths delineated by Stinnett and DeFrain. (See Table 3–1 for a chronological historical presentation of major research done on family strengths.) To emphasize the importance of each of the qualities cited by Stinnett and DeFrain, each quality and any research conducted exclusively on that quality will be discussed in more depth in the following sections.

Commitment and Spiritual Wellness

Commitment is at the core of healthy family functioning, especially for the children (Rampey, 1983). In strong families, members are devoted not only to the welfare of the family but also to the growth of each of the members. Often commitment is tied

TABLE 3–1 *continued*

Study	Number of strengths	Strengths cited
Stinnett and Sauer, 1977	5	1. Mutual understanding and respect. 2. Expression of appreciation. 3. Communication patterns in which problems are openly discussed so that feelings are expressed and not bottled up. 4. Planning and carrying out activities to spend time together. 5. Commitment to religion and the family as first priority.
Sanders, 1979	10	1. Love. 2. Commitment. 3. Effective communication skills. 4. Being a religious person (regardless of specific religion) 5. Understanding. 6. Spending time together. 7. Appreciation. 8. Ego support. 9. Trust. 10. Individuality.
Stinnett and DeFrain, 1985	6	1. Commitment. 2. Appreciating each other. 3. Communication skills. 4. Time together. 5. Spiritual wellness. 6. Coping with crises and stress.

to the spirituality or religiosity of a family (Brigman, 1984) and the resultant lifestyle of that religiosity.

For example, in a national study of professionals who had a graduate degree in an area related to family life, more than two thirds of the respondents stated that religious participation increased family stability (Brigman, 1984). Basic religious beliefs—including forgiveness, reconciliation, the divine value of the individual, love, faith, hope, grace, and parenthood of God—were the most helpful. Religious lifestyle—responsibility, commitment, caring for others, and giving—followed in importance. Also of significance, but to a lesser degree, were shared religious values and observances, shared religious activities, and reverence for the sacredness of marriage.

Similarly, Rampey (1983), in a national study of grown children and their parents, found that the score on the Purpose in Life Test was the strongest single predictor of family success as measured by the Family Success Scale. Perceiving a reason for being in the world—existential meaning—was significantly related to family success, and both parents and offspring who were more religious exhibited clearer purpose in life. Participation in religious groups and organizations was directly related to family success, while the particular religious beliefs had little or no relationship to family success.

Time

As a part and a result of commitment, most families agree to spend time together. In general, healthy families tend to spend more time together than do dysfunctional ones. The importance of time was pointed out as early as 1962 by Otto, who listed sharing leisure-time activities and playing/working together as two of the five strengths he had found in healthy families. Later, Stinnett and Sauer (1977) found members of strong families were willing to spend time with each other, but often had to schedule such time and limit those activities they deemed unnecessary. This could be considered an example of what Satir (1972) terms family engineering, in which the marital coalition modifies the family environment to maximize satisfaction by taking responsibility for making things happen. Spending time together includes all types of activities from the routine (eating meals together) to the once-in-a-lifetime (a special family vacation trip).

Families who perceived themselves as having higher levels of family strengths participated in more leisure activities together. Lynn (1983) found a direct relationship between strong families and participation in hobbies and most other types of activities: cultural, joint, mass media, outdoor, parallel, social, and sports. Leisure activities cited as most strengthening for the families in Lynn's study were church attendance, completion of chores and projects together, and traveling, including vacations. According to Sanders (1979), the most frequent activity engaged in by strong families was spending time outdoors.

While spending time together as a family is important, it is also crucial for a family to have a circle of friends who influence and support each other's children throughout their growth and development. Zimmerman and Cervantes (1960), in the first published study on successful families, linked a family's success—measured by the continuance of the children in high school—to the degree of similarity and intimacy formed among couple friends of the parents. Surrounding the household with friends who share similar ideals and values also led to the implementation of such ideals and values in the children. Such friendships were based on shared values and interests and not governed by gain of an economic, social, or political nature. In working with families, therapists may encounter severely dysfunctional families who have withdrawn from community activities and have few, if any, family friends. In such cases, the therapist needs to encourage family members to begin developing friendships with other families who share their interests and values.

Appreciation

In strong families, the marital partners tend to build the self-esteem of their mates by mutual love, respect, compliments, and other signs of appreciation. In unhappy marriages, spouses think that their self-esteem is attacked by their partners (Hicks & Platt, 1970; Mathews & Milhanovich, 1963; Wills, Weiss, & Patterson, 1974). Learning how to give sincere appreciation effectively is a key to healthy family functioning, but it is not presently taught in school curricula (Stinnett & Sauer, 1977).

Communication

In addition to communication patterns of appreciation, strong families tend to express their feelings and thoughts when problems arise rather than avoiding conflict and discussion of the issue (Stinnett & Sauer, 1977). Typically family members would discuss the conflict, express their feelings, and then wait until later when angry feelings had subsided to propose solutions and reach a decision. Overall, communication patterns in the family are more positive than negative—that is, more expressions of appreciation and responses that indicated to the family member that the family member is loved.

Coping Ability

Many of the strengths already discussed all play a role in how well the family copes with stress or crisis. The family's coping ability is especially important to the therapist because families usually seek therapy when they are struggling with stressful events.

In strong families and marriages, coping with crisis is used to promote family and individual growth. These families reframe the situation, perceiving the positive characteristics of the event (Mackinnon, Mackinnon, & Franken, 1984; Stinnett et al., 1981; Stinnett, Knorr, DeFrain, & Rowe, 1984). During times of crisis—such as serious illness or surgery, the death of an immediate family member, marital problems, and problems with a child's behavior—successful families most often share the crisis by working together (typically laboring manually), staying by family members, talking about the crisis openly among family members, listening to each other, generally depending on one another, and being especially thoughtful toward each other. Hence, they perceive the family itself as the major resource in the crisis. Religious involvement—praying and having faith in God—also helped the successful families cope more effectively with the crisis, as did a commitment to the family.

In addition, family members, close friends, and relatives helped the family in crisis, most frequently by giving emotional support. According to Stinnett et al. (1981), the simple presence of people was more important than anything they said. A touch or caring gesture meant very much to family members, as did financial or physical assistance. Talking about one's own problems or similar crises, or in any way criticizing those people involved was not helpful. Clichés often were wooden and detrimental. Thus, it can be deduced that having a kind heart and a gentle, calm, caring manner is of crucial importance for a family therapist who is working with a family in crisis.

The therapist also serves an important role in assisting the family in reframing a crisis or stressful situation as more positive. Positive outcomes typically perceived by healthy families in or after crisis include feeling closer together as a family because of sharing the pain of the crisis; becoming aware of their own individual strengths;

gaining maturity; appreciating other family members more and improving relationships with them; learning more about the problems of life such as alcoholism, illness, and death; and improving their spiritual life (Stinnett et al., 1981).

Models Based on Family Strengths

The research on family strengths is exemplified by The Building Family Strengths (BFS) Model. This model was formulated by the Center for Family Strengths as part of a federal grant to develop and disseminate a family enrichment program. Entitled "Building Family Strengths," the program began certifying national trainers for each state in 1986. In turn, these trainers educated facilitators in each of their states to utilize *Building Family Strengths: A Manual for Families* and a set of exercise cards that could be used by families when they returned home from enrichment sessions.

The BFS model is symbolized by the circle of power (Figure 3–1). Here, the circle of power represents the family systems concept of circularity, in which each factor influences every other factor. The outer circle symbolizes the commitment that holds the family together in wholeness. It includes commitment to the family and to the growth of each family member. Within the inner circle is wellness, an optimistic belief in the positive effects of human interaction. Because of this belief, family members can trust themselves, each other, and people outside the family. Each of the circle's four arrows represents a strength: communication, time together, appreciation, and ability to deal with crisis, conflict, and stress. The shaded space between the arrows represents the unique strengths of particular families and their special way of implementing the strengths of the model within their own cultures, as there is no one way but many paths to becoming strong families.

While the research from the Center for Family Strengths is significant, the contributions of Otto (1962), who produced a sizable body of research over more than a

FIGURE 3–1 Building Family Strengths Model

From *Building Family Strengths: A Manual for Families* (p. 8) Achord, Berry, Harding, Kerber, Scott & Schwab, 1986, Lincoln, NE: The Center for Family Strengths.

decade, cannot be ignored (Table 3–1). Otto, considered "the Father of Family Enrichment," played an important role in the development of family life education and developed one of the first premarital inventories (Otto, 1951). Convinced that families could take responsibility for building their own strengths, Otto (1964) cautioned therapists about their interventions and encouraged them to build upon the strengths of the families with whom they worked.

Otto (1963) maintained that family strengths were the final result of 12 dynamic, constantly changing, interactive components: (1) meeting the spiritual, emotional, and physical needs of the family; (2) hearing the concerns of family members; (3) communicating; (4) providing security and encouragement; (5) maintaining growth-promoting relationships both within and outside the family; (6) creating positive relationships in the community, especially in the neighborhood, school, and local and state governments; (7) parents growing as people with their children; (8) seeking and accepting help when needed; (9) flexibly performing family roles; (10) respecting the individuality of family members; (11) using a crisis or detrimental experience to grow; and (12) being loyal to the family while cooperating with other families. Otto used these criteria to assess families who were entering treatment. During therapy, they served as a frame of reference to assist families in developing their strengths.

Cross-Cultural Studies on Family Strengths

Are there additional strengths that diverse American ethnic families possess? Do differences in family strengths exist across cultures?

Among American ethnic groups and emigrants to the United States, respect for elders was a valued family strength. Abbott and Meredith (1986) interviewed Chicano, American Indian, black, Hmong Asian refugee, and white parents. In comparison to the white control group, members of these ethnic groups emphasized respect for elders as a strength and financial security. It was essential that the head of the household have a job or a way of financially supporting the family. If this occurred, there was increased respect for elders in that family. Porter (1981) also found that parents highly valued the respect shown to them by their children. They also expected obedience from their children.

Results of a similar study (King, 1980) with strong black families nationwide indicated that black families exhibited the same characteristics as strong white families—namely, commitment, religion, love, communication, and building/supporting the egos of family members. Two major strengths distinguished the sample from other groups: members of these black families were very religious, and the strength of the parent-child relationship, especially the mother-child dyad, was the strongest in the family. Typically, these families liked to spend their time together by playing games, attending church, going to movies, and eating together.

Internationally, black South African families were found to be community-minded (Weber, 1984). They looked out for each other and were not as individualistic as their Western counterparts. They were tolerant and accepting of each other, valuing an illegitimate child as much as any other child and taking in children when they had problems. The patience, tolerance, and good humor of black South African families were definitely strengths.

The parent-child relationship, especially the mother-child dyad, is very strong in healthy, black families according to King's (1980) research.

Swiss and German families considered spending time together to be more important than did Austrian families (Stoll, 1984). Religious orientation was relatively unimportant as a strength to this sample. This may be due to religion being a more personal or individualized matter in Europe rather than a family or group-oriented one.

Expression of affection and love and understanding each other were strengths identified in Latin American countries (Casas, 1979). Children were valued; men often married to have children. Strong families were perceived to have parents who focused their energies on providing good education and opportunities for their children. Most families visited with the extended family weekly or even daily. The extended family provided feelings of belongingness, affection, friendship, and enjoyment of good times together.

Although there are many cross-cultural similarities in the above research, the importance of culture as a distinct variable affecting family life is emphasized. A family therapist must be sensitive to the context set by the clients' culture. Asking questions about how family roles are perceived in a given culture and how things are done helps the therapist to see the family from a broader perspective. This spirit of respectful curiosity is often called *cultural calibration,* in which the counselor asks the clients what a specific situation means in their culture.

For example, in the case of black families it would be important to ask what it means to have a child in that community. A strong maternal-child bond is often considered a strength in the black community, and clients may not want it to be weakened according to the dictates of systems theory. Another example might be the meaning of the extended family to people from Latin America. A couple from Latin America presenting with difficulties with in-laws may need to be asked what this means in their culture. It is a far more serious problem in Latin American cultures than in most American subcultures. Seeing the world through the eyes of clients who come from different subcultures and cultures is a continuing challenge for family therapists.

Other Research on Family Strengths

Other research on family strengths has dealt with particular types of families. In addition to the main strengths found in all families, additional unique strengths were found for specific types of families. For example, families of professional women had three strengths specific to their dual-career lifestyles (Knaub, 1985): independence, financial reward, and time in which goals and interests were shared. The family scheduled time to be alone as a couple, for each parent to have special time alone with each child on a routine basis, and time for family travel, special holiday activities, and vacations.

Creating a supportive environment was the key predictor of family strengths in remarried families (Knaub, Hanna, & Stinnett, 1984). Income was also helpful. One area where family members desired changes was that of relationships with the stepchildren. Therapists working with blended families need to provide support for couples as they work through issues related to the children—a focus of most clinical work with stepfamilies.

In families with children, love was identified as the factor that contributed most to the strength of the relationships (Strand, 1979). Children felt good about themselves when parents complimented them. The ability to listen to the child was the factor that made communication good between parent and child. Children felt comfortable in sharing their problems with parents who listened.

Smith (1983) studied families of business executives who had mean incomes over $150,000 and had been together almost 30 years. Most of these executives were in their fifties, worked nine to twelve hours per day, and spent more than 70% of their time on career concerns. Both spouses were satisfied with their abilities to express affection; to share feelings, especially dependency needs; and to become emotionally close. The executives tended to use physical activity and relaxation to deal with career stress. Sometimes, however, there was spillover that negatively affected the marital satisfaction of their partners, even though techniques such as listening, being supportive, and talking it out on the part of spouses were effective in helping the executives deal with stress.

Couples who were in long-term marriages reported high levels of marital satisfaction and satisfaction with their parenting, household responsibilities, and roles (Mackinnon, Mackinnon, & Franken, 1984). Husbands were more satisfied with the marital relationship than their wives. In comparison to other couples, these were more satisfied with their health and the health of other family members; their sexual relationship, including both sexual behavior and expression of affection; the management of their financial affairs; and the personality of the marital partner.

TIMBERLAWN PSYCHIATRIC RESEARCH FOUNDATION

While the above research on family strengths is helpful for the marital and family therapist, the conclusions are based on the results of survey instruments. Rather than relying on such self-report data as earlier researchers had done, Lewis, Beavers, Gossett, and Phillips (1976) observed and recorded how healthy families functioned by videotaping the interactions of healthy families (volunteers who had no family member identified as emotionally ill) over a 7-year period. The results of their research, sponsored by the Timberlawn Psychiatric Research Foundation, were published in *No Single Thread: Psychological Health in Family Systems*.

This monumental landmark study was unique in its focus on studying and filming the processes by which families dealt with diverse assigned tasks. In addition, the group of healthy families had been matched with a group of families who had an emotionally hospitalized adolescent to compare the differences in functioning. Instead of the presence of one unique variable discriminating healthy families, the role of numerous variables interacting and influencing each other was emphasized.

Optimally Functioning Families

According to the research, the optimally functioning families had expectations that human interaction would be caring both inside and outside the family—a view of the world as a friendly place. They respected the different perspectives of the family members and tolerated individual differences. Many options were explored in approaching problems. In particular, a high level of initiative was demonstrated by the healthiest families. They were not a passive lot!

The parental coalition exercised clear power, but not in an authoritarian way. Children voiced their opinions, and contextual factors were used to determine which spouse would be in charge of what function. The individuals in the healthiest families were the most autonomous. Children learned to share both their thoughts and feelings openly, accepting responsibility for their own thoughts, feelings, and actions.

In healthy families, members perceived the family accurately in terms of how others saw the family (a congruent mythology). The overall mood of the family was warm and caring. Optimally functioning families openly shared their feelings. Although positive, affectionate feelings were shared more often than negative ones, they

Dr. Robert Beavers has applied the research on healthy family functioning completed at the Timberlawn Psychiatric Research Foundation in Dallas, Texas, to the development of an approach to marital and family therapy. (Courtesy of W. W. Norton & Co.)

were able to express anger and resolve conflicts. Spontaneity and humor were present. Family members were not blamed. There was a tendency for the healthiest families to be able to talk about death and dying in a personal way.

Case Studies of Healthy Families

Beavers (1977), a psychiatrist and researcher on the Timberlawn team, wrote the classic study, *Psychotherapy and Growth: A Family Systems Perspective,* which highlighted the diverse ways of being healthy. In optimal families, there was a clear yet flexible structure. Change was not threatening to the family members. All the children gave their input regarding family plans. Negotiations were enjoyed and feedback was welcome. Human biological drives were normal. For example, anger was a signal that a change needed to be made, and sexual interest was positive. In fact, the frequency of sexual intercourse on the part of the parents accurately predicted the emotional health of their children. Since there is no one way to be healthy, case studies of two optimally functioning families follow, showing diverse but optimally healthy families.

The Jones family included parents over 30 and three children aged 14, 13, and 11. In this family, the members supported each other and a sense of "we-ness" was evident. Few oppositional exchanges were noted in their interactions. In fact, their interaction was easy and they were clearly happy, although they did not initiate challenges for themselves. They believed in authorities outside the family and saw them as benevolent. They were verbally open, with a warm, feeling tone. The parents were an effective coalition with no child being favored over another. The father was the leader, but he showed respect and interest in his wife, and did not attempt to dominate or subjugate her. The family was involved in organized sports. The parents enjoyed adulthood and therefore encouraged their children to engage in some grown-up activities.

The Smith family also included parents in their thirties with three children 9, 13, and 14. In this case, the father was an aggressive businessman who set the mood for the family interaction. The younger children were aggressive like their father. The oldest child was somewhat quiet. Overall, the family members responded warmly to each other, although there were some complaints about the father's dominance. The family experienced a high level of anxiety, but operated effectively, using the anxiety to motivate action. The oldest child tended to withdraw moderately in response to anxiety but was not scapegoated for being different from other family members. Diverse viewpoints in the family were respected. Mr. Smith shared his ideas with the family in an enriching, intellectual atmosphere and responded to their statements. He encouraged his wife to further her education, believing that her activity in the world strengthened the family. Communication was direct and open. There was a strong parental coalition and much physical touching in a warm and caring way. Unusually high levels of spontaneity were present in the family. Each family member was a strong, separate individual with autonomy presumed. The Smith family was able to deal with moderate friction constructively, while being involved in the outside world.

Both the Jones family and the Smith family were optimally functioning families according to the research of Beavers (1977). In other words, there are many ways to be healthy, not just one way. As optimal functioning increased, the families showed more diversity and spontaneity while maintaining similar patterns of overall strength.

Family Style: Centrifugal versus Centripetal Tendencies

Families can be classified according to their centrifugal or centripetal tendencies. Spinning outward under stress, that is, finding satisfaction in activities and relationships beyond the family, is a centrifugal style, similar to the centrifuge in the medical laboratory that spins blood samples. Spinning inward under stress, that is, seeking gratification within the family, is a centripetal style, similar to huddling or clinging together in an earthquake (Stierlin, 1974; Stierlin, Levi, & Savard, 1973). Beavers (1982) developed a systems model (Figure 3–2) for assessing families using degree of family style (centrifugal, centripetal, or mixed) and level of competence (optimally functioning, adequate, midrange, and severely dysfunctional). Centripetal families tend to emphasize positive feelings while denying or repressing negative ones, which provides the cement holding them together. Centrifugal families tend to be comfortable with angry feelings, stimulating the outward movement of the centrifugal style.

FIGURE 3–2 A systems model combining continua of family competence and style, leading to seven family types

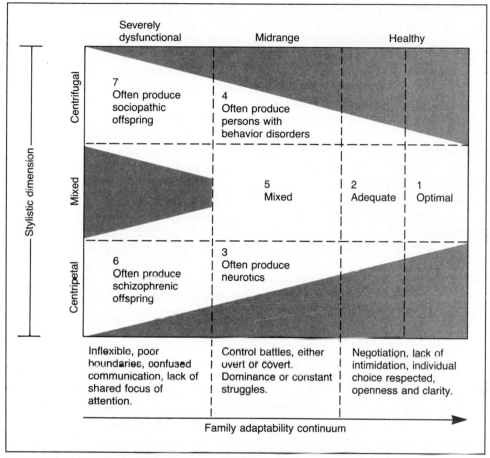

"Healthy, Mid-range, and Severely Disfunctional Families," by W. R. Beavers, from *Normal Family Processes* (p. 58), F. Walsh (Ed.), 1982, New York: Gulford Press. Reprinted by permission.

Families with centripetal styles have difficulty in letting children leave home. Centrifugal families may push offspring out of the nest before they are well-differentiated.

Healthy Couples

Beavers described the characteristics of healthy couples in his book *Successful Marriage: A Family Systems Approach to Couples Therapy* (1985). Healthy couples possess health-promoting beliefs. They believe in relative truth, subjective reality, the benign quality of the motives of family members, the rewarding nature of human interaction, a systems perspective, and meaning or purpose in life. There is a small power difference between them which is overtly observable. Each person is able to own and share feelings, thoughts, and wishes, which helps establish clear boundaries that may merge during passionate, ecstatic, or angry moments. The couple operates in the present, and autonomy is respected. Healthy couples can plan something together, negotiating skillfully to resolve differences. Positive feelings are often shared, including good humor and fun.

All couples have spin-outs—patterns in which a behavioral sequence on the part of spouse A triggers a maladaptive behavioral sequence on the part of spouse B, which influences spouse A to intensify the initial behavioral sequence that bothers spouse B. Such circular patterns lead to discouragement in both spouses. Healthy couples can become aware of their spin-outs and learn conscious spin-ins—behaviors that will reduce the probability of the maladaptive behavior pattern in the other spouse. For example, spouse A may share feelings of anger, to which spouse B withdraws, which influences spouse A to attack in an intensified hostile manner—a spin-out. Spouse B can learn to repeat what spouse A has said in an empathic mode (instead of withdrawing), which leads spouse A to feel understood and less angry. Spouses usually use the same maladaptive patterns and switch roles. For example, spouse B may share angry feelings, to which spouse A withdraws, and then spouse B attacks. Therefore, if a spouse understands the basic spin-out, appropriate behavioral sequences can be learned that will be effective for both spouses—spin-ins. Marital and family therapists, especially in the early phases of treatment, can uncover the spin-out that a couple is exhibiting in the therapy session and teach an appropriate spin-in, an effective strategy for developing rapport and trust in the therapeutic process. The healthier the couple, the better able they are to become aware of spin-outs and to use a behavioral response to spin in.

Healthy Black Families

In a study completed at Timberlawn Psychiatric Research Institute by Lewis and Looney (1983), *The Long Struggle: Well-Functioning Working-Class Black Families,* the sample consisted of 18 families referred by a black ministerial group in Dallas as being healthy families. All were two-parent, working-class families. The researchers found great variability among the families and concluded that black families were heterogeneous in function and structure. The most competent families raised autonomous children, provided emotional support for the development of the parents' personalities, shared power, were close without losing their ego boundaries, solved problems through negotiation, had a strong parental coalition, communicated clearly, responded to each other, expressed feelings openly, were moderately empathic, and did not exhibit chronic conflict. They were able to resolve the continuous conflict that every individual faces between the need to build a personal identity and the need to relate intimately with selected significant other human beings.

Competent, working-class black families were also compared with their middle-class white counterparts from a prior study. Researchers concluded that what appeared to work best for middle- and upper-middle-class white families also appeared to work best for working-class black families. The study emphasized that the interactional processes of the most competent families were similar across socioeconomic levels and racial lines.

Successful Families

Beavers and Hampson (1990) have developed a model of family assessment and intervention based on the research at Timberlawn and the Southwest Family Institute. In their book entitled *Successful Families,* they present nine groups of families that are found at different points on the health-illness continuum with specific interventions suggested for families in each diagnostic group. Families are typically assessed using the Beavers Interactional Scales for competence and family style based on a videotape of their 10-minute interactions attempting to decide what they would like to change in the family. In addition, family members may be asked to complete the Self-Report Family Inventory Version II (SFI).

The field of marital and family therapy has been hampered by a lack of a diagnostic system similar to the *Diagnostical Statistical Manual-Revised* (DSM-III-R), which is used for individuals. The major contribution of *Successful Families* is its attempt to provide a comprehensive system of family diagnosis and recommended treatments tailored to each diagnosis.

THE CIRCUMPLEX MODEL OF OLSON

Olson is noted for his method of classifying families entitled the Circumplex Model (Olson, Russell, & Sprenkle, 1980; Olson, Russell, & Sprenkle, 1983; Olson, Sprenkle, & Russell, 1979). Families are assessed on two dimensions: cohesion (degree of closeness) and adaptability (ability to change). A third dimension of family communication is a facilitating dimension, enabling families to make progress on the central dimensions of cohesion and adaptability. Olson developed FACES I, FACES II, and FACES III (the Family Adaptability and Cohesion Evaluation Scales) to measure levels of family cohesion and adaptability.

Considering scores on cohesion and adaptability, three family types emerge: Balanced, Midrange, and Extreme. Further differentiating the family types, Olson visualized four Balanced types of families in which their scores on cohesion and adaptability fell in the middle, eight Midrange types of families in which a score on one of the dimensions was in the middle but at an extreme on the other dimension, and four Extreme types in which scores on both dimensions fell at extremes—a total of 16 family types.

Over the life span, Olson et al. (1983) found that cohesion was highest in the earliest stages of the family life cycle. It declined during the adolescent family stage, reaching its lowest point during the launching family and increasing in the later stages of the family life cycle, but it never reached the level of cohesion found in the earliest stages. Wives tended to perceive the family as having more cohesion across the life span than did their husbands. Smaller decreases in adaptability did occur over the life span, with husbands reaching their lowest scores during the adolescent stage. Wives reached their ebb at the launching stage. Adaptability increased again in later stages but did not reach the levels of the earliest stage of the family life cycle.

In this landmark study, families at each of the four stages of the family life cycle—young couples, families with young children, families with adolescents, and older couples—were sampled, a total of 2,692 individuals representing 31 states. The

FIGURE 3-3 Functional levels of cohesion and adaptability across the family life cycle

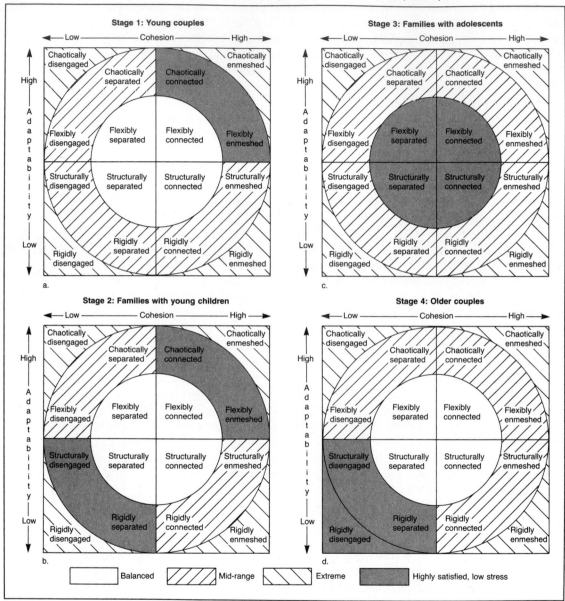

From *Families: What Makes Them Work* (pp. 196, 199) by Olson, McCubbin, Barnes, Larsen, Muxen & Wilson, 1983, New York: Sage Publications, Inc. Reprinted by permission.

results showed that different types of families functioned best at different stages of the family life cycle, although as a total group across the life span, the Balanced family types tended to function better. Different levels of cohesion and adaptability were more functional at diverse stages of the family life cycle.

The young couples with no children who functioned best were Extreme types in the upper right quadrant of Figure 3–3a. They had high levels of cohesion (very connected) and adaptability (very flexible). Couples at this stage of the family life cycle have time to be closer, without the interference of children. They can have less structured and more flexible life-styles.

As children were born, less flexibility and more structure occurred. The families who were optimally functional tended to be Midrange types, either chaotically connected or flexibly enmeshed, or more structured (structurally disengaged or rigidly separated). When the first child was born, the family was appropriately enmeshed around nurturing the infant, working on the developmental task of incorporating the baby into the family. This led naturally to a chaotically connected or flexibly enmeshed family type. As the infant grew into a toddler, the parents had less time for each other, reducing their cohesion. The roles of mother and father became more differentiated as the need for structure to raise the child increased, fostering a structurally disengaged or rigidly separated type.

At the stage of Families with Adolescents, Balanced family types functioned best. The continuous average levels of cohesion and adaptability helped the family to deal with the *sturm und drang* created by adolescents in the family. Families tended to use all their resources to deal with their teenagers, utilizing the family strengths of family pride, adolescent-parent communication, and family accord.

With older couples whose children had been launched, the Extreme family types of rigidly disengaged, rigidly separated, and structurally disengaged were the happiest couples, even though they had higher stress. The Balanced couples relied on spiritual support to cope with problems and experienced less stress. With age, perhaps, people become more comfortable with established routines and less close in defense of loss.

Over the entire life span, the most useful coping strategy was obtaining spiritual support. Reframing, the internal strategy of redefining a negative event in a manner that made it more manageable and acceptable, was the next most useful coping skill. Informal support groups of neighbors and friends were used more often than formal helpers such as agencies, physicians, or psychologists. Passive appraisal (believing that some things would take care of themselves) was generally not very useful, except for older couples who were less hurried. Older couples tended to use spiritual support more than younger couples. Wives tended to use informal support groups more in the young couple stage and the older couple stage. Older couples tended to use more formal helpers, probably due to health problems. There were many discrepancies in the perceptions of the family members, indicating that asking one person about the family may not give a realistic view.

STREIT'S MODEL

In conducting a study of 6,000 teenagers in Pennsylvania with Oliver in the early 1970s, Streit (1987a, 1987c) found a significant relationship between family percep-

Love	Positive evaluation, sharing, expressing affection, emotional support.
Loving Control	Intellectual stimulation, being child-centered, possessiveness, protectiveness.
Control	Intrusiveness, suppressing anger, control through guilt, strong parental direction.
Hostile Control	Strict discipline, punishment, nagging.
Hostility	Irritability, negative evaluation, rejection.
Hostile Freedom	Neglect, being ignored.
Freedom	Extreme freedom, lax discipline.
Loving Freedom	Moderate freedom, encouraging being sociable, encouraging independent thinking, being treated as an equal.

TABLE 3–2 Perception clusters

From *Through my Child's Eyes* (p. 3) by F. Streit, 1987, Highland Park, NJ: Peoplescience. Reprinted by permission.

tions and drug abuse. When measuring the perceptions of how close they felt to their families, those teenagers whose scores indicated that they were not too close or not close at all to their families had the highest probability of drinking alcohol, using drugs, or committing crimes. Questions were not asked directly; but rather measured through an instrument entitled *Perceptions*. Another instrument has also been developed by Streit (1987b) to assess children's perceptions of love in the family.

The way in which the child viewed the parents was measured on eight perception clusters (Table 3–2). When the children perceived their parents as loving them, whether it was love, loving control, or loving freedom, they did not use drugs or chemicals of any type (Figure 3–4). This model clearly delineates healthy versus

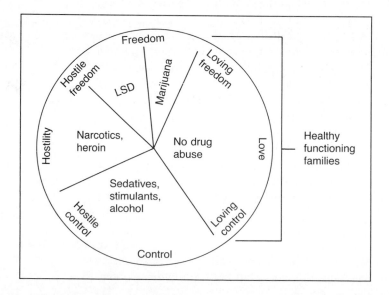

FIGURE 3–4 Drug use and children's perceptions of their families

From *Perception of Love Kit T-203* (p. 4) by F. Streit, 1987, Peoplescience. Reprinted by permission of author.

dysfunctional families from a phenomenological point of view, that is, based on the personal views of the teenagers in those families.

Based on the assessed perceptions, parents can work toward changing their children's perceptions by actions, motivation, timing, choice, and benefits. According to Streit, parents must first do something, such as listening, touching, giving, telling, hugging, buying, nurturing, feeding, or kissing. Children will then assess the motivation of the parent. For example, if an increase in allowance is given near a parent's birthday, a child may wonder if the increase was granted because the child had done a consistently excellent job on chores or because the parent wanted the child to buy a more expensive birthday gift. Next, the timing of the action is important. If a mother runs up to kiss her son in front of his pals, her timing is inappropriate. The child will then wonder why the parent chose to do it. Lastly, the child wonders who will benefit. Parents who always sacrifice may be perceived by the child as inducing guilt to control the child. Weighing alternatives and choosing to interact with a child at an appropriate time for the benefit of the child because of what the child has done or said will lead to increased perceptions of love for the parent on the part of the child.

Streit (1987d) developed an instrument to measure representational systems (the feeling, visual, and auditory modes of neurolinguistic programming) so that family members could make contact more effectively. He has also constructed measures of the expectations that parents have for their children and those that their children have for them (Streit, 1987e). When these are analyzed and openly discussed, family members become closer. In particular, Streit (1987f) has formulated a package of inventories to determine the expectations, perceptions, assessment, and desired changes of single-parent families. By discussing their expectations and perceptions, they can decide what changes need to be made. Such a process helps family members adjust to a divorce.

McMASTER MODEL OF FAMILY FUNCTIONING

The McMaster Model of Family Functioning (MMFF) has been developed over a 25-year period and is still in the process of revision at Brown and McMaster universities. Based on systems theory, the MMFF views the family as an open system composed of other systems, such as the married couple and the individual, and interfacing with yet other systems, such as the community and the school. Epstein, Bishop, and Baldwin (1982) caution that judgments of dysfunction or health based on the model should take into consideration the culture of the clients, because what is normal is relative to the culture in which a client functions and in which clients were raised.

The major assumption of the MMFF is that the primary function of today's family is to meet the biological, psychological, and social needs of its members. To do this, families must be able to deal with tasks in the Hazardous Task Area (crises), the Developmental Task Area (transitions of individuals and the family over time), and the Basic Task Area (housing, food, transportation, and money or income).

MMFF contains six dimensions of family functioning—problem solving, communication, role allocation, affective responsiveness, affective involvement, and behavioral control. All families have problems; however, healthy families tend to solve most of their problems, while dysfunctional families solve few of them. Instrumental prob-

lems such as a means of income for the family, clothing, food, housing, and transportation typically need to be dealt with before affectional problems such as depression can be handled. With the first dimension of problem solving, there are seven
steps in the MMFF decision-making process: (1) identifying a problem, (2) communicating to the appropriate people about the problem, (3) developing alternatives for
action, (4) deciding on an alternative, (5) taking action, (6) checking the action while
it is taking place, and (7) evaluating the success of the action.

The dimension of communication emphasizes clear and direct communication in
both affective and instrumental areas. Healthy families can tell an interviewer very
specifically how they allocate roles when dealing with the third dimension of roles. In
the healthiest families allocation is made according to interest and skills with role
sharing taking place.

The dimension of affective responsiveness means that family members can express
welfare emotions (warm, caring feelings) as well as emergency feelings such as anger
or fear appropriate to the level of the stimulus (neither over- nor under-reacting).
Empathic involvement is the most effective type of affective involvement (the fifth
dimension of the MMFF). With the last dimension of behavioral control, a flexible
approach, in which feedback is taken into consideration in the formation of negotiated
rules, is most effective.

THE FAMILY PARADIGM OF REISS

Oliveri and Reiss (1982) used card sorts (that is, decks of cards with symbols or words
on them that family members sort) to measure the family paradigm, the basic assumptions that the family has about the world. In their original research, they found that the
most important variable was how the family approached the testing situation. They
could differentiate families who had a schizophrenic child (the laboratory was threatening to the ties between family members), those who had delinquent offspring (the
laboratory was a place to exhibit distance from each other), and those who had
neither (they saw the laboratory experience as a challenging game).

The various problem-solving styles exhibited by families were measured on three
dimensions: (1) configuration, (2) coordination, and (3) closure. Configuration is a
family's view of whether the world is a masterable place. Coordination means that
family members obtain feedback from each other because they believe that people,
especially family members, can see the environment in the same way. Closure refers
to the amount of time that family members wait for input before reaching a final
solution. Those families who delay the most tend to see the world as a new and fresh
place.

The results of Oliveri's and Reiss's study indicate that families who arranged the
cards with family figures on them in nonstereotypical ways were high on configuration and coordination. They saw the uniqueness of their own families. Those families
that brought strange figures close were high on configuration, seeing the world as a
manageable place and being able to act independently within kinship ties. Those
families that included cards with inanimate objects in their task were high on delayed
closure and also had large networks of kin. They liked feedback from others and social
interaction.

AN INTEGRATIVE DELINEATION

Having reviewed the material on healthy family functioning, key points can be emphasized in the following compilation (Table 3–3). First of all, commitment is a key variable in family success. In my experience as a therapist, if one partner is not committed to the relationship and wants out, the marriage cannot be saved. Sometimes when dating, individuals can check out the patterns in a person's family of origin. Typically, if divorce is present in the family of origin, it has a higher probability for the child when he or she marries because the parents have modeled their behavior and expectation that marriage is not a life-long commitment. Of course, some individuals may stay in marriages because they vowed never to divorce due to the pain they experienced when their parents divorced.

Commitment involves a promise and dedication not only to the institution of marriage but also to the relationship with the spouse, which includes a deep level of emotional attachment (Lauer & Lauer, 1986). Often people who have been brought up in religious environments are socialized to believe in the stability of marriage and family. Commitment means that people are willing to endure and work through tough times. Commitment requires acceptance and patience. Its rewards include a stronger relationship which has more meaning, security, support, and a sense of survival regardless of the difficulties faced. People in relationships where there is a high degree of commitment can feel secure, which frees energy for the development of the self as well as the relationship.

Successful marriages also require commitment to separateness and togetherness, a reconciliation of seeming opposites—the commitment to the growth of each person

TABLE 3–3   Toward Healthier Family Systems: Characteristics of healthy family functioning

1. Commitment.	13. Couple has couple friends.
2. Meaning/purpose in life.	14. Time together.
3. Positive *weltanschauung*.	15. Enough income to meet survival needs of family.
4. Can talk about death openly.	16. Career transitions are effectively made.
5. Initiates—Takes responsibility.	17. Health.
6. Instills culture and wants to pass it on to children.	18. Conscience and behavioral discipline.
7. Affectionate, sensual, sexual relationship between spouses.	19. Use of mature defense mechanisms.
8. Love.	20. Altruistic.
9. Control/authority clear in family.	21. Reframes crisis into opportunity.
10. Communicates effectively.	22. Humor.
11. Negotiates conflicts.	23. Seeks help when needed.
12. Members support each other.	

Different generations of a family share a meal around the dinner table.

and to the enhancement of the relationship (Fields, 1986). In addition, as children enter the family, commitment means support of the growth and education of these children to become separately functioning human beings.

Healthy families have dreams, sometimes created in earlier generations. They have images of what they would like to become. The family fulfills a symbolic meaning function for the individual, and family members have well-defined purposes in life. They have expectations for each other. Often there is involvement in activities of religious institutions which encourage the development of a purpose in life.

There is a positive *weltanschauung* in healthy families. The world is viewed as a friendly place. Family members expect satisfaction from interactions with other family members and people outside the family.

The healthier the family, the more family members can talk about death openly. Often belief in a religion, especially one that emphasizes love, caring, forgiveness, the worth of the individual, and an afterlife, helps families deal with death. Participation in the activities of a religious organization often provides a community of friends who help family members face such issues.

The family initiates and takes responsibility for preventing and solving problems. They create their life together, which requires choice, planning, and action.

In healthy families there is creation of family traditions. Parents want to inculcate the best parts of their culture of their family of origin. They choose unique traditions for the family with the feedback and input of all family members.

The spouses in healthy families have an active, satisfying sex life. They are affectionate and sensual. The best predictor of the emotional health of the children is the sexual relationship of the parents. Touching, such as hugging, kissing, or massage, is encouraged in the family.

Each person perceives that they are loved in a healthy family. Love means something different to each person. Daily behaviors demonstrate that each individual is loved, and these differ from person to person.

There is a clear chain of command in a healthy family. Parents typically function as a flexible coalition, receiving feedback from the children in order to make the rules. Rules are consistently enforced. Roles are clear and based on the interests and skills of the family members. Some family members may like to cook and are better at it than others, so they may cook more frequently, for example. Often there are shared roles where more than one person does something. Most typically, there are complementary roles with a small or nonexistent gap in the power distribution.

Healthy families communicate effectively. Family members can own and state their own thoughts and feelings. They can see the world from other family members' points of view and empathically respond. Feelings of hurt or anger are shared when they are experienced or as close to the time as possible. Parents listen to children and compliment them. There is confrontation, when appropriate. Lots of energy is present in healthy families: They're spunky. People say what they think and feel.

Conflict management skills are important in families. Spouses can compromise, capitulate, agree to disagree, generate new alternatives—negotiating their conflicts. They can identify their spin-out and spin-in patterns and the needs underlying these patterns so that direct requests can be made.

Members support each other in healthy families. They compliment and give verbal, sincere appreciation to other family members. Sometimes they will do things for each other or give each other little gifts.

The couple has couple friends whom they enjoy. They spend time together, perhaps going out to dinner, watching ball games on television, or talking together. The children in these families are brought up in a community of friends (the adult couples who are friends of their parents) with similar values.

Healthy families spend time together. They have to plan and engineer what they will do. They like vacations together, movies, talk time, playing, hiking, or outdoor activities like boating, sports, playing, hobbies, doing chores together, and exercising. Typically time is set aside for the spouse, separate time for each child, and time for the family as a whole.

Many of the above processes will be strained if there is not enough money to provide for the survival needs of the family—housing, food, clothing, and transportation. Funds would be needed for growth. However, concerns for financial prestige may be detrimental to family functioning.

In healthy families, individual family members sort out priorities and make career transitions effectively. Individuals are encouraged to follow their interest patterns. Women may work full-time, part-time, or not at all because of their interests and what they see as their purposes in life. Men and women may experience crises at mid-life or other transition points, and these crises are managed successfully.

Healthy families take the initiative to plan vacations and other time together.

Physical health is important for functional families. Spouses take responsibility for their own health and have regular check-ups. Family members exercise, eat appropriate diets, and manage their lifestyles effectively.

Each family member develops behavioral discipline. Children are taught values and have a sense of conscience. Family members have effective habits, routines, and behavioral patterns. There is an absence of addictive or compulsive behaviors. Family members work toward using more mature defense mechanisms. Spouses understand their own personality styles and those of their mates. Family members understand each other's idiosyncrasies.

Healthy families are altruistic. They reach beyond themselves into the community to help others.

In healthy families, crises are reframed as opportunities for growth. Family members are able to affirm each other as people of worth during periods of crisis.

There is humor, but not at another's expense, in healthy families. People often laugh at themselves.

Healthy functioning families seek help when they need it. They consult a professional support network about growth, development, and crises. A typical family might have a family dentist, lawyer, accountant, internist, pediatrician, gynecologist, religious advisor, insurance agent, family counselor/therapist, or other specialist as dictated by the needs of the family at a particular point in time.

FAMILY ENRICHMENT PROGRAMS

With the above model of health in mind, it would be a rare family who would have all the above characteristics and processes in place at optimal levels. One trend which is surfacing is the desire for people to enrich the quality of their relationships and family life. The best-educated generation of Americans have high expectations for themselves, their relationships, and their families. They are willing to attend classes, participate in structured enrichment programs, and attend support groups to help them meet their goals.

The Pioneers of Marital Enrichment

In his book David Mace (1983) traces the history of the marriage enrichment movement. In 1943 in London, he and others opened the first marriage counseling center in Europe. After helping to build the marriage counseling movement in England, Mace and his wife moved to the United States. They led their first retreat for couples in 1962 and developed one of the three basic historic models for couple enrichment. During

From Barcelona, Spain, Father Gabriel Calvo is credited with starting the Marriage Encounter Movement, which has spread around the world. (Courtesy of the Association for Couples in Marriage Enrichment)

this same year, a Catholic priest named Father Gabriel Calvo led his first retreat for married couples in Barcelona, Spain. This was the beginning of the Marriage Encounter Movement, which has spread around the globe.

In 1964, Leon and Antoinette Smith began to develop marriage enrichment weekends. These efforts were very successful and led to the development of the Marriage Communication Labs, which were sponsored nationally by the Board of Discipleship of the United Methodist Church.

David and Vera Mace founded the Association for Couples in Marriage Enrichment (ACME) in 1973. ACME, which credentials and trains volunteer couples who lead enrichment groups and also encourages marital support groups, sponsored the first international conference on marital enrichment in Atlanta, Georgia, in April 1988 to celebrate the 15th anniversary of its founding. In 1975 the Council of Affiliated Marriage Enrichment Organizations (CAMEO) was formed. Its constituent members meet every year to share hopes and concerns.

Leon and Antoinette Smith of Nashville, Tennessee, created the Marriage Communication Labs, sponsored nationally by the Board of Discipleship of the United Methodist Church. (Courtesy of the Association for Couples in Marriage Enrichment)

David and Vera Mace founded the Association for Couples in Marriage Enrichment (ACME). They are shown here toasting the first international conference on marital enrichment held in Atlanta, Georgia, in April 1988, celebrating the 15th anniversary of the founding of ACME. (Courtesy of the Association for Couples in Marriage Enrichment)

In 1977, Mace and Mace wrote *How to Have a Happy Marriage* in which they outlined enrichment activities for couples. Their program included three main components: the commitment on the part of both spouses to grow as a couple, communication skills in an effective system, and conflict resolution skills. In particular, they emphasized the ability to negotiate one of three possible solutions: capitulation, compromise, or co-existence (agreeing to disagree).

Mace (1982) focused on the relationship between love and anger in marriage and audiotaped lectures with his wife on the topic. They become angry spontaneously on the tape during the lecture and resolve the conflict. In 1982 Mace also wrote *Close Companions: The Marriage Enrichment Handbook,* a sophisticated volume on the components necessary for healthy change in marital relationships and historical developments in marital enrichment. David and Vera Mace were interviewed in *Wellness Perspectives* about their marriage and life work, providing intimate insight into their interaction. As the pioneer couple to first lead marital enrichment retreats, they have left a significant legacy of writing, professional leadership, and, most importantly, personal role modeling of healthy marital processes. Thanks to their efforts, couples around the world can become members of marital support groups and avail themselves of marital enrichment activities.

Structured Family Facilitation Programs

Hoopes, Fisher, and Barlow (1984) wrote *Structured Family Facilitation Programs,* which teaches professionals to formulate and implement programs of family facilitation. Included are examples of specific programs designed for special populations for family life education, family enrichment, and treatment. An interdisciplinary group of professionals can be trained to deliver facilitation programs to families. There are four stages of program design: (1) preplanning, (2) program development, (3) program delivery, and (4) program evaluation. Knowledge of healthy family functioning can help in designing the goals for such programs. It is particularly important to assess the needs of the target group in establishing the goals of the program. After the program is written, pretest and revise it on the basis of the original feedback. Once it has been piloted, it is ready for packaging and sale. Typically, facilitators are trained to deliver the program. An evaluation of the program and assessment of the various steps in the process are completed.

The Family and Children's Service in Minneapolis and the University of Minnesota Family Study Center were important in the development of the Couple Communication Programs, which are popular and successful marital facilitation programs. Presently, three marital enrichment programs plus a trainer's manual (Miller, Nunnally, & Wackman, 1977, 1979; Miller, Wackman, Nunnally, & Saline, 1981; Miller, Wackman, Nunnally, & Miller, 1988) and one family enrichment program (Carnes, 1987) are available. A professional can complete training to become a Certified Couple Communication Facilitator for these programs.

Bernard G. Guerney, Jr. (1977) wrote *Relationship Enhancement,* which he has utilized to train therapists and families to use in education, enrichment/facilitation, and treatment. The focus of the book is the development of empathic relationships. Four basic skills are taught: the expressive mode, the empathic responder mode, the facilitator mode, and mode switching. He has also written a manual (Guerney, 1986a) to be used with clients and one for therapists (Guerney, 1986b).

Dinkmeyer and Carlson (1984) developed *Time for a Better Marriage* which can be used as a 10-session, structured, conjoint couple group facilitation program or individually at home by a spouse or a couple. The approach emphasizes responsibility for self, encouragement, communication skills, choice, and conflict resolution. Concepts from the Adlerian approach to psychotherapy and experiential/communication theorists such as Satir are evident. Training is available in using this model. Dinkmeyer has also been active in developing programs for teaching effective parenting, especially of teenagers.

Albert and Einstein (1986) have written a structured enrichment program for stepfamilies called *Strengthening Your Stepfamily* which includes a set of at-home activities. The context of creating a stepfamily is explored, especially confrontation of myths and unrealistic expectations, followed by work on the couple relationship, setting up effective roles and relationships in the household, what it means to be a stepchild, and the stepfamily journey. Helping people to create what they want their stepfamily to be can be satisfying.

L'Abate and Weinstein (1987), in *Structured Enrichment Programs for Couples and Families,* suggest the use of middle-level, trained paraprofessionals to deliver structured enrichment programs tailored to the needs of particular target groups. This collection contains 50 structured enrichment exercises to be used at different stages of the family life cycle, to improve various process dimensions of family life, or for diverse types of families grouped according to introductory, intermediate, or advanced levels of skills. In addition, steps are outlined to design and write enrichment programs for diverse targeted families. L'Abate and Young (1987) compiled a casebook to provide examples of how actual enrichment activities worked with various families.

The Building Family Strengths Program, mentioned earlier in the chapter, is a structured family enrichment/therapy program designed to help families grow healthier. Its 10 experiential components can be delivered in flexible formats to suit the needs of the target groups. Based on family strengths research, as well as techniques chosen from the family therapy literature, the program integrates counseling and family enrichment. Professionals can become nationally certified Building Family Strengths Facilitators through the Center for Family Strengths at the University of Nebraska-Lincoln.

These programs of marital and family enrichment represent only some of the experiences that are available to families who have made the commitment to grow and develop over the life span. A marital and family therapist should know about and be able to provide leadership of family enrichment activities.

THE QUADRATIC MODEL OF FAMILY SERVICE DELIVERY

A quadratic model for working with families is shown in Figure 3–5. First, family life education is needed by many families in our society. For example, there are many adults, presently beginning their own families, who were raised in dysfunctional homes due to alcoholism, illness, or other parental problems. In these cases, education about healthy family functioning is needed before long-term changes can occur. Typically, such an approach is predominantly cognitive in nature.

Second, some families may want to improve the quality of their family lives. They participate in experientially oriented family enrichment or family facilitation groups in which process is emphasized. Rather than passively listening to lectures, family members are required to respond and interact through planned exercises, which encourage them to express their own thoughts and feelings. By experiencing the group process, family members can return to their own families and initiate changes in the family process.

Third, there is a need for dealing with crises, represented by diverse family therapy models of treatment. When families are involved in emergency situations, they want help. Strong feelings surface which must be heard but, most importantly, alternatives must be generated, decisions must be made, and *action* must be taken. Although education may be given at this time, families may not be able to concentrate enough to use such information, and experiencing a different process is not possible.

Fourth, to maintain the gains made in family therapy, enrichment groups, and education, support groups provide paths toward wellness. Sometimes such support groups are community-based marriage encounter alumni groups, or they are associated with groups that address special problems of the family, such as Al-Anon.

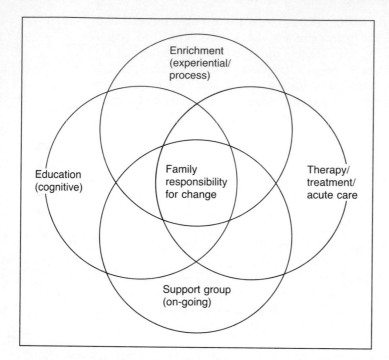

FIGURE 3–5 The Quadratic Model of Family Service Delivery

The most important part of the model in Figure 3–5 is the initiative of the family, the family's responsibility for planning and working a program. Without this crucial component, families can be weakened by the services intended to strengthen them, especially if they learn to be passive recipients. Creating one's own family is a life-long task that is never completely finished. By taking greater initiative, families can make changes and practice new behaviors they have chosen to implement. At any point, a family or family members can decide to avail themselves of education, enrichment, family therapy, or support groups to help them reach the goals they have chosen.

Occasionally, there is overlap because some enrichment programs include education and also aspects of group support. Likewise, family therapy may encompass homework assignments, educational reading or classes, or conjoint couple or family groups that function as support groups. For example, Guerney perceives his relationship enhancement program to be family therapy, but it also provides education, enrichment, and support group functions when delivered in multifamily groups.

Depending upon the predominant mode of functioning of a given family, the family may choose at which point to enter the family service delivery system. For example, an abstract-oriented, highly cognitive couple might feel more comfortable attending lectures on family life or parenting before entering a support group where feelings are shared. A socially adept couple might enjoy a support group such as ACME and may never seek formal therapy or treatment. Marital and family therapists can provide direction to those families who seek their help by encouraging them to become involved in those modes of service delivery that best match the needs and profile of a given family.

SUMMARY

To become an effective marital and family therapist, it is important to form a cognitive map of healthy family functioning, which is the goal of treatment. As families progress in marital and family therapy, they move closer toward healthier functioning. Seven models of healthy family functioning based on research are presented in the chapter: (1) family strengths approaches, including the Building Family Strengths Model from the University of Nebraska-Lincoln and Otto's work as "the Father of Family Enrichment"; (2) optimally functioning families at the Timberlawn Psychiatric Research Foundation; (3) the Circumplex Model of Olson and colleagues; (4) Streit's model; (5) the McMaster Model of Family Functioning; (6) the Family Paradigm of Reiss; and (7) an integrative delineation.

There are many ways, not just one way, of being a healthy family. The unique characteristics and cultural heritage of a given family determine the particular style and strengths of that family, although some key components of family health are found across diverse families. These include commitment; purpose or meaning in life; seeing the world as a positive place; being able to talk about death; taking initiative; affection, including a sensual/sexual relationship between spouses; love; clear lines of authority in the family; effective communication; negotiation; support; time together; sufficient income; effective career transitions; health; appropriate behavior; the ability to reframe crises; humor and other mature defense mechanisms; and reaching out to help others in the community, as well as to seek help for the family when needed.

The current well-educated generation has high expectations for family life and is willing to participate in family enrichment programs to improve their level of family functioning. David and Vera Mace are pioneers in the area of marital enrichment, as are Father Calvo and Leon and Antoinette Smith. The Quadratic Model of Family Service Delivery links family life education, family enrichment, family therapy, and family support groups as components of effective delivery of services to families. The future of family work will highlight the development of support groups for healthy families.

EXERCISES

1. Close your eyes and let memories of your family come to mind. On a sheet of paper, write down as many strengths of your family as you can remember. With a partner, take turns sharing the strengths of your family and any special, warm, positive memories that you choose to share.

2. On a sheet of paper, write down the strengths of healthy families. Share the strengths you have identified in groups of four. Choose a group leader to write down and report to the class the strengths that have been shared in the group.

3. Listen to the audiotape entitled "Understanding Love, Anger and Intimacy" by David Mace. Share with a partner your opinions about how David Mace thinks anger, love, and intimacy are related. How do you think anger should be handled? What does anger mean? Your instructor may discuss these issues and ask for students to volunteer their answers.

4. Write the Association for Couples in Marriage Enrichment (ACME) for information at P.O. Box 10596, Winston-Salem, North Carolina 27108. If your spouse would like to, attend one meeting of ACME and observe what it is like. If you are single, attend by yourself or with a friend.

Chapter 4
Family Development

There is an appointed time for everything, and a time for every affair under the sun.

Ecclesiastes 3:1

THE DIMENSION OF TIME: WHAT IS DEVELOPMENT?

The dimension of time is an important one. Each human being is mortal and has only a limited amount of time on this earth. Development (whether that of the family or the individual) is simply growth and evolution of an organism or system over time.

Typically as people age, they develop and grow, changing in physical size and shape. They evolve—that is, they become competent to perform additional and more complex tasks. In our culture, as with many others, age has become a way of organizing society. Children enter the first grade at age 6, are permitted to drive cars at 16, and at age 18 are considered legal adults in many states, even being able to marry without permission of their parents. These young adults are taller and heavier than 6-year-old children and are capable of holding jobs. They have grown and evolved. Development consists of this basic, continuous yet sometimes discontinuous process of change over the life span. The clock ticks on. The forces of development proceed.

Likewise, families grow and evolve over time. The concept of family development encompasses the growth in membership as well as the changes in structure, tasks, and relational processes of the family over time. Typically families can perform more diverse and complex tasks with the passage of time. Family members age, children grow up, and family development proceeds.

The stair steps of development—changes in physical size and ability to perform more complex tasks.

This chapter focuses on family development. (Development of the individual will be covered in Chapter 5.) This text follows a systems approach: the macrosystems are covered first, followed by the family system and then the individual subsystem. This approach is contrary to the evolution and history of human development theories. Such theories began by focusing on the individual, especially young children, and were followed by theories of family development; however, both individual and family development affect how a particular family functions. Marital and family therapists should be guided by both in diagnosis and intervention.

WHAT IS FAMILY DEVELOPMENT?

Family development is like the changing seasons. What is appropriate in one season is not in another, yet each has its special delights. If a person wore a bathing suit outdoors in January in most parts of the United States, other people would consider this eccentric because the person had not changed to accommodate the shift in the environment. In fact, this person might become ill because of not adjusting to the changes in the season. Yet there are special activities associated with each season that are meaningful to people, such as a white snowy Christmas, a winter dinner shared with friends, the daffodils peeping through the ground in spring, evening baseball games in the summer, football games in the crisp fall air, and turkey at Thanksgiving. Each season is different but special in its own way.

So it is with families. Each stage of the family life cycle is different from the other and unique in its own way, with changes (developmental tasks) that need to be accomplished by the family members if the family is to function in a healthy way. When family members resist the natural changes that are necessary as family members grow and develop, the family will become stuck with symptoms occurring in one or more family members.

A family is continually evolving and changing, meeting increasingly complex developmental tasks faced by the family as a group. For example, after a couple marries, they must negotiate different roles with their parents of origin. On issues upon which there may be disagreement between his family of origin and his new wife, the neophyte husband must learn to support his wife, a difficult task indeed, but one that clearly demonstrates that his relationships with his parents have changed in dramatic ways. If this normal family developmental task is not achieved, the arising conflicts and hurt feelings will affect later stages of family development.

At the next stage of the family life cycle, when the first child is born, the wife will typically become absorbed in caring for the newborn, which can elicit normal feelings of jealousy in the husband. Gradually the wife will learn her new role of mother and become less enmeshed with the child, again giving attention to the husband. The husband, in turn, is also learning his new role of father, which is different from his role of husband and requires the mastery of new and more complex skills. If he has not already renegotiated his relationships with his parents, his parents may interfere with the raising of the child. If the husband listens to the wishes of his parents to the exclusion of the feelings and ideas of his wife, she may feel estranged from him and continue to remain totally absorbed in the child. This creates difficulties for the child, the marital couple, and the family as a whole.

Families who present for treatment may be repeating behaviors that worked at one stage of development but need to be changed to accommodate the needs of children or adults who are now at different stages of human development. For example, a mother who has been effective in meeting the needs of her toddler for clean diapers, talk time, and the monitoring of activities so that the child is not hurt may create tension with her teenager if she continues to monitor activities closely. The teenager will rebel against monitoring and curfews, perhaps becoming involved in delinquent behavior to become an adult (Patterson, 1986). Therefore, it is important for marital and family therapists to know what changes are expected at each stage of the family life cycle. When families present for treatment, the therapist can assess the family to determine at what stage of the family life cycle they are and where they are stuck in their normal developmental tasks.

THEORIES OF THE FAMILY LIFE CYCLE

In the late forties, Duvall and Hill (1948) began integrating the concept of a family developmental task with a stage of the family life cycle—what expected changes will occur in the family over time. Each stage is marked by discrete developmental tasks that must be accomplished effectively if later stages of the family life cycle are to be successful. Each new developmental stage requires adaptations and new responsibilities, creating new challenges and opportunities. For example, according to the eight-stage family life cycle of Duvall, newly married couples must adjust to each other in the marriage, negotiate roles with kin, and deal with decisions and planning regarding parenthood. However, the aging family must deal with the death of a spouse, adjusting to aging, and adapting to retirement.

While Carter and McGoldrick (1980) give credit to Duvall, they propose the addition of a between families stage, consolidating the infant, preschool, and school-age family stages of Duvall into a family with young children stage and combining the postparental and aging family stages of Duvall into one stage, the family in later life. Thus, six stages of the family life cycle emerge in their developmental theory as revised in 1988: (1) between families, (2) the newly married couple, (3) the family with young children, (4) the family with adolescents, (5) launching children and moving on, and (6) the family in later life.

Horizontal stressors include the predictable stressors associated with healthy family development during life cycle transitions and the unpredictable stressors associated with unusual life events such as an illness, accident, or untimely death. Both developmental and unpredictable stress can reverberate throughout the family system.

If the family is already experiencing a high degree of anxiety passed down by previous generations (vertical stress), even a minor horizontal stressor can generate a large disturbance in the family system (Carter, 1978). Therefore, it is particularly important for the marital and family therapist to assess the vertical stressors impinging upon the family at those times when the family is experiencing the horizontal stressors of normal developmental transitions in the family life cycle and of unpredictable life events.

In observing the family life cycle, stages often occur naturally as one member enters or leaves the system. Yet whether or not the family will be able to deal effectively with the new stage is often determined by the ways family members relate. Lyman Wynne (1988) formulated an epigenetic model of family processes to explain the relational changes that build upon one another within a family.

The "epigenetic principle," coined by Singer and Wynne (1965), means that the interactions at any developmental stage are built upon the results of earlier interactions. If previous transactions did not lead to successful outcomes, then subsequent developmental stages will be disrupted because they are built upon a faulty foundation. Biological and behavioral determinants recombine in new patterns at each stage of development which establish the parameters of variability within that stage.

THE FAMILY LIFE CYCLE

The stages of the family life cycle according to Thomas are listed in Table 4–1. The major process of change or transition that family members are required to negotiate at each stage of the family life cycle is also included.

Each stage begins with a dichotomous, discontinuous marker that necessitates distinct changes in the structure and functions within the family. The roles that family members play change dramatically during the transition. Sometimes these markers are additions or deletions of family members, as when a young adult marries or a spouse dies (Falicov, 1988). At other points, the ages of family members or their work statuses are the changes determining the transition and the stage—for example, when the oldest child turns 13 and becomes a teenager or when an adult retires from gainful employment at age 70.

When family members resist these changes and fight the transition, symptoms surface in one or more family members. When family members work on the transition by changing their role behaviors, thoughts, and feelings, individual family members

TABLE 4–1   Toward Healthier Family Systems: The family life cycle

Stage	Process of Change or Transition
1. Independent adult	Take responsibility for living one's own life by learning the role of an adult separate from one's parents.
2. Marital dyad	Establish a marriage by learning the roles of wife and husband.
3. Infant family	Learn the roles of new parents.
4. Preschool family	Learn the educative and emotional roles of parents of toddlers.
5. Grade school family	Change parenting roles to incorporate feedback from the school and community.
6. Adolescent family	Change parenting roles to accommodate the needs for autonomy of the teenager.
7. Launching family	Change parenting roles to support the life choices of the young adult.
8. Mentoring dyad	Change parenting roles to adult-adult mentoring roles and marital relationship to one of increased intimacy.
9. Retired family	Change parental roles to receive from children as well as to give, and increase leisure activities and intimacy in marital role.
10. Elderly family (beyond 80 years of age)	Adjust to death of spouse and living alone.

can develop and symptoms disappear. During any given stage, the family exhibits continuous small, quantitative changes that have been learned in the transition until a new transition triggers the discontinuous change of a qualitative nature associated with a new stage of the family life cycle.

There are specific developmental tasks that should be mastered at each stage of the family life cycle. Like advancing in a career, continuously creating one's family is hard work. The process of raising a family requires the learning of new, ever more complex tasks. These tasks can be subsumed under broad areas of family development.

For example, at each stage of the family life cycle, family changes should be accomplished in a number of areas of development: (1) spiritual (church attendance, involvement in church activities, and meaning/purpose in life), (2) intellectual (formal education, communication skills to express thoughts, logic, and common sense), (3) behavioral (habits such as smoking and drinking, risk-taking behavior, assertiveness, and taking responsibility or initiative), (4) emotional (communication skills to express feelings and personality patterns such as the chronic or consistent use of particular defense mechanisms or coping strategies), (5) imaginal (the "dream" for the family), (6) sensual (touch and massage), (7) sexual development (sex education of the children and maintenance of a warm, sexual relationship between spouses), (8) physical (diet, physical fitness, medication, and state of the body), (9) interpersonal (the interactional patterns between spouses or those child-rearing patterns involved in parenting other family members), (10) social (social activities with relatives, couple friends, and family friends), and (11) financial/career (sources of income derived from work and the planning/management of fiscal resources). The family can move toward health in each of these areas of development at each stage of the family life cycle. The specific developmental tasks in each of these areas of development associated with each stage of the family life cycle can be found in Table 4-2.

At each stage of the family life cycle, assessments can be made as to how the family is progressing on the required developmental tasks for that stage of the family life cycle in a given area of development. These areas of family development can be placed on a Family Health Wheel (Figure 4-1).

In addition, each family member and every family has expectations in the above areas of development. When they meet their expectations, there is congruence, which is defined as health. When there is a large gap between the way the family wants to be and the way it is, there is illness.

When the gap between their ideal goals in diverse developmental areas and their realities is too great, the family is dysfunctional. Just as a person can become healthier by reducing ideal expectations for the self or by growing toward the ideal or a combination of both (usually accomplished through individual self-actualizing therapy), so can a family move toward the healthier pole of the continuum through family therapy designed to reduce the incongruent gap between the ideal family and the real family. The family can confront myths, inaccurate expectancies, and overly high expectations as well as grow toward the ideal in the diverse areas of development. The marital and family therapist can use the Family Health Wheel as a tool in working with families to discuss areas that may not have been volunteered in an intake session. By making explicit the expectations that family members hold in each area of develop-

TABLE 4–2 Stages of family development and associated developmental tasks

1. Independent Adult

   Obtain the first full-time job.
   Set up an apartment.
   Establish and maintain a network of friendships with same-sex peers.
   Develop emotionally intimate relationships involving sexual attraction with peers of
   the opposite sex, leading to a potential marital partner.
   Negotiate adult-adult relationships with parents or significant others who raised the
   person.
   Interact effectively with authority figures at work.
   Maintain collegial relationships with peers at work.
   Maintain a healthy body through exercise and diet.
   Evaluate one's religious upbringing and family values to develop own life code.

2. Marital Dyad

   Adjust to marriage through talking about likes and dislikes, using problem solving to
   resolve conflicts.
   Become established in careers.
   Establish and furnish an apartment or house.
   Decide on who will do what around the house.
   Develop relationships with in-laws.
   Negotiate the "we" of "couple first" with the families of origin and establish couple
   boundary (secrets shared only by couple and not with families of origin).
   Decide on family planning.
   Prepare for pregnancy and parenthood.
   Appreciate and support each other.

3. Infant Family

   Recover from childbirth.
   Breast feed or bottle feed.
   Pay for cost of birth and any equipment or preparation needed in house.
   Establish enmeshed bond between mother and baby in early months, which
   becomes more disengaged over time.
   Encourage expression of normal jealousy on part of father.
   Involve father in caring for child from Lamaze classes through labor, delivery, and
   life at home.
   Spend time with the infant, stimulating emotional, social, and intellectual
   development.
   Share household responsibilities.
   Relate to relatives as parents.
   Create family rituals and routines.
   Appreciate and support each other in parenting roles.
   Maintain employment and stable sources of income, growing in career.
   Spend time reinforcing marital relationship.
   Use family planning.
   Develop relationships with other young mothers and with other couples who have
   infants.

TABLE 4–2 *continued*

4. Preschool Family

Baby-proof the house.
Stimulate the language development of the child.
Meet the emotional needs for touch, affection, and self-esteem expressed by the child within appropriate limits.
Administer discipline and be a "good enough" parent.
Find time for self.
Make time for couple.
Meet costs of family.
Share household and child-care responsibilities.
Interact with relatives.
Advance in career or obtain additional education or training.
Cultivate resources such as doctors, baby-sitters, household help.
Plan family outings and activities.
Answer questions about birth and sex as they arise.
Appreciate each family member.

5. Grade School Family

Support the educational achievement of children.
Participate as a parent in school-related and athletic activities of the children.
Be accepted as a family by the school and community.
Make couple friends.
Bear the costs of housing, food, education, and health of family members.
Parent children, support their self-esteem, and discipline them.
Make couple time.
Create family activities, rituals, and customs.
Encourage and teach effective communication of thoughts and feelings among family members.
Instill values.
Present sex education and answer questions about sex.
Appreciate and support each family member.
Encourage spouse to follow dreams of advancing in career or obtaining additional education and training.
Deal with career ascendancy issues.

6. Adolescent Family

Provide financial support for education.
Negotiate curfews and additional freedom through appropriate rules for adolescents.
Negotiate increased responsibilities for adolescents in relationship to their increased freedom.
Change the relationship with the adolescent to encourage independent decision making.
Discuss sexual issues.
Provide for increased costs of clothing, food, and housing.

TABLE 4-2 *continued*

Adolescent Family *continued*

Discuss the budget to deal effectively with the limitless needs of teenagers influenced by peer acceptance and pressure.

Share household tasks.

Emphasize communication of thoughts and feelings leading to alternatives and conflict resolution to bridge generation gap.

Accept the peers of adolescents but talk about behaviors that may be in conflict with family values.

Be clear about family values.

Talk about the natural consequences of driving while drinking, the use of drugs, becoming drunk, and other delinquent behavior.

Make couple time, but be available in case of crisis (similar to infant family).

Advance in career or obtain additional education or training.

Cultivate network of couple friends and family friends, particularly "polestars."

7. Launching Family

Provide the financial resources to launch the young adults into college, a job, military service, or marriage.

Provide physical space in an apartment or house for young adults.

Provide a stable base for launching through communication in the marital dyad and among family members.

Coordinate household tasks among family members according to age and maturity of children.

Discuss and work with young adults on their future plans, following their lead.

Encourage jobs and ways of earning money to save for the launching transition.

Increase amount and level of work to gain additional income needed at this stage.

Allow young adults to test family values to find their own.

Incorporate new family members and release young adults effectively.

Deal tactfully with situations that may violate family values but are important to the young adult.

Affirm family values while remaining flexible.

Create family rituals for launching.

Deepen relationships with friends, couple friends, and family friends.

8. Mentoring Dyad

Adjust to the physiological changes of menopause and hormone-replacement therapy.

Change diet and implement tailored exercise program.

Renew the couple relationship and develop intimacy.

Maintain old friendships and develop new ones.

Advance and make significant contributions at work.

Cultivate new hobbies and interests in the community.

Listen and be emotionally supportive of the needs and dreams of the spouse and the launched children.

TABLE 4-2 *continued*

Mentoring Dyad *continued*

Provide sponsorship and financial resources such as college expenses when negotiated and agreed upon.

Incorporate new members, such as in-laws and grandchildren, into the family.

Act as a refueling station.

Be available and on standby in cases of crisis.

Take care of elderly parents.

Continue to learn new information for career advancement, self-development, and transmittal to other family members.

Devote time to maintaining kinship ties.

9. Retired Family

Spend time in health-promoting activities, such as exercise and diet.

Adjust to physiological changes due to aging.

Take responsibility for working on any health problems.

Adjust to the loss of work roles.

Cultivate leisure activities.

Spend more time with friends enjoying life.

Imagine dreams and make them realities.

Deal with the death of parents.

Face possibility of death and become more religious, which may not involve increased religious activities.

Budget carefully to conserve financial resources.

Consider selling house or moving to another physical location.

Learn to receive from children as well as to give to them.

Spend substantial time maintaining kinship ties.

10. Elderly Family

Cope with health problems and medical costs.

Maintain companionship and loving, sexual relationship.

Adjust to the death of a spouse and living alone.

Change residences to live in nursing home or with a child.

Value independence while able to be dependent on children.

Reminisce and find meaning through life review.

Remain active in hobbies and interests.

Adjust to the idea of one's own death.

Budget carefully.

Maintain daily routines.

Use a preventive approach to diet, exercise, rest, health check-ups, the monitoring of destructive health habits such as drinking or smoking, and the avoidance of high levels of stress.

Keep in touch with family.

Play role of family patriarch or matriarch by encouraging kinship ties.

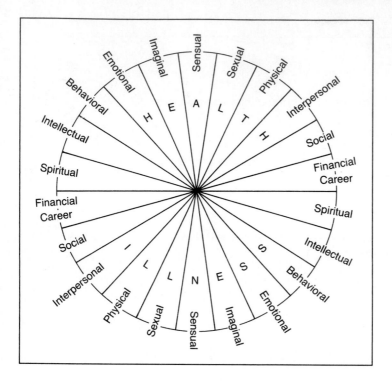

FIGURE 4–1 The Family Health Wheel. The family moves simultaneously toward health or illness in 11 areas of development: spiritual, intellectual, behavioral, emotional, imaginal, sensual, sexual, physical, interpersonal, social, and financial/career.

ment, the therapist can confront unrealistic goals and support growth in those areas where the family wishes to grow.

CO-EVOLUTIONARY HELIX OF THE FAMILY LIFE SPAN

The Family Health Wheel is only one part of a three-dimensional model for the development of the family life span over time. This model is represented by the lightning whelk on the cover of this textbook and in Figure 4–2. On the horizontal axis, the family develops from the stage of independent adult to that of elderly family. Three cross-sections can be visualized as planes moving separately through the family life cycle over time: (1) the Family Health Wheel, (2) the individual developmental stage and tasks of each family member, and (3) the regulation of distance through the use of centrifugal versus centripetal styles and less mature versus more mature defense mechanisms. These factors are normal, intrinsic, predictable elements that naturally affect the family life span on a continual basis.

The cross-sections of the helix and the lightning whelk itself are embedded in culture. Although the developmental tasks are similar at each stage of the family life cycle for all families, the specific ways in which they are implemented differ among families according to cultural influences. For example, the marriage ceremony and the customs associated with it that mark the beginning of the marital dyad stage vary from culture to culture. A Jewish American wedding is said in Hebrew with the custom of

FIGURE 4−2   The Lightning Whelk: A Co-Evolutionary Helix of the Family Life Span

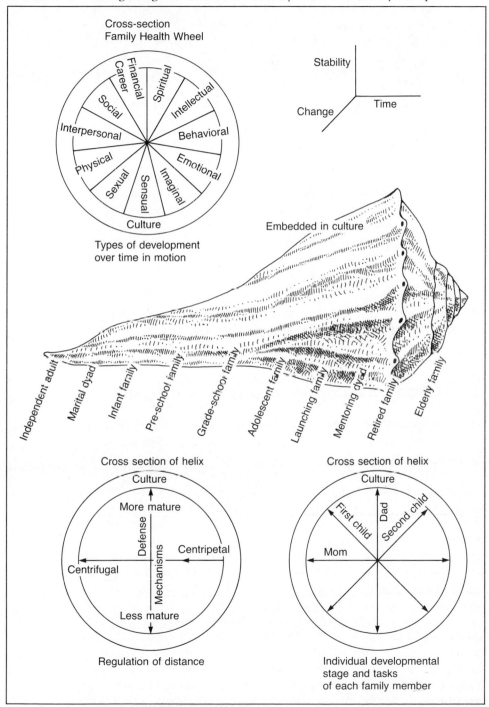

Cross-section
Family Health Wheel

Financial
Career
Spiritual
Social
Intellectual
Interpersonal
Behavioral
Physical
Emotional
Sexual
Sensual
Imaginal
Culture

Types of development
over time in motion

Stability

Change
Time

Embedded in culture

Independent adult
Marital dyad
Infant family
Pre-school family
Grade-school family
Adolescent family
Launching family
Mentoring dyad
Retired family
Elderly family

Cross section of helix

Culture
More mature
Defense
Mechanisms
Centripetal
Centrifugal
Less mature

Regulation of distance

Cross section of helix

Culture
First child
Dad
Second child
Mom

Individual developmental
stage and tasks
of each family member

breaking a glass and saying "mazel-tov," while an Irish American wedding may last an hour or more with a Catholic Mass followed by a reception with ethnic dancing. Yet in both cases the developmental task is the same—the couples make vows of commitment to each other and a long-term marriage.

The Family Health Wheel

Beginning with the first stage of the family life cycle (independent adult), the tasks are clear on the Family Health Wheel. But they expand and become more complex in each area of development in each subsequent stage of the family life cycle until the stage of retired family is reached. In this stage, activities are reduced somewhat and finally become drastically reduced in the elderly family if illness occurs. The circle expands in circumference and becomes broader as the family moves through the stages of the family life cycle as pictured by the increasing spiral or three-dimensional helix within the lightning whelk. Thus, the lightning whelk sea shell represents the three-dimensional family life cycle as the cross-section of the Family Health Wheel moves through time from the stage of independent adult to the stage of elderly family.

The Developmental Stage of Each Family Member

At each stage of the family life cycle, the stage of individual development of each family member can be assessed. The individual development of each family member affects the individual development of the other members and the development of the family as a whole, that is, the family life span. The members of the family are influencing each other and co-evolving together over time. In Figure 4–2, the cross-section of the spiral helix that resembles the lightning whelk contains axes representing the individual development of mother, father, oldest child, second child, and so on, to include all family members.

When assessing the family in the initial session, the family therapist can ask questions to determine the stage of the family life cycle and the stage of individual development of each family member. By observing what family members are wearing and how they are sitting, the family therapist can roughly assess which members are on time in their individual development and those who are off time. A teenager who is dressed like a young child signals a problem in individual development that is impacting the family life cycle. If a family member is delayed in individual development and has not completed the tasks associated with a given stage of individual development, tension occurs and the normal transitions of the family life cycle are delayed.

For example, if a family presents with a 13-year-old daughter who is anorectic, the mother and father typically are overly concerned about the health of the daughter and thus are enmeshed with her. Therefore, the adolescent family stage in which the teenager is granted freedom in relationship to responsibilities is delayed. The parents treat their daughter as though she were a physically ill grade school student. This keeps them together and focused on their daughter rather than using their energy to deal with their relationship and with differentiating in their careers, which are developmental tasks associated with the adolescent family stage of the family life cycle. The longer the daughter's anorexia persists, the more developmental tasks there will be that pile up to be completed by the daughter and her parents when she is better. She will have to learn normal social and assertiveness skills that most pre-teenagers and teenagers were learning when her energy was tied up in her illness. Her parents will need to catch up in their careers and work on making contact with each other and their friends.

Since the development of each family member influences each of the others as they co-evolve through the family life cycle over time, oscillation theory can be applied to the family life cycle. Even as the family moves through a nodal transition of discontinuous change, oscillations between less competent behavior and more competent behavior than warranted by the age of the family members are occurring. Microtransitions requiring change on the part of family members are always happening (Breunlin, 1988) but are intensified at stage markers of discontinuous change.

The Regulation of Distance

A third cross-section of the spiraling helix or lightning whelk consists of the centripetal and centrifugal forces operating in the family and the use of less mature versus more mature defense mechanisms over time. These are methods of regulating the distance among members.

Centripetal and Centrifugal Forces.   In addition to assessing where each family stands on the developmental tasks in each area of family development required at each stage, the therapist should also take note of the family's tendencies either to cling together and enmesh under stress (centripetal) or to separate, with each member rebelling or working on individual developmental issues (centrifugal). Adolescents who run away from home after enduring rejection or neglect and who remain on the street as casual, prematurely independent runaways would come from families in which centrifugal forces are dominant (Stierlin, 1981; Stierlin & Weber, 1989). Likewise, teenagers who do not run away or whose attempts are aborted so they will be found are characteristic of families in which centripetal forces are dominant. In some cases, both centripetal and centrifugal forces are strong in which the adolescent is sent out from the family as a delegate on an unconscious or conscious mission for the family.

Knowing the predominant forces in the family gives the therapist valuable information about how family members may react to the therapy sessions themselves. If the parents spin out centrifugally under stress, they may separate or divorce during the therapy or cancel appointments if the stress becomes uncomfortable. If the parents spin in centripetally under stress, they may exhibit pseudo-mutual or pseudo-hostile ways of relating, having made the commitment to stay together under any circumstances and, therefore, operating under a pact of not expressing true feelings because they view them as endangering the relationship. Such couples may hold hands and appear sweet to each other when hostility is clearly present to an objective observer (pseudo-mutuality) or attack each other while remaining committed (pseudo-hostility).

Certain types of symptoms in teenagers, such as eating disorders and schizophrenia, indicate centripetal forces at work in the family. The adolescent with an eating disorder or a schizophrenic episode may make plans to leave the family but is bound and pulled back in by the strength of the symptoms.

Therefore, when assessing the stage of the family life cycle of a given family, it is important to determine which forces (centripetal, centrifugal, or both) are operating within the family. What is occurring at a given stage of the family life cycle will appear very different to the therapist based on which of the forces are at play in the family at the time.

Rather than label a family as centrifugal or centripetal, it is best to remember that families can oscillate between the two tendencies. Again the image of the three-dimensional spiral or helix applies as the family oscillates between the poles of centripetal and centrifugal forces over time. The opposing forces are reconciled, only to have one pole emerge as dominant.

Combrinck-Graham (1985) connects the oscillation between centripetal and centrifugal forces to a spiral model in which family life cycle stages alternate between those that require close bonding, such as the developmental tasks of the infant family, to those that emphasize autonomy, such as the tasks of the adolescent family. She proposes three complete oscillations in a lifetime—one's own birth and adolescence, the birth and teenage years of one's children, and the birth and adolescent years of grandchildren. A chronic illness or trauma can exert an off-time centripetal pull on the family of adolescents, which can have long-term effects on the degree of differentiation of the teenagers (Rolland, 1988).

At times family members will be close and exhibit strong centripetal pulls, such as during courtship and the first two years of the marital dyad stage. At other times family members will encourage distance, such as the launching family stage when young adults are encouraged to go to college, join the military, or undertake post-secondary training. If these forces are disjointed and off time, additional problems are created for the family. For example, if a young married couple is arguing all the time with one member spending the night in a hotel, the centrifugal forces at work at this stage do not bode well for an effective transition to the infant family stage. The distance is great at a time in the family life cycle when it is normally expected to be closer.

Another way of looking at these forces is to consider the spiraling helix as a repetition of key issues that must be dealt with in life: love/work, separateness/belongingness, differentiation/integration, abandonment/engulfment, and life/death. Although each stage of the family life cycle is unique, many of these same issues recur at subsequent stages. In particular, the optimal distance between marital partners as well as between parents and children is renegotiated at each stage. Whereas marital partners may be close and do many things together when they are first married (during the stage of the marital dyad), they may need more space when the children are teenagers and even more when they are retired (Olson, 1976; Olson, 1988).

Issues of abandonment and engulfment resurface at each stage as family relationships change. These issues are particularly pivotal at the launching family stage, when parents are required to let go. The young adults must separate and become responsible for themselves, abandoning their parents or the values of their parents to some degree. Again these issues recur in the retired family, when spouses must prepare for death and "abandonment" by their partner.

Using More Mature Defense Mechanisms.   Distance is also regulated by the use of defense mechanisms by family members. Defense mechanisms are unconscious ways of coping with anxiety or protecting self-esteem. If a family member utilizes the defense mechanism of projection (blaming) to protect self-esteem, the family member who has been blamed will feel distant from the blamer. If family members and the family as a whole use only those defense mechanisms that increase the distance between members and never use those that reduce the distance such as anticipation of future events or sublimation of desires into socially acceptable channels, the family may fragment and the family life cycle will be delayed. Since the situations faced by family members become more complex over time, more mature defense mechanisms are needed.

Since specific defense mechanisms are defined in Chapter 5, they will be explained only briefly here. According to Vaillant (1977), the least mature defense mechanisms of denial (not being aware of a stressor), distortion (being aware but reorganizing reality to meet inner needs), and delusional projection (seeing others as persecutors) have in common the changing of reality to suit the person using them. If family members use these defense mechanisms, they deny the existence of problems, or they twist reality to such a degree that it is impossible to deal with the problems. Since mastering the transitions of the family life cycle involves solving minor and major problems as they occur, to use such immature defense mechanisms means that major and even minor problems are not dealt with in a timely manner, delaying the family life cycle and hampering the development of individual family members. The defense mechanisms used by individuals can be more detrimental than the real problems to be faced. In addition, using such negative defense mechanisms saps energy that could be used to solve the real problems.

The most mature defense mechanisms are associated with positive feelings and bring human beings closer together. Therefore, although they also use energy that could be utilized to solve problems, the positive reactions of other people toward the person using the more mature defense mechanisms often bolster the self-esteem of the person, increasing the available energy to deal with family problems encountered in a transition to a new stage of the family life cycle. The most mature defense mechanisms, according to Vaillant (1977), are sublimation (expressing aggressive or sexual impulses in socially acceptable ways such as through sports), altruism (doing something to help someone else), suppression (consciously excluding painful impulses from awareness), anticipation (positive planning and expectations about the future), and humor (amusing expressions that reduce tension). Reframing (seeing the positive attributes of a negative situation) tends to be used by people who view stressful activities in more mature ways and who have higher levels of ego development (Labouvie-Vief, Hakim-Larson, & Hobart, 1987).

How families handle the developmental tasks of a given family life cycle stage will be determined to a certain degree by the defense mechanisms that family members use to protect their levels of self-esteem. If family members blame each other by using the defense mechanism of projection, they will damage each other's self-esteem and have less psychological energy to deal with the family transition. However, if they use altruism and anticipation, more positive energy will flow among the members to help them face the real problems.

When a family presents for treatment, the family therapist can assess what the predominant defense mechanisms used by the family are. The therapist can point out the patterns of interaction between family members who use various defense mechanisms. As family members become aware of the patterns, they can learn to stop or restrict the use of certain defense mechanisms. The family therapist can model other more mature defense mechanisms and teach family members how to use them. For example, a homework assignment to plan a family vacation helps family members to experience anticipation and become comfortable with it.

AN ELABORATION OF THE LIGHTNING WHELK OVER TIME

Each stage of the Co-Evolutionary Helix of the Family Life Span will now be discussed. The developmental tasks associated with each stage, as well as how the developmental tasks and stage of each family member affects the transition that is a part of each stage, will be elaborated. The ebb and flow of centripetal and centrifugal forces creating the spiraling life energy of the whelk will emerge because closeness is evident in some stages, alternated with greater distance in others as family members push outward. In addition, the complexity of the family issues faced increases over time. To cope, the family and its members adapt by learning to use more mature defense mechanisms.

The Stages of the Family Life Cycle

Independent Adult.   The family life cycle begins with the formation of a single-person family. For example, the United States Census Bureau uses the one-person household as one of its categories in compiling national statistics related to the family. In fact, one of the fastest growing segments of our population is the single-person household.

The affluence of America in the 1980s has made possible the exodus of young adults to housing of their own. With more than 1 million students graduating from colleges each year to pursue employment or further graduate training, a pool of potential yuppies with the highest starting salaries in history fuels the single-person housing market.

The affluence and radical social changes of the past decade have greatly influenced the family life cycle. During and even after World War II, young working adults lived with their parents in extended family structures because the cost of living in separate apartments was prohibitive, and such housing was either not available or difficult to find. Gutman (1976) traced earlier census records and found that young adults in families from Italian and other ethnic groups tended to live in extended families in the large urban areas of the North such as New York City. Daughters left such homes only by marriage.

Today, with the effects of the women's liberation movement being experienced by this generation of young women, there is an emphasis on becoming independent, being one's own person who is capable of holding a job, and maintaining a separate residence. The high divorce rates affect young women psychologically: they acknowledge the probability that they will be taking care of themselves at various points over the life span and need to feel secure about making it on their own.

In addition, the expectations of young adult males have changed. In surveys about the ideal spouse, young men decades ago always chose physical beauty as the highest priority for their ideal wife. Recent surveys have shown that intelligence has now become the highest priority, although attractiveness is a close second. Most young males are reacting to the "new economics," which fosters dual-career marriages to achieve the material goods and housing associated with middle-class respectability. In addition, this generation of young men may be more egalitarian, wishing to participate more intimately in the marital relationship and the raising of their children. As the song that Peter, Paul, and Mary sang in the sixties says, "The Times They Are A-Changin'."

Young adults begin their treks as wage-earning adults responsible for their own needs in the 11 areas of development mentioned above. There are certain developmental tasks associated with this first stage of the family life cycle. For example, independent adults must have jobs or other sources of income. Budgeting of this income entails learning to plan and to balance a checkbook. Buying and maintaining a car or planning transportation via mass transit or a car-pool system is often a key to maintaining employment. To keep jobs, independent adults must interact effectively with authority figures and maintain collegial relationships with peers in the work environment.

Cooking or buying cooked meals is a necessary task for independent adults on their own. Washing and ironing or arranging to have it done are tasks required of the individual in a single-person family. All household cleaning must be done by the individual in the single-person household.

In addition, when a person lives alone, the individual must reach out to make friends to fulfill needs for intimacy. Same-sex friends, especially a close best friend, are particularly important. Boundaries must be negotiated with families of origin, extended family, friends, and others to establish the individual as a separate independent unit.

Independent adults want to be physically attractive to the opposite sex to date and find a suitable mate. They watch their diets and exercise to maintain healthy body images. They establish routines and monitor behaviors such as drinking that might interfere with their plans for the future. They imagine a dream for their lives—who and where they would like to be.

Often the single person dates to meet interpersonal, emotional, social, and possibly sexual needs. Participating in community groups focusing on art, music, theater, business, or computers allows the single person to express intrinsic interests while meeting social needs. The individual may attend college, graduate, or continuing education classes to advance at work and to receive intellectual stimulation. The person may attend a church, synagogue, temple, or other religious center to meet spiritual and social needs.

Marital Dyad. When two independent adults become attracted to each other, they date over a period of time. If their relationship is comfortable, meets their needs, and is a match between the socioeconomic and other characteristics of their families, they may choose to marry. Often the individuals have established themselves in careers, have dated different partners to know what they want in a spouse, and are ready to settle down. The wedding ceremony is the marker for the beginning of the marital dyad stage of the family life cycle.

The wedding ceremony is the marker of the beginning of the marital dyad stage of the family life cycle.

Marriage is a relationship that is romantic and intensive at the beginning. It becomes an extensive relationship involving others, such as children and grandchildren, concentrating on the solving of problems that arise (Ables with Brandsma, 1977; Lederer & Jackson, 1968). During the courtship phase, partners are on their best behavior, wanting to please and often idealizing each other. This pattern typically continues through about the first 1½ to 2 years after the wedding, which corresponds to the marital dyad stage of the family life cycle. During this honeymoon phase, the spouses slowly begin to see each other as they really are. By the end of the honeymoon phase, spouses usually focus on wanting their needs met and are more interested in what they are receiving rather than what they are giving. If they have learned to negotiate so that the needs of each partner are met, their marital relationship will grow and deepen.

The developmental tasks associated with the marital dyad stage of the family include adjusting to marriage by negotiating differences, deciding on roles (who will do what), establishing a home, forming a couple boundary (secrets that are shared only by the couple), developing relationships with in-laws, renegotiating relationships with the families of origin, learning to appreciate each other, working out a satisfactory sexual relationship including deciding on family planning, making couple friends, and continuing to establish careers. The married couple talk about their shared dream of the future—what has meaning for them. Often they join a church, synagogue, or other religious group that provides support for and challenge to their values.

They begin to work toward their dream in the many areas of development. Perhaps one spouse wants to acquire further education while the other seeks a particular career. They learn to support each other in such endeavors, encouraging each other to grow and develop. They share a wide range of deep feelings with each other—both fears and joys. They express affection toward each other and touch each other often.

They want to look attractive for each other. They exercise and plan healthy leisure activities that allow them to relax and recharge. They establish their routines, especially concerning meal times, work hours, and bed times. Each partner asks what the spouse needs to feel loved and fills those needs when possible. When behaviors of either person interfere with the relationship, the partner expresses annoyance and makes requests for change. The marital dyad practices fair fighting by learning to manage conflicts. Each partner can ask forgiveness and begin again.

Infant Family.   The beginning of the infant family stage of the family life cycle is marked by the birth of the first child. During pregnancy, the couple prepares for parenthood by attending Lamaze classes together, reading books on parenting, decorating the nursery, and talking about what it will be like to be parents. The more of the birth experience that the couple can share (labor, delivery, first weeks at home), the better the bonding between the infant and the new parents and the stronger the couple bond. Some additional developmental tasks include recovering from childbirth, learning to breast feed or bottle feed the baby, and paying for the birth and preparations.

In particular, it is essential for an enmeshed close bond to occur between the mother and the baby at birth and during the first few months of life. It is normal for the father to become jealous of the new baby during this time. Gradually the mother becomes involved with the father again as he, too, works on establishing a relationship with the child. To bridge this transition effectively, it is important for each spouse to be able to share deep feelings and to understand those of the partner.

Typically there is a religious ceremony such as a circumcision, baptism, or christening to celebrate the birth of the child. The marital dyad begins to renegotiate their relationship with the families of origin because they are now parents. From this day forth, they create family rituals and routines. They appreciate and support each other in their parenting roles. The new parents develop relationships with other young couples with children. The new mother looks to other young mothers for support and friendship.

During this stage of the family life cycle, another important task is the maintenance of employment and a stable source of income that provides security so that appropriate caretaking can occur. Parents should spend quality and quantity time playing with the infant to catalyze emotional, social, and intellectual development. Allocation

The infant family brings the first child home from the hospital.

of household responsibilities should be renegotiated in light of the additional work necessary to take care of an infant.

Time and attention should also be focused on reinforcing the marital relationship. The couple should hire a trained baby-sitter or ask a new grandparent to keep the child so they can spend time alone together by going out to dinner or other leisure time activities that will strengthen their relationship.

Preschool Family.   When the first baby walks, the family moves into a new stage, the preschool family. A toddler has special needs. For example, to protect the toddler, all unsafe objects must be put away. The house must be baby-proofed. Parents need to spend time talking to and reading to the child. The child needs touch, affection, and praise to bolster self-esteem.

In particular, the toddler is curious and wants to explore, but always wishes to return to the mother for reassurance. Setting limits can be difficult. A mother should encourage the independence of her child but discipline the child when dangerous situations arise. Being a "good enough" mother by encouraging refueling and appropriate discipline requires a difficult balance. Making friends with the mothers of other toddlers allows mothers to share their feelings about parenting with others in similar situations, providing emotional support during this time.

The parents of toddlers need to talk about discipline to provide consistency and continuity. They also need to discuss household and child-care responsibilities as they change over time. For example, who will take care of the sick toddler? A network of resources will need to be developed, such as doctors, baby sitters, and cleaning personnel.

During this time parents, especially mothers, often experience stress because of the lack of time for self and for the couple. Using "mothers day out" programs and other resources can help to reduce tension. If a mother also continues to work full-time, she will have many demands on her limited physical energy. Therefore, planning energizing, leisure-time activities for self, the couple, and the family as a whole is a key developmental task.

Grade School Family.   When the first child enters school, the grade school family stage begins. The school and community affect the family. If the child has not been cared for and disciplined appropriately, teachers will involve the parents, giving them feedback and guidance to change. One key developmental task at this stage of the family life cycle is to support the educational achievement of the child. Parents often help the child with homework and participate in the school-related activities of the child. Neighborhood athletic teams also provide opportunities for the child to compete and the parent to cheer. Most of all, the family wants to be accepted by the school and the community.

Costs rise as the child grows up. Additional food, education, health care, and participation on athletic teams or various lessons such as music or art require additional funds. Parents continue to develop their careers and increase their incomes. Career ascendancy issues surface as to whose job is the most important. In this stage of the family life cycle, it is important for each spouse to encourage the other to follow a personal dream for career advancement, further education, artistic expression, or another special goal.

The parents act as leaders in coordinating household responsibilities among family members. Each family member should complete tasks and participate in the process of selecting responsibilities. Chore charts on which children receive stickers or points for completion of tasks may be used. Often family meetings are held on a regular basis, which teach effective communication of thoughts and feelings. Children participate in the planning of family vacations, activities, and traditions. They learn to negotiate and compromise. Parents instill values and guide their children. They provide sex education and answer the questions their children have about sexual matters. The family may participate in religious services and activities. Parents appreciate each other and their children, supporting self-esteem. They discipline their children, providing appropriate limits.

The married couple makes couple friends who have similar-age or older children. Such friends become a network of supportive adults who provide role models to the children. The spouses learn to give priority time to their relationship on a regular basis. Each spouse also develops separate interests as an individual, demonstrating to the children that differences not only can be tolerated but actually are also to be celebrated.

Adolescent Family. When the first child turns 13, the family has moved into the adolescent family stage. Often dramatic changes have begun to occur even earlier. Female children may have their first menstrual periods at age 10 or 11, experiencing physiological changes that can affect moods. Parents should talk to their children about sex and the physical changes to be expected as part of growing up.

Teenagers of both sexes are concerned about how they look. The opinions of peers become more important than those of parents. Money required for clothes can become exorbitant unless limits and a budget are set.

Most of all, teenagers want freedom and autonomy. They want to be treated as adults, even though they often think and act more like children. Parents need to implement curfews and enforce them. A dialogue occurs between parents and adolescents in which the teenagers learn to negotiate increased freedom in relationship to increased responsibilities.

In addition, parents must continue to discuss budget matters with their teenagers to deal with the limitless requests for clothes, vacations, and activities generated by the adolescent peer group. Often teenagers obtain their first part-time jobs, but care must be taken to ensure that the number of hours worked will not detract from their achievement at school.

An Austrian family enjoys a vacation at a state resort on the Osiachersee. An example of an adolescent family enjoying friends together.

At this stage of the family life cycle, parents feel pressure for additional sources of income, regardless of their affluence. The cost of providing clothing, food, housing, education, and leisure activities increases dramatically. Parents may invest additional time and effort in their careers and/or in obtaining further education to advance in their careers. Parents may also experience mid-life issues themselves, making it more difficult for them to remain a stable force against which teenagers can rebel appropriately. For example, when family members are surveyed about satisfaction with their families, husbands will typically be most satisfied, wives less satisfied than husbands, and teenagers the least satisfied of any family members (Olson et al., 1983).

Parents must learn to talk with teenagers about the natural consequences of behaviors such as drinking while driving, using drugs, and other behaviors. Family expectations and values should be stated clearly. Parents should encourage teenagers to make independent decisions, teaching them a decision-making process in which they express their thoughts and feelings openly, generate alternatives, analyze consequences, and resolve conflicts. Also, parents need to talk to their adolescents about career plans and any education required to implement those plans. Teenagers are least likely to become involved in alcohol and drugs if they have their own career plans and know that their families expect them not to use drugs or drink to excess. Similar to the infant family stage, parents in the adolescent family stage must be available in a crisis. Teenagers must know how to reach their parents in an emergency.

At this stage of the family life cycle, it is extremely important for the parents to make couple time. Often they may be dealing with the illness or death of their own parents and mid-life issues. They need time to share deep feelings with each other. In addition, teenagers will divide and conquer if they think parents are at odds about a given situation. Parents can profit immensely from marital enrichment and/or marital support groups. Continuing to cultivate and maintain a network of couple friends and family friends, especially polestars (people who have recently raised teenagers and can give pointers and support) is important.

Launching Family. The first child's high school graduation is the marker for the transition to the launching family. In earlier decades when less than 10% of those graduating from high school went on to college, high school graduation signified the completion of formal education and a major achievement of the family. In this technological society where most high school graduates attend college or undertake some post-secondary training, graduation from high school is the first of a series of markers that indicate that a child has been launched. In some states more than one third of the students never complete high school, so it is still an event of which any family can be proud.

The launching family requires additional financial resources. If a child sets up an apartment, parents often help the child to move and decorate. If a child goes to college, the parents may provide part or all of the college expenses, even when the child works during the summers. If a daughter marries, the parents typically pay for most of the expenses; the average wedding in the United States cost $10,000 in 1988. Parents during this stage of the family life cycle try to find ways to increase their incomes. If they have saved money in a launching fund for their children during

A formal family portrait may be taken when the last child graduates from high school. The launching family has many events to celebrate.

earlier stages, the financial pressure may not be as great. They also encourage their children to work and to save their money to implement their future plans.

At this stage it is important for parents to remain flexible. New members may be incorporated into the family through marriage; other young adults leave home. Parents reaffirm their values but are also willing to talk and deal tactfully with situations that are important to the young adult. Young adults will test family values to clarify their own.

Parents need to talk with the young adult about plans, but they should follow the lead of the young adult. Children are sensitive about whether or not they are following the dreams of their parents or their own personal dreams. There is a fine line between encouraging young adults to make plans and supporting them in those plans and being perceived as making the plans for the young adults, viewed as controlling behavior to manipulate children to be what parents want them to be rather than what the children want to be.

Many strong feelings arise for both parents and children during this stage. When people can continue to communicate, the developmental tasks will eventually be achieved. The parents should plan time for themselves to deepen their relationship and to talk about issues. This strong marital coalition provides a stable base from which the children can be launched. Close couple friends and family friends provide enjoyable times to help the spouses release tension. They are also sources of advice and comfort. Leaving home is one of the most difficult transitions, requiring all the skills learned at earlier stages.

Mentoring Dyad. When the last child marries or leaves home to work and live in a separate apartment, the mentoring dyad stage begins. Now that the married couple is alone in the house, they often find that they are strangers. One of the central developmental tasks is the renewal of the marital relationship and the development of intimacy. A couple may attend a marriage encounter workshop or join a marital support group if they have not done so before.

Often by this stage the wife has become menopausal and must deal with physiological changes. In consultation with her doctor, she weighs alternatives such as hormone replacement therapy, choosing appropriate dosages of natural estrogen and progesterone. A hormone deficiency may influence the woman's moods, which can affect her relationship with her husband (Lederer, 1984).

Also at this time the wife may decide to assert herself and become more dominant in the world by increasing her involvement in work. On the other hand, the husband may choose to lessen his commitments and to put more time into leisurely pursuits and his relationships. The couple requires time and energy to adjust to these changes.

Much preparation goes into the marriage or launching of the last child. The house is busy with activity and also serves as a refueling station for the launched children. They come to visit, wanting emotional and often financial support for their life decisions.

Grandchildren are often born during this stage of the family life cycle. The couple serves as a mentoring dyad, capable of giving advice, emotional support, help with the baby, and financial backing when necessary.

In addition to mentoring launched children, the couple also checks on aging parents who may require assistance. The health of their aging parents often reminds the couple to take better care of themselves through exercise, diet, and regular check-ups. Often the woman will have some type of surgery during this stage of the family life cycle. She increases her contact with female friends. The couple is extremely busy with their jobs, friends, launched children, grandchildren, leisure activities, church groups, and hobbies. They make time to meditate on priorities and to grow spiritually.

Retired Family. When one or both of the spouses retire from their careers, the retired family stage begins. Life is still busy for the married couple; however, more time is spent in health-promoting activities such as exercise and diet. Partners take responsibility for working on their health problems and for adjusting to the physiological changes due to aging. They spend more time with friends to enjoy life. In fact, marital satisfaction at this stage in life has been found to be related to time spent enjoying couple friends. In addition, hobbies and other leisure activities take a great deal of time. Spouses at this stage also keep in contact with their parents, children, grandchildren, and other relatives, maintaining kinship ties. Partners still have dreams and make plans to implement them.

Often at this stage spouses may care for elderly parents or for the boomerang generation of children who return home after a divorce, bringing along several grand-

When one or both of the spouses retire from their careers, the stage of the retired family begins. Yet life is still busy for the married couple. David and Vera Mace look into each other's eyes, enjoying this stage of family development. (Courtesy of the Association for Couples in Marriage Enrichment)

children. The caretaking role of the wife may be intensified if she is needed to care for an elderly parent or in-law. Spouses may have to deal with the death of parents and learn to face their own deaths. Typically people strengthen their spirituality even though they may not increase their involvement in religious activities. In particular, parents learn to receive from their children as well as to give.

Because of reduced income, carefully budgeting financial resources is an important developmental task. The couple may decide to sell their house to increase their cash flow.

Elderly Family. When people reach 80 in our society, the probabilities are greater that they will have health problems that will interfere with the quantity and quality of their lifestyles. The elderly family stage of the family life cycle typically begins when an older person in this age range loses a spouse. The partner must adjust to living alone. In facing the death of the spouse, partners deal with the ideas of their own deaths. Often a decision must be made to place this elderly partner in a nursing home. The elderly family must cope with such costs and any medical bills incurred.

Most of all, the elderly person wants to remain as independent as possible, even if financially and emotionally dependent on children. The elderly individual often will reminisce and talk about past times, reviewing life to find its meaning. The person keeps in touch with family and often plays the role of matriarch in her family.

Daily routines become extremely important. Much time is spent in preventive health approaches such as exercise, rest, diet, physicals, monitoring of drinking, and stress reduction. In particular, keeping a best friend can mean the difference between life and death. If this is an opposite-sex companion, a loving sexual relationship may also develop. Spending time with friends becomes the best preventive medicine in the form of social support. Often the person attends funerals of friends, prays for them, and prepares for death.

Divorce and Remarriage: The Slinky Effect

With divorce and remarriage, the "slinky effect" occurs. In the Co-Evolutionary Helix of the Family Life Span shown in Figure 4–3, a member of a stepfamily can be viewed as having one foot in one stage of the family life cycle with the previous family and one foot in another stage with the new family. Therefore, the person is working on the family transitions associated with each family and with double the amount of work tied to developmental tasks.

Such a situation can create role strain. For example, a man who divorces his first wife when he is 40 years old and has two teenage children will have all the financial

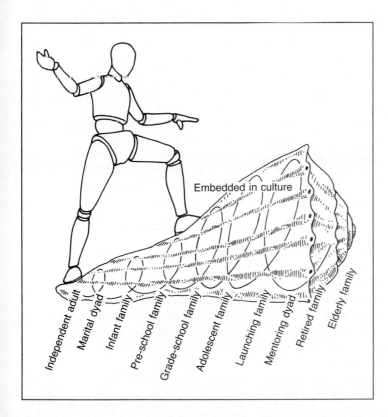

FIGURE 4–3   The slinky effect: double the developmental work

and emotional responsibilities associated with fathering teenagers while he may also be supporting a new wife in her first pregnancy. In addition, the man will be dealing with his own individual developmental work related to mid-life transition. On a given weekend, he might be called upon to take his teenagers shopping when his new wife would like him to stay at home and help her paint the new nursery—activities that require financial resources to be divided among the two families. All the while, he may prefer to work in his garden and refresh his reduced energy at mid-life to meet the week ahead. A high level of interpersonal skills is needed to communicate with the old and new family members, which can be emotionally draining, to say the least.

It is important for a marital and family therapist to assess the slinky effect with the partners in a remarried family. Discussing the developmental tasks associated with the family life cycle of each family (the previous and the current) often helps the families make sense of what is happening to them. Family members can express the feelings of being pulled in two or more directions and the subsequent dissipation of energy. When family members are able to honor their obligations to the previous family, it often helps them to be better parents in the new family and a positive, snowball effect can occur. However, if either family does not understand what is expected of family members because of the slinky effect, resentment and tension can occur. This can create pressure in the new family or, in the worst extreme, actually fragment it.

The slinky effect can also occur with a newly divorced parent. The individual is faced with dealing with the developmental tasks of the independent adult stage of the family life cycle, while also handling the developmental tasks associated with the grade school family stage of the family life cycle since the person is raising an 8-year-old child. Therefore, there can be role strain because the individual has a foot in both stages of the family life cycle at the same time.

The Effect of the Number of Family Members

Each stage of the family life span becomes more complex as the number of children in the family increases. The interactions of the life spans of the individual family members as they move in time through the family life cycle increase as the number of children increases. This is due to the permutative increase in the number of relationships as family members are added. Rather than being a simple arithmetic increase as with the number of family members, the increase in relationships is multifold. Duvall and Miller (1985) propose the following formula: $x = (y^2 - y)/2$ (p. 32).

For example, if a married couple has a child, the family increases in membership by one person, but the relationships increase from one between the parents to three (one between the child and the mother, one between the child and the father, and one between the parents). If a couple has five children, the number of relationships is 21. It takes much more time and energy to maintain and stimulate growth in 21 relationships. The parents in large families have a great deal of relationship work to do and need a high level of interpersonal relational skills just to keep the family going, let alone evolving to higher levels of development.

In addition, each of the family members may be at a different stage of individual development, which is difficult to keep straight. One child may be an infant needing constant attention, while another may be a teenager who needs a great deal of free-dom within limits. If the mother treats both children the same, there will be problems. The teenager would resist any constant attention, while the infant would feel ne-glected if given only limited attention. Parents need to treat the relationship with each child differently.

Just as the number of children affects the complexity of the stage of the family life cycle, so does an increase in the number of other family members. For example, if an elderly parent comes to live with a family that has five members, the number of the relationships in the family increases by five as each person forms a relationship with the added family member.

In one case in which a parent with Alzheimer's disease came to live with the family, the adopted, youngest child developed symptoms. The grandparent had formed re-lationships with the other natural children in the family but rejected the adopted child. This relationship created stress for the child, who acted out in school and became a problem for the whole family.

Single-Parent Families

A single-parent family may result from divorce or separation, the death of one parent, separation due to war, or having a child out of wedlock. Hill (1986) studied the family development of three types of single-parent families—the divorced who never re-marry, the divorced who remarry, and the widowed who remarry.

Divorce was more likely to occur when the oldest child was entering school and one or more younger siblings were at home needing care. The divorced mother was usually required to go to work. Even then income suffered and the family typically moved to another household. Divorced, single mothers looked enviously at those mothers who were not divorced and who were able to buy homes and other house-hold goods.

Typically the mother remarried in the middle of the school-age period and expe-rienced the transition of reconstituting the family, often becoming a stepparent—a second disruption during the same stage of family development. In nuclear families, the school-age period is usually the most stable, allowing time for the development of close relationships with children. In comparison, single-parent families have experi-enced two major transitions. In addition, a high percentage have another child by the second spouse. This prolongs the parenting period by 13 years in remarried families, nearly half of which return to single-parent status due to a second divorce.

In the single-parent families where the mother does not remarry, she is finished with launching children by the age of 43 if black, and 47 if white. On the other hand, those in which the parents remarry and have children experience more disorder and transitions. The widowed families in which the parent remarries have the lowest rates of divorce. The marriage usually takes place later in the family life cycle, when the children are in adolescence.

Hill (1986) recommends that preventive efforts be focused on the preschool family and the adolescent family prior to the decision to divorce or remarry. By understand-ing the developmental consequences of divorce and remarriage, parents may be in a better position to make decisions to which they will remain committed.

Socioeconomic Factors

The family life span presented in this text is that of middle-class families. Poverty greatly affects the family life span. In fact, one concern in the United States is the proliferation of part-time, low-paying jobs rather than full-time jobs with fringe benefits that will support the development of a family. Fewer people at the lower end of the economic stratum will be able to have and support intact families. Maintaining a family may become a status symbol in the decades to come.

Fulmer (1988) compares the stages of the family life cycle of low-income families with professional families (Table 4–3). There are more negative events in poor families, leading to four times the amount of depression. When poor families are isolated from their kin or in nonreciprocal relationships with their kinship network, more symptoms occur in children. Families in which there is conflict between the natural mother and the caretaker, such as the grandmother or the aunt, have more symptomatic children, as do underorganized families.

It is difficult to maintain a marriage in poverty. Single mothers who marry often divorce. As in any remarried family, the children can be the greatest source of stress, especially when they do not accept the stepparent. Intact families in poverty are rare and special.

Cultural Influences

The cultural group in which a person is socialized influences expectations for the family life cycle. The Co-Evolutionary Helix of the Family Life Span is embedded in culture. Behaviors considered normal in one culture may seem odd or even maladaptive in another (Usher, 1989). For example, the Japanese upper-class practice of potential brides formally applying to marry eligible bachelors may seem strange to Westerners. The would-be brides submit lengthy application forms, including pictures of the woman in a kimono, in Western dress, and with a dog. Also, a woman's family history going back at least 600 years must be attached as well as recent dental X-rays and reports of medical check-ups. In the Japanese culture, family pride is passed on to the next generation and divorce is taboo, so such an application process makes sense.

It is important for marital and family therapists to continue to question their personal assumptions of what is normal and the cultural beliefs that they bring to therapy sessions. By knowing themselves, therapists are better able to understand how their own biases may affect and even interfere with treatment.

Often therapists err by overdoing (being too courteous or friendly) or by underdoing (being disrespectful of cultural differences in the family life cycle) (Lappin, 1983). Searching for the strengths within a family's culture that are resources for positive change and using those strengths to involve family members in solving their own problems means that the therapist does less and leaves the family's culture intact and the family stronger as a result of therapy.

Qualities that personnel in minority agencies thought were important in cross-cultural counseling are found in Table 4–4. *Cultural questioning* (asking the family members for help and to serve as guides to their culture, particular customs, expec-

TABLE 4–3 Comparison of family life cycle stages

Age	Professional Families		Low-Income Families	
12–17	a. b. c.	Prevent pregnancy. Graduate from high school. Parents continue support while permitting child to achieve greater independence.	a. b. c.	First pregnancy. Attempt to graduate from high school. Parent attempts strict control before pregnancy. After pregnancy, relaxation of controls and continued support of new mother and infant.
18–21	a. b. c.	Prevent pregnancy. Leave parental household for college. Adapt to parent-child separation.	a. b. c.	Second pregnancy. No further education. Young mother acquires adult status in parental household.
22–25	a. b. c.	Prevent pregnancy. Develop professional identity in graduate school. Maintain separation from parental household. Begin living in serious relationship.	a. b. c.	Third pregnancy. Marriage—leave parental household to establish stepfamily. Maintain connection with kinship network.
26–30	a. b. c.	Prevent pregnancy. Marriage—develop nuclear couple as separate from parents. Intense work involvement as career begins.	a. b.	Separate from husband. Mother becomes head of own household within kinship network.
31–35	a. b. c.	First pregnancy. Renew contact with parents as grandparents. Differentiate career and child-rearing roles between husband and wife.	a. b.	First grandchild. Mother becomes grandmother and cares for daughter and infant.

From "Lower-Income and Professional Families: A Comparison of Structure and Life Cycle Process" by R. Fulmer, in *The Changing Family Life Cycle: A Framework for Family Therapy* (2/e) (p. 551) by E. Carter and M. McGoldrick (Eds.), 1988, New York: Gardner Press. Copyright © 1989 by Allyn and Bacon. Reprinted by permission.

tations, rules, rituals, language, roles, etiquette, and values) shows respect and a willingness to risk making contact (Montalvo & Gutierrez, 1983). In this way, a family therapist can discover the expectations for the family life cycle in the given culture and simultaneously offer help through the process.

Each culture has its own customs.

For example, McAdoo (1988) points to the importance of the extended family in the social mobility and family life cycle of black families. Looking at patterns of social mobility, she found that levels of education peaked for families at the time of highest mobility. Usually, family members credit the financial or child-care help received from the extended family as the means by which they were able to achieve middle-class status. By cultural questioning, a marital and family therapist can find out about the nature of the extended family for a given black family and what strengths may be mobilized through the kin network to help the family in crisis. For additional information about family therapy with black families, see the work of Boyd-Franklin (1989), Hines (1988), Hines and Boyd-Franklin (1982), and Pinderhughes (1982).

The effects of various cultures on the family life cycle are discussed by McGoldrick (1982, 1988), who also edited a landmark book entitled *Ethnicity and Family Therapy* in 1982. It includes chapters on family therapy with different ethnic groups. Since the family is the main transmitter of culture in any society, it is important for marital and family therapists to know about the characteristics of ethnic groups and how these might affect family therapy. Experiencing diverse cultures through travel and cross-

TABLE 4-4 Qualities important to cross-cultural counseling

1. The ability to ask questions about another culture and still observe appropriate boundaries.
2. The ability to listen with understanding, not just to express one's own feelings.
3. Sensitivity to the kinds of questions that may be offensive to minority persons.
4. The ability to accurately interpret people's moods and body language.
5. The ability to project feelings of respect.
6. The ability to relate on a peer level without introducing elements of power into the relationship.
7. The ability to identify with poverty.
8. The ability to avoid making value judgments.
9. The ability to share in social experiences.
10. The ability to avoid intellectualizing.
11. An interest in understanding the language of the culture.
12. A willingness to participate in the culture, not just to observe it.

From "An Experiential Approach to Cultural Awareness in Child Welfare," by L. Wilson and J. W. Green, 1983, *Child Welfare, 42*(4) pp. 309–310. Reprinted by permission.

cultural friendships can strengthen the flexibility needed to be a family therapist. Montalvo and Gutierrez (1983, 1988) caution that an interinstitutional perspective, that is, how cultural characteristics are interacting with the systems of the host culture, is most important in dealing with families from other cultures. It is at these points of intersection that interventions are most helpful to ethnic families.

Culture does influence the family life cycle. A culturally conscious family therapist remains curious and respectful about the expectations of the particular culture of client families, mobilizing the strengths of the culture that surface in the process of therapy.

Milestones of Family Life

Regardless of the culture or the structure of the family (nuclear, single-parent, extended, or other), there are naturally occurring milestones of family life that can be celebrated. Milestones are events that mark transitions or passages in family life (Table 4–5). In the Co-Evolutionary Helix of the Family Life Span, not all families have all of these milestones, but when a family reaches any of these milestones, it is a cause for celebration. By creating rituals linked to these milestones, families can establish family traditions and foster closeness.

Throughout history, most religions have developed ceremonies and rituals to celebrate these family milestones and demonstrate the family's appreciation to God for having reached the milestone. In addition to these formal religious ceremonies, which hold significant meaning for families and their members, families can create their own customs and rituals which children and other family members grow to expect as they

TABLE 4–5 Selected milestones of family life

1. Moving to the first apartment as an adult.
2. The first full-time job.
3. The first meeting (especially important in Japan and to Japanese Americans).
4. Engagement (an engagement party).
5. The marriage ceremony.
6. The birth of the first child (christening ceremony) and each child thereafter.
7. The first child enters school, and the start of school for each child thereafter.
8. The tenth wedding anniversary.
9. The first child becomes a teenager (bar mitsvah, bat mitsvah, confirmation ceremonies), and each child thereafter.
10. The first child graduates from high school, and the graduation of each child thereafter.
11. The first child is launched (enters college, the military, or post-secondary, vocational-technical education) and each child thereafter.
12. The twenty-fifth (silver) wedding anniversary.
13. The completion of any educational degree by any family member.
14. The first child marries (marriage ceremony), and the marriage of each child thereafter.
15. The first grandchild is born (baptismal or christening ceremony), and the birth of each grandchild thereafter.
16. A parent dies (funeral ceremony).
17. Retirement from work role (a retirement party).
18. Special birthdays, such as 70, 80, 90, and 100 (parties to celebrate aging).
19. The fiftieth (golden) wedding anniversary.
20. Death of the spouse (funeral ceremony).

become an ingrained part of the family context. In celebrating the joy and sadness of family life, represented by the milestones, family members learn to share their deepest feelings and thoughts, evolving together over time.

In working with families it is important to ask them what milestones they have passed and how they celebrated them. Such a procedure encourages family members to focus on the strengths of the family. Every family has strengths and milestones of which to be proud.

Milestones occur naturally, and family members in most cases cannot stop milestones from happening. For example, a child becomes a teenager even if he or she is still acting like a 5-year-old. Often in celebrating a milestone, family members reflect upon what behaviors are expected of them and change their perceptions and behav-

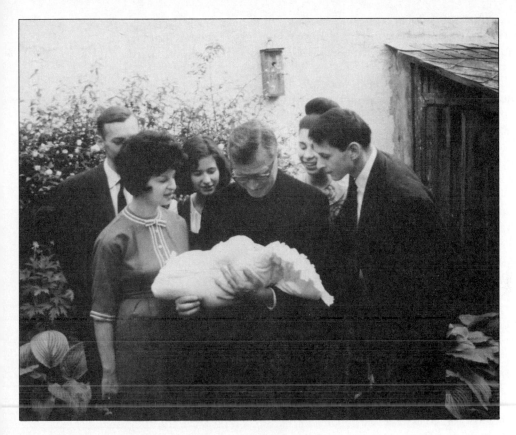

The baptism of the first child is a milestone of family life.

iors, developing as a result of the celebration of the milestone. Creating one's own family traditions can be one of the most rewarding and fun parts of family life. Building upon milestones, the family can plan other activities such as family vacations, leisure-time activities, and community and church involvement.

SUMMARY

In Part One, the macrosystems or contexts of marital and family therapy (the health-care setting and the history of marital/family therapy) are considered first, followed by the family as a system and then the individual subsystem—from larger macrosystems to the family system to smaller subsystems. This particular chapter focuses on the family system over time—family development. Development means the growth and evolution of an organism over time.

In the 1950s, Duvall created the concept of the family life cycle—what expected changes will occur in the family over time—and elaborated eight stages of the family life cycle. Carter and McGoldrick created a six-stage model in the 1980s. To represent the families of the 1990s, Thomas presents 10 stages of the family life cycle: independent adult, marital dyad, infant family, preschool family, grade school family, adolescent family, launching family, mentoring dyad, retired family, and elderly family (Table 4–2).

The Co-Evolutionary Helix of the Family Life Span, represented by the lightning whelk on the cover of this text, is a model that explains family life from birth to death. Spiraling through a process of differentiation and integration (change and stability), family members evolve together over time, affecting each other. The horizontal axis represents the stages of the family life cycle. Three cross-sections move through the family life cycle over time: (1) the Family Health Wheel, (2) the individual developmental stage and tasks of each family member, and (3) the regulation of distance through the use of centrifugal versus centripetal styles and less mature versus more mature defense mechanisms. The model is embedded in culture.

The slinky effect occurs when people divorce. For example, a member of a remarried family can be viewed as having one foot in one stage of the family life cycle of the previous family and one foot in another stage of the family life cycle of the new family. Therefore, the person is working on the family transitions associated with each family and has double the amount of developmental work.

Other variations of the model occur based on the number of family members, single-parent status, socioeconomic level, and culture. Within the Co-Evolutionary Helix of the Family Life Span, milestones of family life occur, from moving into the first apartment as an adult to the marriage ceremony, the birth of a child, the marriage of a child, and the death of a spouse.

In working with families, it is important to assess at what stage of the family life cycle the family is, the Family Health Wheel (development in 11 areas—spiritual, intellectual, behavioral, emotional, imaginal, sensual, sexual, physical, interpersonal, social, and financial-career), the developmental stage and tasks of each family member, how the family regulates distance through the use of centrifugal and centripetal forces and more mature versus less mature defense mechanisms, any slinky effects, and variations of the model due to family structure, socioeconomic level, or culture. Most importantly, encouraging family members to talk about the milestones of family life which they have achieved emphasizes the strengths of the family, freeing energy for use in present and future family transitions.

EXERCISES

1. Read the following vignettes of actual families and assess at what stage of the family life cycle they are according to Thomas.

Vignette A

After 24 years of marriage, Marilyn and Michael Haywood find themselves alone in the house after their daughter Megan married John Hunter. They join a marriage encounter group to make deepened contact with each other again and to create how they would like the rest of their lives to be.

Michael has decided to cut back on his work commitments and to put more time into leisurely pursuits; for example, he would like to better his golf game. He would also like to spend more time with Marilyn. In contrast, Marilyn has decided to leave her job at the hotel to set up her own catering business. She feels more assertive and wants to be in charge. Marilyn has dealt successfully with menopause. She experimented with three different regimens of hormone replacement therapy over the last year until she found the one that fit her best. She wants new challenges.

The Haywood house serves as a refueling station. Megan and John come to visit for a week, wanting support for their decisions to go back to graduate school. Marilyn and Michael agree to help them with part of the tuition and to be there for them if a financial or emotional crisis occurs.

Vignette B

LaTannia and Michael Jones are having trouble with their daughter, Donna. She becomes irritable and begins to cry over the slightest thing. She is more interested in what her peers think than what her parents say. Since her first menstrual period at 11, she has been primping more and more each day, often disappearing for hours in the bathroom by herself. Now that she has turned 13, she wants to be treated like an adult with increased freedom and a later curfew.

LaTannia and Michael are concerned that Donna's behavior sets a bad example for her younger sister, Cheryl. They set a curfew for Donna and ground her if she stays out later. They place responsibility on Donna by encouraging her to generate alternatives, make decisions, and own the consequences of these decisions.

Michael and LaTannia invest more time in their careers. They feel pressure for additional sources of income because costs have increased for the family. In particular, mid-life issues absorb their individual energy and affect family life.

Vignette C

Millie lives alone now that Harold has passed away. He had taken medication for hypertension for many years and died suddenly of a heart attack. The first year after his funeral was difficult for Millie. She found herself remembering the good times that they had together, like the celebration of their 50th wedding anniversary, and she cried easily.

Gradually she has returned to the activities that she has enjoyed over the years. At age 83 she continues to sing in the choir, be a member of the garden club, and be active in the church. Most of all, she enjoys the companionship of her female friends. They have traveled together to Europe and China, which has helped her to regain her spirits. Recently, with the encouragement of her friends, she was elected president of the local American Association of Retired People (AARP) group.

Vignette D

Abdullah and Leila Azimi are excited about their son's entrance into first grade. They want their son, Mohammed, to succeed. They attend parent meetings at his school. In addition, Abdullah coaches the neighborhood softball team, of which their son is a member. Leila times events for Mohammed's swim team.

Leila decides to return to school to renew her nursing license in order to advance at work. At the same time Abdullah is asked to be a partner at the accounting firm. They notice that they are fighting more than usual about who should do what. Career ascendancy issues about whose job is most important lead to long talks into the night. They decide to take a weekend vacation every other month to give themselves time to enjoy each other. They also decide to meet for lunch once a week and to continue their walks every other day.

2. What is the slinky effect? Take turns with a partner explaining it.

3. Draw a picture of the Co-Evolutionary Helix of the Family Life Span and its cross-sections. Take turns with a partner explaining your diagrams. What do *co-evolutionary, helix,* and *family life span* mean? How does the *family life cycle* fit in?

4. Audiotape an interview with the oldest member of your family. Gather information about major family life cycle transitions, how the family worked on these issues, and how various family members dealt with these major family transitions. Some of these tapes will be shared with the class with the permission of the interviewer and the interviewee at the discretion of the instructor.

Chapter 5
Individual Subsystems Over Time

Hold fast to dreams
For if dreams die
Life is a broken-winged bird
That cannot fly.

Langston Hughes—"Dreams," 1979

There are many theories of how human life unfolds. Theories of individual development can be classified into four categories: (1) individual variability, (2) life event, (3) life span, and (4) stage theories. In this chapter selected theories of each type will be elaborated (Table 5–1), and an integrative theory, a Co-Evolutionary Helix of the Individual Life Span, will then be presented. The implications of these models for marital and family therapy will be emphasized throughout the chapter.

INDIVIDUAL VARIABILITY THEORIES

Most theories emphasizing individual variability evolved in reaction to stage theories. Throughout individual and family development, people formulate ideas of where they should be and what they should be doing according to age. These expectations can affect life satisfaction. For example, if a man believes that he should be well established in his career by the age of 35 and he has not held a full-time job by that age, he may think that he has not met the expectations for his age group. This may lower his self-esteem, which may lead to reduced life satisfaction and possible depression. Likewise, a woman who is married and has launched three children by the age of 50 may think that she has met the expectations for her age group, evaluate herself

TABLE 5–1 Theories of development of the individual subsystem

Individual Variability

The unique strengths of the individual are more important than age or life events.

1. *Neugarten's social clock.* Individuals can create their own expectations for their own lives.
2. *Vaillant's work on adaptation.* Everyone encounters obstacles in life. How people adapt is most important.

Life Event Theories

Events that occur or don't occur for people determine the life course more than age.

1. *Lowenthal and associates.* The events experienced are more important than age.
2. *Gutmann.* Becoming a parent is the most distinguishing life event.
3. *Schlossberg's transitions.* Any nonevent or event that results in change requires a process of adjustment—assimilation and appraisal.

The Life Span Perspective

People are developing in many areas at the same time from birth to death, in both continuous and discontinuous ways.

Stage Theories

There is an inherent ground plan for human beings that unfolds over time according to age.

1. *Classic stage theories.* Well-known theories, based on the experiences of their authors, typically focused on what proceeds in one type of development sequentially according to age, such as Freud's theory of psychosexual development, Piaget's theory of cognitive development, or Kohlberg's theory of moral development.
2. *Research on adult development.* Theories of adult development are recent and based on research with adult populations. Sheehy, Levinson, and Vaillant are some of the key contributors.

The Co-Evolutionary Helix of the Individual Life Span

Integrates the diverse types of theories into one broad model with implications for marital and family therapy.

1. *The individual life span.* Process of differentiation and integration from birth to death.
2. *Embedded in gender.* Life proceeds differently for women and men.
3. *Embedded in culture.* The expectations of a particular culture affect the life course of an individual from that culture.
4. *The individual life cycle.* There are 10 stages according to age—infancy, early childhood, middle childhood, adolescence, early adulthood, young adulthood, middle adulthood, later middle adulthood, older adulthood, and elderly adulthood.
5. *The Health-Illness Wheel.* Movement toward health or illness occurs in the nine domains of spiritual, interpersonal, intellectual, behavioral, emotional, sexual, sensual, physical, and imaginal development.
6. *The life structures of self, career, and family.* Triggering events, themes, stages, and impacts of changes in development affect the meaning of these life structures as they interact over time.

positively, and feel a sense of life satisfaction. People often approach high school reunions and college reunions with feelings of uneasiness, wondering how they will compare to others in their age group.

Neugarten's Social Clock

Neugarten and Neugarten (1987) found that changes in modern American society have altered the meanings of age. For example, a young-old person may be anyone from 55 to 85 who is retired, healthy, financially sound, politically active, and involved in community and family life. More than at any other time in history, expectations need not be bound by age restrictions. One person may work until 80 years of age, while another chooses to retire at 50. Friedan (1989) predicts an age revolution in which those Americans older than age 60 begin to dictate the terms for their own lives to actualize their potentials in unique and innovative ways, rather than being bound by social imperatives to act in a stereotypical manner.

Bernice Neugarten's (1964, 1968, 1976, 1979) theory of human development is by far the most popular individual variability theory. Her theory delineates three types of time: historical, biological, and social.

Historical time refers to the period in calendar years that is common to a given cohort of society. For example, people who began working during the Great Depression in the 1930s tend to be more fiscally conservative as a group. As times change, the expectations of a given cohort are modified. For example, since more married women with children are currently working, their daughters will have fewer conflicts over working than did their mothers, most of whom had no such role models.

Biological time is represented by physiological changes that happen at certain points in time, such as puberty and menopause. Given that these changes occur naturally, they are typically not under the physical control of human beings. However, people can influence their attitudes toward these biologically inevitable events. For example, women may choose to minimize the importance of menopause because they are focused on launching children.

Social time consists of those expectations that people create in their minds for age-appropriate behavior. Often called the "social clock," these expectations can be altered by the individual. Just because most people have their first child before 30 does not mean that a woman who wants to have a first child at 40 must perceive this as inappropriate for her age. Of course, she will be limited by her biological clock and may not be able to have a child if early menopause or a hysterectomy occurs at 40.

Neugarten also holds that differences among people become greater with age; a "fanning out" occurs. Due to the choices that people make and the way in which one decision builds upon another, two people who begin with similar backgrounds, such as siblings, may be completely different from one another by old age. For example, one may choose never to fly on an airplane, while another chooses to fly to Europe, China, and around the world. One chooses to be a homemaker; the other chooses a dual-career lifestyle. One finds her first full-time job after 50, while the other advances to an executive position. They are more different than they are alike by age 55.

In addition, new patterns have emerged for the timing of key life events. Neugarten and Neugarten (1987) term this lack of connection between age and life events as "the fluid life cycle" (p. 30). For example, more individuals stay single. More women choose to be mothers for the first time at 40, while others do so at 14. People become grandparents at many different ages. Men choose second careers and go back to school anywhere from age 18 to age 80. Serial divorces and marriages occur more frequently. More children are raised in two-parent, then single-parent, then two-parent homes. Because of this fluidity, it is difficult to make predictions for individuals according to age, and individuals more often choose the expectations that they wish to adopt for their given age.

In the same way that changes in society have affected expectations for individuals, they have also changed expectations for families as well. The boomerang family, in which already launched adult children return to live with their parents after a divorce, often bringing several children with them, has begun to occur more frequently. With longevity increasing, a "sandwich" generation of middle-aged couples who are simultaneously launching adolescents and taking care of elderly parents has arisen. The increase in the rate of divorce has created more single-parent homes than ever before.

Today, people are less able to predict what will happen to their families. When family events do not proceed according to traditional expectations, family members often experience stress (Hagestad, 1986). Since people are less able to predict what will happen to them as individuals over their life spans or as families, some feel confused and insecure. They do not seem to know where they are or what to expect (Rosenfeld & Stark, 1987). Yet the uncertainty about expectations can mean greater freedom and fewer stereotypes for present-day individuals and their families. Rather than being constrained by rigid expectations linked to age, they can create life styles based on their interests, values, and commitments, limited only by factors such as their physical health and financial resources.

Vaillant's Work on Adaptation

Vaillant (1977) conducted a follow-up study of a group of college men over a 35-year period. Even though all had achieved distinction in their careers and 90% had maintained stable families, not one had had a smooth, easy life course. They all had experienced problems and road blocks in life. Therefore, how men adapted to the problems of life became the focus of the study. Vaillant concluded that the lives of individuals were most affected by the interaction between their continuous relationships with other people and the adaptive defense mechanisms they used. Thus, a human being co-evolves with family members over time in a web of family relationships.

In addition, the defense mechanisms used by human beings affect their long-term adjustment and their relationships with other people. It was much more damaging to be in a disturbed family, where a parent was alcoholic or mentally ill, than it was if a parent died or an isolated trauma occurred. Eighteen defense mechanisms were identified by Vaillant and are covered in Chapter 8 on psychoanalytically oriented family therapy. In comparing the best outcomes with the worst, the men with the best outcomes used more of the mature defense mechanisms and less of the immature and psychotic ones.

Men did change over time. Dramatic qualitative changes occurred at various points in the adult life cycle; however, human life was more than a rigid sequence of stages with predictable outcomes. The trajectory of a given human life was determined more by the human being than by external forces. Mental health did exist and consisted of inner satisfaction, play, career achievement, mature defense mechanisms, and a good marriage.

LIFE EVENT THEORIES

Various approaches to human development can be placed under the category of life event theories. Lowenthal and her colleagues focus on life events as marking stages, not age. Gutmann emphasizes parenthood as a major life event. Schlossberg (1984), in highlighting the process of transitions related to life events, developed a framework for counselors to use in assisting clients to work through transitions.

Event Not Age

In a longitudinal study conducted by Lowenthal, Thurnher, and Chiriboga (1975), four subject groups were constructed on the basis of proximity to key life events: high school seniors, just marrieds, middle-aged parents, and couples near retirement. In studying human adjustment to life events, they found that the degree of perceived control and the subject's evaluation of events were more important to adjustment than chronological age. If people modified their thought processes, they could change the meaning of the event and aging in general, which led to better adjustment. Those in mid-life had the most stress, as well as the least sense of control, leading to poor adjustment. This was particularly true for women at mid-life. Lowenthal and her colleagues recommended that women should be educated and prepared for postparental stages such as the empty nest syndrome. Role flexibility, a perception of control, and high self-esteem resulted in more successful adjustment.

The Parental Imperative as a Major Life Event

David Gutmann (1985) maintains that parenting is a major life event that significantly affects the personalities of those who become parents. When women and men become parents, their sex roles become more stereotypic. Wives bear the children, nurse, and provide emotional security for them; husbands provide physical and financial security. Each gender lives out the unexpressed aspects of their personalities through the activities of the other.

Becoming a parent is a major life event that causes people to dampen some of their potentialities in favor of those that will most help their children—"the parental imperative" (Gutmann, 1967, 1985). In the second half of life, the psychological postures of the sexes reverse. After children are launched, both women and men can live out all their possibilities again.

Schlossberg's Transitions

Schlossberg (1984) maintains that it is not as important to know a person's age as it is to know what transitions the person has experienced in life and is facing at the present. She defines a transition as "an event or nonevent that results in change in relationships, routines, assumptions, and/or roles within the settings of self, work, family, health, and/or economics" (p. 43). There are four types of transitions: (1) anticipated transitions (expected life events such as working at the first job, marriage, parenthood, or retirement), (2) unanticipated transitions (unexpected events such as a car accident, serious illness of a child, divorce, or job loss), (3) chronic hassle transitions (on-going difficulties that require adjustment such as concern with weight, sexual incompatibility in marriage, or an antagonistic relationship with an employer), and (4) nonevent transitions (events originally expected but that do not occur, such as not marrying, being infertile, or living to be 100).

Adults are continuously in transition. Their reactions to these transitions are dependent upon the context and impact of the transition. Transitions include the processes of assimilation and appraisal. During assimilation, when the transition seems overwhelming and pervasive, disruptions occur and changes are made. Finally, the transition is integrated. During appraisal, adults evaluate the results of the transition and the resources used.

To explore, to understand, and to cope are the three main goals of counseling people in transition (Schlossberg, 1984). Therapists need to learn from the client about the specifics of the transition, the particular coping resources of the client, and where the client is in the transition process by what the client is experiencing. To obtain this knowledge, the counselor uses attending and listening skills to facilitate the development of a safe, holding environment.

The counselor identifies themes, uses interpretation, and confronts myths or unreasonable expectations. Through the use of these skills, alternative perspectives are provided to the client, reframing the meaning of the event. Through this process, the client gains an understanding of the transition and makes meaning of it.

After the thoughts, feelings, and meanings of the transition have been processed, the counselor can use influencing skills to assist the client to work through a problem-solving/decision-making sequence, to encourage the use of coping skills and model them, and to motivate the client to structure support among friends and relatives. Various techniques can be employed to aid clients in gaining a sense of control in the transition, taking action to change the situation, or modifying the meaning of the situation.

Life transitions become growth experiences when people choose to share feelings and thoughts. Avoiding them and holding them in can lead to physical illness and a martyr stance toward life. The choice rests with the individual to choose to risk sharing or to deny the problem. It is not the ambivalent, mixed feelings of transitions that lead to insanity but rather the process of denying, avoiding, and holding them in.

THE LIFE-SPAN PERSPECTIVE

Life-span psychology is the study of stability and change in multidimensional development from birth to death (Baltes, 1987; Baltes, Reese, & Lipsitt, 1980). Both creative (discontinuous) and cumulative (continuous) processes are at work at every period of human development, and people gain at the same time that they are losing. For example, various types of development are proceeding concurrently in the human being. Some may be increasing while others are decreasing.

The Health-Illness Wheel presented in Chapter 1 is an example of the life-span perspective. Movement toward illness or health continues simultaneously within each

TABLE 5–2 A comparison of developmental stage theorists

Freud: Stages of Psychosexual Development	Erikson: Stages of Psychosocial Development	Piaget: Stages of Cognitive Development
Oral	Basic trust versus mistrust (0–1)	Sensorimotor period (0–2)
Anal	Autonomy versus shame, doubt (1–3)	Preoperational period (2–5)
Phallic	Initiative versus guilt (3–6)	Concrete operations period (5–11)
Latency	Industry versus inferiority (6–12)	
Genital	Identity versus role confusion (13–22)	Formal operations period (11–adulthood)
	Intimacy versus isolation (22–30)	
	Generativity versus stagnation (30–50)	
	Ego integrity versus despair (50–Death)	

of the nine developmental domains. At any time, physical development may be moving toward illness while intellectual development is moving toward health.

Rossi (1980) has applied life-span concepts to the lives of women. Since the development of women is more variable than that of men and transitions for women are unevenly distributed by age (Reinke, 1985; Reinke, Ellicott, Harris, & Hancock, 1985), a life-span approach deserves particular attention when looking at women's lives and when counseling women clients.

STAGE THEORIES

The most popular theories of human development are stage theories, which hold that human growth and changes proceed in an orderly fashion through distinct periods of time, typically associated with age. Each stage is considered to be a critical period for mastering given developmental tasks.

With other species, the concept of critical period connotes a limited time frame in which a physiological change takes place rapidly. If the change does not occur then,

Kohlberg: Stages of Moral Development	Loevinger: Stages of Ego Development	Kegan: Stages of Self Development (A Helix Model)	Ivey: A Spherical Model of Development
Level I: Preconventional	Presocial	Incorporative	Sensorimotor (images)
Stage 1: Heteronomous morality	Impulsive	Impulsive	Concrete operations (belief)
Stage 2: Individualism, instrumental purpose and exchange	Opportunistic	Imperial	Formal operations (abstract thinking)
	Conformist	Interpersonal	
	Conscientious	Institutional	Dialectics (knowledge)
Level II: Conventional	Autonomous	Interindividual	
Stage 3: Mutual interpersonal expectations, relationships and interpersonal conformity			
Stage 4: Social system and conscience			
Level III: Postconventional or Principled			
Stage 5: Social contract or utility and individual rights			
Stage 6: Universal ethical principles			

it will never happen. Likewise, with human beings there are sensitive periods during which certain social/emotional/intellectual skills can be learned. If they are not, it may be difficult to learn these skills at a future time (Havighurst, 1972).

Classic Stage Theories

Selected classic stage theories are presented in Table 5–2. Most stage theories focus on one type of development, for example, emotional or cognitive development. A short summary of selected theories important to marital and family therapy is presented here.

Freud (1915–17) was the first to propose stages of human emotional development. He believed that the first 5 years of life determined what occurred later in adulthood, including marriage and family life. Personality consists of the id (the source of unconscious instincts that operates according to the pleasure principle), the superego (the conscience), and the ego (the rational administrator that makes logical plans to meet the needs of the superego, the id, and the real world, and that operates on the reality principle).

Jung (1933) was a follower of Freud but broke with him in 1913. He thought that Freud emphasized the first 5 years of life too much and that attention should be paid to adult development. The age of 40 was the critical point that divided human life into two halves. The second half of life was focused on individuation—owning all of the parts of the self and becoming truly oneself, a process of intrapsychic change. During this time people were focused on reconciling the polarities within them, in particular, the animus (male) and anima (female) archetypes. Men would own their expressive, creative, caring parts during the second half of life, and women would identify with the assertive, instrumental parts of their personalities if they had not been expressed during the first half of life. Jung was the first major stage theorist to focus on adult development, thereby providing a bridge from Freud to the work of later theorists such as Erikson.

Erikson (1963, 1968, 1978) was a poet turned psychologist who was deeply affected by his own mid-life transition; therefore, he believed that human beings continued to grow and evolve throughout adulthood. At each stage he postulated a conflict to be worked through—a struggle between opposites that has to be resolved if the individual is to move to the next stage of development.

According to Jane Loevinger, the ego of an adult can continue to grow and develop over the life span. Few people move through all of the stages of ego development to the highest stage, which is represented by Maslow's self actualizing person. Most adults are found in the conformist, conscientious-conformist, or conscientious stages of ego development. Loevinger (1976) developed measures of assessing ego development. In testing married couples, Heidt (1984) found that if one spouse moved to a higher level of ego development over time, pressure would be experienced in the marriage if the other spouse did not also develop to that level. The frequency of divorce increased as the gap in the levels of ego development of the spouses increased.

Piaget (1952) watched the development of his own children, taking copious notes of what they did and said. His theory is important to family development because it emphasizes evolution of the human organism. Human beings become more complex over time by changing their intellectual structures as a result of experiences within the family social environment. Kegan (1982) combined Piaget's cognitive developmental approach, which focuses on the processes of thinking, with neo-Freudian theories that explain emotional development. Therefore in his theory both thinking and feeling have equal importance in the development of the self.

The infant reaches out to grasp at the environment, and thus recruits attention from caretakers. She is trying to be recognized by others—the start of a life-long movement to be recognized and to in turn recognize others. The child's basic survival depends on being able to attract the care and attention of another human being. By this single act of grasping, the infant creates meaning, a physical, social, and survival activity.

A human being moving forward can only see the old identity as no longer the self. Through interaction with the old identity (object), she accepts the new identity. By this recurring process of differentiation and integration of what is self and what is object, the self grows and develops over time. In this way, a person who is 60 can reflect on life, see the old self at 30, and say that was an immature self and not the self now. Progress in evolution has been made.

Every human being wishes to belong and to be separate. There is a continual tension between independence and inclusion. At each stage of self development a temporary balance is achieved by favoring inclusion or independence. Over the life span, there is a back and forth motion between the two which is best represented by a helix.

There are advantages and disadvantages of marital relationships between people at different stages (see Table 5–2). For example, a stable relationship may exist between one partner at the interpersonal stage and one partner at the institutional stage. Neither evolves developmentally, however, because the opposite pole of inclusion or independence is met by the partner. When a need is met externally by a spouse, the capacity to meet it is not developed internally. For example, if a husband handles all the finances, the wife may not learn to balance a checkbook until after his death. Such marriages may have difficulty assimilating the evolution of one or both partners and may break up when one chooses growth over the marriage. The marital therapist can reframe the conflicts between the couple as the tension of the growth process in each. Providing a holding environment for both partners to express their thoughts and feelings about what is happening to them as people and to the marital relationship is an important role for the therapist.

Likewise, two partners who are at the institutional stage may have difficulty achieving intimacy with each other, which is an integral part of moving to the interindividual stage. Each may experience the expression of bottled-up feelings as overwhelming, a loss of the self. To become intimate requires a certain amount of spontaneous craziness, which may be frightening to those people at the institutional stage. Either partner may leave the marriage in an effort to continue personal growth. The marital therapist may encourage the spouses to plan time together for sharing dialogue. A reciprocity in which each partner can be held and hold in return allows for both dependence and independence for both spouses, stimulating further evolution to the interindividual stage.

Ivey (1986) proposes a three-dimensional spherical model of development in which all aspects of development (images, beliefs/actions, abstract thinking, and knowledge) are available at the same time. He matches therapeutic techniques and modalities to each of the developmental dimensions. Ivey considers family therapy one of the psychotherapies of choice for clients who are functioning at the level of dialectics. The family therapist can assess which developmental dimensions are being experienced least by given family members, creating a blocked or "stuck" family. For example, a well-educated, professional couple may need encouragement to play more sensorimotor games with their child. They can read and understand the abstract ideas about parenting, but they may have trouble touching, spontaneously playing with, and enjoying the child.

Stage Theories of Adult Development

Most of the classic stage theories focused on childhood. For generations people believed that once they were adults they stopped growing. Most theorists did not search for changes in adult development or pay much attention to the stages of adulthood. However, in the 1970s some researchers began to study the stages of adulthood in more depth. Research on adult development is presented in Table 5–3.

TABLE 5–3 Research on adult development

Sheehy, 1974, 1981	Smith, Cardillo, and Choate, 1984	Levinson and others, 1978	Gould, 1978
Pulling up roots, 16–21	Early adult transition, 20–21	Childhood and adolescence, 0–22	Leaving our parent's world, 17–22
Trying twenties, 22–27		Early childhood transition, 0–3	I'm nobody's baby now, 22–28
Catch 30, 28–33	Age 30 transition, 27–33	Middle childhood transition, 5–6	Opening up to what's inside, 28–34
Mid-life passage, 34–39	Midlife transition, 37–43	Adolescent transition, 12–13	Mid-life decade, 35–45
Frantic forties, 40–45,	Age 50 transition, 47–55	Early Adulthood, 17–45	
Half-century reckoning, 46–51	Late adulthood transition, 64–69	Early adult transition, 17–22	
Freestyle fifties, 52–55		Entering the adult world, 22–28	
Selective sixties, 56–63 and 64–69		The age 30 transition, 28–33	
Thoughtful seventies and Proud to be eighties, 70 +		Settling down, 33–40	
		Middle Adulthood, 40–65	
		Mid-life transition, 40–45	
		Entering middle adulthood, 45–50	
		Age 50 transition, 50–55	
		Culmination of middle adulthood, 55–60	
		Late Adulthood, 60	
		Late adult transition, 60–65	
		Late Late Adulthood, 80	

Deadline Decade { Frantic forties, 40–45, Half-century reckoning, 46–51

Comeback Decade { Freestyle fifties, 52–55

Sheehy's Passages.   Gail Sheehy (1974) wrote the first book focused entirely on adult development. *Passages* divides the years from 16 to death into periods, each of which begins with a transition, or passage. Sheehy's work is of particular importance to marital and family therapists because it is based upon biographical interviews with 115 people, most of whom were couples and many of whom were interviewed together. Her goals for the project were (1) to assess the inner changes each individual had experienced in life, (2) to compare the development of men and women, and (3) to study predictable critical turning points for couples.

Sheehy found that typically women and men were at completely different places during the identified passage. Rarely were they experiencing the same feelings, thoughts, or needs, which therefore exerted pressure on the marriage. If the spouse could not understand and empathize with the different and strong feelings of the partner, the partner might feel misunderstood and unloved, precipitating the consideration of divorce. It is important for the marital and family therapist to normalize such differences as healthy, explaining that conflict between spouses and the sexes is to be expected as a normal part of adult development. Teaching spouses how to listen effectively to each other (without maintaining that there is only one right way to feel) is necessary if the couple is to traverse the passage successfully. Many couples who present for marital treatment are in these passages working on Sheehy's "predictable crises for couples" (p. 15).

One of Sheehy's (1981) major contributions is "the sexual diamond" (Figure 5–1). This figure clearly shows the results of Sheehy's research with couples and individuals concerning sex roles. At age 18, men and women are more similar. As they age, men become more instrumental over time and women become more expressive. By midlife, men and women are almost completely different from one another. A cross-sexual shift begins to occur after the age of 40 as women become more assertive and seek mastery and power, and men become more expressive and interested in relationships. Men and women become more alike again by age 60 as they both have integrated into their personalities the traits usually attributed to the opposite sex.

Sheehy (1981) also conducted research on the sources of well-being for human beings. Based on one of the largest samples ever used in research on the life cycle (60,000 responses), she concluded that the following five characteristics were linked to well-being by adult respondents across all occupational groups: (1) meaning in life; (2) at least one major transition that was handled in a creative, unique, or personal way; (3) a lack of feelings of disappointment with life or of being unfairly treated; (4) the attainment of several important long-term goals; and (5) being pleased with personal development and growth. The highly educated group had additional characteristics of being loved mutually, having more friends, being cheerful, being insensitive to criticism, and not having major fears. Married people were happier than single people. Older people as a group were more satisfied than younger people.

Most importantly, Sheehy (1981) found that a willingness to risk was a necessary aspect of successfully working through a passage of adult development. The process of a successful passage included anticipation (an image of having succeeded), separation and incubation (relinquishing an old identity), expansion (continued risk-taking behavior), and incorporation (integration of new behaviors and rest/relax-

FIGURE 5–1   Sheehy's sexual diamond

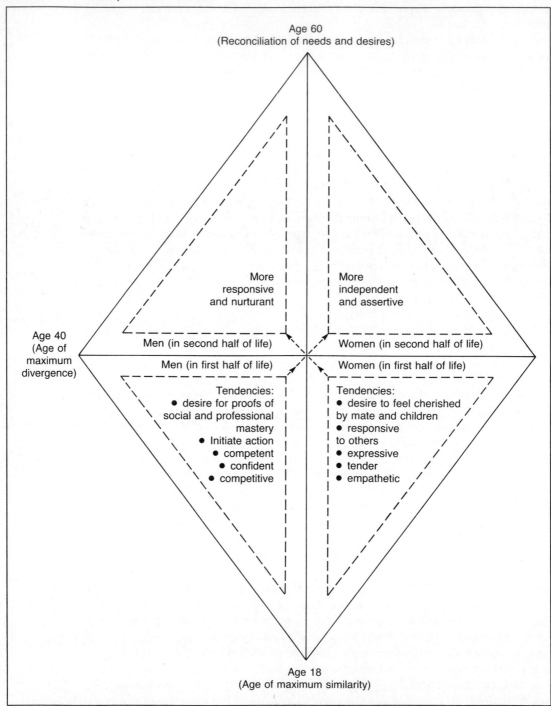

From *Passages* (p. 185) by G. Sheehy, 1981. New York: Morrow. Reprinted by permission.

ation). Usually a passage required external changes, that is, taking action in the environment, but such changes were always preceded by inner changes in attitudes and perceptions.

Levinson's Men at Mid-Life. Through extensive biographical interviewing of males aged 35 to 45, Levinson proposed four eras of the lives of men. Each stage lasted about 25 years, had required developmental tasks, and built upon the previous stage in a hierarchial, sequential, and orderly manner. There were alternating periods of structure building and structure changing—stability and change. Major periods of transition overlapped the stages. During these transitions, men actively reviewed their lives, making changes in the life structures of occupation and marriage. A major transition took a minimum of 3 years to a maximum of 6 years of effort.

In particular, the tasks of the mid-life transition included re-evaluation of the past, alteration of the life structures, and individuation. The process of individuation at mid-life entailed the reconciliation of opposites—the polarities of "young/old, destruction/creation, masculine/feminine, and attachment/separateness" (Levinson, p. 197). Being able to integrate the generativity of youth with the finality of old age is the fundamental polarity underlying the others.

People can remain young at heart, depending upon the choices they make in resolving this polarity. For example, men typically plan the legacy that they will leave, their special claims to immortality. They also face their own destructiveness and experience the pain of guilt for the people whom they have harmed at earlier stages of development. They often express these feelings through creative endeavors, thereby transforming the destructiveness into a positive life experience. Men struggle to integrate their feminine characteristics at mid-life—the empathic, caring, expressive modes of their existences. Relationships with the marital partner, children, parents, and friends take on a new, more important meaning. Finally, men learn to be attached to the external world and simultaneously to be separate from it. They can invest full participation in worldly commitments only to return home to the enjoyment of meditation and inner play.

The work of Levinson and his colleagues has important ramifications for marital and family therapists. When men find themselves in the major transitions of the life cycle, especially at mid-life, they reappraise their marital and family relationships. During these periods, they are more likely to enter marital or family therapy to evaluate their relationships. A wise marital and family therapist can point out the alternatives of divorcing, staying together and keeping things as they are, or changing the nature and quality of the present relationship while keeping it intact. At these points, men are more amenable to making changes in themselves and their relationships. They can learn new behaviors and re-create their current relationships, especially when they integrate the more expressive feminine parts of themselves. This is a process of hard developmental work, but also part of the normal transitions of adult development. For relationships to remain stable and intact, they must change and renew themselves, a paradox of adult development.

Gould's Transformations. Gould (1978) compiled the basic concerns of each age group. He describes the assumptions and the sentences people say to themselves as the restlessness arises at the beginning of each transformation. As a person becomes more independent at each stage of adult development, childhood feelings are triggered. The process of working through these feelings and thoughts, leading to the re-definition of the self, is called transformation.

GENDER DIFFERENCES IN DEVELOPMENT

Carol Gilligan (1982) critiqued most of the studies of adult development as being focused on male samples. Since male identity is based on achievement and separation, these concepts have been held up as the models for adults of both sexes. She maintains that only half the story has been told.

Women build their identities upon the blocks of relationships and intimacy. They view moral dilemmas by a different yardstick, one of care and responsibility. They develop by continuing in relationships with their mothers, with whom they remain both separate and attached at the same time. Men, on the other hand, must clearly separate from their mothers to show that they are male and different from them. The quality of a woman's life satisfaction is most directly related to affiliation rather than achievement, even when she is a successful achiever (Sheehy, 1981).

Belensky, Clinchy, Goldberger, and Tarule (1986) indicate that women tend to remain silent or to listen to others. They learn by experience to talk to other women who may be older, but with whom they can identify. The styles in which women talk and interact in the family (the politics of family life) shape their ways of knowing. Eventually they learn to rely on themselves and listen to their inner voices.

Josselson (1987) conducted a longitudinal study of college women. Her research is of particular interest because it is the first longitudinal study of adult development conducted using female subjects exclusively. Using a method of identity-status research that had been developed by Marcia (1966), she placed female interviewees into the following four identity classifications:

1. **Foreclosures** were living out a dream from childhood and made commitments without a crisis period.
2. **Identity Achievements** sifted through options and chose their own life plans.
3. **Moratoriums** remained ambivalent about life choices.
4. **Identity Diffusions** did not integrate experiences to connect them but rather fluctuated with environmental demands.

Each pathway had pathological and healthy aspects. For example, Foreclosures could be considered rigid or loyal; Identity Achievements, prematurely committed or self-directed; Moratoriums, indecisive or flexible; and Identity Diffusions, irresponsible or creative.

At follow-up, Josselson (1987) found that women had developed through anchoring with other human beings, either in the family of origin, through their own husbands and children, in careers, or through friends. Women developed a sense of identity in a web of relatedness. They were most vulnerable when crises occurred in their relationships. The Foreclosures emphasized security in relationships, safety, and family closeness. They were hard working, capable, and responsible with high standards and difficulty with peer relationships. The Identity Achievements valued their capabilities to make a difference in the world. They were proud of themselves and their accomplishments. Their independence was based on support from a male significant other.

Although society values the pathway of Moratorium for males, this pathway was not found to be productive for females. Those who made decisions—the Foreclosures and the Identity Achievements—had greater life structure and were more content with their lives. In particular, the pathway of Identity Diffusion—no crises and no commitments—led to inconsistent and sometimes tragic outcomes. Thus, it is important to identify the process as early as possible and prevent it by encouraging decision-making and risk-taking.

Work did not appear to be the primary identity for most of Josselson's female subjects. The development of these women tended to be grounded in a balance between self-in-relation and self-in-world. Josselson (1987) concluded that "communion, connection, relational embeddedness, spirituality, affiliation—with these women construct an identity. This is not to suggest that women cannot succeed, achieve, wield power, or govern nations as well as men. They can and do. Rather, it is to emphasize that such activities will have a place in an identity that is uniquely female in form" (p. 191).

THE HUMAN LIFE CYCLE: AN INTEGRATED APPROACH

The stages of the individual human life cycle are presented in Table 5–4. The tasks to be accomplished in each area of development by women and men at each stage of the human life cycle and the implications of those tasks for marital and family therapy are also included.

A CO-EVOLUTIONARY HELIX OF THE INDIVIDUAL HUMAN LIFE SPAN

The lightning whelk on the front cover of this text is a symbol of the individual human life span (Figure 5–2, p. 154). A gift from the ocean, the lightning whelk has much to tell us about human life. Human life is a process of differentiation and integration over time, representing three dimensions of the helix, the spiraling whelk. Human life is a living system operating on the principles of anamorphosis and homeostasis. Through change, stability is maintained over time. Human beings are meaning-making organisms who continue to create purposes for their existences until they die.

A Co-Evolutionary Helix of the Individual Life Span is a theoretical model that integrates human life cycle theories, life event/transition theories, life-span theories, and individual variability theories. There are ten stages of the human life cycle in the model based upon age: infancy, early childhood, middle childhood, adolescence, early adulthood, young adulthood, middle adulthood, later middle adulthood, older adulthood, and elderly adulthood. Each stage builds upon another. There are transitions at the beginning of each stage: walking—gateway to the world, entering school, puberty, early adult transition, age 30 transition, mid-life transition, age 50 transition, retirement, and the 80th birthday. During each stage, people function qualitatively differently from the way they did at earlier stages.

TABLE 5–4   Toward Healthier Family Systems: The life cycle of the individual human being (pp. 146–153)

Infancy (Birth–12 Months)

1. Receive affection, touch, talk, and social interaction from caregiver. When these needs for touch and social interaction are met, the baby learns that the external world is a positive place and that people can be trusted.

2. Receive food, liquid, and comfort from caregiver. When these nutritional needs are met, the infant experiences rapid physical growth, the largest amount at any stage, and the maximum number of brain cells.

Female	Male
Female babies tend to vocalize more; therefore, parents talk to them more.	Male babies tend to "fuss" more and be held more.
	They may have circumcisions.

Implications for Marital and Family Therapy

Normally, the relationship between the mother and the infant is very close and enmeshed during the first 4 months of life. A maternity leave is helpful at this time (Brazelton & Yogman, 1986). It is important for the husband to bond with the child during this period; paternity leave is also encouraged. A family may present for treatment because the husband is jealous of the baby. This is normal, and these feelings will subside as the mother spends more time with her husband after the fourth month and as he bonds to the baby.

Early Childhood (12 Months–5 Years Old)

1. Become independent and explore while parents set appropriate limits.
2. Grow intellectually through sensorimotor experiences and talking with caregiver(s).

Female	Male
Often reinforced for staying indoors near their mothers.	Often reinforced for being outside alone and involved in physically active, creative play.
Toys usually relate to housework or child care, such as dolls or mini-household appliances.	Socialized for independent problem-solving role.
Socialized for nurturing role.	

Implications for Marital and Family Therapy

Mothers present with questions about parenting, especially setting limits. This period is the most restrictive one for mothers, leading to "cabin fever" and higher rates of depression and anxiety. Encourage the woman to make friends with other mothers so that they can watch and work with their children together. Ask the mother to hire a babysitter and plan time for herself to enjoy, to have an interest/hobby, or to work—a separate sense of self apart from the baby. Behavioral parent training approaches can be useful.

TABLE 5–4 *continued*

Middle Childhood (5–13 Years of Age)

1. Acquire academic, social, and extracurricular skills.
2. Develop sense of right and wrong—a conscience.

Female	Male
Girls are reinforced for being neat but often receive negative feedback about their school work.	Teachers tend to call on boys more (Sadker & Sadker, 1986).

Implications for Marital and Family Therapy

Parents often present for family therapy when a child is not doing well academically in school or is overly aggressive with classmates. A referral may be necessary to have the child tested to rule out learning disabilities. Sometimes the parents differ on how they think the child should be disciplined or are arguing a great deal with each other in front of the child. Behavioral parent training approaches can be useful to teach parents how to design contracts with children to reinforce them for desirable behaviors.

Adolescence (13–18 Years of Age)

1. Period of rapid growth, especially height, second only to that in the first year of life.
2. Sexual maturation.
3. Use of logic and abstract thinking; can do advanced problem solving and understand literature.
4. Develop sense of identity.
5. Develop autonomy by using freedom appropriately and taking responsibility for one's actions under the supervision of parents.
6. Learn to drive a car and obtain a driver's license.
7. Begin dating relationships with the opposite sex.
8. Peer pressure may influence the use of drugs and alcohol; differences between the sexes in rates of use are decreasing.

Female	Male
Growth of breasts, vagina, labia, uterus, pubic hair, and axillary hair.	Growth of scotum, testes, penis, prostate, seminal vesicles, pubic hair, and axillary hair.
Menarche—first menstrual period (10–16).	Voice deepens.
Critical body fat percentage and weight necessary before menstrual period can occur.	Beard grows.
If a female chooses to begin sexual activity, there is a high probability of pregnancy within the first 6 months of such activity.	Nocturnal emission and spontaneous ejaculation.
	Identity focuses on achievement/independence.
	Rate of marijuana and cocaine use slightly higher for boys.

TABLE 5–4 *continued*

Implications for Marital and Family Therapy

Families typically present when an adolescent is in trouble. A teenager may be pregnant, drinking heavily, using drugs or arrested for delinquency. Families who are very rigid and who are "stuck" in an earlier stage of close monitoring of a child will need to become more flexible, using input from their teenagers to form the rules while consistently enforcing the rules once they are made. On the other hand, families who are extremely permissive will need to set rules and be prepared to deal with the normal testing behavior of teenagers.

Early Adulthood (18–28 Years of Age)
The Leaving Home Transition (18–22 Years of Age)

---

1. Move away from home.
2. Less financially dependent upon parents.
3. Greater autonomy in roles.
4. Work in a job, enter military service, attend college/post-secondary training, or get married.
5. Negotiate adult-adult relationships with parents based on adult identity.
6. Work on developing deeper relationships with people of the opposite sex.
7. Form dream of self in the world.
8. Provisional or firm commitments on life structures (occupation and/or marriage/family), May be stable in one, but transient in another, stable in both, or unstable in both.

Female	Male
May marry, or develop career first and then marry.	Cultivate mentor, often of same sex.
Obtain education or training to hold job.	The vision of "The Dream" is powerful at this stage.
Wedding takes planning and cooperation of both families.	Choose a career.
Can prepare for natural childbirth by attending Lamaze classes with spouse.	Obtain education or training for first job.
Cesarean interventions are being used frequently in the United States (Strickland, 1988) and require a recovery period.	Marry during this stage or wait until later.
	Attempts to form such life structures not completely satisfactory the first time because it takes practice.
Postpartum depression can occur after childbirth.	Period of crisis is experienced.
Most women prefer to have babies before 30, although an increasing minority are doing so after 30.	New commitments are made to change the structures.

TABLE 5–4 *continued*

Implications for Marital and Family Therapy

Families often present during the leaving home transition of the young adult. This period is one of the most tense for the parents and the young adult. During this anxiety-producing time, symptoms often surface. For example, a schizophrenic child may experience the first hospitalization. Eating disorders may appear for the first time.

The basic underlying developmental issues of separating and becoming an independent adult while renegotiating adult-adult relationships with parents should remain central. The family therapist needs to continue to support the differentiation of the young adult from the family in a socially appropriate way so that the young adult can stand alone successfully. Symptoms should be dealt with, but in ways that emphasize movement away from the family, with appropriate support, rather than increased enmeshment with the family.

Young Adulthood (28–38 Years of Age)
The Age 30 Transition

1. Life becomes more serious. During the age 30 transition from 28 to 32, people review what they have done with their lives and what they want to do. They carefully evaluate what parameters of life are nonnegotiable; for example, the biological clock limits childbirth. They choose new directions that have not been taken previously.

2. An integrated life of work, family, leisure, friends, and community in which goals and aspirations are met is difficult to attain before 35 (Sheehy, 1981).

Female	Male
Women who have not married often find mates and have children before time runs out.	Build upon previous life structures.
Women who have married and have had children may return to school to prepare for new careers now that the children are in school or go to work full-time.	Advance in careers based on past accomplishments. May go to graduate school or another training program that will help in career advancement.
The last child in each family is typically born before the mothers turn 35.	If not married, men often feel pressure to marry; can see women as separate persons rather than as objects.
	Men want to establish niches and make it in the larger world. Implementing "The Dream" and external advancement are key goals. By the late thirties, many men peak in achievement.

Implications for Marital and Family Therapy

Dual-career couples may present for treatment when considering a job move to another state for which they may wish to consider a commuter marriage pattern (each living in a separate residence). Role stress and role allocation issues may occur. In particular, career ascendancy issues may surface when the man is absorbed in following "The Dream." A couple may present to discuss infertility issues or whether or not to have a child. Families may seek treatment if their school-age children are not achieving in school.

TABLE 5–4 *continued*

Middle Adulthood (37–47 Years of Age)
The Mid-Life Transition (37–40 years of Age)

---

1. The mid-life transition prompts an intense life review. Individuals build on past choices or take entirely new paths.

2. The "shadow" side of the personality is explored and integrated. People often admit their weaknesses and explore them.

3. Physical fitness and diet become important as people experience some loss in vigor.

Female	Male
Women who have focused on children may be launching them and finding energy in new career options or deeper career commitments.	The search for the "Holy Grail." Loss of the heroic self.
May pursue "The Dream" with confidence.	Grieving over loss.
May become more assertive over time.	Incorporate the neglected parts of the self.
May go back to school to implement earlier frustrated career plans.	Recognize limits and gain more daily enjoyment from actual life experiences rather than imagined conquests.
Women who have experienced the nurturing sides of themselves at earlier stages will now explore their instrumental, assertive sides. Single career women may make contact with their nurturing sides and mentor others in their careers or marry in their forties. A few women may even have their first child after 40.	Men focus on the legacies they will leave.
	If a failure is experienced at mid-life, the mid-life transition may be traumatic.
	Major polarities, such as old/young masculine/feminine, belongingness/individuation, and creative/destructive, are integrated.

Implications for Marital and Family Therapy

Married couples may present for treatment due to the husband's attempts to regain his power and youth by having an affair and/or marrying a younger woman. When a spouse is experiencing a traumatic mid-life crisis, the partner is shocked by the abrupt changes in the spouse. Families may present when children are having problems in teenage or launching years while their parents are preoccupied with mid-life concerns.

Later Middle Adulthood (47–62 Years of Age)
The Half Century Transition (47–50 Years of Age)

---

1. This stage is often experienced as the last chance to reach those goals not previously sought or attained.

2. Implementing a plan of diet and exercise to maintain health and fitness is important.

3. A search for greater spirituality and union with God is an integral part of this stage.

4. Typically the sexes are at vastly different places.

TABLE 5–4 *continued*

Female	Male
Peri-menopause is the cessation of progesterone and occurs 1 to 2 years before estrogen decreases and menstrual periods stop. Ovulation and menstruation cease at menopause when both estrogen and progesterone dramatically decrease.	A man may see himself as successful if he enjoys a job at which he excels, has a wife whom he loves, and has a sense of humor.
Adjustment to hormone replacement therapy— the use of natural estrogen every night accompanied by natural progesterone 12 to 15 days per month (Cutler, 1988).	Men often become more nurturing and oriented toward relationships as they age.
Hormone replacement therapy prevents osteoporosis (bone loss), hot flashes (sudden sweats, most often occurring at night which interrupt sleep and can produce depressed feelings in some women due to sleep loss), atrophy of the vagina, and depressed mood in women prone to depression.	A man may retire early and go into business for himself or spend his time in volunteer community activities and with friends and family.
Women often become more assertive with age.	Men enjoy mentoring their children.
Depression at this stage is linked with the increased caretaking roles of caring for elderly parents or in-laws, children, and spouse. If the spouse caused stress, there was a significant increase in depth of depression. A work role had a positive outcome for health, even when other roles were combined (McKinlay, McKinlay, & Avis, 1989).	Being able to receive from children rather than give may feel awkward for men during this stage.
Sexual intercourse with the spouse on a regular basis is linked to higher hormone levels and greater physical well-being (Cutler, 1988).	

Implications for Marital and Family Therapy

Married couples may present for treatment of a conflicted relationship. The family therapist should check out possible symptoms of peri-menopause and menopause, making referrals for possible hormone replacement therapy. Often women do not know about peri-menopause and menopause, but are just aware of increased irritability or fluctuating moods that are affecting the marital relationship (Lederer, 1984). If a woman has had a hysterectomy within the last two years, feels depressed, and is not on hormone replacement therapy, she should be referred to a gynecologist for possible hormone replacement therapy. The rate of depression is twice as high among women who have had hysterectomies (McKinlay, McKinlay, & Avis, 1989).

TABLE 5−4 *continued*

Older Adulthood (62−80 Years of Age)
The Retirement Transition (62−70 Years of Age)

---

1. If a person is healthy, there is energy available to be invested in church, community, leisure, and even work pursuits.
2. A diet tailored to the particular needs of the individual is important with an individualized exercise plan.
3. The individual at this stage often functions as the scribe of the family, keeping everyone in contact.
4. There is an increased interest in spirituality.
5. Marital satisfaction is directly related to time spent with couple friends.

Female	Male
Longevity is greater for women as a group, yet they have more surgical operations than do men (Strickland, 1988).	Men usually retire and shift their energies into leisure activities, politics, hobbies, or community affairs.
Women in good health will often work throughout this stage, since their life span is longer. They may form their own businesses or make major contributions in other work roles.	They prepare for their own deaths, but live each day to the fullest.
Some women travel extensively at this stage, taking cruises and seeing the world.	They may travel at this stage of life.
Women keep in touch with their children and parents, maintaining kinship contacts.	Some men have open heart surgery or cancer operations.
A woman may be asked to take care of an aging parent or in-law.	Men are sensitive and caring.
	They keep in contact with the children.
	They can become more dependent on their wives.

Implications for Marital and Family Therapy

Couples may present for marital therapy to adjust to the husband's retirement. A homemaker who has not worked still has her job of keeping the house clean and cooking the meals. Having her husband home around the clock can interfere with her routine and her lifestyle. Likewise, a woman who continues to work when her husband retires may feel pressure from him to organize more social activities and travel plans than she wishes. Couples may also enter treatment to deal with decisions concerning who takes care of an elderly parent or in-law. In addition, if a divorced child returns with several children (the boomerang family), advice may be sought.

The cross-section of the whelk, focusing on the Health-Illness Wheel, is a life-span approach designed to take into account the effects of individual variability and unexpected events in various areas of development. Some examples are losses in meaning (spiritual), educational degrees (intellectual), behavioral addictions (behavioral), nervous disorders (emotional), the person's unique dreams of what life can be (imaginal), therapeutic massage (sensual), marital sexual relationships (sexual), medical problems (physical), and relationships with parents, spouse, children, friends, employer, and co-workers (interpersonal) as they affect the individual life cycle determined by age. These types of development are co-evolving, affecting each other as they move toward health or illness—a life-span approach.

TABLE 5—4 *continued*

Elderly Adulthood
(The 80th Birthday and Beyond)

1. Concerns about health predominate. People who take responsibility for their health by following an appropriate exercise and diet plan under the advice of their physicians tend to be more active and feel better.
2. Often there is an interaction effect among medications that must be checked.
3. People prepare for death and face their own mortality. They deal with the loss of the spouse and of friends.
4. Life review occurs to find meaning in one's life and to know that one made a difference.
5. Friends and a social network are particularly important at this stage.
6. Elderly adults are interested in sex and enjoy sexual relationships.
7. Lack of finances or fear of loss of finances can occur.
8. People are happier if they continue a forward direction in life by making future commitments.

Female	Male
Women become more domineering and assertive (Brim, 1976).	Men become more affiliative and sentimental (Brim, 1976).
Women can live alone successfully, valuing their independence.	Relationships with grown children are related to life satisfaction.
Women can continue hormone replacement therapy, which reduces the probability of urinary incontinence. Kegel exercises help.	Widowers often remarry within a year.
	Prostate problems need to be checked out.
	Impotence can become a problem.

Implications for Marital and Family Therapy

The main presenting complaint at this stage is grieving over the death of a spouse. In married couples, the impotence of the male can be a cause for concern. Checking the number of medications being taken can be important, as drug interaction effects can be occuring. Referral to one physician to coordinate all medications is helpful. A family may present to discuss placement of an elderly parent in a nursing home versus living with them. Adjustment to a chronic illness or health concerns may also be reasons for entering treatment.

The cross-section of the whelk that focuses on the life structures of self, career, and family allows for the impact of life events and individual variability in achievement in each of these structures as they influence the individual human being proceeding through the stages of the human life cycle based on age. In each structure there are movements toward change and stability characteristic of systems.

One point is clear: All these dimensions of the whelk (the individual life cycle, the Health-Illness Wheel, and the life structures of self, career, and family) generate transitions that need to be worked through if a person is to grow and develop over the life span. The individual life cycle speaks to the discontinuity of the changes, leaps to new ways of processing experience, and provides an orderly sequence. The Health-

FIGURE 5-2   The Lightning Whelk: A Co-Evolutionary Helix of the Individual Life Span

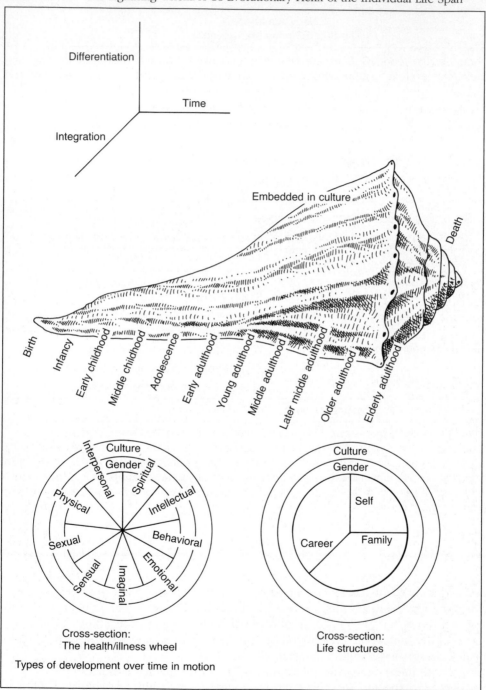

Illness Wheel and the life structures of self, career, and family include the life events over a life span and individual variability that can trigger this sequence earlier than expected, add to the overload of transitions that must be worked through simultaneously, or provide sources of energy to be drawn upon when a transition is affecting one or more areas of development.

The transition process is similar across transitions, as pointed out by Schlossberg (1984) and Hopson (1981). A process of differentiation (taking action) and a process of integration (making meaning) are required to handle a transition successfully. There is, however, a component of uniqueness associated with each transition in the individual life cycle. First, people experience a transition as something never encountered before and different from anything that they have managed previously. From the first day of the transition, they are operating at a different level of development, a leap into the unknown. Usually people think they are the only ones going through the transition. They often feel isolated and afraid to share their feelings because they fear others might consider them crazy or strange.

Therefore, one of the values of the individual life cycle is normalizing what occurs naturally at each transition and stage of the life cycle. People can be educated about what to expect and discuss it openly because everyone goes through similar changes. For example, people can learn about the restlessness of later middle adulthood, when people view the time remaining as their last chance to make unfulfilled dreams realities, and recognize it as normal when it occurs. If a man has dreamed of his own business, he may leave his comfortable job with all its benefits to risk starting his own firm. A woman who has secretly dreamed of moving into a management position may apply for a promotion. At this stage, women can be educated about menopause and hormone options such as natural progesterone and natural estrogen (Cutler, 1988; Hargrove & Abraham, 1982). They can look at fitness, diet, and other alternatives to hysterectomy and other female surgeries. The aggressive drive to operate in the external world that arises for females and the warm, caring trend toward affiliation in males are seen as normal developmental changes at this stage.

The strength of the strivings that emerge from nowhere—the vague uneasiness and rumblings within—herald the beginning of yet another transition in the human life cycle, which may or may not be triggered by a specific event. These strivings provide support for the existence of a ground plan for the human organism. For example, in the United States, middle-class adolescents often have three free meals a day, their own rooms, an allowance, the use of a car or their own cars, access to a telephone or their own phone, free designer clothes and other amenities. Why would they want to leave home? Only a developmental ground plan that creates from within a restless yearning to be on one's own could provide the impetus for leaving such a comfortable environment.

Embedded in Gender

The human life span is affected by the sex of the individual. The Lightning Whelk: A Co-Evolutionary Helix of the Individual Life Span is embedded in gender. The context—that is, the social groups in which the person grew up—affect the sex roles with which the individual has been socialized. A living human system is interacting with the environment; they are co-evolving. Therefore, the individual learns a sex role through interactions with the environment, or context. The nature of a person's sex role will often affect career choices, the kind of person to marry, the friends with whom one feels comfortable, and other aspects of a person's life.

In addition to the socially learned sex role, the biological development of women and men is different. Women can bear children and nurse them. Each woman must face the biological clock and decide whether or not she will have a child. A man can physiologically father children into his seventies or eighties. He has more options, such as marrying a younger woman if his first wife is infertile and he wants children. In contrast, the female biological clock set by Mother Nature has a limit between the ages of 40 to 45.

Goldner (1988) has said that generation and gender are the two variables that form the basic structure of the family: There are people of different ages in the family and parents of different genders. In this way, the children learn the instrumental skills that are used more often by men and the expressive communication skills that are used more often by women. Likewise, children learn what is expected of adults because their parents are older than they.

Embedded in Culture

The Lightning Whelk: A Co-Evolutionary Helix of the Individual Life Span is embedded in culture. Expectations emanate from the culture in which we are socialized. Some expectations are carried down through the generations via stories. For example, in Appalachia people expect strangers to be untrustworthy. They remember the following story, passed down from generation to generation.

> Years ago when the first ship landed on this continent, men were lost. One man wandered on foot, walking through brush and overgrowth deeper and deeper into the forest and higher and higher into the hills. One day he came across a clearing where he rested. Suddenly from behind a tree, a fierce animal sprang toward him. He wrestled with it but was losing his strength, when a "hairy thing" beat the monster away. He followed the "hairy thing" to her cave, where he became comfortable through the cold and dark winter. He cared for the "hairy thing" and in the spring a baby was born to the man and the "hairy thing." The man began to teach the "hairy thing" English words so that she could say "baby." And although he missed the intellectual companionship and customs of his native land, the man was happy with "hairy thing" and the baby.
>
> One day a group of explorers from his homeland came to the cave. The man did not realize how much he missed his culture until he saw his countrymen. They told him that there was a place for him on their ship home but *not* for the "hairy thing" and the baby because they would not fit in. For days the man was in anguish. Then on the day that the other men were due to leave, the man arose early and went with them. When the "hairy thing" awoke, she carried the baby, tracking the man through the wilderness until she reached the shore where she saw him on the ship as it sailed away. She ran into the water, holding the baby above her head and crying loudly, "baby, baby, baby." As the ship disappeared below the horizon, she tore the baby in two. Clinging to the hairy part as her own, she proudly said, "I am Appalachia," as the water crept above her head. (Adapted from a story recorded by the WPA Writers Project.)

Children play in Austria. There are different expectations for clothes from one culture to another.

Such a story emphasizes pride in the Appalachian culture and the expectation that strangers, even though warm and friendly, are not to be trusted. Expectations can be very powerful and are passed down through the generations via stories and tales. This particular story shows the influence that the culture has on the choice of a marital partner and the early adulthood transition. Cultural expectations can impact on every stage of the individual life cycle. They can affect the career chosen, the family size, even aspects of the personality.

The Life Cycle Within the Life Span
The point at the left of the whelk represents the birth of the human being, and the tip on the far right of the whelk denotes the person's death. Between these two points, the stages of the human life cycle based on age unfold over time. The number of changes

and activities and the stability of the individual increase over time, peaking in older adulthood at retirement. They remain high until elderly adulthood, where they may be reduced only by poor health.

People's activities and accomplishments peak at retirement (which may occur at a later and later age), followed by a full and active life similar to early and middle adulthood. The slope of the whelk mirrors this continued rate and peak of activity until the rings of elderly adulthood at 80, 90, and 100 lead to the end point of death and return to the sea.

Qualitative changes occur at each stage. For example, adolescents can think abstractly about broad, general concepts, while children in early childhood are learning how to talk and could never think in such abstract terms about ideas. Women in their 40s and 50s become dominant and assertive while their husbands enjoy relationships with friends and family, becoming more spiritual in orientation as the sex roles reverse during the postparental years of middle adulthood. Inner activities increase with age as people in middle and later middle adulthood learn to reconcile opposites, a process that is not understood by people in early and young adulthood.

When treatment begins, the marital and family therapist can assess the stage of the life cycle for each family member. The therapist can use the areas of strength of the family members as shown by their successful developmental changes to assist those who are "stuck," unable to move forward on their developmental trajectories.

The lightning whelk represents the human life span, from birth to death.

The Health-Illness Wheel

Cutting a cross-section of the whelk, the Health-Illness Wheel, composed of various types of development, moves from birth to death. At any given stage of the individual life cycle, the types of development on the Health-Illness Wheel can be measured. Spiritual, intellectual, behavioral, emotional, imaginal, sensual, sexual, physical, and interpersonal development can be assessed. At certain stages of the family life cycle some types of development will increase more than others. However, each human being is working on all these areas of development to a greater or lesser degree at the same time, which is one of the key elements of a life-span perspective.

For example, an adolescent is trying to make meaning (spiritual) out of the sexual maturation that she has experienced. Is she a child or an adult? Who is she? How should she act? What does being a woman mean in her culture? She notices that she is able to think in abstract terms to answer some of these questions and can logically consider the consequences (intellectual). She finds herself acting more grown up (behavioral) even though inside she is feeling awkward and unsure of herself (emotional). Dreams of marrying and having a child come to her mind as she realizes that she is physiologically capable of motherhood (imaginal). She would like to be touched and held (sensual). She is attracted to boys for the first time (sexual). She now has breasts that require a bra; She has shot up almost 4 inches in height and has regular periods every month (physical). She is particularly concerned about how she is perceived by her peers and cannot understand why her parents are so old-fashioned and restrictive (interpersonal). She is making progress in all these areas at the same time, although more in some than in others. The areas of development are co-evolving and being affected by each other.

The lightning whelk represents a living human system. As the Health-Illness Wheel moves from birth to death over time, the various types of development on it move toward health or toward illness. Each is a subsystem with forces of growth (health) and decline (illness). Such antithetical movements are the system processes of anamorphosis and homeostasis.

Life Structures

The life structures of self, career, and family also move from birth to death over time. They co-evolve, interacting with each other and with the stage of the individual life cycle. Sometimes a person can experience an accomplishment in one of the life structures that can offset a failure in another. Each is a system that develops through processes of change and stability, part of the larger human system represented by the lightning whelk. All grow and decline within the contexts of gender and culture.

On rare occasions, an individual can experience simultaneous positive changes in self, career, and family, leading to a peak experience in life. For example, a professor might go to Europe as a consultant (career domain), take the children along to show them the world (family domain), and gain confidence in independent action through planning and carrying out the trip (self domain)—a peak experience. Later, when under stress, this professor can draw upon memories of the trip to renew vitality from the wellspring of the peak experience.

The timing of the trip should be based on an understanding of the critical times in the life cycles of the children. For example, if it had been planned later, they might not have wanted to go because of commitments related to the young adult transition. Planning goals that interface more than one domain can be risky, but can also lead to peak experiences in which the interaction and synergy across domains lead to indescribable levels of satisfaction and well being.

Sunny Hansen (1988) has developed integrative life planning, which focuses on roles, contexts, and developmental domains. She is particularly interested in the relationships among work, education, family, and leisure. One analogy that Hansen uses to illustrate the process of integrative life planning is quilting. Each person is a quilter who chooses different pieces of work, education, family, and leisure. The pattern of the quilt will be unique based upon the way in which the quilter integrates the contexts, chosen roles, and developmental domains. Eliza Calvert Hall, a Southern writer referred to as Aunt Jane of Kentucky in honor of her folk wisdom, captures Hansen's idea well (Figure 5–3).

In formulating a model for working with adults, Okun (1984) proposes a model of a life system composed of the systems of the individual, family, and career that are together most, but not all, of the life system within the contexts of social, cultural, political, and economic systems. Her conceptual model integrates systems theory and

FIGURE 5–3   The analogy of the quilt

Did you ever think, child, how much piecin' a quilt's like livin' a life? And as for sermons, why, they ain't no better sermon to me than a patchwork quilt, and the doctrines is right there a heap plainer'n they are in the catechism. Many a time I've set and listened to Parson Page preachin' about predestination and free-will, and I've said to myself, "Well, I ain't never been through Centre College up at Danville, but if I could jest git up in the pulpit with one of my quilts, I could make it a heap plainer to folks than parson's makin' it with all his big words."

You see, you start out with jest so much caliker. You don't go to the store and pick it out and buy it, but the neighbors will give you a piece here and a piece there, and you'll have a piece left every time you cut out a dress, and you take jest what happens to come. And that's like predestation. But when it comes to the cuttin' out, why, you're free to choose you own pattern. You can give the same kind o' pieces to two persons, and one'll make a "nine-patch" and one'll make a "wild-goose chase," and there'll be two quilts made out o' the same kind o' pieces, and jest as different as they can be. And that is jest the way with livin'. The Lord sends us the pieces, but we can cut 'em out and put 'em together pretty much to suit ourselves, and there's a heap more in the cuttin' out and the sewin' than there is in the caliker.

Eliza Calvert Hall
Aunt Jane of Kentucky
1899

developmental theory. Three overlapping circles within the larger circle represent the three domains of individual development, career development, and family development that are interacting with each other within socioeconomic, cultural, and environmental contexts.

In contrast, the present model defines interactive self, career, and family subsystems, which travel over time through the individual life cycle to comprise the life span of the individual. The interaction between development in each of these subsystems and life-cycle development is only one of four interactive dimensions that comprise the present model. The triggering event in the system, the effect of changes in the Health-Illness Wheel on a given system (changes in types of development toward health or toward illness), and the unique themes of that system are integral aspects of each type of life structure: self, career, and family.

Self.   The self is the source of meaning. In adult life the self coordinates the making of meaning. In the later stages of adulthood in particular, the self is involved in a dialectic with itself and others in the making of inner meaning. As a person becomes more independent, the person can paradoxically become more interdependent on another human being.

The self has likes and dislikes, interests, and ways of enjoying leisure. The self is creative, reaching out to explore the environment. The self in the present reflects on the self of yesterday, last week, or last month and knows that it is now "not me." Like a snake that sheds its skin to grow and develop, the self renounces its former condition to accept and renew itself as it is in the present. Through this process of differentiation and integration, the self develops (Kegan, 1982). The tension between the activity of this actualizing principle and the force toward stabilization is the balance found in any living system, including this self system.

When thinking of the life structure of the self moving from birth to death across the life cycle of the individual, four dimensions of the self are considered concurrently: (1) Kegan's stages of self-development, (2) a triggering event in the self system, (3) the Health-Illness Wheel (changes in various types of development over time) as it impacts on the functioning of the self system, and (4) unique themes of the self. Transitions can occur related to all four of these dimensions that should be worked through. The marital and family therapist can assess these dimensions as part of the intake process.

First, the stage of self-development of the system can be assessed. At what level of Kegan's system is the person functioning? If the person is in transition from one stage to another, individual, marital, or family therapy can be particularly effective in facilitating the process of change.

The second dimension that can be assessed is the presence of a triggering event in the self system. For example, a suicide attempt is a triggering event in the self system that impacts the self most directly and then produces ripple effects in the career and family systems.

The most difficult developmental work we will ever do is the inner work we do on ourselves. The third dimension to be assessed is the impact of the Health-Illness Wheel (the various types of development) on the self system. For example, we have the capability of changing our life purpose and the meaning we attach to events. We can change our thoughts and even our ways of knowing. We can decide to behave in different ways, such as being assertive or not drinking alcohol. We can become aware of our feelings and the patterns of interaction that trigger them. We can generate our own dreams of a better future and make them realities. We can enjoy a therapeutic massage, a warm bath, or sexual intercourse with our spouse. We can become aware of bodily sensations, the health of our bodies, and what our bodies are telling us. We can decide to improve our levels of physical fitness. We can become aware of our patterns of interaction with our parents, spouse, children, employer, co-workers, and friends. We can change these patterns if we want to. In all of these areas we can become more ourselves. When changes occur in any of these areas of development, the self-concept and self-esteem are typically affected. These changes represent transitions to be bridged.

The self uses defense mechanisms to protect and regulate self-esteem. The defenses that worked well as a child usually become barriers to the advancement of the adult (Gould, 1978). If the child learned to blame his sister for his mischief to avoid his mother's punishment, the man may create barriers for himself when under stress at work by blaming his female co-workers for his own mistakes or blaming his wife at home for something that happened to the children. Projection or blaming worked when he was a child but is now hampering him at work and in his close relationships. A marital and family therapist can assess what defense mechanisms a person is using and can help that person become aware of defensive patterns and generate alternative ways of responding. Such defense mechanisms are examples of emotional development that is measured on the Health-Illness Wheel.

The fourth dimension is the unique theme about the self. A 50-year-old can look at baby pictures and say, "That is no longer me," but the themes of that particular infant persist throughout the life span. The self of a particular person is unique with special themes that weave their way across the life span, intensifying with time, until the core is reached. The self becomes more itself with age. People begin to live life more on their own terms rather than by conforming to what "should" be done. Neugarten's fanning does, indeed, occur: older people differ from each other more than babies differ from other babies. These themes represent meaning to the individual, and change in these themes is a transition that needs to be worked through.

Career.   Aggressive strivings can be expressed in socially acceptable ways through a career. A career is more than a job. There is typically a commitment to education or training to prepare for it, to continue to be current, and to make a contribution. A career becomes more complex at each successive stage of the individual life cycle. Skills are required to maintain a career. Particularly important are interpersonal skills, such as assertiveness, goal-setting, persistence, frustration tolerance, appropriate attitudes toward authority figures, and cooperation with clients or colleagues.

There are career development theories about how people choose careers and improve them over time. Theories of career development have changed a great deal since Ginzberg and associates (1951) postulated three stages between the ages of 6 and 18, with no change after the age of 18. The job market is dramatically different now. The average person at age 18 in the United States today can expect to have 10 different full-time jobs before retirement. In addition, more is known now about transitions in adult development, such as the mid-life transition, when people are expected to assess their careers and move toward changing them by applying for promotions or by re-creating their present positions (see *The Plateauing Trap* by Bardwick [1986]).

Holland (1973) has left a legacy of research and data on the personality traits of individuals and the characteristics of their careers. He classifies both jobs and personalities into six categories that can be shown on a hexagon: investigative, artistic, social, enterprising, conventional, and realistic. Individuals who take his self-scoring Self Directed Search can then match their personality categories with lists of jobs within the same categories. When people have high scores in one or a few categories, they typically stay in the career with those codes for a long time.

Roe's (1956) theory of career choice states that people choose careers that match their childhood patterns of parent-child interactions. People whose parents were overprotective or demanding of achievement typically choose careers where they receive recognition from others. People who experienced neglectful or rejecting parenting patterns often go into scientific or mechanical careers where they find satisfaction from working with things rather than people. People who were accepted as children usually go into careers where there is a balance between interest in people and in things.

Super, Stavishesky, Matlin, and Jordan (1963) linked the self-concept with career choice. People implement their self-images in their careers (Super, 1957). This life-long process has five stages (and many substages): (1) growth, birth to 14; (2) exploration, 15–24; (3) establishment, 25–44; (4) maintenance, 45–65; and (5) decline, 65 to death. One of the strengths of Super's theory is its focus on the process of career development and choice over the entire life span.

Thomas (1976) proposed a cognitive, actualizing theory of career development called the Contributing Person Model. Composed of domains of Self, Vocademic Studies, and Career Decision-Making, the model emphasized the inherent growth potential of human beings to reach out and act upon their environments. For example, children will continue to "work," even when they receive no toys as rewards. There is a basic human orientation toward curiosity, activity, and growth. The person takes the initiative to assess Self, Vocademic Studies (careers and educational programs to prepare for them), and Career Decision-Making skills and attributes. Based on the assessment, the person decides on a tentative career and a plan of preparation for that career. Using skills from the Career Decision-Making domain, the individual takes action to implement initial steps in the plan. This process continues over the life span as the person assesses self, present career, and other career options to measure the congruence, implementing action steps to produce balance in the interactive tension among the Self, Vocademic Studies, and Career-Decision-Making domains. Thomas et al. (1974) also wrote four volumes to educate counselor educators in using competency-based modules to train graduate students in career counseling.

When thinking of the life structure of career as moving from birth to death across the life cycle, several aspects of career are considered concurrently and can be assessed when conducting intake interviews with individuals, couples, and families. First, the stage of career development of the individual can be evaluated. This is best done by asking questions about satisfaction with present career, what is liked and disliked about it, future career goals and jobs in the past, basically: Where are you now? Where would you like to be? Where have you been? Circular questioning of the spouse and family members can also be used (the Milan approach) by asking the wife how she perceives the relationship between her husband and his job, then each child. In this way, the family therapist can discover whether or not the future is seen as a time of increased career growth, exploration, stabilization, maintenance, or decline. A change in career stage represents a transition that needs to be worked through.

The second dimension of career to be assessed is the presence of a triggering event. Has the person recently been fired or laid off because the company is closing? Did the person recently receive a promotion, or was the person passed over? Was there a recent change in employer? Even a promotion can have significant effects. A triggering event in the career life structure of the father or mother has an interactive effect on the family life structure, and the reaction must be integrated.

The third dimension of career which influences the individual is the impact of changes in areas of development on career functioning (the Health-Illness Wheel). For example, a physical illness or injury could make it more difficult to work 40 hours a week. The reaction to such a change in physical development is a transition needing work.

The fourth and final dimension of the life structure of career is unique themes. Each person is different. Sometimes it is the motive for working, such as the desire to earn money, help disadvantaged youngsters, or be in control, that represents the meaning attached to the career by the individual. If this meaning has been disturbed in any way, the reaction to such a loss or change is a transition that needs to be worked through.

Family.   As the family structure moves from birth to death, four comparable aspects are considered concurrently and can be assessed when conducting an intake interview with an individual, couple, or family: (1) stage of family development, (2) triggering family event, (3) the impact of changes in areas of development of the individual (the Health-Illness Wheel) on the family, and (4) unique family themes.

To determine the stage of family development, questions can be asked about the ages of family members and any changes in membership. It is important to ask about prior marriages and children from other marriages because one or both spouses may be involved in different stages of development with two different families (the slinky effect discussed in Chapter 4). From this information, the marital and family therapist can determine if the family is undergoing a transition from one stage to another and is stuck along the way.

The second dimension of the family life structure is the occurrence of a triggering family event. This can be a milestone for a family member, such as graduation from high school or the funeral of a parent. Perhaps one member of the family is in trouble, such as a teenager or parent addicted to alcohol or drugs. If a family member is not

*The life structures of self, career, and family co-evolve in the individual from birth to death.
The spiral helix of the lightning whelk represents the interaction among these subsystems.*

discussed, it may be because of a triggering event. By asking questions about reasons and timing for entering treatment, a triggering family event will often be shared.

The third dimension of the family life structure to be assessed is the impact of changes in the areas of development of the individual on the family (the Health-Illness Wheel). For example, a baby may now be crawling a little bit more each day, and her parents are having a difficult time adjusting to a baby-proof house.

The fourth dimension of the family structure is the presence of unique family themes. Sometimes a family has a sport that they all enjoy, like swimming, so they are a swimming family. Maybe both grandparents on each side of the family were alcoholics, and this family is proud that the family members are not. Perhaps someone committed suicide several generations ago, and family members are still feeling the repercussions. Such themes can be identified through preparing a genogram (see Chapter 9).

FIGURE 5–4   Assessment form (based on the concept of the lightning whelk)

Self

1. Stage of life cycle based on age of family member:
2. Any triggering events:
3. Impact of Health-Illness Wheel on self:
4. Theme(s):

Career

1. Stage of career development based on age of family member:
2. Any triggering events:
3. Impact of Health-Illness Wheel on career:
4. Theme(s):

Family

1. Stage of family life cycle based on ages of family members:
2. Any triggering events:
3. Impact of Health-Illness Wheel on family:
4. Theme(s):

Key Strengths

Problems

Suggested Interventions

Interaction Among Self, Career, and Family.   There is interaction among the life structures of self, career, and family as these subsystems co-evolve in the individual from birth to death. The pulsating spiral helix represents the interactive movement among these subsystems.

If a man's career is in a slump, he often will be having marital problems as well. In addition, his self-esteem may be affected. Just as an individual might have a peak experience through the interaction of positive changes in each of these life structures which is greater than the sum of the subsystems, feelings of intense sadness may result if negative changes are occurring in all of these life structures.

Implications for Marital and Family Therapy.   The stage of life, the life-cycle transition, the individual variability and triggering life events in self/career/family, and the individual variability and triggering events noted in the types of development found in the Health-Illness Wheel generate transitions that create the pressure, motivating individuals to enter treatment. The marital and family therapist can use the Lightning Whelk: A Co-Evolutionary Helix of the Individual Life Span to assess the strengths of the individual, the nature of the transitions, and the areas where the individuals are stuck in their developmental work (Figure 5–4).

Practitioners can use the skills developed for particular life-cycle transitions and stages to deal with the content and process of particular transitions at specific stages of the individual life cycle. They can also look at triggering single life events and the unique themes of given individuals that influence these individuals, creating stress. Therapists can use the generic process of meaning making associated with transition work to facilitate their movement through the transition in a successful manner.

SUMMARY

Recent books and conferences have emphasized the role of the individual subsystem in the family system. Marriage and family therapists have been encouraged to take the individual subsystems into consideration when diagnosing and treating couples and families. The effectiveness of therapeutic outcomes improves over the long-term when the components of individual subsystems in the family are considered.

This is easier said than done, however, because of the many theoretical explanations of how life unfolds. Since the beginning of time human beings have asked themselves, "What is life all about?" These theories of individual development, such as individual variability, life-event, and stage theories as well as the Lightning Whelk: A Co-Evolutionary Helix of the Individual Life Span, are summarized in Table 5–1 for review.

There are differences in development for men and women—gender differences. In particular, the works of Josselson, Gilligan, and Belensky point out that women develop a sense of identity in a web of relatedness. Making commitments is particularly crucial for women, whose biological clocks may rule out options. Ambivalence can lead to diminished life structures and less satisfaction. Culture also dramatically affects individual development over the life span.

Thomas proposes the Lightning Whelk: A Co-Evolutionary Helix of the Individual Life Span as an integrative model that incorporates individual variability, life event, life span, and stage theories within gender and cultural contexts. On the horizontal axis are the ten stages of the human life cycle—infancy, early childhood, middle childhood, adolescence, early adulthood, young adulthood, middle adulthood, late middle adulthood, older adulthood, and elderly adulthood. The developmental tasks of each stage and their implications for marital and family therapy can be reviewed in Table 5–4. The cross-section of the individual Health-Illness Wheel with its nine areas of development (spiritual, intellectual, behavioral, emotional, imaginal, sensual, sexual, physical, and interpersonal) moves through the human life cycle over time, and so does the cross section of the life structures of self, career, and family. In particular, an assessment instrument using the model has been developed to plan interventions for marital and family therapy.

EXERCISES

1. Interview middle-aged or older adults and ask them about the transitions they have made in adult life. What was the role of the family in these transitions? How did the family help or hinder the individual self in transition? How did the transition of the individual affect the person's family? The person's career?

2. Write down a major transition in your own life, how your family was involved in the transition, and how your transition affected the family. Share your writing with a partner in class. Voice your appreciation of the actions of any family members or other people during your transition. How did the life structures of self, career, and family interact during the transition?

3. Refer to the opening quote on page 130. Close your eyes and visualize yourself having accomplished a goal or being in a different role 5 years from now. Share your "dream" with a partner while your partner plays the role of counselor by giving only supportive responses, such as "You can do it." Reverse roles. If your instructor directs, process with the class how it felt to be supported in a transition plan.

4. Take turns conducting an intake interview with a partner using the lightning whelk assessment as a guide. Complete the form linking strengths to possible ways of attacking problems through interventions (Figure 5–4).

5. Draw a triangle on a piece of notebook paper. Write "Self" on the top corner, "Career" on the bottom left corner, and "Family" on the bottom right corner. The triangle represents a quilting piece that makes up the quilt of your life. In each corner, jot down goals or dreams you have for each life structure of self, family, and career. In the middle, draw a symbol that represents you and where you are now in life. With a partner, take turns sharing the meaning of your symbol and your goals in each life structure. (Similar to a technique developed by Hansen [1988].)

PART TWO
THE THERAPEUTIC PROCESS
BASED UPON THEORY

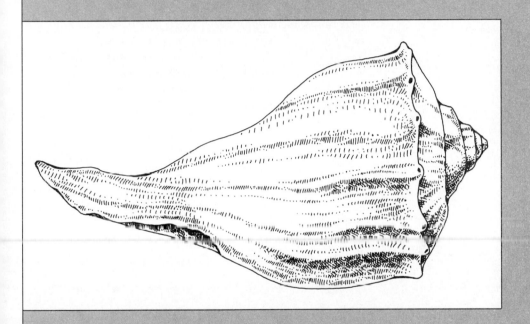

Chapter 6
The Challenge of Integrating Theory and Practice

There is something obscure which is complete
before heaven and earth arose;
tranquil, quiet,
standing alone without change,
moving around without peril.
It could be the mother of everything.
I don't know its name,
and call it Tao.

Lao-tzu—Ta Te Ching, 1937

In becoming a family therapist, one must begin somewhere. In the world of nature, baby sharks are born alive and begin to swim immediately on their own, to be devoured by their mother if swimming near her. However, with the great majority of species in nature, offspring begin their lives in a protected atmosphere of nurturing by their mothers, and after having learned the lessons of survival, they are then encouraged to risk a life apart. Like fledgling birds that are pushed from the nest to fly for the first time, beginning family therapists learn all they can from books, professors, supervisors, and others before plunging into the abyss of the family system in their first initial interviews.

In contrast to individual psychotherapy, in which practitioners can adopt more passive interactional styles and survive (even with effective therapeutic outcomes in many cases), marital and family therapy, regardless of approach, requires action and direct control of the session on the part of the therapist (Napier & Whitaker, 1973; Whitaker, 1976). Otherwise the family will take over, fights will escalate, and neophyte therapists may wish that they had become engineers or computer programmers—occupations in which the levels of emotional intensity are typically not great. Haley

(1969) so aptly stated the following motto in "The Art of Being a Failure as a Therapist:"

> *The Five B's Which Guarantee Dynamic Failure:*
> *Be Passive*
> *Be Inactive*
> *Be Reflective*
> *Be Silent*
> *Beware. (p. 61)*

More importantly, a family in crisis needs reassurance that their therapist does, in fact, know what he or she is doing (Napier, 1976; Haley, 1980). Therefore, the therapist must have a meaningful game plan or abstract mental file of what constitutes family intervention before engaging a family in treatment (Freed, 1982). Such an abstract map is often called a theory. Having a personal theory of family therapy provides necessary self confidence to the beginning therapist, even if the theory evolves to something quite different within a few months or years, based on actual experience with clients.

WHAT IS A THEORY?

A theory is a set of interrelated, abstract ideas that describe and explain a phenomenon. Using a theory, a professional can generate hypotheses or educated guesses about what will happen in the future. These predicted outcomes can be tested. The results can then be used to revise the ideas that constitute the theory. Like a mental road map, a family therapy theory allows us to plan where we would like a family to be and to evaluate the usefulness of the map (Friesen, 1985).

Deductive versus Inductive

More often in the social sciences, theories are developed inductively, that is, based on observations of people in the real world. For example, Piaget observed his own children and took copious notes on exactly what they said and did. Studying these observations, he formulated his theory of cognitive development, or how human beings learn to think over time. Another example of an inductive theory is that of Freud's theory of psychosocial development. Freud saw disturbed individuals face to face on an individual basis over long periods of time. Using his clinical experience with these patients, he generated the abstract ideas of the stages of psychosocial development—the oral, anal, phallic, latency, and gential stages—his psychosocial theory of development which has dominated the mental health field for a century.

Factors That Influence the Development of Theories

There are many factors that influence the development of a theory of family therapy. First of all, ideas of what constitutes a healthy family evolve from the culture in which the theorist is raised. For example, the concept of libido (sexual energy), which is one of the tenets of Freud's psychoanalytic theory of personality, was created in a Germanic culture where people were interpersonally reserved and not sexually permissive. Therefore, repression of sexual energy could lead to maladjustment, according to Freud's view. In the Milan School of Family Therapy, the role of the therapist is that of an objective, neutral authoritarian which corresponds to the role of the medical doctor in Italian culture, the authority figure who knows best and has the magic power to cure.

Theories also develop out of work with target groups. For example, Minuchin (1974) developed his structural theory while working with the families of juvenile delinquents and also families in the inner city. The ideas that form the concepts of his theory are based on his actual experience and research with these target groups, so his theory can easily be applied to work with these populations.

Finally, a theory of family therapy emanates from the personal philosophy and life history of the proponent of the theory. If an individual sees human beings as good, neutral, evil, or a combination thereof, this perception affects the theory of how people behave in families. A person's determination of what the good life is, in turn, influences what that person projects as positive outcomes for family therapy. The world views of the theorists affect their theories.

INTEGRATION OF THEORIES

There are many theories of family psychotherapy. Most developed separately and have strong advocates. Therefore, often a practitioner who espouses one theoretical position will not accept another professional who holds another view. Yet each theory represents but one view of reality. Two people can look at the same field, and one may see the grass while another focuses on the trees, yet the reality of the field is greater than both the grass and the trees.

Because I taught in Japan for 3 years, Oriental ways of thinking have meaning for me. In Chinese philosophy, there is the Tao, which cannot be defined by words but approximates the ultimate reality of nature symbolized by drifting, coursing water (Watts, 1975). Tao encompasses the forces of two opposites—the yin and the yang. The yin corresponds to the passive, negative polarity and the yang to the active, positive polarity—the opposing characteristics of weak and strong, darkness and light, or the sunny and shady sides of a hill. The art of living is seen as balancing both, because one does not exist without the other, rather than banishing or ridding oneself of one or the other as some Western philosophies dictate. In the representation of the tao or t'ai chi (Figure 6–1), the black area that corresponds to the yin (passive traits) has a small circle of white (active traits). Likewise, in the yang (the white area of the circle representing creative characteristics) there is a small circle of black corresponding to the receptive traits (Stone, 1986). Thus the presence of both yin and yang in a person makes the balancing of the chi possible. The Tao is cyclical in motion with the parameters represented by the yin and the yang. Too much yang in a cycle becomes yin and vice versa, two aspects of the same whole. The martial art of akido and the physical discipline of t'ai chi are means of balancing the yin and the yang.

The approach of this book, which focuses on helping families to become healthier over the life span, is a continual spiraling interplay between health and pathology: a reconciliation of opposites. The practitioner of family therapy, especially the beginner,

FIGURE 6–1 Tao/t'ai chi

needs to be aware of both polarities, learning to balance both within the context of professional work. Repeated attempts to force health will create pathology. In order to be healthy, families must be at least a little bit sick. To be human is to live with paradoxes, the most penetrating of which is the inescapability of death; yet its recognition makes the present more meaningful. Physicist Fritjof Capra (1982) applies the "new" physics to psychology and medicine in *The Turning Point: Science, Society, and the Rising Culture* and indicates that a holistic approach mirrors the discoveries of modern physics in which the interrelatedness of systems is paramount.

In the Taoist way of looking at the world, a thing exists in relation to other things. The moon needs the sun and the stars as much as it needs its own parts. Light would not be light without the eyes to see it. From this point of view, the theories of family therapy, although contradictory and opposite to each other in many ways, add to the existence of each other and "need" each other for their existence, being pieces of reality, parts of the ultimate reality of a meta-theory of family therapy yet to be uncovered in the search for ultimate reality, the Tao. Thus, as each theory proclaims its own reality, there is a mutual interdependence among them. Professionals adhering to diverse theories of family therapy often have more in common with each other than with mental health professionals who conduct only individual therapy. After grappling with family process and content, their dialectical discussions may lead to greater understanding of their own positions through comparison and contrast: Their theoretical positions at the extremes are part of the continuum of the greater whole.

WHAT IS YOUR PERSONAL THEORY OF FAMILY THERAPY?

As one human being, an individual is limited by the construction of reality to which the person subscribes—the values, beliefs, thoughts, feelings, and actions that one owns as part of the self (Keeney, 1987). These act as a filter or pair of glasses through which the individual sees the world (Dell, 1987). In *Aesthetics of Change,* Keeney (1983) states that human beings experience the world through a dialectical process between the abstract thoughts in their own minds that they have created and the manner in which their senses take in data. He relates the dialogue of the therapist who asked the epistemologist how he could know. The epistemologist replied, "Kuan Tsu once said, 'What a man desires to know is *that* (i.e., the external world). But his means of knowing is *this* (i.e., himself). How can he know *that*? Only by perfecting *this*'" (pp. 200–201).

By constructing your own personal theory of family therapy, which you will use with your future clients, you are working on *this,* that is, yourself. By adopting certain theoretical ideas, you will be screening out others. Liddle (1982) points out that in adopting a theoretical position, some data that are not in agreement with that position will be ignored and go unnoticed. Yet the opposing theoretical position will still exist in its own right and represent a partial reality and limited applicability as well (Capra, 1975).

ATTEMPTS TO CLASSIFY AND INTEGRATE THEORIES

The main task of the second generation of family therapists is now in progress—to classify and integrate the unique approaches that have developed during the first 25 years. More than 50 citations were located on the topic of classifying and/or integrating theories of family therapy: A book could be written on this single topic alone. The number of articles and books on the subject reflects the importance and concern attached to this topic by researchers and leaders in the field.

Three systems of classification and integration of theories have been selected for elaboration here: those of Sluzki, Schultz, and L'Abate. In addition, a new model is proposed based upon the work of Kegan (1982).

Sluzki's Classification System

Sluzki (1983) classified the systemic models of therapy (brief, structural, strategic, and Milan) into three groups: (1) the process-oriented group, (2) the structure-oriented group, and (3) the *weltanschauung* or world-view group. Sluzki placed the brief family therapy school (Watzlawick and others) into the process-oriented category because the therapists in this school focus on interactional sequences that are repetitive in nature which can be observed in operation or process during the therapy session (interpersonal feedback loops). Two models belong to the structure-oriented category: the structural school (Minuchin) and the strategic school (Haley), because there is an emphasis on hierarchies and boundaries in both of these approaches to family therapy. The systemic approach of the Milan team fits the world-view group because therapists in this school focus on the cognitive maps that families bring to treatment.

Such a classification permits clinicians to perceive the differences of the approaches within the overall framework of similarity. When Sluzki classified the theories, he made no attempt to carry the process one step further—that is, to integrate the theories into a model for selecting techniques for clinical practice with particular families. His classification system is helpful as a guide to learning the systemic models because it points out differences among theories emanating from similar theoretical roots.

A Second-Order Model by Schultz

Schultz (1984) proposed an innovative second-order model for integrating family therapy theories based upon level of psychopathology in the family system (Figure 6–2). Using Vaillant's (1977) four levels of psychosocial functioning, Schultz suggested that transactional theories of family therapy (Singer, 1977; Wynne, 1977) would be more appropriately used with families with psychotic levels of functioning, structural approaches (Minuchin, 1974; Minuchin and Fishman, 1981) with those families performing at immature levels of functioning, and strategic theories (Watzlawick, Weakland, & Fisch, 1974; Haley, 1973) with families functioning at neurotic levels. Families presenting with a schizophrenic member would be functioning at psychotic levels. Delinquent behavior, addictions, acting out, character disorders, and psychosomatic complaints would be characteristic of the immature level. Inhibitions and acting in would indicate the neurotic level of functioning. The developmental family life cycle model represented another dimension in the second-order integrative model, since regardless of the level of psychological functioning the members of the family would still need to move through stages of their own individual life cycles as well as those of the family life cycle.

When the symptoms of family members represented different levels of functioning, Schultz (1984) would intervene with the therapeutic approach applicable to the lowest level of functioning. As treatment proceeded and level of functioning increased, techniques corresponding to the next higher level of functioning were used. The systemic model of the Milan School was useful with schizophrenics. Bowen's model would be applied to families falling between psychotic and immature, often labeled as borderline in functioning. Behavioral approaches would be used with families functioning at the immature level, and cognitive behavioral approaches and psychoanalysis would be used with neurotics. The developmental dimension was applied with all

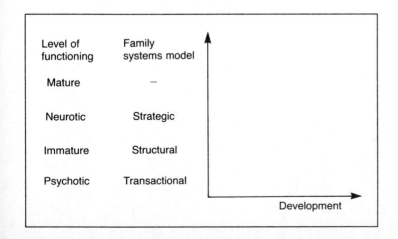

FIGURE 6–2 The second-order integrative model of Schultz

From *Family Systems Therapy: An Integration* (p. 289) by S. J. Schultz, 1984, New York: Jason Aronson, Inc. Reprinted by permission.

families. In crisis intervention, strategic techniques would be used with all families to return them to pre-crisis levels of functioning. In addition, Schultz would place Figure 6–3 in a third dimension represented by extra-familial stress.

A case example of part of an interview in which Schultz's model is used and explained is quoted verbatim here:

> Taken from the first of the six initially-contracted family sessions, these . . . depict an exercise in parenting for the executive subsystem and illustrate the application of transactional, structural, strategic, and developmental models, guided by the second-order model described above.

> (The oldest child John was absent from the previous session because of a fight he had had with Mrs. Bach in which he reportedly either threw a knife at his mother or attempted to choke her. The couple was given the task of bringing him to this session, which they did. In discussing the fight and its aftermath—John took the car in violation of a directive from his father and then left home—it became clear that Mrs. Bach thinks that her husband is too harsh with John, whereas Mr. Bach believes her to be too lenient. The therapist discovered that, in the case of the present incident, father assigned a tough punishment which mother undercut. As a result, there have been no consequences at all for John's behavior. The supervisor phones in, telling therapist to have father and mother come up with a suitable consequence for John's actions.)

> T: What needs to happen now is, the two of you need to come up with one consequence that both of you can agree to impose on John for what happened. I mean, what appears to us is that John directly disobeyed you a number of times and he went off with the car and ran away and so on and so forth. And basically what John is saying is "Well, not much happened. Business as usual.". . . the two of you do need to impose some kind of consequence. And it needs to be something you can both agree to. So the task for the two of you now is to come up with, with one consequence for that. . . .

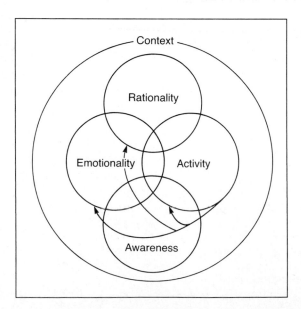

FIGURE 6–3   The Eclectic E-R-A-Aw-C Model of L'Abate

From *Systematic Family Therapy* (p. 143) by L. L'Abate, 1986, New York: Brunner/Mazel. Reprinted by permission.

M: All right. Let me say something to that, John, since grade, from sixth to ninth grade, has watched very little TV. Because every time he was deprived of TV. Four weeks, six weeks. He was grounded. It doesn't work. . . . The problem is lack of communication. What you say may help temporarily, perhaps. Maybe. It does not help the problem. I know.

T: What I'm saying. . . .

M: (Interrupts.) It's not a good way to go.

T: (Continues.) What I'm saying is that, in essence John has learned that he doesn't need to obey you. I. . .

M: (Overlaps and drowns out therapist's words.) He also has learned that, he has learned so many other things, which are much . . . more important. Obeying is of little importance right now . . . he will move out. He's almost eighteen. And we at eighteen can't impose our will all that much anymore. My parents could on me, sure, and even on my three brothers. At eighteen I think we can try to communicate a different way and not say "If you don't do this, you can't do this." I think that's past. We can do that with Eric and Rita yet. When you're almost eighteen, that doesn't work. You know that. You were eighteen at one time. (And mother displays her power by turning therapist into a child and speaking to him in a very patronizing way.)

T: Do you, a, see a basic issue of responsibility being involved here? Both for John living in your house and for you as parents? (Here therapist shifts his frame a bit, from obeying and the consequences of John's misbehavior to responsibility.)

M: Uh-hum.

T: That's really what I'm talking about.

M: So, Frank (father) and I are talking about one punishment to impose on John and that's it? That will solve the whole thing?

T: . . . No, no one solution is going to solve the whole thing.

F: . . . I think this is a step, a, I think what's happened, I don't think you. . . . (To mother) I think the article which you read a long time ago about authority and violence, remember? That's what. . . . We have, because of our problems, lost authority in the family. And the result of that is violence. . . . And I think in order to maintain that there's a family unit going and there's equal responsibility on all family members. That's not going to solve, not going to make us love each other, you know . . . all of a sudden. I think we need, need to play our roles for a while so we can get along. But I think we need to play our roles in a way that there is some kind of order. And one of the things that needs to be done is that when we tell John "You bring home that car. You have no business taking that car. You have no business choking your mother." A, that should be obeyed, at that point. As long as he lives in this house as part of the family unit. If he doesn't live in the house anymore, he's not part of the family unit, then it will be up to him to come to us if he wants to. But at this time he is still part of the family unit and he still has to abide by certain rules and responsibilities for this family. . . . (Transactionally, father's speech shows some communication deviance that interferes with the listener's ability to share a focus of attention with him, chiefly commitment problems—abandoned and unstable remarks—and turn-taking difficulties—monopolizing the floor.)

F: (Continues above speech) I really feel, I don't want to be the one to hand out the punishment. I think the punishment should come from both of us. At this point you feel you should not give any punishment because John's going to be gone in a few months anyway. Now, that's, I don't see that at all. I don't see that's the logical approach. (Here father rather succinctly and directly points out the couple's failure as an executive subsystem.)

F: (Continues above speech.) And I don't think John feels comfortable with the fact that he can get away with anything he wants to. I, a, in the long run he won't feel comfortable.

Nobody feels comfortable in that sort of situation. You wouldn't either. If you could get away with anything you wanted to at any time, you wouldn't feel comfortable either. You would feel "Somebody's playing games with me. Why would they do that to me, that I can do whatever I want?" (Now father ups the ante by using the technique mother used above on therapist, attempting to make her a kid alongside John.). . .

This segment nicely illustrates the interplay among the four first-order models. The Bach family has all the earmarks of immature-level dysfunction: acting-out adolescents, alcohol abuse, some physical violence, and chronic unresolved marital conflict. Following the second-order model, the main therapeutic work is structural. But higher-level models (strategic, in this case) apply as well. The therapist always works within some frame and always has the task of getting the family to join him in the frame. And as in all cases, the developmental model is crucial as this family faces the task of emancipating the children. . . .

Although chronologically the children (particularly John) are approaching the age of emancipation from the family when they will be out from under parental control, developmentally this family is much younger. The Bach family is struggling with issues of limit setting and family structure it should have settled years ago. Had this been done, the parents could now be granting to John the kind of autonomy appropriate for a soon-to-be 18-year-old. If John is to become emancipated properly from the family and go off to be a truly autonomous individual, his family must first reorganize itself along generational lines. There has to be a generational hierarchy in the family before this hierarchy can be relaxed. Elsewhere in our work with this family, we learned what is likely to happen if things do not change soon: John is already planning to leave the family as soon as he is 18, to get away from the chaos and conflict at home. This would be a less-than-desirable emancipation, one which would likely compromise this young man's psychological functioning in the future. (pp. 300–305)

L'Abate's Eclectic Systematic Model of Family Therapy

L'Abate (1986) integrates family therapy theories according to an eclectic E-R-A-Aw-C model (see Figure 6–3), which states that family therapy interventions can be made in five distinct but interrelated domains: emotionality, reasonability, activity, awareness, and context. The family's most accessible domain needs to be worked on first, moving toward the least accessible modes of experiencing. L'Abate assumes that deficits occur in a developmental sequence, with emotions being the least accessible and actions being the most accessible. Therefore, L'Abate would encourage a therapist to use homework assignments or prescriptions (manipulating behavior) before focusing on rationality, and then moving toward an emphasis on emotions, which constitutes intimacy. By affecting one domain, another domain is influenced due to the interrelated and overlapping nature of the domains.

L'Abate (1981) gives the example of a married couple who presented with a problem of excessive quarreling. Encouraged to fight more (prescription) or to fight on alternate days with a different partner starting the fight on each day (ritual), the couple fought less and experienced less stress. Therapeutic interventions then focused more on the rational development of priorities, congruence, and self-definition before moving on to the use of "I" statements to express emotions leading to the development of intimacy.

In *Systematic Family Therapy,* L'Abate (1986) further refines the model, connecting it with various schools of family therapy. In contrast to his earlier formulation, activity is represented by the behaviorists (Jacobson, Liberman, Patterson, Stuart, Thomas, and Weiss) rather than by the structural and strategic schools (Minuchin, Watzlawick, Haley, Madanes, and Selvini Palazzoli) which represented the activity domain in the original theory and now represent the context domain in the revised model, with Adler and Alexander included in this domain. The domain of emotionality is represented by the humanistic and experiential theorists including Gordon, Guerney, Levant, Whitaker, Napier, Satir, Duhl, Constantine, and Kempler, while the rationality domain is represented by the psychoanalytic theorists including Ackerman, Bowen, Boszormenyi-Nagy, Framo, and Stierlin. The awareness domain, which focuses on bodily sensations, is best represented by the Gestalt theorist (Perls) and by Watts, Selman, and Eastern philosophers.

In his eclectic model, L'Abate proposes four stages of family treatment: engagement, skill training, termination, and follow-up (Table 6–1). In the initial stage, therapeutic interventions from the context domain (such as prescription of the symptom) and from the activity domain (such as behavioral contracting) are used to promote change through homework assignments. In the intermediate stage of treatment, interventions from the rationality domain are emphasized as clients see the interactional patterns that are creating problems in their relationships through interpretation and by the use of genograms to analyze themes intergenerationally. Present issues are also the focus at this stage. Finally, in the termination stage the emotionality domain takes precedence as intimacy issues, feelings of abandonment and loss, and possible future

TABLE 6–1 Systematic family therapy

Stages	Major Therapeutic Emphases	Interventional Modality	Task Assignments
1. Engagement	Crisis resolution Symptomatic relief Relationship building	Contextual activities "Change" activity Past issues	Prescriptions of symptoms Individualized homework Depression SHWAs Homework Assignment Sheet
2. Skill training	Negotiation learning Emotional give and take	Rationality "growth" Present issues	Negotiation-SHWAs Homework Assignment Sheet
3. Termination	Resolution of unfinished business Intimacy issues Loss and leaving	Emotionality "being" Future issues	Intimacy SHWAs Homework Assignment Sheet
4. Follow-up	Maintenance of gains Spread to other positive behaviors	Multiple modalities	Checkups and evidence of improvements

From *Systematic Family Therapy* (p. 38) by L. L'Abate, 1986, New York: Brunner/Mazel. Reprinted by permission.

problems are dealt with. In the fourth stage of follow-up, several or all of the modalities are used to support the gains that have been made by the family.

By the sheer volume of his work, L'Abate has played and will continue to play an important role in the development of family therapy and, in particular, family psychology (L'Abate, 1983; L'Abate, 1985). His attempts to devise an eclectic meta-theory approach to family therapy, although far from perfect, provide professional modeling of behavior which hopefully other theorist/clinicians will emulate. The field of family therapy and the broader culture need a meta-theory from which to operate, to approximate more fully the broad perspective of ultimate reality, the Tao. In addition, L'Abate's work on family enrichment (L'Abate & Weinstein, 1987) and marital enrichment (L'Abate & McHenry, 1983) coupled with his approach to family therapy (L'Abate, 1986; L'Abate, Ganahl, & Hansen, 1986) integrate family life education, family enrichment, and family therapy approaches—an important but difficult task that few family therapy professionals attempt.

The Lightning Whelk: A Co-Evolutionary Helix of Family Therapy Theories

The lightning whelk is a symbol for a three-dimensional developmental method of classifying family therapy theories (Figure 6–4). This classification is based upon the assumption that human beings co-evolve in their environments (culture) to a higher form of life over time.

Human beings evolve from embeddedness to successive qualitative differentiations of the self from others—an increasing distinctiveness over the years that is also integral to increased relatedness (Kegan, 1982). To the degree that we are able to move away from embeddedness, creating our diverse existences, we are able to share and be close to other human beings—a paradox of human life.

On a 105-degree day, the mimosa trees reach for the sky. They do not rigidly stay as they are, but instead grow toward the sun, initiating and moving toward a higher evolutionary form. Nature is active and moving.

Human beings are active, making meaning through the process of differentiation and integration—the Piagetian processes of assimilation and accommodation. In the process of emerging from embeddedness, a human being experiences a loss of the "old self." Therefore, with each evolutionary step forward, pain and loss are associated with the growth. Yet the organism continues to move toward greater coherence through a process of defending, surrendering, and finding a center again, with plateaus of equilibrium along the way in which a new structure is operative.

According to Kegan (1982), there are six qualitatively different stages (incorporative, impulsive, imperial, interpersonal, institutional, and interindividual). There is a lifelong tension, a creative motion between belongingness and autonomy. A person wants to experience both communion and agency.

In the Lightning Whelk: A Co-Evolutionary Helix of Family Therapy Theories (Figure 6–4), theories of family therapy are matched to the developmental stage of the individuals in a family. Individuals and families can move from one dichotomous stage to another (Table 6–2) by holding on (the process of confirmation), letting go (the process of contradiction), and then staying put to allow for reintegration (continuity).

FIGURE 6–4 The Lightning Whelk: A Co-Evolutionary Helix of Family Therapy Theories

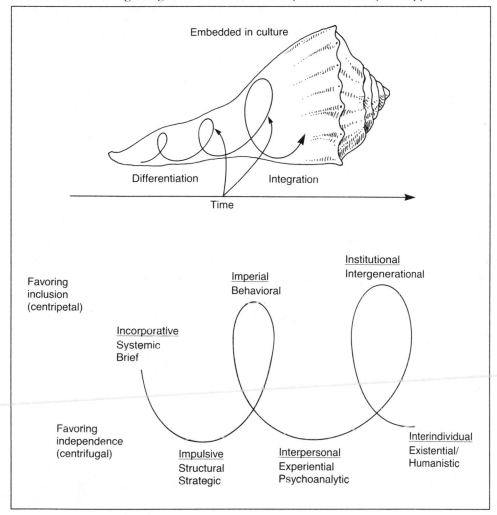

For example, at the lowest level of differentiation are schizophrenics. Systemic therapy and brief therapy have been found to be effective with schizophrenics and others who are functioning at extremely low levels of differentiation—the stage of incorporation. Such families tend to huddle during crises in a centripetal fashion. At the next level of balance are anorectics and drug abusers. Structural and strategic family therapy have been effective with these clients, who are functioning at the impulsive level of balance. They have a centrifugal manner of dealing with emergency situations in the family.

Going up the developmental scale, at the next level of balance or imperial stage are clients with behavioral problems. Behavioral family therapy will be the most effective here. These families become more enmeshed under stress using a centripetal style.

6

TABLE 6–2 Theories of family therapy and levels of evolutionary balance

Evolutionary Balance and Psychological Embeddedness	Culture of Embeddedness	Function 1: Confirmation (Holding On)
(0) INCORPORATIVE Embedded in: reflexes, sensing, and moving. (Systemic & Brief)	*Mothering culture.* Mothering one(s) or primary caretaker(s).	Literal holding: close physical presence, comfort, and protecting. Eye contact. Recognizing the infant. Dependence upon and merger with oneself.
(1) IMPULSIVE Embedded in: impulse and perception. (Structural & Strategic)	*Parenting culture.* Typically, the family triangle.	Acknowledges and cultures exercises of fantasy, intense attachments, and rivalries.
(2) IMPERIAL Embedded in: enduring disposition, needs, interests, wishes. (Behavioral)	*Role recognizing culture.* School and family as institutions of authority and role differentiation. Peer gang which requires role-taking.	Acknowledges and cultures displays of self-sufficiency, competence, and role differentiation.
(3) INTERPERSONAL Embedded in: mutuality, interpersonal concordance. (Experiential & Psychoanalytic)	*Culture of mutuality.* Mutually reciprocal one-to-one relationships.	Acknowledges and cultures capacity for collaborative self-sacrifice in mutually attuned interpersonal relationships. Orients to internal state, shared subjective experience, "feelings," mood.

*Ideas contributed by Mauricia Alvarez.
From *The Evolving Self: Problems and Process in Human Development* (pp. 118–120) by R. Kegan, 1982, Cambridge, MA: Harvard University Press. Adapted by permission.

Function 2: Contradiction (Letting Go)	Function 3: Continuity (Staying Put for Reintegration)	Common Natural Transitional "Subject-Objects" (Bridges)*
Recognizes and promotes toddler's emergence from embeddedness. Does not meet child's every need, stops nursing, reduces carrying, acknowledges displays of independence and willful refusal.	Permits self to become part of bigger culture, i.e., the family. High risk: prolonged separation from infant during transition period (6 mos.–2 yrs.).	Medium of 0–1 transition: *blankie, teddy,* etc. A soft, comforting, nurturant representative of undifferentiated subjectivity, at once evoking that state and "objectifying" it.
Recognizes and promotes child's emergence from egocentric embeddedness in fantasy and impulse. Holds child responsible for his or her feelings, excludes from marriage, from parents' bed, from home during school day, recognizes child's self-sufficiency and asserts own "other sufficiency."	Couple permits itself to become part of bigger culture, including school and peer relations. High risk: dissolution of marriage or family unit during transition period (roughly 5–7 yrs.).	Medium of 1–2 transition: *imaginary friend.* A repository for impulses which before *were* me, and which eventually will be part *of* me, but here a little of each. E.g., only I can see it, but it is not me.
Recognizes and promotes preadolescent's (or adolescent's) emergence from embeddedness in self-sufficiency. Denies the validity of only taking one's own interests into account, demands mutuality, that the person hold up his/her end of relationship. Expects trustworthiness.	Family and school permit themselves to become secondary to relationships of shared internal experiences. High risk: family relocation during transition period (roughly early adolescence, 12–16).	Medium of 2–3 transition; *chum.* Another who is identical to me and real but whose needs and self-system are exactly like needs which before *were* me, eventually a part *of* me, but now something between.
Recognizes and promotes late adolescent's or adult's emergence from embeddedness in interpersonalism. Person or context that will not be fused with but still seeks, and is interested in, association. Demands the person assume responsibility for own initiatives and preferences. Asserts the other's independence.	Interpersonal partners permit relationship to be relativized or placed in bigger context of ideology and psychological self-definition. High risk: interpersonal partners leave at very time one is emerging from embeddedness. (No easily supplied age norms.)	Medium for 3–4 transition: *going away to college, a temporary job, the military.* Opportunities for provisional identity which both leave the interpersonalist context behind and preserve it, intact, for return; a time-limited participation in institutional life (e.g., 4 years of college, a service hitch).

TABLE 6–2 *continued*

Evolutionary Balance and Psychological Embeddedness	Culture of Embeddedness	Function 1: Confirmation (Holding On)
(4) INSTITUTIONAL Embedded in: personal autonomy, self-system identity. (Intergenerational)	*Culture of identity or self-authorship* (in love or work). Typically: group involvement in career, admission to public arena.	Acknowledges and cultures capacity for independence; self-definition; assumption of authority; exercise of personal enhancement, ambition or achievement; "career" rather than "job," "life partner" rather than "helpmate," etc.
(5) INTERINDIVIDUAL Embedded in: interpenetration of systems. (Existential Humanistic)	*Culture of intimacy* (in domain of love and work). Typically: genuinely adult love relationship.	Acknowledges and cultures capacity for interdependence, for self-surrender and intimacy, for interdependent self-definition.

The next neo-Piagetian developmental stage is the interpersonal. The experiential school of family therapy would help clients to become aware of their feelings and to express them, as would psychoanalytically oriented family therapy focusing on the interpretation of the defenses so that aggressive and sexual feelings can be expressed appropriate to the social context—characteristics of this stage of development. A centrifugal style is used by these families when confronted with internal or external stressors. At the next stage, human beings identify and achieve for their institutions. Intergenerational approaches such as Bowen's style of family therapy with its genograms and emphasis on the family of origin would be effective. Families functioning at the institutional level use a centripetal style under stress, wanting to be included.

The highest stage of development is the interindividual where people dialogue with each other. The existential/humanistic family therapy approaches encourage the therapists and the participants to be themselves in all of their spontaneity. These families use a centrifugal style under pressure. To move from one level of balance to another, family members confirm, contradict, and reintegrate what has been learned—a process of differentiation and integration which parallels the centripetal/centrifugal forces in the family.

If you review the diagram of family functioning according to Beavers (1977), there is a great degree of overlap between the results of his research and the Lightning Whelk: A Co-Evolutionary Helix of Family Therapy Theories. For example, the spiraling helix appears similar in shape to the two-dimensional figure that represents the results of his research.

In Beavers' model the most dysfunctional families are schizophrenics (who are centripetal) and anorectics (who are centrifugal), which mirrors the incorporative and impulsive levels of balance. In his model, the midrange centripetal families have

Function 2: Contradiction (Letting Go)	Function 3: Continuity (Staying Put for Reintegration)	Common Natural Transitional "Subject-Objects" (Bridges)*
Recognizes and promotes adult's emergence from embeddedness in independent self-definition. Will not accept mediated, nonintimate, form-subordinated relationship.	Ideological forms permit themselves to be relativized on behalf of the play between forms. High risk: ideological supports vanish (e.g., job loss) at very time one is separating from this embeddedness. (No easily supplied age norms.)	Medium of 4–5 transition: *ideological self-surrender (religious or political); love affairs protected by unavailability of the partner.* At once a surrender of the identification with the form while preserving the form.

behavioral problems (see the use of behavioral family therapy at the imperial level of balance in the Lightning Whelk: A Co-Evolutionary Helix of Family Therapy Theories). The centrifugal midrange families have neurotic problems that are typically treated by experiential and psychodynamic approaches. The adequate families in the Beavers model would be able to profit from intergenerational approaches, making meaning from differentiating themselves from their families of origin. The most optimally functioning families would be encouraged to grow through the existential/humanistic schools of family therapy in which there is a dialogue—a dialectical process of formulating meaning among the participants which encompasses the ability to talk about death, one of the distinguishing features of the healthiest families.

Doherty, Coangelo, Green, and Hoffman (1985) analyzed 13 models of family therapy on the family FIRO issues of inclusion, control, and intimacy. The intergenerational approaches were rated high on inclusion, as was the only behavioral school in the list. Brief therapy was rated second on inclusion but lowest on intimacy. Existential, experiential, and psychoanalytic schools of family therapy were rated highest on intimacy. Only with the schools of strategic family therapy and structural family therapy were the results incongruent with the proposed model.

The Lightning Whelk: A Co-Evolutionary Helix of Family Therapy Theories classification can also be used as a way of integrating theories and techniques for professional practice. The model can be used to effect such an integration in a number of alternative ways. For example, the neo-Piagetian developmental stage of the family could be assessed and the techniques of family therapy could be selected based on the developmental level of the family. Another approach would use a circular interview with circular questions or an intake interview format from the brief therapy model with all families. After the first prescription, the therapist could judge by the reaction of the family (similar to de Shazer's style of cooperation) what should be done next. In fact, the styles of cooperating advanced by de Shazer (1985) correspond to confirmation (performing the requested task), contradiction (doing the opposite of the requested task), and reintegration (doing nothing, being vague, or doing something a little different from what is expected). Another way of perceiving the family's response would be to decide the family members' developmental levels. If they were at a higher level of balance, then techniques should be selected from that level.

Yet another way of using the family response would be to stay at that level (brief and systemic techniques) until the problem was resolved. If other problems arose, as they tend to do in about half of the family therapy cases, techniques associated with the next higher developmental level could be used. For example, Stanton (1981) integrated structural and strategic techniques by using structural techniques initially to develop rapport. Then the strategic approach was used until the symptom was reduced, and structural techniques were instituted again. Therefore, using the Lightning Whelk: A Co-Evolutionary Helix of Family Therapy Theories, the therapist could begin with techniques from the lowest levels of development until change occurred, then move to working on the next stage of development as the clinician saw movement and if the family wished to, by using the family therapy techniques associated with that stage.

Another approach that has been very successful for psychoanalysts over the years has been to screen clients very carefully. For example, it is estimated that only 25% of those presenting for treatment could profit from psychoanalytically oriented treatment. If a family is at a lower level of development where they may not profit from psychoanalytic treatment the family can be referred to a family therapist who uses techniques from the Milan school of family therapy or one who practices techniques that would match the developmental level of the clients.

Yet another approach would build an integrative practice model in which the clinician would use systemic circular questions with all new clients to form a hypothesis, prescribing a positive connotation in the first session. Then if the prescription were carried out well, some strategic boundary-making hierarchical techniques would be applied in that session with a strategic directive to implement at home. Behaviorally oriented skill-building exercises would be utilized in subsequent sessions. As the family made progress, experiential techniques such as family sculpture or gestalt exercises could be used with psychodynamic interpretations to stimulate catharsis and abreaction. As family members became interested in their families of origin through working through psychodynamic issues, genograms could be assigned. As sessions with the family continued, it would become more and more a team effort among equals.

Lebow (1987) makes recommendations concerning how to create your own integrative approach to family therapy. Four examples of personal integrative theories of family therapy have now been presented, and you are asked to create your own personal theory of family therapy.

CONSTRUCTING YOUR PERSONAL THEORY OF FAMILY THERAPY

Now that you have seen how others have attempted to integrate family therapy theories and techniques to create their own approaches, you are ready to risk the task of integrating theories yourself—a challenging and enjoyable task. Aradi and Kaslow (1987) maintain that one of the best ways to integrate components of diverse theories in family therapy is to analyze the theories, your own personality, and the family with whom you are working according to explanatory, diagnostic, therapeutic, prognostic, and evaluative power. (Table 6–3 has a self rating of the therapist on these variables.) In other words, where does the dysfunction exist (in the individual, interactionally, or both), and is it due to the past in an absolute way, to the present, or to the future in a relative way (explanatory power)? What is the role of assessment and diagnosis in the therapeutic process (diagnostic power)? How does the therapy bring about change? For example, is it brief or protracted, with specific or general goals, structured with the therapist responsible for change or with the family active in pursuit of their own change (therapeutic power)? What is the view of human nature and the course of the presenting problem (prognostic power)? How can the approach be evaluated, and what research is available concerning its efficacy with diverse target groups (evaluative power)? Can this style of therapy prevent future problems; that is, has the functioning of the family been improved or have only symptoms been reduced (preventive power)?

For family therapy to have the most efficacious outcome, there must be a match among the characteristics of the theory, the needs of a particular family, and the congruence of a given theoretical approach with the personality of the therapist. In order to accomplish this delicate match, a therapist should have self knowledge. You may wish to use the self-rating form that Aradi and Kaslow (1987) developed to think about yourself and how you stand personally on these key issues. Such an introspective process will help you to be a better therapist and also to assess families in a more effective way.

In reviewing all of these efforts to classify and integrate the healthy diversity of family therapy, Liddle (1982) proposes that the family therapist find a mountain top where one can contemplate and take stock. In so doing, the family therapist can formulate an epistemological declaration, that is, the personal theory that guides clinical decisions for that practitioner. For example, the family therapist should clarify how human nature is viewed and therapy is defined, the goals of therapy, the role of the therapist and how the therapist defines and brings about change, a personal definition of healthy and dysfunctional families, and how the personal approach to therapy will be evaluated.

Using these suggestions in the following chapters, the various theories discussed in this book will be presented and compared according to the following outline:

1. historical development of the theory,
2. healthy family functioning in the model,
3. key theoretical concepts associated with the theory,
4. the goals of treatment,
5. the use of diagnosis/assessment,
6. the role of the therapist,
7. techniques associated with the therapeutic approach,
8. how the initial session proceeds,
9. how therapy progresses, including any stages if proposed,

TABLE 6–3 Self rating form: Matching the personality of the therapist with diverse theories

Explanatory Power

Dysfunction Exists Within the Individual	—————— Both ——————	Dysfunction Exists Interactionally
Past Focused	————— Present Focused —————	Future Focused
Dysfunction is Absolute	——————————————————————	Dysfunction is Relative

Diagnostic Power

Assessment is:

Absent	————— Intermittent —————	Ongoing
Informal	————— Both —————	Formal
Separate from Therapy	——————————————————	Integral to Therapy

Diagnosis is concerned with:

| Absent ——— | Discrete _____ Behaviors | Behavioral _____ Patterns | Unifying Constructs |

Therapeutic Power

Treatment Should be Brief	————— Length Determined ————— by Patient Need	Treatment Should be Protracted
Process is Specific, Structured	——————————————————	Process is Left Open to the Therapist
Therapist is Responsible for Change	————— Both Together ————— Are Responsible	Family Responsible for Change
Therapist is Non-Directive	———— Style is ———— Varied	Therapist is Directive
Therapist's Actions Planned	——————————————————	Therapist's Actions Spontaneous
Insight Necessary	——————————————————————	Insight Unnecessary

From "Theory Integration in Family Therapy: Definition, Rationale, Content and Process" by N.S. Aradi and F. W. Kaslow, 1987, *Psychotherapy*, 24, p. 604. Reprinted by permission.

10. how therapeutic outcome is measured in the model, and,
11. contributions and limitations of the given theoretical model.

Based on an elaboration of each theory, readers are encouraged to study and understand each theory, celebrating the uniqueness of each. You will also be encouraged to practice selected techniques of the various theories with fellow classmates and families. The challenge to you is to then find a mountain top, create your own personal theory of how you will work with your target group of families, and write this down to form the basis of your professional functioning with families.

Tables 6–4 and 6–5 compare the various theories of family therapy on a number of these dimensions. They will also be useful as references in formulating your own approach to marital and family therapy and to study and understand the content and process of the various theories. Regardless of what theory you select to adopt or

TABLE 6–3 *continued*

Main Goals:

| Personal _____ | Feeling _____ | Improved_____ | Problem |
| Growth | Happier | Functioning | Resolution |

Prognostic Power

Natural Course
of Dysfunction:

| Deterioration ——————— | Unknown/No Change ——————— | Improvement |

View of Human
Condition:

Pessimistic ———————	Neutral ———————	Optimistic
Therapy is Not Necessary	——————— Unknown ———————	Therapy is Necessary
for Improvement		for Improvement

Evaluative Power

Approach is Nonquantifiable	_____	Approach is Quantifiable
Empirical Research	_____	Empirical Research
is Not Valued		is Valued
Approach is Not	_____	Approach is
Research-based		Research-based

Preventive Power

Ignored ———————	Addressed Indirectly ———————	Addressed Directly
No Ideal Model	_____	Promotes an Ideal
of Health Promoted		Model of Health

whether you create an eclectic approach to your work with families, a firm grounding in the stages of the family life cycle and the development of the individual over the life span is needed to effectively work with families.

After a therapist has developed a theory to guide intervention with families, it will feel awkward and uncomfortable to use at first. Over time, the skills required by the nature of a given theory will become automatic, and the therapist will be able to use the self more effectively to catalyze growth and change in clients. It is by being a human being with all the vulnerability inherent in this label that true intimacy and effective outcomes are encouraged in our clients (Kaslow, Cooper, and Linsenberg, 1979). Whitaker (1976) gives a set of rules for therapists to continue to grow as human beings, a necessity if we are to be effective as therapists:

1. Relegate every significant other to second place.
2. Learn how to love. Flirt with any infant available. Unconditional positive regard probably isn't present after the baby is three years old.

TABLE 6–4 A comparison of the distinctive features of eight approaches to family therapy

Theory	View of Healthy Functioning	History and Key Proponents	Major Theoretical Concepts
Experiential-Humanistic	Health is a continuous process of becoming. By validating growth, family members are transformed and developmental delays wither away.	Virginia Satir, "the Columbus of family therapy," developed the first program for training family therapists. Kantor, Lehr, the Duhls, and Whitaker are key proponents.	Self esteem, maturation, and communication theory undergird Satir's approach. She emphasizes each person taking responsibility for self.
Psychoanalytic	Family members can see each other as they really are, not as distorted figures from the past. Spouses in a healthy marriage oscillate between self interest and concern for the partner. Parents seek to be "good enough."	Nathan Ackerman headed first family treatment program at the Jewish Family Service in New York. Alfred Adler started child guidance clinics in Europe. Kirschner & Kirschner as well as Scharff & Scharff are couples who have become key figures recently.	Key concepts include anxiety/defense, defense mechanisms, introjects, transference/counter transference, object relations, dipoles/conflicts, and stages of psychosexual/object relations/ego development. Ackerman is noted for the concept of scapegoating.
Intergenerational Family of Origin	While staying in contact with the family of origin, an individual can assert self and detriangle, according to Bowen. Family members dialogue and earn entitlement through care, which frees them to differentiate (Nagy). Spouses have priorities of self, spouse, and children (Framo). They have adult-adult relationships with their own parents.	Murray Bowen hospitalized the families of schizophrenics and based his theory on this research. Boszormenyi-Nagy and James Framo studied the families of schizophrenics at the Eastern Pennsylvania Psychiatric Institute.	Self-differentiation, triangulation, emotional cutoff, and multigenerational transmission process are Bowenian concepts. Nagy's contextual therapy emphasizes relational modes, the ledger of entitlement, loyalty, justice, merited trustworthiness, accountability, and exoneration across generations.

Major Techniques	Goals of Treatment	Role of the Therapist
Experiential therapists use metaphor, reframing, humor and "I" statements. Satir is noted for communication stances, family sculpture, family reconstruction, the parts party, and awareness enhancement.	As a result of family therapy, members of the family can express their feelings and thoughts more effectively, leading to greater intimacy. They become more mature and responsible for their choices.	The therapist models healthy expression of feelings and thoughts, checks out meanings with family members, listens, observes, questions, analyzes patterns of communication, and teaches family members to understand the family.
Free association, formation of a therapeutic alliance, interpretation of conflicts/defenses/patterns of interaction, expression of a theme, and working through are major techniques. Ackerman counteracted scapegoating, exposed family secrets, used confrontation, and tickled the defenses of family members. Adler used early recollection, family constellation, typical day, and the family council.	Increased ego strength gained through insight is a goal of treatment. Most proponents seek internal changes in the object relations of the individual family members toward a more mature developmental level and greater differentiation.	The therapist plays the role of a "good enough" parent by providing consistency while maintaining balance between nurturing and setting/maintaining limits—reparenting.
Both Bowen and Framo work with couples. Genograms, detriangling, and person-to-person relationship are Bowen's major techniques. Nagy uses siding, rejunction, crediting, and motivation for the use of resources. The family of origin session is a distinctive technique of Framo.	Greater differentiation of the self in the family of origin is the main goal. Ties across generations are reopened and renegotiated so that individuals gain greater autonomy.	Bowen establishes a person-to-person dialogue with one spouse while the other observes. Nagy holds each family member accountable, focusing on the intergenerational ledger of justice. Framo and his opposite-sex cotherapist work with the couple alone to prepare them for the couples group therapy and the meeting of each spouse with the respective family of origin.

TABLE 6—4 *continued*

Theory	View of Healthy Functioning	History and Key Proponents	Major Theoretical Concepts
Behavioral	Reciprocity occurs in the marital relationship. Spouses can identify what is going on in the relationship and negotiate changes.	Gerald Patterson and Jim Alexander are noted for behavioral parent training. Richard Stuart focuses on behavioral marital therapy. Aaron Beck created a cognitive behavioral approach to marital therapy.	The behavioral exchange model of marriage in which spouses reciprocate appetitive and instrumental behaviors, Stuart's "Principles of Relationship Change," and the cognitive mediation model of marital interaction are key theoretical concepts.
Structural	Healthy families restructure themselves over time in order to adapt to stressors.	Salvador Minuchin worked with the families of delinquents, economically disadvantaged families, and psychosomatic families. The Philadelphia Child Guidance Center has been main training center. Maurizio Andolfi is in Rome, Italy.	Family structure including boundaries, enmeshment versus disengagement, subsystems, alignment, and power are key concepts.
Brief	The properties of communication are appropriately applied via healthy communication patterns.	Don Jackson established the Mental Research Institute in Palo Alto, California. Paul Watzlawick and Steve de Shazer are key figures.	Don Jackson is noted for the concepts of homeostasis, rules calibration, and the typology of marriage. The concepts of first order change and second order change (change of change) are characteristic of Watzlawick. De Shazer focuses on ecosystemic epistemology, isomorphism, and a binocular theory of change.

Major Techniques	Goals of Treatment	Role of the Therapist
Major techniques of behavioral marital therapy include behavioral assessment, positive and negative reinforcement, contracting, communication skills, decision-making skills, negotiation of role responsibilities, conflict management strategies, and cognitive restructuring.	Family members learn how to maintain desired behavior while eliminating undersirable behavior.	The therapist is a behavioral scientist, an expert, model, and educator who establishes rapport, conducts a behavioral assessment, and designs behavioral programs acting as a coach to reinforce their implementation.
Techniques include joining, enactment, reframing, relabeling, restructuring, the family lunch, and challenging the communication rules and structure of the family.	Changing the hierarchies and boundaries, that is, the structure of the family, is the key goal of structural therapy.	The therapist is very directive, but is emotionally responsive, "joining" the family by exaggerating the feeling tone of the family or using personal information to make contact.
Jackson used the quid pro quo, relabeling, and prescribing the symptom. Watzlawick utilizes reframing, paradoxical interventions, and directed behavior change. De Shazer developed the written compliment, the clue, the confusion technique, the crystal ball, and skeleton keys.	There will be a change in behavior. The presenting problem will be resolved through second-order change. Jackson emphasized that interactional patterns change through changes in the rules, and de Shazer maintains that this occurs through altering the world view of the family in subtle ways so that solutions to the problem evolve.	The therapist is the directive expert, asking questions, collaborating with the client on goals, planning between and during sessions to select techniques tailored to particular clients, and using dirctive interventions which often are paradoxical.

TABLE 6–4 *continued*

Theory	View of Healthy Functioning	History and Key Proponents	Major Theoretical Concepts
Strategic	The family changes its structure and organization over time, especially when launching a young adult. The couple works on becoming more intimate in their relationship and exerting appropriate power through the parental hierarchy.	Jay Haley and Cloe Madanes lead practice and training groups in Washington, D.C.	Haley's key concepts include the perverse triangle, the double bind, and power in the family. Madanes developed helpfulness as power, the symptom as a metaphor, and cyclical variation maintaining incongruous dual hierarchies.
Systemic	At each new stage of the family life cycle, the family system makes a quantum leap to a different way of functioning.	Mara Selvini Palazzoli established a center in Milan, Italy, to treat the families of anorectics. Luigi Boscolo, Guilana Prata, and Gianfranco Cecchin joined her. American proponents are Penn and Hoffman.	Coevolution, cybernetics of cybernetics, the time cable, discrimentation of differences, and discontinuous changes are major theoretical concepts.

3. Develop a reverence for your own impulses, and be suspicious of your behavior sequences.
4. Enjoy your mate more than your kids, and be childish with your mate.
5. Fracture role structures at will and repeatedly.
6. Learn to retreat and advance from every position you take.
7. Guard your impotence as one of your most valuable weapons.
8. Build long-term relations so you can be free to hate safely.
9. Face the fact that you must grow until you die. Develop a sense of the benign absurdity of life—yours and those around you—and thus learn to transcend the world of experience. If we can abandon our missionary zeal we have less chance of being eaten by cannibals.
10. Develop your primary-process living. Evolve a joint craziness with someone you are safe with. Structure a professional cuddle group so you will not abuse your mate with the garbage left over from the day's work.
11. As Plato said, "Practice dying." (p. 164)

SUMMARY

The role of the therapist in marital and family therapy is an active, directive one in comparison to the therapist's role in many approaches to individual psychotherapy.

Major Techniques	Goals of Treatment	Role of the Therapist
Straightforward directives, indirect directives, and ordeals are Haley's key techniques. Madanes is noted for the technique of pretending.	Solution of the presenting problem is the main goal of diverse strategic therapies with the exception of the problem-solving therapy of Jay Haley, which also aims to change the structure of the family.	The therapist is very emotionally reserved and directive in the session, does not share personal information, and remains aloof and detached.
The generation of systemic hypotheses, circular interview, circular questions, problem-focused/pattern-focused positive connotations, and rituals are major techniques.	The Milan team wants to stimulate changes in the cognitive maps of family members so that the family will find its own way of solving the problem.	The therapist maintains a neutral stance. A team observes from behind a two-way mirror and consults with the therapist.

Therefore, a game plan or theoretical approach is needed so the therapist can be active and directive in the initial contact, based on a cognitive map of projected treatment and outcomes.

A theory describes the nature of a phenomenon from which hypotheses can be generated. There are many diverse theories of marital and family therapy. Many attempts have been made to classify and integrate them. Examples include the systems of Sluzki, Schultz, L'Abate, and Thomas.

This chapter encourages you to construct your own personal theory of family therapy. An overview of all of the theories of marital and family therapy considered in future chapters is contained in Tables 6–4 and 6–5. Theories are compared on: (1) view of healthy functioning, (2) history and key proponents, (3) major theoretical concepts, (4) major techniques, (5) goals of treatment, (6) role of the therapist, (7) diagnosis/assessment, (8) nature of initial session, (9) stages of therapy, (10) therapeutic outcome, (11) dysfunction, and (12) contributions/limitations.

TABLE 6–5 **A comparison of other characteristics of eight approaches to family therapy**

Theory	Diagnosis/ Assessment	Nature of Initial Session	Stages of Therapy
Experiential-Humanistic	In the here and now of the session, Satir assessed the rules, communication patterns, and self esteem of family members.	Satir conducted a family life chronology. Humanistic therapists tend to be spontaneous and experiential, using intuitive processes to make contact with the family.	The stages of therapy for Satir are making contact, chaos, and integration.
Psychoanalytic	Through asking open-ended questions and observing the interaction of family members, the therapist assesses the theme, level of anxiety, defense mechanisms, patterns of interaction, any binding or expelling, and stages of psychosexual/object relations development.	A history of the family of origin of each parent is taken in front of the family. Information about the presenting problem, prior attempts at treatment, and a detailed developmental history of each individual are obtained.	Establishment of a therapeutic contract, development of a therapeutic alliance, working through, and termination are the four stages.
Intergenerational Family of Origin	Bowen uses genograms to determine the process and structure of three generations of the family. Boszormenyi-Nagy assesses facts, psychology, patterns of transaction, and relational ethics through siding with each family member in turn. Framo asks open-ended questions and observes interaction in the session to ascertain the effects of the family of origin on present functioning.	Bowen asks each spouse to talk directly to him. The therapist asks questions of each spouse to obtain information for a genogram.	As each spouse uses material from the genogram, Bowen prepares each for visits to the family of origin and terminates therapy after each spouse has processed detriangulation in the family of origin. Framo also terminates when spouses have debriefed after each has completed the family of origin session.

Therapeutic Outcomes	Dysfunction	Contributions/ Limitations
Increases intimacy in the family. Lack of documented outcome studies.	Symptoms are messages that can tell how family members are hurting each other, blocking growth.	Emphases on holistic growth across areas of development for each family member and the family as a whole, on expression of feelings, and on action-oriented techniques are key contributions. Lack of outcome studies is a limitation.
Internal changes in the introjects and object relations of the family members occur, so that family members can become closer to the real selves of each other. Spontaneity of the approach does not lend itself to controlled studies. Lorna Benjamin's SASB system offers promise for the future.	Family members are fixated at early stages of the development of object relations. They interact with current family members as though they were important figures from the past such as "critical parents."	First books in the field of family therapy were by Midelfort and Ackerman. The application of object relations theory to family therapy is a significant contribution, especially to long-term marital therapy. Limitations include the lack of outcome studies and the linear nature of the analytical model.
Greater differentiation in the family of origin leads to increased intimacy in the current family of procreation. Bowen, Nagy, and Framo worked with the families of schizophrenics on federal grants; therefore, their approaches did lead to improvement in schizophrenic patients who participated in family therapy.	Individuals are enmeshed in their families of origin and are not able to assert their own feelings, thoughts, and needs. The ledger of justice may also be unbalanced.	The emphasis on contact with the family of origin is a major contribution of these approaches. Genograms have been adopted across theories as a valuable technique.

TABLE 6–5 *continued*

Theory	Diagnosis/Assessment	Nature of Initial Session	Stages of Therapy
Behavioral	A behavioral assessment is conducted of a child, family, or married couple.	The therapist asks questions to obtain information about the antecedent and consequent behaviors of the presenting problem. A detailed behavioral analysis of the problem is made, focusing on problem resolution.	Stages include establishing rapport, behavioral assessment, application of positive reinforcement, communication skills, contracting, decision-making, managing anger/conflict, and relapse prevention.
Structural	Through directing family members to talk to each other and enactment, the therapist observes and draws diagrams of the present family structure (diagnosis) and proposed family structure (treatment plan).	The therapist encourages the family to interact with each other during the session and observes the patterns. The therapist "joins" with the family and may direct an enactment of the problems in the session.	Overlapping in every session, stages include joining, creating transactions, restructuring, and constructing alternative realities.
Brief	Open-ended questions are asked about the problem and the behaviors maintaining it. The interactional patterns of the family are observed in the session to assess whether or not paradoxical or direct interventions would be most effective.	Open-ended questions are used to obtain information about the problem while the therapist observes the communication patterns of the family. The problem is reframed, and a directive or paradoxical intervention is used.	There are six stages which are accomplished in 10 sessions or less: (1) explanation of treatment (2) defining the problem, (3) analyzing the maintaining behaviors, (4) formulating goals, (5) implementing interventions, and (6) termination.

EXERCISES

1. Turn to the person next to you when your professor says to do so. Take turns asking and answering the following questions. Your professor may prefer that you write out the answers to these questions and turn them in.

   a. What is a theory?
   b. Compare a deductively generated theory with an inductively generated theory.
   c. What factors influence the development of a theory?

Therapeutic Outcomes	Dysfunction	Contributions/ Limitations
Reduced problem behaviors, absence of new symptoms, and an increase in desired behavior occur for behavioral parent training, behavioral marital therapy, sexual therapy, and cognitive behavioral approaches with documented outcome studies, a strength of behavioral approaches.	The give and take in the relationship(s) is unbalanced. Undesirable behaviors are more frequent than desirable ones.	Emphasis on research with effective outcomes in behavioral parent training, behavioral marital therapy, sexual therapy, and the cognitive behavioral therapy of couples and families is key contribution. The development of a sequence of treatment is a contribution. Linear emphasis sometimes leads to recidivism.
Amount of outcome research is impressive. Reduction in symptoms and changes in underlying family structure documented for delinquency, anorexia nervosa, psychosomatic illnesses, asthma, pain, and alcohol and drug addiction.	Families who rigidly adhere to the same structure and rules rather than changing over time.	Noted for his emphasis on action in the session and for expanding family therapy to delinquents, anorectics, and substance abusers and to families from diverse cultures.
Research consists of following up clients to determine whether or not the presenting problem has been resolved. More than two thirds of those responding confirmed that the problem had been resolved.	When dysfunctional patterns of communication are repeatedly and redundantly used by family members, symptoms appear in at least one of the family members.	Major contributions include basic research on human communication, the application of cybernetics to communication within the family, an explanation of dysfunctional communication processes, and the development of paradoxical techniques after reframing the problem. Self-report outcome research is a limitation.

d. What is the Tao and how does it relate to the process of integrating theories?

e. What is Schultz's second-order model for integrating theories in family therapy?

f. What is L'Abate's eclectic systematic E-R-A-Aw-C model for integrating family therapy theories into a coherent framework? What are the stages of his eclectic systematic family therapy model? How does therapy work with a real couple?

g. What model does Thomas propose for classifying and integrating family therapy theories?

2. Count off into dyads. The first partner should ask the second partner the following question: "If

TABLE 6–5 *continued*

Theory	Diagnosis/ Assessment	Nature of Initial Session	Stages of Therapy
Strategic	At what stage of the family life cycle is the family "stuck"? At what stage of the individual life cycle is the individual family member "muddled"? The hierarchy is also assessed to determine how power is being used so that strategies can be designed to help the family.	There are five stages of the initial session in Haley's problem-solving therapy: (1) social stage, (2) problem stage, (3) interaction stage, (4) goal-setting stage, and (5) task-setting stage.	Problem-solving therapy occurs in stages until the presenting problem is resolved and other problems that arise that people want to work on are resolved as well.
Systemic	A telephone chart is used to assess the family to generate tentative hypotheses prior to the initial session.	The therapist asks circular questions. The therapist meets with the observing team to obtain a prescription, which is delivered to the family at the end of each session.	Ten sessions spaced one month apart comprise the typical contract. The same stages occur in each session— circular questioning while observers watch through the two-way mirror, a conference with the observers to identify the nodal rule and to write the prescription, and delivery of the prescription, which may be a family ritual. Selvini Palazzoli designed specific set universal prescriptions for each of the 10 sessions.

you want to practice family therapy with people, why is having a theory of family therapy important?" The second partner should answer the question as fully as possible. The first partner should then contradict every argument the first partner has made. The first partner should then counter every opposing view which the second partner has brought up. The exercise is most effective when people really argue the issues and become involved. After the sequence has been completed, it should be repeated, switching roles.

Therapeutic Outcomes	Dysfunction	Contributions/ Limitations
Single case studies of successful strategic therapy have been published. Three follow-up studies by Haley demonstrated that more than two thirds of the cases had successful outcomes, with a lower success rate for drug and alcohol cases.	The family does not change its structure and organization over time, leading to symptoms in a member. The power hierarchy in the family is disturbed and malfunctioning.	Haley made significant contributions to the development of the theoretical concepts regarding communication, which undergird most of family therapy. He emphasized the discontinuties in the family life cycle and power hierarchies in the family. His clear writing about the step-by-step sequence of doing family therapy is a key contribution. He developed innovative techniques or strategies for effecting change in families, a major contribution of all strategic therapists.
Single case studies of therapeutic outcome have been presented and published, but no outcome studies of a statistical, rigorous nature.	A nodal family rule blocks change and keeps the family mired in dysfunctional feedback loops.	The in-depth analytic and systemic training of the family therapist is a key contribution. The congruity between theory and practice—that is, logic and hypotheses—has added to the field. The development of innovative techniques such as the circular interview as well as the use of therapist/observer and co-therapy teams are major contributions. More rigorous scientific research of outcomes is needed.

3. Complete Aradi and Kaslow's self rating form (see Table 6–3) by circling the words that represent where you stand on each of the theoretical issues stated on the form. Write a summary of your position on each of these issues. Turn it in to your instructor, if you are directed to do so. As you read each of the theories in the book, rate them on the same form. At the end of the course, you can see which theory best matches your position on these essential theoretical issues. It would not be unusual to change some of your positions as you move through the course and dialogue with your professor, fellow students, and the author.

Chapter 7
The Experiential Humanistic Schools

A human being is like a seed planted below the dark earth.
As the seed sprouts, it struggles painfully over time,
To push through the restricting and compacted clay,
Reaching toward the light, shooting up in growth,
Flowering and bearing fruit, to send its seeds forth.
Through the pain of change, comes the joy of becoming—
Being all that is possible, satisfied in self, fruition
and generation.

Michele Thomas

OVERVIEW

Experiential humanistic approaches to family therapy are characterized by (1) a philosophy of growth, (2) an emphasis on expression of feelings and meanings, (3) the therapist sharing personal feelings and thoughts in the therapy session, (4) processing pain as a natural part of any growth, (5) action-oriented techniques within the therapy session, (6) encouragement of the process of communication and resolution of conflicts among family members, (7) grieving loss or death, (8) an orientation toward increased health across a number of areas of development, leading to wholeness or balance, and (9) each person taking responsibility for self. This chapter will present the work of the following theorists who are experiential humanistic in orientation: (1) Satir, (2) Kantor and Lehr, (3) the Duhls, and (4) Whitaker.

VIRGINIA SATIR

Historical Development
Virginia Satir was originally trained as a social worker, with a heavy emphasis on individual psychoanalytic theory. She entered private practice in 1951, after 6 years of teaching school and 9 years of clinical work in an agency. Satir (1986) noted that her work with family units evolved from her treatment of a schizophrenic young woman

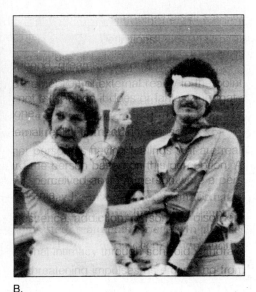

A.   B.

(A) Virginia Satir is often called "the Columbus of family therapy" because she developed the first family therapy training program in the United States. (B) Satir is particularly noted for her use of experiential activities. For example, she used ropes to represent relationships and sometimes used blindfolds so that participants could fully experience their senses. (The name Virginia Satir and her works and photographs are the copyrighted and trademarked properties of Avanta Network, Inc. © 1989 Avanta. Used with permission. All rights reserved.)

whose mother threatened to sue Satir when the young woman improved. Satir heard the double message of threat/cry for help and responded to the mother's plea for assistance by inviting her into the therapy. Before her shocked eyes, the schizophrenic woman who had made progress regressed to her former level of functioning, at which point Satir began to work with both women in treatment until they could make contact and communicate congruently. When each family member entered therapy in turn, the other members regressed to their original states. Eventually, the whole family achieved a balance by working together in therapy. At follow-up, Satir found that the family's improvement was maintained over time, and her approach to family therapy was born.

During 1955, Satir taught family dynamics to psychiatric residents at the Illinois State Psychiatric Institute at the request of Dr. Gyarfas. The following year, she visited Murray Bowen, who was conducting research at the National Institute of Mental Health with the families of schizophrenics. In 1956, Satir also read Don Jackson's article about the etiology of schizophrenia, and in 1959, while visiting California, she contacted him. He invited her to make a presentation to his research group in Palo Alto. On the day she delivered the presentation, Jackson asked Satir to join him and Jules Riskin to establish the Mental Research Institute (MRI).

At the MRI, Satir (1965) developed the first family therapy training program in the United States. Her first book, *Conjoint Family Therapy* (1964), is considered a landmark text in the field and is still used in training family therapists today. Satir not only wrote but traveled extensively around the world, conducting workshops on family therapy and forming her own training group, the Avanta Network (1987). She is often referred to as "the Columbus of family therapy." Following Satir's death in 1988, special tributes were paid to her work. For example, *The Family Therapy Networker* devoted a special issue to Satir (Andreas, 1989; Corrales, 1989; Duhl, B., 1989; Duhl, F., 1989; Nerin, 1989; Simon, 1989). The American Association for Marriage and Family Therapy commemorated her contributions at their convention in October 1988.

Satir's work is noted for its emphasis on the expression of feelings. She combined concepts from communication theory with the humanistic Rogerian concept of self-esteem and the psychoanalytic approach of how awareness of patterns learned in the family of origin can lead to change. Satir's approach is experiential, involving families in exercises and activities during the session.

Satir's training workshops have impacted a much larger national audience than any other family therapy models (Kolevzon & Green, 1985). This impact is due to the match between traditional individual psychoanalytically oriented therapy models and Satir's psychodynamically informed family therapy approach. It may be easier for a traditional individually oriented therapist to adopt Satir's approach to working with families. In addition, Satir's model simulates a universal, healthy growth process. This makes its implementation more familiar and comfortable for a wider group of therapists and clients. It is especially practical for private practice, where practitioners want to treat individuals and families. Satir's approach is very adaptable.

Key Theoretical Concepts

Family Theory.   The relationship between marital partners is of utmost importance to the family (Satir, 1964). If it is pained, symptoms will develop in a spouse or child who is an identified patient. People with low self-esteem choose each other as marriage partners because they can more easily merge into one, not seeing how they are different. After the marriage, when they notice differences, they are neither able to negotiate the differences nor to support each other's self-esteem. They married to obtain a care-taker and mind-reader, not a person capable of making independent decisions. When children begin to make decisions, each parent sees them as potential allies and asks them to side against the other parent. If the children do this, they may lose the other parent. The parents live for the children. The children are seen as extensions of the parents, following the rules of what the family wants the children to be. They suffer low self-esteem and conflicted male-female relationships.

To develop normally, the children require validation of growth by the parents in a matter-of-fact manner. When children are encouraged to ask questions, their self-esteem is increased. When parents model a satisfying male-female relationship and acknowledge their children as masterful, sexual human beings, children acquire self-esteem.

Self-Esteem.   One of the most important concepts underlying all of Satir's work is the concept of self-esteem. Self-esteem means self-worth, the value that each person assigns to self at any given time. Satir (1972a) likened it to a pot that sat on the front porch of her family home when she was growing up. At times there was more in the pot (high pot) than at other times (low pot). Satir thought that the amount of self-esteem of the individuals involved was a key factor in what happened both between them and inside of them. Low self-esteem describes people who feel low but act as if those feelings do not exist. They maintain doubt about their value, even when they experience success. People with high self-esteem can directly share when they are feeling low and do not have to hide such feelings. They know the feelings are temporary and will dissipate when the environmental situation improves.

Satir (1972a, 1972b) maintained that self-esteem is learned in the family from nonverbal behaviors and remarks parents make in interaction with children. For example, children receive messages about self-worth from family interaction at the dinner table. Certain methods of discipline can affect self-esteem, as children learn to feel guilty and ashamed. Even as adults, self-esteem can be influenced by the comments of employers and co-workers, as well as those of our family members. Since self-esteem is learned, adults can raise levels of self-esteem. The reader is referred to *Self Esteem* (1970), Satir's poem on this topic.

Maturation.   Satir (1964, 1983) defined maturation as the state where an individual is completely in charge of self. The mature person makes choices, owns them, and takes responsibility for outcomes. Decisions are based on accurate and realistic appraisals of the context, others, and self. A mature person expresses self directly to others, is aware of the internal self (what is being felt and thought at any given moment), and treats other people as unique and different from self—worthy of exploration and learning. A mature person deals with situations as they are, rather than how they are expected or wanted to be, and sends, receives, and checks out meanings with other people.

Communication Theory.   Communication is the verbal and nonverbal behavior between people that conveys meaning. By analyzing the communications of an individual, a person can determine the interpersonal functioning of that individual (Satir, 1964, 1976, 1983). People who often overgeneralize, using "always" and "every" and either/or dichotomies such as "right/wrong" or "enemy/friend," function at lower levels of interpersonal functioning. Rather than asking open-ended questions to obtain clarifying information when asked to take a stand on a position, they will simply agree or disagree. If they are asked questions about the message they sent, they become defensive and will not answer, holding to their position. They often connect thoughts that make sense to them but fail to communicate their messages directly. They expect others to receive and understand, even if nothing has been said, and the receiver is often left guessing about the meaning of these messages.

Communication has two levels: the denotative level (content) and the metacommunicative level (message about the message). The content is usually expressed verbally, while the metacommunication is generally expressed nonverbally, although sometimes it is also verbalized. People cannot *not* metacommunicate. Nonverbal behaviors such as gestures, posture, tone of voice, and facial expressions send metacommunications automatically. A verbal metacommunication can be sent about the relationship between the sender and the receiver. For example, the sender says, "I was just joking." The receiver takes in the frown and loud voice (nonverbal metacommunication) along with this verbal metacommunication. When they are discrepant, as in this case, the receiver usually believes the nonverbal metacommunication: The sender was angry at the receiver. However, when the metacommunications do not match, it is helpful to comment on the discrepancy or incongruence between what the person is saying and doing and to ask for clarification by a process of checking it out with the other person. For example, in the above situation the receiver would say, "You said that you were joking, but you seemed to be frowning and talking in a loud voice, like you're angry with me. What do you really mean?" Another way of checking a communication out, when it seems like the sender is commanding an action from the receiver, but it is unclear, is to ask, "Is there something that you would like me to do for you?"

Patterns of Communication.   In *Peoplemaking*, Satir (1972a) discussed four communication stances—placator, blamer, computer, and distractor. These patterns of communication are used when people feel threatened and want to protect self-esteem by not sharing true reactions. Such patterns block real contact between people. Satir describes physical positions that represent each of the dysfunctional styles of communication.

The placator agrees with whatever the speaker says, even though the placator may actually not like what the speaker has proposed. Inside the placator feels worthless if the speaker leaves. The physical position taken by the placator is to kneel on one knee with a hand reaching out for help. Often this communication stance has been used by women, but it is not their exclusive domain.

The blamer disagrees with the speaker and tells the speaker that she is definitely wrong and whatever bad that has happened is the fault of the speaker. Pointing one's finger with the other hand on the hip is the physical position of the blamer. The blamer's body says that the blamer is in charge. Inside the blamer feels unsuccessful and lonely.

The computer is ultra-reasonable and uses logic instead of feeling words. Sitting rigidly with hands together on the lap is the typical physical position of the computer. The computer's body says that she is calm and cool. Inside, the computer feels vulnerable.

The distractor uses irrelevant words leading away from the topic. The distractor's physical position is angular and off balance. Inside, the distractor thinks that nobody cares.

The optimal healthy communication stance is the congruent communicator, where balance is achieved (Corrales, 1989). Internally, all parts work together (feelings, images, words, and sounds) to support the external senses. The person is aware and in touch with all of the facets of the self and can give accurate information as well as take in realistic perceptions of other people and the external world.

View of Healthy Functioning

Human beings are good. By validating growth, a person is transformed and developmental delays wither away. Influenced by Rogers and other existential phenomenologists, Satir is concerned about the views people have of their places in the world (the *weltanschauung*), especially as expressed by the roles they play within the family.

Satir's therapeutic model is oriented toward growth and wellness:

> At this time, I see that my therapeutic task lies in reshaping and transforming into useful purposes the energy bottled up in a person's or a family's demonstrated pathology. This is in contrast to my earlier belief that my task was limited to exterminating the pathology. I refer to my present approach as a health-oriented approach, although it is really more than that. I call it the Human Validation Process Model. (Satir & Baldwin, 1983, p. 207)

Satir (1986) used the analogy of a wheel as a person. The spokes represent various parts of the individual, and the rim represents the boundary of self (Figure 7–1). In Satir's Human Validation Process Model, the hub represents potential wellness. The symptom is a means by which the individual tries to express health. In this model, the therapist looks for the strengths in each of the parts (spokes) of the individual. The focus is upon the life force as manifested in each component of the total individual. By contrast, in a pathology-extermination model, the hub would represent the symptoms or pathology, and the therapist would view all the parts of the individual only in relationship to the pathology. In such a case, even if the symptoms are eradicated, the person still has not addressed the key issues of growth that are inherent in long-term health.

Satir's levels of health are included in Table 7–1. There is a separate specialist for each dimension. For example, there is a clergyman for the spiritual dimension, an educator for the brain, a psychotherapist for emotions, and a physician for the body. Satir maintained that a therapist should attend to all eight dimensions with every member of the family. All eight parts add up to a separate self, but the self is always

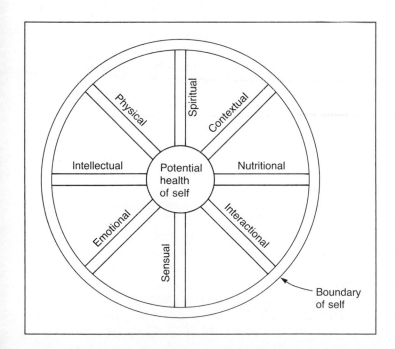

FIGURE 7–1 Satir's eight levels of health and of self

From "A Partial Portrait of a Family Therapist in Process" by V. Satir in *Evolving Models for Family Change: A Volume in Honor of Salvador Minuchin,* H.C. Fishman & B.L. Roseman (Eds.), 1986, New York: Guilford Press. Adapted by permission.

TABLE 7–1 Toward Healthier Family Systems: Satir's levels of health

Spiritual. The individual's relationship to the life force that created all living things.

Contextual. An individual's surroundings such as colors, sounds, temperature, movement, space, light, form, and time.

Nutritional. Food, liquids, and vitamins that furnish energy.

Interactional. Relationships with other people that meet the social needs for love and respect.

Sensual. Data from the five senses filtered through the lenses of expectations and past experiences.

Emotional. The right side of the brain (including the glands and nervous system) that influences feelings.

Intellectual. The left side of the brain representing logic by which human beings process facts, draw conclusions, and do research.

Physical. The human body.

From "A Partial Portrait of a Family Therapist in Process" by V. Satir in *Evolving Models for Family Change: A Volume in Honor of Salvador Minuchin* (pp. 278–293), H. C. Fishman & B. L. Rosman (Eds.), 1986, New York: Guilford Press. Adapted by permission.

greater than the sum of them. Satir (1986) proposed the formula: "A (body) + B (brain) + C (emotions) + D (senses) + E (interactions) + F (nutrition) + G (context) + H (soul) = S (self)" (p. 287). She strongly believed that a therapist should determine what message each symptom sends regarding each of the eight levels.

The Therapeutic Process

Goals of Therapy.   For Satir, increased maturity was the primary goal of therapy (Satir & Baldwin, 1983). In family therapy, her main aim was to integrate the growth of each family member with the integrity and health of the family system. In particular, she wanted: (1) to assist the family to gain hope, awakening dreams of what the future can be like; (2) to strengthen the coping process and the coping skills of family members; (3) to bring into awareness that individuals can make choices and take responsibility for the outcomes of those choices; and (4) to develop health in the individual family members and the family system.

In Satir's model, symptoms are like signal lights pointing the way to some form of starvation, injury, or disharmony. One task of therapy is to decipher the message of the symptoms and to find out how family members hurt themselves and each other, blocking growth. Then Satir would focus on releasing and redirecting blocked energy by facilitating the development of increased self-esteem, improved communication *by insight!* skills, and more tolerant rules as these interface with the levels of self. Using the

Human Validation Process Model, Satir's goals are holistic. As blocked-up energy is transformed, symptoms atrophy and wither away.

Role of the Therapist. Therapists who have adopted Satir's therapeutic style perceive the role of the therapist to be that of a modeler, attender, composer, and analyzer, in that order (Kolevzon & Green, 1985). A modeler participates, uses reality testing (checking out), models effective communication and what it means to be human, and is supportive. An attender listens, questions, observes, and is consistent. A composer is comic, casual, and teaches. An analyzer interprets and reflects. When comparing across theoretical groups, therapists trained by Satir valued the roles of the therapist as facilitator and risk-taker with greater family participation more than did therapists of the other theoretical orientations. Family role structure was also valued, but not as much as in the structural and strategic schools.

The Use of Diagnosis and Assessment. Satir would assess the family system and its rules, the self-worth of each family member, and the communication patterns among family members (Satir & Baldwin, 1983). A family system may be open, closed, or a variation in between. Closed systems comply with rigid rules, which are followed even when they violate the needs of the human beings within the family. Such a system focuses on power, dependency, conformity, obedience, and guilt. No changes are allowed. People in closed systems seek more and more reinforcement from outside the system in order to feel comfortable with themselves. Eventually one or more individuals reach the limits of their coping abilities and the system breaks down, with one or more people exhibiting symptoms. In contrast, an open system is flexible. Each individual feels control and responsibility for what will happen in the future. Open systems change with the context. In such systems the full range of feelings including anger, fear, hope, and frustration are expressed and accepted.

Satir would assess the rules of the family. Satir would examine the flexibility or rigidity of the rules (whether or not they change according to the situation at hand). She discovered the rules regarding negotiation of differences, affection, the keeping of secrets, and the sharing of thoughts and feelings. She would pay particular attention to the rules dictating how anger is communicated.

Satir assessed the self-worth of each family member by observing nonverbal communications with other family members and by listening to what they say to each other. Something becomes a problem if an individual feels ashamed or worthless as a result. For example, misplacing one's car keys may be inconvenient, but it is not a real problem until the person feels guilty or ashamed about it or tells herself that she is worthless because of it. When such thoughts and feelings are generated, the individual may begin to placate, blame, distract, become super-reasonable, drink, run away, or carry out some other defensive move in order to defend the self and keep others from knowing about the feelings. Satir would continually assess the communication stances that family members use most often, with whom, and under what conditions. Congruent healthy people share their feelings of helplessness and thoughts that say it was a dumb thing to do, laugh at themselves, and accept their humanity. They do not hide true reactions. Everyone loses or misplaces car keys at some point, and the inventor who creates a fool-proof system for reducing such losses will become an instant millionaire.

Nature of the Initial Session.   Satir would make contact with each family member by introducing herself and finding out the name of each person. In some cases, she would go around the circle, saying a few words to each person and often touching.

In the early phases of the development of her style, Satir (1967) generally used a history-taking intake procedure for the initial session, which followed a set format (Table 7–2) and was called the Family-Life Chronology. In front of the children, Satir asked the parents how they met and about their courtship. Since most couples have many of their happiest memories associated with their engagement, wedding, and early marriage, the interview focused on the positive aspects of the past, reducing the anxiety of the couple and the children, who were usually very curious about the lives and history of the parents. The chronology went back in time to how each parent was raised and their perceptions of family members in the family of origin. Efforts were made to alternate questioning and to interrupt when answers became too long or when one person attempted to monopolize the interview. From the family of origin, Satir moved through and up to the time of marrying the spouse and what each family thought about it, then asked about each spouse's expectations for marriage. During this time Satir was analyzing how each spouse expressed self, what models were present earlier in life, and what roles the person was currently playing.

Then Satir asked about early married life, the birth of each child, and expectations for parenting. She asked each child how the child saw the parents and their relationship with each other. Satir continually encouraged open, clear communication of thoughts and feelings by all family members, stating that therapy is a safe place to share. She ended the family chronology on a hopeful note, setting the tone for future sessions.

Stages of Therapy.   According to Satir and Baldwin (1983), there are three stages of intervention in the Human Validation Process Model of Satir: (1) making contact, (2) chaos, and (3) integration. These stages are present in each interview and in the therapy as a whole.

At the beginning of the first session, Satir would shake each person's hand and focus her full attention on that person as they introduced themselves. She would validate the individual's uniqueness in some way. This basic process of connecting with each person and listening attentively to the person raises self-esteem and fosters hope. In the first stage and throughout the therapy, Satir was nonjudgmental and accepting of what family members revealed. The therapist legitimizes all feelings. This is particularly important in the first stage, where the main task is to create a safe environment in which family members will open up and share themselves. During this first phase the therapist has already begun to model communication skills for the family. Family members are encouraged to observe and report what they see in a nonjudgmental way. Satir may have taken 45 minutes to an hour just for the opening process. She simultaneously assessed the family as she developed a sense of trust with them. Rather than focusing on a problem, she would ask each person about hopes and expectations for the therapy, not spending too much time with any one member.

TABLE 7–2 Main flow of family-life chronology *— past & current*

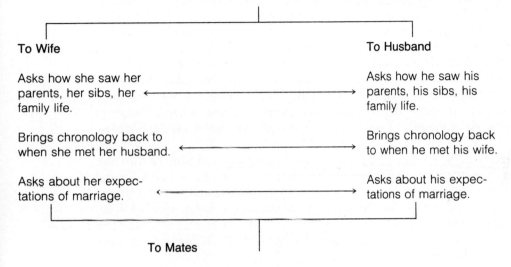

To Family as a Whole

Therapist asks about the problem

To Mates

Asks about how they met, when they decided to marry, etc.

To Wife

Asks how she saw her parents, her sibs, her family life.

Brings chronology back to when she met her husband.

Asks about her expectations of marriage.

To Husband

Asks how he saw his parents, his sibs, his family life.

Brings chronology back to when he met his wife.

Asks about his expectations of marriage.

To Mates

Asks about early married life. Comments on influence of past.

To Mates as Parents

Asks about their expectations of parenting. Comments on the influence of the past.

To Child

Asks about his views of his parents, how he sees them having fun, disagreeing, etc.

To Family as a Whole

Reassures family that it is safe to comment.

Stresses need for clear communication.

Gives closure, points to next meeting, gives hope.

From *Conjoint Family Therapy* (p. 135) by V. Satir, 1967, Palo Alto, CA: Science and Behavior Books. Reprinted by permission of the author and publisher.

Usually Satir would begin to intervene in this first phase and may have conducted a family sculpture. She would ask open-ended questions about feelings in this first stage, but never pushed family members beyond the level of their defenses. She by-passed anger and aimed for developing positive contact in the initial stage of therapy.

In the second stage of therapy, chaos and disorder are the characteristic features as family members risk the unknown by sharing the hurt and pain underlying angry feelings and becoming vulnerable. Satir would support the person as the fear of potential loss of love was faced in revealing the self. She would combine toughness with empathy and pushed only after the therapeutic alliance was well established. Satir also supported all other family members simultaneously. Issues would emerge spontaneously in the therapy as Satir drew upon her many skills, selecting the most appropriate to use at a given time. This stage is very unpredictable, as family members open up and work on issues in a random order. People may feel stuck and hopeless in this stage.

The third stage of the therapy is characterized by integration or closure on the issue that arose in the preceding stage. There is a willingness to change and hope on the part of family members. Often this stage is emotionally more restful than the others. Family members work together to plan actions to implement what has been resolved. As in other stages, Satir would act as a teacher, interjecting cognitive information. The cycle of stages will repeat itself each session and throughout the therapy until the family is ready for termination.

Application: Major Therapeutic Techniques
Satir used the following techniques (Satir & Baldwin, 1983):

1. *Family sculpture*. A family member is asked to show the relationship to one or more other family members using bodily positions and gestures to represent degrees of closeness and communication patterns. When movement is added, a family sculpture becomes a stress ballet.
2. *Drama*. Family members are asked to act out a scene in the life of the family or an individual.
3. *Metaphor*. A word is used to represent another idea, and the idea is discussed by analogy. For example, Satir would use the term "pot" as a metaphor for a person's self-esteem and asked how full a person's pot was at a given time.
4. *Reframing*. Labeling positive intentions behind problematic behaviors and positive by-products of such behaviors.
5. *Humor*. Often the positions of a sculpture will lead to laughter. Satir would use a light touch of humor to keep a relaxed atmosphere for learning.
6. *Touch*. Satir often used touch with family members, shaking hands with each at the beginning of therapy. She was careful not to violate the boundaries of individuals, as some people consider touch a violation. She said there is often a subliminal invitation from the person asking to be touched. This may have occurred when she was working verbally with another family member, and the touch acted as a nonverbal support and involvement to the other family member.

Intimacy is respecting the distances between people, touching when invited, and honoring boundaries.

7. *Communication stances.* Satir would ask family members to participate in an exercise in which each person takes the physical position of a certain stance: placator, blamer, computer, distractor, and a congruent person. Family members share feelings associated with using various stances and with responding as recipients to stances. In this way, family members increase their awareness of effective communication and learn how to become congruent.

8. *"I" statements.* Satir would encourage family members to own their feelings. Often people use passive forms such as "It is confusing." Satir modeled the active form, "I am confused," in family therapy and developed exercises in which family members practice such "I" statements.

9. *Simulated family.* Workshop participants are often asked to form simulated families in order to learn about family systems and communication stances.

10. *Ropes as therapeutic tools.* Ropes, representing relationships with other family members, are tied to the waist of each member until each has as many ropes as there are family members. The other ends of the ropes are tied to each of the other family members. All the family members become aware of how they are connected and how tension is created in the ropes. Often entanglements occur. The therapist asks family members how they are able to reduce the tension on the ropes in order to untangle. When they can verbalize how they are able to do this with the ropes, the learning can easily be transferred to everyday life.

11. *Anatomy of a relationship.* The unconscious contract in a marriage is made overt through sculpture and role play. Alternative possibilities for contracts are enacted, and the spouses are asked to comment on them. For example, if a woman married her husband because she wanted a person to lean on, she will be asked to stand behind her husband, hold his neck, and lean against him. Both are asked to verbalize their feelings. Then she is asked to intensify the action and lean even more. Then both are asked to express their feelings. The roles may then be reversed. Satir also used this technique to find out how each spouse saw the current relationship and how each spouse would like it to be.

12. *Family reconstruction.* This unique technique is considered to be most representative of Satir's philosophy and theory of change. The star of the reconstruction (the central character or client) discovers the origin of distorted learnings, about the parents as people, and the separate self. The star had prepared a chronological account of family events (who was there, what was happening, the setting, time, and place) from the birth of the first grandparent to the present time. Satir, as a guide, would use this calendar during the reconstruction to ask the star about events. The star had also prepared a family map, which included three generations (grandparent, parent, and present generation) with names of family members and five or six adjectives describing each member's personality. The star may also have prepared in advance, or with the guide, a circle of influence. This is a circle with the star in the middle and a spoke for each relationship important to the star while growing up. The thicker the spoke, the more important the relationship. The guide develops a trusting relationship with the star by talking about what the star

has prepared and spending time together. The guide determines what scenes will be enacted by the group (of 15 or 20) in the actual reconstruction. At least three scenes are included in almost every reconstruction: (1) the family history of each of the star's parents, (2) the story of the relationship of the star's parents from meeting to the present, and (3) the birth of the children to the star's parents, especially the star. The guide may add other scenes as well.

13. *Parts party.* This experiential exercise is directed toward helping individuals increase awareness of the parts of themselves and how to use them in an integrated manner. It involves at least six people. The guide asks the individual to furnish the names of six to ten males and females in the public spotlight who either repel or attract the individual and who are considered interesting to invite. These personalities are described in one adjective with other members playing personality characteristics represented by the adjective. The experience is divided into four phases: (1) meeting the parts, (2) observing the conflict and competition among the parts, (3) transforming the parts, and (4) integrating the parts.

As the individual watches, the guide freezes the parts into clusters; for example, Johnny Carson's humor talking to Albert Einstein's intelligence. This process is repeated several times, and parts talk about the conflicts and competition among them. Each part is also asked to take turns dominating. The parts are eventually asked to cooperate and then circle the host, who accepts them formally and expresses feelings about them several times.

14. *Awareness enhancement.* Since Satir's style of therapy emphasizes awareness of feelings, over the years she developed exercises in which people who participate learn to use their senses more effectively and to become more aware of their feelings. In particular, she is noted for the development of triadic experiential exercises in which an observer watches two participants interact and gives them feedback about their interaction.

DAVID KANTOR AND WILLIAM LEHR

Historical Development

Kantor and Lehr (1975) developed a theory of family process that has influenced experiential family therapy approaches. The theory was based upon a study of normal and disturbed families in their homes. The 19 families studied lived in Boston or attended the clinics of the Boston State Hospital. More than half were classified as normal (there was no record of a disturbance that required hospitalization for any family member). Participant observers lived with the families and collected first-hand data about the communication patterns, norms, culture, and styles of the family. In addition, microphones installed in the homes recorded the conversations of family members, and three interviews were held: one with the total family, one with each subsystem of the family, and one with each individual. Administration of the Thematic Apperception Test accompanied the individual interview.

From the analysis of these data (see their book, *Inside the Family*), the importance of space to a family became evident. The spatial metaphor is the basic way in which Kantor and Lehr described the family. Space is used by the family to regulate closeness and distance among family members and to mark the territory of the family from the rest of the community. Because of the importance of the variable of space in their work, Kantor and Lehr impacted the development of many experiential family therapy techniques that utilize space, such as family sculpture and other action-oriented techniques.

With Fred Duhl and Bunny Duhl, David Kantor initiated the Boston Family Therapy Institute. More recently, Kantor established the Family Institute of Cambridge to train family therapists and to encourage research on families. The link between research and practice continues in Kantor's work.

Key Theoretical Concepts

Kantor and Lehr (1975) are most noted for their explanation of family systems and family types—their Theory of Family Process Types. For example, family systems can be closed, open, or random. A therapist may think that a given client family is pathological when their style is just different from that of the therapist's family. An elaboration of some of the main theoretical concepts of Kantor and Lehr follow.

Family System.   A family system is a set of different people who are related to each other via reciprocal causal effects. Each component is related to the other components in a stable way over any given period of time. The feedback loop undergirds goal-seeking activity, which is a characteristic of family systems.

Subsystems.   There are three subsystems of the family system: the personal, the interpersonal, and the family unit.

Interface Phenomena.   An interface is where two or more subsystems or systems meet. Family activities, by their very nature, include interfaces between the family unit, the interpersonal subsystem between each two people in the family, and the personal subsystem of each family member. When one family member is participating in a family activity, that family member is simultaneously (1) a self with individual needs, desires, and self-interests; (2) a member of an interpersonal subsystem with each person in which there are responsibilities for maintaining relationships with every other family member; and (3) a member of the family unit in which the person has certain obligations.

In analyzing problems in a family system, it is important to look at family strategies in terms of the interactions at various interfaces. For example, Melody, a vivacious teenager, may be told by her mother to be home at a certain time. Her father concurs, but the tone of his voice conveys the self-interest of his personal subsystem. He secretly envies the freedom of his teenage daughter. Melody returns home late, following the covert message of her father rather than the overt message of her mother. The concentric circles (family-unit, interpersonal, and personal subsystems) and interface phenomena are extremely useful concepts to therapists who are assessing family process.

Distance Regulation.   The most important key differentiating concept in the model of Kantor and Lehr (1975) is the concept of distance regulation. Each family member has an optimal distance (degree of closeness each desires) which is a goal in any given interpersonal relationship and in the family as a whole. Strategies, dimensions, family types, and selection of a role to be played are all means by which family members monitor the distance among them, so that it is neither too great nor too small. When a person marries an individual from another family type who is accustomed to a different degree of distance, conflicts automatically occur: When the distance is optimal for one spouse, it will be uncomfortable and stressful for the other. Forming a new family involves talking about and negotiating optimal distances and how they will be regulated.

Strategies.   Strategies are processes of repeating interactional sequential patterns. Strategies are collaborative and purposive patterns of movements toward goals made by members in a family system. Family members are aware of their parts in the sequences, although some freedom is allowed, and they share responsibilities for the outcomes of strategies.

Target Dimensions. (Goals) sought by family members are called target dimensions. They include affect (nurturance and intimacy), power (deciding what is wanted and the capability to get it), and meaning (a philosophy that explains reality and our identity in it).

Access Dimensions.   Energy, space, and time are the access dimensions, that is, the physical means through which family members mark paths for attaining goals or targets.

Family Process Types.   Each family has a style that signals its members how to regulate distance. The three family process types are random, open, and closed.

The core purpose of the closed family system is to achieve stability through tradition. Family members seek stable affect over time through being faithful in their relationships, even when apart or in conflict. Sincerity, tenderness, durability, and fidelity are important goals of closed family systems. People care deeply but do not show it, remaining composed. In a closed system, the parents are the authorities and do not argue in front of the children. Parents believe in discipline and preparation. Unity, certainty, and clarity provide meaning in a closed family system. Space is fixed. For example, certain rooms may be off limits and are only used with the permission of the parents. Time is regular in a closed system, with meals and bed times set at the same time each day. Energy is steady in the closed family system, and fueling is prescribed. For example, family members are required to go to church and allowed to go to a movie, but are not permitted to go out on Sunday evening. Closed system families can obtain high rates of fueling (gaining psychological supplies) if they consistently go to rich sources.

The core purpose of the open family system is to achieve adaptation through consensus. The affect ideals for the open family system are emotional responsiveness and authenticity. Although closeness is encouraged, distancing of a temporary nature is allowed to relieve the discomfort of too much closeness. Family members have latitude to make choices. Family members talk about family and individual goals and resolve conflicts. Parents argue in front of their children to act as a model for resolving conflict. Cooperation and allowance for individual differences are valued. Concerned about the past-present interface and the future-present time interface, family members focus on relevance (what works in the present). Relevance, tolerance of individual differences, and affinity for and liking others in the present have meaning for open family systems. The use of space is regulated by group consensus, so there are many guests and friends visiting in diverse parts of the home at any given time. Time is variable. For example, dinner may not be at the same time every night, but will vary according to the schedules of the individuals and the consensus of the group. Access to energy targets for fueling are flexible. Family members try to think of new and different activities that will charge up their energy supplies and are encouraged to do so as long as they do not infringe upon the activities of others in the family.

The core purpose of the random family system is to achieve exploration through intuition. The affect ideal of the random family system is spontaneity. Feelings are passionately expressed. Humor, whimsicality, or the ecstasy of rapture are preferred over planned experiences. Power is interchangeable among people. There is free choice. Challenging occurs when anyone takes the lead. Creativity, originality, diversity, and ambiguity are valued above all else. Space is dispersed, with much attention given to tailoring living areas to match the interests of the individual who inhabits that area. Time is irregular. There is no set dinner time, and some members may not eat with the family at all. Parents are inconsistent with permission, one time refusing it, another time granting it. Energy is regained through spontaneous, diverse means. Therefore, fueling fluctuates, being quite high at one time, quite low at another.

Parts to be Played.   There are four parts to be played by family members or members of any social group: mover (the person initiating a social action), follower (the co-mover who responds by showing agreement with the mover or with the opposer), opposer (the co-mover who challenges the mover), and bystander (the co-mover who observes the action of the mover but neither agrees nor disagrees with it). The power of the mover depends on the responses of the co-movers. In other words, there can be no chief without Indians, who either follow or resist the actions of the chief or at least participate in the rituals of leadership by observing. A family in which each of its members can play all of these parts at different times has more resources available when crises occur. If family members are permitted to play only one part each, flexibility is not there to use in times of emergency.

Enabling Family.   In an enabling family system, a balance in distance regulation is maintained in such a way that no one subsystem is repeatedly, systematically, and consistently denied the actualization of its goals.

In summary, each person carries an internal image of the appropriate distance regulation mechanisms to use in forming a family. Sometimes ironic displacement occurs when destructive consequences happen as a result of the family strategies used to maintain distance. All are part of an overriding family theme that emanates from past generations. For example, if a grandfather was orphaned and a son was also orphaned, an abandonment theme may be very strong in the family.

The Therapeutic Process

At the Boston Family Therapy Institute, Bunny Duhl and Fred Duhl experimented with techniques that used space and time in innovative ways. They developed an approach to family therapy called Integrative Family Therapy (Duhl & Duhl, 1981). In the initial session in this style of therapy, they listen to the family story and evaluate the nature of the triggering event and the degree of pain in the family. They note the stage of family development, the degree of novelty permitted in the family, the feeling state, how information is accessed, and the flow of relating in the family. They review the resources of the family system and the time, space, and energy used by the family. They look at the attributes of each family member. Goals, hypotheses, and assumptions are formulated on the basis of the initial assessment, the family resources, and the attributes of the individuals in the family.

Interventions are selected to achieve the goals and might include home visits, the use of puppets, the use of magic wands and fantasy, family sculpture, metaphors, and opening up access to information so that parents talk to their children about the feelings and meanings associated with the triggering event over a period of time based upon the developmental levels of the children. The outcome is then evaluated.

The analogy of the tool box is useful. The therapist selects a "tool" or technique to fit the specific nature of the family's problem. It is the responsibility of the therapist to develop additional creative techniques, to add innovative tools to the tool box over time.

Application: Major Therapeutic Techniques

Sculpture. In 1973, Duhl, Kantor, and Duhl wrote "Learning, Space, and Action in Family Therapy: A Primer of Sculpture," a classic article in the field of marital and family therapy that explains the theoretical rationale and specific directions for sculpture. The therapist is the monitor, who is in charge of the process. The client is the sculptor, who shares the content. The actors are chosen from the group by the sculptor based on their similarities to the personalities of the original family. The members of the group are the audience, observing the sculpture.

First, the monitor asks the sculptor to choose the actors from the group. Each actor asks questions of the sculptor to obtain the information necessary to play the role in the sculpture. The sculptor gives each actor a gesture to use that is characteristic of that family member and places each actor in a particular space. Then the monitor encourages the actors to silently move in space while the sculptor observes. The monitor may ask some actors to move closer or farther apart or to intensify gestures. The monitor controls the sculpture and stops it before feelings overwhelm the sculptor.

In turn the monitor asks each actor for feelings experienced in the role, while the sculptor observes. The multiple perceptions of reality are emphasized. The audience is asked for feedback about their observations. Finally, the monitor composes a metaphor or image that represents the meaning of this family. For example, the monitor

Bunny Duhl is known for her use of metaphors and other creative techniques, such as the vulnerability contract. (Courtesy of Bunny Duhl.)

might say, "This family reminds me of a cage of tropical birds, preening their feathers to look good and squawking with no one listening."

Sculpture can be done with the actual family. In this case, each family member, in turn, places the other family members in positions according to the directions of the therapist. The therapist may ask each family member to place other family members based on the patterns of intimacy in the family (who is close to whom) or of power (who makes the decisions in relationship to whom). The multicentric aspects of family life are emphasized as each family member sculpts the family in a different way. The underscoring of multiple truths, with no absolute, is very therapeutic for the family.

Metaphor. One characteristic technique of experiential humanistic approaches is the use of metaphor, although metaphors are sometimes used by family therapists of other theoretical persuasions as well. A metaphor is a way of talking about one thing which represents another and interacting with a symbol, a process that can be particularly effective when the original topic is difficult to discuss.

Bunny Duhl (1983) explains in detail the various creative tools that she has developed over the years at the Boston Family Institute. One of her most recent is the metaphor of the "toy" (Duhl, 1987). Each person is asked to visualize his- or herself as a toy and is asked questions about size, shape, movements, and noises. Then the toys act out their motions, finding other toys whose motions complement or hinder. After each exercise, Duhl asks the participants about their feelings as they experienced their toys. Next she adds noise to the motion and processes this dimension. Finally, she asks each toy to write an ad in an effort to sell itself. Volunteers share their ads with the group. People learn about their strengths and their patterns in their relationships by implementing the toy metaphor.

Vulnerability Contract. One technique that represents Bunny Duhl's work at its best is the Vulnerability Contract, designed to increase the intimacy of a couple (Figure 7–2). Each spouse is asked about the worst things that happened to the person and the sequence of events that occurred after that. As each spouse shares, the empathic therapist validates the pain. The therapist asks the partner how much the partner knew and what information was needed and lists the worst situations on the Vulnerability Contract Form.

Then each partner is asked to share upsetting present-day situations. These can often be linked to the worst situations that have been recorded and are familiar patterns. The therapist repeats the same steps used for the worst situations and records the situations under "vulnerabilities."

Next the therapist asks each spouse questions about the internal states experienced in response to the worst situations and the vulnerabilities. Sometimes a person experiences a tightening of the stomach. Another's heart may pound. The spouse may have sweaty palms or a quaking voice. These internal signals are recorded on the form. When people learn to recognize these internal cues, they gain freedom to make choices about external responses.

Then each spouse is asked what specific overt behaviors are used to defend the self. Like the quills of a porcupine, these external signals protect self-esteem but often keep people away, thereby reducing possibilities for intimacy. The partner is asked to add any behaviors not already volunteered. The therapist asks how effective these behaviors have been in working through the vulnerabilities or in obtaining what is wanted. Usually both spouses begin to see that "quills" do not take away the underlying pain or help them to obtain what they want from the environment.

The therapist then asks each spouse how each would like it to be—what would happen in what sequence. Often people do not believe or trust that other people can meet their needs because their own parents did not. Each spouse is asked to share how the person will alert the partner to personal feelings of vulnerability and what the spouse would like the partner to say or do in response. The partner can agree to do

FIGURE 7—2 Vulnerability contract form

"Worst Things":

Origins (Contexts and Conditions)

Vulnerabilities:

Internal Signals:

External Signals:

Contract:

1. If I am aware first that I'm feeling vulnerable,
   I can:

   And then I want you to:

   And then I will:

2. If you are aware first that I seem vulnerable,
   I want you to:

   And then I will:

   And then I want you to:

From *The Vulnerability Contract: A Tool for Turning Alienation into Connection, with Couples, Families and Groups* (Appendix) by B. S. Duhl, 1976, paper presented at First International Family Encounter. Reprinted by permission.

this or can generate an alternative acceptable response. The spouse also states what the person would like the partner to say or do if the partner notices the spouse's vulnerability first. The spouse then specifies what the person will do and what the person will want the partner to do in response. If the partner agrees, this becomes the contract, which is then recorded by the therapist on the Vulnerability Contract Form. If not, alternative behaviors are selected that are acceptable to both spouses.

Through this process, spouses notice the unique uses of space and time. One person may want to be held silently. Another may say that the partner should point out the vulnerability. The spouse will acknowledge the vulnerability, but may not discuss it then, negotiating a time out for a period up to 24 hours. Some people want to get to the heart of the issue immediately and cannot wait at all to discuss it. The differences of each spouse are understood and valued.

The success of the Vulnerability Contract depends upon its continued and repeated use over a period of time so that new patterns become entrenched and old ones fade away. Sometimes both spouses become vulnerable at the same time. They need to be able to say that they are at a bad place together, owning the pronoun "we," and working from there.

CARL WHITAKER

Historical Development

Carl Whitaker was born on a dairy farm in New York state (Neill & Kniskern, 1982). Early on he became accustomed to the Calvinistic work ethic as he helped his father on the farm. Shy, sensitive, and asthmatic, Carl moved with his family to the city where he began his high school years. He became friends with the valedictorian, who was also the most socially adept boy in his class. Through this friendship, Carl overcame his isolation and culture shock. The themes of rejecting isolation, forcing growth, and accepting the curing power of relationships have followed him throughout his life.

Whitaker had an innovative mix of training and experience in medicine, psychiatry, and psychology, working with diverse ages and problems. He completed medical school, and in the last year of his residency in obstetrics and gynecology he decided to switch to psychiatry with adults in a state hospital setting. He then accepted a child psychiatry fellowship where he used play therapy with young clients in a child guidance center. In 1941 Whitaker completed a master's degree in psychology, submitting a follow-up study of chronic alcoholics. He then worked at a home for delinquents.

During World War II, Whitaker went to Oak Ridge, Tennessee, acting as a therapist at the facility where the first atomic weapons were developed. The work load was extremely heavy, with 12 or more patients a day in half-hour sessions. Since he had such a short time with each patient, Whitaker began to do co-therapy with John Warkentin so they could discuss what would work best with each client. This also permitted a splitting of administrator/therapist roles, which simulated the interaction between two parents. Co-therapy became a characteristic of Whitaker's style that he has retained throughout his career.

It was at Oak Ridge that Whitaker experimented and refined the use of his primary process, the spontaneous unconscious, in therapy. One day in the office a schizophrenic patient saw a baby bottle that had been used with a child patient. The adult began to suck it eagerly (Whitaker & Keith, 1981). Whitaker became the symbolic "mother" for the patient, encouraging him to continue to suck the bottle of milk. After 12 days of therapy sessions with bottle-feeding, the patient gave up his hallucinations and was eventually able to go back to work. Whitaker was successful with other patients using this technique, but the bottle-feeding technique eventually became empty and useless because Whitaker as a person had grown to a different stage himself. He began to realize that the most effective interventions were congruent with his own growth process at a given time. Whitaker believes it is the responsibility of the therapist to continue to grow and develop toward higher levels of integration as a human being in order to help others.

At the age of 34, Whitaker went to Emory University to head the Department of Psychiatry. As he attempted to implement innovative changes, administrative support dissipated. Finally, he and his faculty left to establish the Atlanta Psychiatric Clinic, and Whitaker never again chose to function in an administrative role. He perceived himself as making a difference by helping people through individual psychotherapy. Three mornings a week he discussed the nature of psychotherapy with Thomas Malone, and they co-authored a book (Whitaker & Malone, 1953).

Whitaker and his group often worked with schizophrenics. They found that the patients improved, only to regress when they had contact with their families. Whitaker began to use co-therapy teams to work with the families of schizophrenics, which kept the therapists from becoming enmeshed with the families.

After working with families, Whitaker became bored with doing therapy in Atlanta and accepted a position to teach family therapy in the Department of Psychiatry at the University of Wisconsin, from which he retired from full-time teaching to serve as Emeritus Professor and to write extensively (Whitaker, 1976). During this time, Napier with Whitaker (1978) wrote *The Family Crucible,* which describes therapy sessions with one family.

Key Theoretical Concepts

Symbol World.   All human beings have the basic impulses of rage, sexuality, and loneliness. They must deal with universal issues such as their own deaths. Symbols range from abstract universals characteristic of all human beings to symbols that have meaning only for a particular family, such as the family myth.

Symbolic-Experiential Therapy.   Using a metaphor, Whitaker and Bumberry (1988) compare symbolic experiential family therapy to the telephone lines, water pipes, and gas mains of a city—the infrastructure. The impulses and symbols that flow through the infrastructure affect the surface life of the city in a pervasive way. By participating in symbolic experiential family therapy sessions, family members become comfortable with their impulses and can integrate them into everyday life. The therapist focuses on experiencing and discussing these symbols and impulses in the therapy session. The family will need to make decisions about how they will live. Life involves decisions and struggle. The therapist cannot do it for them: They will need to work at it themselves.

View of Healthy Functioning

Whitaker thinks that there are no individuals (Whitaker & Bumberry, 1988). Each person is only a fragment of some family. Life and pathology are interpersonal in nature. The family is the source of energy and life.

The family and its members grow continuously throughout life, experiencing increased belongingness and individuation. The more family members risk involvement, the greater freedom they have to be individuals. Likewise, the more individuated family members are, the closer and more intimate they can be with each other, creating an intensified sense of togetherness.

Health is a continuous process of becoming. The journey is never finished (Whitaker & Bumberry, 1988). Therefore, the healthy family is always changing and in motion. Rules serve as guides, helpful to the process of growth in healthy families rather than as ways of keeping things as they are. The structure of healthy families separates the generations. Parents have responsibility and authority, although experimenting with roles in a playful way is encouraged. Scapegoats rotate in healthy families and triangles fluctuate. Each family member can join, then leave, and then rejoin the family. When a person can freely leave, the individual can then choose to belong, giving meaning to life. As the family moves through the family life cycle, the family changes. Crises are opportunities for growth. People in the family are free to express hate and love. Issues are discussed and people grow through encounters.

Whitaker and Bumberry (1988) see healthy marriages as a blending of cultures—two foreign ones from the families of origin into a new one. The new family is different from the families of origin, yet the best aspects of the culture of each family of origin are kept and transmitted to the next generation. This is hard work because it involves sharing and struggling over time. In healthy marriages, spouses value differences and use them effectively to grow by recognizing, accepting, respecting, enjoying, and valuing them.

In parenting, the health of the child is dependent on the relationship between the parents. If the child's parents care for each other and model a loving yet confrontive human relationship in which they can grow as individuals, the child will thrive.

The Therapeutic Process

Goals of Therapy. The goals of treatment in family therapy are to simultaneously increase the perception of belongingness on the part of family members and the freedom for each family member to be a separate individual (Whitaker & Keith, 1981). Family therapy aims toward increased craziness on the part of family members and the family as a whole—creativity and spontaneity.

To accomplish this overall goal of increased belongingness and individuation, therapists attempt to do the following: (1) expand the symptoms, escalating interpersonal stress; (2) develop a sense of family nationalism; (3) improve relationships with past generations of the extended family; (4) increase contact with the community and its members, in particular, the cultural group; (5) understand expectations of the family and family boundaries; (6) increase the separation between generations; (7) encourage the family and its members to learn to play; (8) provide a model of a continuous cycle of joining, separating, and rejoining; (9) confront the myth of individuality; and (10) encourage family members to be more who they are. Goals in symbolic-experiential therapy are process goals. Only when family members ask are treatment goals shared and then within the context of the specific questions of the family.

Role of the Therapists.   One of the distinguishing characteristics of Whitaker's therapy is his use of a co-therapist, usually another male. Augustus Napier and David Keith have often done co-therapy with Whitaker. Whitaker views this as essential to the therapy process, as it prevents the therapist from becoming enmeshed in the family. Co-therapy also models a healthy parental coalition and gives each therapist someone to talk with regarding the family, just as parents discuss how they will discipline and rear their children.

Therapists are caring and confrontative in a way that encourages growth in the family and its members. They integrate love and hate (which are complementary feelings, not opposites), challenging the family to grow. Most of all, therapists use their personalities in sharing their internal symbolic activity with the family. Therapists do not betray themselves. They maintain personal integrity and respect the strengths and resources of the family.

Use of Diagnosis and Assessment.   Assessment is conducted simultaneously with the therapy, not as a separate process. A definite attempt is made to involve extended families in the initial session. If this is not possible, information about the families of origin is requested in the initial interview. The process of assessment begins with the initial phone contact and continues throughout the initial session. If families are particularly guarded, assessment continues for three or four sessions.

Whitaker begins with the father, internally comparing him to what Whitaker thinks a father does and is. This subjective process uses Whitaker's introjected father figures as a yard stick against which to measure the client father. The interpersonal and intrapersonal functioning of each family member is assessed through their responses in the sessions. The quality of the relationship between the parents is evaluated through their comments and interaction in the actual interviews.

Nature of the Initial Session.   Often when clients call for initial interviews, a battle for structure ensues as the family proposes what will be done at what time. The therapist makes a counterproposal, outlining what the therapist thinks is needed before therapy begins. Family members often try to set up appointments and types of relationships that are unrealistic or will be countertherapeutic. For example, one spouse may ask for an individual appointment. Whitaker will not see individuals, only families when all of the members are present.

In the beginning of the initial session, Whitaker establishes personal contact with the family (joining) and states ground rules and his expectations for the family. He explains that he is like a coach to a team and the family members are the players, a metaposition to the family. The players make their own decisions about their lives. He tells them that he wants to hear about the pain of the family and its members, but clearly states that he will be tough as well as caring.

Whitaker begins the first session by asking the father to tell him how the family works and asking the mother to understand about his interaction with the father. He then asks about both families of origin. He then highlights the interactive nature of relationships—how people mutually create relationships by what they say and do. The symptoms are reframed to emphasize the mutual responsibility of both parties. They are expanded so that the scapegoat is no longer the only one associated with the problem.

Often there is a battle for initiative in which the family becomes quiet and asks the therapist to do their work for them. The therapist resists because the family is capable of struggling and growing. They do not need a therapist to do this for them. When the therapist deals effectively with the battles for structure and initiative, a therapeutic alliance is formed with the family.

Stages of Therapy.   Since creativity is emphasized, therapy sessions are unpredictable. Especially in early sessions, the therapists establish a menu by asking questions about all kinds of taboo primary impulses such as tendencies toward murder, extramarital affairs, suicide, and death. No topic is off limits. This sets the tone for the family members to bring up anything that comes to mind. Family members learn to see family interaction from another perspective and realize they have the power to create and work on their relationships, to be authors of their own life scripts.

Often the relationship between the parents is one of the primary targets of the work. Whitaker and Bumberry (1988) maintain that men are raised to relate to objects such as cars, computers, and activities—not to intimacy in close relationships as women are. The therapists show that relationships are bilateral. Each person can change the relationship by what is done and said. By withdrawing and assuming that a relationship is only unilateral, the spouse sentences the relationship to deterioration. By involvement and hard work, relationships can improve.

If an impasse occurs, a consultant is invited into the next session to furnish a different perspective. This also contaminates the fantasy that the therapists can cure by magic rather than by the hard work of the family members. When the family substantially increases the use of its own resources, trusting thoughts and feelings, they are ready to terminate.

Application: Major Therapeutic Techniques

Joining.   The therapist makes contact with each family member, beginning with the most distant, typically the father. If the therapist forms a relationship with the father, the family usually stays in therapy.

Homework.   The only assignment is to refrain from discussing therapy and relationships between sessions and to stop being therapists to each other.

Use of Self.   One of the main characteristic techniques of symbolic-experiential therapy is the use of the self by therapists. Therapists are in touch with themselves and share their personal processes with the family. They never betray themselves by losing themselves in the family.

Additional Techniques.   The following techniques are often used: (1) redefining symptoms as attempts to grow; (2) encouraging family members to talk about fantasy alternatives (such as how one spouse might kill the other); (3) converting an intrapersonal problem to an interpersonal stress by the use of fantasy (such as what the other family members might do if one family member committed suicide—the therapist initiates the fantasy and asks the suicide-prone individual to complete it); (4) increasing and exaggerating the pain of a family member; (5) playing with children in the interview; (6) using feelings to confront people (such as telling parents to "bug off" when they interrupt the play between the therapist and one of the children); (7) sharing spontaneous primary process suggestions as they arise; (8) playing with family roles (encouraging family members to reverse roles); and (9) seeing love and hate not as opposites, but as yoked feelings.

THERAPEUTIC OUTCOMES

Johnson and Greenberg (1985) found that an experiential approach that focused on the emotions underlying the patterns of interaction exhibited by marital couples was significantly more effective than a problem-solving approach of a cognitive-behavioral nature in increasing intimacy and marital adjustment and reducing targeted complaints. However, both approaches were better than the control group, which received no treatment at all. Even 8 weeks after termination, significant differences were found in satisfaction and cohesion at follow-up. At a later point, Johnson and Greenberg (1988) studied the process that led to this effective outcome. They found that the most successful therapy sessions were those that contained the highest levels of experiencing, coupled with interactions that were more affiliative and autonomous in nature. These were the only outcome studies found. Experiential humanistic approaches are noted for their vigor, not their rigor.

CONTRIBUTIONS AND LIMITATIONS

One of the main contributions of the experiential humanistic approaches is their emphasis on holistic growth across areas of development for each family member and for the family. Life is a struggle and relationships are hard work, but through communication, creativity, and responsibility, people can gain a greater sense of belongingness while becoming separate individuals.

Another contribution is action-oriented techniques, such as sculpture, communication stances, family reconstruction, metaphors, the vulnerability contract, and other creative, innovative uses of space and time. Humor and spontaneity are cherished in these approaches.

The emphasis on feelings and primary process is another main contribution of experiential humanistic styles of marital and family therapy. Feelings can be openly expressed and validated, leading to better integration of impulses.

In these approaches, the therapist is encouraged to share personal feelings and reactions directly with family members, which is very different from other approaches. The therapist is a growing human being in process, a facilitative model for the family.

One key limitation is the lack of outcome studies documenting the success of such approaches. There is a dearth of research by proponents of experiential humanistic approaches. These therapists tend to be innovators, constantly creating new tools for their tool boxes, but they may not be emphasizing quantitative analytical research.

SUMMARY

This chapter focuses on experiential humanistic approaches that encourage growth: Satir, Kantor and Lehr, the Duhls, and Whitaker. Virginia Satir, "the Columbus of family therapy," developed the first family therapy training program in the United States. Her first book, *Conjoint Family Therapy,* is still used as a text for training in marital and family therapy. Satir's approach to therapy, the Human Validation Process Model, emphasizes feelings. She looked for and affirmed the health of the total self through validation of the spiritual, contextual, nutritional, interactional, sensual, emotional, intellectual, and physical strengths of the unique person the client is.

David Kantor and William Lehr wrote *Inside the Family,* which emphasizes the importance of space to the family as a means of regulating closeness and distance among members. Each family has a style that signals its members how to regulate distance: random, open, and closed types of family systems. Family members can play four parts: mover, follower, opposer, and bystander. The work of Kantor and Lehr influenced the development of experiential family therapy techniques such as family sculpture and other action-oriented techniques.

Bunny and Fred Duhl proposed Integrative Family Therapy and, with Kantor, wrote one of the first articles on how to conduct family sculpture. Bunny Duhl is noted for her creation of metaphors and the development of the Vulnerability Contract.

Carl Whitaker uses a co-therapist, which allows him to freely share his primary process (gut feelings) openly in family interviews while still staying in touch with reality. Spontaneity is one of the main characteristics of his clinical interviews with families and one of his main goals for the family.

EXERCISES

1. Close your eyes and become aware of your thoughts and feelings. Satir (1972a) uses the metaphor of a pot for self-esteem. How full is your pot at this moment? On a sheet of paper, write down your thoughts and feelings regarding your present level of self-esteem. What sentences are you saying to yourself about yourself? Where do you think these come from? What could you say to yourself to improve your self-esteem?

2. In the section of this chapter on communication patterns, Satir's communication stances are explained. Read that section again for this exercise. Satir said that there are five communication stances: placator, blamer, computer, distractor, and congruent communicator. Your professor will ask you to count off into groups of five or to make a group of five with those nearest to you. Your instructor will pass out a piece of paper to each person which states the roles each will play in what order. Your task will be to plan a family vacation. When your professor tells you to begin, play your role using body positions and words. When your professor tells you to stop, take turns sharing your thoughts and feelings about how it felt to play your role and to be in a relationship with people playing the other roles. Repeat this process, playing the roles on your sheet of paper

as many times as your professor tells you to do so while your group plans a vacation. We all use these patterns in our daily lives. Which one(s) do you use the most? If time permits, your professor may ask people to share their reactions with the class on a voluntary basis. This is a variation of an exercise developed by Satir (1972).

3. Refer to Table 7–2, Main flow of family-life chronology (Satir). Outside of class, make arrangements to meet with your simulated family from exercise 2. Taking turns, practice asking the questions of the family-life chronology of Satir of your family members, playing the role of the family therapist. Your professor may want to videotape you playing the role of the family therapist with your simulated family.

After you have practiced, find a volunteer family and obtain their written permission to audiotape a family-life chronology session with them, with yourself in the role of the family therapist. Listen to your tape, and write down 10 strengths and 3 areas needing improvement. If your professor asks you to do so, hand in your audiotape and your written comments to your professor to obtain feedback.

4. The professor will ask for volunteers from the class to participate in a family sculpture. In par-

ticular, one student volunteer is needed who is willing to have his or her family sculpted and who will also play the role of sculptor. There will need to be as many student volunteers as members of the person's family, with volunteers staying with their gender roles. The student sculptor will meet with the professor to prepare for the sculpture before the next class. The professor will play the role of the monitor, managing the sculpture and giving feedback and guidance to the sculptor throughout the process. It is also helpful to read "Learning, Space, and Action in Family Therapy: A Primer of Sculpture" by Duhl, Kantor, and Duhl (1973).

5. Kantor and Lehr (1975) state that there are four parts to be played by family members or members of any social group: mover, follower, opposer, and bystander. Your professor will direct you to find your simulated family or count off into groups. Your professor may pass out slips of paper with your roles and their order written on them, or the professor may give you oral instructions. If not, in your group choose the part which you most like to play in your family. Your task as a group is to choose a specialized topic of interest within marital and family therapy to study as a group during the semester. Playing your role, interact as a member of the group to complete the task. How did you feel playing your part? How did the parts other people played affect the completion of the task? Repeat the task choosing a second topic or by choosing a different part to play. How did you feel playing your part? How did you feel being in a relationship with persons playing other parts? If you have also completed the exercise on the communication stances of Satir, how do they compare to the parts of Kantor and Lehr? How are they alike, and how are they different?

Chapter 8
Psychoanalytically Oriented Family Therapy

The essence of object relations theory is quite simple: We relate to people in the present partly on the basis of expectations formed by early experience.

Michael P. Nichols

An Austrian physician named Sigmund Freud has been a dominant force in mental health treatment for nearly 100 years. Through his clinical work (called psychoanalysis), his lectures, and his books, he has deeply affected the training of mental health care professionals. For example, Virginia Satir received training in ego psychology, which greatly influenced her theoretical approach to family therapy.

Freud saw patients on a one-to-one basis, developing the clinical research method. However, his assumptions about human nature and theoretical concepts were eventually applied to families by the early pioneers of family therapy: Nathan Ackerman and John Elderkin Bell.

Various neo-Freudian theorists disagreed with Freud's theory or built upon it in innovative ways. For example, Adler emphasized social interest, led the movement to establish child guidance clinics in Europe, and supplied a theoretical bridge to the development of family therapy. Neo-Freudians of the object relations school such as Klein, Mahler, and Fairbairn stated that a human being lives to relate to another human being or object. They provided the basis for the proliferation of psychoanalytically oriented couple therapy and the recent development of object relations family therapy by Scharff and Scharff.

PSYCHOANALYTICALLY ORIENTED FAMILY THERAPY

Historical Development

Freud is credited with developing a method of working with maladjusted individuals (called the clinical method of observation), based on his one-on-one experience with them. According to Freud (1900, 1920, 1923, 1926), man is full of libido, a static amount of sexual energy. Human beings consist of structures: the id, the ego, and the superego. The id operates on an unconscious pleasure principle. The ego is the organizer and operates on the basis of the reality principle. The superego is the conscience and represents moral sanctions and "shoulds." Tension occurs when the id seeks a pleasure that the superego does not permit. Much libidinal energy can be tied up in these conflicts. The ego will rationally mediate with the environment, leading to a compromise acceptable to both parts and freeing libidinal energy for use by the human being.

There is an on-going dialectic in each human being between Eros, the life instinct, and Thanatos, the death instinct. Freud's theory gradually accented the ego more and more. Human beings are often at the mercy of their instincts, but through psychoanalysis their egos can be strengthened and their drives reduced. Freud's theory emphasizes drive reduction. Aggressive and sexual impulses are destructive unless tamed through psychoanalysis.

Freud believed that the first 5 years of life were most important. Human beings developed through psychosexual stages: oral, anal, phallic, latency, and genital. If the child's needs were not met at a given psychosexual stage, the child would become fixated at that stage and remain fixated throughout adult life. Through psychoanalysis, an adult could work through the fixation and move through the remaining psychosexual stages.

Key Theoretical Concepts

Regardless of the particular mode or style of psychoanalytically oriented therapy, there are certain key concepts that apply (Table 8–1). A discussion of selected concepts follows.

Introjects From Early Childhood. One key characteristic of psychoanalytically oriented therapy is its emphasis on the past, especially what occurred in childhood between the child and significant others (particularly parents and parent-figures). Through interaction in dyadic relationships within the first 5 years of life, the child develops expectations of what will happen in current relationships with significant others, including the therapist.

In the initial interview, therapists should explore and discuss what transpires between the client and the therapist, what happens between the client and key significant others in present relationships, and the patterns as well as expectations that were generated in important relationships with parenting figures in childhood (Strupp & Binder, 1984). Such areas of inquiry form a therapeutic triangle (Figure 8–1).

TABLE 8–1 Selected key theoretical concepts of psychoanalytically oriented therapy

Observing Ego. The part of the patient's ego that forms a reality based alliance with the therapist and objectively evaluates situations (Sullivan, 1953, 1954).

Experiencing Ego. The part of the patient's ego that relives maladaptive patterns in the therapy session by misconstruing interactions with the therapist (Sullivan, 1953, 1954).

Free Association. The patient's spontaneous sharing of anything that comes to mind.

Resistance. The use of defenses to keep repressed material from entering consciousness.

Reality Testing. The process of checking out perceptions to objectively discriminate between what is emanating externally from what is originating internally.

Interpretation. A statement made by the therapist linking a conflictual pattern expressed between the patient and therapist to a similar pattern that either occurred in early childhood interaction with the parents or is currently occurring between the patient and a significant other.

Working Through. The process of the patient becoming aware of the unconscious patterns from early childhood (transference) and how they affect the relationship with the therapist and with significant others—considered to be the most important component of intensive psychoanalytically oriented therapy.

Conflict. The desire to perform exclusive actions simultaneously.

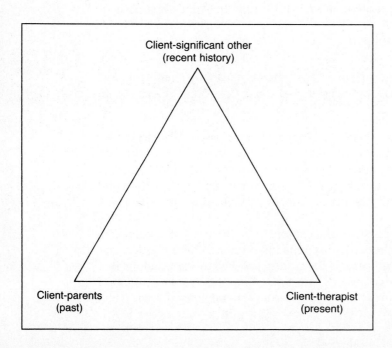

FIGURE 8–1   The therapeutic triangle of dyadic interactional patterns

Not only do reoccurring patterns emerge, but theorists such as Klein, Mahler, Winnicott, Kohut, and Kernberg also maintain that an actual intrapsychic structure, called an introject, is present. In England, Klein (1948) observed the transactions between mothers and infants from birth through the early years. Through interaction with the mother or main care-giver, the infant uses fantasy to pass through stages of the development of part objects and self parts until whole objects are internalized as separate from the internal representation of self. These internalized objects or introjects constitute the intrapsychic apparatus that the child and adult use to form close relationships with others.

For example, Miller (1984) cites a case of a woman with the problem of ruining her relationships with men. She was happy to be with a man for a short time, only to immediately begin to search for his weaknesses, pointing them out at the first chance. Although she vehemently maintained that her main goal in life was to marry and have children, she defeated her plans by repeating this pattern with every potential suitor. Eventually she evidenced the same pattern with her male therapist, criticizing him at every turn, until it was obvious that he did not want to continue treating her. In her second analysis, the therapist encouraged the woman to talk about her relationship with her father, especially any memories of interaction in early childhood. In dreams, the woman remembered her father happily playing with her for hours, only to turn against her, shaming and hitting her without warning. The woman had internalized this pattern as an introject, using it to interact with men in her current life.

Such a pattern was also reenacted with her second therapist, who looked at the pattern and discussed it with her in light of her early childhood experiences. She realized that her father had been the toy of his divorced parents. They only saw him when each wanted to, not when he needed them. She forgave him when she understood that this introject was all he knew from his own parents. Through forgiving her father and accepting the weaknesses of her male therapist, she gradually changed her pattern of relating to men, becoming more tolerant and forgiving of them.

Benjamin (1974, 1979) developed a computer program to implement her model of Structural Analysis of Social Behavior (SASB) in which a therapist can actually see the behaviors of the parent toward the self of the child, the responses of the self of the child toward the parent, and the intrapsychic introject that comprises the behaviors of the other turned toward the self. Such computerized pictures of the introjects can also be helpful in both individual and family therapy. A therapist can learn to use the antithesis of a negative introject as an antidote to effect change in the intrapsychic introject. For example, if family members have blamed the patient and the patient has introjected this interpersonal interaction pattern toward self, the therapist can use the opposite behavior of friendly listening, inviting the client to move toward a constructive introject of listening and exploring the inner self.

The uses of the SASB system have been expanded to coding the free associations of clients, which produce the patterns of family dynamics experienced by the child—introjects (Humphrey & Benjamin, 1986). By coding one telephone call from a mother, nonclinicians were able to code the comments defining the family dynamics between the mother and daughter that had led to suicidal ideation in the daughter. The computer printout of the interpersonal patterns of other, self, and introject included alternative possible therapeutic interventions to use in individual or family therapy. Computers are beginning to play an important role in diagnosis and treatment planning (Greist et al., 1984).

Transference and Countertransference.   Each person carries intrapsychic introjects formed from their interpersonal interactions with parent figures. The therapist attempts to remain a neutral blank slate upon which the client can transfer or project the intrapsychic introjects that can then be analyzed and worked through with the therapist. For example, if the patient had a critical parent, the patient may see the therapist as being critical of the patient, even if the therapist has not been. This process is called transference and is the heart of any psychoanalytically oriented therapy.

The therapist's internal reactions to the projection of the introjects is called countertransference. For example, a therapist may be a caring person who likes other people to see him in a supportive, warm light. When the client accuses the therapist of being cold and critical, the therapist may become angry. In some approaches, the therapist becomes aware of countertransference but never shares any emotional reactions with the client. In others, the therapist rationally controls acting upon countertransference feelings (for example, becoming angry back at an angry client), but will share some reactions that may help the client to grow or to find the theme of the therapeutic session or of the therapy itself.

For example, a therapist notes feelings of sexual attraction but does not share these with the client, realizing that the client's pattern is to elicit sexual feelings from men as she did with her father. Instead, he asks the client about her relationship with her father. Ackerman (1966) shared selected countertransference reactions that he thought would be helpful to clients. As an example, he might say that he feels blocked because he cannot get a word in edgewise. He asks the parents if the child's talking ever bothers them in the same way and inquires as to how they feel about it.

The therapist also helps family members to see how their intrapsychic patterns are being translated into present interpersonal interactions with family members. By becoming aware of the patterns, family members can begin to sort out the reality of the situation and the real selves of family members in contrast to the fantasy roles that they have assigned to them. Interactional patterns in the family thus become more reality based.

Anxiety and Defense.   Anxiety is tension. From a purely Freudian view, when the superego, ego, and id are in conflict, anxiety results. When anxiety increases, the ego uses unconscious mechanisms to reduce the anxiety so that the ego is not overwhelmed. From a theory of self psychology, such defense mechanisms protect the level of self-esteem.

Defense mechanisms are unconscious ways of coping with anxiety or protecting self-esteem. Everyone uses them to some degree. However, since they all distort reality if overused, they can lead to poor life adjustment.

Vaillant (1977) classified defense mechanisms in four levels: psychotic, immature, neurotic, and mature (Table 8–2). In his longitudinal follow-up study of men, Vaillant (1977) found that men with the best life adjustments used more of the mature and neurotic defense mechanisms and less of the immature and psychotic defense mech-

TABLE 8-2 Defense mechanisms classified according to Vaillant's four adaptive levels

Defense mechanism: Unconscious way of coping with anxiety or protecting self esteem.

Level	Definitions
I. Psychotic	(Common in childhood, dreams, and psychosis.)
Denial	Grossly impaired perception of external reality to the point of saying something does not exist when it does or fantasizing that a person exists when dead or gone.
Distortion	Rearranging external reality to meet inner needs.
Delusional projection	Perceiving another person as having feelings that are really one's own and acting toward the person based on this perception. Anger or hatred toward a person is perceived as if the person were a persecutor, as in paranoid schizophrenia.
II. Immature	(Common in adolescence, addiction, personality disorders, and depression.)
Fantasy	Avoiding interpersonal intimacy through schizoid withdrawal or fantasy.
Projection	Seeing one's own threatening impulses as emanating from others.
Hypochondriasis	Transforming negative feelings toward others, which arise from loneliness, aggression, or bereavement, into self reproach and then worry over one's health and complaints of somatic illness, fatigue, and pain.
Passive aggressive behavior	Defiant resistant behavior expressed indirectly or toward oneself.
Acting out	Expressing sexual or aggressive impulses or wishes through action to avoid dealing with the affect and tension that accompany them.
III. Neurotic	(Common in most people.)
Intellectualization	Thinking about wishes in logical, emotionally bland ways and not acting out.
Repression	A memory lapse of thoughts although the feelings remain in consciousness, such as weeping and forgetting for whom one is crying.
Reaction formation	Expressing the opposite feeling or impulse.
Displacement	Discharging energy meant for a threatening target toward a safer one.
Dissociation	Cutting off feelings or thoughts from the rest of the personality by drastic, temporary changes in one's personal identity.
IV. Mature	(Common in normal, healthy adults.)
Sublimation	Redirecting aggressive or sexual impulses to express them through socially acceptable channels such as sports.
Altruism	Directing energies toward services for others.
Suppression	Consciously excluding painful impulses from awareness.
Anticipation	Goal-directed planning for future discomfort, such as surgery or death.
Humor	Expressing feelings and ideas directly without hurting self or others.

From *Adaptation to Life* (pp. 80, 383–386) by G. Vaillant, 1977, Boston: Little, Brown. Adapted by permission.

anisms than did men with poor life adjustments. Those using less mature defense mechanisms had over 600% more time in the hospital over a 25-year period than those using mature defense mechanisms. By age 55, none of those using mature defense mechanisms were dead or chronically disabled, while half of those who used immature defense mechanisms were dead or chronically disabled.

One goal of psychoanalytically oriented family therapy is to increase the use of mature defense mechanisms by family members. As the therapist uses educative responses and points out defenses by using interpretation (linking the patient's behavior in the session to protection of self-esteem in a collaborative manner), family members become more aware of unconscious defense mechanisms at work and can learn to analyze and consciously control them.

Ego Development.   Loevinger (1976) devised a theory of ego development in which human beings grow and develop and use more adaptive ego defensive mechanisms over time, moving to higher stages of ego development. Few people move through all of the stages to the highest stage, which is represented by Maslow's self actualizing person. Most adults are found in the conformist, conscientious-conformist, or conscientious stages of ego development.

Dipoles That Lead to Conflicts.   Psychoanalytic theory is composed of dipoles, opposites such as the urge to die (Thanatos) and the life force (Eros) that exist simultaneously in all human beings. We all love and hate at the same time and harbor ambivalence toward those we hold close in intimate relationships. At the heart of many marital and family problems is the inability to face and integrate differences.

People often marry others thinking that they share the same values. After the illusions wear off, people begin to notice that they are different. They may use defense mechanisms such as denial to deal with difference, or they may learn to not only accept but to celebrate differences. Reconciling opposites and learning to live with ambivalence represent higher levels of ego development. An effective psychoanalytically oriented family therapist points out differences in an accepting and positive manner, celebrating them.

In *Unifying Individual and Family Therapies,* Allen (1988) defines self sacrifice as camouflaging on a consistent basis the true characteristics of one's own nature in order to fit a role that makes others in the family or society feel more comfortable. Camouflaging is destructive not only to that individual but also to the other family members and to society at large. One of the dipoles that needs to be reconciled in human life is how to belong while being an individual, or as Freud said, "*zu lieben and zu arbeiten*" — to love and to work.

One key goal of psychoanalytically oriented family therapy is to encourage the individuation of each family member. Paradoxically, as individuation increases, the ability for closer relatedness increases (Simon, Stierlin, & Wynne, 1985). Stierlin, Rucker-Embden, Wetzel, and Wirsching (1980) coined the term "related individuation" to describe the principle that higher levels of individuation require and permit higher levels of relatedness. By individuation, they mean both self-demarcation and self-differentiation. In self-demarcation, a person can recognize the external world as separate from the internal world and the expectations of others as separate from one's expectations for self. Self-differentiation is the cultivation of individual tastes and interests as well as the creation of psychological boundaries. A person can clearly state feelings, expectations, and needs, owning them by using "I" statements. By being able to be separate individuals, people can risk coming closer to others without losing the self. In fact, people in close relationships can co-evolve: that is, grow as individuals through their relatedness, moving toward higher levels of ego development through increased reconciliation of opposites.

Another set of opposites dealt with in psychoanalytically oriented family therapy is abandonment-engulfment. People in a close relationship can experience loss if the other person leaves or dies (abandonment). People often stay in a painful relationship because they do not want to deal with loss or feelings of abandonment. Others experience a fear of being engulfed as they move toward intimacy (Beavers, 1985). They fear merging with the other person in such a way that they will lose themselves.

Normally, people in close relationships both cling and distance to a degree to deal with the opposites of abandonment-engulfment. However, with individuals who have been fused in symbiotic relationships in their families of origin without well-defined boundaries, these feelings are very strong, causing serious difficulties in close relationships. They act as though they cannot live without the person and then abruptly leave the relationship when they begin to feel smothered. Such individuals also have fears of destroying others, of going berserk, of sexual promiscuity, and of the people upon whom they have projected their anger and other feelings. They have a deep sense of emptiness (Beavers, 1985).

Living life through polarities can sacrifice the true self. People who have higher levels of individuation match their behavior in any one of the dipoles to the circumstances of the current situation. Those with lower levels of individuation may behave at one extreme and quickly switch to its opposite. In addition, people may use compulsive behavior to keep their true selves in line. In order to inhibit the spontaneity of the true self, a person compulsively repeats behavior that is toward the opposite end of the dipole from the real self.

View of Healthy Functioning

Based on the work of Stein and research conducted on healthy families, Kirschner and Kirschner (1986) developed an integrative family therapy approach that combines psychodynamic and systemic models, called Comprehensive Family Therapy (CFT). In CFT, a pattern of healthy family processes is used as a means of family assessment to aid in treatment planning (Table 8–3).

From a psychodynamic point of view, when the married couple is functioning well in these processes, healthy parenting is fostered. Parents are required to be "good enough" parents, providing the limits of discipline and the emotional nurturing that children need. Single parents must play both roles effectively while pursuing their own growth as human beings in the areas of dating and work.

The Therapeutic Process

Goals of Therapy. The goals of psychoanalytically oriented family therapy aim toward making conscious those unconscious patterns from the family of origin (object relations) through interpreting patterns of transference and countertransference. This

TABLE 8–3 Toward Healthier Family Systems: Healthy family processes from a psychodynamic view

1. Each spouse moves forward, progressively facing more difficult challenges as an individual in the marriage and in child rearing. Through struggling with these more complex tasks, the spouse's ego strength is increased, and the spouse moves to a higher stage of ego development.

2. Process of progressive abreactive regression in the marriage: Through a dialectical process oscillating between self-interest and concern for the partner, between progressive and regressive trends, a spouse grows in the marriage. The spouse reaches out to act in the world and looks to the partner for validation (progressive trend). If the spouse received deficient parenting, the partner may need to help the spouse through reparenting to succeed in the world—similar to a parent helping a child to ride a bicycle. When the spouse succeeds in the world, the spouse feels gratitude toward the partner and spends more time with the partner in becoming more intimate (regressive trend). In addition, there is fear of losing or being abandoned by the partner. The spouse returns to the partner for nurturance. Filled with gratitude and love, the spouse encourages the growth of the partner and validates the actions of the partner in the world in a similar reciprocal process.

3. In the regressive phase, each spouse acts as a therapist for the other, listening to deeper and deeper thoughts and feelings related to fears of engulfment and abandonment. The patterns from the family of origin (object relations) are worked through, so fewer and fewer misperceptions remain to interfere with individual functioning.

4. When marital interaction is optimal, the married couple can act as a team to parent the child. Parents fulfill the needs of their children including food, shelter, clothing, safety, self-esteem, belongingness, and self-actualization.

5. In parenting, the same-sex parent typically acts as the disciplinarian and programmer setting limits, and the opposite-sex parent functions as the facilitator, listening to the feelings of the child while also telling the child that the same-sex parent loves the child. The opposite-sex parent acts as a mediator with the spouse, privately listening to blocks in relating to the child that go back to early childhood interactions and encouraging and supporting the spouse's relationship with the child.

6. Parents are flexible and can change roles in relation to the child, one being the disciplinarian and the other being more supportive.

7. In single-parent families, the parent performs both the same-sex and opposite-sex roles, being sure to err on the side of objectivity rather than reactivity, listening to the feelings of the child, and providing an emotional anchor for the child. In addition, it is important for the single parent to reach out to the community so that the child has relationships with other adults. Most importantly, the single parent needs to develop in the areas of dating and work, so that the parent continues to grow, which leads to healthier parenting.

From *Comprehensive Family Therapy: An Integration of Systemic and Psychodynamic Treatment Models* (pp. 21–46) by D. A. Kirschner and S. Kirschner, 1986, New York: Brunner/Mazel. Adapted by permission.

leads to increased awareness and reduction of these blocks to relatedness. People learn to become strong, separate individuals capable of sharing deep feelings and thoughts with other family members, increasing their sense of belonging within the family.

Role of the Therapist. In psychoanalytically oriented approaches, the therapist plays the role of a "good enough" parent, providing effective reparenting for the members of the family, especially for spouses who have received deficient parenting. Limits are established and maintained through discipline as well as constancy, and emotional needs are met through nurturing. By modeling appropriate instrumental and affective behaviors, the therapist supports and encourages effective parenting of the children by the spouses.

Use of Diagnosis and Assessment. Patterns of optimal family functioning can be used by the therapist as a diagnostic tool to develop a treatment plan. The therapist assesses each family member's unique strengths and deficits, tailoring the treatment plan to reparent each person, just as a parent rears each child somewhat differently.

Other important characteristics that are evaluated in early sessions are the boundaries of the individuals and the family and how these are affected by stress. In some families, members distance during stressful periods, while in others, family members cling together, tightly enmeshed. Stierlin et al. (1980) look for signs of the binding or expelling mode. Where binding is the problem, family members are very important to each other. There may be Id-binding (children who have been spoiled and become tyrants as teenagers), ego-binding (where the distorted ego of the parent is imposed upon the child), or superego-binding (the child is overly loyal to the family). With the expelling mode, massive deprivation of the child exists, and such an adult tends to emphasize autonomy and work, fearing closeness and relationships. Children are often delegates, unconsciously fulfilling missions for the family. Information about such centripetal and centrifugal forces in the family needs to be obtained to facilitate treatment planning (Stierlin, 1974).

In psychoanalytically oriented family therapy, assessment of ego functioning, object relations, and defense mechanisms is an on-going part of the therapy. As the family deals with diverse stressors during treatment such as the separation of a child, lower levels of functioning may occur. The clinician should be prepared to tailor the treatment plan to the functioning of the family at a given time, providing more of a supportive, holding environment when they are under extreme stress and providing active interpretation of defenses and patterns of object relations at other times.

Nature of the Initial Session. Scharff and Scharff (1987) have developed a psychoanalytically oriented family therapy called object relations family therapy. An initial session is usually begun by greeting the family and sharing any information the therapist has learned over the telephone or from the referral source. Toys are placed in the center of the treatment room to create a home atmosphere in which play is encouraged. The therapist provides a safe emotional holding environment and asks how each member sees the problem, encouraging interaction. Then the therapist assesses the object relations, psychosexual stages, common defense mechanisms, and

Dr. Jill Savege Scharff and Dr. David Scharff of Washington, D.C., are noted for their book entitled Object Relations Family Therapy, *in which their psychoanalytically oriented approach to family therapy is elaborated. (Courtesy of the Washington School of Psychiatry.)*

any shared family anxiety from observing the interactions of the family (Ables with Brandsma, 1977; Blanck & Blanck, 1974). Usually the therapist attempts a trial interpretation to determine the family's suitability for the working through phase (Scharff & Scharff, 1987). In developing a formal treatment plan, strengths and resources are considered, as well as weaknesses and ability to tolerate frustrations.

Typically the psychoanalytically oriented therapist asks a number of questions, both in the initial session and throughout therapy. In addition to questions about the presenting problem ("What brings you here?" "What is the reason for seeking therapy now?"), a therapist will ask about a history of relationships including the marital and sexual relationship, the patterns from the family of origin, the current relationship with parents, those with children, any close friendships, previous therapy relationships, and work and leisure patterns (Scharff & Scharff, 1987). Framo (1982) considers the quality of the sexual relationship to be a prognostic indicator, but often spouses will not be completely truthful about their sexual relationship in the initial session. Questions are also usually asked about deaths in the family and family of origin, other significant losses, and major disruptions such as serious illnesses or job losses.

Stages of Therapy. Stages of psychoanalytically oriented therapy include (1) establishment of a therapeutic contract (frequency of meetings, cost, and rules for missed appointments), (2) development of a therapeutic alliance (the establishment of rapport with each member of the family so there are no favorites), (3) working through (defenses and resistances of family members are discussed and understood; object relations from the family of origin are played out and talked about, leading to increased understanding of any "interlocking pathologies"; transference and counter-transference patterns are interpreted), and (4) termination (issues of loss and separation resurface and are dealt with).

NATHAN ACKERMAN

Historical Development

The most noted early psychoanalytically oriented family therapist was Nathan Ackerman, often called the "grandfather of family therapy." In 1958, Ackerman wrote *The Psychodynamics of Family Life: Diagnosis and Treatment of Family Relationships,* the second book in the field of family therapy, which focused on his theoretical positions. In 1962, using his excellent writing and editing skills, Ackerman joined Don Jackson to produce *Family Process,* the first journal of family therapy (Ackerman, 1970). He eventually left the Jewish Family Service to found the Family Institute in New York City, which exists today as the Ackerman Institute. Bloch and Simon (1982) have released a selection of Ackerman's papers, *The Strength of Family Therapy,* in commemoration of his 1971 death.

Key Theoretical Concepts

The major theoretical concepts of Ackerman are contained in Table 8–4. He is particularly noted for formulating the concept of scapegoating (Ackerman, 1967).

The Therapeutic Process

Role of the Therapist. Ackerman saw the role of the family therapist as a dyadic reciprocal one. The therapist became aware of his own thoughts and feelings in reaction to the projections of the intrapsychic events of individual family members (countertransference) and shared emotions and thoughts that would lead the family to health. The self of the family therapist was like a finely tuned musical instrument for the family to play, with the therapist expressing both the theme and particular feelings, thoughts, and patterns helpful to the family. Ackerman risked sharing himself, but only in a way that was helpful to the family. He was an observer and a participant, as Sullivan (1953, 1954) would say, using his objective observing ego to make comments describing what his experiencing ego was thinking and feeling. Ackerman was outspoken, open, spontaneous, and caring as a person and as a therapist. Through his example, family members would often open up, discussing issues they had been avoiding for years.

Ackerman (1966, 1982) summarized the functions of a family therapist as follows:

1. The therapist develops communication and empathy between the therapist and the family members, as well as among the family members themselves.
2. The therapist uses rapport to clarify and point out the main conflicts and coping mechanisms of the family by counteracting the defenses of displacement, rationalization, and denial of conflict; by bringing hidden conflicts into the open; by linking intrapsychic conflicts to their enactment; and by neutralizing scapegoating.

TABLE 8—4 Key theoretical concepts and techniques of Ackerman

Theoretical Concepts

Complementarity. Complementarity is circular support within the family in which members encourage each other's creative development, satisfy needs, find solutions to conflicts, support self-esteem, and support defenses against anxiety.

Conflict and Coping. Each family has its own style of dealing with conflict. Healthy families perceive differences as a source of growth, and dysfunctional families see them as threats, using splits and alignments, such as scapegoating, to deal with conflict.

Symptom. A symptom is a maladaptive behavior—a compromise for unresolved conflict.

Defense. A defense is used to reduce excessive anxiety that threatens to overrun the ego and take over the symptom.

Growth. Growth is a positive, progressive force leading to greater maturity based upon the resolution of conflicts and problems associated with previous life stages.

Scapegoating. In this process, family members are selected by unconscious shared emotional processes to play the roles of persecutor, scapegoat, and rescuer. Members can play different roles at different times. One person (persecutor) attacks another (scapegoat) as the cause for tension in the family. Another person (rescuer) "heals" or "rescues" the scapegoat.

Techniques

Live History. Ackerman observed the family's interaction in the session as an expression of the background and history of the family. He used no standard set of questions in the initial interview nor formal intake procedure.

Focus on Strengths. Ackerman believed in health and focusing on the strengths of the family. He thought that it was not enough to be a blank screen; the therapist should inject feelings that the patient needs to experience in order to get well.

Family Secrets. When family members become silent about an issue, it usually has pathological meaning. People say more by what they do not say than by what they do say.

Confrontation. The therapist observes family patterns of complementarity, conflict, and coping as well as the symptoms, defenses, and areas of growth of the family. The therapist points out ineffective patterns of coping and defenses that block growth on the part of family members.

Counteracting Scapegoating. The therapist labels scapegoating as a way of reducing anxiety in the family and focuses on the underlying conflict supporting the scapegoating pattern.

Tickling of Defenses. This technique encourages family members to communicate at deeper levels and consists of pointing out the discrepancies between the verbal rationalizations of family members and their non-verbal behaviors, often at unexpected times in the therapy sessions.

Harmony Among Parts or Balance. Ackerman emphasized the ability of each family member to pull oneself together into one piece—a growing harmony of expression in words, feelings, and bodily movements and integration of oneself into social roles.

From *The Psychodynamics of Family Life: Diagnosis and Treatment of Family Relationships* (pp. 41, 61–62, 85–86, 100–104) by N. Ackerman, 1958, New York: Basic Books. Adapted by permission of Basic Books.

3. The therapist plays the role of a parent by being emotionally supportive and nurturing as well as controlling the amount of danger or risk.
4. Using confrontation and interpretation, the therapist undermines resistances and reduces the intensity of anxiety, fear, guilt, anger, shame, and conflict.
5. The therapist acts as a reality-testing machine for family members.
6. The therapist is an educator and model of healthy family functioning.

Nature of the Initial Session.   In typescripts of Ackerman's family therapy sessions, it is clear that the beginning of every session and every initial session was unique. He went wherever the family led him, commenting on what he observed. There was neither a set list of questions nor a standard history. In fact, even when being televised with a family, he adamantly refused to be briefed in advance. He maintained that the family would spontaneously share the most important parts of their individual and collective histories—those that were affecting the present interaction—or would show by their repetitive avoidance the crucial importance of certain topics.

Ackerman's interviews conveyed the depth of emotion to which he guided the family within a session. While following the family, he analyzed the family conflicts and the intrapsychic organization of each family member. By asking open-ended questions and making interpretations of what he observed, he guided the family to discuss deeper and deeper currents of the primary emotional process. By the end of the hour session, he had often touched on one of the key conflicts causing the distress.

Application: Major Therapeutic Techniques

The main techniques used by Ackerman can be found in Table 8–4. He was a master therapist—a pioneer in family therapy.

JOHN ELDERKIN BELL AND THE EVOLUTION OF GROUP FAMILY THERAPY

Prior to World War II, most individual psychotherapy was psychoanalytically oriented. After World War II, there was pressure to apply psychodynamics to group psychotherapy as an economical way of treating returning veterans and chronic patients, such as schizophrenics (Bell, 1975). The next development was the application of psychoanalytic theory to group therapy for natural groups such as families. More recently, such therapeutic approaches have been expanded to multi-family group psychotherapy.

John Elderkin Bell, a psychology professor at Clark University, began to see the entire family as a group in 1951. He presented a report about family group therapy to fellow psychologists in 1953, but it was never published in a national journal. However, because of his early involvement in treating families, Bell is considered a pioneer in the field. His monograph, *Family Group Therapy,* published in 1961, is a founding manuscript in the field of family therapy.

Bell (1972) saw the family as a social group. He applied the principles from the social psychology of groups and psychoanalytically oriented group psychotherapy to the treatment of families. His approach drew from: (1) early work by Bales (1950, 1955), which emphasized the balance sought in groups between implementing the group task and meeting the affiliative needs of the members; (2) concepts from

Lewin's (1951) field theory; (3) the theory of Bion (1961) that dependency, fight-flight, and pairing are the main components of group interaction; and (4) the role of inclusion, control, and affection in the development of a group, as postulated by Schutz (1960)—presently used in his marital therapy assessment instrument, the MATE (Schutz, 1967, 1976). Although Bell applied such social psychology literature to group family therapy, he used such psychoanalytic techniques as interpretation in sessions with families.

In England, Robin Skynner, a psychiatrist well-versed in the theory and use of group psychoanalysis, applied his knowledge to the treatment of married couples and families. He credits his mentorship by Foulkes (1948, 1964), who led his completion of group analysis, as having major impact on the development of his approach. Foulkes and Anthony (1957, 1965) led groups as if they were open systems even though they did not reconcile systems theory with linear psychoanalytic thought in their writings.

Skynner (1976) integrated systems theory with psychoanalytic stages of development (combining the Freudian psychosexual stages with Erikson's psychosocial stages), the phases of object relations (according to Klein), and the developmental stages of group process. Members of groups at first tend to depend on the leader, just as a child in the oral psychosexual stage is dependent upon the mother. After a period of time, resistance appears, and the group members are critical of the leader, just as the child resists toilet training during the anal stage of psychosexual development. In the final developmental stage of group process, the members of the group take more responsibility in a cooperative mode, and the leader serves as a resource, just as the mother plays this role with her child in the genital stage of psychosexual development.

In addition to the intellectual awareness fostered by psychoanalytic techniques, Skynner's approach is based on the implementation of a corrective experience—a nonverbal action that may be accompanied by words, as is often seen in effective group therapy. One characteristic of his approach is his theoretical discussion of gender and sex roles and their effects on marriage and the family. Skynner links pathology in the parents with sexual and marital problems, leading to developmental arrest in the children (according to Erikson's psychosocial stages).

Skynner begins a session as an unstructured group, only introducing himself and meeting other family members. He asks an open-ended question such as "I understand from your phone call that you're having a problem with one of your children. Can you tell me about it?" He follows the lead of the family members and clarifies points that they make, expanding the presenting problem to deeper and deeper levels, noticing who does not speak and what is not said. Questions are then asked to obtain specific information about how, when, and where the problem occurs, patterns of family transactions in managing the symptoms, and how various family members feel about the problem. Questions about interactional patterns in the family of origin and the childhood of the parents will be asked when they have bearing on the natural evolution of the interview.

With about 20 minutes left in the hour session, Skynner has usually gained some insight to make sense out of the session. If the family is educated and articulate, Skynner may share his insight directly by revealing his own fantasy about what is going on and asking the help of the family members in understanding it. If the family needs more direction, Skynner will prescribe an action and, serving as conductor, use his influence to alter the family system directly. Skynner's approach exemplifies the best in the integration of systems theory, group process, and psychoanalytic techniques.

ADLER AND HIS FOLLOWERS

Historical Development

Alfred Adler (1870–1937) was a physician in Vienna, Austria. He was a colleague of Sigmund Freud for more than 8 years and served as president of the Vienna Psycho-analytic Society, which Freud founded. Freud expected strict conformity to his psychoanalytic doctrines, which led Adler to resign from this association in 1911 because he disagreed with Freud on several key issues. In 1912, Adler formed the Society for Individual Psychology, consisting of a number of former members of Freud's association (Dinkmeyer, Dinkmeyer, & Sperry, 1987).

In contrast to Freud, who focused exclusively on individual treatment and emphasized little or no contact with the family members of those in treatment, Adler was concerned with the social institutions that affected children, especially the family and the school. He thought many of the problems that adults brought to therapy were due to inappropriate parenting practices and that changes to a more democratic society had created a mismatch between autocratic parenting and how children actually live within a democratic society. He established a child guidance center in 1922, which led to the eventual creation of 31 centers, most of which were housed in public schools and staffed by psychiatrists trained by Adler. Groups of parents listened to lectures and watched Adler work with volunteers from the audience. Although Adler did not work with individual families, as is now done in family therapy, his emphasis on parenting and the involvement of family members led the way to the use of eclectic techniques and experimentation that fostered the development of the family therapy movement.

After the *Auscluss,* the Nazis occupied Austria and closed the centers. In 1937, Rudolf Dreikurs, a follower of Adler's, emigrated to Chicago, where he began a class for parents at Abraham Lincoln Center in 1939 (Sherman & Dinkmeyer, 1987). After 3 years and the establishment of a number of classes, the center was used as a base for the development of a child guidance clinic. Other centers and clinics were established. The Individual Psychology Association of Chicago was founded in 1947. The Community Child Guidance Center of Chicago was established one year later, eventually sponsoring the creation of new centers across the United States, Europe, Israel, and Canada.

Dinkmeyer applied the work of Adler and Dreikurs to his work with children (Dinkmeyer et al., 1987). Through his writings and the development of instructional kits such as DUSO (Developing Understanding of Self and Others), Dinkmeyer has popularized Adlerian approaches to parenting such as STEP—Systematic Training for Effective Parenting (Dinkmeyer & McKay, 1982)—and STEP/Teen (Dinkmeyer & McKay, 1983). An Adlerian approach to marriage enrichment—Training in Marriage Enrichment (TIME)—was also developed by Dinkmeyer and Carlson (1984). Most recently, Sherman and Dinkmeyer (1987) have developed an Adlerian approach to integrating family therapy systems.

TABLE 8–5 Principles of Adlerian psychology

1. All human beings have feelings of inferiority stemming from early childhood. People act to overcome these feelings of inferiority to obtain feelings of perfection or superiority.

2. All human beings strive to reach an ideal self, which is fictional and in the imagination as a goal to be obtained in the future. Therefore, the future determines the present.

3. Most psychological goals are not known to the self. Adlerian therapists point out the client's purposes and make them known.

4. Human beings have holistic natures with various aspects (emotional, physical, intellectual, unconscious, conscious), all moving toward the ideal self.

5. Human beings subjectively perceive the world and relationships with others through their own apperceptive schema.

6. By understanding the relationships that a person has to others, one can begin to understand the person. To contribute to society, a person must be educated to exhibit and value social interest.

7. Problems of an individual human being become problems for the society and social group.

From *Guiding the Family: Practical Counseling Techniques* (pp. 7–11) by B. B. Grunwald and H. V. McAbee, 1985, Muncie, IN: Accelerated Development. Adapted by permission.

Key Theoretical Concepts

Although he agreed with Freud that what happened to the child in the first 5 years of life could significantly influence outcomes in adult life, Adler believed that human beings could take responsibility to create their own lives by making choices about what they think and do. He focused on the ego, consciousness, and goals.

The basic principles of Adlerian psychology are contained in Table 8–5. Adler saw human beings as acting to implement a unique ideal self to overcome feelings of inferiority from early childhood. His approach was phenomenological: He saw each human being as viewing the world through a unique filter of experiences and goals.

Dreikurs (1971) made significant contributions to Adlerian theory. He especially focused on parenting and asserted that parents pamper children. Pampered children tend to exhibit disturbing behavior in order to belong to a group. There are four goals for misbehavior: getting attention, power, revenge, and assuming a disability. If a child does not receive acceptance and recognition through socially acceptable means, the child will resort to misbehaviors to gain attention. If this does not work, the child will imitate the authority position of the parents and attempt to gain control. If imitation fails, the child seeks revenge through delinquency of some type. If revenge is ineffective, the child feigns a disability and gives up the struggle.

In Adlerian family therapy and parenting groups, parents are taught to study the motivation of their children and help them to meet their goals in positive ways. By giving children encouragement, parents can help them to grow, to develop social interest, and to be happy, successful adults.

View of Healthy Functioning

The healthy family from an Adlerian point of view uses many democratic processes. Each person plays a different role that contributes to a well-functioning whole. Positions and functions can change over time on the basis of negotiation. Each family member has a voice in decisions. The couple holds meetings to discuss their interests. Family meetings are held to work through family issues. The parents are leaders. Children are expected to carry out chores appropriate to their age levels (Sherman & Dinkmeyer, 1987).

The Therapeutic Process

Role of the Therapist. The therapist is very optimistic and directive, asking open-ended questions, encouraging the family, and modeling the parental role for the adults (setting limits while providing emotional support).

Nature of the Initial Session. Therapists establish rapport, gather information, focus on the main issues, generate alternatives, recommend corrective measures, encourage the family, and summarize the session. To obtain information, the family counselor often asks questions about the family constellation and the typical family day.

In traditional Adlerian family work, the parents were seen separately from the children, who were interviewed after the parents. Often the two interviews were watched by people who had come to observe and to learn how to become better parents. In the recent evolution of Adlerian family counseling to Adlerian family therapy, the entire family is interviewed at the same time.

Application: Major Therapeutic Techniques

Mosak and Shulman (1988) developed the Life Style Inventory to gather information about the family constellation, early recollections, blocks to goals, and strengths of the individual through a structured interview. Such questions can be used to obtain information from individual family members in initial or subsequent sessions (Shulman & Mosak, 1988). Key techniques of Adlerian therapy are contained in Table 8–6.

PSYCHOANALYTICALLY ORIENTED MARITAL THERAPY

One of the major applications of psychoanalytic theory has been the proliferation of psychodynamically based approaches to marital therapy. Most of these approaches are based largely on the work of neo-Freudian object relations theorists.

Key Theoretical Concepts

Object Relations Theory. Object relations is the bridge between individual psychoanalytic treatment and psychoanalytically oriented family therapy. Adults who present for family therapy are often fixated or stuck at an earlier stage of development of the introjects, which interferes with their abilities to form and maintain relationships based on a realistic appraisal of the spouse as a separate and distinct person (object). Various theorists have proposed diverse stages for the development of object relations

TABLE 8–6 Key techniques of Adlerian therapy

Family constellation. Information is obtained regarding the birth order of each family member; siblings; relationships to and between parents; physical, academic, sexual/gender, and social development in childhood; the family climate; additional parental models; and life meanings in childhood. The role of the adult is often formed by the birth order and influence of the personalities of siblings and parents.

Early recollections. Each family member is asked to share eight memories from early childhood, which are analyzed according to theme and developmental maturity. Often family members construct such memories, but they are still very helpful in identifying the unconscious psychological goals of the person and the ideal self.

Typical day. Parents or other family members are asked to detail specific events in a complete typical day.

Encouragement. Techniques are used conveying respect and equality, such as understanding, having faith in a family member, asking for help, using logical consequences, honesty, the right to make decisions, setting goals, the right to give encouragement, consistency, and encouraging words.

Paradoxical intention. The therapist assigns the repetition of the symptom as a homework assignment.

Use of family council. A family meeting is held on a regular basis in which all family members participate in the discussion of issues so that each person's views are taken into consideration in making decisions.

Use of logical or natural consequences. Parents are taught how to use natural consequences with their children without arguing or criticizing them. For example, a child who is continually late may miss going to the movie because the family went on time.

Confrontation. The therapist points out mistaken personal logic.

From *Guiding the Family: Practical Counseling Techniques* (pp. 67–68) by B. B. Grunwald and H. V. McAbee, 1985, Muncie, IN: Accelerated Development. Adapted by permission.

formed by interpersonal interactions with significant others (objects) in early childhood (Table 8–7).

Klein (1948) was the first theorist to espouse object relations theory. In England she observed mother-infant interaction and maintained that infants were oriented toward objects (people) from birth. Rather than mastering id drives, she saw the infant using fantasy to make contact with the mother and the environment by the use of two defense mechanisms (unconscious ways of defending against anxiety): projective identification and splitting.

The baby splits bodily sensations into opposites, such as pain and pleasure or good and bad. Through splitting, the baby can separate an unwanted quality of the self and can divide an object such as the mother into several objects with separate polarized qualities—"a good mother" and "a bad mother."

During the paranoid-schizoid period of development, the infant attempts to become part of the mother's body by using projective identification, in which the self unconsciously transfers a split-off part of the self through fantasy to another object so

TABLE 8–7 The contributions of object relations theorists

Theorist	Contribution
Klein (1948)	First theorist to propose object relations theory. Infant oriented toward objects (people) from birth. Defense mechanisms of splitting and projective identification. Two stages of object relations—paranoid-schizoid position and depressive position.
Fairbairn (1952)	Considered founder of object relations school. Deepest need of all human beings is for a loving parent figure.
Winnicott (1965)	"Good enough mother"—not overly involved but not neglectful.
Mahler (1968, 1975)	Four stages of the development of object relations: autism, symbiosis, separation individuation, and on-the-way-to-object-constancy.
Guntrip (1968)	Explained the development and treatment of the schizoid position.
Kernberg (1975)	Three stages of object relations—fused self-other, separated self-other (either all good or all bad), and object constancy (object is both good and bad.
Kohut (1977)	Mirroring responses by parents in early childhood lead to cohesive self.
Ables with Brandsma (1977)	Applied object relations theory to assessment of readiness for marital therapy and to couples treatment.
Slipp (1984)	Applied object relations theory to diverse patterns of transactions in the family of origin, leading to specific pathological diagnoses and treatment plans for individual and family therapy.
Masterson (1985, 1988)	Development of therapy for borderline patients—confront defenses, work through abandonment depression, and communicative matching for real self.
Scharff and Scharff (1987)	Developed a particular style of family therapy that applies object relations theory to family treatment—object relations family therapy.
Nichols (1987)	Applied object relations theory to family therapy and wrote *The Self in the System: Expanding the Limits of Family Therapy*.

the object is seen as having the unwanted quality, or the self controls the object or merges into the stronger object to avoid feelings of helplessness (a sense of oneness with the object or mother). The infant feels omnipotent and is part-object re-lated—not able to see others as separate, whole, unique human beings.

If an infant does not receive appropriately timed nurturing from the mother, the adult may be fixated at the paranoid-schizoid position. The adult experiences anger toward someone and splits the anger to project it onto the boss, seeing the boss as angry at him rather than vice versa. This protects the person from anxiety and damage to self-esteem at the expense of reality. Another example is the adult who dates someone and idealizes her as a "good mother," then suddenly devalues her as the "bad mother." He is unable to see positive and negative qualities in the same person at the same time.

During the next stage of development according to Klein, the depressive position, the child is able to see others as whole objects. Mother is seen as both frustrating and comforting. The infant mourns its object when out of sight and shows guilt as well as concern for having destroyed the object, if even temporarily. Through projective identification the child sees the mother as omnipotent and idealizes her, attempting to merge with her in symbiosis.

Another object relations theorist who has influenced marital and family therapy is Mahler (1968, 1975). She delineates four developmental stages: autism, symbiosis, separation-individuation, and on-the-way-to-object-constancy. Ables with Brandsma (1977) applied Mahler's theory in their approach to marital therapy, especially in establishing contraindications for marital treatment. They indicated that couples in which one or both members are fixated at the autistic stage are not candidates for marital therapy because it would be too anxiety-producing and too threatening to their self-esteem. Such couples use the defense mechanism of projection (blaming) almost continuously and have splitting defenses. Likewise marital therapy is contraindicated for the symbiotic couple in which one spouse calls the other 20 times a day to be sure that the spouse is there. However, marital therapy can produce positive outcomes for couples at Mahler's separation-individuation stage. Spouses fixated at this stage can form object relationships, that is, endow another human being with object libido.

The Application of Object Relations Theory to Marriage

People actually marry individuals whose object relations are familiar, even though they may be painful. For example, a woman grows up with a narcissistic father who must always be right and win every argument. Her father blames everyone else for any problems he might have (projection). However, he is kind to her, much more so than her mother, and she idealizes him, consulting him about every decision. When this woman attends college, she meets a man who seems very strong to her. He can argue any issue and put anyone down, except her. She is very attracted to him. At an unconscious level he may have similar introjects to her father and function at the same level of object relations. It is not until after they are married that she becomes upset when her husband blames her for every family problem.

Psychoanalytically oriented marital therapists might label such a couple as an example of "interlocking pathologies" (Ackerman, 1956). The man may be classified, according to the DSM III-R, as having a narcissistic personality disorder, while the wife may be diagnosed as having a histrionic or borderline personality disorder, depending upon the consistency of her defenses. He married her because he needed someone to gratify his narcissistic self object and to see him as a father object prior to marriage. After about 2 years, however, she expressed some differences, and she became a bad object for him, a critical mother. Therefore, he blamed her to protect his self-esteem from perceived criticism, at which point she perceived him as a bad father object from whom she wanted to escape by divorce. As long as both played out their pathological patterns during the romantic illusion stage of marriage, they were inseparable (interlocking pathologies). Such a couple may separate, but they are more likely to repeat the patterns from their families of origin, living out their object relations as a "gruesome twosome," stuck together by painful but familiar patterns.

Major contributors to psychoanalytically oriented approaches to marital therapy are presented in Table 8–8. Dicks (1967), a psychiatrist at the Tavistock Clinic in London, began his work with married couples at a special unit established at the clinic just for couples. He explained interlocking pathology through the use of object relations theory. His model of marriage was comprised of three marital levels or subsystems: (1) the public subsystem, (2) the central ego subsystem, and (3) the unconscious subsystem.

The public level includes the cultural components and values associated with education and social class that are readily apparent to the average person. People tend to marry at similar social levels. The second level, or central ego subsystem, consists of the conscious expectations the mates have for the marriage based on personal experiences. The third level, or unconscious subsystem, is comprised of part-objects and split-off parts of the selves of the spouses—negative aspects of their object relations. It is this third level that corresponds to Ackerman's theory of interlocking pathology.

For example, a woman who has learned to fear the expression of angry feelings never asserts herself. Her husband is very assertive and, at an unconscious level, she continues to see herself as a "good girl" who never becomes angry. This system may work well temporarily, but the longer the couple uses the system, the more dysfunctional it becomes. The wife becomes more passive with time and is unable to deal with her own affairs without the help of her husband. The husband tires of handling all of the confrontations and does not allow himself to be vulnerable, which is necessary in intimate relationships. The personality of each spouse becomes more rigid over time.

The Therapeutic Process

Although there are variations in technique from one psychoanalytically oriented contributor to another, a number of similarities often exist. A discussion of some of these similarities follows, although all contributors to psychoanalytically oriented couples work do not exhibit all of the following characteristics.

Telephone Contact. The tone of the therapeutic relationship is often set by the initial telephone contact, which is often between the spouse requesting help and the therapist, rather than a secretary. The therapist should set limits to clarify the rules and frame of the relationship. For example, a therapist should hold fast to the commitment to only see the couple. The therapist should not see an individual concerning marital problems with the intent of later involving the spouse. In agreeing to do this, the therapist makes a covert pact with the phoning spouse, which undermines the goal of equal alliance with each spouse.

The anticipated frame of the therapy should be clearly stated (cost, frequency, length of session, and required paper work) so that the calling spouse knows what is expected and can decline if such expectations cannot be met. Sometimes therapists will ask about the referral source and any prior history of therapy and request a short statement about the nature of the problem before agreeing to see a couple.

TABLE 8—8 Contributors to psychoanalytically oriented couples therapy

Dicks (1967)	British psychiatrist whose model of marriage included three levels: public, central ego, and unconscious.
Sager (1976)	Popularized idea of each spouse's contract in the marriage on three levels: verbalized, conscious but unverbalized, and unconscious. Each spouse has conscious expectations, biological/psychological needs, and externals to be gained as well as biological/intrapsychic determinants. Encouraged spouses to write down what is desired from the partner and what they are willing to give in exchange, leading to renegotiation of a new contract for the marriage.
Martin (1976)	Asked spouses to share earliest memories and also focused on the contract of the marriage, including the unconscious level of fantasies and dreams.
Ables with Brandsma (1977)	Used object relations theoretical base upon which they build the model of negotiation, communication, and re-education.
Bowen (1978)	Developed the genogram to obtain information about the family history. Believes in multi-generational transmission of problems and themes. Works only with the couple, using the therapeutic triangle in which each spouse talks to the therapist in turn.
Wile (1981)	Saw each spouse as deprived and validated inner experiences so that spouses could make unconscious needs conscious in their direct requests, which reduced the role of collusion.
Paul and Paul (1975)	Emphasized the role of unresolved grieving in marital therapy due to a death that has not been faced.
Framo (1982)	Used couples group therapy to normalize the process of analyzing object relations and to prepare for a family of origin session.
Strean (1985)	Linked mating patterns and common marital conflicts with fixation at diverse, psychosexual stages and specific relationship patterns of treatment for each pattern of fixation, including vignettes of how to handle the psychodynamics of each pattern based on years of clinical experience.
Beavers (1985)	Linked psychoanalytic concepts at the individual system level with systems concept at the marital dyad level with healthy family functioning.
Guerin, Fay, Burden, and Kaulto (1987)	A four-stage method of marital treatment, ranging from low conflict, to significant conflict, to sudden changes/turbulence, to seeing an attorney, which includes specific techniques tailored to the particular stage, based upon Bowenian principles of triangulation.
Nichols (1988)	An integrative approach to marital therapy that combined systems thinking with the object relations schools and social learning theory.

The Nature of the Initial Interview.   Most psychoanalytically oriented practitioners begin the initial interview by establishing rapport with the couple by joint introductions and with a mention of the nature of any telephone contact or referral information that the therapist has gained. An open-ended question may be used to begin the interview such as "Can you tell me a little bit about what brings you here?" Then the therapist, in an unstructured manner, observes who answers the question, who remains silent, who interrupts, and what nonverbal communication occurs.

The therapist can then clarify responses and ask open-ended questions to obtain more information and to balance the involvement of each spouse. The therapist is active and directive, maintaining a safe holding environment for the couple. A history of the relationship may be obtained either by weaving questions in as they relate to the presenting problem or by directly asking questions of each spouse in turn. Questions about the family of origin are asked as they relate to the material discussed.

The therapist often asks the couple to negotiate by discussing expectations, what attracted them, and how the presenting problem relates to their unconscious expectations. By bringing unconscious material into awareness, spouses can negotiate more effectively.

Often the therapist picks up a theme for the session or for the relationship and expresses it as a summary. A trial interpretation may be made linking the presenting problem to patterns in the family of origin.

A review of the frame, including items such as the fee, frequency of sessions, length of sessions, past therapy, and referral source, is made, and dates are set for future appointments.

A psychoanalytically oriented marital therapist conducts an initial interview with a couple.

The Contract.   Most psychoanalytically oriented approaches to couples therapy dwell on bringing unconscious expectations into awareness and encouraging negotiation of shared expectations. Sager (1976, 1981) developed a therapeutic system for making unconscious agreements conscious. He stated that each spouse has a contract in the marriage with three levels: the verbalized, the conscious but unverbalized, and the unconscious. Usually each spouse's contract differs from the other's to some degree and may change over the life span, requiring re-negotiation.

In Sager's approach, each spouse is asked to study a list of expectations of marriage, a list of biological/psychological needs, and a list of externals to be gained. The spouse is asked to write down at the end of each list what is desired from the partner in that area and what the spouse is willing to give in exchange. The therapist orients the couple toward the task of formulating one single contract between them from their disparate individual contracts. Sessions focus on areas of discrepancy between the individual contracts until either compromise is possible or one spouse chooses to meet a need outside of the relationship (Sager & Hunt, 1979).

The Therapeutic Alliance.   In subsequent sessions, the therapist is careful to balance interventions between spouses. The therapist should remain curious about the family background and individual characteristics of each spouse. If the therapist feels bored with either spouse, this may signal that the therapist is allying with one spouse against the other, which will sabotage therapy.

Working Through.   As a couple works in therapy, more and more work is done on introjects from childhood, which are played out in the transactions between spouses in the session. When spouses begin to realize that they project unrealistic patterns onto the spouse, they appreciate the uniqueness of the spouse and who the spouse really is. For example, a wife may learn that she interprets questions her husband asks out of interest as criticism because of a pattern with her father, who constantly found fault with her. She becomes more receptive to her husband's questioning, and the relationship becomes stronger.

Termination.   Issues of separation and loss arise as the termination date of therapy is set. Fears of abandonment surface and are discussed. Since ends typically mirror death, it is not unusual for death of loved ones to be brought up by one or both spouses. Through grieving, the processes of internalization are strengthened.

THERAPEUTIC OUTCOMES

Outcome studies are difficult to carry out in marital and family therapy treatment. This is particularly true for approaches that are spontaneous and tailored to the specific defenses and ego functioning of the family as psychoanalytically oriented approaches are. Without a training manual or set protocol, it is difficult to carry out scientifically rigorous outcome research. No recent journal articles have been found on outcome studies of psychoanalytically oriented marital and family therapy.

The SASB system of Benjamin (1979) offers promise as an assessment tool prior to and following treatment. Perhaps as this is applied more widely and systematically to the actual selection of specific family therapy techniques, meaningful outcome data for psychoanalytically oriented family therapy approaches will result.

CONTRIBUTIONS AND LIMITATIONS

The first books in the field of family therapy—*The Family in Psychotherapy* by Midelfort (1957) and *The Psychodynamics of Family Life* by Ackerman (1958)—were by psychoanalytically trained psychiatrists who applied the concepts of psychoanalytic theory to their work with families. Without the pioneering efforts of the "grandfather of family therapy," Nathan Ackerman, and other psychoanalytically oriented practitioners, family therapy may not have taken hold. They helped to legitimize it as a therapeutic modality within mental health practice, an innovative American experiment that worked.

One monumental contribution that will continue to be an area of future exploration is the application of object relations theory to family therapy. As clinicians become more adept at translating intrapsychic introjects into interpersonal transactions played out in the family therapy session and vice versa, they can assist family members to work through outdated objects and split-off parts of the self to change internal introjects and to accept other family members as they really are rather than as people from the past. Object relations theory provides a bridge between individual and family treatment that makes sense and works.

One of the more recent contributions has been the application of psychoanalytically oriented approaches to marital therapy, especially in long-term treatment. Often as the relationship improves between spouses, the problems of children in the family abate.

One of the main limitations of psychoanalytically oriented approaches to family therapy is the emphasis on an analytic linear model. Although a number of theorists maintain that they have combined psychoanalytic concepts with systems theory, there is still an emphasis on the intrapsychic make-up of the individual in psychoanalytically oriented approaches. Proponents of these approaches claim that changing such internal processes in the individuals is the only way to long-lasting change in the family as a whole. Other approaches may show impressive short-term results, but family members regress after a period of time because their internal introjects have not changed.

Nichols (1988), Allen (1988), and others strongly recommend that the self be seen as a subsystem of the family. In this way, psychoanalytic approaches to marital and family therapy that also combine a systemic view of the family can be viewed as true systems theories.

Another limitation is the lack of recent specific outcome studies of particular psychoanalytically oriented approaches to marital and family therapy. Since the approach is often tailored to the specific level of ego functioning of the family, it is difficult to specify a particular protocol and link outcome with a routine treatment regimen. The work of Benjamin (1979) may be helpful in future outcome studies of psychoanalytically oriented approaches.

SUMMARY

Psychoanalytically oriented approaches to marital and family therapy focus on the past, especially what happened in early childhood between the child and the parents or caregivers. Through interactions with each parent in the family of origin, the child forms introjects of the self and the objects, such as parents, that comprise the intrapsychic structure and serve as mechanisms by which the individual creates relationships through transactions in the present with family members and the therapist.

Psychoanalytically oriented therapists often make interpretations—statements connecting patterns of interaction with family members in the session to interactional patterns with the parents in early childhood and with the therapist. Such interpretations lead to insight and are one of the main sources of healing.

In the 1950s, the "grandfather of family therapy," Nathan Ackerman, a child psychoanalyst, started the first fully licensed mental health unit for families in the United States at the Jewish Family Service in New York City. He is noted for the following concepts: complementarity; conflict and coping; scapegoating; and symptom, defense, and growth. In his therapy, as in all psychoanalytically oriented therapy, each session has a theme, and often there is a theme for a family that is consistent across sessions.

John Elderkin Bell, a psychology professor at Clark University, was a pioneer in the field who applied the principles of group analytic therapy to family treatment. Robin Skynner, in England, also developed a solid family therapy approach, integrating group treatment concepts with systems theory.

Alfred Adler emphasized responsibility and choice in moving toward the self ideal to compensate for feelings of inferiority. In 1922 he began the first child guidance clinic. Dreikurs brought Adler's approach to America, where it flourished in Chicago and was exported around the world. Recently, Don Dinkmeyer has applied their work to the development of Adlerian family therapy, which emphasizes encouragement. Some techniques include the family constellation, early recollections, typical day, and the family council.

Based on her research on mother-child interactions, Melanie Klein proposed object relations theory. Her theory states that infants focus on people (objects) from birth. They make contact with their mothers through fantasy by using projective identification (merging into the mother) and splitting ("good mother" and "bad mother"). If infants do not receive appropriate nurturing, they remain fixated at this low level of object relations in adult life. Scharff and Scharff are noted for object relations family therapy. Many psychoanalytically oriented marital therapists have based their clinical work on object relations theory.

The goal of psychoanalytically oriented marital and family therapy is to make the unconscious patterns of object relations conscious so family members can become aware of them and can choose to change them. The therapist plays the role of the "good enough" parent to provide effective parenting for family members who have deficits in object relations.

EXERCISES

1. Your instructor will divide the class into pairs. When the professor directs you, turn to the student next to you and explain the Progressive Abreactive Regression (PAR) model of healthy marital functioning proposed by Kirschner and Kirschner in *Comprehensive Family Therapy*. Reverse roles and listen as your partner explains the model to you. What is a healthy family from a psychoanalytically oriented perspective?

2. Probes or open-ended questions are one of the key tools used by psychoanalytically oriented therapists. During this exercise, you will practice asking open-ended questions. Count off according to the instructions of your instructor. One person will play the role of therapist. Two people will play the role of a married couple. The fourth person will be the observer. The couple should make up a presenting problem for marital ther-

apy. The "therapist" should begin to ask open-ended questions (see sections in this chapter on initial sessions) while the observer takes notes on the Observer Form provided by the instructor. The best sessions focus on one or two main themes. Follow the instructions of your professor. When the instructor says to stop, the observer should share feedback about the open-ended questions. If time permits, rotate into other roles as directed by your instructor.

3. In the following case studies, identify the level of anxiety, the defense mechanisms being used, the object relations, the stage of psychosexual development, and the theme for each family member. Design a tentative treatment plan in each case.

Case #1. Geraldine was a social worker who worked with victims of sexual abuse. She presented with her ex-husband, Fred, because they were considering remarriage. When Dr. Thorne asked Fred to share a history of their relationship—how they met, dating, what had created problems—Fred refused to talk. Geraldine spoke for him, saying that they had met at a bar, had dated for about 2 months, usually dancing at a local bistro, and that Fred's drinking had caused the break-up of the marriage. However, Fred was a good provider and the best man she had ever had. Fred refused to comment. Geraldine said that she was jealous and wondered who Fred had been with since their divorce. Fred did not speak. Sex had been great with Fred. Geraldine would tie him to the bed post and found it exciting. Fred said nothing. Geraldine had been raped by neighborhood boys when she was a young teenager, but did not trust her mother enough to tell her. She said that Fred was the youngest child in the family and was worshiped by his mother. His dad was an alcoholic who never talked much.

Case #2. Juanita had been divorced three times. Now, at the age of 43, she brought her fourth husband, Harold, in for marriage counseling because she wanted to make this one work. She complained bitterly about her past. She could not understand how she had chosen such selfish men. When she was a child, her parents gave her anything she wanted. She was the apple of their eyes. A history of her relationship with Harold revealed that he was a wealthy businessman who had provided well for every physical need. Now that they had been married 2 years Harold had asked her to entertain a few of his business

friends and their wives with the help of their servants. In addition, he was talking about having children. Now that the romantic illusions had worn off, Juanita saw these as intolerable demands and wondered if she had married another selfish man. Harold was the oldest child in his family. When his father died, he had taken care of his mother and stepped into his father's shoes. He never expected anything in return from his mother, who was so withdrawn in grief that she could not function, but it would be different with his wife. Meekly, he told Dr. Thorne that he would understand if Juanita left him and wondered what he could do to keep her.

4. Your professor will model several trial interpretations for you. When making interpretations, think of a triangle that links patterns from early childhood with patterns toward present significant others with patterns toward the therapist. An interpretation is a statement which connects any two points of the triangle or all three.

Picture yourself as the therapist doing marital therapy with the following couple. What interpretations might you make?

Mrs. Dunn came from a family in which her father continually blamed her mother for everything that didn't go well. No matter what her mother did, her father would chastise her. Mr. Dunn is a meek and gentle man who has been married to Mrs. Dunn for 30 years. In the middle of the session, Mr. Dunn sits back quietly and tunes out. Suddenly Mrs. Dunn attacks him verbally saying, "Pay attention. You're ruining this therapy just like you do everything in our relationship. It's all your fault that our marriage has become what it is." She then turns to you and says, "I knew we should have gone to the more expensive therapist. I can tell that you don't know what you're doing to let him just sit there. Do something."

5. On a piece of notebook paper, write down four of your earliest memories. If none come to mind, construct some plausible events. Analyze the themes of these early recollections. What do they have in common? Do they give you hints about the theme or meaning of your life? If your instructor directs, turn to the student seated next to you and share whatever you would like to share. You may choose not to participate in this exercise.

Chapter 9
Intergenerational Theorists

*The one most important goal of family systems therapy is to help family members toward a better level of "differentiation of self."
. . . In any course of therapy it has been routine to encourage each spouse to work systematically toward the differentiation of self in the family of origin.*

Bowen, 1978, pp. 529-30.

Certain marital therapists who were originally trained psychoanalytically or psychodynamically have made profound impacts on the field because they have linked the resolution of marital difficulties to differentiation from and direct work with the family of origin. For this reason, the unique therapeutic approaches of Murray Bowen and James Framo are highlighted here. Bowen restricted his work to couples therapy. Framo sees couples, encouraging them to move toward couples group therapy in preparation for each spouse's individual meeting with the family of origin. Although Boszormenyi-Nagy's contextual therapy can be applied to individuals, couples, or the whole family, it is also considered in this group because of its characteristic emphasis on themes of justice emanating from the family of origin and past generations.

MURRAY BOWEN

Historical Development

While he was affiliated with the Menninger Clinic as a psychiatrist, Murray Bowen became interested in and observed informally the families of his patients (Kerr, 1981; Kerr & Bowen, 1988). In 1954, he went to the National Institute of Mental Health in Washington, where he was funded to conduct research on the families of schizo-

Dr. Murray Bowen created the genogram, an effective technique for studying the families of origin of a couple during marital therapy. (Courtesy of Andrea Malony-Schara)

phrenics. Bowen called his theory family systems theory, but it is not related to Bertalanffy's general systems theory. In treating family systems with a schizophrenic member, Bowen requested that the families move into the hospital setting and live there. Observation and treatment of the family unit living at the hospital formed the basis of his conceptualizations of the family system as a natural system and how it changes to a more open system with stronger, healthier individuals.

After the completion of the grant, Bowen continued his research on an out-patient basis at Georgetown University. In 1978, he wrote *Family Therapy in Clinical Practice,* a compilation of his research papers and clinical work with families over a 20-year period, which demonstrates the evolution of his family systems theory from 1957 to 1978.

Key Theoretical Concepts

Bowen theory contains two main variables: degree of anxiety and degree of self-integration. Most organisms can adapt to acute anxiety of short duration. However, chronic anxiety over long periods of time can lead to differentiation of self or to physical illness, emotional symptoms, or social delinquency. This anxiety is infectious and can spread to other members of the family. People can seem normal at one level of anxiety and ill or abnormal at more intense levels of anxiety.

Self-Differentiation.   People can be categorized on a continuum according to the amount of fusion between thinking and feeling. At one end of the continuum is fusion (whatever intellectual functioning of which the person is capable is dominated by emotion). At the other pole is differentiation (intellectual functioning is relatively autonomous even in periods of crisis). Distinguishing differentiation from the intellectualization often found in neurotics, Bowen said that the solid self is formed by the calm use of logical reasoning over time for the decisions of life rather than inconsistent, random verbalizations that sound like intellectual thought but are not.

Bowen observed whether an individual said "I feel that" rather than "I think" when asked for an opinion or belief and ranked the person on a scale from 0 to 100. Those who responded "I feel that" are focused more on the feeling state, the pseudo-self, and relationships. They have lower scores on the scale and are capable of making only vague long-term goals. Such people focus on keeping harmony in their present relationships which are dependent, have failed and moved from one crisis to another, or have given up.

At the next level of differentiation, people use another authority to back up their opinions rather than holding to an "I" position. At the next level of good differentiation people have more of a sense of solid self. They can participate in emotional situations because they know they can use logical reasoning to extricate themselves if necessary. They may have times in which they are lax and let emotion take over as an automatic pilot, but if trouble develops, the solid self can take over, lessen the anxiety, and prevent a life crisis.

These individuals can follow their own independently chosen life goals. In contrast to "rugged individualism," which Bowen views as a psuedo-self fighting against fusion, well-differentiated individuals are aware of the relationship system and other human beings around them.

Triangulation.   When a two-person dyad is calm, it is stable. However, when anxiety arises, a vulnerable person is involved to form a triangle, the smallest relationship system that is stable, according to Bowen (1978). When tensions become too great in this triangle, others are recruited to form interlocking triangles. Usually a triangle is made up of two people who are close and a less close outsider. Under moderate stress, two sides of the triangle are comfortable and one is conflicted. If the triangulation pattern is repeated in a family, family members take on fixed roles in response to each other rather than differentiating as separate people.

The mother-father-child triangle is the most common example of this in the family system. Conflict and tension between the parents may result in the most vulnerable child being triangled in the system. For example, when mom cannot solve an on-going problem with dad, she begins to confide in her youngest son about how awful dad is. At first, the son refuses to listen, but after a time, he listens and finally begins to take mom's side in the arguments between mom and dad. The son is triangled in the system and begins to function only as a role, not as a separate person.

The concept of triangulation in the family system has been useful for explaining many symptoms in the family. For example, Kellerman and Kellerman (1985) point out that a bottle of alcohol can be triangled between a husband and wife (Figure 9–1). When problems arise, the couple do not know how to resolve them. They bicker continuously, which is painful for the husband. He drinks to reduce the tension and numb the pain, triangling the bottle into the marriage.

A daughter can be triangled between her father and mother. When they fight, she intervenes, trying to stop them. In addition, she can be fused to one of her parents such as her mother (see Figure 9–1). When her parents are in conflict, her mother experiences pain and the daughter hurts, too, without her mother ever talking to her about it. Such fused triangulations can be excruciating.

Nuclear Family Emotional System. In one generation, the family emotional pattern can be described by the "nuclear family emotional system" according to Bowen (1978). Two people meet and marry, developing emotional patterns between them based on the levels of differentiation from their families of origin. The manner in which the courtship and marriage planning process is carried out predicts the degree of future problems. Human beings tend to choose marital partners who are differentiated at the same levels.

Most adults have the closest relationships during the courtship phase. At the time of the marriage, two pseudo-selves merge into a common self. The less differentiated the people are, the greater the degree of fusion. One becomes more dominant and the other more adaptive. If both attempt to be dominant, conflict arises. If both attempt to be adaptive, no decisions can be made.

Fusion creates anxiety, as one or both spouses experience a sense of loss of self. Ways of reducing this anxiety include emotional distance, marital conflict, sickness of one spouse, and projection of the anxiety and difficulties to one or more of the children. Although marital conflict may appear painful to the spouses, it requires much emotional intensity and reduces the anxiety, often preventing problems in the children. Sometimes the anxiety is relieved by one spouse becoming ill and the other spouse taking care of the person. These marriages are enduring. If the spouses are harmonious and healthy, often the anxiety is reflected in the serious impairment of a child, as in the case of autistic children. If problems shift from one method to another, the probability of major dysfunction is lessened. If the family projection process is focused on one member, a lower level of differentiation is passed on to the next generation.

Emotional Cutoff. All human beings have unresolved attachments to parental figures, but if people handle separating from the families by running away, isolating and withdrawing, or denying the importance of the family of origin, an emotional cutoff has occurred. The therapeutic task is to modify this cutoff into a logical, step-by-step self-differentiation from the family. The more emotional contact between generations, the fewer symptoms there are for both generations, especially if a person has worked and continues to work at differentiating the true self in the family of origin.

Multigenerational Transmission Process. Bowen (1978) theory maintains that the emotional adjustment of the family is transmitted across generations. A child who has

FIGURE 9–1 Examples of triangles

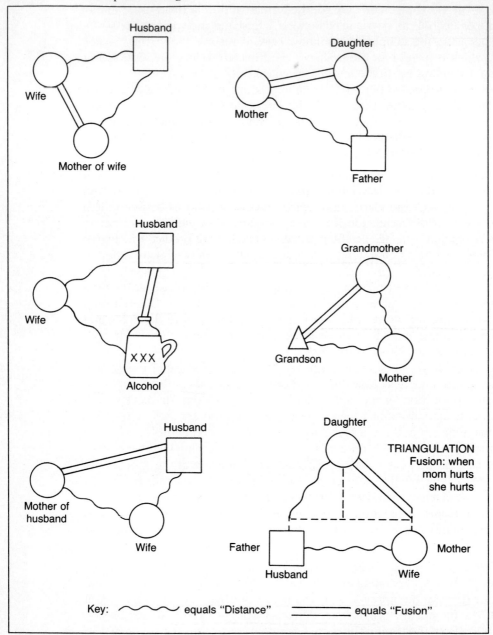

From *Diagrams of Triangles* by E. Schroeder, 1987, Rutgers Univ.: Summer School of Alcohol Studies. Adapted by permission.

been the focus of the projection process of the family has a lower level of differentiation from the family, usually a poorer adjustment to life, and will usually cut off (have no contact with the family), providing an even lower level of differentiation in the next generation. After many generations of this pattern, a schizophrenic will appear, representing the lowest level of differentiation. Likewise a child who has not been the object of the family projection process will usually have a higher level of differentiation, which will be passed on to the next generation of the family.

Children who are only slightly involved with the parents exhibit levels of differentiation similar to those of the parents. Consistency of emotional functioning across generations is typical. Individuals with higher levels of differentiation will usually come from family lines where people have been successful and well differentiated.

Sibling Positions. Bowen (1978) adopted Toman's work (1961) on the personalities of people born in different birth orders. Some of the characteristics usually attributed to people born in various sibling positions include the following:

1. Only: high achieving, feelings of being special, center of attention, does not need to share, very serious, relates easily to adults, experiences no competition, learns to use creativity in time alone, isolated, lonely, more introverted, less of an opportunity to gain social skills, often triangled into parental conflict, focus of realistic/unrealistic parental expectations.
2. Oldest: overachieving, perfectionistic, responsible, rescuing, wants to please parents and often fulfills their needs, jealous of siblings (especially those of same sex), difficult to express own needs, may minimize feelings, may put others first, compliant/rebellious, relationships are easier with adults, acts an example.
3. Middle: thinks that parents did not give enough love, seeks approval, may not feel "good enough," feels compared to siblings, often in middle between parents, may be born a sex different from what parents had wanted, seeks more attention by proving oneself.
4. Youngest: feels loved, sometimes spoiled, protected, receives more because family was usually better off, feels closer to and responsible for parents, identity issues, self-centered, jealous, outgoing, fewer photographs than other siblings, always the "baby" of the family (Schroeder, 1987b).

Marriages have a higher probability of long-term stability if a person marries a partner from a compatible birth order, such as an oldest son with a younger sister marrying the youngest daughter with an older brother (see Toman, 1988).

If a child's personality does not meet the characteristics typically determined by birth order, Bowen postulated that it was due to the family projection system. For example, an oldest child who has been triangled between the parents may have more of the characteristics of a youngest child. This provides a guide as to how the projection process is transmitted across generations. A calm oldest child who functions responsibly bodes well for future generations.

View of Healthy Functioning

Families become healthier when individual family members are able to differentiate as separate selves while staying in contact with the family ego mass. This means that each child develops a person-to-person relationship with each parent. The child shares thoughts and feelings about the self in the relationship with each parent. The parent also communicates introspective, personal thoughts and feelings about the self rather than about a third person or an object. Both spouses develop such a person-to-person relationship with each other.

In addition, as an individual family member focuses on career plans and pursuing life goals, that is, the essence of differentiation, the individual can "detriangle" and remain emotionally disengaged to the negative reactions of other family members. Such negative emotional reactions on the part of other family members are to be expected and are signs that the individual is actually differentiating.

Regardless of age, the more an individual can differentiate in the family of origin, the better adjusted that person will become, as will the other people who are in meaningful relationships with that person. Work on the primary triangle (parents and child) reverberates through the system of interlocking triangles that comprise the family emotional system, leading to higher levels of differentiation in the individual family members within the triangles.

The Therapeutic Process

Goals of Therapy.   The main goal of Bowenian therapy is to assist one or more members of the family to move to a greater level of self-differentiation.

Role of the Therapist.   To Bowen, emotional triangles were basic. Therefore, he preferred to work with the couple alone, forming a triangle composed of the therapist and the two spouses. He encouraged each spouse to detriangle by establishing a person-to-person relationship with the therapist in front of the observing partner.

The spouse learns to communicate thoughts and feelings about the self separately by saying "I feel" and "I think." Rather than talking or gossiping about a third person, the spouse focuses on self and the relationship of the self to the therapist.

Use of Diagnosis and Assessment.   The family evaluation interview is conducted with one family member or the married couple. The format of the interview has three parts: (1) the presenting problem, (2) the nuclear family, and (3) the extended families. Historical data are collected in each of these areas (Kerr, 1981; Kerr & Bowen, 1988). From analyzing patterns, the therapist can determine how any undifferentiation was handled in the extended families—that is, through marital tension, the dysfunction of a spouse or a child, or other means.

Nature of the Initial Session.   Typically the initial session consists of the family evaluation interview. In the beginning, it is important for the family therapist to listen as the family members tell their story about the symptoms. Questions can be asked to clarify information and to obtain the exact details. The attitude of the therapist should be one of curiosity and wanting to learn from the family. By the end of this part of the session, the therapist will typically know why the family is seeking treatment at this time, the family member who has initiated the referral and her reasons for doing so, the symptoms and their course, and how each family member sees the problem and the reason for being in therapy.

A Bowenian therapist works with a couple. One characteristic of Murray Bowen's therapy is that he works only with the couple in the therapy session. No other family members are present.

A history is gathered in the second part of the session, beginning with the first meeting of the husband and wife, their courtship and marriage, birth of each child, job histories, geographical moves, and other changes up to the present time. Such information gives the therapist an idea of the present level of anxiety of the family, changes in the family, past and present amounts of stress, and how the family emotional system functions.

The third part of the session consists of a survey of both the paternal and maternal sides of the extended families of each spouse. First, information is obtained on dates of births and deaths, occupational and educational histories, dates of all marriages and divorces, health histories including any causes of death, and geographical locations of the siblings, their children, and the parents. Next, similar data are obtained on the grandparents, their children, and any first cousins. These data are typically organized in a family diagram called a genogram.

Stages of Therapy.   From the beginning, the therapist is responsible for the tone or emotional level of the session, keeping it lively but not overly emotional where spouses may become defensive and reactive. The therapist alternates asking questions of one spouse and then the other, especially about any thoughts and feelings being experienced in the session in reaction to what the other spouse has said to the therapist. The therapist is careful not to react to what is said, remaining objective and detriangled from the emotional system of the family.

Information for a genogram may be collected in the first session or later in the therapy after the intake process has been completed. The genogram can be referred to at various points in the middle stage of therapy as spouses tie their present patterns to past themes in the family of origin and previous generations.

The therapist uses "I" statements to emphasize positions in the therapy. The therapist is not on the fence but rather takes stands with the couple.

As therapy progresses, the therapist encourages each spouse to make trips home to differentiate self in the family of origin. The progress of therapy can be judged on how long the spouse is able to stay detriangled in the family of origin, that is, own a separate thought or feeling and not back down when the family reacts negatively. The spouse remains objective and is no longer drawn into the family emotional system.

Application: Major Therapeutic Techniques

Bowen preferred to work with the couple, using the therapist to complete the triangle and reduce the tension between the couple and in the family as a whole. He found that when the married couple make a project of themselves, other problems in the family improve, such as those of a child.

Genograms. Bowen (1980) is credited with developing the genogram, a map representing the process and structure of at least three generations of a family (Figure 9–2). In order to create a genogram, Bowen gathered such information as the names of family members and the dates of important life events from the marital couple in the initial session. According to Bowen (1980), a complete genogram should include:

1. All family members' names and ages
2. Dates of significant life events (births, marriages, deaths, etc.)
3. Notes explaining significant events
4. Data on several generations

McClure and Milardo (1986) created a genogram exercise for students to use in marital and family therapy training classes. In *Genograms in Family Assessment,* McGoldrick and Gerson (1985) created an expanded list of questions to use in a genogram interview as well as ways of interpreting the information. An example of a completed genogram (Jane Fonda's genogram) is found in Figure 9–3.

It is important for future family therapists to know and understand their families of origin so that they are aware of the "emotional baggage" they carry. A lack of awareness of such baggage may interfere with their ability to work effectively with clients in the future. It is recommended that each student complete a genogram (Table 9–1) and analyze it (Table 9–2). Emphasizing the strengths of past and present generations, especially the themes that motivated family members to reach beyond themselves, can build self-esteem. Often, in order to obtain needed information, relatives must be contacted. One family member usually functions as a family scribe or historian, keeping track of such information. Calling or writing the family member who functions in this role is usually the quickest, most efficient way to complete the family history. If you interview family members in person, you may wish to audio- or videotape them.

Alex Haley (1976) popularized the family history in *Roots,* encouraging others to write histories of their families. One example of a published family history is *In Search*

FIGURE 9–2 Key to the use of the genogram

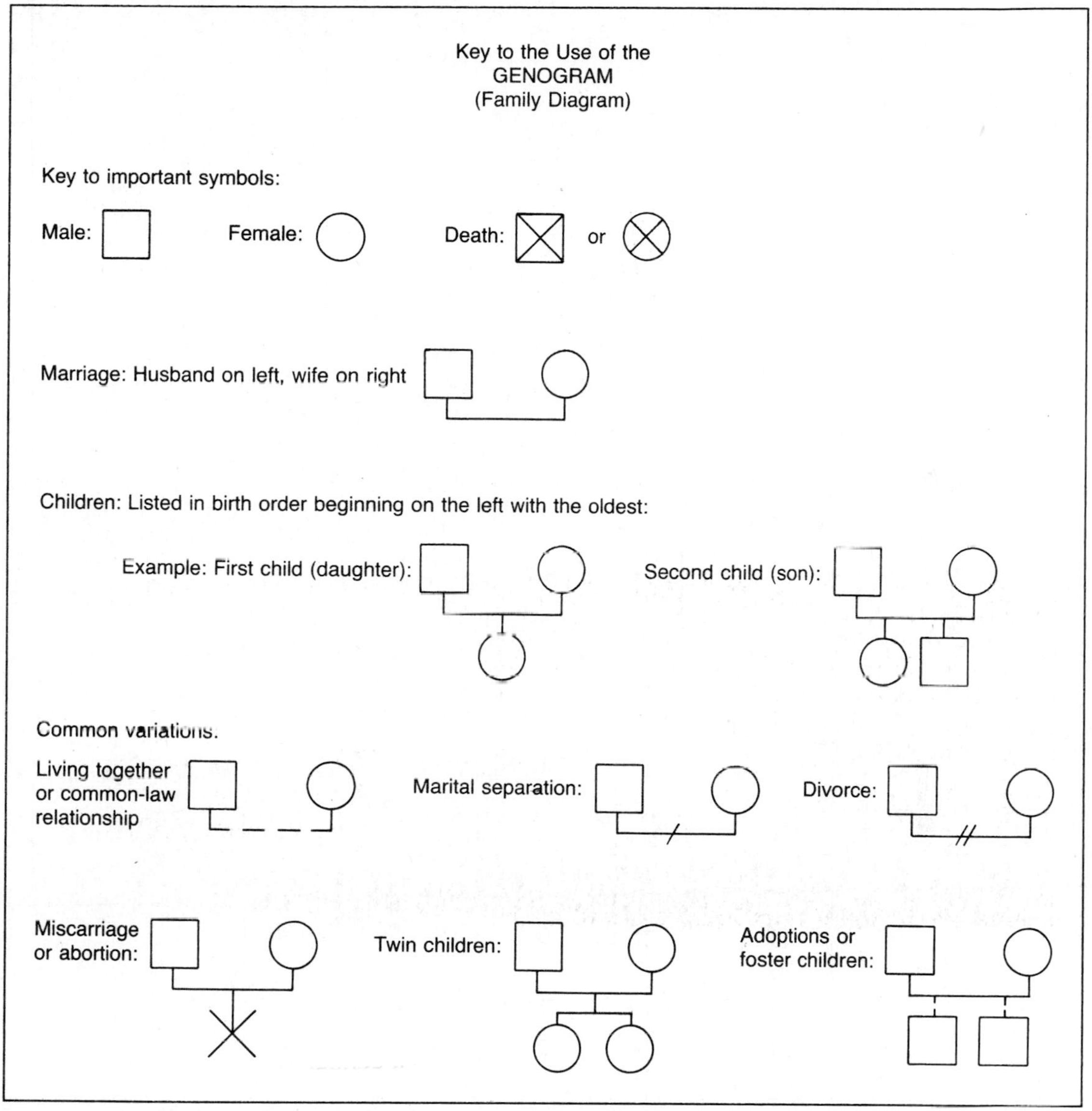

Copyright: Murray Bowen, M.D., 1980. For permission to reproduce the Key to the Genogram, write to M. Bowen, M.D., Georgetown University Hospital, Washington, D.C. 20007.

of Kith and Kin: The History of a Southern Black Family by Barnetta White (1986). Many families are investing in a video camera to record family events (family history in the making): the renewal of marriage vows, holidays, family celebrations, weddings, births, baptisms, and wakes. For example, I audiotaped an interview with my grandmother before she died at the age of 101, a special treasure for our family.

FIGURE 9–3 Jane Fonda's genogram

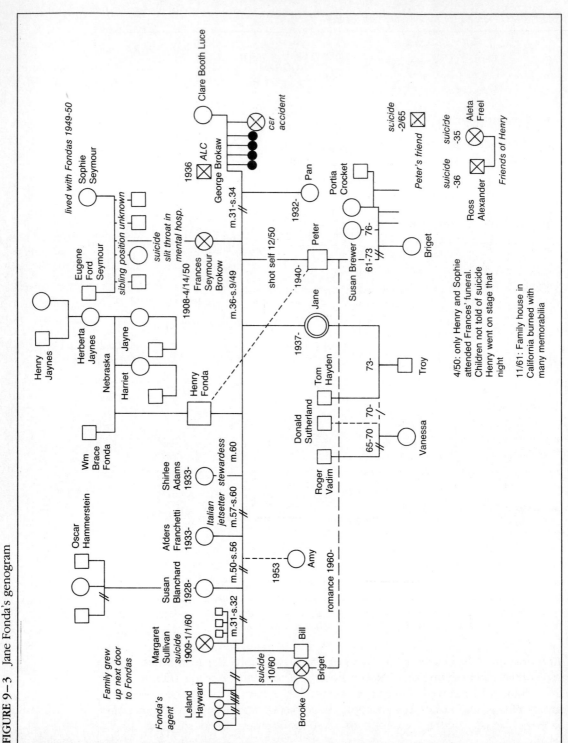

FROM *Genograms in Family Assessment* (p. 24) by M. McGoldrick, M.S.W. and R. Gerson, Ph.D. 1985, New York: W.W. Norton & Co. Reprinted by permission. Copyright © 1985 by Monica McGoldrick and Randy Gerson.

TABLE 9–1 Questions to use in a genogram interview

1. Can you tell me the names and ages of the family members for at least three generations on both sides of the family who are presently living?

2. When were these individuals born, married, separated, or divorced? Give specific dates including day and year, if possible.

3. Who passed away in the family? When? Of what? When were they born, married, separated, or divorced?

4. What jobs did family members hold?

5. What were the educational levels of family members?

6. What were the ethnic/cultural and religious backgrounds of family members? How have these traditions been passed on in the family?

7. Where did family members live? In what city and state? When and where did they move? For what reasons?

8. How did people get along in the family? Who was close to whom? Did anyone *not* speak to another family member? What happened in these cases?

9. Which family members were very successful at what they did?

10. Which family members used alcohol or drugs, were arrested, had mental problems, committed suicide, or had other serious problems?

11. What illnesses are found in the family? How did family members cope with them?

12. Can you tell me any special life events that happened—positive, neutral, and negative?

13. Are there any stories that have been passed down through the generations in our family?

14. Are there any family themes that seem to repeat in our family?

15. As an elder of the family, is there any advice that you would give to me as a younger member of the family?

Sexual Genogram.   When a sexual problem is one of the main presenting problems, a sexual genogram technique is used to elicit additional information through very pointed questions given as a homework assignment to the couple. A sexual genogram should be used after rapport has been established, when no crisis is in effect, and when one of the main goals of the marital treatment agreed upon is the treatment of sexual problems in the couple. Hof and Berman (1986) have tailored Bowen's genogram technique to work with sexual dysfunctions by developing a list of specific questions to obtain sexual information and a therapeutic process to accompany them. A list of the questions is included in Table 9–3.

Each spouse typically writes the answers to each of these questions privately at home and decides what will be shared at any given time in a therapy session, maintaining individual control. The spouse is asked to record any dreams, feelings, or thoughts that arise as the questions are answered. Spouses are encouraged to approach their families of origin individually (face to face, if possible) to make gradual,

TABLE 9–2 Questions to answer in writing a genogram analysis

1. How healthy were family members in your genogram? What were the most common health problems on each side of your family and in your family of origin? What did family members do to prevent or treat such problems?

2. What type(s) of family structure (single parent, nuclear, extended) were repeated in your genogram?

3. What family themes have been carried down through the generations?

4. What occupations occur most frequently in your family?

5. What stages of the family life cycle have been easier for your family to cope with? Most difficult?

6. What life events have affected family functioning throughout the generations of your family?

7. Where are triangles present in your genogram? Where are relationships close, distant, conflicted, or fused? Where are there emotional cut-offs?

8. What patterns are repeated, such as educational or work success, religious commitment, alcohol or drug use, or other behaviors?

9. How large were the families in your genogram? Do some families stand out as larger or smaller when looking at the genogram? What stresses might have occurred due to family size or family imbalance?

10. Since you are a dynamic, active organism according to systems theory, what could you do to change any patterns that disturb you? What would you like to pass on to your children some day?

respectful requests for information such as, "What did your parents or others teach you about sexuality when you were a child, and what did you think I should know or think about it?" Confrontations are discouraged. Spouses are encouraged to share what they have learned and how it might help to resolve the sexual problem.

Person-to-Person Relationship.   The therapist establishes a relationship with each spouse in which the spouse shares thoughts and feelings about the self directly with the therapist while the partner observes. In this way, the spouses begin to develop a person-to-person relationship in their marriage rather than an emotional divorce. Each person learns to focus on self rather than talking or gossiping about a third person. In our society, most people are not used to talking about their innermost thoughts and feelings. They become anxious after only a few minutes. It is difficult to establish and maintain a person-to-person relationship, but such a relationship is the key to a higher level of differentiation.

Detriangling.   The process of remaining objective in response to the family ego mass is called *detriangling*. Being able to share one's thoughts and feelings without becoming defensive or putting down the views of others is one example of detriangling. The person remains calm in response to reactions by other family members.

A family poses for a family picture during the Christmas season, a common family tradition on holidays. Three generations of the family are together. Often such a time is a good opportunity to obtain information for a family history.

JAMES FRAMO

Historical Development

James Framo is a psychologist who worked closely with Boszormenyi-Nagy for 13 years on a research project using family therapy in the treatment of schizophrenia. Framo has contributed to the field of family therapy since the late 1950s. In 1982, he published a collection of selected papers, entitled *Explorations in Marital and Family Therapy*. Like Bowen and Boszormenyi-Nagy, Framo emphasizes the influence of the family of origin in his approach.

Key Theoretical Concepts

Although he is knowledgeable and trained to do psychoanalytically oriented therapy, Framo (1981) does not like his theory to be placed within this category. He views psychoanalysis as a linear, closed system (the psychoanalyst treats the patient in a vacuum, as though what is going on in the external world has no effect), whereas his

TABLE 9–3 Questions used to obtain information for a sexual genogram

1. What are the overt/covert messages in this family regarding sexuality/intimacy? Regarding masculinity/femininity?

2. Who said/did what? Who was conspicuously silent/absent in the area of sexuality/ intimacy?

3. Who was the most open sexually? Intimately? In what ways?

4. How was sexuality/intimacy encouraged? Discouraged? Controlled? Within a generation? Between generations?

5. What questions have you had regarding sexuality/intimacy in your "family tree" that you have been reluctant to ask? Who might have the answers? How could you discover the answers?

6. What were the "secrets" in your family regarding sexuality/intimacy (e.g., incest, unwanted pregnancies, extramarital affairs, etc.)?

7. What do the other "players on the stage" have to say regarding answers to the above questions? How did these issues, events, and experiences impact upon him/ her? Within a generation? Between generations? With whom have you talked about this? With whom would you like to talk about this? How could you do it?

8. How does your partner perceive your family tree/genogram regarding the aforementioned issues? How do you perceive it?

9. How would you change this genogram (including *who* and *what*) to meet what you wish would have occurred regarding messages and experiences of sexuality/intimacy?

From "The Sexual Genogram" by L. Hof and E. Berman, 1986, *Journal of Marital and Family Therapy, 12*(1), pp. 39–47, The American Association for Marriage and Family Therapy. Adapted by permission.

family of origin approach is an open systems approach, which emphasizes the connection between intrapsychic and transactional factors.

Intrapsychic conflicts that originated in the family of origin are replicated in present transactions with significant others in the current family. The link between intrapsychic and family transactions is the object relations of family members, the introjects that they carry from their interactions with parents in the families of origin.

A summary of the key tenets underlying Framo's theory follows:

1. Framo subscribes to the object relations of Fairbairn rather than to Freud's structural view of instinctual gratification as the basis for human motivation. All human beings need an object, that is, an intimate social relationship with another human being—the fundamental motivation in life.

2. Infants internalize representations of the mother (both good and bad) as introjects. Father introjects, split-off parts of the self, and other objects are added or altered through childhood experiences.

3. People choose mates because they can recover a lost part of the self that had been split off but can be re-experienced through projective identification or they can obtain a good parent object. After the marriage, negative split-off parts of the self or painful bad parent introjects may be projected onto the spouse, creating conflicts.

People marry individuals whose object relations permit them to recreate unresolved conflicts in the family of origin.

4. Parents project introjects onto their children.
5. When an adult meets with the family of origin, misperceptions in the introjects are more easily changed. People realize that the parents are not as they remembered. They begin to see their parents as real people, and they can make peace with them before they die.

View of Healthy Functioning

Framo (1981, 1982) was very interested in what constituted healthy functioning in married couples and in families. His views are contained in Table 9–4.

TABLE 9–4   Toward Healthier Family Systems: Framo's principles of healthy marital and family functioning

1. Spouses have separate senses of self, which they developed before leaving their families of origin, and can choose when to be dependent on a spouse. The autonomy of each family member is encouraged.

2. Spouses understand their introjects from their families of origin and know the irrational expectations that they brought to the marriage. They have accepted disenchantment with romantic love and value mature love, which is based on reality, not idealization.

3. Spouses have realistic expectations of their children and of each other. They perceive each other as "real" people.

4. Even though they are different people, spouses can meet each other's realistic needs.

5. Spouses and family members can communicate clearly and honestly with each other to resolve problems as they arise. They can handle crises flexibly.

6. Spouses enjoy sex with each other more and more.

7. Clear generational boundaries exist within the family.

8. The strongest loyalty is to the family of procreation (one's marriage partner and children) rather than the family of origin.

9. Spouses have definite priorities in this order: (1) self, (2) spouse, and (3) children. However, children are not excluded from having relationships with both parents. Being close to one does not mean that the other parent becomes jealous or alienated.

10. Spouses enjoy their work, their children, and life in general. Affection and warmth are expressed between spouses, between spouses and children, and among children.

11. Each spouse has an adult-to-adult relationship with each parent and encourages relationships between the grandparents and their grandchildren.

12. The family is open to involvement outside the family with friends and outsiders, who are permitted inside the family.

The Therapeutic Process

Framo has developed a treatment sequence that uses different techniques at each stage of treatment. Based on his writings (1976, 1981, 1982), the following sequence is summarized, highlighting the specific techniques associated with each stage:

1. *Emphasis on couples therapy*. If the whole family presents focused on the problem of a child, Framo may see the entire family and obtain information from each family member, but will move to couples therapy as soon as possible.

2. *Initial assessment*. Several couples sessions are held with a co-therapist of the opposite sex. Interventions are not made during these assessment sessions. Rather open-ended questions are used to obtain information from each spouse in turn about the following: source of referral; nature of the presenting problem; demographic data such as occupation, age, date of marriage, ages of children, and any prior marriages; nature of and outcomes of any previous therapies; reason for choosing mate; family's reaction; fight style of the couple; whether they love each other; whether the relationship was ever good; the degree of commitment; the sexual relationship; the family of origin; and current relationship with siblings and parents.

   The therapist will then ask about the couple's goals for the therapy to assess their motivation. Often they will interact with each other, giving the therapist an opportunity to observe how they relate. Framo audiotapes all sessions so that couples can listen at home and learn from them when they are not as emotionally aroused.

   The therapist explains the expectations for therapy; that, in addition to individual sessions with the couple, the spouses will participate in couples group therapy to prepare for a session in which they will meet with their families of origin near the end of therapy.

3. *Co-therapy with the couple*. The focus of this stage of therapy is to build a trusting relationship with the couple and to demonstrate the link between the transactions of spouses, their object relations, and families of origin. The co-therapists seek to establish relationships with each spouse and to meet the individual goals of each spouse as well as their own goals. The co-therapists use questioning, reflecting, supporting, challenging, confronting, disagreeing, directing, and even some self disclosure where helpful to the spouses. Each spouse begins to see how certain expectations and patterns of behavior are carried as introjects and projected onto the spouse. As this link becomes established, couples begin to understand the importance of understanding and meeting with the family of origin. Typically such sessions are scheduled weekly with co-therapists of opposite sexes.

4. *Couples group therapy*. After the co-therapy sessions have ended, the couple joins a group of three couples to prepare for the family of origin meeting. Initially resistant couples become less apprehensive as they observe other couples linking the current patterns in their relationship to their families of origin. They see these couples graduate and return to the group to tell about the family of origin session and how helpful it was for them. Traditional couples techniques to encourage communication, fair fighting, negotiation, and work on differentiation are used during this phase.

5. *Family of origin session*. In the family of origin session, only the individual spouse and the co-therapists participate. Care is taken to neither devalue nor blame the parents in any way, as everyone loses when this occurs.

The co-therapists usually set the tone by stating that all families have problems and that the purpose of the session is to assist family members to learn more about each other as people and to handle their concerns regarding other family members. Co-therapists usually establish rapport by asking family members from out-of-town about their trip to the institute.

Then the co-therapists turn the session over to the clients, who bring up unresolved issues. Sometimes parents bring up issues of what life was like in their families of origin. Audiotapes of the session are made. Co-therapists mediate, asking questions for clarification, summarizing, and slowing down the pace of the expression of feelings to keep family members from becoming overwhelmed.

6. *Termination of treatment*. Usually individual sessions are held with the spouse or the couple after the family of origin session, or the spouse returns to the couples group to process what happened. These sessions are audiotaped so that the other spouse can listen and not feel left out. After each spouse has completed processing the family of origin work, treatment is terminated.

IVAN BOSZORMENYI-NAGY

Historical Development

According to Boszormenyi-Nagy with Krasner (1986) in *Between Give and Take: A Clinical Guide to Contextual Therapy,* Boszormenyi-Nagy was one of the pioneers of family therapy. He founded the Department of Family Psychiatry of Eastern Pennsylvania Psychiatric Institute of Philadelphia in 1957, one of the earliest family therapy treatment and training centers in the United States. He required family therapy there as part of the treatment regimen for all schizophrenic patients.

Boszormenyi-Nagy, born in Hungary, followed his interest in schizophrenia by completing medical school and his psychiatric residency (Van Heusden & Van Den Eerenbeemt, 1987). During his residency, he was influenced by the psychodynamic and relationship-oriented approach of his mentor, Kalman Gyarfas, under whom he worked when he relocated to the United States in 1950.

Boszormenyi-Nagy founded a school of therapy called contextual therapy, named for its emphasis on the multigenerational perspective (context). Whether one client or a whole family is being seen, the emphasis is on the ever-changing ethical connections between people and their relationships (context) (Van Heusden & Van Den Eerenbeemt, 1987). The therapist takes responsibility for and always considers the consequences of the therapy for all those in close relationships with the client(s).

Although not formally trained as a psychoanalyst, Boszormenyi-Nagy exhaustively read psychoanalytic literature and used object relations theory, especially the work of Fairbairn, as one basis for the development of contextual therapy. The promotion of self-differentiation, ego strength, and the maintenance of a stable feeling of self-esteem for each family member are the goals of contextual therapy (Simon, Stierlin, & Wynne, 1985).

Another influence was phenomenologist Martin Buber's work, entitled *I and Thou* (1958), which presents dialogue as the model for all close interpersonal relationships (Van Heusden & Van Den Eerenbeemt, 1987). Boszormenyi-Nagy believes that successful outcomes depend upon the therapist's facilitating or catalyzing dialogue between an individual and significant others. The dialectic that occurs between two people in a personal relationship is one of receiving through giving care to the other.

Boszormenyi-Nagy was also a part of the early research on schizophrenia. He directed a therapeutic research project on schizophrenics and their families for more than 6 years (Boszormenyi-Nagy, 1965b). He was affected by the work of Bowen, Wynne, Jackson, and others (Boszormenyi-Nagy with Krasner, 1986). He is knowledgeable about systems theory and believes that the individual is a system—not only a psychological system, from an object-relations point of view, but also from a broader ethical perspective. The individual system is interconnected with other individual systems—a network of multi-individual systems—with the family system having properties of its own, all linked by the unifying ethical dimension of give and take in relationships.

Some authors contend that Boszormenyi-Nagy integrated psychoanalytically oriented therapy with phenomenology, although others maintain that he reconciled the psychoanalytic object relations school with general systems theory. Boszormenyi-Nagy himself stated, "I consider that the new paradigm in my approach is the unifying view of the ethical dimension as the basis of relationships. Relational ethics is a human universal which does not depend on particular value systems, but on the fairness of the distribution of merits, benefits and burdens" (Van Heusden & Van Den Eerenbeemt, 1987, p. 7).

Key Theoretical Concepts
Some key contextual theoretical concepts are defined in Table 9–5. A discussion of others follows.

Ledger of Justice. A multigenerational structure of expectations and actions (Boszormenyi-Nagy & Spark, 1973), sometimes called the ledger of merits, is the accounting of debts and merits accumulated on each side of a dyadic relationship. One source of merits is ontic versus functioning relatedness, or owing for one's very existence. Children are indebted to their mothers for their very being (Boszormenyi-Nagy, 1965a). Such an existential debt exists even if the mother does not function in caring for the child.

In symmetrical relationships among equals such as between marital partners or close friends, to the extent that an individual receives positive benefits from another's contribution, the person becomes indebted to the individual, who is entitled to merit on that side of the ledger. In an asymmetrical relationship, such as between parent and child, a parent cannot expect to be repaid for the care given to the child, but the child is required to repay the debt by caring appropriately for the next generation, attempting to do so in an even better way. In addition, a child may earn merits by caring for a parent, especially in old age.

TABLE 9–5 Key concepts of contextual therapy

Merited trustworthiness. Mutual consideration of the true self-interests of each family member, and trust toward each family member based on the care each has exhibited.

Accountability. An existential concept stating that regardless of one's attitude, one is liable for the consequences of one's actions or inactions (Boszormenyi-Nagy with Krasner, 1986). In particular, one is responsible for dialogue in a relationship, in both its self-validating and self-delineating aspects.

Justice. The distribution of material resources and the immaterial resources such as protection, love, and recognition of the family in an equitable manner to its members, horizontally in the present generation and vertically across generations (Simon et al., 1985). Parents may give resources to their children, but children also give affection and joy to their parents, and years later they may take care of both the physical and psychological needs of their aging parents. The therapist facilitates equity discussions to bring into the open questions of justice among family members.

Exoneration. A child's effort to forgive parents for past emotional debts. Any attempt to forgive a parent, even if it is rebuked, frees the adult child to exhibit positive behavior in relationships with others.

Intersubjective fusion. Symbiotic families in which subject-object positions are not clear; members are trapped in "we-ness" of the family and do not experience themselves as separate.

Adapted from *Between Give and Take: A Clinical Guide to Contextual Therapy* (pp. 35, 413–422) by I. Boszormenyi-Nagy with B. R. Krasner, 1986, New York: Brunner/Mazel.

Entitlement. Not to be confused with a feeling of entitlement, it is a guarantee of merit for caring, such as parenting or the repayment of parenting. It has the additional benefit that people experience freedom to the extent that they are able to earn entitlement. Responsible caring and autonomy go hand in hand. A dialectical synthesis of altruism and selfishness, caring and self-gain, allows people to experience personal enjoyment. They use their capabilities to succeed at work, to risk trusting in future relationships, to be assertive, to mentor future generations, to be free of psychosomatic symptoms, and to enjoy and value emotional satisfaction of the partner as well as the self. A relationship can be defined as mutually interlocking individuation (Boszormenyi-Nagy with Krasner, 1986).

Destructive entitlement occurs when (1) a child has not received appropriate parental nurturing, (2) the child's need for trust is exploited, (3) mistrust is returned for trust, or (4) the child is blamed for what happens in adult relationships. Such a child may act overentitled, as though the world or other people in relationships owed the child a debt.

Delegation. The parents or grandparents expect a child to fulfill a certain mission for the family. In return, the child gains self-esteem. (Delegation is the term for this coined by Stierlin, 1974.) For example, one child may function as a scapegoat (a delinquent or alcoholic) in order to keep his parents together by their ministering to the child. The child is given credit (merits) for performing such services for the parents, which often frees the child to become more autonomous. A contextual therapist would ask the child what the child has done to help the parents recently.

Loyalty. A triadic configuration in which an individual prefers one person, based on earned merit, and does not prefer another. For example, a man may experience a loyalty conflict when his mother asks him to run an errand for her at the same time that his wife wants him to attend a concert. Both women are loyalty objects for him. His mother has spent time parenting him, earning merit in his eyes, and his wife has taken care of him in the marriage, also gaining merit. He will suffer from split loyalties. When split loyalties occur for a child, such as in a divorce situation where the child is asked to choose which parent with whom to live, the child will exhibit symptoms, often psychosis.

Relational Modes. Boszormenyi-Nagy (1967, 1987) is noted for proposing relational dyadic modes in a hierarchy, from least to most optimal ways of delineating self. Of particular importance to marital therapy are two forms of dyads, represented in Figure 9–4: dialogue and mutual projection (Boszormenyi-Nagy, 1965a). In the dyad as dialogue, the partners can use each other as subjects or as objects. For example, a

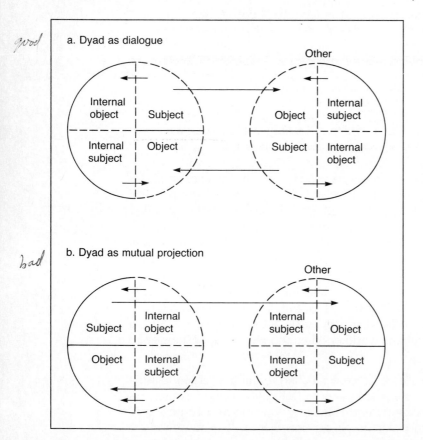

good

bad

FIGURE 9–4 The dyad and the internal dialogue

From "A Theory of Relationships: Experience and Transaction" by I. Boszormenyi-Nagy in *Intensive Family Therapy: Theoretical and Practical Aspects* (p. 48) by I. Boszormenyi-Nagy and J.L. Framo (Eds.), 1965, New York: Harper & Row. Reprinted by permission.

husband listens to his wife, passively being her object, as she, the subject, talks about her day. She, in turn, listens to him tell about his day, acting as his object. This is the optimal relational mode, leading to increased self-differentiation.

On the other hand, when a dyad is mutual projection, neither sees the other's real self. Rather, each sees only one of their own internal introjects transferred or projected onto the partner. Mutual projection is the least effective way of attaining self-differentiation because it is based on illusion, not reality.

When people fall in love they often unconsciously look for someone who will match their internal introjects. They then project split-off parts of the self onto the beloved. For example, the "good mother" introject is projected onto the girlfriend. Often a suitor will ignore the real-life attributes of the girlfriend—the real self. After 2 years of marriage or less, the husband begins to see how his wife is different from the ideal mother. In some cases, the husband may then project the "bad mother" introject onto the wife. He may divorce her for another woman, only to repeat the pattern of idealization followed by devaluation (splitting defenses).

Mutual projection is used by people who are fixated at lower stages of development in object relations, when as infants they did not integrate the good and bad aspects of the mother as one object. When mutual projection occurs, splitting defenses are operational so that the individual does not see the other's real self, only the idealized illusion. The "good parent" introject has been projected or transferred to the partner. Then when the other's real self is perceived, often the "bad parent" introject will be transferred or projected to the other, leaving the remaining introject of the "good parent." This leads to greater self-esteem for the individual. By perceiving the partner as the "bad parent," the individual plays the role of "good parent," self-righteously upbraiding the partner for faults, leading to a feeling of superiority.

Although many people do not use extreme splitting defenses of idealization (placing the person on a pedestal) and devaluation (throwing the person on a garbage heap), everyone in close relationships uses a degree of projection. One premise of psychoanalytically oriented therapy is that people often marry individuals who match their introjects to recreate unresolved conflicts within the family of origin. For example, a man is raised by his divorced mother, whom he loves very much. She works very hard and has high expectations. It seems that he can never meet her expectations, regardless of how much he excels. He meets a very capable woman, falls in love, and marries her. Whenever the wife asks questions about what he does at work, he becomes defensive and withdraws. Instead of perceiving her as the interested partner she is, he sees her as his critical mother, whom he can never please. By involving himself in a dialogue with his wife, and with the therapist and his wife, he becomes aware of the pattern he projects from his childhood.

View of Healthy Functioning

Families that reopen dialogue about merits and debts in both current and multigenerational relationships move toward health. Through dialogue in dyads and in family meetings, as well as in contextual therapy sessions, individuals are able to earn entitlement through care, which frees them to separate and individuate.

In dialogue, family members move toward seeing each other's real selves. Rather than making a marital partner or family member fit the internal introjects and meet psychological needs, an individual becomes aware of the patterns being repeated from the family of origin and accepts that person's real self.

The Therapeutic Process

Goals of Therapy.   The main theme of contextual therapy is that disturbances in families and in individuals are expressions of imbalance in entitlement and fulfillment—giving and taking—especially in emotional caring. Contextual therapy aims to balance the multigenerational ledger of merits through a nondirective dialogue that promotes mutual trust, understanding, and responsibility.

Role of the Therapist.   The therapist takes an active position and is responsible for sequentially making each family member accountable. The therapist excludes no one from accountability, not even an absent family member (Boszormenyi-Nagy, 1981). Care is taken to inquire about three generations as the opportunity arises, even if all are not represented in the session.

Use of Diagnosis and Assessment.   According to Boszormenyi-Nagy and Ulrich (1981), there are four aspects of relational reality to be assessed in developing a treatment plan: (1) facts (including genetic endowment, ethnic origin, health, divorce, death, or other acts of fate), (2) psychology (intrapsychic or object relations factors), (3) patterns of transaction (role assignments and observable repetitive behaviors between family members), and (4) relational ethics (balance of fairness between people over the long term, in which the interests of each are considered by the others). Of these, the most important dimension is relational ethics.

The contextual family therapist assesses the ethical dimension of the relationships within the family in the initial session. The indebtedness and entitlement of each family member are evaluated as each shares a personal view of the family's ledger of merits. Assessment continues throughout therapy. In contrast to Bowen and Framo, who hold sessions separate from therapy to evaluate presenting families, Boszormenyi-Nagy views assessment as a part of the total process of relating to the family in a trustworthy manner.

Nature of the Initial Session.   The tone of the initial session is set by the telephone call referring the family. It is helpful for the therapist to say that the distinguishing features of contextual therapy are that family members can help to heal each other and that action is emphasized.

The contract takes into consideration the effect of the therapy on all members of the family. The therapist asks all family members to attend the initial session, but if they cannot, the therapist will still see those who attend. Often this is more considerate of the needs of all family members, because a person who attends alone may want to talk about a secret—for example, an extramarital affair.

A history is taken, including the four aspects of relationships: facts, psychology, interactional patterns, and relational ethics. This includes any triggering trauma and histories of health, prior treatment, and families of origin. Based on the patterns of behavior exhibited between family members themselves and with the therapist, the therapist assesses the level of object relations of the parents and the roles that each member plays in the family. If there is an emergency such as sexual abuse of a child, risk of suicide or homicide, or other possibilities of violence, the therapist takes action by involving appropriate members of the family and hospitalizing an individual when necessary.

The overall attitude of the therapist is extremely important in contextual therapy. The therapist should convey a sense of relational ethics, that is, concern for all family members, their individuation, and their relatedness. The therapist encourages family members to open dialogue, always keeping control of the session and validating the worth of each family member.

The therapist is the catalyst, but the actual work occurs in family meetings held at home, family rituals, and spontaneous happenings during the week between therapy sessions. The therapist in the session stimulates spontaneous generation of alternatives, actions, and problem-solving by planting seeds such as handling transference dynamics, teaching, and using spontaneous responses.

Stages of Therapy.   Contextual therapy is designed as intensive long-term therapy for individuals and families. It is not unusual for a family to work in treatment for 3 or 4 years. Contextual therapy can be brief as well. However, it takes a very well-trained therapist to lead the family to deep levels in a short time.

The strengths of contextual therapy lie in its contribution to theory. Those who practice contextual therapy must also be well versed in psychoanalytic theory and practice, with significant amounts of individual supervision of their work. Therapists should have completed therapeutic experiences to understand the relational ethics of their own families and how that may facilitate or impede their work with families.

Contextual therapy progresses through the same stages of treatment as other forms of psychoanalytically based family therapy. First, the therapeutic contract is established, including frequency of meetings, cost, and rules for missed appointments. Rapport is then established with each family member in order to develop the therapeutic alliance. The longest and most difficult stage is that of working through, in which defenses and resistances are interpreted and patterns of object relations are discussed as they are played out in transactions between family members in the therapy session. Finally, the issues of loss, separation, and abandonment are discussed as they surface during the termination stage.

Application: Major Therapeutic Techniques

Therapeutic techniques are based upon multidirectional partiality; that is, therapists relate empathically with each family member, understanding each member's ethical viewpoint as if it were their own. Efforts are aimed toward making overt the invisible loyalties that bind family members together between and across generations.

Siding.   The therapist asks each family member about contributions to the family, expounding on the viewpoint of that person and taking the side of the person. It is essential to the success of contextual therapy that the therapist side with each family member, even those not present, so that multidirectional partiality is maintained.

Rejunction. Family members rejoin the mutual dialogue in an effort to gain entitlement. Intention is the first step. Often members have given up on attempting to earn merit in the family and trust is low. When one family member begins to try again, other members of the family are affected. Reaching out to work on a relationship makes a difference.

Crediting. The therapist credits a family member for what they have done to help the family. The therapist begins with the family member who has been hurt the most (the delinquent or scapegoat). The therapist will ask the person, "In what ways have you helped your parents recently?" Even a child or adolescent who has exhibited the most rebellious behavior can point to the role of listening to mom when she complains about dad or acting as a referee for parental feuds (parentification), which reduces the energy available to the child to work on differentiation.

Motivation for the Use of Resources. The therapist encourages mutual accountability to replace mutual blame (Boszormenyi-Nagy with Krasner, 1986). A person might say, "Now that the family is in this predicament, what can each member do to turn the situation to the family's favor?" A family member who is filled with resentment might be encouraged to be accountable, so that the person might say, even though he resents the spouse, "What action can I take to make the situation better?"

THERAPEUTIC OUTCOMES

It is important to keep in mind that the works of Bowen, Boszormenyi-Nagy, and Framo were funded through research grants, mainly for the study of schizophrenic patients and their families. The development of their approaches was based on this research and did lead to improvement in the schizophrenic patients who participated in family therapy. Framo (1982) makes the point that outcome studies are affected by how effective outcome is defined. Is the case successful only if a schizophrenic family member stays out of the hospital, only if the family's distress is reduced, only if there is increased differentiation on the part of family members, or only if there is greater social involvement in the community? For example, an innovative suggestion for evaluating Bowenian family therapy is that of Novotny (1987), of the Menninger Foundation, who suggests that clinicians carry out their own Bowenian plan for differentiation from their families of origin, similar to self-analysis, and gauge the utility of Bowen's approach on the effectiveness of their personal outcomes.

CONTRIBUTIONS AND LIMITATIONS

The development of the genogram by Bowen and application of other family-of-origin techniques and concepts are major contributions. Increasingly, genograms are being used routinely by many practitioners regardless of orientation. The themes and problems that emanate from the family of origin shed light on the presenting problem of the family. As family members understand the patterns of their families of origin, they are able to take steps to differentiate from them, while increasing their capacity for closeness.

One of the main limitations of psychoanalytically oriented approaches to family therapy has been the emphasis on an analytic linear mode. A number of theorists maintain that they have combined psychoanalytic concepts with systems theory. However, there is still an emphasis on the intrapsychic make-up of the individual in psychoanalytically oriented approaches, and proponents of these approaches maintain that changing such internal processes in the individuals is the only way to long-lasting change in the family as a whole. Other approaches may show impressive short-term results, but they are not long lasting, and family members regress after a period of time because their introjects have not changed.

SUMMARY

Distinctive work built upon a psychoanalytic base has been made by intergenerational family theorists such as Murray Bowen, James Framo, and Ivan Boszormenyi-Nagy. All three were pioneers, conducting research on the families of schizophrenics and the treatment of schizophrenia. Bowen's approach is the best known because of his extensive training efforts and his creation of the genogram technique, a map representing the process and structure of at least three generations of a family. Concepts of his that have been adopted by other approaches include self-differentiation, triangulation, nuclear family emotional system, emotional cutoff, and multigenerational transmission process. He also emphasized the birth order of individuals in a family, finding this particularly important in satisfactory marital functioning. Bowen worked with one couple at a time, taking turns speaking directly with one spouse while the other observed.

James Framo uses an innovative step-wise approach in which he assesses a couple, works with the couple through a number of sessions, and includes the couple in couples group therapy in preparation for a session of each individual spouse with the family of origin, followed by termination. He uses a co-therapist, usually of the opposite sex. The focus of therapy is changing the introjects or object relations of the spouses through face-to-face discussion with the members of the family of origin. When distortions are removed, spouses can see each other as they really are.

Boszormenyi-Nagy works with couples or entire families. He emphasizes accountability and justice across generations, as recorded in the ledger of justice. Merited trustworthiness is a sense of trust that develops toward each family member based on the care each has exhibited. Entitlement is a guarantee of merit for caring. People earn freedom to be autonomous to the extent that they are able to earn entitlement. Boszormenyi-Nagy is noted for his relational modes and his emphasis on the dyad as dialogue—ways of explaining internal introjects and how they affect relationships. He developed a treatment plan based on facts, psychology, patterns of transactions, and relational ethics. His techniques include multidirectional partiality, siding, rejunction, crediting, and motivation for the use of resources.

EXERCISES

1. Construct a one-page genogram using at least three generations on each side of your family. Look at the example of a completed genogram (see Figure 9–3) and Tables 9–1 and 9–2 as well as Figure 9–2 to help you with your task. You will probably need to call or write relatives who can give you the needed information. When you go home for the weekend or a school holiday, interview a parent or relative, using the list of questions in Table 9–1.

After you have diagrammed your genogram, but before you have written your analysis of it, choose a partner from the class with whom to discuss your genogram and the questions from Table 9–2. Make an appointment outside of class and spend at least one hour, with each person talking about the genogram and obtaining feedback from the partner (total time—2 hours).

Based on your own analysis of the genogram and feedback from your partner, write an analysis of the genogram in flowing essay paragraphs by answering the questions from Table 9–2.

2. Count off in threes according to your instructor's directions. One person should volunteer to play the role of the therapist in each group, with the other two playing the married couple. The "therapist" should pretend to be Murray Bowen, conducting a family history interview with a couple.

The therapist should complete a genogram on the couple. Write down the information for the genogram as you interview. Rotate until each person has played the therapist.

3. Carry a small note pad with you for one week. When you talk with friends or teachers, count how many times you say "I feel like" or "I feel that" and record the number in your notebook. Based on your data, where would you place yourself on Bowen's scale of self differentiation? What could you do to become more differentiated?

4. The instructor will number the four corners of the room. When the instructor indicates, all oldest children should proceed to corner #1, all middle children to corner #2, all youngest children to corner #3, and all only children to corner #4. The task of each group is to generate a list of questions to be asked of the family in the initial session according to the contextual therapy approach of Boszormenyi-Nagy. Each group will share their list with the class.

Chapter 10
Behavioral and Cognitive Approaches to Marital and Family Therapy

On caring days couples <u>are asked to act "as if" they cared for one</u> <u>another</u> in an effort to elicit more frequent small, specific, and positive investments by both spouses in the process of building a sense of commitment to their marriage.

Stuart, 1980a, p. 193

OVERVIEW

This chapter focuses on behavioral approaches to parent training, marital counseling, and sex therapy. In particular, recent contributions of cognitive behavior therapy to family therapy and marriage counseling are emphasized. The theme of healthy functioning is stressed in the chapter, as it has been throughout the text.

Behavioral approaches to marital and family therapy developed later than other styles. Originally, behaviorists conducted basic research with animals to discover how they learned. It was not until the late 1960s that behavioral researchers began experimentation on an extensive basis with applications for children. Thus behavior modification, the treatment of human beings by the use of behavioral learning principles, was born (Thomas, 1970).

As researchers began to work with children, they had to have contact with parents. They found that behavior modification with children would not work if it were confined to the research facility. Children went home to the environment created by their parents, and the problems recurred. Experts such as Gerald Patterson and others in the Oregon group began to teach parents how to implement behavior modification programs with their children at home. Behavioral parent training (BPT) was established and became popular in the 1970s, continuing to the present day. Alexander and Parsons (1982) integrated behavioral parent training and systems concepts to devise an approach called functional family therapy.

As it became clear that distress in the couple created problems for the children, researchers collected data on married couples within families. Behavioral marital therapy (BMT), or behavioral couple therapy as it came to be called (Jacobson, 1981), was initiated. Pioneers in BMT include psychologist Richard Stuart and psychiatrist Robert Liberman.

Masters and Johnson (1970) established a center in St. Louis for research on sexual response. They began training therapists, using behaviorally oriented techniques, to provide treatment for sexual dysfunctions. Today sexual therapy is considered to be one of the major contributions to family therapy made by behaviorists.

Cognitive behavioral researchers have expanded the definition of behaviorism from a focus on overt, observable actions to include the words people say to each other and to themselves. These practitioners have developed specific techniques for confronting irrational ideas espoused by family members. Of particular importance is the contribution of Aaron Beck (1988), who has applied cognitive behavioral techniques to marriage counseling.

Common to all of these behavioral approaches to marital and family therapy is a view of human beings as neutral black boxes influenced only by environment. Their behavior is determined by responses to their own actions. They react to stimuli—rewards, punishments, or contiguous events—in predictable ways based on learned behavioral chains.

Since maladaptive behavior is learned, it can be unlearned. Learning continues until human beings die, so there is hope that adaptive behaviors can be taught and substituted for inappropriate behaviors. In addition, the scientific method can be applied to the analysis and treatment of human problems. In behavioral marital and family therapy, family members, in collaboration with the therapist, can specify clear behavioral goals, analyze the antecedents and consequences of behavior, and change the contingencies within the family environment.

BEHAVIORAL PARENT TRAINING

View of Healthy Functioning
A behavioral model of healthy parenting is included in Table 10–1. Appropriately timed rewards contingent upon desired behavior increase positive behavior. By contracting, parents can teach children the process of negotiation.

The Therapeutic Process

Goals of Therapy. The goals of behavioral parent training (BPT) are: (1) to teach the client new adaptive behaviors to increase the child's repertoire of desirable behaviors, and (2) to weaken or decrease maladaptive or undesirable behaviors.

Role of the Therapist. In behavior modification, the therapist acts as an expert and model who can assist parents in identifying behaviors and designing contingencies. The therapist establishes rapport, analyzes the behaviors parents or family members want to change, assists in designing a behavioral management program, and acts as a coach to reinforce parents as they implement the program.

TABLE 10–1 Healthy parenting

1. The child has a healthy repertoire of behaviors and is continually learning new ones from the parents.

2. Parents act as behavioral engineers and models to teach their children through behavioral management programs and contracting.

3. Parents receive from their children what they give.

4. There is behavioral reciprocity in parent-child interactions in that high rates of positive behaviors on the part of parents toward their children lead to high rates of positive behaviors on the part of children toward their parents.

5. Time outs from positive reinforcement are contingent upon undesirable behaviors.

6. The behaviors of the larger social system interact with those of the child and the parent-child dyad. The school, community, and court system provide learning environments for children and adolescents.

Adapted from "Behavioral Parent Training" by S. B. Gordon and N. Davidson in *Handbook of Family Therapy* (pp. 519–523) by A. S. Gurman and D. P. Kniskern (Eds.), 1981, New York: Brunner/Mazel.

Use of Diagnosis and Assessment. In BPT, the therapist teaches parents how to conduct behavioral assessments. They learn to observe and record data, measure baselines, implement behavioral management programs that include positive reinforcers, and collect data to determine how well the program is working.

Therapists typically administer questionnaires before and following treatment. In addition, parents observe and record behaviors during and after treatment. Observers are often used to record behaviors as well so that objective feedback can be obtained concerning the effectiveness of the training program.

Gerald Patterson

At the University of Oregon, Gerald Patterson (1968) worked with more than 100 problem children and their families. He wrote a programmed text, *Living with Children,* for parents to use in teaching children adaptive behaviors, while reducing problem behaviors. Patterson and Gullion (1968) revised this text to include short forms with concise instructions for parents to use with their normal, healthy children. Most recently Patterson has focused on the conduct disorders of pre-adolescents and adolescents (see Patterson & Forgatch, 1987; Forgatch & Patterson, 1989).

Patterson teaches parents about social learning and positive and negative reinforcers. For most children, rewards of candy, money, food, and toys serve effectively as positive reinforcers. Social reinforcers such as smiles, pats on the back, praise, kisses, approval, and attention also function as positive reinforcers. Parents must be very careful regarding the timing of the reinforcement. It should be given immediately after the desired behavior. If the reinforcement is given at the wrong time, it may actually reinforce an undesirable behavior (such as whining).

Parents are then taught to observe, count, and record the child's behavior. One effective technique in changing undesirable behavior is the use of time out, a form of punishment in which a child is isolated from positive reinforcement in a quiet room for a short period of time. Time outs can be used to shape the behaviors of normal children as well as the maladaptive behaviors of problem children. Time outs are best accompanied by a retraining program in which rewards are given when the undesirable behavior is absent for an agreed-upon period of time or if a competing new desirable behavior occurs several times a day. Such parent training programs have been successful (Patterson, Chamberlin, & Reid, 1982).

Patterson (1975a, 1975b) refined his approach and applied it to the total family. He encourages families to use a technique called contracting, in which a written contract, outlining desired and undesired behaviors, and the contingencies or consequences of such behaviors, is agreed upon by all members. Contracts can be used for children and with married couples. With children, contracting works on a 10-point system. Parents count and record the frequency of occurrence of undesirable behavior, then contract with the child to promote desirable behavior. The child is given points for exhibiting not only the desirable behavior but also for exhibiting encouraging steps leading up to it. When the child accumulates 10 points, parents reward the child with positive reinforcers such as toys or special privileges.

In contracting with married couples, the process of negotiation is particularly important and should occur as problems arise by arranging a place and time to discuss problems before they become large or out of proportion. The person initiating the negotiation describes the behavior that is creating the problem and how the person feels in response to the behavior. The partner listens and then paraphrases what the person has said, ending the first part of the process.

Later, at a mutually agreed-upon time, the couple meets. Each points out and records on paper desired behaviors of the partner that would make life more satisfying, while the other person listens. Aversive comments should be recorded, and when an agreed-upon limit is reached, the negotiation session should be terminated. Beginning with the first item on the list, each person attempts to exchange items. After the parties agree to exchange certain behaviors for others, they reach consensus on the consequences, both positive and aversive, that will occur contingent upon the demonstration of the behavior. Each signs a written contract to show agreement.

Jim Alexander

Jim Alexander has conducted research on delinquent teenagers for more than 10 years at the University of Utah, combining behavioral approaches with systems theory to create functional family therapy (Alexander, 1973; Alexander & Barton, 1976, 1980; Alexander & Parsons, 1973, 1982; Barton & Alexander, 1977a, 1977b, 1981). In the initial session the therapist asks what type of interpersonal function a given behavior plays in a family: merging, in which closeness is the intent; separating, in which independence is the aim; or midpointing, in which both merging and separating are present (for example, double dating, which permits independence while allowing some intimacy). The functional family therapist observes the interactional behavioral sequences in the family and the thoughts and feelings expressed by family members in the initial session to assess the functions of their behaviors (Alexander & Parsons, 1982).

The functional family therapist enters the family by: (1) clarifying the meaning of the behavior of each family member, (2) relabeling any blaming behavior, (3) pointing out the interdependence of the behaviors and feelings of family members (focusing on interactions and relationships), (4) determining the functions of the behaviors of family members, and (5) assigning homework. After the initial session, the therapist analyzes the family on these five dimensions and plans tentative goals.

Specific techniques are recommended for dealing with diverse family structures. For example, Alexander and Parsons (1982) suggest a negotiated quiet time of 30 minutes for working single parents, during which the parent relaxes and the children are quiet. The parent then meets with each child individually to deal with requests and give needed attention. Where there is two-parent contact in a single-parent family, recommendations include cooperation by the parents so that the non-custodial parent emotionally supports and appreciates the custodial parent, and the custodial parent provides structure for the non-custodial parent's new role.

As one of the best-known researchers in family therapy, Alexander (1988) encourages further research on the process of family therapy. He developed an Anatomy of Intervention Model (AIM) which delineates five phases of therapy: (1) introduction, (2) assessment, (3) motivation, (4) behavior change, and (5) termination. Each phase has different goals, central tasks, needed skills of the therapist, and therapeutic activities or techniques. A therapist must be able to exhibit both relationship skills (warmth, integration of behavior and feelings, humor, non-blaming, and self-disclosure) and structuring skills (self-confidence, directiveness, and clarity) to effectively treat a family.

BEHAVIORAL MARITAL THERAPY

View of Healthy Functioning

The behavioral model of a healthy functioning marriage is contained in Table 10–2. In successful marriages, the spouses expect to receive at a high level, so they give at a high level. Spouses work hard to maximize mutual benefits while reducing individual costs. Spouses are able to observe and to objectively identify what is going on in the relationship, including consequences that reinforce both positive and aversive behaviors. They understand and emotionally support each other and can communicate at deep levels. Together the spouses can negotiate, solve problems, and manage conflicts that arise (Jacobson, 1981; Weiss, 1978).

The Therapeutic Process

Goals of BMT. The goals of BMT are: (1) to create and maintain the positive expectancy that spouses can function as positive reinforcers for each other in a collaborative reciprocity; (2) to conduct a behavioral assessment of the marriage and teach spouses how to assess the behavioral interactions in their relationships; and (3) to implement behavioral learning principles in the marital relationship such as communication skills, problem-resolution competencies, behavioral exchange, contracting, negotiation of rules and roles, and managing conflict.

Role of the Therapist. The therapist is a behavioral scientist who analyzes the difficulties of the couple. The therapist also functions as an educator and role model to teach the spouses to assess their relationship, to implement strategies of behavioral change, and to use resources to strengthen the relationship.

TABLE 10–2 Toward Healthier Family Systems: A healthy marriage from a behavioral view

1. Reciprocity occurs in the relationship. There is a positive expectation that the spouse will return positive reinforcement at a high rate.

2. Positive interactions between spouses greatly exceed aversive ones.

3. Each spouse in the relationship perceives greater positive benefits from staying in the relationship than individual costs.

4. Affectionate, tender, emotionally satisfying behaviors such as companionship, affection, sex, consideration, couple activities, and communication are exchanged at a high rate in the marital relationship.

5. Instrumental behaviors such as financial planning, household management, parenting, and employment/education are exchanged at an acceptable rate.

6. Spouses can observe and objectively identify what is going on in the relationship, including consequences such as positive reinforcers or aversive behaviors.

7. Spouses can understand and emotionally support each other.

8. Spouses can communicate at deep levels.

9. If inequities occur in their relationship or as natural changes happen in the family life cycle, they can negotiate behavioral changes in the relationship.

10. Spouses are able to formulate and change the rules of their relationship and negotiate the instrumental roles that they will play as part of the relationship.

11. Spouses can use problem-solving skills.

12. Spouses can handle conflict effectively, using it to grow in the relationship by making changes as needed.

Use of Diagnosis and Assessment. Behavioral marital therapists use assessment prior to initiating therapy, during the initial session, throughout the therapy process, at termination, and often in a follow-up many months after therapy has terminated (Jacobson, 1981). Because of the emphasis on research within behavioral approaches, many questionnaires are distributed and outcome is assessed by various types of measures. For example, the Spouse Observation Checklist (Weiss & Perry, 1979) asks spouses to list the frequencies of behaviors that are pleasing or displeasing (Jacob & Tennenbaum, 1988).

One important characteristic of BMT is the behavioral analysis of the marital interaction of the couple. All behavioral marital therapists conduct some form of behavioral assessment during the initial phases of treatment and evaluate how the behavior is changing throughout treatment and at termination. One of the pioneers of BMT is Robert Liberman (1970), who uses behavioral assessment in his BMT approach.

Liberman (1975) completes the following steps in performing a behavioral analysis: (1) specifies the therapeutic goals in terms of target behaviors and how they will be measured; (2) takes a baseline of the present rate of the behaviors in the relationship; (3) sets up cues for desirable behaviors and withdraws cues for undesirable behaviors, showing spouses how to do this for each other; (4) locates positive and negative reinforcers; (5) educates the spouses on how to use the reinforcers in their relationship; (6) shapes the target behaviors by rewarding successive approximations of the behaviors; (7) fades out cues in sessions to encourage generalization; (8) reinforces gains on an intermittent schedule of reinforcement; and (9) keep updated records of sessions.

Nature of the Initial Session.   Bornstein and Bornstein (1986) divide the initial session into opening remarks, the presenting problems, a developmental history of the relationship, a cross-sectional history, an initial intervention, and closing remarks. In order to establish rapport, the therapist makes a few opening remarks regarding what the couple can expect from the session. The therapist will then ask an open-ended question such as "What brings you here?" By observing who speaks first and how the response is conveyed, the therapist gathers data for an assessment.

Usually angry or hostile remarks are made by one or both spouses, so the therapist should intervene and redirect the interview by asking specific questions about the presenting problem. The therapist should move quickly here so that spouses do not become bogged down in lengthy litanies of the problems in the relationship. A brief overview can be expanded in later sessions as the focus shifts to specific problems.

In the initial session, the most time should be spent obtaining a developmental history of the relationship. Questions such as the following are helpful in taking this history:

What was attractive to you about each other when you first met?
What were some of the best times that you remember?
When and how did you decide to marry?
What were the wedding and honeymoon like?
What was your relationship like in those early years?
What do you think changed things?
How do you see your future?

In addition to a developmental history, the therapist should gather a cross-sectional history by asking such questions as "What is a typical weekday like for each of you?" and "Could you tell me about an average Saturday or Sunday for you?" By listening to the content and observing the process, the therapist can piece together a picture of the benefits and costs in the relationship.

Where time allows, it is often helpful to perform an initial intervention by focusing on some small, annoying behavior that a spouse would like to have changed. A simple homework activity can be assigned which, if implemented, will instill hope in the therapeutic process.

Finally, it is appropriate for the therapist to summarize what has occurred in the session, repeating the concerns of each spouse, stating a few tentative goals that have been discussed, and giving feedback about the interactional style of the couple. Such a procedure provides closure for the couple. In addition, the number of assessment sessions remaining, appropriate fees, and any expectations for the next session should be outlined. The therapist should gain the commitment of the spouses to complete the assessment questionnaires prior to the next session.

In the next session, after the self-report instruments have been completed, Bornstein and Bornstein (1986) give the couple feedback on their strengths and weaknesses. An explanation of the treatment process is stated, along with an estimated number of sessions required and a discussion of fees. The goals of treatment and the ground rules are spelled out clearly, gaining the consensus of the couple through discussion and agreement.

Richard Stuart

In 1969 Richard Stuart, a psychologist and the most noted of the behavioral marital therapists, wrote the first journal article on behavioral marital therapy, entitled, "Operant Interpersonal Treatment for Marital Discord." He integrated the social exchange theory of social psychologists such as Thibaut and Kelley (1959) and the contracting of Lederer and Jackson (1968) with behavioral learning principles to formulate his own model of marital therapy.

Key Theoretical Concepts. Stuart developed a set of principles of relationship change which undergird his work with couples (Table 10–3). Some of these principles include the "change-first" principle, in which Stuart encourages each person in

Dr. Richard Stuart is a psychologist who is credited with writing the first journal article on behavioral marital therapy. (Courtesy of Richard B. Stuart)

the relationship to take responsibility for changing first rather than waiting for the partner to change. He advises each person to act according to the "as if" principle, as though a person expects the partner to act in a reciprocal manner and responding to positive behaviors in kind, and to be interested in the improvement of the relationship. Stuart maintains that relationships operate according to the "all win" principle: One person can gain only temporarily unless both partners gain.

The Therapeutic Process. As an illustration of the stages of behavioral marital therapy and its typical techniques, a summary of Stuart's approach is discussed. The sequence of his intervention techniques across therapy sessions includes: (1) completion of inventories and the presentation of the ground rules for therapy, (2) the "caring days" exercise, (3) communication skills, (4) contracting, (5) decision-making skills, (6) conflict management skills, and (7) prevention of relapse.

Completing inventories and presenting ground rules. In addition to using a pretreatment orientation tape at the beginning of treatment, Stuart (1973) administers his Marital Pre-Counseling Inventory and other instruments to assess the marital relationship. He states the expectations for treatment and spends time establishing rapport with the couple. Unlike previously mentioned therapists (Bornstein & Bornstein, 1986; Jacobson, 1981; Jacobson & Margolin, 1979), Stuart does not believe in taking a developmental history of the relationship (1980b, 1980c). He is interested only in what the spouses volunteer that may be interfering from the past. He emphasizes the present relationship and what problems each spouse would like to change.

"Caring days." In this exercise, each spouse is asked to state exact behaviors the partner should show in order for the spouse to know that the partner cares. In other words, each spouse is required to clearly state, "I feel loved when you. . . ." (Achord et al., 1986) and to request small behaviors that can be accomplished on a daily basis. For example, one spouse may feel loved when the partner gives a hug upon awakening in the morning, while the other feels loved if the partner asks how the spouse is feeling at the breakfast table each morning. Rules include that the requested behaviors must be small and exhibited at least daily, have not been the cause of recent conflicts, are not chores, must be positive, and are very specific. A spouse may or may not agree to demonstrate the behavior. For example, an individual who has an intense fear of touch may say so and indicate that touching is something that the person cannot give at this point.

After the spouses have agreed to 18 items between them, the items are marked on a chart (forms are available from Research Press) posted in the home, so that the recipient of the behavior can mark the date upon which the behavior was received. The couple can add a few items each week. Out of the 18 behaviors, each spouse is asked to commit to giving the spouse 5 or more of these behaviors on a daily basis. Stuart (1980a) calls the couple several days after the session to reinforce or prompt the continuation of the 5 required behaviors a day.

In marriages in which couples use such instrumental behaviors for exchange, there is often an absence of affection and companionship that is killing the marriage. Requiring each spouse to state how he or she will know that the partner cares by specific affectionate behaviors is crucial to the success of the exercise and the subsequent

TABLE 10–3 Principles of relationship change

I. In understanding relationships:
   A. *The open-system principle.* All relationships change constantly as a result of reactions to external demands and shifting desires on the part of all people in the relationship. Therefore, change is the norm of all relationships.
   B. *The best-bargain principle.* The behaviors that all parties in relationships display at any given moment represent the best means that each person believes he or she has available for obtaining desired satisfactions.
   C. *The instability principle.* All relationships are intrinsically unstable in that any party may decide that the reward-cost balance of opting out of the relationship may be greater than the reward-cost balance of remaining within it.

II. In changing relationships:
   A. *The change-first principle.* To overcome polarities in relationship struggles, all parties must assume the responsibility for changing their own behavior first in order to prompt behavior changes in others.
   B. *The positive-change principle.* Relationships can be changed best through a search for positive behaviors that can take the place of (i.e., provide the satisfactions earned by) negative exchanges.
   C. *The small-steps principle.* Complex relationships can be changed only through small, planned, sequential steps.
   D. *The as-if principle.* To prompt the initiation of small, assertive, positive changes, it is important for each person to act as if the others have a definite interest in promoting relationship change.
   E. *The fear-of-change principle.* In virtually all areas of human behavior, it is wise to expect that people will be fearful of change even if by any objective standard that change is toward the relief of pain and the provision of pleasure. Therefore, some resistance to all change efforts is to be expected and cannot be taken as a negative sign.
   F. *The testing principle.* All parties can be expected to test especially the most positive of changes in order to make certain that they can be trusted over time. Testing takes the form of a time-limited return to earlier behaviors that can be overcome by reaffirmation of the desire for change.
   G. *The predictability principle.* Relationships produce more comfort and more freedom for all principals when their norms are expressed as rules.

From *Helping Couples Change: A Social Learning Approach to Marital Therapy* (pp. 370–371) by R. Stuart, 1980, New York: Guilford Press. Reprinted by permission.

marital therapy. When couples resist the exercise by not doing it, the therapist must confidently reiterate the value of the exercise and expect that it will be done by the third session. Such an approach strengthens the couple's view of the therapist's expertise and commitment to the success of the marital therapy. Nichols (1984) cautions that exercises to increase reinforcement reciprocity are contraindicated for couples in

TABLE 10–3 *continued*

H. *The principle of irreversibility.* No act of any kind can ever be completely withdrawn, nor will it ever be completely forgotten. Therefore, tact and timing should be the benchmarks of all behavior.

I. *The all-win or no-win principle.* In every bargaining situation in all relationships, no person can make more than a temporary gain unless all parties win.

J. *The principle of shared responsibility.* All parties to the relationship are jointly responsible for everything that happens between them, good or bad; and therefore, all parties must participate in any successful effort to promote relationship change.

K. *The principle of behavioral essence.* We are all what we do in the eyes of others. Therefore, we are "loving" only if we act in lovable ways; we are "trustworthy" only if our behavior supports this label, etc.

L. *The principle of the urgent present.* It is necessary to concentrate attention on the present, forsaking the opportunities to exact penalties for the past in all efforts to promote or maintain relationship improvement.

III. In understanding and changing communication:

A. *The principle of constant communication.* One cannot not communicate, as every behavior, verbal or nonverbal, expresses both a specific content and a comment about the relationship between the parties.

B. *The principle of level consistency.* Because all communications have at least two levels, and because communicators often attend more closely to one level as opposed to the other(s), there are frequent inconsistencies between the varied levels of each communication.

C. *The principle of the whispering words and shouting gestures.* When there are inconsistencies between the levels of the messages expressed, the nonverbal message almost always has a greater impact than the spoken message.

D. *The princess-and-the-pea principle.* Any negative dimension of any communication is likely to have a greater impact than the sum total of all of the positive dimensions of the communication.

E. *The ownership principle.* It is important to take active ownership of every message sent whether in the form of a statement or in the form of a question, for that is the only way to enter into responsible communication.

F. *The principle of incomplete communication.* Because one can never be sure that the message sent is the message that will be received, no communication cycle is complete until the message is sent and acknowledged.

---

complementary relationships in which one individual is dominant and the other is submissive.

Communication skills. Stuart (1980a) teaches couples to listen; to make constructive requests using "I" statements; to give positive feedback, complimenting a spouse on a particular positive behavior immediately after it has occurred; and to use clarification questions to check out nonverbal and verbal behaviors.

Contracting. Using a win-win approach, Stuart (1980a) encourages the couple to negotiate a holistic, therapeutic marital contract. Each spouse is required to make requests of the other for specific positive behaviors. The other spouse rephrases the requests and asks for clarification of meaning. After reaching consensus, they record the requests in contract form and sign it. About one half of the couples in treatment renegotiate the contract at least once.

Decision-making skills. Stuart (1975) asks each spouse to identify those areas where the person exercises power and those areas where the person ideally would like to exercise power. The spouses then negotiate who will control what area, under what conditions, and in what situations. Spouses may use a powergram to discuss those areas that each controls alone, that each controls after consulting the other, and that they control equally. Desired patterns can be requested, and different patterns of authority can be negotiated.

Conflict management skills. It is easier to prevent conflicts if couples know how to communicate and to allocate decision-making within certain specified roles. If couples have negotiated effective reactions to potential triggers in their relationship, they are more apt to respond with an appropriate response, which will reduce tension and avoid conflict.

Stuart (1980a) emphasizes the importance of keeping the discussion confined to the present, rather than expanding to related incidents or issues from the past. Conflicts are easier to resolve if they are broken into small steps or issues that are dealt with in sequence. The stages of conflict include trigger, reflex, fatigue, commitment, reconsolidation, and rapprochement.

At first an individual automatically feels reflexive anger in response to a trigger but can pause to decide what or how much to express. To manage the feeling level, spouses can be taught relaxation exercises and the expression of assertive responses rather than aggressive ones. To manage the nonverbal or verbal actions taken, spouses can be taught to own their anger, express respect for the spouse, state a threat in terms of what the person will do to whom if certain things do not happen, and request a reasonable change. The spouse may then respond by owning anger, restating what the spouse would like to have happen, and checking it out with the spouse.

During the commitment stage, the angry spouse often withdraws. It does not help for the other spouse to withdraw; rather, the other spouse should be willing to listen, with either partner being able to reach out to the other. Most couples set up a system of signals so that each will know when the other is ready to problem solve and reconsolidate. Rapprochement occurs when one of the spouses states what has been learned and what behavior will change in the future, acknowledging the requested change made by the partner.

Maintenance of therapeutic outcome. Stuart (1980a) proposes a model for the maintenance of therapeutic outcome which includes the following components: (1) explaining the rationale for each intervention and the principles of relationship change; (2) modeling techniques during the therapy that the clients themselves can apply in the future in their relationship; (3) teaching spouses how to assess marital interaction and change the relationship so that they can continue these processes after termination; (4) helping spouses to anticipate predictable relapses (progress occurs with a peak, then a deep valley of testing, followed by another higher peak and a shallow valley, ending with the highest peak); (5) identifying supports in the environment by encouraging the couple to spend one hour a month together assessing the relationship, rewarding each other for the gains that have been made, and making new requests for additional desirable behaviors; and (6) equipping the couple with stabilizing maneuvers, such as a written summary of the interventions used and the changes made by each spouse and the completion of an experiential "what if" exercise.

BEHAVIORAL SEX THERAPY

Many couples who present for marital therapy have sexual problems. It is important for marital therapists to know the phases of normal sexual functioning, to be able to assess sexual functioning for possible sexual dysfunctions, and to have available a list of medical specialists to whom clients with particular sexual dysfunctions can be referred. With some sexual complaints, it is crucial to refer the individual or couple to physicians. For example, painful intercourse (dyspareunia) in females can be the result of a yeast or other type of infection or due to the reduction in the production of hormones by the ovaries at peri-menopause or menopause, necessitating hormone replacement therapy. Additional training specifically in sex therapy should be obtained by marital therapists who wish to provide treatment in this area or to specialize in sex therapy.

View of Healthy Functioning

The Diagnostic and Statistical Manual of Mental Disorders—Revised incorporates a combination of the pioneering work of Masters and Johnson (1966, 1970) and that of Kaplan (1974, 1979) in defining the normal healthy sexual response in human beings (Table 10–4). They state four phases: appetitive (fantasies accompanied by a desire for sexual intercourse), excitement (physiological changes in the sex organs accompanied by sexual pleasure), orgasm (a climax of sexual pleasure with a release of tension accompanied by contractions), and resolution (muscle relaxation).

Sexual activity can be the ultimate symbol of human love when it is the expression of an intimate and caring relationship. However, if there are conflicts in the relationship such as unresolved anger, the enjoyment or ability to function sexually can be affected.

Initial Interview

In every initial interview in marital therapy, some questions should be asked about the sexual activity of the couple. Such open-ended questions as "How often do you have sexual intercourse?" "How satisfied are you with your sexual activity?" and "What do you like about your sexual activity and what do you dislike?" often elicit lengthy responses from the couple. This information may not have been volunteered in the first encounter, but it is vital to the overall treatment plan.

In addition, asking questions about alcohol and drug use and medical problems are important in the initial interview. Chronic alcoholics often experience sexual dysfunctions due to nerve damage (in some cases, irreversible). Individuals who drink too

TABLE 10–4   Toward Healthier Family Systems: Phases of normal sexual response

I. Appetitive

Fantasies about sexual activity accompanied by a desire for such activity.

II. Excitement

Physiological changes in the sex organs accompanied by sexual pleasure.

In the female, swelling of the breasts and external genitalia occurs, coupled with vaginal lubrication, vasocongestion of the pelvis and the labia minora, and widening and lengthening of the innermost part of the vagina. The outer part narrows to form an orgasmic platform due to vasocongestion and pubococcygeal muscle tension (PC muscle).

In the male, swelling of the penis results in an erection and secretion by the Cowper's gland.

III. Orgasm

A climax of sexual pleasure with a release of tension accompanied by contractions of the reproductive organs in the pelvis and the perineal muscles.

In the female, contractions of the vagina occur.

In the male, ejaculation of semen occurs in response to contractions of the urethra, prostate, and seminal vesicles.

Generalized muscle contractions often occurs in both females and males.

IV. Resolution

Muscular relaxation with a sense of well being.

Physiologically females may be able to be stimulated immediately, while males are refractory to further stimulation for a period of time (varies from male to male).

From *Diagnostic and Statistical Manual of Mental Disorders—Revised* (p. 291), 1987, Washington, DC: American Psychiatric Assoc. Adapted by permission.

much in an evening can expect to feel uninhibited sexually, but they will probably not be able to perform effectively. Certain illnesses such as diabetes in men can dramatically affect sexual response, as can pelvic surgery in women if key nerves have been severed.

If a specific sexual problem surfaces in response to general open-ended questions, obtaining a specific history of the sexual problem is indicated. A marital therapist might ask such questions as "When did you notice the problem for the first time?" "What happened immediately before the problem occurred and immediately after?" "What did each of you do to try to correct the problem, and what happened each time?" and "What do you think is the cause of the problem?" If it appears that the sexual problem is the main presenting problem, the therapist can set treatment goals with the couple directly related to the sexual problem.

In any case, a thorough assessment of the marital relationship should be made in the initial session to determine any other problems that may be of primary importance or tangential to the sexual problem. Questions are asked about the current relationship to explore five areas: (1) inclusion, control, and intimacy, (2) behavior, thoughts, and feelings, (3) communication skills, (4) decision-making and problem-solving skills, and (5) conflict management. After this information is obtained, the expectations concerning the original marital contract are discussed, including goals, needs, and external factors. Finally, the relationships in the family of origin are explored (Hof, 1987).

Definitions and Treatments of Sexual Dysfunctions

The diagnosis of a particular sexual dysfunction may be made, based on information received in the initial and additional sessions. Table 10–5 includes the diagnostic criteria for diverse sexual dysfunctions and suggested treatments for each. In all cases, a diagnosis of a sexual dysfunction is made only if the criteria occur when another clinical syndrome is not present.

When physical components have been treated or ruled out, the therapist must decide if treatment of the particular disorder falls within the therapist's education, training, and experience. If so, the therapist will work out a treatment plan with the couple and proceed. If not, the therapist may need to refer the couple to other specialists or clinics.

Since the program at the Masters and Johnson Institute in St. Louis, Missouri is a prototype of sexual dysfunction treatment programs, its components will be discussed here. Masters and Johnson (1970) require both spouses to attend the entire 2-week program. One of the basic premises at the Institute is that the marital relationship is the patient. Both spouses are involved in conjoint treatment, because it is impossible to have a married partner who is not implicated in some way in the sexual inadequacy. The couple works with two co-therapists, one of each sex. For the first 3 days of the program, an extensive sexual history of each partner is taken by the same-sex therapist in front of the spouse and opposite-sex therapist. There is an extensive physical examination, including a medical history. At the end of the third day, the co-therapists summarize what has been learned and permit the spouses to ask questions.

The couple is assigned a non-genital sensate focus exercise for homework. The spouses are instructed to take off their clothing, and one spouse, designated by the therapist, begins to touch the body of the other spouse in ways designed to evoke sensual pleasure, while the other spouse receives and enjoys the pleasure. Then the roles are reversed, and the exercise is repeated. Since genital touching and intercourse are forbidden, the exercise increases both positive feelings and effective communication.

On the fourth day, the couple is assigned the genital sensate focus exercise. The genitals and breasts are included in the parts of the body touched by the partner in the exercise, but no intercourse is permitted. During the fourth day, couples also receive instruction in basic anatomy and physiology. From the fifth day through the end of the 2 weeks, the couple participates in activities specifically tailored to treat their specific dysfunction (see Table 10–5).

TABLE 10—5 Types and treatments of diverse sexual dysfunctions

I. Sexual Desire Disorders

Hypoactive Sexual Desire Disorder: Persistent absence of sexual fantasies and impulses.

Treatment: Sequence of behavior modification of avoidance behaviors, sensate focus exercises, giving permission to enjoy sexual sensations, assigning sexual fantasies, and focusing on sexually stimulating fantasies or materials.

Sexual Aversion Disorder: Persistent avoidance of genital sexual contact.

Treatment: Sensate focus exercises and systematic exposure to sexual situations.

II. Sexual Arousal Disorders

Female Sexual Arousal Disorder: In a female, persistent inability to have lubrication and swelling of the sexual organs or lack of sexual pleasure or excitement during sexual intercourse.

Treatment: A sequence of sensate focus exercises, nondemand coitus, coitus to orgasm, and Kegal's exercises for the PC muscle.

Male Erectile Disorder (Impotence): In a male, persistent inability to have or maintain an erection or lack of sexual pleasure or excitement during sexual intercourse.

Treatment: A sequence of erotic pleasure (without erection), no orgasm with erection, orgasm with erection outside the vagina, penetration without orgasm, and coitus.

III. Orgasm Disorders

Inhibited Female Orgasm: A persistent absence or delay of orgasm in a female who has experienced normal arousal and excitement. For some women orgasm is achieved by clitoral stimulation by their partner, and this is normal for them.

From *Diagnostic and Statistical Manual of Mental Disorders— Revised,* 1987, Washington, DC: American Psychiatric Assoc. Adapted by permission. Also from *The Illustrated Manual of Sex Therapy* (2/e) by H. S. Kaplan, 1987, New York: Brunner/Mazel. Adapted by permission.

Kaplan (1979) has developed techniques for dealing with sexual desire disorder. With hypoactive sexual desire disorder, behavioral techniques are used to deal with the avoidance, fantasies as well as sensate focus exercises are assigned, and permission is given to enjoy sexual activity. With sexual aversion disorder, a spouse must learn to relax using relaxation exercises as well as sensate focus exercises and is gradually and systematically exposed to sexual situations over a period of time while remaining relaxed. With sexual desire disorders, Kaplan (1979) emphasizes that psychodynamically oriented therapy, which focuses on the underlying conflicts, is needed in addition to the behavioral sexual exercises.

COGNITIVE BEHAVIORAL APPROACHES

One puzzling occurrence in sex therapy and marital therapy is that sometimes, even when married couples or families make positive progress as measured by objective

TABLE 10–5 *continued*

Treatment: A sequence of masturbation, clitoral stimulation with the partner leading to orgasm, orgasm within intercourse, and a bridge maneuver if orgasm does not occur with intercourse.

Inhibited Male Orgasm (Retarded Ejaculation): A persistent inability to ejaculate within the vagina.

Treatment: Behavioral shaping of closer approximations to ejaculation within the vagina. The wife may be encouraged to stimulate her husband to orgasm while he is distracted by erotic fantasy. A male bridge maneuver may also be used.

Premature Ejaculation: A persistent ejaculation when slight stimulation occurs, so that the male ejaculates upon or immediately following penetration of the female.

Treatment: Squeeze method of Masters and Johnson or the Stop-Start technique as developed by Kaplan.

IV. Sexual Pain Disorders

Dyspareunia: In females or males, recurrent genital pain during, before, or after sexual intercourse.

Treatment: In females, treatment by a gynecologist of non-venereal yeast or fungus infections or the prescription of estrogen for women in the peri-menopause or menopause. Use of sensate focus exercise to lengthen foreplay, thereby increasing lubrication.

Vaginismus: In a female, involuntary muscle spasms of the vagina that interfere with sexual intercourse by blocking penetration.

Treatment: Systematic desensitization and hypnosis to treat phobic avoidance. In-vivo desensitization and insertion of finger or spouse's finger or gradually larger objects under the supervision of a gynecologist. Analytic and supportive work may also be needed to reduce phobic avoidance prior to this procedure, if hypnosis or systematic desensitization have not reduced the fears of penetration.

---

observers, on marital satisfaction scales or comparable instruments of satisfaction in family life they report the same low level of satisfaction recorded prior to treatment. Unfortunately, their thoughts or attitudes toward the marriage are better predictors of self-reported satisfaction and marital longevity than their improved behaviors. Ingrained cognitive processes appear to be central to marital dissatisfaction and surprisingly independent of actual skill in communicating and solving problems. Couples who are excellent communicators and solve many practical problems may not stay together because of the attitudes and cognitions they have toward marriage in general and their partners in particular.

Key Theoretical Concepts

Cognitive Mediation in Marital Interaction. Epstein, Schlesinger, & Dryden (1988) developed a model of cognitive mediation of behavioral exchanges in marriage that explains this phenomenon. The wife thinks that her husband should always pay attention to her. She then talks to her husband, who thinks to himself that he wants to pay attention to the end of the television program, which exercises his right to be an autonomous individual, and he does so. His wife says to herself that he did not pay attention to her; therefore, he is inconsiderate, does not love her, and probably wants a divorce. She feels angry and depressed but afraid to say anything. She withdraws. The husband says to himself that his wife has withdrawn; therefore, she is cold and unloving, a hard woman who is difficult to please. He withdraws. The wife sees that her husband has withdrawn and says that he is rejecting her because he wants to leave her like her father left her mother. She feels angry. She packs her bags and leaves before he has a chance to leave her.

Such a scenario seems somewhat unrealistic, but divorce papers have often been filed over such trivial matters. The meaning that an individual spouse attaches to the trivial behaviors of the partner can affect subsequent reactions to the partner, creating distress and lowering marital satisfaction. Often themes of malicious intent, lack of love, and lack of respect are cognitions contributing to marital distress. In Figure 10–1, each person is attempting to read the partner's mind. The inaccurate thoughts or cognitions they are saying to themselves are affecting the relationship, leading to distress.

Types of Cognitions.   In marital and family interactions, a number of diverse cognitions can mediate an individual's behavior (Table 10–6). When these cognitions are positive and collaborative, there will be a positive behavioral exchange in the marriage and within the family. When cognitions are negative or extremely rigid, interaction may deteriorate between the spouses and within the family.

Causal attributions are related to marital satisfaction (Holtzworth-Munroe & Jacobson, 1987). Spouses satisfied with their marriages attributed the causes of positive events to the global, voluntary, internal, stable characteristics of their partners and negative events to situational, unintentional, involuntary, or unstable factors— relationship-enhancing attributions. For example, a wife might say that her husband surprised her with flowers because he is a caring, thoughtful man, but he was late for supper because the car unexpectedly broke down.

With distressed spouses, opposite, distress-maintaining attributions occur. The positive behaviors of the spouse are attributed to unstable, situational, involuntary, or unintentional factors, while negative behaviors of the spouse are viewed as stable, intentional, internal, global, and voluntary.

In such situations, spouses often perceive that nothing can be done to change the attributions and behaviors. Learned helplessness sets in, similar to the rats who were shocked every time they pushed a lever to obtain food pellets and learned to apathetically huddle in their cages rather than try to obtain the pellets when the shock was turned off (Seligman, 1975). Couples become involved in apathetic competition waiting for each other to make the first move, expecting aversive consequences if action is taken to initiate change in the behaviors in the relationship (Seligman et al., 1988). They believe that, regardless of what is done, negative consequences will result. Therapists are encouraged to directly chal-

FIGURE 10–1 Mind reading and distorted cognitions lead to distress in relationships

TABLE 10—6 Types of cognitions

Perceptions	Identifying and judging events and people through sensory information. Cognitive distortions are inaccurate perceptions of events.
Beliefs	Probabilities from a subjective point of view that a person or event has a particular characteristic. Many beliefs can be organized into a belief system such as the self-concept, which consists of the probabilities of certain characteristics being found in the self.
Attributions	Causes assigned to the occurrence of an event or characteristics assigned to an individual.
Expectancies	Predictions about the likelihood of the occurrence of events based on what has happened in the past—expectations. Self-fulfilling prophecies can happen as a result of negative expectancies.
Values	Standards of behavior, priorities in life, or key life goals.
Expectations	A person's subjective estimates that events will occur in the future—expectancies.
Reactances	Tendencies of human beings to defend the behaviors that they are competent to perform if they choose to—personal behavioral freedoms.

lenge the expectations undergirding the learned helplessness (Hollon & Garber, 1980).

Cognitive Mediation in Healthy Family Functioning.   In healthy families, perceptions tend to be positive but not absolute. People are seen as they really are—human beings with imperfections and foibles who are still lovable in spite of, and sometimes because of, their faults (Table 10–7). People talk to each other rather than attempting to read each other's minds. Family members attribute positive characteristics to other members and expect that other members will exhibit positive behaviors toward them.

An Afro-American Cognitive Expectancy Approach.   In working with members of minority groups, especially black students and urban families, it is important to engender positive expectations and confront negative expectancies (Thomas, 1986). The saga of Afro-Americans has been a history of struggle against negative expectations and oppression. Arriving as slaves on American shores, the original ancestors of the current black community passed on their history through the oral tradition: stories and speeches that contained messages encouraging the positive expectancies necessary for survival. The image of "the dream" flows from the souls of Afro-Americans and is interwoven throughout their literature. One of the most famous examples is the speech by Dr. Martin Luther King, Jr., which states:

> I say to you today, my friends, that in spite of the difficulties and the frustrations of the moment, I still have a dream. It is a dream deeply rooted in the American dream. . . . With

TABLE 10—7 Toward Healthier Family Systems: Cognitive mediation in healthy families

1. Perceptions are realistic: Situations are neither minimized nor maximized. Positive behaviors are noted and not disqualified. Negative events are taken in stride as a part of life without linking them to negative expectations.

2. Perceptions are relative rather than absolute. Both the positive aspects of negative situations and the negative aspects of positive situations are recognized.

3. People talk to each other to find out each other's perceptions of situations.

4. Family members attribute positive characteristics to other family members and to themselves.

5. Family members believe that other family members have positive intentions even if their behaviors are negative.

6. Family members expect positive behaviors from other family members and, therefore, exhibit increased positive behaviors themselves because they expect that these behaviors will be reciprocated.

7. Family members have a shared dream of what family life can be like, target goals, expect positive results, take initiative and work hard to make the goals realities, and deal with failures along the way by processing the event and deciding what to do differently in the future, expecting the future to be better.

8. Parents expect that their teenagers will be able to handle the responsibilities inherent in increased freedom.

9. Parents expect their adolescents to use personal judgment in handling life situations rather than automatically obeying the parents.

10. Family members negotiate requests and leave much freedom for each family member to decide when, where, and how any given agreed-upon behavior will be carried out, reducing reactance.

---

this faith we will be able to hew out of the mountain of depression a stone of hope. (King, 1972, p. 872)

Personalizing this dream is the life work of each human being. What unique meaning does life have for this particular individual? How will this person make a difference? Such philosophical questions underlie motivational interventions with Afro-American clients (Thomas & Dansby, 1985). Brainstorming alternative positive possibilities for the person's future undergirds therapeutic endeavors.

When people are apathetic, the doughnut analogy can be used very effectively. In slang, it is stated as follows: "It is important to keep your eye on the doughnut, not the hole, 'cause if you get part of the doughnut it is better than all of the hole." Such an image can help to engender positive expectancies in Afro-American clients.

Using black literature such as the work of Martin Luther King, Jr. (see Washington, 1986) as an ancillary to treatment can be a powerful means of encouraging positive expectations. One poem that is particularly motivating was written by Dr. Benjamin E. Mays (1969), one of King's mentors at Morehouse College:

It must be borne in mind that the tragedy in life doesn't lie in not reaching a goal.
The tragedy lies in having no goal to reach.

It isn't a calamity to die with dreams unfulfilled, but it is a calamity not to dream.

It is not a disaster to be unable to capture your ideal but it is a disaster to have no ideal to capture.

It is not a disgrace not to reach the stars but it is a disgrace to have no stars to reach for.

No failure but low aim "Is Sin." (p. 120)

Thomas and Dansby (1985) say, "Whether or not success or failure is the outcome, in following the dream one is involved with life—living it to the fullest and these memories can never be taken away. . . . The only person who can take away a person's 'right to aspire' is the self" (p. 404).

It is by taking action, by *doing,* that people create their roles in American society. In the United States in the early part of this century, there were no black professional athletes, opera stars, or political leaders. The power of action is exemplified by the words "keep on keeping on" from black culture. Afro-Americans have motivated themselves to exhibit the behaviors necessary to be the "first" in these fields, to expend the effort required to accomplish these triumphs. They held positive expectations for their dreams, which triggered the positive emotions necessary to generate the often grueling behaviors over a long period of time needed to be successful in these areas.

Thomas, Moore, and Sams (1980) created "dream exercises" to motivate clients to set goals and to take risks, focusing on their dreams. Indigenous literature by Afro-American writers as well as paperback texts on encouragement (Dinkmeyer & Losoncy, 1980; Losoncy, 1977, 1980) can be used as bibliotherapeutic adjuncts. The "dream exercises" emphasize self-supportive statements that have been found to significantly increase mood and performance (Raps, Reinhard, & Seligman, 1980). The goal is to encourage the internalization of positive self-talk.

Resistance to goal setting is explored to expose negative cognitions. Clients can be taught a process of analyzing and refuting these cognitions.

Finally, failures are dealt with only after they occur. Teaching the client the process of attribution is crucial. Attributing failure to global ("I am totally incompetent"), stable ("I was and always will be incompetent"), and internal ("It is all my fault") factors leads to depression, whereas specific ("I had no control over the tornado—it was a unique situation"), unstable ("Tornadoes only come once in a lifetime"), and external ("I am not responsible for the luck of the weather") attributes are less likely

The five children in this family are all doctors—four medical doctors and one dentist. This family is an example of a strong family that values achievement in the professions—setting goals, taking risks, and working hard to make their dreams become realities. (Courtesy of Billy Easley)

to create negative emotional reactions. The therapist should be supportive of global, stable, internal attributions for success.

The Therapeutic Process

Cognitive behavioral marital therapy is the systematic use of cognitive and behavioral techniques in a process of:

1. Exposing and confronting irrational ideas that underlie the presenting problems,
2. Exposing and altering the thoughts that keep spouses from changing in the directions desired by their spouses,
3. Teaching functional analytical skills related to relationships, and
4. Teaching behavioral skills in assertiveness training, communication, problem solving, and conflict management where deficits exist.

The meaning that a spouse assigns to a behavior by the partner is explored and modified through discussion, using logical analysis, the generation of alternative explanations, and the substitution of positive self talk. Where additional behavioral relationship skills are needed, they are taught.

As is customary with behavioral approaches, there is a thorough assessment prior to beginning therapy. With cognitive-behavioral approaches, such an assessment may include the Relationship Belief Inventory (Eidelson & Epstein, 1982), the Irrational Belief Test (Emmelkamp, Krol, Sanderman, & Ruphan, 1987), the Maudsley Marital Questionnaire (Arrindell, Emmelkamp, & Best, 1983), a measure of the attributional style of individual family members, an instrument to assess communication skills, and a subjective baseline measure of the cognitions and attributions exhibited by the family members in the initial interview as assessed by the clinician.

In cognitive restructuring, family members are encouraged to become observers of their own interpretations of family events and to develop skills to test the validity of these interpretations through collecting and processing data (Epstein et al., 1988). Often therapists distribute handouts and give mini-lectures on how cognitions affect emotions and behavior. In a collaborative Socratic approach, family members are asked open-ended questions to assist them in discovering inconsistencies or inaccuracies in their thought processes for themselves. They internalize the process of asking themselves these same questions in future family situations as a form of reality testing to influence their cognitions, emotions, and behaviors in these situations. Such questions include: "What did you think when she did that?" "What does that mean, if that were true?" "What do you believe might happen?" and "How accurate do you think these thoughts are?"

Automatic thoughts can be neutralized not only by logical analysis but also by generating alternative thoughts or explanations for a given event. For example, a wife may say, "My husband is late. Therefore, he does not love me." She can analyze the logic of her statement by thinking of the years they have spent together and generating alternative reasons for his lateness, such as car trouble or a long meeting at work.

Beliefs are more difficult to modify. Weiss (1984) uses a list of universal truths about relationships as a means of eliciting material from the couple about the beliefs affecting their relationship. Contrary to the myths identified by Lederer and Jackson (1968), such sentences focus on the positive beliefs that lead to successful interpersonal interactions. He then encourages the spouses to analyze how their beliefs differ from these universal sentences.

Family members in collaboration with the therapist may brainstorm the advantages and disadvantages of a certain belief and write them down (Epstein et al., 1988). Then the therapist can guide the couple in writing a revised form of the belief. For example, in response to a spouse's allegation such as "You do not spend enough time with me," Revenstorf (1984) states that cognitions that can be used to replace distorted thoughts include self-reinforcement ("Although it is difficult, I can handle this situation"), distraction ("I will go shopping until he is in a better mood"), displacement back to the spouse ("He has had a bad week; how could I help him to feel better?"), devaluation ("She does not mean it"), and normalization ("It is normal to have arguments in marriage").

The therapist interrupts negative marital interaction in the therapy session and makes contact with one spouse while the other observes. The therapist asks what the spouse is feeling, requests the client to focus on body sensations, and encourages the client to express feelings using "I" statements. Often the therapist asks the spouse to visualize any situations from childhood that come to mind. The therapist helps the spouse to think about such events in a different way, relabeling them.

The other spouse observes and begins to realize that many of the thoughts and the feelings interfering with the relationship go back to childhood experiences and are not a reflection on the observing spouse. The spouse can then assign attributions to the spouse's reaction other than malicious intent.

Spouses can be taught self-instructional techniques for altering distorted cognitions and negative attributions. One way of teaching positive self-talk can be accomplished by assigning logs as homework for each spouse (Epstein et al., 1988). Each person is asked to record dysfunctional emotions, thoughts, and behaviors, as well as positive reinforcing self statements to be substituted for distorted cognitions.

Aaron Beck (1988), noted for his development of cognitive therapy for treating depressed individuals (Beck, Rusch, Shaw, & Emery, 1979), has successfully applied it to the treatment of marital distress in his book, *Love Is Never Enough*. Beck's model

Dr. Aaron Beck is known for the development of cognitive therapy for depression, which has now successfully been applied to marital therapy in his book, Love Is Never Enough. *(Courtesy of Jerry Bauer)*

is cognitive behavioral in orientation with the following components: (1) motivating change; (2) reinforcing commitment, loyalty, and trust; (3) increasing behavioral expressions of love; (4) changing cognitive distortions; (5) improving communication skills; (6) solving problems through management of conflict; (7) troubleshooting; (8) dealing with anger and hostility; and (9) special problems.

Beck's strategies to deal with anger encourage each spouse to look internally for automatic thoughts that trigger the anger and to generate rational responses to combat these anger-provoking sentences. People choose to increase their anger. Therefore, they can also choose to decrease it. In dealing with anger, it is important to keep it in the present and not to bring up grievances from the past. Insults and attacking the mate's vulnerable points such as weight or job status only lead to intensified feelings of hurt and anger.

THERAPEUTIC OUTCOMES

In reviews of prior BPT research, behavioral parent training was found to be effective (Gordon & Davidson, 1981; O'Dell, 1974; Patterson et al., 1982). More recently, BPT was a successful treatment for the obsessive compulsive disorder of a 9-year-old child (Dalton, 1983), for the management of angioneurotic edema in a 16-year-old hospitalized female (Zimmerman & Elliott, 1984), and for encropresis and enuresis in a child (Wendorf, 1984). Rios and Gutierrez (1986) register concern that most BPT outcome studies have been done with middle-class samples. They recommend the expansion of the BPT intervention model to an ecobehavioral one, which would target broader contextual variables in the greater society and include an instructional component to teach low-income mothers how to reduce their insularity.

Ulrici (1983) found that functional family therapy had a 0% recidivism rate for juvenile delinquents whose families completed therapy. Barton and Alexander (1982) sequentially conducted six research studies with delinquents using the functional family therapy model and found them to have a substantially low recidivism rate and less contact with courts than delinquents treated with other approaches.

Jacobson, Follette, and Elwood (1984) reported that 16 controlled outcome studies of behavioral marital therapy had been conducted since 1976, probably more than any other marital therapy approach. In analyzing data from 148 couples from 4 other studies, Jacobson, Follette, Revenstorf, and colleagues (1984) found that more than 50% of married couples improved with usually no deterioration; the relationships of one third became non-distressed. Hahlweg, Revenstorf, and Schindler (1984) and Hahlweg, Schindler, Revenstorf, and Brengelmann (1984) completed the Munich Marital Therapy Study, a controlled outcome study that showed that the average couple treated with BMT was better than approximately 90% of wait-listed controls. Hahlweg and Markman (1988) performed a meta-analysis of studies of behavioral marital therapy and found that gains were usually maintained and were equal for both American and European couples. Training in problem solving was found to be very effective with distressed couples, with gains maintained in two thirds of the couples after one year (Jacobson, 1978b, 1978c, 1981). BMT programs that included behavior exchange and communication skills led to improvements in marital satisfaction (Jacobson, 1977, 1978a). In fact, Jacobson, Schmaling, and Holtzworth-Munroe (1987) found no differences at 2-year follow-up among the results of a component of communication/problem-solving, behavior exchange, and a complete multi-component BMT treatment protocol. However, in a laboratory study, nearly one third of the participating couples did relapse after 2 years (Jacobson, 1989). Barlow, O'Brien, and Last (1984) found behavioral couples treatment to be effective in the treatment of agoraphobia.

Heiman, LoPiccolo, and LoPiccolo (1981) reviewed the outcome research on sexual dysfunction and cited various rates of success for diverse sexual problems. In particular, behavioral treatment of premature ejaculation had a high success rate (90–95%), followed by female primary orgasmic dysfunction (85–95%). Schover and LoPiccolo (1982) found that gains made in treating sexual desire disorders with behavioral sex therapy were maintained at follow-up. Libman, Fichten, and Brenden (1985) found that different formats were equally effective in the delivery of behavioral sex therapy. In fact, Morokoff and LoPiccolo (1986) found that 4 sessions with minimal therapist contact were just as effective as 15 sessions of behavioral sex therapy with therapist involvement.

Cognitive restructuring has been found to produce effective outcomes when used alone (Emmelkamp et al., 1988; Emmelkamp, Van Linden Van Den Heuvell, Sanderman, & Scholing, 1988; Epstein, Pretzer, & Fleming, 1982; Huber & Milstein, 1985) and as part of a behavioral marital therapy treatment program (Baucom & Lester, 1986; Jacobson, 1984). Cognitive-behavioral approaches are particularly applicable to married couples and families where outbursts of anger and violence have been a problem. The therapist explores the thoughts and feelings preceding the violence, encouraging the spouse or parent to identify anger-provoking thoughts, analyze the reality of the ideas, and substitute self-generated realistic soothing sentences (Arias & O'Leary, 1988; DiGiuseppe, 1988; Morton, Twentyman, & Azar, 1988). The therapist can tie the thoughts into images from childhood, relabeling the early experiences where appropriate.

Leslie & Epstein (1988) have found cognitive-behavioral family approaches to be very effective with remarried families. With blended families, it is very therapeutic to question family customs and create new ones. Through family therapy sessions, the therapist teaches the process of analyzing the antecedents of behavior and the thoughts and meanings of other family members so that family members can do so at home. Other applications have been made to the families of older adults (Qualls, 1988), addicted individuals (Schlesinger, 1988), suicidal and depressed people (Bedrosian, 1988), and adults with sexual dysfunctions (Walen & Perlmutter, 1988). All of these approaches share an emphasis on cognitive restructuring, coupled with training in the particular behavioral skills needed by family members to overcome the difficulty, which include assertiveness training, communication, problem-solving, or conflict management.

CONTRIBUTIONS AND LIMITATIONS OF BEHAVIORAL MODELS

One key contribution of behavioral approaches to marital and family therapy is the emphasis on research. There are many studies of effective outcomes in behavioral parent training, behavioral marital therapy, sexual therapy, and the cognitive behavioral therapy of couples and families. Because behaviorism started with the study of animals in research laboratories, its scientific emphasis on research has made an impact on marital and family therapy.

Another main contribution of behavioral approaches to marital and family therapy is the development of a sequence of treatment based on a theoretical model. For example, in behavioral marital therapy, a couple is assessed prior to treatment, and rapport is established. Then they are asked to complete an exercise to increase the positive behavioral exchanges. Focus shifts to communication skills, contracting, problem-solving skills, and managing conflict. Treatment ends with an emphasis on how to maintain gains and an evaluation of treatment. A couple can be shown what to expect and what the phases of treatment are. Understanding the sequence of treatment often motivates couples to remain in treatment until termination in order to acquire the use of specific interpersonal skills. Sequences of treatment are also clearly delineated in behavioral parent training and sex therapy.

Behavioral marital and family therapy approaches can also be credited with the development and refinement of specific techniques such as contracting in BPT and BMT, sensate focus exercises for the treatment of sexual dysfunctions, and cognitive restructuring techniques. In addition, exercises for increasing positive behavioral exchanges between spouses such as the "caring days" exercise of Stuart and the "love day" of Weiss are unique treatment tools in the marital and family literature, most of which is focused on resolution of presenting problems rather than on widening the array of positive alternatives available for use.

The most notable limitation of behavioral approaches to marital and family therapy is that they are linear. They address the behaviors of individuals who pursue goals in logical ways. The family is not viewed as a separate system with properties of its own. Based on behaviorism, the world view is mechanistic and reduces complex phenomena to their basic elements (Leslie, 1988). Behaviors can be reduced to an S-O-R model. People respond (R) to stimuli (S) that are processed within the individual (O). Such a model is linear and unidirectional.

Bandura (1977) questions the S-O-R model and maintains that human beings are capable of self direction as well as self regulation, and are able to move in more than one direction. He proposes reciprocal determinism in which S, O, and R are interdependent. Behavior in Partner A is a stimulus to thoughts in Partner B, which activate emotions and behaviors in Partner B, which are stimuli for Partner A. However, such a revised concept of S-O-R remains reductionistic even though it is no longer unidirectional.

Behavioral approaches fall short when intervention is needed at the family level (Leslie, 1988). From their theoretical base, such a level does not exist. The emergent properties of the family as a unit are neither recognized nor treated. Only the behaviors of individual family members and their cognitions (in the case of cognitive-behavioral approaches) are logically explored with the goal of changing the behavioral contingencies and gaining insight (in the case of cognitive-behavioral approaches only). By contrast, systems approaches use paradoxical interventions to manipulate change in the total family system without insight as a goal.

Another limitation is the recidivism rate one year after therapy with most behavioral approaches (Epstein & Baucom, 1988). Including a cognitive restructuring component greatly decreases this rate. In some cases, behaviors have improved as measured by objective observers, but people continue to report low pre-treatment levels of satisfaction with relationships. Psychoanalytically oriented proponents would maintain that people may learn to exhibit corrective behaviors for a while, but over time their true personalities will re-emerge. Lasting change occurs only when insight into the deep psychological needs of family members is gained and individual family members change ingrained personality styles and/or have identified needs met in other selected ways.

SUMMARY

Behavioral approaches to marital and family therapy include: (1) behavioral parent training (BPT), (2) behavioral marital therapy (BMT), (3) sex therapy, and (4) cognitive behavioral therapy (CBT). All of these share the application of behaviorism to the treatment of human problems.

Gerald Patterson conducted behavior modification research with children and found that it was more effective to train the parents to monitor a behavior management program with their child (BPT) than to work with the child directly. Jim Alexander implemented behavioral programs for the treatment of juvenile delinquents, involving the total family in functional family therapy.

Richard Stuart conceptualized a number of relationship principles. He developed a sequence of interventions to be used in behavioral marital therapy: (1) completing inventories and explaining expectations, (2) the "caring days" exercise, (3) communication skills training, (4) contracting, (5) decision-making skills, (6) conflict-management skills, and (7) maintenance of therapeutic outcome.

Masters and Johnson applied behavioral techniques to the treatment of sexual dysfunctions in 2-week treatment programs at their institute in St. Louis. In particular, they created sensate focus exercises in which both spouses are encouraged to touch each other in turn with sexual intercourse not permitted, thereby reducing performance anxiety while increasing pleasure. Helen Kaplan identified disorders of sexual desire and developed therapeutic techniques for treating both hypoactive sexual desire disorder and sexual aversion disorder.

Cognitive behavioral therapy is the combination of cognitive restructuring with behavioral skills training. Cognitive restructuring is the process of teaching a couple or family members how to analyze perceptions, values, beliefs, and attributions and gather information to test their validity. When clients are able to use self-talk to counteract these cognitions, they can control emotional reactions and behaviors. Aaron Beck, Neil Jacobson, and Norman Epstein are prominent figures in this area.

EXERCISES

1. What is a healthy marriage from a behavioral point of view? If your instructor directs, turn to your partner and share your answer.
2. Liberman (1975) is a pioneer in the behavioral assessment of marriages. Given the following case, what steps would you use to conduct a be-

havioral assessment of the couple? What would your tentative treatment plan be, including goals and objectives?

Mr. and Mrs. Stone have been married for 15 years, in which there has been much strife and conflict. Mr. Stone is very sensitive to any lessening of affection and can become somewhat paranoid at times, even though he has never been psychotic. Mrs. Stone is very disorganized and not a very competent homemaker and mother to their three children. They blame each other for their marital unhappiness, depreciate each other, withdraw, and sulk.

Write down the steps you would take to assess this couple and at least one possible treatment plan, including goals.

3. One of the techniques for which Richard Stuart is most noted is "caring days." If your instructor has formed "families" in your class, carry out this exercise with your "family." Otherwise you should complete the exercise with your own spouse if you are married or with your roommate(s) if you live in a dormitory or apartment. Please read the instructions for the exercise that are given in the section on Richard Stuart (p. 293). Your instructor will pass out forms that you can use to record the caring behaviors you receive from your spouse on a daily basis. If you are completing the exercise as a "family" in the class, you can record the initials of the person who gives you the caring behavior. On a separate sheet of paper write down your thoughts and feelings in response to the exercise after you have completed it.

4. In the following cases, diagnose the type of sexual dysfunction present and possible alternative ways that it might be treated.

Vignette #1.

Fred had been married and divorced before. He presented with the complaint that his new wife, who had given birth to their daughter more than a year ago, was dissatisfied with their sexual relationship and was thinking of divorce if Fred did not do something to correct the problem. Fred loved his wife and little girl very much and wanted to save his marriage. Every time he and his wife had sex, he would become easily aroused, and although he would try to hold back, he would reach a climax immediately upon entering his wife's vagina. Which common sexual dysfunction is this, and how is it treated?

Vignette #2.

Alice has been married for 13 years and has one child. In the intake interview, it became apparent

that one of the main presenting complaints of her husband, who was ready to divorce, was their sexual problem. Even when he would approach her after a romantic dinner and affectionate attention, he could not physically enter her. Painful contractions blocked entry. What sexual dysfunction is present, and what steps should be taken to treat it?

Vignette #3.

Harold experienced intense anxiety when he dated women. He felt pressure to have sex with them but was not really interested. He liked the companionship, but beads of sweat would begin to form on his forehead and the back of his shirt would be wet by the end of a date. In talking, he shared vague memories of a traumatic event when he was 7. He was not sure if his father had raped his mother in front of him, or if he had been raped by his father or mother. Memories were confusing and often blank. What type of sexual dysfunction is this, and what are the various ways of treating it?

Vignette #4.

Henrietta was crying more often than usual. She and her husband Bill presented for marital counseling. In the intake interview, it was learned that sex was painful for Henrietta. Even when Bill spent a long time in affectionate foreplay, Henrietta did not feel lubricated. Looking toward her 50th birthday, Henrietta did not know what was wrong. She seemed depressed and irritable with Bill all of the time. She and Bill wanted to work on the relationship. What sexual dysfunction is present, and what steps should be taken to see that it is treated?

5. Choose a dyadic relationship in which you have contact at least weekly. Keep a log of negative feelings you experience in the relationship. Also write down any thoughts that were going through your mind immediately prior to the negative emotions. Write an antidote sentence, that is, a positive sentence which substitutes for and counteracts the negative cognition. Analyze the log on a weekly basis during the semester to identify the key sentences which repeat again and again in this close dyadic relationship. Be prepared to repeat the antidote sentence in response to the faulty cognition the next time that it occurs.

Chapter 11
The Structural School

O Chestnut tree, great rooted blossomer,
Are you the leaf, the blossom or the bole?
O body swayed to music, of brightening glance,
How can we know the dancer from the dance?

W. B. Yeats, 1928, p. 60.

This chapter focuses on the structural school of family therapy and its founder, Salvador Minuchin. As healthy families develop over the life span, they change their structures. Those families that hold rigidly to the same structure produce symptoms in at least one of their members. Minuchin's background, key theoretical concepts, view of healthy functioning, therapeutic process, major techniques, therapeutic outcomes, and contributions/limitations are presented in this chapter.

SALVADOR MINUCHIN

Historical Development

In contrast to most of the family therapy approaches that were developed to treat the families of schizophrenics, the original work of Minuchin, Montalvo, Guerney, Rosman, and Schumer (1967) was based on a grant from the National Institute of Mental Health to conduct research on poor, inner-city families who have raised at least two delinquent children and to create a theoretical approach that had positive therapeutic outcomes with such families. In these families, the aggressive dimension is particularly intense in an either/or framework. Family members equate violence with power. Either the therapist is powerful or not, and a therapist may be perceived as being powerful and violent. On the other hand, if the therapist intervenes in a quiet, calm manner in therapy, the family members may think that the therapist is not powerful and that nothing has been done to help them. Children raised in these families use projection as their main defense mechanisms, blame others for what has happened, react immediately with high intensity and defuse rapidly, are not able to remember and talk through an event after it happened, and participate in an event without recognizing or experiencing their own participation. Minuchin found that dramatic, active interventions were necessary to be effective in conducting therapy with these families.

Another distinguishing characteristic of Minuchin's work is its emphasis on the effect of culture on the family. Minuchin emigrated from Argentina after working in Israel, so making contact with clients from other ethnic backgrounds was a very natural part of his work. In *Families of the Slums,* the research team of Minuchin et al. (1967) includes transcripts of family sessions with black families and the families of Puerto Rican and other ethnic groups. A classic in the field, this book is still as readable and current today as it was in 1967.

Minuchin was originally trained as a child psychiatrist, and he became interested in involving families in the treatment process in order to help their children. He became director of the Philadelphia Child Guidance Clinic, where he surrounded himself with an intelligent, challenging group of professionals such as Braulio Montalvo, Harry Aponte, Jay Haley, and Bernice Rosman. Montalvo, Minuchin, and Haley used to chat about family therapy on their way to work in the morning in the same car. Both Minuchin and Haley credit each other's influence in the development of the structural and strategic schools, respectively.

Therapists came from around the world to work and study under Minuchin. Marizio Andolfi came from Italy to study this American phenomenon of family therapy. He returned to Rome to found the Family Therapy Institute and to begin and eventually preside over the Italian Society for Family Therapy (Andolfi, 1979, 1980; Barrows, 1981).

Minuchin remained at the Philadelphia Child Guidance Center for 10 years before leaving to devote himself to the research and treatment of psychosomatic children and their families. Even today the Philadelphia Child Guidance Center is one of the best training centers in the United States for learning family therapy through its internship, externship, and continuing education programs.

Although he was one of the key contributors to the theory of family therapy, Minuchin admitted to downplaying theory when he first began to train therapists. He saw it as an impediment to beginning therapists, who might become inhibited by the theory and distracted from their observation and interaction with the family (Minuchin & Fishman, 1981). Now he believes in the importance of theory and would indoctrinate students with more theory before introducing them to families, placing himself in a position midway between the experiential and Milan systemic therapies.

Because of his orientation to what worked with families and to action, there is not much mention of the philosophical nature of man as good, evil, or some combination thereof in his early writings. In later work, Minuchin (1974) clearly defines his approach as different from psychoanalysis. He sees man as a social being whose per-

Dr. Salvador Minuchin was born in Argentina. His style of family therapy, structural family therapy, has been adapted for use with families from many cultures. (Courtesy of Salvador Minuchin)

ception of reality has both external and internal components. He relates a parable of Ortega y Gasset in which a famous explorer in the Arctic pushed his team of sleigh dogs in order to make rapid progress north in search of the North Pole, only to find when he stopped that night to check his bearings that he was farther south than when he had started in the morning: He had been advancing north on a mammoth iceberg that was being carried south by a strong ocean current. Man's reality is based not only on individual perceptions but on environmental interactions. By changing the environment, especially the social environment, people will experience reality differently.

In addition, there are strong developmental assumptions in his work, based on his education in child development during his child psychiatry training. Minuchin sees children as capable of mastering their developmental stages if impeding family structures are unbalanced and changed. The family can deal with the tasks of a given developmental transition in the family life cycle when their structure is more appropriate to accommodating the growth of the children and other family members.

Key Theoretical Concepts

Minuchin et al. (1967) elaborate theoretical concepts relating to the structure and the communicational and the affective systems of the family. Seven of the 12 experimental families in *Families of the Slums* were single-parent families. The parent could nurture but could not provide executive guidance, although the parent functioned as a regulator or monitor of the pathways of communication.

Communicational System.   The families in Minuchin's study were "noisy": Family members continued to talk when other members were talking. Rarely did family members listen to other family members. Topics were changed frequently. Rarely was one theme developed until the problem was resolved. The activity level of members was high, with movement and action prevalent. If there were spouses, they rarely talked to each other. Content of communication focused on "don'ts," the dangerous world outside the family, and power transactions.

Affective System in the Family.   Disciplining the children typically was related to the internal anxiety of the parent and not to the behavior of the children. The child who misbehaved may not have been touched, although the child nearest in proximity to the mother may have been spanked. Children were socialized to make contact through anger first. Anger would melt to nurturance if a child realized that positive responses were acceptable. Love often meant total giving in concrete terms, an all-or-nothing perception. For example, a mother who gave her child her last nickel was faced with an enraged child because he could not have another, and therefore he was unloved.

Family Structure.   Family structure is the set of demands or codes that organize the transactions that occur to fulfill the functions of the family (Minuchin, 1974). An example of a structure in the broader society would be the chain of command in the military establishment, which organizes how a general will speak to a private and vice versa. The family structure is, therefore, the chain of command in the family that determines the operational transactions to carry out the functions in the family. For example, the family structure determines that a mother will tell her daughter what time her curfew is as a way of carrying out the parenting function in the family.

The boundaries of a system or subsystem are the rules that define who is a participant in that system or subsystem and who is not and how people in the system or subsystem participate. For example, a father might say to the oldest daughter (Figure 11–1), "If your younger sister goes out of the back yard, come tell me and I will do something to stop her."

Boundaries lead to greater differentiation, because there are special demands inherent in belonging to a particular system or subsystem. For example, negotiation skills among peers are learned in the sibling subsystem and will occur if parents do not interfere by crossing the boundary into the sibling subsystem.

For families to function smoothly, boundaries must be clear. People need to know to whom to go for what. In describing boundaries, Minuchin is noted for the concept

F	Parental subsystem
– – – – – – –	
C	Sibling subsystem

FIGURE 11–1   Clear boundaries separating subsystems

From *Families & Family Therapy* (p. 53) by S. Minuchin, 1974, Cambridge, MA: Harvard Univ. Press. Adapted by permission.

FIGURE 11−2   Boundaries

Diffuse boundaries	Clear boundaries	Rigid boundaries
· · · · · · · · · ·	− − − − − − − −	_____
Enmeshment		Disengagement

From *Families & Family Therapy* (p. 54) by S. Minuchin, 1974, Cambridge, MA: Harvard Univ. Press. Adapted by permission.

of enmeshment versus disengagement (Figure 11−2). Parent-child interaction can vacillate from over-controlling enmeshment in which the child looks only for parental cues before communicating or acting to the disengagement of withdrawal by the parents in which they leave the field or leave the family entirely (Minuchin et al., 1967). Sometimes in rigidly organized families, behavior at one end of the continuum of enmeshment versus disengagement predominates. An enmeshed family responds with excessive intensity and speed. A disengaged family does not respond, even when a response is needed.

In *Families of the Slums,* the husband-wife subsystem among the poor most often functioned only as a parent subsystem. Because of low self-esteem and a lack of identity, the husband and wife gained all of their identity from being parents. If the therapist made any statements about their parenting, they saw the therapist as making critical comments about the self. Parents fluctuated from being autocratic, dominant controllers to helpless, ineffective victims.

In families from low socioeconomic levels, Minuchin found that the sibling subsystem often unified to rebel against the directives of the parents. One child was often the parentified child, responsible for parenting the other children. There were problems in communication between the parental subsystem and the sibling subsystem.

Alignment is the agreement of two or more family members. There are several types of alignments: the stable coalition, the detouring coalition, and triangulation (Figure 11−3). In a stable coalition, two or more family members are in agreement against another family member in an inflexible, recurring manner, regardless of what the family member does. This occurs when one parent elicits the support of a child to continually reinforce opposition to the other parent. The child needs both parents and suffers in the long run. When two family members reduce the stress between them by agreeing that a third member has a problem with which they will give help or for which they will attack the family member, a detouring coalition is formed. For example, a child may be scapegoated to reduce the tension in the marriage and keep the family together through the joint efforts of the parents to help or attack the scapegoat. In triangulation, two family members each seek to join with the same family member to oppose the other—for example, each parent seeks the attention of the same child to oppose the other parent. The child is caught in the middle, using up valuable energy that could be better used in self-differentiation.

Power is the ability to get something done. In the family it means who can get whom to do what in what way. For example, mom may have the power to keep her

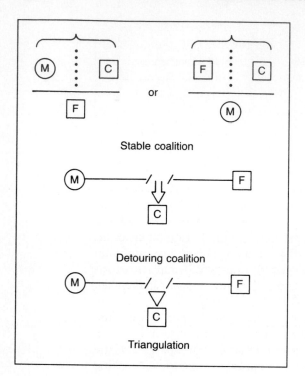

FIGURE 11–3 Types of alignments

asthmatic child from playing outdoors by giving the verbal order, but the child has power through the dependency created by coughing and wheezing to be able to stay up past bedtime to watch television. The child exerts power through illness and its associated dependency. Dad may have power and the last word in financial matters and mom in decorating the house and other housekeeping concerns. It is important through observation and questioning to find out who has the last word in disciplining the identified patient. For example, if one parent disciplines but the other does not agree and instead allows the child to do what is prohibited, the permissive parent has become more powerful.

These concepts can be illustrated with an actual family. The Allan family is comprised of Mr. and Mrs. Allan, the older child—a daughter named Joyce—and the younger child—a son named Harold. Harold is a 17-year-old heroin addict. In the first therapy session, Harold sits near his mother on the couch, and his father sits in a chair near the therapist. Mrs. Allan tells the therapist how concerned she is about Harold and his drug use. Harold responds to what his mother says by interrupting her. Mr. Allan says nothing. Harold and his mother are enmeshed. The mother is closer to Harold than she is to her husband—a dysfunctional boundary.

In the interview it becomes apparent that when Mr. Allan disciplines Harold in the session, his wife intervenes. She says that Mr. Allan is too strict with Harold. Mrs. Allan is aligned with her son against Mr. Allan.

Mrs. Allan gains power by passively not carrying out or supporting her husband's efforts at disciplining their son. Mr. Allan has told his wife not to give Harold any money. After agreeing with this plan, Mrs. Allan unconsciously leaves her purse containing a large sum of money on the table when she knows Harold will be in the house alone. She passively gains power by permissively supporting Harold's drug habit in an indirect manner. Harold, too, becomes powerful through his dependency on heroin. He is able to blackmail his father into a late curfew because Mr. Allan is afraid of triggering his son's drug use. Mr. Allan gives direct orders and appears to be the most powerful; yet Mrs. Allan and her son gain the actual power through the symptom.

View of Healthy Functioning

Change is a part of life. Families will be required to change to adapt to external stress in the larger social world that is encountered by the whole family, such as a tornado that strikes the town in which the family lives, and to external stress experienced by one family member, such as the loss of a job by the mother or father. In addition, families must deal with internal stress from normal developmental transitions in the family life cycle, such as a young adult leaving home for the first time, and to internal idiosyncratic stressors, such as the aging of a mentally retarded child (Minuchin, 1974). Healthy families restructure themselves over time in order to adapt to stressors. They can mobilize alternative patterns of interaction when the level and type of stress require it. The family adapts to stress to maintain continuity of the family over time.

The need for treatment occurs when families rigidly hold to transactional patterns rather than changing to adapt to the stressor. For example, if a family has two children, one 6 years old and one 16, and if the parents adhere rigidly to the same rules for the teenager that they have for the 6-year-old, the teenager will rebel. The parents will need to generate rules that allow greater autonomy for the teenager such as a later curfew, even though the current rules worked well when the teenager was a younger child.

The Therapeutic Process

Goals of Therapy.   The goals of structural family therapy are to resolve the presenting problems and to change the underlying structure of the family (Aponte & Van Deusen, 1981). By bringing about changes in the structure of the family, the presenting problems are often resolved. In later work, Minuchin and Fishman (1981) added the goal of changing the family's construction of reality, the world view of the family.

Structural family therapy emphasizes action over insight. In particular, action occurs in the session. By restructuring the transactions directly in the session, change in the family structure occurs. Through homework assignments, families continue changes through action.

Role of the Therapist.   The therapist takes an active, directive stance in structural family therapy. The therapist is friendly in making contact with each member of the family, asks open-ended questions, gives orders, directs enactments, gives homework assignments, and can be very theatrical at times.

In structural family therapy, co-therapists are usually not used, which makes it more cost effective for the consumer and more widely adaptable to agency and private practice settings. Sometimes the therapist may use a one-way mirror to allow siblings to view the interaction of their parents, but typically a consultant is not used behind the one-way mirror. Sometimes subsystems of the family are seen concurrently, such as seeing the spouses without the children or the children without the parents. Sometimes groupings are seen to work out a problem that must be handled before family therapy with the entire family can proceed.

Stanton (1981) suggests that the role of the therapist vary in order to accommodate both structural and strategic approaches to family therapy. Initially the therapist would join the family, assess and diagnose it, and attempt to restructure it. If the structural techniques are not working due to intense resistance on the part of the family or the therapist becomes confused, having been pulled in by the family through a fascination with content, then strategic disengagement is indicated, with the therapist becoming very detached. Following the success of the strategic techniques, the therapist would then revert to the use of structural techniques in a therapeutic role that was more engaged and warm.

Use of Diagnosis and Assessment.   During the session, the structural therapist often directs the family members to talk to each other about the presenting problem. By observing how they interact and who talks to whom, the structural family therapist analyzes the structure of the family and can draw a map of the structure of the family, including boundaries and subsystems. The therapist will interrupt transactions and direct one family member to stop talking and listen while another family member talks to the family member indicated by the therapist.

An example of such a diagnostic intervention, called enactment, is as follows:

Therapist: Now that you have told me a little bit about the problem with your son, Mrs. Carmichael, I'd like you to turn to your husband and talk with him about the problem.

Mrs. C: But we've done that at home, and we never seem to get anywhere.

T: This is different because I'm here to be your coach, to help when I see that you might need it. Turn to Mr. Carmichael and talk to him about the problems with Billy.

Mrs. C: John, Billy has failing grades at school, and he's running around with a bad crowd now.

Billy: Hell, Dad, don't listen to her. She just wants to keep me under her thumb. I'm a guy and guys will be guys, right Dad?

Mr. C.:   Joan, Billy's just like me when I was in the neighborhood.

Mrs. C.:   On the yard, the teacher thought he had some crack, so I'm worried that he's lying to us.

Billy: Oh, Ma, I just want to be one of the gang.

T: Mr. and Mrs. Carmichael, how do the two of you handle Billy's horning in on your discussion and interrupting?

In this case there was a diffuse boundary between Billy and his dad; they were enmeshed, interacting more like friends than father and son. A diagnosis of the family structure can be seen in Figure 11–4 with a proposed changed structure—one of the goals of treatment in this family.

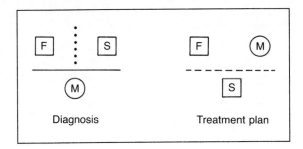

FIGURE 11–4   Map of diagnosis and treatment plan

In addition, by asking open-ended questions the therapist obtains information about the presenting problems (in this case, failure at school, the adolescent peer group, and possible drug use) to form a hypothesis about present transactional sequences in the family, the presenting problem, and the structure that may be maintaining it. Immediate goals are determined for the intervention in the session in light of broad long-term goals for the therapy. The therapist intervenes to change the patterns and to control extraneous variables that might affect the intervention. Based on the reactions of the family members (feedback), the steps are repeated (problem, data, hypotheses, goals, intervention, and feedback) (Aponte & Van Deusen, 1981).

According to Brown and Samis (1987), structuralists assess each family on six dimensions: (1) boundary quality, called ambience, such as diffuse (permeable), clear (semipermeable), or rigid (impermeable); (2) flexibility (ability to change their structure to meet the needs of an individual member); (3) interactional patterns of the spousal, parental, and sibling subsystems; (4) the stage of family development; (5) how a symptom serves to maintain homeostasis; and (6) the context in which the presenting problems happen (stressors both internal and external impinging upon the family). Figure 11–5 contains typical symbols for diagraming families using the structural model, an example of a healthy binuclear family structure, and several types of dysfunctional family structures, which will be discussed here.

Using the six criteria for assessment, the structural therapist diagnosed the Peterson family as a healthy binuclear family (see Figure 11–5a). Both parents had remarried and each parent had a close relationship with the new spouse. There were clear boundaries between the parents and children, with the spouses spending time together by themselves and also spending time with the children. When one spouse was ill, the other would cook and help the other spouse, a sign of flexibility. The parents of the children, although no longer married, communicated about discipline and other matters relating to the children. The parental subsystem was functioning well. The children could love and care for both parents without feeling guilt or being attacked by the other parent. There were problems in the family, as any normal family has. The parents and spouses were able to deal with the changes and problems associated with new developmental stages of the family life cycle as each child grew and matured. When symptoms appeared, they did not last long because the parents and spouses talked about them, resolved differences, and worked out solutions. Stressors affected this healthy binuclear family, but family members did not ignore them. They dealt with them through a process of negotiation, compromise, and action.

FIGURE 11–5 Family diagrams

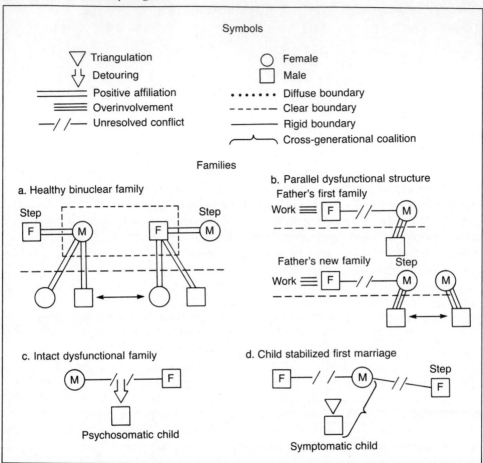

From "The Application of Structural Family Therapy in Developing the Bi-nuclear Family" by N. Brown and M. Samis, 1987, *Mediation Quarterly,* No. 14/15, pp. 53–64. Adapted by permission.

Examples of several dysfunctional families are also represented in Figure 11–5. In one dysfunctional pattern (see Figure 11–5b), the father of a 10-year-old boy had never been involved very much in the parenting of his son. When he divorced and remarried his present wife (4 years after the divorce), he began to bring his son over and leave him with his new wife, repeating the pattern of not spending much time with the boy. When the father began to have problems in his second marriage, he no longer picked up his son; when the relationship improved after several years, he again wanted to have his son visit. The father had restructured his new family to parallel his first family where he was never very involved with the child (Brown & Samis, 1987).

In an intact family with a psychosomatic child with diabetes mellitus (Figure 11–5c), there was a detouring coalition in which the tension was reduced between dad and mom when the child became ill and they were drawn together to help the child. In another dysfunctional pattern (Figure 11–5d), a 10-year-old would go to his father's empty house after school to surf in the nearby ocean. The boy was failing in school and fighting with peers. The mother blamed the father's underinvolvement; the father blamed the mother's parenting for the difficulties. Both would compete for awards as best parent in the eyes of the child, who was triangled between the parents. When the stepfather tried to become involved with the boy to help his stepson out, the mother entered a stable coalition with her son against the stepfather, which was similar to the coalition present before the divorce (the coalition then opposed the biological father).

The six criteria are helpful in developing a treatment plan. Where there are coalitions, attempts will be made to increase the involvement of the disengaged dyads while decreasing the involvement of the enmeshed coalition. Highlighting the developmental transitions of the family and the individuals in it will help to clarify where and in what direction freed-up energy needs to be expended. When the role of the symptoms is clarified, other therapeutic strategies can be devised to insure that the needs of the family being met by the symptoms are met in other ways.

O'Sullivan, Berger, and Foster (1984) asked therapists to conduct structural assessments of families to include (1) stage of the life cycle, (2) a structural map of the family, (3) a description of the problem, (4) any triangles around the problem, and (5) treatment goals. The authors were encouraged by the results and concluded that the study provided support for many categories of structural concepts in family therapy and the usefulness of it for family assessment.

Nature of the Initial Session.   The following outline of an initial session is based on a key source (Minuchin, 1974).

1. Plan—The therapist is encouraged to read any background material available on the family prior to the first session. In this way alternative hypothetical structural diagnoses may already be in mind, which will sensitize the therapist to look for certain patterns in the initial session. In addition, the therapist will know the names of the family members and have enough chairs for them in the session room.
2. The family therapist is a host and should aim to put the members of the family at ease during the initial interview.
3. Where are people sitting?—At the beginning of each session, the therapist notes the physical position of each family member in the room—who sat by whom. For example, if there is a stable coalition between mother and her daughter, they may sit next to each other and father may sit by himself, or a scapegoated child may sit off in a corner away from the rest of the family.
4. Join each member of the family—The therapist makes contact with each member of the family individually in a process of joining. Often this is done by asking each member to state what they think the problem is. Typically the therapist will begin by addressing the parents or executive subsystem first, to accord it more honor and power. The therapist uses self to make contact in any way possible. Joining is an attitude that is conveyed by the therapist through different behaviors that let a

family know they are understood and the therapist is working with them and in their interest.

A therapist may join in a close position by confirming a feeling word that a person has said such as, "You feel sad and depressed that Sally is sick"; by describing a transaction in a nonjudgmental manner; or by stating a negative behavior but negating responsibility for that behavior such as, "You're late, but how did your parents teach you that?" A therapist may also use joining techniques such as tracking, mimesis, and accommodation, which are explained later in this chapter.

5. Watch spontaneous transactions and point out their pattern. The therapist may comment on transactions in an objective, nonjudgmental manner, especially when they give information that leads to a tentative diagnosis of the family structure and the presenting problem.

6. Direct an enactment of the presenting problems in the session. For example, the therapist may direct the couple to discuss their spending habits with each other while the rest of the family watches, or ask a parent to discipline a child in front of the family in the session.

7. State an alternative transaction when a transaction is not working. For example, the therapist may give a mother suggestions on how to discipline a child when everything she is doing in the session is not working out.

8. Select one focus based on the transactions that have been observed and the data obtained. Such a focus will include one structural goal and a therapeutic strategy for reaching that goal. In developing one theme, one circumscribed area is explored in depth. An informal diagnosis takes place using the six criteria of quality of boundaries, flexibility, transactional patterns, developmental stage, function of the symptoms, and context.

9. Restructure the family. This can be done by delineating boundaries (psychological distance is created between subsystems by asking members of one subsystem to talk to each other and to sit by each other). The duration of interaction between members of a subsystem may be lengthened (a mother may be encouraged to play with her daughter for 10 minutes using puppets), or the therapist can unbalance the system by aligning with one family member, alternating alignment, ignoring a family member, or forming a coalition against a family member.

10. Use intensity to challenge the perceptual reality of families. For the therapist's message to be heard, often the family must be "hit over the head." Such intensity can be accomplished by repeating the message over and over again, repeating isomorphic transactions (indicating to an adolescent to keep her door closed while sleeping, buy her own alarm clock, wake herself up, and remember that she now is an adult), changing the time (increasing the length of time that two family members talk to each other or slowing down the speed of the session), changing the distance or position of family members (directing family members to change chairs to sit beside each other in subsystems), and resisting the family pull.

11. Encourage a changed world view through reframing the problem. The punctuation of events occurring between family members can be challenged as a "dance"

in which one moves in one direction, influencing a movement in the other, which influences a movement in yet another—the complementarity and circularity of the "dance." The therapist can help the family to change and construct its world view through the use of universal symbols, expert advice, and the reframing of family truths.

12. Look for the strengths of the family and point these out. Ending the session in a positive way can be particularly meaningful.

13. Repeat any steps in this process until progress and closure have been made on the area of focus.

14. Give a task assignment to be done at home to reinforce changes made in the area of focus.

Stages of Therapy. Typically, structural family therapy proceeds through mini-stages of joining, reading the family structure through creating transactions, changing the family structure through restructuring, and constructing alternative realities. In a single session a structural family therapist might use all of these in sequence many times. In addition, each process overlaps to some degree: By restructuring, the therapist may also be joining the family at the same time; by joining the family, the therapist may be creating a transaction, and so on. The advantage of these cyclical, overlapping stages is that the family experiences success, even if they do not return to therapy after one or two sessions. The typical duration of structural therapy is six to ten sessions over 2 to 3 months, although some psychosomatic families have continued for 7 months or more.

Application: Major Therapeutic Techniques

Joining. Each family has a characteristic mood. Joining means acting out the mood of the family. If a family is depressed, the therapist may become "very sad" and exaggerate her "depression," which lightens the mood of the family (Minuchin et al., 1967).

In later work, Minuchin (1974) and Minuchin and Fishman (1981) expanded the definition of joining to mean making contact with each member of the family. Mimesis is one way of joining in which the therapist becomes like the family by using and sometimes exaggerating the same content or behavioral manner of communicating. For example, the therapist could communicate with the same feeling tone as the family (a sad tone), speak slowly if the family members do, use gestures like the family does, appear as reserved as the family, or talk about personal experiences that are similar to those of the family. This definition of mimesis is similar to the original definition of joining in Minuchin's early work. Sometimes joining is accomplished through confirmation of a family member by using a feeling word to reflect an expressed or unexpressed feeling of that family member or by a nonjudgmental description of the behavior of the individual. A therapist may also join the family by tracking the interactions of family members, that is, by observing the transactions and letting the family know that they are heard by rephrasing statements of family members or describing the transaction. In addition, the therapist can join by accommodation to the transactional patterns of the family; for example, asking the father to speak first in a clearly patriarchial family.

Enactive Formulation.   The therapist will attempt to slow down the interaction in the family and to reduce the noise. Directives are used by the therapist such as, "We cannot hear each other because of the noise of the children. Do something to make your children less noisy. Make it happen." The therapist will *do* something when also verbally making a point, such as changing seats while saying "I feel left out here" (Minuchin et al., 1967). These enactive formulations occur relatively early in a session, usually within the first 10 minutes. They demonstrate that the therapist can speak the same action-oriented language that the family does. In later work, Minuchin defined this term as enactment, encouraging family members to carry out the action in the session. Through the use of enactments, the family structure could be restructured (Minuchin, 1974; Minuchin & Fishman, 1981).

Challenging the Communication Rules of the Family.   The therapist sets up a new set of rules for communication in the session, thereby challenging the rules of communication of the family. Each member is asked to single out a person to whom they are talking and demand that the person respond. Since some families don't really know how to communicate using words, they also need to be rewarded for using them for problem-solving. Most interactions are based on relationships rather than content in dysfunctional families, so efforts are made to clearly discriminate between content and relationship messages. For example, the therapist might indicate that she can't hear a family member because the person is always yelling so the therapist doesn't listen (Minuchin et al., 1967).

Reframing.   In reframing, a positive connotation is given to a negative behavior (Minuchin et al., 1967). For example, a mother may yell at her son to do his homework. The "yelling" on the part of the mother is reframed as "concern" about her son. Reframing is an important interpersonal skill, as there are advantages and disadvantages of every behavior. By accepting the behavior, the person will often decrease the behavior.

Relabeling.   In the blaming projective stance typical of families in treatment, an adjective that is positive in connotation is substituted for an adjective that is negative in connotation. For example, the wife screams at the husband that he is "controlling." The therapist relabels by saying that the husband is "overburdened."

Challenging the Structure of the Family.   The therapist may choose to obey the pathways in the family, disobey the pathways but in an implicit manner, disobey but in an explicit way, or eliminate the pathway entirely (Minuchin et al., 1967). For example, the mother may never talk to the father directly but only to the son, who then talks to the father. The therapist may talk directly to the father or may ask the mother to talk directly to the father. The therapist will work directly with the interactional patterns that are exhibited in the session. An observer may watch through a one-way mirror and come into the room to state observations about the interaction or one family subsystem may be asked to watch another subsystem through the one-way mirror as it communicates. Minuchin believes very strongly that the parental coalition should be one focus of the therapeutic work, but he also works with other subsystems, including the sibling subsystem and the individual subsystem of the identified patient. For example, members of the community, such as the elders of a minority community, are brought into the therapy to assist in the therapy.

Restructuring.   The process of changing the structure of the family is called restructuring. Restructuring can be accomplished through enactments, delineating the boundaries (creating psychological distance between subsystems by physical distance or verbal interactions between members of a subsystem in the session), unbalancing (by affiliating with one member more than others, by alternating alignments, or by forming a coalition with some family members against another family member), and complementarity (pointing out the movements in the "dance" between family members and suggesting a contract to learn new steps or sequences that better meet the needs of family members).

An example of the structural technique of restructuring is presented here from Umbarger (1983, p. 104):

Therapist:	Mrs. Darcy, I would like for you to sit over here next to me, relax for a while, and let Sid talk to his father.
Mother:	No, . . . he's afraid of his father. They. . . .
Son:	I never talk to him, no, I never. . . , No, I never. . . .
Father:	Oh, I always let his mother handle him. She. . . .
Mother:	I understand Sid better, so we agree that. . . .
Therapist:	(Interrupting everyone) You're all so cozy about this, that Sid and his father never talk. It's like a rule you have: Sid is to be afraid of his father. I want to break that rule. Go ahead, Mr. Darcy, ask Sid about coming to the hospital's day program.
Son:	(To the therapist) I think I'm getting sick, my stomach hurts. I need something to eat. Are my ears funny to you? Are you laughing at me?
Therapist:	Your ears are for listening to your father. That's the only task now, for the two of you to talk together. For five minutes only. Your mother is prohibited from talking, so you are on your own. (To the mother) If you interfere, I will ask you to leave the room for five minutes. If you can't let them have five minutes without you, especially with me right here, then your family is really stuck. . .
Son:	I don't know what to say to him.
Therapist:	That's all right, 'cause during this stage of things, your father is going to take the lead. Go on, Mr. Darcy. Help your son get going.
Father:	Oh, he's my baby. He knows I won't hurt him. Right, Siddy dear? (Blows a kiss to his son.)
Therapist:	Now you are acting like your wife, you are keeping her right here so she is still having to work with her son. Don't baby him like your wife does. He's not a baby. (To Sid) They make you a baby, and you make them successful at it by acting dopey. (To the father) Try it again. We still have a few minutes left before your wife comes back to take over.

In the above interview, the therapist is using the techniques of restructuring, including enactment (requesting the parties to actually do something in the session; in this case, the son was asked to talk to his father) and delineating boundaries (requesting that the mother leave while the son talks to the father will promote distance between the mother and the son while strengthening the relationship between the father and the son; in addition, the mother cannot interfere in the relationship with the father and son so the boundary will be clear between them). Restructuring techniques are characteristic of structural therapy and are the main sources of assistance to families in pain.

Task Setting.   The therapist gives a homework assignment that will reinforce the restructured transactions learned in the session.

The Family Lunch.   Minuchin, Rosman, and Baker (1978) developed a technique for working with anorectic families in which the therapist actually eats with the family and enacts the parents attempting to force the anorectic to eat.

THERAPEUTIC OUTCOMES

The amount of research that has been done using the structural model of therapy is impressive. Positive therapeutic outcomes have been documented for the treatment of delinquency, including aggressive "acting out" behavior (Minuchin et al., 1967); anorexia nervosa (Minuchin et al., 1975; Minuchin et al., 1978; Rosman et al., 1975); the psychosomatic illnesses of children (Sargent, 1983a, 1983b), including diabetes mellitus (Minuchin et al., 1975); chronic or intractable asthma (Minuchin et al., 1975); psychogenic pain and abdominal pain (Berger, Honig, & Liebman, 1977; Liebman, Honig, & Berger, 1976); drug and alcohol addiction (Davis, Stern, & Van Deusen, 1977; Zeigler-Driscoll, 1977, 1979); heroin addiction (Stanton et al., 1979); and elective mutism (Rosenberg & Lindblad, 1978). However, most of these studies used uncontrolled designs except for the drug, alcohol, and heroin addiction studies. The majority of the patients in these studies demonstrated positive outcomes, as measured by reduction in presenting symptoms. In addition, rigorous measures were used in the above studies to measure family functioning pre- and post-family therapy using multiple methods, such as structured tasks in which families were asked to interact, a family apperception technique, a stress interview, the L'Abate Family Assessment Battery, questionnaires, and diverse rating scales. Family functioning improved significantly in all of the studies.

Recent case studies (Carlson, 1987; Fulmer, Cohen, & Monaco, 1985) demonstrate the applicability of the structural model of family therapy to the treatment of school-age children with learning disabilities and academic problems. School psychologists and those who conduct full-scale psychological assessments of the child for educational remediation have used structural family therapy to modify the family structure, thereby reducing the academic problems in the child. Ross, Phipps, and Milligan (1985) report a successful case in which structural techniques were used to eliminate the symptoms of irritable bowel syndrome in an adolescent who was adjusting to the divorce of her parents. Cohen (1982) reports the effective use of structural approaches when working with cancer patients and their families.

Ko (1986) presents a case study in which she adapted structural therapy techniques for use with a Vietnamese extended family who had recently emigrated to Canada and was experiencing "culture shock." She joined the family by passing messages through the male patriarch, the father of the patient's husband, thereby gaining the support of the extended family for the therapy rather than offending the family head by involving only the nuclear family. The technique of utilizing symptoms was used during the first session in which the in-laws were involved in order to gain their support in encouraging their son to spend more time with his wife. This helped all of them adjust better to the new environment and the physical break-up of the extended family in Vietnam and in Canada.

In addition, the technique of strengths was used to encourage the client to recognize her strengths, thereby strengthening her self-esteem. Her increased self-confidence helped her to baby sit in her home, thereby gaining income and respect from her husband and her in-laws. The therapist also helped the in-laws to make

Structural family therapy has been adapted to therapeutic work with clients from many diverse cultures.

contact with community resources that would provide services, thereby reducing the pressure on the son to provide all of these for his parents. The client had been depressed and ready to leave her husband before therapy; however, she now accompanies her husband to the home of his father, who still remains the patriarch of this Vietnamese family.

Care must be taken in applying structural therapy cross-culturally. The therapist must make efforts to understand the culture and to adapt the techniques to the given culture. When this is done, the therapeutic outcome is much better than when individual therapy is used, especially for those cultures in which the extended family is the norm rather than the exception.

Structural family therapy was developed to treat children by including their families in the treatment process; therefore, structural approaches are best used when the identified patient is a child or adolescent. The structural model is effective for treating delinquency and acting out behaviors of adolescents; substance abuse of children and teenagers; anorexia nervosa; psychosomatic disorders of children such as chronic asthma, diabetes mellitus, and irritable bowel syndrome; school problems and learning disabilities of children; with the families of cancer patients; and in cross-cultural settings, with due care to adapt the approach to the culture of the presenting family.

In the case of heroin addiction and other types of substance abuse the structural approach has been found to be effective even when the client is an adult no longer living at home. The involvement of the parents of drug addicts in their twenties and thirties in structural family therapy has led to effective outcomes.

With adults from other cultures and diverse ethnic groups, structural family therapy has led to positive outcomes. Care must be taken to perceive the world through the eyes of the family. The *weltanschauung* of the presenting family may be very different from that of a typical middle-class American family. In *Ethnicity and Family Therapy,* Falicov (1982) gives specific suggestions for tailoring the initial structural therapy interview to the needs of Mexican families; Jalali (1982), Moitoza (1982), and Welts (1982) describe adaptations of the structural model for use with Iranian, Portugese, and Greek families, respectively. McGill and Pearce (1982) state that the use of the model is contraindicated for British families. Jung (1984) uses structural family therapy in working with Chinese-American families, which works well because it matches the hierarchical nature of the Chinese culture.

Boyd-Franklin (1987) states that structural family therapy can be effective in the treatment of black families, in combination with other approaches. Black and Hispanic families were part of the original sample used in the research upon which the structural school is based. The action orientation toward solving problems through changing the structure of the family empowers black families and meets their therapeutic needs for concrete results. The family is engaged in the process immediately in the initial session. In addition, the structural model includes techniques for working with three-generational families. Here, the grandmother is taught to help her daughter to be a better parent by creating a parental executive subsystem in which the grandmother is a partner. Clearer boundaries are also formed with the parental child who takes care of younger children due to economic necessity. The parental child reports to the mother, who takes full responsibility for the parenting, allowing the parental child to enjoy being part of the sibling subsystem while remaining a junior executive.

Boyd-Franklin (1987) has found structural family therapy to be effective in the treatment of black families, in combination with other approaches.

Boyd-Franklin (1987) further suggests that the expansion of the structural model to that of the ecostructural (see Aponte, 1986; Auerswald, 1968) encourages the therapist to move outside the family to the interactions with the systems and agencies that impact the lives of many black families. She also encourages the use of genograms to support the efforts of black clients to heal cutoffs so that they can profit again from belonging to the extended family network. In addition, care should be taken to develop trust through structural interventions that work before attempting any paradoxical strategic techniques with black families, since they may bring with them a suspicion of the system and treatment personnel. Straightforward structural techniques that effect change will be more acceptable, with a higher probability of black families remaining in treatment. Aponte (1986) reports a successful case using an ecostructural approach with a poor black family where the mother was a single parent raising six children and two grandchildren. Such an approach focuses on the strengths of the individuals, the family, and the community, using any or all as needed by the particular family. Boyd-Franklin (1987) emphasizes that such an ecostructural approach is useful because any family therapists who wish to be effective in working with black families need to view the context of therapy more broadly and to expand their roles as therapists.

Structural family therapy is particularly appropriate for families in the process of divorce or of building a remarried, binuclear family. In *Family Kaleidoscope,* Minuchin (1984) presents typescripts of his work with a single parent and her children who are in the process of divorce and with a blended family in which the stepfather and stepson are conflicted. The original sample upon which Minuchin's theory is based was composed of a number of single-parent families; therefore, from its very inception his approach was developed to work effectively with this target group. Brown and Samis (1987) elaborate on the application of structural family therapy theory and techniques used by mediators in formal divorce mediation. Fulmer (1983) used the structural approach in working with the unresolved mourning by the family members in family systems with a single parent.

Russell, Atilano, Anderson, Jurich, & Bergen (1984) studied the process of family therapy to determine which intervention strategies were linked to the positive therapeutic outcomes of increased life and marital happiness. They found that husbands in particular gained the most from the restructuring of dysfunctional boundaries in the family. Both husbands and wives profited from enacting transactions among family members in the therapy sessions. Wives were happier when symptoms were broadened and reframed. This study clearly supports the effectiveness of the active interventions associated with the structural approach to family therapy.

CONTRIBUTIONS AND LIMITATIONS

Minuchin expanded the use of family therapy as a treatment modality to delinquents, anorectics, psychosomatic children, and the families of substance abusers. Rather than being restricted only to the families of schizophrenics, family therapy became accepted as a normal treatment of choice for many of the problems faced by children and their families. With adaptations, his work provides a model for use with minority and cross-cultural populations, groups who were often not considered by other approaches to family therapy.

Noted as an outstanding and gifted clinician, Minuchin pioneered active therapeutic techniques for engaging families in the process of therapy. Through enactments, family members would interact in the sessions, showing the transactions that were creating blocks to the growth of the family and the differentiation of its members. By restructuring transactions in the session, family members could learn new and effective ways of interacting. These active interventions have been linked to effective therapeutic outcomes in therapy sessions (Russell et al., 1984).

Minuchin also provided leadership for the research needed to document the effective outcomes of the structural school. His method of diagraming the family system structure made a significant impact on the process of diagnosis in family therapy.

The limitation of the structural school, if one were forced to select one, would be a weakness in the generation of abstract theory or theoretical concepts. Minuchin's earlier work contrasts with later studies, and it is difficult to follow the development of diverse concepts and techniques. This may be due to a creative spiral effect in which earlier work catalyzed later work in a dialectical way, similar to the kaleidoscope in his book, *Family Kaleidoscope* (1984). After all, an artist grapples with creation and does not need to explain his art work—it stands for itself.

SUMMARY

Salvador Minuchin developed the structural school of family therapy based on his work with juvenile delinquents and their families from low socioeconomic levels and psychosomatic families who had children who were diabetic, asthmatic, or anorectic.

An outstanding clinician, Minuchin is most noted for his use of action in the family session through enactments of interactions.

Minuchin believes that the reality of human beings is based not only on their individual perceptions but on environmental interactions. By changing the environment, especially the social environment of the family structure, people will experience reality differently. Important theoretical concepts include family structure, boundaries, subsystems, the continuum of enmeshment versus disengagement, alignment, and power.

The goals of structural therapy are to resolve the presenting problem, change the underlying structure of the family, and reframe the family's construction of reality or world view. Change is a natural part of life. Families restructure themselves to adapt to changes in the family life cycle and the life cycle of the individual as well as to stressors affecting an individual family member or the family as a whole. When families rigidly hold to the same transactional patterns rather than changing their rules, symptoms appear and treatment is needed.

Minuchin developed a system for diagraming the structures of families that can be used effectively in diagnosis and treatment, which are integrated processes. The role of the therapist in structural therapy is an active one, a director of the family drama. Some of the techniques of the structural school include joining (making contact with each member of the family through confirmation, tracking, accommodation, and mimesis) and restructuring (which can be done through enactments of transactions in the sessions, tasks assigned for homework, reframing, relabeling the symptom, using intensity, unbalancing, and seeing the strengths in families). Joining, restructuring, and reframing are cyclical and overlapping, occurring from the first minute of the first session throughout the therapy so that progress is made in every session, which typically is focused on one interactional theme.

EXERCISES

1. Draw structural diagrams to represent the following family structures (include parental, spousal, and sibling subsystems where appropriate), even though such diagrams only represent tentative hypotheses until the therapist actually observes the transactions between family members in the therapy session.

a. The Fredericks family is composed of the mother, Sally, and the children: Maria (age 13), John (12), Kitty (6), and Gloria (4). Most of the time, Sally leaves Maria in charge while she works, but sometimes she says that John will be the boss while she is gone. The father, Bill, drives a cab. He has not seen the children in the year since the divorce. John has developed an embarrassing problem of encopresis (having bowel movements in his pants). Sally is dating a man named Herman, who has no in-

terest in the children. Your diagram should show a proposed structure that would provide a direction for treatment.

b. Mom goes to work, and grandmother comes to keep the children—Mark (5 years old) and Peter (2 years old). Mom does not want to talk about how to discipline the children with her mother. Sometimes grandmother spanks them. Sometimes their father does. Sometimes their mother does. One time grandmother gave them candy after they did not pick up their toys as their mother had directed. Draw a second diagram that shows an alternative hypothetical family structure to aim for in treatment.

c. The Gonzales family consists of the mother, Rosita, and her husband, Raoul. They have six children: Maria (age 18), Jose (16), Juan (12),

Lolita (10), Rosario (8), and Raoul Jr. (6). Raoul Jr. has developed a school phobia. As the youngest child, he has received a great deal of special attention. Rosario carries him around most of the day. Rosita works and is busy with housework when she returns home. When Rosita tries to discipline Raoul Jr., his father intervenes because his namesake is a special person to him, and Rosita sides with her father to protect Raoul Jr. from her mother, who she thinks does not love Raoul Jr. like she does. If her mother did really love him, he would not be afraid of school.

2. The structural technique of joining is very useful in therapy. Your instructor will divide the class into groups of four. In your group, take turns playing the role of the therapist joining a three-member family—two parents and a child. Each person should have 5 minutes. Your instructor will call time after each 5-minute segment. Be sure to reread the sections of the chapter on theoretical concepts, techniques, and initial interview in preparation for this exercise. Remember that joining means making contact with each individual family member. For example, you could introduce yourself and then in turn request the name of each person, beginning with the parents, and then ask each person, "What do you think the problem is?" or "What do you expect to gain from this therapy?"

3. Another structural therapy technique that is very useful is enactment. In a group of four people, take turns playing the role of the therapist and direct an enactment. The most common method is to ask the parents to talk together about what the problem is, noting what the other members do and commenting on the transactional patterns that occur in an objective, nonjudgmental way.

4. Relabeling means substituting an adjective with a positive connotation for an adjective with a negative connotation that has been used about a person in the session (Minuchin et al., 1967). For example, a wife may scream at a husband that he is "controlling," which is relabeled as "overburdened." The following is a list of adjectives that have negative connotations to many people in our society. On the line to the right of the adjective, write down a positive adjective that would describe the same behavior.

Domineering _____
Picky _____
Messy _____
Perfectionistic _____
Wasteful _____
Weird _____
Rebellious _____
Shy _____
Gossipy _____
Bossy _____
Hysterical _____
Nosey _____
Stubborn _____
Passive-aggressive _____

5. Reframing is the process of giving a positive connotation to a negative behavior (Minuchin et al., 1967). For example, a mother may yell at her son to do his homework; the "yelling" on the part of the mother is reframed as "concern" about her son. On the line to the right of the negative noun, write down a positive behavior that could be an advantage or an underlying meaning of the negative behavior.

Yelling _____
Teasing _____
Fighting _____
Ridiculing _____
Being late _____
Talking back _____
Contradicting _____
Lecturing _____
Smothering _____
Laughing at or
   making fun of _____
Ignoring _____
Punishing _____
Criticizing _____
Belittling _____
Saying you'll do
   something but
   not doing it _____

6. Often a structural therapist will use reframing to redefine or relabel a symptom by indicating the function it plays. For example, the symptom of being anorectic may be relabeled as "being helpful by holding your parents together" or as being

"King Kong" (the anorectic is powerful through the illness just as King Kong is). Relabel the following symptoms by writing a reframed statement on the line to the right of each one.

Taking drugs _____
Being anorectic _____
Failing in school _____
Losing a job _____
Fighting _____
A relationship
  breaking up _____
Needing space _____
Physically abusing
  a spouse _____
Depression _____
Hallucinations _____
Arguing _____

7. Often in life our greatest strengths are also our greatest weaknesses. For example, the very persistence that allows an executive to lead a group until a major project is completed can be viewed as stubbornness by his wife and children when he will not change the family vacation plans based on their feedback.

An accountant who earns a high salary because she can find errors and attend to detail may be considered "picky" by her family when she constantly checks to make sure that the stove is turned off and other details are taken care of before the family leaves the house. Lawyers who win big fees because they can argue well and are logical may be difficult to live with because they are uncompromising and not empathic as spouses. Strengths can indeed be considered weaknesses. Likewise, our weaknesses can be reframed as strengths.

Many weaknesses that we perceive in other people are positive qualities that have been used to the extreme. This extreme can be viewed as negative. However, this negative quality can be reframed or redefined in the positive. For example, a "loud" child may just be "enthusiastic," or a "stingy" individual may be very "thrifty." By reframing, a person can reduce the extremes of the behavior. If you see the goodness in a person and share your perception, the relationship is reframed and redefined in a positive way—a self-fulfilling prophesy.

Find a partner whom you do not know, or follow the directions of your instructor to obtain your partner. The first partner will be asked to complain. Close your eyes and picture the person about whom you are going to complain. Take a moment or two to imagine all those traits and behaviors that annoy you. Open your eyes.

When your instructor says, "Go," complain about the traits and behaviors of this person to your heart's content while your partner listens, until your instructor says to stop (2 minutes).

Your partner now has the task of reframing all those negative adjectives and behaviors into positive ones about the same traits. Begin when your instructor says "Go," and continue until your instructor says "Stop" (2 minutes).

Now the partner who complained is asked to "brag" about the same traits and behaviors of the same person. You can use any words or ideas that your partner created in the reframing process and any that you generate on your own. Brag about those same traits and behaviors until your instructor says "Stop" (2 minutes).

Now reverse roles and repeat the exercise.

Your instructor may ask for volunteers to share their feelings about this exercise. Did you notice any changes in your thoughts and feelings about the person whom you complained and bragged about?

Chapter 12
Brief Therapy

Be Spontaneous!

Watzlawick, Weakland, and Fisch, 1974, p. 64.

This chapter focuses on communication approaches to family therapy, especially styles of doing brief therapy. Based on research on the processes of communication in the families of schizophrenic patients, these approaches include the work of Jackson, the techniques developed by Watzlawick and his colleagues at the Brief Therapy Center, and the contributions of de Shazer. All use techniques based on communication. Attaining healthy patterns of communication is an important goal of treatment.

It must have been exciting to have participated in the birth of family therapy at one of its major birthing sites—the Mental Research Institute (MRI) in Palo Alto, California, during the 1950s and 1960s. In the original works of Jackson, Satir, Bateson, Watzlawick, Weakland, Haley, Sluzki, and Beavin, the excitement of the intellectual challenge of these strong individuals from diverse disciplines comes to life. Their cross-disciplinary, cooperative endeavors set the tone for the future development of family therapy.

Jackson (1968a) details how it all began in his foreword to two volumes of papers produced at the MRI. It was a dreary day in January 1954 when Jackson, a noted psychiatrist, delivered the Frieda Fromm-Reichmann lecture at the Veterans Administration Hospital in Palo Alto, California. Gregory Bateson, a famous anthropologist was in the audience, and he came up afterwards to introduce himself and to indicate that the topic of the lecture, homeostasis, was definitely of interest to him. He and his colleagues (Haley, Weakland, and Fry) were conducting some communication research on the language of schizophrenics. Jackson (1968a) stated, "From that moment on, I became more closely related to the social sciences than to medical psychiatry, I have never regretted this decision" (p. v).

Jackson became enamored with research, serving as a consultant to the Bateson project. He started a research foundation for the behavioral sciences with private funding in November 1958. The Mental Research Institute (MRI) operated under the auspices of the Palo Alto Medical Research Foundation. With four staff members—Jackson; Virginia Satir, a social worker; Jules Riskin, another psychiatrist; and a secretary—the first grant (focusing on the study of schizophrenics and their families) was obtained in March 1959. According to Bodin (1981), the Bateson Project, separate from the MRI, also received funding for a similar project on schizophrenia and the family in 1959. The following year, Satir received a 2-year grant from the Hill Foundation of Minneapolis for the first family therapy training project in the United States. In 1962, the NIMH awarded its first formal training grant in family therapy to Satir for a 5-year period. Satir is credited with formulating the first family therapy training program in the country.

Three important pioneers in family therapy joined the MRI during the 1960s: Haley, Weakland, and Watzlawick. Jay Haley, who later became a research associate at the MRI after the Bateson project phased out (Bateson became bored with schizophrenia and went to the South Pacific to study the communication patterns of porpoises), was a communications analyst, not formally trained as a psychologist or psychiatrist. John Weakland received his training in chemistry and chemical engineering at Cornell University. After practicing as an engineer for 6 years, he returned to graduate school to study sociology and anthropology under Bateson, following him to Palo Alto to work on the original research grant and then becoming a research associate at the MRI. Paul Watzlawick, an Austrian, joined the MRI in 1961 after having completed two doctorates, one in linguistics/literature and one in psychology. He had taught at the National University of San Salvador, lecturing in psychology.

The Brief Therapy Center of the MRI opened in 1967 with Richard Fisch, a psychiatrist, as its director. Arthur Bodin joined Watzlawick, Weakland, and Fisch. At the Brief Therapy Center clients were seen for a maximum of 10 sessions, focusing on the quick and effective resolution of the presenting problem.

Two volumes of papers were edited by Jackson (1968b and 1968c), but he died suddenly before the work was published. Watzlawick and Weakland (1977) edited *The Interactional View: Studies at the Mental Research Institute, Palo Alto, 1965–1974,* which included most of the major research papers completed at the Institute after the first two volumes were printed. Jackson had been a popular and dynamic leader who was sorely missed as federal monies became tighter. John Bell became the second director of the MRI, obtaining a grant to study families with older members. Riskin, Cummings, and Sluzki became directors of the MRI over the years. The Mental Research Institute remains one of the key centers in the United States for training therapists in the art of family therapy and the skills of family research. Currently there are opportunities for year-long externships in family therapy (including one available for training Spanish-speaking therapists) as well as short-term workshops and other continuing education activities at the MRI.

VIEW OF HEALTHY FUNCTIONING

Although communication theorists (Watzlawick, Beavin, & Jackson, 1967) believe that the human mind exists, they limit their approach to observable inputs and outputs of the "black box"—that is, to communication. Human beings are neutral black boxes that can be studied only in terms of their communications, which are the observable functions of the mind.

The study of human communication is the study of meaning (semantics) and content (syntax) and their effect on behavior (pragmatics). Human beings exchange information with their environments—that is, they communicate. Therefore, human beings can be studied through the science of cybernetics, the functions of communication as information exchange, regulation, control, and information processing. Human beings are neither good nor evil but rather neutral systems of communication.

Positive feedback leads to a loss of stability. Information is used to increase the deviation from a set point. Constantine (1986) uses the analogy of two people who have separate controls for their electric blankets but the controls are reversed, so when the husband turns his side up, his wife's becomes hotter. Then she turns hers down because she is too hot, which means he becomes colder. Therefore, they end up quarreling as the problem is amplified rather than decreased. Negative feedback leads to a steady state of the organism. Information is used to reduce the deviation in output from a set point, just as a thermostat provides information to turn on or off the furnace in order to keep the room at the same temperature.

Redundancy is the occurrence of repeated behaviors, phenomena, or events. Patterns of interaction may be studied in the family since family behaviors tend to repeat themselves in similar patterns over time, according to the principle of redundancy.

Communication theorists focus on the present patterns of interaction between family members in the here and now. For example, the axioms of communication listed in Table 12–1 were developed from research on communication. All human beings communicate according to these properties of communication. When they are incongruently applied, dysfunctional communication results.

DON D. JACKSON

Historical Development

As the founder and director of the Mental Research Institute, Don Jackson led the establishment of family therapy as a treatment modality. As a psychiatrist, he was vitally interested in the etiology and treatment of schizophrenia, writing two books on the subject: *The Etiology of Schizophrenia* (1960) and *Myths of Madness* (1964). But he is remembered best for his contributions to marital therapy, most notably the "quid pro quo" (meaning "this for that" in Latin), which is a negotiation technique that has been adopted by most schools of marital therapy as an integral part of modern-day treatment. According to Broderick and Schrader (1981), Jackson originated the term *conjoint therapy* in 1959 to define a therapist treating the husband and wife together in

TABLE 12–1 Toward Healthier Family Systems: The properties of communication

1. A person cannot *not* communicate.

2. The smallest unit of communication is a message or a communication. A sequence of messages sent and received between people is called an interaction.

3. Each message has a report aspect (the informational content) and a command aspect (statement of relationship). The report aspect supplies the data, and the command aspect supplies the instructions or meaning of the data.

4. The report aspect is the verbal part of a message, and the command aspect is the nonverbal part conveyed by voice tone, voice inflection, gestures, posture, facial expression, and context.

5. The command aspect permits a person to communicate about the communication, which is a metacommunication. People are then talking about the relationship between each other.

6. Punctuation of a communicational sequence is how it is organized by the receiver. For example, two people have a marital conflict. The husband sees the wife nagging first and then he withdraws, whereas the wife sees the husband withdraw and then she criticizes him. They have each punctuated the same communication sequence differently.

7. There are analogic (relationship) ways of communicating and digital (content) ways of communicating. Digital ways are verbal, have a higher degree of complexity, are logical and abstract, and have adequate syntax but no semantics. Analogic ways define the nature of the relationship, are ambiguous, and have adequate semantics but no syntax.

8. All interactions are either complementary (based on differences) or symmetrical (based on equity). An example of a complementary interaction would be as one person in the interaction becomes more assertive ("one up" position), the other becomes more submissive ("one down" position). Dissimilar behaviors elicit each other in an interlocking relationship fit. An example of a symmetrical interaction is competitive boasting. Escalation may occur in symmetrical relationships, and rigidity can happen in complementary relationships.

From *Pragmatics of Human Communication: A Study of Interactional Patterns, Pathologies, and Paradoxes* (pp. 48–70) by P. Watzlawick, J. H. Beavin, and D. D. Jackson, 1967, New York: W. W. Norton & Co. Adapted by permission.

the same room. In addition, Lederer and Jackson (1968) wrote *The Mirages of Marriage,* one of the best volumes available on the nature of marriage. It is still in print more than 20 years after Jackson's death.

Key Theoretical Concepts

Jackson viewed the family as a rule-governed cybernetic system. He is credited with developing the concept of homeostasis as it relates to family systems.

Homeostasis. The tendency of pathological systems to rigidly adhere to the status quo, is called homeostasis (Jackson, 1977a).

Rules. Governing principles, which organize family life so that family members repeatedly behave in certain prescribed ways when interacting with each other across most content areas, are defined as rules by Jackson (1977b).

Calibration. The process of defining the rules of the relationship is calibration. By defining and redefining the rules, the family can control positive and negative feedback in the system and regulate the homeostasis, similar to the way a person turns the thermostat up or down to control the furnace and to regulate the temperature in a room.

The Therapeutic Process

Goals of Therapy. Jackson intended to change the behavior, that is, the interactional patterns of the families that he treated. By encouraging families to change the rules governing their relationships (a process of recalibration), interactional patterns would change.

Role of the Therapist. Jackson was a very directive expert, exuding confidence in what he was doing. He asked questions of each family member and observed who talked to whom. He used the directive techniques of prescribing the symptom and relabeling.

Use of Diagnosis and Assessment. In the face-to-face interview with the family, Jackson observed the interactional patterns in the family to determine who was communicating to whom in what way. Often he would permit family members to use inappropriate communication styles so as not to embarrass them early in treatment and, more importantly, to accurately assess the family rules.

Nature of the Initial and Subsequent Sessions. Jackson would see the family members together, which was quite a departure for his day (see Jackson & Satir, 1968). He would ask open-ended questions about the presenting problem, being careful to observe the communication patterns of the family—who said what to whom. He would encourage the family members to recalibrate the system by redefining the rules. This was particularly important as the couple discussed what they were trading in the marriage—the quid pro quo. Often the symptom would be relabeled and prescribed. The family would change its behavior and thereby change its rules of operation.

Application: Major Therapeutic Techniques

Quid Pro Quo. In this technique the therapist asks each spouse what is needed from the other and finds out what the other partner is willing to give. The spouses trade, negotiating a bargain or new rule for their relationship (Jackson, 1977b).

Relabeling.   Positive characteristics of a symptom are emphasized in this technique. For example, arguing may be relabeled as caring on the part of the family members because people typically argue only with those to whom they are emotionally attached.

Prescribing the Symptom.   The therapist directs the family members to continue, usually to increase the interactional pattern, which is the main symptom. For example, Jackson would often relabel arguing as a sign of caring, directing couples to increase their arguing to a specified number of times between sessions to show their caring for each other. Since the couple wanted to prove the therapist was wrong, that, in fact, they did not care for each other, they would typically fight less, thereby improving their relationship.

Some guidelines for prescribing are given by L'Abate, Ganahl, and Hansen (1986): (1) prescriptions should be utilized cautiously and with sensitivity; (2) acting out behavior such as sexual behavior or substance abuse should not be prescribed; (3) suicidal behavior should not be prescribed; (4) destructive behavior should not be prescribed; (5) detracting from the self-esteem of a family member is off limits; (6) discounting feelings should not be prescribed; and (7) downplaying the importance of the functioning of a family member to the rest of the family should not be encouraged.

As the therapy begins, the behavior is reframed by relabeling the behavior. Then the relabeled behavior is prescribed. An example of a dialogue in which the therapist relabels the symptom and then prescribes it follows:

Therapist:	It seems obvious that this family has a need to shout at each other and argue much of the time. This shows great strength of character. Fighting for what you think is right and being right is an important family value. It also provides a way for family members to get together and really feel one another's presence. Of course, there is a price to pay. It is possible that the arguing may get in the way of the family's functioning and performance of necessary activities. Perhaps we can find some way to confine the fighting to a specific time of the day so that it will cost less and still accomplish the useful things you get out of fighting.
Mom:	What do I do in the meantime? If I ask Cathy [her daughter] to set the table for dinner, she's always too busy.
Therapist:	You will have to find some way to put off the argument until your "FFT."
Dad:	What is "FFT"?
Therapist:	Family Fighting Time! I recommend at least one hour of FFT per day. You should set up the FFT to be held at least one hour after dinner, to allow for your dinner to be digested.
Mom:	How do we have dinner when nobody ever helps?
Therapist:	I would suggest that you each get a small notebook to make notes for FFT so that you won't forget to fight about everything that comes up. Can you [Mom] figure out a way to put off the argument until FFT?
Mom:	Well, I could set the table, as usual.

Therapist:	Or . . . you might consider calling the family in to dinner after you've set only one place for yourself. Of course, you would only serve yourself in that case. [The therapist is testing the resistance.]
Mom:	I couldn't do that!
Therapist:	You'll just have to find some way of putting off the fight until FFT.

In summary, it would be well for you to follow these rules:

1. Family members will find some way to postpone all arguments until FFT, even if it means giving in that one time.
2. Family members will make comprehensive notes so that they won't forget the smallest detail to fight about.
3. The family will spend the entire hour of FFT each day screaming and arguing with each other as loud as they possibly can. It will be important to make your points, so remember to refer to your notes. If you run out of things to fight about, you may have to invent some—just be sure to use up the entire hour.
4. If someone starts in with you (pushes your button), rather than retaliating simply ask them to save it for FFT. Then you both must make notes in your books.

The hour will take place in the living room with the entire family present so you can fight with anyone you need to. Put on all the lights to see each other well. There will be no interruptions of the fighting and no competition with records or T. V. or telephone. It's important that you carry out this assignment. I'll see you next week. (Peckman, 1984)

PAUL WATZLAWICK

Historical Development

Paul Watzlawick, an internationally known lecturer and best-selling author, is the professional at the Brief Therapy Center of the MRI who has written the largest number of books and presented the most training events. His book, *The Situation Is Hopeless but Not Serious* (1983), is a humorous exposé on the logical thought processes that lead to each of the major mental illnesses. Most recently Watzlawick (1988) has written another paradoxical book, this time dealing with utopian problems that need comparable super-human solutions—*Ultra-Solutions: How to Fail Most Successfully*.

Key Theoretical Concepts

First-Order Change.   Change within a system with the structure or rules of the system remaining the same is first-order change. For example, when a person is dreaming, actions could change from running to fighting to loving but the individual would still be dreaming. Based on negative feedback, first-order change occurs in a continuous manner and is typically quantitative or more of the same (Watzlawick et al., 1974).

Second-Order Change.   Change of change or a change in the rules regulating the internal order or structure of the family is second-order change. For example, a change from dreaming to waking would be a second-order change—a change to a different state or to a different logical level. Based on positive feedback, second-order change occurs in an abrupt, discontinuous manner and is qualitatively different, like a leap to something new (Watzlawick et al., 1974).

Typically people seeking help have attempted to solve ordinary difficulties in life by repeating the same solutions—first-order change. The attempted solutions make the problem even worse, and they come to a therapist because they are stuck in a pattern of repeating solutions that do not work. Likewise, they may have ignored a problem that really did need their attention, and the problem has grown worse because no solutions have been attempted when they were needed.

The Therapeutic Process

Goals of Therapy.   The goal of brief therapy is the resolution of the presenting problems through second-order change. Therefore, there will be an observable change in behavior. In other words, the symptoms will disappear. Brief therapists do not see much use in working toward insight.

Role of the Therapist.   The therapist asks open-ended questions about the problem and collaborates with the client to formulate goals. The therapist puts planning and effort into the selection of specific interventions tailored to the idiosyncratic needs of the particular clients. Such planning occurs between sessions and typically includes members of the team who have observed the family sessions, although it may also occur in the session as the therapist formulates an appropriate intervention to be used during that session. The therapist is directive in using such interventions as paradoxical instructions and directed behavior change.

Use of Diagnosis and Assessment.   At the Brief Therapy Center, a client calls a secretary to set up an appointment. No information is taken over the telephone. At the initial visit the client fills out a short form with demographic information and a written consent form for taping and observing of the sessions. No psychological testing is conducted.

The assessment is problem focused and occurs during the first session. Typically goals are formulated and stated no later than the second session. By inquiring about the problem, the therapist makes an assessment about what behaviors are maintaining it.

In the approach of Fisch, Weakland, and Segal (1982), an assessment is made over the telephone. For example, if parents call to make an appointment for a reluctant teenager, the therapist asks them to come in alone to work on ways of motivating their son for treatment. Or a client may say that information can be requested from a previous therapist rather than going over the information again. The therapist responds that better use could be made of the information if the therapist could talk with the client first to obtain a fresh view of the problem. The therapist takes every opportunity to exercise control in this early stage of therapy.

If a family session is requested, the therapist may ask what the main problem is and may have a family session only if it appears that the problem involves the entire family. Otherwise, the session is with the individual, the couple, or the couple with a child who is having the problem, in contrast to most approaches to family therapy. In addition, a prospective client may call for a last-minute appointment on the same day, saying that his schedule is unpredictable and regular appointments cannot be made. After asking if the client is in crisis, the therapist may turn the client down but ask him to call again, indicating that such short notice probably would not work out and that it is only fair to indicate that impossible odds are being set up if the client wants to work on a problem without planning appointments.

Typical questions asked to assess and define the problem include: (1) Who referred you? (2) What previous treatment have you had? (3) What was the treatment like? (4) What brings you to treatment with this therapist at this time? (5) What is the nature of the problem? (6) Because of the problem, what are you doing now that you would stop or do in a different way? (7) What does the problem interfere with your doing right now? (8) How have you been trying to deal with the problem up to now? How have other family members dealt with it? (9) What minimum change would show you that some progress forward has been made? (Weakland, Fisch, Watzlawick, & Bodin, 1974). The therapist carefully observes how the family members interact as they answer these questions during the session.

Fisch et al. (1982) very carefully assess the patient's position in the first few sessions. This gives clues to whether a client would profit better from a direct order or a paradoxical one. For example, if the client is very compliant (exact words of agreement by the client to what the therapist says and a more passive stance), a more direct, straightforward intervention is indicated rather than a paradoxical one, which is more appropriate for a resistant client (one who qualifies what the therapist says and never quite agrees or openly debates what the therapist says). The therapist must listen carefully to avoid making statements that might strongly oppose the views that clients bring to the session to minimize resistance and to maintain therapeutic maneuverability.

Nature of the Initial Session.   The therapist asks questions about the presenting problem and about behaviors that might be maintaining the problem. Often specific behavioral goals are reached in the first session, and if not, then by the second session. Reframing and paradoxical interventions are typically used in the sessions.

The following is an example of a questioning sequence in which the therapist asks about the problem, reframes it, and uses a paradoxical intervention or prescription.

Patient:	My main problem is that I'm depressed most of the time. It has its ups and downs—at the worst, I'm still just able to do my job, but nothing else; at the best, I still don't feel good.
Therapist:	You say depression is your main problem. Anything else?
Patient:	Yes—I don't have any lasting relationships with men. They're all brief and unsatisfying.
Therapist:	Could you describe that a bit more specifically?
Patient:	Well, when I'm feeling relatively OK, I'll take some action to find somebody. I may go to a bar and meet a man there.
Therapist:	Then what?

Patient: After we get acquainted, we may go home together. But it never lasts long. After a few days or a week—a couple of weeks at most—I don't hear from him anymore. And if I call him, he puts me off. Then I wonder what's the matter with me, and I get depressed again. This happens over and over.

Therapist: Are you depressed right now?

Patient: Yes—and I'd like to feel better.

Therapist: I can understand that, but I have to tell you that it really would not be a good thing for you to start feeling better, less depressed, right away. Let me explain why, since I know this may seem contradictory to you because you came here to get over your depression. You see, you have another problem: In some way—it's not yet clear just how—at this point, you don't know how to handle your relationships with men so that they work out to your satisfaction. In that particular area, you must lack some social skill you need. So, if your depression were to get better right away—before you have time to find out what you need to handle things better—then you would be in serious danger of getting involved with another man, only to have it end badly soon. And then you'd feel even more depressed.

Patient: Well, I can sort of see that, even though I'd like to feel better.

Therapist: Of course you would, but right now it's too big a danger for you. In fact, I'm concerned that if you got to feeling even a little better, you might be tempted to go out looking, and fall into a bad relationship despite what I've explained to you. So let me suggest a way to prevent that. If you should feel an urge or need to go out, OK, you may have to. But you definitely should do something to make yourself less attractive, so as to prevent or at least slow down this quick involvement in relationships—until we can get an idea of what you need to have them work out better. You don't have to do very much. If you do go out, you could just make a black mark somewhere on your face—as a sort of blemish. (Fisch et al., 1982, pp. 1–3)

Stages of Therapy.   There are six stages of brief therapy (Weakland et al., 1974): (1) introduction and explanation of what the treatment system is like; (2) obtaining information about the problem and defining it; (3) analyzing what behaviors on whose parts are maintaining the behavior; (4) formulating goals for treatment; (5) choosing and implementing interventions; and (6) termination. These stages are accomplished over a maximum of 10 sessions.

Application: Major Therapeutic Techniques

People make their problems worse by repeating solutions that do not work. Thus, a paradox and a positive feedback loop are created in that the more they do, the worse it gets. An example of a paradox that becomes the problem is the directive, "Be spontaneous." The more one attempts to force oneself to be unstructured, the more structured one becomes. The directive is a paradox because a person cannot comply with a rule that is a structured activity and also emit spontaneous activity that is unstructured and non-rule-compliant—they are mutually exclusive opposites. An example of a paradox in which the solution has become the problem is shown in Figure 12–1. The wife's efforts to "train" her husband to be a man are having the opposite

FIGURE 12-1   "I was a fool to marry you—I thought I could train you to become a real man!"

Illustration by A. A. Wood is reproduced from *Change: Principles of Problem Formation and Problem Resolution* (p. 65) by P. Watzlawick, J. H. Weakland, and R. Fisch, 1974, New York: W. W. Norton & Co. Reprinted by permission. Copyright © 1974 by W. W. Norton & Company, Inc.

effect, as can be seen by his posture in the cartoon. To use a brief therapy approach, the therapist must find out what attempted solution has become the problem, and then a paradoxical intervention is designed to undo the solution that has not worked—in essence, a counterparadox.

Successful Reframing.   In order for the counterparadox prescription to work, however, it must be reframed to be acceptable to the client or clients who will be asked to carry it out. In brief therapy, reframing is the changing of the meaning of a behavior or a situation without changing the concrete "facts" of the situation (Watzlawick et al., 1974). Thus, the attitude of the family is altered. This may be conceptual in that ideas are changed, emotional because feelings about the event are changed, or a combination of these. For example, look at the glass in Figure 12–2. What do you see?

If you said that the glass was half full, you perceived the glass differently from a person who said that the glass was half empty. The concrete facts are still the same: The same amount of fluid was in the glass when both individuals perceived it. Yet the "frame" (Bateson [1955] is credited for coining the term) that each individual brings to the task is quite different. Some would label one frame as optimistic and the other as pessimistic. In therapy with depressed patients, therapists often attempt to change the frame from a pessimistic one to an optimistic view.

Reframing is based on a constructivist perspective of reality (Coyne, 1985). In other words, people create their own reality (Watzlawick, 1976, 1978, 1984). This phenom-

FIGURE 12–2   What do you see?

enological view of reality is the basis of many, if not all, types of psychotherapy. For example, the wife of a stroke victim might be told that her husband's stubbornness is his way of maintaining his self-respect and sense of dignity. After such a reframe the wife may be told to nurture his self-respect with pessimism about his readiness to do small tasks. The reframe of his stubbornness has given her a rationale or viewpoint that makes her change of behavior in response to the therapist's directive have meaning. She can back off from her efforts to coerce him, yet it will make sense due to the reframe. The facts of her husband's illness have not changed, but the meaning of both of their behaviors in this factual situation have changed. Therefore, for most directive interventions to work, whether or not they are paradoxical, they must be reframed to have meaning within the client's frame—a mediational linkage of the client's frame to new behavior expected of the client.

For it to be successful, the social context must be taken into consideration in the process of reframing (Coyne, 1985). For example, most parents know that it is the God-given right of every teenager to protest the rules, orders, and directions of the parents. Therefore, when clients present with difficulty in being firm with their adolescents, it is important to couch any therapeutic work with the social reframe that protesting and other outrageous behavior on the part of the teenagers is a sign of progress. Otherwise, the parents might discard the planned homework assignment, thinking that it did not work.

Paradoxical Interventions.   These interventions are directive instructions to implement a paradox or contradictory behavior. Twelve types with examples are given in Table 12–2.

Fisch et al. (1982) suggest the following main paradoxical interventions: (1) deliberately directing the client to bring about a symptom, which works with most types of problems with bodily functions (for example, direct a client to stay awake when insomnia is the presenting problem); (2) exposing the client to a feared problem while restraining the completion or the mastery of it (for example, direct the client

TABLE 12–2 Types of paradoxical interventions

1. *Less of the Same.* Clients are instructed to do less of certain behaviors to achieve the same goal. For example, a couple who wants to be independent of their parents are told to do nothing when their parents come to visit. The parents will then tire of doing everything.

2. *Making the Covert Overt.* The father is told to give his daughter 10 cents every time she is arrogant to her mother, making overt what he was covertly doing, so the teenager stopped her attacks on the mother.

3. *Advertising in Contrast to Concealing.* In his public address, a man states how anxious he is and that his nervousness will in all likelihood overwhelm him. The problem goes away when he advertises it.

4. *Small Causes Make Big Differences.* By instructing a person to change one small behavior, a larger cognitive map will change. For example, a perfectionistic woman is told to make one small mistake on purpose each day.

5. *Bellac Ploy.* When a boss puts a woman down in front of other employees, she is encouraged to call him aside and tell him that when he does that it really turns her on sexually. Then she immediately leaves the room. The behavior of the boss stops.

6. *Using Resistance.* The directive, "Go slow." Also stating all of the positives in a person's life and asking, "how could you change?"

7. *Not Challenging Accusations nor Denials.* The therapist tells a person to not drink but pretend to be drunk on some days and to drink and appear sober on some days and for the other spouse to judge whether or not the person has been drinking and write it down.

8. *Sabotage, in a Nice Way.* Parents request the expected curfew time and say that there is nothing that they can do to make the teenager keep it, and then they walk away. At the curfew time, they are instructed to lock all doors and windows and get up to open them when the teenager comes in, apologizing to the teenager and going to bed without asking any questions.

9. *Inattention Can Have Its Consequences.* A teacher who has been giving a student a great deal of attention is requested to give the student the same amount of attention that she gives everyone else. The student will then do more work to gain attention.

10. *Study.* A student is told to write two papers: one in which the student attempts to obtain a C-minus and one in a typical style done at the last minute that aims for a higher grade. In another variation, a student is told that if studying is not done by a set time, the student is not permitted to do any studying or even look at books for the rest of the evening.

11. *Handling Utopias.* If a client has broad goals, the therapist suggests even more grandiose goals. The client will then typically focus on smaller goals.

12. *"Devil's Pact".* The therapist obtains the agreement or disagreement to carry out a therapeutic plan before he tells the client the nature of the plan.

From *Change: Principles of Problem Formation and Problem Resolution* (pp. 116–57) by P. Watzlawick, J. H. Weakland, and R. Fisch, 1974, New York: W. W. Norton & Co. Adapted by permission.

with writer's block to write one page and do no more); (3) taking a position of one-down in control issues (for example, not engaging the teenager in a fight about doing homework by asking the mother to say that she doesn't know if her daughter's homework is done or not, but would the daughter like to watch a good show that's on television with her?); (4) directly requesting (for example, gentle indirect requests are reframed as destructive, leading a child toward failure in life, and direct requests are benevolently reframed as sacrifices); (5) confirming the suspicions of the accuser (for example, a husband was told to admit to being no fun and that it was too late to change); (6) a "U-turn" (for example, the therapist realizes the intervention isn't working because the client is complaining; therefore, the therapist agrees with the client and takes the opposite paradoxical position); and (7) giving suggestions on how to worsen the situation (for example, stating that if the client follows the advice given, the situation will become worse; tell the person to analyze the behaviors of others and attribute a hostile motivation if the client wishes to become angrier).

STEVE DE SHAZER

Historical Development
The work of Steve de Shazer (1982, 1985, 1988), director of the Brief Therapy Center in Milwaukee, Wisconsin, is an innovative form of brief therapy that typically lasts five sessions. Although de Shazer says that his ideas have evolved historically from the contributions of Milton Erickson, Gregory Bateson, and the brief therapists of the MRI, they are very different in key ways. First of all, there is a different theoretical episte-mological basis for de Shazer's work, an ecosystemic epistemology that includes a binocular theory of change. In practice, de Shazer maintains that the process of change may be similar in each case. Making one small change by using a "skeleton key" that is not directly related to the idiosyncratic presenting problem may unlock the door to the problem because a solution evolves. He emphasizes a vision of the future with crystal ball techniques and focuses on past successes, using a cooperative relationship that has been built with clients. He is more interested in how family members will know that a problem has been resolved than the details of the complaint or past solutions that have not worked. De Shazer gives much credit to his wife and colleague, Insoo Kim Berg, who brainstormed ideas, dialogued with him, and participated as the conductor or member of the therapeutic team.

Key Theoretical Concepts

Ecosystem. Bateson (1972) defined ecology or ecosystem as the survival unit, which is the larger system, not the species or the individual, in which the individual lives. All individual organisms are in reciprocal relationships with each other within the eco-system.

Ecosystemic Epistemology. This term was coined by Keeney (1979) and means that all individuals in the unit of survival participate reciprocally in the process of knowing. De Shazer (1982) applied this concept in a particular way to his style of therapy—the therapist-conductor of the family session, the members of the therapeutic team behind the mirror, and the family were all participants co-evolving a reciprocal joint reality. The behavior of the family was affected by the behavior of the team, and the behavior of the team was affected by the behavior of the family members, as was that of the conductor of the session, all of whom were now members of a suprasystem. Therefore, there was a reciprocal, mutual process of thinking and deciding—an ecosystemic epistemology.

Binocular Theory of Change.   According to de Shazer (1982), the pattern that the team presents to the family is very similar to the present pattern of the family, yet a little different. Therefore, the family recognizes it as their pattern and takes it into the present pattern rather than creating a new pattern. However, since it is slightly different, their original pattern is changed without the family realizing it. It is analogous to the picture that each eye takes when you look at a mountain. The brain processes the two images of the two eyes from slightly different angles to form a third image, which now has depth because it is binocular.

Cooperating.   The response of the family to the pattern, the behavior or set of behaviors that the family evokes in response to the pattern of the team, is called cooperating. The team then analyzes the pattern of behavior and designs an intervention that mirrors the behavior but yet is a little different. The family carries out the intervention, owning it as their own behavior. Therefore, if the family reacts in a paradoxical manner, the prescription of a counterparadox would be an appropriate intervention because it mirrors the behavior of the family yet is somewhat different. The binocular theory of change represents a rationale for the use of paradoxes as well as other innovative interventions such as stories or straightforward directives. This theory is similar to the Piagetian process of accommodation when a schemata in the mind is naturally altered when the mind encounters something that is very similar to a schemata but slightly different, such as a new type of dog. Such an additive process contrasts with assimilation in which a new schemata is created, which is more confusing and unsettling for the organism that reviews previous schema to see where something fits before creating a new schemata.

The Therapeutic Process

Goals of Therapy.   The goals of de Shazer's brief therapy are to alter the world view of the family in subtle ways and to change their behavior so that a solution to the problem evolves, and the problem is resolved.

Role of the Therapist.   The therapist, who is the conductor of the family session, asks open-ended questions and takes a noncritical stance toward the problem, the individual family members, and the world view of the family. The team members observe interactional sequences and diagram them. They construct a message or compliment and clue (explained later in this chapter). Then they consult with the conductor, who may add or change it in some way. The conductor is then very directive with the family, reading the message and clue in the role of an expert.

De Shazer (1985) maintains that a team is not needed to implement this type of brief therapy. If an individual therapist were using this style alone, a break would still be taken for the construction of the compliment and clue. The therapy would resume after the break. Another possibility would be to deliver the compliment and clue at the beginning of the second session, but such a process would not be as effective. Even if the compliment and clue given in the first session were not completely on target, it would still be better to close with the presentation of the message and clue so that feedback could be obtained about the family's response to the intervention in the second session.

Use of Diagnosis and Assessment. Two types of assessment are very important in this approach to therapy: a sequential map and a decision tree. First of all, a sequential map is formulated to represent the interaction of the family members and their frames. This is very helpful in reframing what is going on and in writing the message. For example, the husband asks the wife if she loves him, and she remains silent because she views this as nagging her. He then asks her again because he feels even more insecure than before, at which point she becomes silent because she is angry at being pressed. This sequence could be punctuated in another way with the wife's silence coming first. In addition, the neurolinguistic style of each person in the transaction typically is included on the map, and a reframe is added as it is developed by the team.

Another form of assessment that is idiosyncratic to this style of therapy is the decision tree related to the family's responses to the message and the clue (Figure 12–3). Based on the binocular theory of change, the decision tree pictures the alter-

FIGURE 12–3   Selection of next intervention based on family's style of cooperating

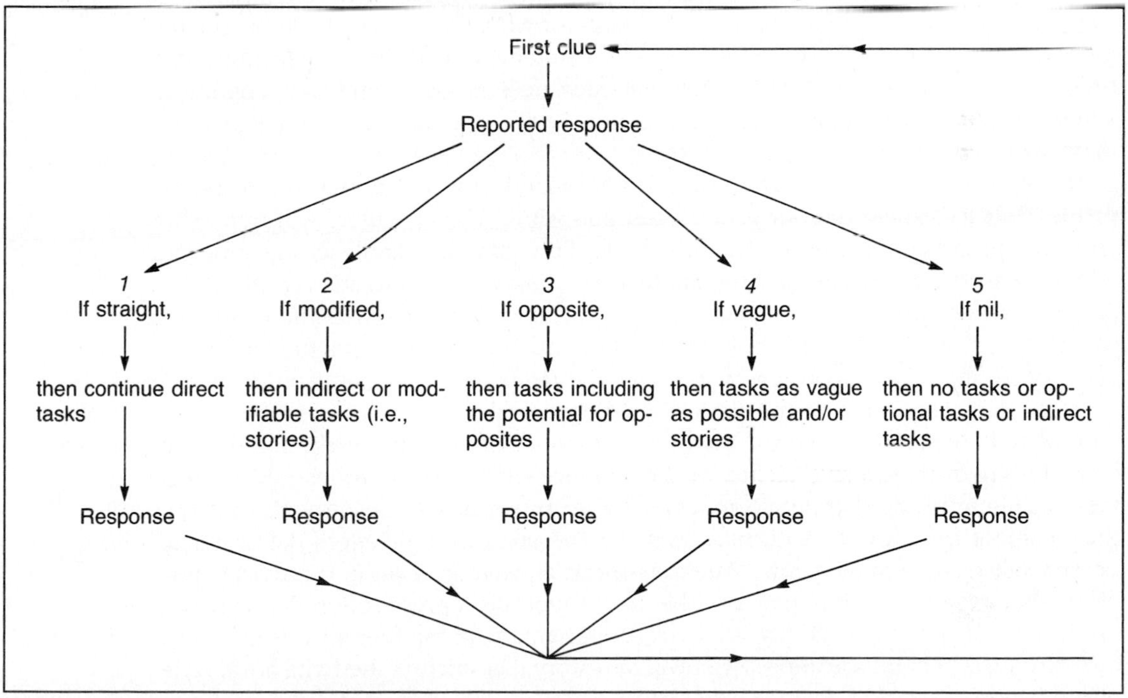

From *Patterns of Brief Family Therapy: An Ecosystemic Approach* (p. 68) by S. de Shazer, 1982, New York: Guilford Press. Reprinted by permission.

native interventions to be used with the family in the future in response to their style of cooperating with the initial intervention. If they followed the direct task, another direct task will be given in the next session. If they modified the direct task, a modifiable task will be given after a story that mirrors the family situation has been presented. If they did the opposite of the task, a paradoxical prescription will be designed for the clue in the next session. If their response was vague, a vague task or a story by way of analogy will be given. If they did nothing, they will be congratulated on doing so. Another experimental task will be given, and if they do not do this after the next session, only a reframe will be done as the message with no clue in the following session. This sensible procedure is a way of integrating the many diverse options the clinician has into an intervention that will work with a particular family.

Nature of the Initial Session.   The therapist who interacts directly with the family in the session is called the conductor. Other therapists observe behind a one-way mirror and consult with the conductor during a consulting break (about 40 minutes into the one-hour session). Each therapy session is divided into six phases: planning before the session, prelude, collecting data, designing an intervention during the consulting break, delivering the message, and studying the effects of the message.

During the 10-minute prelude, the conductor refrains from asking any questions about the problem. Instead, every effort is made to ask casual questions about the social environment of the family—where a person works or goes to school, the neighborhood the family lives in, and their religion—piecing together an idea of how the family sees their world. Concurrently behind the mirror, the team members are taking notes about who talks to whom, who talks for whom, who talks the least and the most, and the favorite phrases of each person. Using the categories of neurolinguistic programming, the nature of the verbs that each person uses—auditory, cognitive, kinesthetic or visual—is recorded. These notes will help the team to match their message to the world view of the family.

During the next phase of data collection, the conductor asks about the problem, that is, "What problem can our group assist you with?" The observers will note who answers this general question, which has been directed to the family as a group, and any process that evolves around the family's deciding who should answer. After one person answers, the conductor asks each family member in turn, with the observers noting the responses. Then the conductor asks about the solutions that the family has tried, obtaining details about them and what the family wants to gain from therapy.

Based on observation of the interaction between the conductor and the family members, the team maps the interactions and frames being used by the family. The team designs a message and a clue for the conductor to deliver to the family. During the consulting break of about 10 minutes, the team members consult with the conductor about the message and may revise it. The conductor practices the message before delivering it to the family. The message is an isomorphism of the world view of the family and its current pattern. The clue is typically a prescription that is based on the team's view of the family's style of cooperating with the therapist. It may be a direct request, a paradoxical prescription, or a story that mirrors the behavioral style of the family.

As the conductor delivers the message, the team watches, writing down their observations of the family's reaction to both the message and the clue. If the family disagrees with the message, a team member may call the conductor to suggest additional wording for the message. After the family leaves, the team meets to discuss the reactions of the family and to predict whether or not the family will come back, and if so what the team thinks the family will do with the task. This is written in the session notes for comparison with what actually happens during the second session.

Stages of Therapy.   The next session uses the same format, except that the data collection focuses entirely on how the family handled the assigned task. Based on their mode of cooperation, a more specific message and another clue are designed. This process is repeated in subsequent sessions. Most people indicate that their problems have been solved in fewer than six sessions.

Application: Major Therapeutic Techniques

Compliment.   The compliment is a written reframed message. In the first part of the message the team praises the family for the strengths that they observed in the family. In the second part of the message a difference is included and previous behavior is given a different meaning. An example of a compliment follows:

> First of all, we are impressed with all the fine details you've given us about your situation. Most families we've met are nowhere near as observant of these details. Your descriptions have been very helpful to us. It's clear to us that you are both loving and dedicated parents who've been resourceful in trying to find ways to solve the problem. Another unusual thing struck us: You seem to care a lot about how the other parent treats the boy. Many parents would only be interested in the boy's difficulties. (de Shazer, 1982, p. 44)

Clue.   The intervention that mirrors the behavioral responses of the family is called the clue. If the family operates using double binds or paradoxes, then the intervention would be a counterparadox. If the family behaves in a straightforward manner and takes direction well, the prescription of a task to be completed would constitute the clue. An example of a clue that would be repeated after the above compliment is as follows:

> Between now and the next time we meet, the team would like you each to observe what happens when you are alone with Jimmie and he misbehaves like this. And we would like to know some other details. When during the week—which days and what time—does Jim most frequently misbehave while both of you are there? (de Shazer, 1982, pp. 44–45)

Confusion Technique.   In de Shazer's (1982) technique, each family member is asked in detail about all of the differences between them, especially as they relate to goals in therapy, and the therapist admits confusion without reaching any resolution of the differences.

Crystal Ball.   Perhaps in an hypnotic trance, the client is asked to use four crystal balls in succession over a period of sessions, as related by de Shazer (1982). In the first session, the client is asked to visualize and experience at its fullest a pleasant memory from an earlier period of life that was long ago forgotten. The client is asked to describe the memory in detail, especially anything that other people are doing. Then the client returns the memory to wherever it was before the session, and the sequence of the first crystal ball ends.

In the second session, the client is asked to use another crystal ball to remember and experience a recent event that has been surprisingly forgotten, an event that the client wants to remember more vividly. Typically the client recalls some success. The client is asked to describe the behavior of the other people at the event and the behavior of the client in the situation. This, too, is returned to memory. In the third, the client is asked to look into the future and to "remember" coming back to tell the therapist that the problem has been resolved. The client is asked to describe this scene in detail. In the fourth, the client is asked to remember how the problem was resolved. The client is asked to describe how other people behaved and what the client did. The client is asked to come back to the present, and the topic is changed away from the crystal ball and the problem.

Past Successes.   The therapist compliments the client on particular past successes but does not directly link this to the resolution of the present problem (de Shazer, 1982).

Skeleton Keys.   These formula interventions, or stock prescriptions, can be used with many different types of problems (Table 12–3).

THERAPEUTIC OUTCOMES
Weakland et al. (1974) maintain a rate of significant success at the Mental Research Institute, stating that in 75% of a sample of 97 cases the problem had been resolved and remained so at follow-up. De Shazer (1985) followed up 88 new clients seen at

TABLE 12–3 Skeleton keys

1. *Write/Read/Burn.* On odd numbered days of the month, the client is to spend one hour writing about all of the bad and good times that the client experienced with the ex-spouse. On even days of the month, the client is expected to spend one hour reading what has been written and then burn it.

2. *Structured Fight.* To decide the order of the fight, toss a coin. The winner complains for 10 straight minutes. The other person also gets a turn for 10 minutes. Ten minutes of silence is respected before the coin is tossed for a second round.

3. *Do Something Different.* The therapist directs the client to do something different related to the specific problem situation between now and the next session.

4. *Overcoming the Urge.* Clients who are tempted to eat too much or to return to drinking alcohol or taking drugs are directed by the therapist to observe whatever they are doing when they overcome the desire to indulge.

5. *Intervention for the Initial Session.* Clients are asked to pay attention to whatever is occurring in their lives (in marriage, family, or a relationship) that they would like to have continue so that they can tell about it in detail in the next session.

From *Keys to the Solution in Brief Therapy* (pp. 120–137) by S. de Shazer, 1985, New York: W. W. Norton & Co. Adapted by permission.

the Brief Therapy Center in Milwaukee using a six-question survey identical to that used at MRI, except that one question had been added to determine if using the standard initial intervention of asking people what they would not change had made any difference. Overall, he found that 72% thought the main complaint was better, while 82% of those using the standard initial intervention thought that the complaint was better.

Bodin (1981) reported the results of the evaluation of a grant for psychotherapeutic services to policemen and their families in which the MRI approach was used. On goal attainment scales (questionnaires asking if goals had been reached) an 82% success rate was obtained (90 of 110 cases were closed because goals had been reached). Only a short questionnaire was sent out by both the MRI and the Brief Therapy Center, compared to the outcome research of the structural school where many assessment instruments of family functioning or stress interviews were given prior to the initiation of therapy and afterwards.

Such rigorous designs, of course, could interfere with the treatment modality in brief therapy. For example, if a family were required to take several instruments such as FACES III and the Wellness Inventory as well as a stress interview and/or a structured family task, the number of sessions for pretest and posttest might be longer than the therapy, confounding the research results because the researcher would not know if the family thought the problem was better due to the therapy sessions, the interaction, or doing something different as required for the pretest/posttest assessment. Data from external, objective third parties showing that the problems of the treated families were better were not found.

However, case studies of the effectiveness of brief therapy are available. Friedman and Pettus (1985) report successful case studies of the treatment of the families of a Jewish adolescent, an Italian-American teenager, and a Greek young adult. They suggest that brief therapy is very appropriate for Greek ethnic families and/or other ethnic families in which there is an expectation of concrete, immediate results. Morawetz and Walker (1984) discuss their use of brief therapy in their book, *Brief Therapy with Single-Parent Families*.

Golden (1983) developed a checklist for school counselors to use in deciding which families could be most effectively helped by brief therapy of no more than three conferences in the school setting. If there is an identifiable environmental stressor, the misbehavior of the child is recent, the boundaries/hierarchies/communication in the family are effective, the family can agree on what the problem is, and the family can follow through with assigned tasks, the family would be an appropriate case for the elementary school counselor. Families who do not meet the criteria should be referred to agencies and private practitioners.

CONTRIBUTIONS AND LIMITATIONS

The basis for much of what we presently know as family therapy according to the "systems" model originated with the research and practice at the MRI by such notables as Jackson, Bateson, Satir, Haley, Watzlawick, Weakland, Fisch, Bodin, Beavin, Sluzki, and others. Major contributions to family therapy include basic research on human communication and the application of the concept of cybernetics to communication within the family; an explanation of dysfunctional communication processes, especially those occurring in the families of schizophrenics; and the development of innovative techniques such as the quid pro quo, the prescription of paradoxes after the behavior has been reframed, and techniques focusing on the future and on strengths.

The limitations of brief therapy approaches include the weaknesses of their research designs. Follow-up studies have been conducted consistently, but they have involved only very short client self-report instruments. Also, there have been few attempts—the exception is the study by Golden (1983)—to assess families to refer those who might be more effectively treated by other approaches and retaining those most likely to profit from this short-term approach. A set of criteria could be developed for such a purpose.

SUMMARY

Don Jackson founded the Mental Research Institute (MRI) in Palo Alto, California, after becoming intrigued by the communication research of Gregory Bateson. He brought together many talented individuals from diverse backgrounds to study a variety of topics, most importantly the communication patterns used in the families of schizophrenics, and to treat them together as a family unit. A psychiatrist, Jackson is credited with applying the concept of homeostasis to family systems. He encouraged families to redefine their rules and recalibrate the family system through the techniques of relabeling and prescribing the symptom. He also coined the term *conjoint therapy* for his work with married couples, for whom he developed the quid pro quo technique of trading this for that within the marriage relationship.

Paul Watzlawick developed a style of brief therapy based on the concept of second-order change, or change of change. He reframed problem behaviors and prescribed paradoxical interventions or counterparadoxes to achieve remission of the symptom within 10 sessions. Examples of counterparadoxes that have been adopted and found useful across theoretical approaches include "go slow," "beware of the dangers of change," exposing a person to a feared situation with no expectation of completion or mastery, and assigning a symptom when a bodily function is the problem, such as assigning an insomniac the task of staying awake.

Steve de Shazer directs the Brief Therapy Center in Milwaukee, Wisconsin, where he has developed an approach to brief therapy embedded in an ecosystemic epistemology. The therapeutic team participates in the suprasystem, which includes the family. Based upon a binocular theory of change, interventions are designed using the concepts of isomorphism (a compliment, which is a type of reframe, should be similar to the world view of the family with only a little difference) and cooperating (a clue is a prescription of a task similar to the behavioral pattern that the family uses to "cooperate" with the therapist with a little difference). De Shazer has developed some innovative future-oriented techniques focused on people's strengths, such as the crystal ball exercise, skeleton keys, strength exercises, and an initial session intervention requesting people to observe and report on what they do not wish to change.

1. Count off in threes according to your instructor's directions and take turns playing the role of the marital therapist, using the quid pro quo technique. First ask one "spouse" what is needed from the other spouse. Be sure to interrupt and cut off any attempts on the part of one spouse to blame the other spouse for not having met past needs. Ask the other spouse what is requested from the first spouse. Find out how each spouse feels about meeting the need or if the spouse can meet the need. The dialogue is more important than the agreement, as this is the process of recalibration, redefining the rules for the marital relationship. Therefore, do not permit either spouse to agree too quickly to do something that cannot be done or that is not wanted. Be active and intervene. Restate what each spouse is requesting and what the other spouse is willing to give. Encourage exploration of thoughts and feelings about each request. When a bargain is reached, it may be written down or remembered because it is repeated orally several times by the therapist and each spouse until it is clearly understood.

2. In an earlier chapter, you practiced relabeling symptoms. Now you are being asked to prescribe the symptom after it has been relabeled. (See the guidelines in this chapter for using relabeling and prescribing the symptom.) Given the following case, write down the exact words that you would use to prescribe the symptom for this couple.

   Jane Henderson reported in her second family therapy session that everyone in her family is always bickering. Every interaction seems to result in an argument, ending up with loud shouting. No one is ever violent in the sense of hitting another family member, but Jane is discouraged about the whole process. Her husband, Ted, and the children (Henrietta, Kyle, and Bob) all agree. As their therapist you have perceived this style of interacting in the first session as everyone interrupted and tried to out-talk the other until they were shouting by the end of the session.

3. Connect all of the dots shown in Figure 12–4 in this exercise by four straight lines without lifting your pen from the paper (Watzlawick et al., 1974, pp. 24–25). Your instructor has the solution to this exercise.

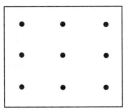

FIGURE 12–4   A reframing puzzle

4. Given the following client presenting problems, reframe the previous solutions that have not worked and create a paradoxical intervention for each—that is, a prescription of a paradox that will help the client.

   a. Neil is a graduate student who is having trouble writing his master's thesis. Time is running out. He is very anxious and perfectionistic about it and would like it to be the best thesis ever completed at the university. He has cut out all of his activities just to work on it, but so far has not been able to write one word. Write down the specific dialogue you would use if you were Neil's therapist.

   b. Janie can't sleep. She is getting married in 2 weeks and is so excited. She knows that she needs her sleep. She has tried a warm bath, hot milk, reading a book—nothing seems to work and she hasn't slept through the night in 2 weeks. She has bags under her eyes and is frantic about it. What would you tell her? Write down the exact dialogue you would use as Janie's therapist.

   c. From the comments of the Jones family in their initial session, they appear somewhat hesitant and even a little resistant to following a doctor's advice. Their daughter is bulimic, and they have been asked to eat breakfast together as a family each morning and supper together as a family each evening. You decide to use the "go slow" restraining paradoxical intervention or prescription with them. Write down exactly what you would say if you were their therapist.

   d. Mr. and Mrs. Brown are having trouble with their son, who will not keep his curfew even though they have grounded him and taken away the car keys at various points. They dread each evening because it typically ends up in an argument with their son after he returns later and later each night. How would you reframe this situation and convince Mr. and Mrs. Brown to use a paradoxical intervention? Write down the exact dialogue you would use. The above dialogues can be shared in groups or in a class discussion, or your instructor may ask you to turn them in.

5. Given the following case study, write a compliment and a clue according to de Shazer's method as though you were a member of the therapy team behind the one-way mirror. The message should point out strengths of the behavior that the family has presented and a subtle difference that sets the cue for the clue. The clue should be a written prescription of a behavioral pattern that is similar to what the family is already doing, but a little bit different. It is often helpful to diagram the behavioral sequence including motivations, which makes it easier to reframe the motivations in constructing an appropriate compliment.

Charlie is 10 years old. When he misbehaves, his father steps in to yell at him. The mother was raised in a family where people were taught not to raise their voices at any cost. When the mother hears the father yell, she tenses up. When his father yells, Charlie cries and runs to his mother. The mother criticizes her husband for yelling at Charlie. The husband argues with his wife and yells at her. He resumes yelling at Charlie. The mother goes to the bedroom, withdrawing from the scene.

6. Assume that the family did the opposite of what you requested them to do in the clue you created for them. They come back to the second session and you ask them how it went. They detail exactly how they did the opposite because they knew that what you had told them to do would not work. Design a second compliment and clue for this same family based on their style of cooperating with you.

7. Form a group according to the instructions of your professor. Take turns sharing your behavioral diagrams, compliments, and clues from Exercises 5 and 6 with each other. Be sure to point out the strengths of different ways of wording the compliment and clue, refraining from any critical comments.

Chapter 13
Strategic Therapy

When a therapist sees himself [herself] as being in a position of power, she [he] can directly tell a client or a family what to do to solve the problem. When a therapist is not certain that his [her] directives will be followed, he [she] is better off using an indirect approach to influence people.

Madanes, 1984, p. 188.

OVERVIEW

Strategic therapy has a number of meanings and can encompass diverse styles of conducting family therapy. Gregory Bateson, the noted anthropologist, formed a research group of Jay Haley and John Weakland, with Don Jackson and William Fry as part-time consulting psychiatrists to study communication. This group existed from 1952 to 1962 and is credited with discovering the double bind concept. Bateson's group declined to be a part of the Mental Research Institute (MRI) and did not want people to confuse their group with the MRI.

This original research undergirded many approaches to family therapy—Satir's communication/humanistic/ego psychology approach, the brief therapy approaches discussed in Chapter 12, and the strategic as well as systemic approaches. For this reason, some authors have grouped all of these approaches under the heading of communication approaches. However, as they have developed over the years, there are a number of differences among these approaches.

In a stricter classification system, Jackson's approach would be called a communication approach; Watzlawick's, a brief therapy approach; the approaches of Haley and Madanes, strategic approaches; and the Milan School, the systemic approach. Yet many authors would group all of these approaches as strategic approaches because they all focus to some degree on the resolution of the specific presenting problem through the use of strategies. Many strategies are paradoxical in nature, such as the prescription of the symptom that has been reframed. These approaches are then often contrasted with the structural school of Minuchin in attempts to integrate the two approaches or further delineate differences (Andolfi, 1986; Fraser, 1986; Friesen, 1985; Scott, 1982; Stanton, 1981 and October, 1981). MacKinnon (1983) contrasts the strategic approach of Haley and Madanes with the contributions of the Milan School.

The definition of *strategic family therapy* in this book will be limited to the work of Jay Haley and Cloe Madanes. Those who adhere to the tenets of the Milan School have been classified as systemic therapists, including Mara Selvini Palazzoli, Guiliana Prata, Luigi Boscolo, Gianfranco Cecchin, and the American proponents of their work, Peggy Penn and Lynn Hoffman. With this historical clarification, the work of the strategic therapists follows.

JAY HALEY

Historical Development

In studying therapists, it is often helpful to point out their differences in style or personality. The danger in such an approach is that it may detract from the unalterable fact that the individual is an outstanding and gifted therapist. With this caution in mind, the uniqueness of Jay Haley is explored.

The humor and clarity of Haley, especially his delightful book of essays, *The Power Tactics of Jesus Christ and Other Essays* (1969), provides a reward or incentive during the research necessary for a book like this. For example, his humorous classification of models of family therapy taken from this book of essays has become a classic in the field—"The Chuck It and Run School," in which the therapist leaves the room to observe the family discussing their problems; the "Stonewall School of Family Therapy," in which the therapist charges at the family to effect change; and "The Great Mother School of Family Therapy" that sees positive interactions among all family members at all times (1969, pp. 86–94).

Haley could be called "the great communicator." In fact, he was hired as an expert in communication (his terminal degree is a master's degree in communication) by Gregory Bateson in 1952 when he launched his landmark study of communication, which included the study of the communication processes of schizophrenic families. As a result of that original grant, Haley became interested in studying the hypnotherapy communication processes of Milton Erickson, about whom he has written a number of books (Haley, 1963, 1967, 1973).

Erickson's work is not presented as a separate theory here because he worked mainly with individuals and is probably best known for his work with hypnotherapy. Haley (1963) details Erickson's style of directive therapy in the third chapter of his first book, *Strategies of Psychotherapy,* from which the school of strategic family therapy received its name. Haley goes on to apply three major aspects of Erickson's work to family therapy in a later chapter of the same text: (1) emphasizing the positive (Erickson tended to accept wherever the patient was—for example, if the patient was short, Erickson might comment on the advantages of being agile and small); (2) using ambiguous directives phrased so that they were difficult to resist, such as directing

Jay Haley is often called "the great communicator" because of his prolific and clear writing in the field of family therapy and his original research on communication, especially the concept of the double bind.

people to express their feelings by saying something like, "It's important to understand the real feelings underneath all this, so let's attempt to express them now;" and (3) encouraging or directing usual or routine behavior so that resistance is shown through change. (An example would be directing a person who wastes time and stays away from people to continue to do so at the library, being sure to waste time and make contact with no one. Usually when a person exhibits these routine behaviors—procrastinating and withdrawing—but in a different setting, the behaviors become boring, and the person may start to read a magazine and end up with a new hobby or a new friend met at the library as a change to the self-imposed boredom.)

Haley's next book, *Uncommon Therapy* (1973), was devoted totally to the work of Erickson and defined *strategic therapy* as the approach in which the therapist took an active and directive role, initiating what occurred in the therapy. The therapist should identify workable problems, set goals, select interventions tailored to the particular clients, analyze responses to the interventions to assist in the development of future strategies, and measure outcome in terms of whether the goals have been met and the problem is resolved. The strategic therapist must be extremely sensitive to the patient, responding not only to the patient but also to the social context in which the patient operates, including family, work, and community.

Haley (1973) compiled case studies of Erickson's work and presented them according to the stages of the family life cycle—from the courtship period, how a young adult changes, the effects of marriage, childbirth, typical problems that families face in raising children, launching children which includes weaning parents, and growing older. This family life cycle developmental framework has continued to be an essential component of strategic family therapy. Strategies are chosen to fit the transitions of the family life cycle and the phases of the individual life cycle.

In 1962, Haley joined the staff of the Mental Research Institute, where he worked until 1967, when he left to join Minuchin at the Philadelphia Child Guidance Center. He remained in Philadelphia until 1976, when he left to assume a faculty position at the University of Maryland Medical School and to found the Family Therapy Institute with his wife, Cloe Madanes. Since Haley spent almost 10 years in direct contact with Minuchin, conversing with him and other structural therapists, his therapeutic approach does show the influence of the structural school in its observation of hierarchies and interactional patterns within families.

Key Theoretical Concepts

The Perverse Triangle.   In a perverse triangle relationship structure, two people who are on diverse levels of a hierarchy establish a coalition against a third person (Haley, 1967). Typically this is a cross-generational coalition in which one parent and one child align against the other parent, or a grandparent and a child form an alliance in opposition to a parent. Haley (1976) believes that the degree of severe disturbance of a symptomatic family member is determined by the number of perverse triangles in which the person is entrenched.

Double Bind.   No matter what a person says or does, the person cannot win in a double bind (Bateson, Jackson, Haley, & Weakland, 1956). This pattern is most characteristic of the families of schizophrenics and other rigidly organized family systems.

Power in the Family.   In pathological family systems, there is a strong pull to keep things the way they are—the status quo or homeostasis. When a normal developmental transition occurs, such a family attempts to rigidly hold to current rules and interactional structures rather than changing them. There is a struggle for the power to make the rules. The question of "who makes the rules in this family?" becomes all important. Haley very clearly puts the parents in charge of their children and of this crucial rule-making function (Haley, 1980).

In assessing the problem in the initial session, Haley focuses on the interactional sequences around the problem, linking these to the structures in the family: the hierarchies, triangles, and coalitions in the family and who holds the power. In *Problem-Solving Therapy,* he elaborates on a step-wise therapeutic process in which the family's organization is changed to a more normal but still abnormal organization, and then to a more normal organization, at which point the problem is resolved. Hoffman (1981) views Haley's tracking (in the ongoing assessment of the family) and step-by-step stages of the changing of these organizational sequences as perhaps his most characteristic contribution to theoretical conceptualization in the field.

Family Life Cycle Transitions.   At the points in the normal family life cycle where members enter and exit the system, the family is under stress to adapt to a new structure. If the family does not change, one or more members typically will become symptomatic. Haley (1980) is particularly concerned with the transition in which young adults leave home.

View of Healthy Functioning

As individuals pass through various stages of development, they change and mature. Likewise, families must change their structure and organization over time as they enter new stages of the family life cycle. One of the most difficult stages of the individual life cycle is leaving home and becoming an independent adult. Similarly, the stage of launching young adults into the world is one of the most difficult for the family to surmount.

Haley (1976) assumes that the problem does not emanate from the individual but rather from the social situation in which two or more people are interacting with each other. A problem is a sequence of behaviors between several people that is repeated until it is crystallized. The therapist becomes part of the problem through the interactions in therapy.

The Therapeutic Process

Goals of Therapy.   The goal of treatment is to solve the presenting problem of the family. The problem is defined as the sequence of behaviors between family members within a social context. It is the therapist's responsibility to plan interventions that resolve the problem within the social context of the client.

Another goal of treatment is to help the family members move to the next phase of the family life cycle and their own individual life cycles. The stage of leaving home for the young adult is a particularly difficult one for the person and for the family.

Use of Diagnosis and Assessment.   The therapist determines at what stage of the family life cycle the family is stuck, and at what stage of the life cycle the individual is muddled. The therapist observes the sequences of communications and other behaviors between people. In this context, a symptom such as depression is a means of communicating with family members. The symptom metaphorically and analogically expresses not only a problem but its solution. The therapist analyzes the hierarchy of the family to determine if there are any cross-generational coalitions and conflicts among the executive hierarchy of the parents. Such an assessment is done as part of the initial session by observing the interactions among the family members and is continuous throughout further sessions.

Role of the Therapist. In Haley's approach the therapist is very active and controlling, at points almost selling a directive or ordeal. The therapist is in charge, powerful, and in control. Again the term *power* is linked to Haley's strategic therapy. The therapist asks many open-ended questions, takes an objective stance, encourages family members to interact by acting like a director in a play, sets goals with the family, gives orders to different family members in the session, and delivers directives of various types to be completed between sessions—a very active, powerful role.

Nature of the Initial Session. In *Problem-Solving Therapy,* Haley (1976, 1987) explains in clear, concise language what a beginning therapist should do and avoid doing in the initial session with the family. The secretary obtains the following information when setting up the appointment: names, telephone numbers and addresses of relevant family members, a list of those living in the house and their ages, family members' employers and types of employment, the referral source, the length and types of any previous therapies, and a couple of sentences about the nature of the presenting problem. The therapist calls the family member back to confirm an appointment and to ask that all of the family members come. Haley (1987) thinks it is imperative that all of the family members living in the same house come to the initial session. After that, he may ask only those directly involved with a particular problem to come, but it is easier than starting out with a few members of the family and then asking the rest to come later.

The initial session is divided into five stages:

1. The social stage, in which the therapist talks to each person, asking the name and obtaining a response from each person similar to a hostess or host encouraging guests to feel comfortable. The therapist looks at the seating arrangement that the family has chosen, mentally drawing tentative hypotheses, and also matches the mood of the family in vocal tone and gestures.
2. The problem stage, which the therapist begins by asking formal questions about the problem.
3. The interaction stage, in which the therapist asks family members to talk with one another about the problem. The therapist observes who talks to whom, who remains silent and who interrupts whom, but does *not* share any tentative hypotheses with the family.
4. The goal-setting stage, in which the therapist finds out what changes are expected by family members as a result of therapy, specifying these in clear behavioral terms.
5. The task-setting stage, in which the therapist gives the family a directive. It may be practiced in the session, but it is more often a homework assignment to be completed at home between sessions. An appointment for the next session is set during this stage as well as indicating which family members are to return to the session.

Haley (1987) recommends that the therapist start the session by making the therapist's position clear, that is, sharing what the therapist already knows about the situation. For example, a therapist might say, "From my short, 5-minute telephone conversation with Mrs. Oaks, I understand that Tommy is having trouble in school, so I have a general idea of the problem, but I particularly asked each of you to come today so I could find out your own ideas about the problem." Another variation would be to say something like, "I wanted all of the family to come today to get everyone's opinion about what is going on." Then the therapist makes contact in the social stage with each person.

As the therapist moves to the problem stage, considerations of hierarchy are important. Typically initial formal questions about the problem should be addressed to the adult who appears to be the least involved with the problem. The family member who seems to have the most power to influence the family members to return to the next session should be treated with the most respect and concern. For example, if the father were involved in his work and more peripheral in the family, the first question might be directed to him in order to "hook" him into the therapy, while the mother is treated with more respect and concern because she can influence the family members to come to the sessions. Such balancing is necessary, or the family may be lost to treatment. Typical questions that the family expects in the initial session and that therapists most often direct to family members are "What's the problem?" or "What do you see as your problem here?" or "What problem brings you to therapy right now?" Usually each child is asked in turn what the problem is in the child's view, ending last with the child who has been labeled as having the problem. Haley (1987) cautions that when a therapist feels nervous, questions should be directed toward the parents and not toward the identified patient.

In the strategic approach to family therapy, the therapist listens, restates the problem, and asks open-ended clarifying questions as family members speak during the problem stage. No effort is made to ask family members how they feel about the problem, to reframe the problem, or to give advice. If one family member interrupts another, the therapist should observe this and note it mentally. The second time it happens, the therapist should intervene by telling the person interrupting that that person will also have a turn and encourage the person who has been interrupted to continue talking. The therapist should pace the interview so that everyone does have a turn in this stage to state opinions about the problem, continuing to move to another family member until all family members have been heard, rather than returning at any point to one who has already spoken. Such a procedure permits the problem to be expressed metaphorically.

In the interaction stage, the therapist directs the family members to talk to each other about the problem by saying something like "Now I'd like for you to talk to each other about the problem." Typically, family members may begin to talk to each other but then shift and attempt to talk directly to the therapist. At this point the therapist should intervene by redirecting the family members to talk to each other by saying something like, "I hear what you're saying, but it's very important that you talk to your husband about it right now." In addition to redirection responses, the therapist should be ready to jump in to encourage a third person to help two family members who may be talking but getting nowhere. During the interaction stage it is most helpful to have the family members actually do in the session whatever the problem is. For example,

A strategic therapist uses straightforward directives with a couple.

if fire-setting is the problem, the therapist will encourage the family member to set a fire in the ashtray; if disciplining a child is the problem, the therapist will ask the parents to do so in the session. Beginning therapists should start by having the family talk about the problem, moving to more action-oriented techniques as their confidence increases with experience.

In the goal-setting stage, the therapist asks what changes would signify progress for the family members. Here the inquiry is not metaphorical but rather concrete, behavioral, and specific. The therapist will need to know how many times the present behavior is being exhibited and what goal the family would view as a step in the right direction. Open-ended questions such as "when," "where," and "how often" are used to pinpoint the exact nature of the problem and the specific goals sought. At the end of this stage, the therapist summarizes what the expected changes are. For example, the therapist might say, "Tommy has a grade of F right now in all of his subjects. The goal is for Tommy to raise these grades to Cs by the end of this 6-week period so that his grades for this 6-week period are listed as Cs on his next report card." This represents the therapeutic contract and includes behaviors that can be counted, measured, and observed.

In the task-setting stage, the therapist uses a directive especially tailored to the nature of the particular problem and of the characteristics of the family. Directives may be straightforward or indirect. Since most of the change in strategic therapy is attributed to these directives, how to design them will be discussed at length in the technique section of this chapter. After the directive is given, the next appointment is set. Strategies are discussed for encouraging an absent member to attend. The therapist typically says that therapy will continue only until the problem is resolved. Sometimes families want a specific contract for a set number of sessions, so the therapist may say that they will meet for six sessions and decide at that time if more sessions are needed.

In *Leaving Home: The Therapy of Disturbed Young People,* Haley (1980) focuses on young people with serious diagnoses such as heroin addiction, schizophrenia, and delinquency who are trying to leave home. In such crisis situations, the initial session must be even more action oriented. The therapist clearly states at the beginning of the interview, "From everything I have heard, this teenager is now out of control. As her parents, you're going to have to take action. This session will be focused on what you are going to *do* about the situation." The only exception is a suicide threat or attempt, when Haley (1987) states that it is more important for parents to show their concern. In this case, decisions must be made concerning hospitalization or a possible suicide watch by family members. Such a threat should never be taken lightly or be underestimated.

Stages of Therapy. Problem-solving therapy occurs in stages until the presenting problem is resolved and other problems that people want to work on are resolved as well. For example, Haley (1987) will change a pathological organizational sequence to a less pathological one and then to a more normal organizational sequence. As this proceeds in a step-by-step fashion over a period of sessions, the presenting problem will be resolved. However, another problem that was underlying the symptom may arise, and this will then be dealt with in the therapy until it is resolved as well.

For example, a woman presented with the complaint of anxiety. The therapist told her a story about how a teenager had been helped to rid himself from the physiological difficulty of bedwetting due to following a similar procedure, and she was prescribed an ordeal in which she had to wash and wax the floor in the middle of the night every time she encountered anxiety during the day. The anxiety disappeared. However, the woman became very angry with her husband and wanted to leave him. Haley then worked with them in marital treatment, and the husband in individual work, until the difficulties were resolved. Therefore, although the therapy may be brief as in "brief" therapy, the number of sessions can vary a great deal depending upon the resolution of the presenting problem and other problems that may surface. The frequency of sessions is often varied as progress is made and as the needs of the family dictate.

Application: Major Therapeutic Techniques

In strategic therapy, the predominant technique is the use of various types of directives. Often called prescriptions, directives are orders that the therapist gives either in a direct or an indirect way, hoping for either compliance or its opposite, rebellion, respectively. Directives help people change their behavior with each other, thereby changing their subjective reality. They also intensify, for better or worse, the relationship with treatment personnel, especially the therapist (Haley, 1987).

The delivery of the directive or prescription is often just as important as the exact nature of the directive itself (L'Abate, Ganahl, & Hansen, 1986). For example, the therapist should decide what degree of pressure will be most appropriate for this family. The therapist can ask the permission of the family directly or indirectly, which applies little pressure. Next, the therapist can suggest directly or indirectly, and more pressure is applied. Finally, the therapist can prescribe when no consent is obtained from the family, when consent is requested after the prescription has been presented, when such consent is requested before the prescription is presented to the family, or clearly stated sanctions may be imposed if the prescription is not carried out—the most pressure (Bodin, 1981). According to L'Abate, Ganahl, and Hansen (1986), if a family is rigid and more resistant, a more permissive, hesitant style is more effective. For example, the therapist would say, "I'm not quite sure whether or not you are ready to do this. What are your ideas on this?" (indirect permission) or "You'll probably think, 'Dr. Thomas is crazy' when you hear what I'm going to ask you to do, but even though it sounds absurd, I'd like you to give it a try" (indirect suggestion). With an underorganized, chaotic family, a more certain, authoritarian approach will bear more fruit—"This technique has worked for more than a hundred families I've used it with, and I think it can make a big difference for you, too. Don't be upset if it doesn't work exactly right at first—that may mean I gave it to you too soon or it was too hard. Just be sure to come to the next session to say how it did and didn't work for you."

Consent can be sought after giving the directive such as, "Mrs. Calvani, do you agree to carry out the plan? How about you, Charlie?" or "Would you prefer to implement the plan on Monday, Wednesday, Friday or Tuesday, Thursday, Saturday, Mrs. Calvani? How about you, Charlie?" In a variation on the devil's pact described in the previous chapter, a therapist can obtain agreement from the clients prior to telling them what they will have to do. For example, "Now, there is a special plan that I know will work to make things better for your family, but I'd like your agreement that you will promise to carry out the plan before I tell you what it is. You'll have to trust me a bit on this, but life is full of risks. Will you agree to implement the plan?" Such an approach is used typically as a last resort when the person has made no movement when other techniques have been tried and is very stuck and afraid to take risks.

In addition to the actual delivery of the directive, the therapist should decide about sharing the reason for the task. In some cases, it is helpful to explain the conceptual, theoretical basis for assigning the task (for example, "Sally appears isolated in this family and this task will help her to feel less alone and more a part of this family"). Sometimes this is withheld but shared when clients ask about the rationale. In other cases, a plausible reason is given but not the real reason (for example, "Teenagers like Sally need the guidance of their parents.")

Straightforward Directives. An order or request in which the therapist actually wants the family members to carry out the task is called a straightforward directive. Typically, the therapist perceives that she has more power and authority to get things done and that the family will comply and carry out orders. One example of a straightforward directive is coaching.

One straightforward directive is telling someone to stop a behavior. For example, if the mother keeps on interrupting her son in the session when he talks to the therapist, the therapist might tell her to stop, or the therapist may stand up, saying

"Stop" while waving her hands. The therapist could also tell the son and the father to prevent the mother from interrupting them. Often the support of other family members is needed to stop the behavior over the long term.

To motivate family members to follow advice or change to a new sequence of interaction, the therapist can state that the task will help them to get what they want from the therapy, or each family member can be told how that person will gain from doing the requested task. The therapist can encourage family members to talk about what has not worked. Then often they are more ready to listen to the directive that the therapist proposes. In addition, the therapist could encourage the family members to talk about how desperate the situation looks or future dire projections and agree with their analysis if action is not taken. The therapist can encourage family members to do small tasks in the session—for example, asking a mother to help her son with a task during the session. When this goes well, she'll be more apt to follow through with a directive outside the session. The directive should be tailored to fit a particular family based on what they have said in the session and what the therapist has observed.

The instructions should be very clear when giving a directive, such as, "I want the family to do the following: You are to. . . ." Being very precise in giving the actual instructions is very important, because if a family returns without doing the task, the therapist will not know if they were resistant or if the instructions were vague and unclear. Everyone in the family should be involved in the task to be accomplished. The family members should be asked to review their parts in the task after the therapist has given the directive. Even a discussion of ways family members might attempt to avoid the task will help with its implementation.

Haley (1987) lists 18 examples of straightforward directives that he recommends. Some examples of his straightforward directives can be found in Table 13–1.

During the next session, the therapist should always ask if the family did the task. If so, they should be congratulated. If not, the therapist can apologize by saying, "I guess I didn't understand you or the situation to have asked you to have done it—I'm sure you would have followed through otherwise." Another tougher approach is to say that doing the task was important and that they lost out by not doing it. When they talk about problems during the session, the therapist should repeat that they would not have those problems if they had done the task. If they ask for another chance to do the task, it should be denied, stating that the opportunity is gone. By taking this hard line, the family will be more likely to carry out the directive the next time. Haley (1987) recommends that the therapist not easily forgive family members who do not do tasks and that noncompliance should never be downplayed.

Another straightforward directive that does not appear so is the use of metaphor. A metaphor, like a story, tells about something that is similar to something else. For example, when a couple is having sexual difficulties but is embarrassed to talk about them, the therapist may ask them to talk about their eating together—how one may like to eat quickly while the other likes to savor each bite. As they talk about how they like to eat together they are really talking about their sex life. Then, the therapist will give them a straightforward metaphor directive to take each other out on a date to eat together (a metaphor for having sexual relations together).

TABLE 13–1 Straightforward directives

Situation	Directive
1. Marital Boredom	*To Husband:* "I want you to do something nice for your wife that will surprise her."
	To Wife: "I want you to graciously accept whatever your husband does."
2. Mother Enmeshed with Son	*To Father:* "I want you to do something with your son that is minor that your wife would definitely not approve of."
	To Son: "I want you to do something with your father that your Mom wouldn't want you to do."
3. Mother Who Treats All Children the Same Regardless of Age	*To Mother:* "I want you to set and keep a different bedtime for each one of your children, even if they are only 20 minutes apart."
4. Father Defending Bedwetting Daughter Against Wife	*To Father:* "I want you to wash the sheets every time your daughter wets the bed."
5. Family Members Interrupting Each Other Constantly	*To Family:* "I want you to pass a hat around the group, and only the family member holding the hat can talk," or "I want only the family member to talk who is sitting in the assigned 'Speaker's Chair.'"
6. Daughter Interrupting Parents	*To Parents:* "I want you to talk without your daughter interrupting you."
7. Father Cuts in When Mother and Daughter Are Talking	*To Mother and Daughter:* "I want you to talk without father interrupting you."
8. Couple Who Don't Openly Express Affection for Each Other but Want To	*To Couple:* "I want you to express your affection openly from 7:00 P.M. to 9:00 P.M. three times this week to teach your children how to express affection."
9. Unemployed Person	*To Person:* "I want you to go through with a job interview at a place where you definitely don't want the job."
10. Mother Helpless at Disciplining Children	*To Father:* "I want you to educate your wife about how to discipline the children. Let's begin right now here in the session."
11. Mother Does Not Understand How Her Child Thinks	*To Mother:* "I want you to hide this toy where your child will find it within 10 minutes but more than 5 minutes."

From *Problem-Solving Therapy for Effective Family Therapy* (2e), (pp. 84–89), by J. Haley, 1987, San Francisco: Jossey-Bass. Adapted by permission.

Indirect Directives. An indirect directive is an order or request that the therapist does not want the family members actually to carry out, but rather for change to happen more spontaneously. An example of an indirect directive would be the therapist restraining the family from changing by saying, "Go slow."

Haley (1987) gives eight stages for the use of indirect or paradoxical directives: (1) establish a relationship with the family; (2) define the problem very clearly; (3) set specific goals; (4) offer a rationale to make an indirect directive reasonable within the framework of a plan for treatment; (5) subtly disqualify any family authority on the topic; (6) give the paradoxical directive; (7) observe what happens and continue to support the direction of the paradoxical directive; and (8) be puzzled by any improvement, avoiding credit for any improvement at all costs.

The context and preparation for the use of paradoxical or indirect directives is important. They are not "shotgun" interventions but rather well-planned directives within a broader context. Often behaviors must be reframed before a paradoxical directive is given. Therefore, in addition to motivating family members, deciding on how the directive will be delivered, and what rationale will be given, in most cases the behavior must be reframed prior to assigning it as an indirect or paradoxical intervention. Reframing, discussed in Chapter 12, is stating the positive meaning of a present symptom.

Ordeals. An ordeal is a directive in which the therapist tells the client to do something that is more severe than the symptom after it has appeared. Typically the ordeal is something that is good for the person such as exercise, housework, reading, or some other type of self-improving activity, but an ordeal may also be a sacrifice for someone else.

In *Ordeal Therapy. Unusual Ways of Changing Behavior,* Haley (1984) delineates six steps in the process of ordeal therapy: (1) the problem must be defined clearly; (2) the person must be motivated to get rid of the problem; (3) the therapist needs to select an ordeal; (4) the directive that is the ordeal should be assigned with a rationale; (5) the ordeal is to continue until the problem behavior is gone; and (6) the ordeal occurs in a social setting.

An ordeal can be straightforward. For example, a man who became nervous when he began to speak on his television show was told he had excess energy and was required to set his alarm for the middle of the night, do an exercise 100 times and then go back to bed, at which point the anxiety disappeared. An ordeal can be paradoxical. A person must deliberately do one symptom if another occurs. For example, a client was anxious about writing and was blocked. He was also shy about dating. The ordeal was the paradoxical directive that on the day after he was not able to write he must make a date with a girl for the next week. He wrote a page every day.

CLOE MADANES

Historical Development

Cloe Madanes received her "Licienciada" degree from the University of Buenos Aires, Argentina, in 1965, having majored in psychology. She is co-director of the Family

Therapy Institute in Rockville, Maryland, with her husband, Jay Haley. Particularly adept at working with children and their families, she has developed innovative techniques that use fantasy, play, and metaphor to reorganize incongruous dual hierarchies in the family. In addition to chapters on comparing theoretical approaches to family therapy and the strategic approach, her first book, *Strategic Family Therapy* (1981), contains an excellent chapter on working with married couples to overcome dual hierarchies and power issues.

Key Theoretical Concepts

Helpfulness as Power.   Madanes (1981) is most noted for her analysis of power in the family. An individual human being is a part of the smallest unit with independent intelligence—the family. The behavior of one family member is determined by the interpersonal influence of another. Power can be benevolent when it is used for kind and helpful ends or malignant if used to achieve hostile, exploitative goals. For example, a hypnotist has subtle interpersonal influence that affects the unconscious of the client so that warts disappear. Even more subtle and powerful is the interpersonal influence of one family member upon another. Children may be powerful through helpfulness, a way of protecting or helping a parent by exhibiting a symptom. This encourages parents to forget their own difficulties for a while and feel needed by a sick child—an illusion of power and superiority, even though they are not able to cure the child.

   In fact, the child plans ahead to fulfill the task of helping the parent, just as a beetle plans ahead in depositing its larvae in the limb of a mimosa. The child is part of a family system that has its own purpose.

Incongruous Dual Hierarchy.   Symptoms take place in a malfunctioning organizational structure. For example, a child who is exhibiting disturbed behavior is in an inferior position, as any child would be, but simultaneously is also in a superior position because the child is protecting the parents by having the symptom. Therefore, the child is in a powerful position in relation to them because they cannot change the symptom and make the child better. In a healthy hierarchy, the parents are in a superior position but relinquish more and more power as their children grow older. When the children go out in the world on their own, there is increasing equality between children and parents.

   Likewise, a spouse who develops a symptom is in an inferior position in which the superior mate helps and protects the spouse. At the same time the spouse is in a superior position by not being cured by the mate, who is in an inferior position as an unsuccessful helper. In a healthy marital relationship, spouses typically carve out areas of dominance and responsibility in which each spouse is superior in several areas and inferior in other areas. They complement each other because where one is superior, the other is inferior. Therefore, the spouses both experience power, dominance, and responsibility, but in different areas.

The System of Interaction as a Metaphor.   The sequence of interaction that results in a symptom is often a metaphor for a similar interaction between two other family members. For example, when a father comes home from having trouble on the job, his wife comforts him. When the daughter has an asthma attack, the father comforts his daughter. The system of interaction between the father and daughter resulting from the symptom is a metaphor for the interaction between the wife and the husband.

In addition, the discussion of the child's symptom and the interaction around the symptom mirror the discussion of the interaction around the father's problem. Therefore, if the therapist discusses the interaction around the child's symptom at a metaphorical level in therapy, the father's problem is also being worked on. In this way sometimes marital problems of a couple are being worked on at a metaphorical level at the same time that the system of interaction around a symptom of the child, the presenting problem, is being dealt with.

The Symptom as a Metaphor.   A symptom may be a metaphor in itself. For example, a headache can be a metaphor for another internal pain, or a headache could be a metaphor for another family member's fear or pain. A child could have a headache when the mother is feeling afraid.

Cyclical Variation Maintaining Incongruous Dual Hierarchies.   The focus of interaction may shift from a symptomatic child, to a parent's problem, to an ill spouse with the incongruities in the hierarchies and the helplessness being maintained. The symptoms come and go in cycles, but the incongruous hierarchies and helplessness remain the same.

View of Healthy Functioning

All families evolve through developmental stages. Healthy families change their structures at key transition points in family development. In addition, family members know the hierarchy in the family; it is clear. Both the structures and hierarchies in healthy families are socially sanctioned (Stanton, 1981). Healthy families do not focus very much on themselves or on gaining insight. They are just involved in life, making it happen. Positive metaphors are present in their interaction.

When the family attempts to remain the same in its structure as it progresses to a new stage of the family life cycle, the members of the family experience pain, especially the individual family member who is trying to become independent. For example, parents may try to remain organized in a pattern of focusing all of their energies on doing everything for their children rather than changing to emphasize the development of their relationship with each other, the new two-person structure that evolves as the last child leaves home (Madanes, 1980).

When the structure does not change appropriately over time as the family moves through the stages of the life cycle, patterns of communication in the family will also be affected because of a disturbed hierarchy. The teenager appears to be in a superior position to his or her parents when, in fact, he or she is not even taking care of himself or herself—definitely an insecure, inferior position.

The Therapeutic Process

Goals of Therapy.   As a strategic therapist, Madanes seeks to resolve the presenting problem by using diverse strategies tailored to meet the needs of a particular family. In addition, hierarchies will be clarified and no longer incongruous. Family members will not need to "protect" each other any more in order to be in powerful positions through their helpfulness or helplessness. The family and its members will be freed up to develop competencies considered normal for their ages.

Role of the Therapist.   The therapist asks open-ended questions and obtains information about the problem and the concerns of the family members. Usually another therapist is used behind the one-way mirror to give objective feedback about the interactional sequences of the family. Directive strategies are designed and given to the families to effect change. Based on the response of the family members to the strategies, new strategies are devised until the presenting problem is resolved. Madanes has found humor to be effective in her work with families and that it can be a part of the therapist's role.

Use of Diagnosis and Assessment.   Diagnosis is accomplished through implementing an intervention. By the interactions of the family members in reaction to the intervention, the therapist learns about the problems of the family. Therefore, every intervention is a form of assessment, and every attempt at diagnosis has treatment benefits (Stanton, 1981). The strategic therapist learns by doing.

In addition, the sequence of interactions among family members is observed carefully by the therapist. These interactional sequences are continually assessed throughout the course of therapy.

As mentioned earlier, the therapist considers at which developmental transition point the family is stuck. Rigidity in structure is noted. Dual hierarchies are explored. Helpfulness as power is checked in both the behavior in the session and in the reports of family members about what happens at home. The use of the symptom as a metaphor can tell the strategic therapist about the nature of the family's problem.

Nature of the Initial Session.   Madanes uses an initial session similar to that of Haley. A sequence in the session leads to the setting of goals. Typically, a strategy is employed at the end of the first session.

Stages of Therapy.   The strategic therapist tailors each intervention to the goals of the family. Based on the sequence of interactions in response to a given intervention, another intervention is designed and implemented. The family changes until the goals are met. If new goals surface as the therapy progresses, they are targeted and reached.

Application: Major Therapeutic Techniques

Pretending   In one technique developed by Madanes (1980, 1981), the therapist directs the child to pretend that he or she has the symptom. The parent or other relative involved with the child can also be directed to pretend to assist the child when the child pretends to have the symptom. For example, in one successful case (Madanes, 1980) the therapist directed a child who had presented with a recurring stomachache to pretend to have this problem. The grandmother, who would hold the child in her arms while praying the rosary for him and putting oil drops in his nose, was directed to pretend to do these same things. The child even brought her the pretend rosary beads and oil. The pretend interventions were prescribed for 7 days. At the end of the time, the boy's stomachaches did not recur. The pretend exercise allowed the boy to receive the affection and nurturance of his grandmother, which she enjoyed giving, but without the symptom. In carrying out the directives, the child and grandmother realized at an intuitive level that they could still be affectionate without the symptom being present.

Since symptoms can also be hypothesized to be ways that the child is protecting one or both parents, another pretend intervention is to direct the parent or parents to pretend to be helpless and need the child's protection or assistance while directing the child to pretend to help the parents when they pretend to need help. In the case of a family who presented for treatment because of the headaches of the 7-year-old son, the father, a recovering alcoholic, was having trouble at work and was disillusioned because his manuscript of a novel had not been sold. The parents could not discuss the father's pain. Since the headache was viewed metaphorically as the pain of the father, the therapist directed the father to pretend to have a headache when he came home from work each night. The therapist directed the son to attempt to cheer his father up by playing with him and to determine if his dad had a real headache by asking him about his day at work and what he was feeling. The father was directed to discuss make-believe problems at his job while mother and daughter pretended to fix dinner. There was some improvement within a week, and the intervention was continued for 3 weeks until the boy had no more headaches. The boy had protected his father at the unconscious level by having a problem that required his father to stay together emotionally in order to help his son. The pretend interventions made the covert protection overt because the boy was now openly helping his father, even though it was a pretend exercise.

How to Choose a Strategy. Madanes (1984) discusses how to choose the right strategy for a particular family with a given problem. Nine dimensions are important to consider in designing a strategy: (1) voluntary versus involuntary behavior (reframing an involuntary problem as voluntary can make a big difference); (2) power versus helplessness (family members who have symptoms can be in very powerful positions in the family); (3) equality versus hierarchy (does a dual hierarchy exist?); (4) love versus hostility (a client's hostile behavior can be reframed as motivated by love); (5) altruism versus gain (a disturbed behavior can be reframed as protecting the parents—an altruistic motive rather than one of self-interest); (6) literal versus metaphorical sequences (the sequence of interaction around the symptom may be a metaphor for similar interaction among other family members); (7) dependence versus freedom (dependence on parents can be reframed as being all alone in the whole world, and a person claiming to be free may be told that the person is, indeed, very dependent upon the children or spouse); (8) resistance versus commitment (restraining and other types of paradoxical interventions are useful with resisting families); and (9) weakness versus power of the therapist (straightforward directives are most useful when the therapist is in a powerful position, and indirect or paradoxical directives are most effective when the therapist is in a weak position of power in relation to the family).

Using the above dimensions, the therapist can then choose among 10 strategies that Madanes (1984) recommends (Table 13–2). If a therapist is definitely in a position of authority and power with a given family, then straightforward directives should be

TABLE 13–2 Strategies

Strategy	Example	Dimension
1. Telling parents to direct the child to have the problem on purpose or a symbol of the problem, and the parents will monitor it to be sure that it is done properly.	In the case of firesetting, the uninvolved father was directed to tell his child to set five fires a day and put them out under the father's supervision.	Used when hostility is a benefit of the symptom a) Problem becomes voluntary b) Parents no longer helpless c) Clear hierarchy encouraged
	In the case of a girl masturbating in public at school, the parents were directed to buy a rocking horse and direct their daughter to ride it under their supervision three times a day, taking turns in the supervision of the half-hour sessions.	Symbolic rocking was substituted for masturbation a) Problem became voluntary b) Parents were in charge and no longer helpless c) Hierarchy was encouraged d) Metaphorical rather than literal
2. Prescribing "pretending" to have the symptom.	Therapist directed parents to direct daughter to pretend to have an epileptic seizure and to comfort her when she pretended.	Used when affection is benefit of symptom, and it is voluntary or involuntary a) Problem became voluntary b) Parents no longer helpless c) Parents in charge in hierarchy d) Girl gained love and affection without having symptom
3. Prescribing "pretending" the function that the symptom plays.	If a child is afraid, a parent is directed to pretend to have a fear, and the child is directed to protect and comfort the parent	Makes overt parent's covert need for help a) Child is no longer helpless b) Parent gains affection and love c) Problem becomes voluntary
4. Directing a reversal of the hierarchy in the family.	The child is directed to be in charge of a given parent's happiness because that parent needs to be taught.	Used when parents complain about their children being out of control while the parents present as helpless, on drugs/alcohol, or delinquent.
5. Paradoxical contract—tying two problems of two family members together.	Father agreed to cooperate. His daughter who was anorectic agreed to eat if he did not drink a drop of alcohol. If the father drank, he would sacrifice his daughter; if he did not, he would rescue her.	Both family members gave up their symptoms and demonstrated their power.

6. Directing which family members will have the presenting problem.

Therapist requests family members to take turns having the symptom for a specified period of time so client can pursue other interests or take a vacation.

a) Equality versus hierarchy
b) Power versus helplessness

7. Prescribing the problem and changing the context a little.

A spouse is directed to have the symptom at a set time in a set place for a set period of time, and the other spouse is directed to react in a particular way. For example, husband is told to share his pain about an affair his wife had 30 years ago from 7:45 to 8:00 a.m. every morning, and she is only to say "I'm sorry."

a) Metaphor is used
b) Love versus hostility is involved

8. A paradoxical ordeal — the consequences of a compulsive behavior be what it is intended to avoid.

In a couple where the wife was a compulsive cleaner, the couple was directed that if the wife cleaned after 5:00 p.m. (except for one half hour to do dishes) her husband was to make her lie down in bed with him to watch television for the rest of the evening, and if she cleaned before dinner, the husband was directed to make her go out to a restaurant with him alone

Used with compulsive symptoms where family members want to solve the problem, but have failed to do so on their own.
a) Voluntary versus involuntary
b) Love versus hostility
c) Altruism versus gain

9. An illusion that there is no alternative.

A woman with many options is encouraged only to do what she is doing half well, being a half-devoted wife.

a) Independence versus freedom
b) Gain versus altruism

10. An illusion that one is all alone in the whole world.

Tell the family that the symptomatic young adult is all alone in the big world — the youth is an orphan, abandoned and rejected by the parents.

a) Independence versus freedom
b) Gain versus altruism

From *Strategic Family Therapy* (pp. 65–94) by C. Madanes, 1981, San Francisco: Jossey-Bass. Also from *Behind the One-Way Mirror: Advances in the Practice of Strategic Therapy* (pp. 152–185) by C. Madanes, 1984, San Francisco: Jossey-Bass. Adapted by permission.

used. On the other hand, if the therapist is uncertain about whether or not the family will follow directives, more indirect approaches should be utilized. When the presenting problem is analyzed according to the nine dimensions, the strategy that best matches the dimensions represented by the problem can be used. The specific strategy will be tailored to the unique characteristics of a particular family and their problem. How the therapist thinks about the problem is crucial to its successful resolution. The approach of Madanes (1984) helps therapists in their processes of thinking about cases.

THERAPEUTIC OUTCOMES

Haley (1980) maintains that formal, rigorous therapy outcome research is lacking for the strategic approach to family therapy due to the shortage of research funds to support well-designed studies with matched control groups. However, he presents results of less-rigorous research that is suggestive evidence of the efficacy of the strategic approach. A study of 14 schizophrenic families yielded a failure rate of 29%, meaning that the young adult was either rehospitalized or was a failure in life. The follow-up was conducted by their therapists anywhere from 2 to 4 years after therapy concluded. Haley mentioned that the community can definitely have an effect on the outcome if employment is difficult to obtain in a poor, urban area.

The second sample that Haley (1980) discussed was comprised of patients at the Family Therapy Institute (19% failure rate of rehospitalization) and the Department of Psychiatry at the University of Maryland (22% failure rate of rehospitalization) with a follow-up of 3 to 6 months. These groups included anorectic, suicidal, psychotic, violent, alcoholic, drug addicted, phobic, and exhibitionist patients. The failure rate was higher for drug/alcohol cases, with a 50% rate of rehospitalization.

There have been a number of case studies of the effective use of strategic therapy. In fact, the books by Haley and Madanes are full of reports of specific cases in which the techniques have been used successfully. Stone and Peeks (1986) describe a school counselor's prescription of an ordeal with a senior, male, high school student with a behavior problem with whom other counseling techniques had not worked. After obtaining the agreement of the principal to waive the student's suspension if the parents carried out the ordeal, the counselor met with the mother and father. When the boy misbehaved, the teacher would notify the counselor, who would call the father. The father would pick the boy up at school and supervise while his son dug a particular-size hole in the back yard, in which he would deposit one record album and cover it with dirt. The ordeal was evoked three times. After that, the young man never misbehaved again and was able to graduate from high school and adjust effectively in the military, where he was still stable after 3 years.

The counselor thought that the fact that both parents worked together to implement the ordeal was the main source of change. However, there was a clear authoritarian hierarchy set up from the principal to the counselor to the parental coalition to the young man which was also very powerful. Only five sessions, each no more than 15 minutes, were spent with the family in addition to about 3 hours with colleagues in processing permissions and contingencies. This contrasts with more than 10 hours that had already been spent in individual counseling with the young man and 20 hours with his teachers and administrators in meetings about his problems, which had been to no avail. The authors encourage the consideration of strategic techniques for use in school settings as cost-effective measures that may have long-term success.

There have also been case studies using strategic therapy for obsessional disorders. Harbin (1985) reported the successful case of a white female high school student who was 16 at the time of treatment. She was spending around 5 hours per night doing homework and would have uncontrollable obsessional thoughts to the point where she would throw objects in anger or cry. The therapy had three stages over 8 months: (1) focus on the parents jointly enforcing limits on self-injurious behavior; (2) focus on the mother's depression with antidepressive medication and life planning (the mother found a job, since the client was the last child at home and the mother thought she would need a way to fill her time); and (3) the prescription of an ordeal in which the client had to perform a half hour of exercise at midnight in her room if she had experienced obsessional thinking during the day. She became symptom free and had remained so for 12 months.

O'Connor (1983) had five family sessions over 3 months with the family of a 10-year-old boy who was afraid of vomiting. His obsessive thoughts of vomiting interfered with his staying at school. Prescription of the symptom was used, and the boy was asked to set aside one hour per day to do nothing but think of vomiting and vomit if he needed to. In addition, his parents were not to reassure him, but his father was to give him a button to carry with him, which was then changed to a penny and finally to a nickel during the period. Finally, the parents were directed to have one 3-hour date per week without their son along. The boy was directed to take over some household responsibilities appropriate for his age to show that he was becoming more mature. The fear of vomiting disappeared. The boy was able to spend the night at the house of a friend with no problems and to have peers to his home.

O'Connor (1984) reports a successful case in which one interview was held and a follow up after 3 weeks with a 10-year-old girl whose presenting complaint was migraines. A four-pronged intervention was made: (1) the mother was asked if the girl's headaches would bring back her father, to which her mother replied that they would not—it would be up to the adults to work out their own problems; (2) the mother was asked to monitor time, intensity, frequency, and duration of the migraines for 3 weeks; (3) to replace the lost bedtime activities with her father, a new ritual was established: the girl would call her father after she was ready for bed, and then the mother would read her stories and talk to her for 20 minutes; and (4) the girl was asked to recall the image of a favorite stuffed animal, and she agreed to "give away" her headache to her stuffed animal in the way she chose (by touch or another way). The girl's headaches were gone. She said that she had given them to an old doll that she didn't like very much.

CONTRIBUTIONS AND LIMITATIONS

Jay Haley made significant contributions to the development of the theoretical communication concepts that undergird most of family therapy practice. He studied the work of Erickson and adapted his theory and techniques to the development of a separate school of family therapy. He emphasized discontinuities in the family life cycle as producers of stress and symptomatic family members—especially the launching of young adults. His book, *Leaving Home,* is still one of the best sources for treating teenagers and young adults in crisis. Tracking of interactional sequences in the family that represented ineffective hierarchies led him to develop step-by-step procedures to move the family to a less pathological structure and then to a normal structure, often by putting the parents in charge through innovative techniques. Straightforward and paradoxical directives, including the use of ordeals, became characteristic techniques of strategic therapy. Most of all, his clear style of writing, so evident in *Problem-Solving Therapy,* exemplified his major contribution as a communicator of how to do family therapy and enjoy the process. There can be no doubt that he is a master clinician.

Cloe Madanes uses fantasy, play, and pretending in helping parents to help their children. Her concept of power in the family as established by dual hierarchies in symptomatic families, in which a child or spouse might gain power through the helplessness and/or helpfulness of the symptom, led to the development of diverse strategies using metaphor, pretending, prescription of the symptom, and other types of directives to help families re-establish clear hierarchies.

Limitations of the strategic approach include the lack of rigorous research studies with matched controls. There were three follow-up studies (total sample was 42 families seen for an average of 11 sessions each), but only 14 cases were followed for more than 6 months. Although no rehospitalization and not being a failure in life were considered outcome measures, the question remains whether the results are significant from a rigorous research point of view.

In addition, the strategic approach is very pragmatic, using what works in the here and now. Its strength of innovative directives and other strategies tailored idiosyncratically to particular families, by sheer contrast, make its theoretical concepts pale. Its major contributions have been to techniques that work, while theoretical concepts could be broadened and deepened.

Braverman (1986) evaluated Haley's work from a nonsexist perspective and also from a feminist framework. She found Haley's contribution to be nonsexist—that is, one in which the therapist knows and owns personal values. His work encourages no set sex-role behaviors, does not use tests nor labels, expects women to be as independent and autonomous as males, and expects men to be as tender and expressive as females. He accepts alternative lifestyles as healthy, does not label sex-role reversals as pathological, and regards marriage as no better a therapy outcome for a woman than for a man.

However, in reviewing the same work from a feminist perspective, there are limitations to the strategic approach. Both Haley and Madanes use the pronoun "he" when referring to the therapist in their writing, which excludes female therapists. (The *Publication Manual of the American Psychological Association* [1983] recommends the use of the plural subject and verb, using the pronoun "they" as a gender-free form of communication.) In addition, as with all systemic approaches that use reframing, some acts of violence against women such as wife battering, rape, and incest are reframed in a circular manner with no perpetrator responsible in the strategic approach. Bograd (1982, 1984), Dell (1986a, 1986b), and Imber-Black (1986) have all pointed out the difficulty with accepting circular systemic causality in all endeavors—that, in fact, lineal causality—one factor can cause another in a direct line—does exist in the world (as Dell's title, "In Defense of 'Lineal Causality'," so aptly suggests). He cites the example of the German family therapists who said that they didn't believe in lineal causality until the night their spouses shot them. The difficulty arises in how to reconcile these opposites.

In addition, Braverman (1986) and Weiner and Boss (1985) are concerned with the equitable distribution of roles when the hierarchies are clarified. When the system is in transition, the opportunity occurs for a return to an ultra-traditional distribution of role tasks or one based on the skills and interests of the human beings involved in the relationship. Hopefully, strategic therapists will explore these options with their clients. Finally, in a feminist critique of strategic therapy Braverman (1986) questions the role of expert played by the therapist rather than a more equalitarian, symmetrical role with the client. In this category strategic therapy definitely would not meet the criteria of a feminist therapy.

SUMMARY

Jay Haley coined the term "strategic family therapy" for that type of family treatment in which the therapist takes an active and directive role, initiating what occurs in the therapy. The therapist should identify workable problems, set goals, select interventions tailored to the particular clients, analyze responses to the interventions to assist in the development of future strategies, and measure outcome in terms of whether the goals have been met and the problem is resolved. Besides the concept of the double bind, Haley is noted for the theoretical ideas of the perverse triangle (a relationship structure in which two people on diverse levels of a hierarchy establish a coalition against a third person), power in the family, and the importance of family life cycle transitions, especially young adults leaving home. Haley believes that family members struggle for the power to make the rules in the family. He assesses the interactional sequences around the problem, linking them to the hierarchies, triangles, and coalitions in the family, that is, who holds the power in the family. In addition, such struggles become more acute when a person enters or leaves the system, which occurs naturally as the family life cycle unfolds. If a family tries to keep the same structure at these transition points, symptoms will result, especially at the transition when young adults leave home.

The initial session is divided into five stages: the social stage, the problem stage, the interaction stage, the goal-setting stage, and the task-setting stage. The techniques for which Haley is probably most noted are his use of directives: straightforward directives, including metaphor, in which family members are expected to carry out a task between sessions; indirect or paradoxical directives in which the therapist does not want the family to carry out the task but rather for change to happen more spontaneously; and an ordeal (which can be either straightforward or indirect) in which the client is directed to do something that is more severe than the symptom after the symptom has appeared (typically exercise, housework, or a self-improving activity).

Originally from Argentina, Cloe Madanes serves as co-director of the Family Therapy Institute in Rockville, Maryland, with her husband, Jay Haley. She is noted for her innovative techniques for working with children and their families, especially "pretending" directives, in which children may be asked to pretend to have a symptom and their parents pretend to comfort them. From a theoretical point of view, she analyzes helpfulness as power. Often a spouse or child will endure a symptom to help a spouse or parent at a covert level. A child may plan ahead to fulfill the task of helping a parent, as a part of the family with its own purpose. By so doing, an incongruous dual hierarchy is continued, in which the child who is exhibiting disturbed behavior is in an inferior position but simultaneously is in a superior position because the child is protecting the parents by having the symptom. Therefore, the child is in a powerful position in relation to them because they cannot change the symptom and make the child better. The system of interaction can also be viewed as metaphor, in that a symptom may be a metaphor for a similar interaction between two other family members. Madanes devised a set of dimensions that are helpful in affecting the thinking of therapists who are in the process of selecting strategies for use with a family. In addition to pretending strategies, which are her trademark, Madanes emphasizes the use of nine other strategies, some of which are paradoxical or metaphorical.

EXERCISES

1. Given the following cases, design a straightforward directive for use with the family. Write down the exact wording you would use to deliver the directive. What, if any, rationale would you give for the directive?
   a. The members of the Boxley family were always interrupting each other. No one could ever get a word in edgewise.
   b. Helga and Fritz Hitner came for marital therapy because they were bored with their marriage. After asking them many questions, you hypothesized that they, indeed, were in a rut with each one, waiting for the other person to initiate a new activity.
   c. Mr. Tomlison was very close to Charlie, his son. Almost every time Mrs. Tomlison tried to give Charlie chores to do, Mr. Tomlison would interfere, telling Charlie that he did not have to do the chores but needed to watch and help him work on the family cars.
   d. Monica kept on interrupting her parents, Mr. and Mrs. Graber, in the initial therapy session.

2. Given the following cases, design an indirect or paradoxical directive for use with the family. Typically, problem behavior must be reframed before it is prescribed as an indirect or paradoxical directive. What, if any, rationale would you give for the directive? What would the exact wording of your paradoxical directive be?

   a. A wife was complaining about what her husband had done to her by having a short-lived affair while she was abroad with her mother, for which he had asked her forgiveness more than 20 years ago. The husband said that he had been faithful to her for the last 20 years and could take no more of her complaining.
   b. Mr. Henry is depressed since he retired. His wife does not know what to do with him around the house, since she still enjoys her job.

3. Given the following case, design an ordeal for use with the family. Write down the rationale you would use to "sell" the ordeal. What would the exact wording of your ordeal be?

   Harold Tolson had unwanted thoughts (obsessions) that interfered with his ability to study for his high school classes. His parents contacted their internist, who referred them to you. Mrs. Tolson was very close to Harold, who spent most of his time at home, especially since his obsessions were taking so much time that it often took him 5 or 6 hours to study for only one subject. Harold's dad was concerned that Harold's grades were dropping and that he might not be able to attend his college alma mater.

4. Given the following case, design a "pretend" directive for use with the mother and daughter. Write down the exact wording that you would use

to deliver the directive. What, if any, rationale would you give for the directive?

Susie Halifax, who is 10 years old, has been rushed to the hospital five times in the last month in a diabetic coma. She will not follow her doctor's orders for diet and exercise. There is a history of diabetes in the family. In fact, Susie's mother also has diabetes. Mrs. Halifax is an obese, unkempt woman who does not follow her doctor's orders either. When Susie is in the hospital, however, Mrs. Halifax does take the opportunity to see her doctor, whose office is in the same building.

5. When the Kellner family came to therapy, Mrs. Kellner was experiencing panic attacks. Her husband had a new job that was very difficult for him. Their daughter, Marcey, was due to graduate from high school in June. When Mr. Kellner tried to go to work every morning, his wife had an attack. He stayed with her until she calmed down, which took as long as 2 hours. At this point, Mrs. Kellner was afraid to go grocery shopping for fear that she would have a panic attack in the grocery store. Mrs. Kellner had always been a full-time homemaker, enjoying her life very much until the move to the new town where her husband accepted his present job.

Reviewing the strategies which Madanes (1984) proposes, choose an appropriate strategy for dealing with this case. Write down what you would do, that is, your strategy. Then write down the exact wording of what you would say to the family members to implement the strategy which you have chosen.

Chapter 14
The Systemic School of Family Therapy

God, is it true that for you a thousand years are as a minute?
Yes, my son.
And God, is it true that for you a thousand dollars are as a
penny?
Yes, my son.
Then, God, will you give me a penny?
In a minute.

Hoffman, 1983, p. 40.

OVERVIEW

Historically, family therapy began as an American innovation based upon research conducted with the families of schizophrenics at the Mental Research Institute (MRI) in Palo Alto, California, and at other federally funded sites across the United States. European mental health professionals continued to focus on individual psychotherapy, especially the psychoanalytic approaches of Freud and the neo-Freudians. In Italy, one psychoanalyst became dissatisfied with the slow progress of her individual patients and began to experiment with different modes of treatment, including working with couples and families. She read the works written at the MRI and incorporated these theories into her approach.

This chapter focuses on the work of Mara Selvini Palazzoli and her colleagues in Milan. First, an historical account of the development of the systemic school will be elaborated. The key theoretical concepts of the systemic school will then be presented as identified by the American proponents of the systemic school—Lynn Hoffman (1988) and Peggy Penn (1985). In particular, the reconciliation of the opposites of health and dysfunction are emphasized in assisting families to become healthier. A detailed description of the systemic therapeutic process is provided. Finally, the systemic school will be compared with others that use paradoxical techniques, and a summary of the approach will be included.

It is exciting to see how the research and books from the United States have influenced innovative therapeutic contributions elsewhere in the world. Words and ideas can be very powerful in changing people's lives—especially family life.

MARA SELVINI PALAZZOLI

Mara Selvini Palazzoli, a Milanese specialist in internal medicine, became interested in the difficulties of treating anorectic patients (Barrows, 1982). She changed specialties and studied psychoanalysis in Switzerland to become a psychiatrist and psychoanalyst. Her therapeutic techniques did lead to a higher success rate with anorectics, but she gradually became dissatisfied with the treatment, which often required 500 to 600 hours and still left the clients with the desire for a certain ideal weight. In an effort to become more efficient and effective with her patients, she became the first to implement couple therapy and family therapy in Italy (Tomm, 1984a). In 1967, Selvini Palazzoli founded a center for family studies in Milan, still focusing on the use of the psychoanalytic model with families (see Selvini Palazzoli, 1983). She asked Luigi Boscolo to join the staff of the Center after he completed his psychoanalytic and psychiatric training in New York City. As many as 10 professionals constituted the staff

Dr. Mara Selvini Palazzoli is a strong advocate of basic research in family therapy to solve the serious problems of families, such as anorexia nervosa and schizophrenia. (Courtesy of Dan Miller, NYT Pictures)

at the Center during this early period, applying their psychoanalytic backgrounds to work with couples and families.

In 1971, Selvini Palazzoli adopted the views of Americans, especially those of Watzlawick, Beavin, and Jackson (1967), and some of the professional staff left the Center (Barrows, 1982). The four who remained came to be known as the Milan group. These two heterosexual pairs of psychoanalytically trained psychiatrists—Mara Selvini Palazzoli, Luigi Boscolo, Guiliana Prata, and Gianfranco Cecchin—developed their own unique approach to working with families. This team expanded their target group of patients to include schizophrenics. They launched a research project and asked Watzlawick to serve as a consultant. In this capacity, he visited Milan on at least three occasions. During this time the team tried to learn as much as they could about American techniques, including the work of Haley (1963).

The Milan group then isolated themselves for several years, developing their own system of working with families. In 1975, during this period, the team wrote a book (published in English in 1978) entitled *Paradox and Counter Paradox: A New Model in the Therapy of the Family in Schizophrenic Transaction,* which detailed their use of written paradoxical prescriptions called positive connotations, which not only relabeled the symptom but also reframed each family member's behavior around the symptom. These were read to the family during the final phase of the therapy session.

Around 1975, the journal articles of Gregory Bateson and his book, *Steps to an Ecology of Mind* (1972), had profound influence upon the group of professionals at the center. Boscolo, Cecchin, Hoffman, and Penn (1987) state that the Milan group became fascinated with Bateson's concept of cybernetic circularity (the idea that the family system was constantly evolving) and developed an interview method of circular questioning to scan for difference and to tap the pattern of circularity used by the living system of the family. The therapist would remain neutral in an effort to assess the map or belief system of the family. Families appeared stuck because of epistemological errors—that is, an outdated belief system. The Milan group adopted Bateson's adaptation of Russell's logical types. There were two levels of types—action and meaning (Tomm, 1984a). The level of meaning is derived from the context, so special attention was given to the messages sent by behaviors within a context. Goals of the therapist were to develop a hypothesis from the data obtained in the questioning sequence and to introduce new information into the system that would allow families to change their meaning systems. Families learned through the circular questioning and positive connotations (reframing the symptom or inaccurate belief as a solution) as well as the rituals assigned to be completed between sessions. The positive connotation evolved as a reframing of the theme or myth of the family in which all family members participated.

For example, in a videotape, Cecchin interviewed a doctoral student in his thirties who was having trouble completing his studies. In less than half an hour of well-phrased, spiraling circular questions, he came to the knowledge that the man had been born out of wedlock and had been raised by his aunt. When Cecchin asked an open-ended circular question, "How did the clan banish both you and your mother?" there was a change in the client's facial expression and other nonverbal behaviors. It was as though a light bulb of insight had been lit in his mind, and he confessed that he had perceived his mother as having abandoned him all these years. Now he made the connection and realized that they both had been banished. His mother had, indeed, loved him and had followed the advice of the clan that he would be better taken care of by the aunt and uncle, even though it had also been painful for her. The client changed his map of meaning through the circular questioning and positive connotation. Now he was free to become a success as the clan had intended rather than the unsuccessful, rejected child of his mother.

In 1980, the Milan group split apart: Guiliana Prata and Mara Selvini Palazzoli did therapy and research separately from Luigi Boscolo and Gianfranco Cecchin, who specialized in training and therapy and called themselves the Milan Associates. Palazzoli and Prata became interested in finding a universal prescription that would apply to all families. They were intrigued by the seemingly universal positive results to the prescription of telling the couple to do the secret task of leaving a note telling their children only when they would return from going out together. The parents were not to tell the children what they did nor where they went. This universal intervention was based on Ashby's (1954) concept that a strong connection in a changing evolving system has the effect of rupturing repetitive patterns related to that connection.

On the other hand, Boscolo and Cecchin think that interventions should remain flexible, with a number of alternative prescriptions possible. They even divide therapists behind the one-way mirror into two groups—the "O" group and the "S" group. These groups meet separately to generate alternative hypotheses, which are then shared in the post-session. In order to learn this approach, therapists from other European countries and the United States study with Boscolo and Cecchin who host summer training experiences in the lake district of northern Italy (see Boscolo & Cecchin, 1982).

Selvini Palazzoli has continued to grow and change. Most recently she decided to isolate herself with a small research team to concentrate on in-depth research on cases of psychosis. She and her team have developed a model of how psychosis develops (Selvini Palazzoli et al., 1989).

In summary, there are five distinct periods in the evolution of the Milan group (Tomm, 1984a): (1) the founding of the center to study families in Milan by Mara Selvini Palazzoli in 1967; (2) the adoption of the American brief therapy approaches, turning away from psychoanalysis around 1971; (3) the move to meaning indicated by the shift to the applications of Bateson's original research and his adaptation of the logical types of Russell; (4) in 1980, the separation into two groups, one focusing on research and therapy (Selvini Palazzoli and Prata), especially the development of an invariant prescription, and the other emphasizing training and therapy (Boscolo and Cecchin), using flexible interventions tailored to families; and (5) in 1985, Selvini Palazzoli chose to concentrate on research on psychotic processes in isolation with a small team of collaborators which did not include Prata.

The systemic school of family therapy takes its name from the cybernetic systems theory upon which Bateson based his work. Information theory and the theory of games of which Bateson often wrote are important in this approach. Therefore, human beings are in reciprocal interaction through time, becoming each other. When viewing the river, one is the river. People are neither good nor evil. The family is always changing, and its members are connected with each member, influencing each other continuously over time.

The Milan group would be considered the most pure application of the systems work of Bateson, in that every technique or practice is a particular application of his systemic theory. For example, the circularity of systems theory is applied in the circular questioning model developed by the Milan group.

Key Theoretical Concepts

Co-Evolution.   In his book, *Mind and Nature,* Bateson (1979) defines co-evolution as a system of change in which events happen and a process of selection permits only some random events to endure. For example, species A affects changes in species B. The deer tick sucks the blood of mice in the woods, and when the same ticks bite people, the epidemic of lyme disease occurs in humans, leading to illness and possible death. The family is the co-evolutionary ecosystem of the individual. Each family member affects the conditions of growth or decay of all of the other family members over time.

Cybernetics of Cybernetics.   Cybernetics refers to the feedback loops of communication. In cybernetics of cybernetics, the therapy team is part of the co-evolving ecosystem, as is the referral source. They affect each other in circular feedback loops. Interventions can be directed toward the referring professionals and the therapists as well. They are not neutral objects to be ignored but are part of the therapeutic communication system of the family, creating it and being affected by it in circular feedback loops.

The Time Cable.   Time is a very important dimension of the Milan model. Although observing and asking questions about how the problem is serving a function in the present, as do other approaches based on communication theory, the therapists in the Milan group are also interested in what happened in the past and what will occur in the future that may impact the symptom and the family system.

Hoffman (1983) devised the construct of "the time cable" (Figure 14–1) to show how the context of the problem has co-evolved with the symptom over time. The therapists ask questions of difference of each family member for each of the five aspects of time—present (here and now), onset (when the problem first occurred), historical (prior to the onset of the symptom), future (what will happen in the future about this problem), and mythic (family theme, often intergenerational)—and can also ask questions about the referring source and the therapy team related to these aspects of time. Through such questions the therapist obtains the information necessary to formulate a hypothesis. Keeping the image of the time cable in mind allows the therapist in training to remember to ask questions related to all of the subsystems (family members, therapists, referral source) across all five dimensions of time. These are typically done in comparative pairings, so that in asking what it was like when the problem first occurred and how it is now the difference will be highlighted, which

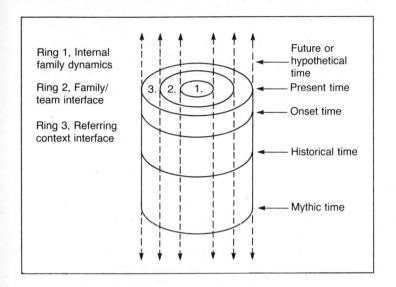

FIGURE 14–1 The time cable

From "A Co-Evolutionary Framework for Systemic Family Therapy" by L. Hoffman in *Diagnosis and Assessment in Family Therapy* (p. 42) by J. Hansen and B. Kenny (Eds.), 1983, Rockville, MD: Aspen Systems Corp. Reprinted by permission.

allows family members the possibility of changing their cognitive maps. In many ways, the most important questions concern mythic time as they access inappropriate cognitive maps relating to the muddle in which the family finds itself. These maps can then be changed by asking questions concerning future time. Family members can change what they do in the future and affect their collective destiny.

Future questions, feed forward, disrupt the rules regulating communication in the family (Penn, 1985). People are free to fantasize and dream about alternative futures, which can unblock the present. In addition, after obtaining information from all of the family members across aspects of time, the clinician can arrive at a problem premise, which is an idea that organizes the behaviors related to the problem. Such a premise can be projected into the future by the use of a future question. Penn (1985) gives the example of a family in which the father of the wife moved in with the family after the death of the mother and took over the vacant father role of the detached husband. The teenager was asked whom she would lean on for help in raising her children—her father or her mother. At this point the husband said in an emotional tone that he hoped that she would lean on her husband. The problem premise had been projected forward into the future so that a new choice could be made, which in turn would influence the present. The use of future questions can be especially important for chronically or terminally ill individuals. Being able to talk about the future helps to change it for the better.

Differences. Bateson emphasized the discrimination of differences, how events are not like each other. The Milan group developed circular questions to point out differences in a nonjudgmental way. A person is asked a question about the problem, now and in the future. This allows the people to think about the differences in the answers. Likewise, asking the same question of two family members will highlight differences. For example, the question of how dad and Bill get along may be answered very differently by Sally, the sister, and her mother. This is very similar to the Piagetian processes of assimilation and accommodation.

Discontinuous Change.   There are two levels of logical types—behavior and meaning. Therapists attempt to affect each one, through rituals of prescribing certain behaviors in an effort to affect the meaning level or through reframing the meaning by releasing new information into the system through positive connotations and circular questions. Change of change occurs in discontinuous steps that are qualitatively different (see Hoffman's [1988] analysis of step functions). Information is more important than behavior in achieving change. The therapist wants to change the epistemology of the family—the family's way of knowing, the cognitive maps that the family members carry with them.

The Diachronic Model of Psychoses.   Selvini Palazzoli's later work (Selvini Palazzoli et al., 1989) reconciled the system with the actions of the individual subject by using a game metaphor. In addition to the influences of the system, a person makes moves in the game comprising strategies similar to a company that has an organizational chart, yet in actuality operates somewhat differently based on the individual players in the positions and their strategies.

There are six stages in the game leading to schizophrenia and other psychotic disorders: (1) a stalemate in the couple's marriage develops (a silent deadlocked battle in which both are provokers—one, active, the other, passive—forever challenging each other but never clearing the air through angry exchanges or negotiations); (2) the child becomes the pawn of the passive parent in the game through implicit seduction and ambiguous promises, even though the parent continues to focus on the other spouse and is only using the child to attack the spouse in a passive, indirect manner; (3) the child exhibits unusual behavior toward the active parent as a means of showing the passive parent how to rebel against the spouse; (4) the passive parent joins with the active parent to punish the child—a "volte face"; (5) recognizing the betrayal and realizing that the passive parent was never really interested in him, the child responds with psychotic behavior; and (6) each spouse organizes around the symptoms of the child by devising an individual strategy, which keeps the game going and reinforces the couple's chronic stalemate.

The Anorectic Process in the Family.   A stalemate is also seen in the marriage of the parents of an anorectic. In this case it most often is a silent husband who appears inadequate in response to the nagging of his wife or a domineering husband with a wife who sees herself as a martyr. One person will nag; the other will either lose his temper and rage at the spouse or become silent. In both cases, the wife harbors resentment toward her husband because he has not fulfilled his fatherly role in an appropriate way. Neither spouse takes a leadership role in the family, each waiting for the other to act in behalf of the family. Each member of the family also reserves the right to reject any offer, even of a relationship.

The six stages of the anorectic process (Selvini Palazzoli, Cirillo, Selvini, & Sorrentino, 1989; Selvini Palazzoli & Viaro, 1988) include: (1) the game of stalemate is played by the parents; (2) the child becomes a pawn in the game of the parents, either through the daughter becoming the special confidante of the mother or the favorite of the father; (3) either the daughter is forsaken by her mother and then indirectly seduced by her father or continues to be her father's favorite in an implicitly incestuous manner; (4) the daughter begins to diet to be different from her mother, who abandoned her emotionally, or as a means of rebelling against her mother; (5) the father joins with the mother—a volte face—and the daughter eats less to rebel against her parents; and (6) the family members adopt strategies designed to keep the system. A special relationship between a child and a parent that is only a way of attracting the attention and affection of a spouse is termed an *imbroglio*.

View of Healthy Functioning

At transitions such as entering new stages of the family life cycle, the rigid family system is not able to transform itself and make a quantum leap to a different method of functioning (MacKinnon, 1983). The symptom is keeping the family system in balance. In order for the system to survive, one of its members is being sacrificed. The challenge to the therapist is to catalyze the family system with new information so that its members will find another way for the system to survive that does not necessitate a symptom in one of its members.

The Milan approach to family therapy works as the reconciliation of opposites—wellness and dysfunction. From the first moment when the family member calls for the appointment, the response is one of detached respect in which the interviewer assumes the stance that the family member is normal and competent, a healthy person. As the first session unfolds, the family therapist again asks questions in a calm manner about the relationships between other members of the family, conveying that family members are capable, well human beings.

In the paradox or other prescriptive intervention, the symptom and the reactions of the other family members are labeled as healthy, and they are encouraged to continue these behaviors, thereby viewing the homeostatic principle of the system as healthy. In this acceptance, the equilibrium can shift toward change, toward behaviors and interactions closer toward the pole of wellness on the continuum from health to dysfunction. Just as in acceptance of self individuals can grow and develop to an increasingly more differentiated self, families whose basic homeostasis with symptomatic behaviors and reactions has been accepted can also grow and change. They are no longer mired in the "stuckness" of their predicament; instead, they are free to use familiar and new behaviors in their repertoire as they move closer to the pole of wellness on the continuum from health to dysfunction.

The Therapeutic Process

Goals for Therapy. No specific behavioral goals are negotiated with the family. Changes in behavior are not goals of the therapy, as they are with brief and strategic approaches to family therapy. Therapists of the Milan group see change as a random, discontinuous process. There is no way to predict the creative, alternative ways that families will find to evolve. The Milan group wants to stimulate change in the cognitive maps of family members so that the family will find its own way of solving the problem (Keeney & Ross, 1985).

Therefore, according to MacKinnon (1983), therapists of the Milan group claim no specific goals. However, they do have a global or general goal of transforming the patterns in the family system.

Role of the Therapist.   The therapist maintains a neutral stance. All of the therapists in the Milan group are psychiatrists who have completed formal psychoanalytic training. A neutral objective posture is the role of a psychoanalyst, except in the stage of working through where it may be more directive. MacKinnon (1983) believes the neutrality in reality is due to the rigorous analytic training that members of the Milan group have completed.

However, from a theoretical point of view the position of neutrality matches the cybernetic construct of Bateson. The aim of the therapy is to present a cognitive map of the family so that it is accepted in the present by the therapists and the family, thereby freeing family members to change the paradigm. Therefore, the family has nothing to resist. If the role of the therapist were directive, then there is a strong possibility that the family would not comply and, in fact, resist the efforts of the therapist. The neutral stance also permits therapists to affect family members more easily with the circular questions they ask. The therapist does not align with anyone. What is said is more likely to be thought about and accepted. Selvini Palazzoli discussed the role of the therapist and her style of therapy with Simon (1987).

One main characteristic of the Milan style of therapy is the use of more than one therapist. One therapist meets with the family while at least one other therapist observes behind a one-way mirror. When a number of people are in the room, as often occurs with family therapy, it is very easy for a therapist to be "sucked in" to the family view and to inadvertently take sides, seeing one member as a hero and another as a villain. The observer provides objectivity and emphasizes the meta-perspective characteristic of systemic therapy.

In the original development of the Milan method, one therapist met with the family while the other three members of the team observed. At various points in the therapy interview, a team member might knock on the door to call the therapist out of the room for consultation. This frequently occurred when the therapist appeared stuck or had become subjectively enmeshed in the family system. In this style of family therapy the therapist routinely will tell the family that the experts who are observing will be consulted at the end of the session while the family takes a break. Then the therapist will return with an expert opinion, which is also based on the feedback and ideas of the team. Often 2½ hours are set aside for each session, with 30 minutes for pre-session team hypothesizing, 90 minutes for the family interview, and 30 minutes for post-session discussion and development of the intervention and announcing the intervention to the family (Campbell, Reder, Draper, & Pollard, 1983).

As the role of the therapist has evolved in the Milan approach of Selvini Palazzoli, the therapist now abolishes reticence and is, instead, very open about directly sharing hypotheses for what is happening in the family. Rather than using paradoxical techniques that make the family wonder if the therapist is playing a game, in recent work Selvini Palazzoli et al. (1989) encourage the therapist to develop a relationship with each spouse. A spouse learns to trust the other spouse and break the marital stalemate in direct proportion to that spouse being able to trust the therapist more and more.

For example, using the Diachronic Model of Psychotic Process, in the second or third session the therapist might share directly with the schizophrenic patient that the patient is responsible for his psychotic behavior and what a waste of a life to keep the parents together. Typically at this point, the schizophrenic patient would then be dismissed from the therapy. In later sessions, the couple would collaborate with the therapist in an attempt to uncover the underlying themes from their families of origin that lead to an emotion such as fear at the heart of the marital stalemate. For example, the husband may be afraid that his wife will be unfaithful. If their son is psychotic, this is one way to keep the wife at home caring for the son.

The therapist uses "to and fro" thinking—thinking in feedback loops that move from the system to the individual and back to the system. Such multidimensional thinking reconciles attention to both the individual and the system. Earlier, the approach focused almost exclusively on the system. Like a detective, the therapist matches important dates when the symptom first appeared with events in the nuclear and extended families to find a clue to the family game.

Use of Diagnosis and Assessment. **Telephone chart.** The telephone chart is an assessment tool developed by the Milan group. Information is obtained from the family over the telephone prior to making an appointment (Blasio, Fischer, & Prata, 1986). In contrast to many other approaches which restrict severely the amount of time spent on the telephone with the family member requesting treatment for the family, the Milan group talks with this family member for at least 15–30 minutes to obtain information necessary to generate a hypothesis before the team meets with the family, to decide whom the family should invite to the first session (usually the person who would be invited, if necessary, is one member of one side of the extended family), to grasp recurring dysfunctional patterns, and to notify the family member of the rules and expectations of the therapy. The role of the family member making the request is considered by the team. For example, if a sibling of the identified patient makes the request, this could be indicative of a dysfunctional pattern in the family in which the sibling is functioning as one of the parents—a parentified child.

The relational chart includes the referring person, caller, reasons for seeking family therapy, family name, telephone number and address, who is living in the nuclear family, a description of the father of the family, a description of the mother of the family, date of their marriage, a description of each of the children in order of birth, other people living in the house, the membership of the extended family on each side, the presenting problem, who should be asked to attend the first session, and the topics that should be addressed in the first session.

All of these facts and perceptions are gathered in a calm, intellectual manner. The client is not permitted to talk just about what he or she wants to discuss. The stage is set for the first session, in which similar types of factual questions will be asked. The interviewer tells the potential client that the team will be consulted and the interviewer will call back with the results. The interviewer and the team discuss the

The relationship between a grandparent and grandchild can be very special and is often linked to emotional survival when children live in an abusive family. By collecting information on the telephone to construct a telephone chart, systemic therapists can decide which grandparents should be invited to the initial session.

telephone chart. Then the interviewer calls the client again to indicate the team's willingness to meet with the family, an appointment time, and whom the family should invite to the first session.

Circular questioning. The role that the symptom is playing and has played in the family system is assessed using circular questions, asking about what was happening among whom prior to the problem occurring, at the time of onset, and in the present (Viaro & Leonardi, 1983, 1986). Liddle (1983) states that the therapist uses circular questioning to find out the reactions of family members and their perceptions of the problem. A tentative hypothesis helps to organize the therapist's approach to the family, with the therapist remaining sensitive to responses from the family that might alter the hypothesis. Circular questions can also be therapeutic when framed to target the systemic hypothesis, especially questions about the future.

Nature of the Initial Session.   Selvini Palazzoli, Boscolo, Cecchin, and Prata (1980a) use the principles of hypothesizing, circularity, and neutrality in conducting the first and subsequent therapeutic family sessions. Usually the therapist in conference with the team, and based on the data obtained from the telephone chart, formulates a hypothesis or educated guess about what is happening at a systems level in the family.

This hypothesis is used as the basis for the questions that are asked in the first session, but the therapist can and often does change the hypothesis during the session (Burbatti & Formenti, 1988).

Using the feedback obtained from the family, the therapist investigates the hypothesis, soliciting information about the relationships in the family, especially difference and change. Like a detective, the therapist explores patterns of circularity, including differences between nonverbal behavior (analogic information) and verbal statements (digital information), the definition of the problem from the phenomenological perspective of each member of the family in a circle, and the presence of various coalitions discovered by asking another member about the reactions of each member of the family to the problem (Penn, 1982). Also included in patterns of circularity are tracking what happened in sequence before and after the occurrence of the problem, asking members to categorize and compare the reactions and behaviors of other members of the family, and gossiping in the presence of the family by asking one family member to comment on the relationship of two other members of the family. Also, questions are asked to obtain comparisons among subsystems of the family and to elicit the perceptions of each member of the family about the pattern of interaction in each relationship.

The therapist maintains a neutral stance. None of the questioning is direct nor is any attempt made to involve the family in uncomfortable patterns of interaction in the actual session. A controlled, intellectual, analytical stance is used by the therapist.

This approach to family therapy, using circular questioning in a detached way, is similar to the short-term, dynamic psychotherapy approach used with individual clients. However, in contrast, there are no interpretations of any type used in the Milan family therapy session, as interpretations would imply judgments of the family. Selvini Palazzoli et al. (1980a) point out that the therapist has established an alliance with each member of the family by asking them questions about the relationships between other members of the family, yet no family member thinks that any special alliances have been formed. The circular feedback loops used with each member of the family are illustrated in Figure 14–2.

Usually the entire nuclear family plus some extended family members from one side of the family are included in the first session. If a family member is absent, questions about the relationship between another family member and the absent member are asked of each member of the family. If a child has functioned as an identified patient for a period of time by being institutionalized, the therapists may ask to see only the parents, working with them through brief therapy to treat the children (Selvini Palazzoli, Boscolo, Cecchin, & Prata, 1974). Sometimes the referring person is invited to the first session and is included in the circular questioning of the session. According to Selvini Palazzoli, Boscolo, Cecchin, and Prata (1980b), even if the referring person is absent, it is important to ask questions of each family member about the relationship between the referring person and other family members. When the referring person is a sibling, a separate initial session is suggested with the referring sibling, who is often a professional in the mental health field (Selvini Palazzoli, 1985).

The interview technique that has evolved in Milan is characterized by its prescriptive interventions at the conclusion of the session (Viaro & Leonardi, 1986). The

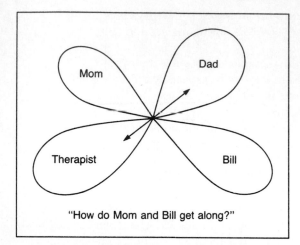

FIGURE 14–2 Circularity of feedback loops: Asking a family member how two other family members relate to each other and repeating the process with each family member until everyone has been asked.

standard techniques are based on the principles of individual competence and reticence. In other words, the way that the therapist asks the questions conveys that the therapist assumes that the family member is normal, has the information, and is competent to answer. The therapist can tell that certain questions are being evaded by the family and, in turn, the therapist keeps information from the family until the conclusion of the session when the prescription is made based on the information that the therapist has collected. This prescription at the end of the session is one of the distinguishing features of the Milan method.

Particularly effective with families of schizophrenics and those with anorexia nervosa, the prescriptive intervention is tailored to change the rules of the family system by focusing on changing the nodal, most basic rule that undergirds the other rules in the system (Selvini Palazzoli, 1978, 1983, 1985, 1987; Stierlin, Simon, & Schmidt, 1987; Weeks & L'Abate, 1982). In a family in which a member has become a schizophrenic, there is much hostile criticism without any clarification as to what the expected appropriate behavior is. Double binds occur often between verbal and nonverbal behavior. Isolating the nodal, basic rule is a spiraling process that occurs in the discussion of the team at the conclusion of the first session. The first part of the intervention is a positive connotation of the symptom and the behaviors of the other family members, that is, a confirmation of the homeostatic principle of the family system. It is in accepting the homeostasis of the system that the system moves in the direction of transformation and change (Selvini Palazzoli, Boscolo, Cecchin, & Prata, 1979).

In interviewing Selvini Palazzoli, Barrows (1982) found that the discussion of the four therapists resembles the Piagetian cognitive developmental process. The collective intelligence of four people is brought to bear on the family system, and the discussions of the four people move through phases of conflict just as a child develops intelligence by accommodating and assimilating differences and similarities, akin to a mathematical process. Each prescription is tailored idiosyncratically to the rules and nature of the particular family seeking treatment. A disagreeable symptom is found agreeable because it carries out the family theme, according to Campbell et al. (1983)

of the Tavistock Clinic in London. The paradox chosen to present to the family represents the functional, nodal interactional double bind that the family finds itself in within its contextual framework. The variable of time is usually contained in the prescriptive intervention, according to Selvini Palazzoli (1975).

An example of a prescription at the conclusion of the first family therapy session occurred with the family of a 10-year-old boy of superior intelligence who was diagnosed as schizophrenic after his grandfather's death and a visit from his aunt.

> "We are closing this first session with a message to you, Ernesto. You're doing a good thing. We understand that you considered your grandfather to be the central pillar of your family [the hand of the therapist moved in a vertical direction as if tracing an imaginary pillar]; he kept it together, maintaining a certain balance [the therapist extended both hands in front of him palms down, both at the same level]. Without your grandfather's presence, you were afraid something would change, so you thought of assuming his role, perhaps because of this fear that the balance in the family would change [the therapist slowly lowered his right hand, which corresponded to the side where the father was seated]. For now you should continue in this role that you've assumed spontaneously. You shouldn't change anything until the next session, which will be January 21, five weeks from now." (Selvini Palazzoli et al., 1978a, p. 81)

Selvini Palazzoli's work has evolved from the use of very specific paradoxical prescriptions tailored to positive reasons for the symptom's appearance in this particular family at this time, to a set of invariant prescriptions that do not change from one family to another (Selvini Palazzoli et al., 1989). For example, all members living in the same household are invited to the initial session, as are relatives from one side of the family, such as the maternal grandparents, if they play an influential role in the workings of the nuclear family. At the end of the first session after the therapist has taken a break to discuss the matter with the team, the invariant prescription is directed to those present who are not members of the nuclear family and is as follows:

> Normally, at the end of a first session, we are able to say whether we believe family therapy is or is not advisable. In this case, however, despite everyone's excellent cooperation (this is said even when there has been nothing but obstinate reticence), we have not come to a definite conclusion and require a further meeting with the family. The next appointment will be on such and such a day at such and such an hour. You will stay home; we will see only the family. We wish to thank you so very much for having come today and for being so helpful. (Selvini Palazzoli et al., 1989, p. 19)

The systemic theorists believe that the patient improves before the next session, sometimes dramatically, because a firm boundary line has been drawn around the nuclear family. The schizophrenic or anorectic child has been reinstated as a member of the nuclear family through this process (Selvini Palazzoli, 1988; Selvini Palazzoli et al., 1989).

Stages of Therapy. Typically Selvini Palazzoli's therapy consists of an agreement for no more than 10 sessions, spaced at least one month apart. After experimenting with different lengths of time, the therapists of the Milan group concluded that this length of time produced the best results. The power to influence change in the family system emanates from the interaction between the complementary subsystem of the family

therapists and the subsystem of the family (Selvini Palazzoli, 1980). It can be dangerous if the family therapist suprasystem becomes too richly joined to the family subsystem.

After the therapeutic intervention, which consists of a written paradoxical comment, a family ritual or a prescription for the family system is made (usually at the end
of the first session). Time must be allowed for the family system to reorganize itself
on the basis of this new information (a cybernetic mechanism). Often families will
call, asking for an earlier appointment, but such an appointment tends to dilute the
effect of the intervention. By having no interaction with the family, the therapists are
able to disconnect and remain objective and constant in their interactions with the
family system, maintaining the complementarity of the family therapist suprasystem to
the family subsystem.

Viaro and Leonardi (1986) state that all families in treatment since 1979 have
received the same prescription in the same sequence:

1. At the end of the second session, the prescription reads that there is a definite
   indication for family treatment with the next session set for a specific time on a
   specific day, and that the children will stay home and only the parents will attend.
2. The third session with the parents alone focuses on asking the parents how each of
   their children reacted to only the parents being invited, how each parent reacted,
   and how they had talked about it, with the prescription that the parents shall
   officially announce to the family and to the family of origin that the doctor has
   prescribed that everything that happens in the treatment sessions will be kept
   secret from all of the other family members. Parents are told to keep hidden
   notebooks in which they record the dates and reactions of family members to the
   announcement of secrecy.
3. The fourth session emphasizes reading the notebooks, after which the parents are
   designated as co-therapists and informers with the prescription that they meet
   alone away from the house for a particular number of times prescribed by the
   therapist. They leave a note for the children that they would not be home that
   evening.
4. At the fifth session, the couple is prescribed a weekend away from home without
   the children, leaving a written note that they will be back on a certain day.
5. The sixth session consists of a prescription of a 10-day to one-month vacation
   without the children.
6. In the seventh and subsequent sessions there are no rigid prescriptions, but the
   disappearances are encouraged as well as other prescriptions suggested by the
   couple or the therapists.
7. The tenth session is the last session, regardless of whether or not the clients ask that
   it continue.

The purposes of these invariant prescriptions and their sequence are: (1) to de-
marcate and strengthen the boundaries of the levels of the system, from the extended
family, to the nuclear family, to the spousal subsystem, and (2) to generate information
that the therapy team can use to determine the family's game and the moves of

individuals within the game. The notes that spouses record concerning the reactions of others to their secrecy and outings provide information that would not be typically shared with the therapist by the family members. Through prescribing action, much is learned about the family's game.

For example, the father in a family may have a painful relationship with his overly critical mother. He refuses to tell her of the secrecy pact because he does not want her to know that he and his family are in therapy, hoping to avoid her critical comments. By telling the therapist that all relatives have been informed about the secrecy pact except his mother, the father gives valuable information about his relationship with his mother and her influence on how the family functions that he would never have voluntarily shared (Selvini Palazzoli et al., 1989).

In particular, the couple's reaction to the invariant secrecy prescription determines the use of one of three alternatives at the end of the fourth session: (1) if compliance has occurred, the prescription will consist of asking the couple to disappear a set number of evenings; (2) if partial compliance has occurred, the secrecy prescription will be repeated; and (3) if compliance has not occurred, treatment will be interrupted, giving a reason tailored to the individual family. "To keep the secret is to get married," say Selvini Palazzoli et al. (1989, p. 48). If a couple refuses to do so, they have defined the relationship with the therapist as a symmetrical one. For healing to occur, the definition of the therapist-couple relationship must change. Therefore, the therapist gives the couple the choice of remaining the same and interrupting treatment or following the prescriptions of the therapist, which defines the therapist-couple relationship as a complementary one. The therapist is in charge, and change occurs.

Most recently, Selvini Palazzoli (Selvini Palazzoli et al. 1989) has gradually begun to use the invariant set of prescriptions less in lieu of specific prescriptions. These prescriptions emanate from their models of psychotic and anorectic processes and are tailored to the specific game being played by the family. The secrecy prescription is still utilized, but as a test of readiness that the couple can, indeed, form a therapeutic alliance with the team and operate as a marital subsystem.

Application: Major Therapeutic Techniques

The Generation of Systemic Hypotheses.   An hypothesis is an educated guess as to the cognitive map or myth (the epistemological error) which the family holds that is keeping them in a stuck place. Anderson and Bagarozzi (1983) give an example of such a cognitive map and how an intervention was tailored to match yet change the family myth.

A hypothesis is based on information obtained in a telephone intake that usually takes about a half hour, a call from the referring person, or any previous sessions with the family. The hypothesis is based on content, behavior exhibited during the interview (especially patterns of interaction), analogic data (any family stories, metaphors, secrets, or cue words), and previous experience of the team.

The principle of hypothesizing leads to generating alternative systemic hypotheses. The therapist continues to ask circular questions, following the logic of the tentative hypothesis. If it is not confirmed, an alternative hypothesis is chosen, and the therapist changes the order of questioning to fit the new hypothesis (Tomm, 1984b, 1985).

There is not one right hypothesis; rather there are many alternative hypotheses, any of which may be useful. The hypothesis that is used to develop a positive connotation should include all members of the family and how their behaviors contribute to the problem (problem-focused positive connotation) or the cognitive map of the family in which all participate (pattern-focused positive connotation). For example, perhaps whenever a family member nears success, the family member does something in order to fail and be able to say, "Poor me. The world's against me." A suitable hypothesis might be that family members carry out self-defeating behaviors in order to huddle together against the world (a cognitive map of the family that will require a pattern-focused positive connotation as an intervention if it is confirmed through the circular questioning). The therapist would not tell the family members the hypothesis. Instead the therapist would ask questions to confirm the hypothesis or to generate another one.

Circular Interview. The principle of circularity (circular causality) undergirds the circular interview. In the circular interview the therapist asks questions of each family member, completing the circle and being careful not to spend too much time with any one person (Fleuridas, Nelson, & Rosenthal, 1986; Tomm, 1984b, 1985; Viaro & Leonardi, 1983). The therapist has generated a tentative hypothesis about what function the symptom is playing in the family, around which questions are asked of each member. The hypothesis makes meaning out of what the family is doing, is a guide for the interview, and can help the family to develop new views of their behaviors, relationships, and beliefs. The therapist asks questions in a logical order so that family members gain by integrating the differences. The therapist listens for the key repeated words of family members and uses them in phrasing questions about the problem and the hypothesis.

Often questions will be asked in a logically opposite manner, especially with sensitive issues. For example, instead of asking "Who was upset with Mary?" a therapist might ask "Who was *not* upset with Mary?" The therapist continues to ask questions until a complete interactional pattern becomes clear. Any gaps are filled in by further inquiries. Questions are not asked randomly but in a logical order. Information gathered in this way leads to the completion of the circle by the end of the interview so that an intervention can be made. The therapist should always take into consideration what not having the symptom will mean to the system as a whole and the members in it.

Circular Questions. Fleuridas, Nelson, and Rosenthal (1986) of the University of Iowa have shared their guidelines for conducting a circular interview, their description and classification of circular questions, and a list of many examples of circular questions (Table 14–1). Questions are asked in four categories: problem definition, interactional sequences, classification/comparison, and intervention. It is important to create a logical arcing effect by asking the same person the same question about the present and the past. Such a process helps family members integrate the differences. This is especially true of future questions when they are alternated with present questions in a logical arc. Since the future has not yet occurred, future questions allow for creativity and do not follow the family rules for communication. Often they can unblock family members who are stuck.

An example of the use of circular questions follows:

Q: Who is most upset by the problem?

A: Mother.

Q: What does mother do about it?

A: She tries to motivate Johnny to go to school.

Q: Who agrees with mother?

A: The school psychologist.

Q: Who disagrees?

A: Father.

Q: Why do you think he disagrees?

A: He thinks they are babying Johnny.

Q: Who feels the same as father?

A: Grandmother. . . .

Q: When did the problem begin?

A: A year ago.

Q: Was anything else happening a year ago?

A: Grandfather died.

Q.   Who missed him the most?

A: Grandmother, then father.

Q: Who was his death hardest on?

A: Mother.

Q: Why do you think that?

A: She and grandmother don't get along and grandmother is now living in our house. (Hoffman, 1983, pp. 44–45)

When you are at home with a spouse or friend, practice using pairs of these questions as you ask about the person's life. The classification/comparison questions are the most difficult to ask in such a conversation because they emphasize difference, and most typical questions in informal conversation highlight similarities between people. Notice that the intervention questions focus on the strengths of families and behaviors that are routine in healthy families. Therefore, focusing family members on positive family goals by asking them questions about them brings about an improvement.

Problem-Focused Positive Connotations.   The systemic school is noted for a type of prescriptive intervention called a positive connotation. In their early work, positive connotations constituted the reframing of the symptom as a solution and how the behavior of each of the family members was connected to the problem. This was accompanied by a directive to the family members to continue to do what they were

TABLE 14–1 Examples of circular questions (pp. 404–410)

I. Problem Definition Questions:
Whenever possible, ask for a description of the specific behaviors which are perceived to be problematic.

General Examples: | *Specific Examples:*

A. Present:
- What is the problem in the family now?
- What concerns bring you into therapy now? or: What concerns bring you here now?
- What is the main concern of the family now?
- What problems do the other children have?
- For children: What changes would you like in your family?

1. Difference
- How is this different than before?
- Has this always been true?

2. Agreement/Disagreement
- Who agrees with you that this is the problem?

3. Explanation/Meaning
- What is your explanation for this?
- What does his behavior mean to you?

B. Past:
- What was the problem in the family then?

1. Difference
- How is that different from now?

2. Agreement/Disagreement
- Who agrees with Dad that this was the major concern of the family then?

3. Explanation/Meaning
- What is your explanation for that?
- What do you believe was the significance of her decision to move out at that time?

C. Future/Hypothetical:
- What would be the problem in the family if things were to continue as they are?

1. Difference
- How would that be different than it is now?

2. Agreement/Disagreement
- Do you agree, Mom?*

3. Explanation/Meaning
- If this were to happen, how would you explain it?
- What purpose would that serve?

II. Sequence of Interaction Questions:
Focus on interactional behaviors.

A. Present:
- Who does what when?
- Then what happens?
- What next?
- Where is she or he when this happens?
- What does she or he do?
- Then what do they do?
- Who notices first?
- How does he respond?

- Ask Daughter: When Mom tries to get Sister to eat (to solve or prevent the presenting problem) and she refuses, what does Dad do? Then what does Mom do? What does Brother do? And what does Sister do? Then what happens?
- When your mom and brother are fighting, what does your dad do?
- Does Dad get involved in that fight or stay out of it? Describe what happens.

Note: The terms "Mom," "Dad," etc. are used in the text. In therapy, the person's name would be used in cases of direct address.

TABLE 14–1 *continued*

General Examples:	Specific Examples:

- When she or he does not do that (problem definition), what happens?
  - When Dad doesn't get involved in their fights, what happens? How does your mom react when your dad doesn't get involved and fight with your brother?

1. Difference
   - Has it always been this way?
     - Has Brother always behaved in this manner?

2. Agreement/Disagreement
   - Who agrees with you that this is how it happens?
     - Who agrees with you that Mother yells at Dad every time he stomps out of the house?

3. Explanation/Meaning
   - What is your explanation for this?
     - How do you explain Dad's tendency to leave home often?
   - What does this mean to you?
     - What does Dad's behavior mean to you?

B. Past:
   - Who did what then?
     - What did Dad do on those days when Brother used to push Mother around?
   - What solutions were tried?
     - How did your folks try to get you to stop? How did that work?

1. Difference
   - How was it different?
     - How was his behavior different? Describe what he used to do.
   - When was it different?
     - When did he do this? How often?
     - When did he change?
   - What else was different then?
     - How did Dad respond to the earlier situation? (Then what happened?).
   - How does that differ from how it is now?
     - How does that differ from how he responds now? (Then what?).
   - Was it more or less then, than it is now?
     - Was he gone more or less often than he is now?

2. Agreement/Disagreement
   - Who agrees with you?
     - Who agrees with Mom that Dad is more involved in the fights now?

3. Explanation/Meaning
   - How do you explain this change?
     - How do you explain this recent involvement?
   - What does this change (or lack of change) mean to you?
     - What does it mean to you that day after day, year after year, things between the two of you have not changed?

C. Future/Hypothetical:
   - What would you/he/she do differently if she or he did (not) do this?
     - What do you think Mom would do if Dad were to ignore Brother?
     - What will Dad do with Brother when Mother begins to work nights?

From "The Evolution of Circular Questions: Training Family Therapists" by C. Fleuridas, T. S. Nelson, and D. M. Rosenthal, 1986, *Journal of Marital and Family Therapy, 25,* pp. 120–125. Reprinted by permission.

TABLE 14-1 *continued*

General Examples:	*Specific Examples:*
1. Difference	
● How would it be different if she or he were to do this?	● How would your parents' relationship be different if your mom were to return to school?
2. Agreement/Disagreement	
● Who would agree with you that this is probably what would happen?	● Do you think your mom would agree that they would probably get a divorce if she were to return to school?
3. Explanation/Meaning	
● Tell me why you believe this would happen.	● Dad, explain to me why you think your daughter and wife both agree that a divorce is likely should your wife return to school.
● How do you think your wife would explain it?	
● What would this mean to you/him/her/them?	● What would a divorce between your parents mean to you?

III. Comparison/Classification Questions:

A. Present:

● Who is closest to whom?	● To whom does Dad show most affection—Mom or Daughter?
● Who is most like whom?	
● Who gets angry most?	● Who is most like Mom of your seven children? Then who?
● Who acts most upset when (the problem) occurs?	● Who acts most upset when she seems uncooperative?
● Who feels most helpless when (the problem) occurs?	● Who is most convinced that something is wrong with his behavior? Who next?
● Who is most involved in this situation?	● And who is least convinced that something is wrong? (Rank order.)
● Then who? (Rank order.)	● Who is the first to help you when you are having trouble with your homework?
● Who helps the (so-called) problem child the most?	● Who spends the most time helping you with your homework? Who spends the least amount of time with you?
● Who is most apt to do what another member of the family does?	● Classify the various members of the family in reference to their tendency to keep their rooms neat. Begin with whoever is the neatest (or the messiest).
● Who generally sides with whom?	● If Mother begins to cry during the session, you may state: Mother seems unhappy. Who is most able to comfort her when she is sad—your dad, your grandmother, your sister, or you? (Then who?)
● Who generally argues with whom the most?	
● Who has the most fun with whom?	
● Who most understands a certain member of the family?	● Who is more attached to Mom—your brother or your sister?
● Who spends the most time with whom else?	● Do you, or does your husband, communicate best with the children?
● Who else feels this way?	● Is your parents' intimate life better or worse lately?
● Who else in the family prefers this?	● Have you felt more like a wife or a daughter in the past month?

TABLE 14–1 *continued*

General Examples:	Specific Examples:

1. Difference
   - How do they differ?
   - How is this different than that?
   - How does your family differ from other families?

   - How does his behavior bother you differently than it bothers Mom?
   - How is Mom's discipline different than Dad's?
   - Is your family as close as other families that you know?
   - Would you consider your parents' marriage to be happier than most?
   - Do the children fight more than most siblings do; less; or are they about average?

   - How does this family differ from your/his/her family of origin?

   - How close is he to the children compared to how close your dad was to you when you were growing up?
   - How do you think you and your spouse's relationship differs from that of your parents?
   - How are you raising the children differently than how your parents raised you?

   - Has this always been true?
   - Was it ever different?

2. Agreement/Disagreement
   - Who agrees with whom about this?
   - Who else believes this is true?
   - Which set of grandparents would be most apt to agree?

   - Who disagrees with Dad the most?
   - Who do you think would agree with you that Dad is closest to Sister?
   - Who in the family agrees with you that Mom is closest to Brother?
   - To Dad: Do you agree with your daughter that your son is closer to your wife when you and she quarrel?

3. Explanation/Meaning
   - What is your explanation for this?
   - Explain to me the meaning of this.
   - Have you thought about why this occurs? What hunches have you come up with?
   - How does (the outsider) explain this?
   - What does this mean to him or her?

   - What leads you to believe that Dad and Daughter are closest in the family?
   - What do you think is the significance of their (or your) closeness?
   - What is your explanation for this difference (or agreement)?
   - What is your reason for his extreme dislike of school?
   - How does the teacher explain this behavior?
   - What does marriage mean to your spouse?
   - How has she or he showed you that this is so?

B. Past:
   - Who was closest to whom before this happened?

   - Before Brother left home, who was closest to Dad? (Rank order.)
   - Was your Mom more on your side in the past than she is now?
   - Who was most pleased with your former therapy? Who next? (Rank order.)
   - Who argued the most with Brother before he went to jail?

TABLE 14–1 *continued*

General Examples:	Specific Examples:
1. Difference • Has this always been true? • How was it different then?	• Has she always demonstrated her sadness this way in the family? • How were Mom and Dad closer before you moved out?
2. Agreement/Disagreement • Do you agree with her that it was different?	• Do you agree with Mom that they got along better before you moved?
3. Explanation/Meaning • What was your explanation for that? • What do you think she or he meant when she or he did/said that?	• How did you explain the distance you both experienced at that time? • What did he mean when he told you that he would never leave you again?

C. Future/Hypothetical:

• Who will be closest then? • Who would show the most anger if ____? • What would happen between the two of you if this were to happen? • Who would be the best companion for whom? • Who would seem the most helpful? • Who would act the most upset if this were to happen? • Who would show the most relief if this no longer happened?	• Who will be closest to Mom when all of you children have grown up and left home? • If the girls were no longer at home, would things be better or worse for you and your husband? • After your wife's (imminent) death, who will take care of your (handicapped) daughter? • If one of you children had to stay home after high school graduation to take care of your parents, who would be the first to volunteer? Who would be the best for your mom? for your dad? • Who would act the most upset if Dad were to come home drunk—Mom or Daughter? • Who would show the most relief if Dad were to quit drinking?
1. Difference • How would that be different than it is now? • How would their relationship be different if ____?	• What would you do differently if Mom and Dad got along? • How would Mom and Dad's relationship be different if you were to leave home?
2. Agreement/Disagreement • Who agrees with her that if this were to happen, they'd be closer?	• Who agrees with Dad that Son would improve if Mom and Dad got along better? • Do you agree with your daughter that you and your husband would get a divorce if she were to leave home?

TABLE 14–1 *continued*

General Examples:	Specific Examples:
• If (teacher, Grandmother, school counselor, etc.) were here, with whom would she agree?	• If your teacher were here, what would she say?

3. Explanation/Meaning
   • What is your explanation for this?
   • What is your reason for the likelihood that this would (not) happen should that occur?
   • What purpose would that serve.

• How do you explain your Dad's guess that if they were to go on a trip, you three children would get along fine?
• Explain why you think they would not get a divorce if you left.
• He just stated that he should run away. What purpose do you think that would serve?

IV. Interventive Questions

Note: Many of the examples above may be an interventive, depending upon the intent of the therapist and the family's frame of reference. Some additional examples appear below.

A. *Present:*
   • What "fun" things do you usually do together as a family?
   • How much time alone do you typically spend together doing something enjoyable?
   • How often do you go out together; alone; as a couple?
   • How much time do you two spend alone?
   • How is she or he going to learn to _____ ?
   • From whom did son/daughter learn to (reframe behavior or intent)?
   • What would be different in your family if I told you that change would be risky now? (Paradox)

   1. Difference
   2. Agreement/Disagreement
   3. Explanation/Meaning

• Ask each of the children: What's something fun that you did with your family this week?
• Have you had some special time alone with your dad lately? What did you do?
• Did your mom and dad get to go out together, just the two of them?
• What do you like to do when your folks go out on a date?
• How do you think James will learn to do his homework on his own? (Do you agree, James?)
• How do you think Karen will best learn to share her feelings? (That's one possibility, any other ideas? Which do you think would be most helpful?)

• From whom did Daughter learn to act so courageous and persistent?
• In what other ways does he show you that he's concerned about the two of you?
• How do you think your mom would respond if I told her that the family is not ready for you to change, and that they need you to stay home from work and school in order to protect them as they grow older?

(The same type of questions suggested above apply to the interventive questions

TABLE 14–1 *continued*

General Examples:	Specific Examples:
B. Past:	
• How did your parents do that in the past?	• How did your parents discipline you in the past? What do you think was most helpful? What have they done with James when he misbehaves? Did that work? The last time that he ran away, what did your mom do? What did your dad do? What do you think helped James the most then?
• What do you think was most effective?	
• Did that work?	
• What did your family do the last time this happened? How did that help?	• When did Carol take on the responsibility of keeping your brothers out of trouble by monopolizing all of your parents' time and attention?
• When did she or he first take on the job of caring for her or his mom/dad/ siblings in this way? (Reframe.)	
• What other creative ways have you found to discipline the children?	
1. Difference	(The same type of questions suggested above apply to the interventive questions.)
2. Agreement/Disagreement	
3. Explanation	
C. Future/Hypothetical:	
• What does she or he need to do to prepare for this?	• What do you think Mother needs to do to prepare for the time James leaves home?
• Who will be the most prepared when this happens?	• What does James need to do?
	• When Mother goes to the hospital, how are each of you going to help in the home? How could Dad help the best? How could James help?
• How will each member help the family when this happens?	
• What would happen if ____?	• What would happen if they grounded him from the T.V. every time he stayed out past his curfew?
• What do you think would be the most effective way to resolve this problem?	• Do you think she would be more willing to share her feelings if you were to: (a) ask her questions about her day, (b) share your feelings with her, or (c) if she were to see you and your wife share your feelings with each other?
• If she or he were to help, how would she do it? Would she succeed?	• If Mom were to try to teach Daughter not to whine and complain, how would she do it? Do you think that would work? How would Dad try to teach her?
1. Difference	(The same type of questions suggested above apply to the interventive questions.)
2. Agreement/Disagreement	
3. Explanation/Meaning	

doing for now. This type of positive connotation can be labeled as a problem-focused positive connotation to distinguish it from the later work of the Milan group in which the focus of the positive connotation was on the pattern or cognitive map of the family and how family members participated in it.

An example of a problem-focused connotation is the following: "It's good that you're hearing voices, Nancy. Your parents have become worried about you so they have been talking more these days. It's good they're talking more so they'll be prepared for when you leave home. What you are doing is good, and I want you to keep doing it for the time being."

Pattern-Focused Positive Connotations.   A positive connotation in which the cognitive map of the family is in error (an epistemological error) is reframed as a solution, with how each family member participates. This is called a pattern-focused positive connotation. It is accompanied by the double-binding restraining caution to continue seeing the pattern as it is, or the problem would occur if the pattern did change.

To construct a pattern-focused positive connotation, the therapist generates a tentative hypothesis and asks circular questions. If the hypothesis is a systemic one and is confirmed, the therapist devises a pattern-focused positive connotation to read to the family in the last part of the family therapy session.

An example of a pattern-focused positive connotation is: "From observing your family we can see that you are very loyal not only to each other but to your clan. Sometimes it seems that when one of you is about to succeed, another family member or the clan asks a favor to check out your loyalty. But how could one belong without this problem?"

Rituals.   After the therapists have detected the rules of the family system, another method that can be used to break up these old rules is the prescription of a family ritual. A ritual is a type of prescription that directs the members of the family to change their behavior under certain circumstances. By changing the actions of the family members, the therapist hopes to change the cognitive map or meaning of the behavior. When prescribing a ritual, the therapist should state a specific time when the ritual is to be carried out.

For example, the therapist might direct the husband to be in charge of the discipline of a child on Monday, Wednesday, and Friday, while the wife will do so on Tuesday, Thursday, and Saturday. They will do it the way they always have done it on Sunday (Selvini Palazzoli, Bocolo, Cecchin, & Prata, 1978b). Each marital partner is responsible for recording any interference on the part of the other marital partner on the days that they are in charge, or this task may be assigned to the identified patient or to one of the children. Such a ritual blocks the usual patterns of interaction in the family and also uses the competition between parents to bring out the "best" techniques of discipline of which the parents are capable. Even if the family does not follow the prescription for more than one day, which occurs often with the most dysfunctional schizophrenic families, the key interactional sequences in the family will surface in the discussions of what each family member had done in relationship to the assignment, which shows the rules of the family game.

Another ritual (Selvini Palazzoli et al., 1978b) used to break up a family myth that had become a rigid family rule of not speaking or acting negatively toward the clan was the prescription of 15 timed minutes on alternate evenings in the privacy of their home of expressing feelings and thoughts about other members of the clan on the part of each family member while the other family members listened, promising to keep these secret from the clan while increasing their helpfulness to the clan. Within 2 weeks there was dramatic improvement in the identified patient in this family. In this way, one side of the conflict is expressed on each day, breaking the double bind, which was the simultaneous expression of both poles of the conflict. Sequencing exercises like this ritual can help to jog the way family members view their rules and create change of change, a change of the rules.

Unlocking the Marital Stalemate.   Selvini Palazzoli et al. (1989) found that at the bottom of the couple stalemate in psychotic and anorectic families was an intense fear of one spouse directed toward the partner. In some cases, it might be an overpowering fear of sexual infidelity on the part of the partner or an intense fear that the partner did not respect or admire the spouse. This strong fear, held by one or both spouses, is deeply concealed and never discussed by the couple.

In the fourth or later sessions, with only the couple present, the therapist can risk unlocking the marital stalemate by sharing his hypothesis about the spouse's intense fear. The reactions of the couple confirm the accuracy of the hypothesis. If on target, the door has swung open, permitting the use of humor to deflate the fear and reveal the nature of the game. Talking about this deepest feeling will reduce its intensity and create greater interpersonal intimacy for the couple, thereby reducing psychotic and anorectic illnesses in the children.

THERAPEUTIC OUTCOMES

Selvini Palazzoli originally worked with anorectics and their families. When she initiated a center to study families in Milan, anorectic patients and their families continued to seek her out. In 1971, this target group was expanded to include schizophrenics. Typically schizophrenics and their families, as well as patients from other rigid family systems with chronic and severe pathology, are the target groups for this approach. Selvini Palazzoli and colleagues (1978a) presented a summary of individual cases where improvement had occurred. Most recently, a report on the outcomes of 290 individual cases, with a large number of clinical diagnoses seen over an 8-year period from 1979 to 1987, was published (Selvini Palazzoli et al., 1989). There were 93 cases of anorexia nervosa and 49 cases of diverse types of schizophrenia. The Milan set of invariant prescriptions were given to the families of 149 of these clients. Effective therapeutic outcomes were found in most of these cases. Selvini Palazzoli and colleagues (1989) are moving away from invariant prescriptions and toward tailoring specific interventions to the particular family system and the individual family members in that system.

Stierlin and Weber (1989) present outcome data on 42 families of anorectics who were followed up at least 2 years after their family therapy had terminated. Typically, symptoms had begun when most of the girls were 14. They had experienced the symptoms for more than 3 years before entering therapy at the age of 18. The families were seen for a mean of six sessions over an 8-month period. Eating behaviors that showed a marked disturbance for 80.95% of the clients at the beginning of therapy were still present in 47.6% of the cases. Around one fourth of the patients had a weight gain large enough to place them in a higher rating category. More than half had a regular menstrual period at follow-up and had individuated to a higher level of functioning.

In a study of 20 families, Bennun (1986) found that Selvini Palazzoli's approach was more effective in bringing about second-order systemic change than a problem-solving approach. Both approaches had similar results in achieving symptomatic relief over the short and long terms as well as in increasing family satisfaction. All of the families had sought psychiatric help through the British National Health Service.

The efficacy of circular questioning was documented in research by Andersen, Danielsen, Sonnesyn, and Sonnesyn (1985). In reviewing six videotaped sessions of family therapy with a man who had fainting spells, circular questioning was linked to shifting relationships in the family. The therapeutic process and circular questioning influenced changes in the family.

CONTRIBUTIONS AND LIMITATIONS

The congruity between theory and practice is one of the strengths and contributions of the systemic school. Every effort was made to carry out Bateson's theoretical schema in clinical practice. The logic of the systemic school borders on the mathematical. The training of the Italians who use this approach is very rigorous and long. Most have completed not only medical and psychiatric training but also 4 years of psychoanalysis and a 3-year training program in family therapy. Because of the depth of the training, the therapists are able to maintain a neutral stance. They have finely tuned analytic skills that allow them to generate accurate hypotheses in a short amount of time, using the logical method and framework of the system, which is one of its most important contributions.

The development of the techniques of circular questioning, positive connotation (particularly of family myths), and rituals are significant contributions of the systemic school. In particular, the highlighting of subtle differences by using circular questions appears to be useful across schools. Positive connotation—in which each family member's behavior or the problem is reframed in terms of the family's myth, showing how each person participates in the process—is a valuable paradoxical technique. Some of the rituals used in systemic therapy appear to be somewhat universal in application, such as encouraging the couple to spend time together according to certain specified conditions and taking a weekend vacation together. It may well be that Selvini Palazzoli and Prata will continue to evolve rituals that will be effective for a wide variety of presenting problems because of the systemic factors undergirding the problems.

The effective use of co-therapy and therapist/observer teams is a contribution of this school. The therapist and team are seen as part of the ecosystem, as is the referral source. The direction of interventions toward the referring professional or the therapy team is an innovation of the Milan school.

The systemic approach requires the use of a one-way mirror and a therapy team, which means it may be expensive or limited logistically. The typical therapist in private practice seeing a full patient case load would not have the time to utilize such an approach, nor would the typical patient be able to pay the costly fees involved (2½ hours × at least 3, if not 4 people = $600 to $800 per visit).

COMPARISON WITH OTHER PARADOXICAL SCHOOLS OF THERAPY

In comparing the systemic school to the strategic therapy approach of Haley and the brief therapy of Watzlawick, the following conclusions can be drawn: (1) the role of the therapist is neutral in the Milan school (Hoffman, 1981), whereas it is somewhat more directive in brief therapy and very powerful in a controlling and active participatory way in the strategic school; (2) a hierarchy is represented in Haley's approach but not in the others (Stanton, 1981); (3) the systemic school wishes to change the cognitive map of the family (Keeney & Ross, 1985), that is, information, rather than focusing on changing interactional behavior (in fact, there are no specific behavioral goals in the Milan approach—Fraser, 1986); (4) in the systemic school, the role of the therapist is aesthetic, versus pragmatic in the strategic and brief therapy schools (MacKinnon, 1983); and (5) systemic family therapy is oriented toward past, present, and future time, whereas the brief therapy and strategic schools are focused on the present (Liddle, 1983). Regardless of these differences, Taylor and McClain (1987) point out that it is important to encourage continuation of effectiveness after the termination of treatment since all of these approaches to family therapy can be short in duration. Giacomo (1986) focuses on the process of hypothesizing, which is very important in systemic, brief, and strategic therapies.

SUMMARY

Mara Selvini Palazzoli began the first center to study families in Italy in Milan in 1967. She recruited a staff of well-trained psychiatrists who were also psychoanalysts to work with anorectics and their families. In 1971, she adopted the American concepts of brief therapy developed at the Mental Research Institute, at which point some staff left. Selvini Palazzoli, Prata, Boscolo, and Cecchin formed the Milan group and conducted family therapy with one therapist working with the family and the other three observing behind the one-way mirror.

In 1975, the Milan group changed direction, focusing on the pure application of the original work of Bateson. They adopted the idea of co-evolution: The family members, the therapist, and even the referring professional were part of the same ecosystem influencing each other over time. Time is very important in the model. Hoffman (1983) developed the construct of the time cable to show that the systemic school asks questions about differences across various aspects of time: mythic, historical, onset, present, and future time. Fastforward or future questions are a useful tool for encouraging family members to create their own futures.

In 1980, the Milan team split into two groups, with Selvini Palazzoli and Prata specializing in research and therapy, and Boscolo and Cecchin emphasizing training and research. At transitions such as entering a new stage of the family life cycle, the rigid family system is not able to transform itself, leaping to a new method of functioning, but instead is stuck, attempting to keep things as they are. The Milan group has no specific goals for therapy other than the metagoal of stimulating change in the cognitive maps of families so that they find their own solutions.

The Milan group developed the principles of hypothesizing, circularity, and neutrality to apply Bateson's cybernetic model to family work. Techniques include the generation of alternative hypotheses, the circular interview, circular questions, the use of problem-focused positive connotation and pattern-focused positive connotation, and rituals. Circular questions are particularly useful in helping clients make connections and can be adapted for use across family therapy theoretical orientations. The systemic model has been developed for use with schizophrenics and anorectics.

EXERCISES

1. Pretend that you are the therapist for the Won family. You call them back to confirm the appointment. What types of questions would you ask Mrs. Won when you return her call? What is your rationale for asking each question?

2. Given the following case with the following information from a telephone contact, what would your tentative hypothesis be? Write down 10 pairs of questions (for example, before/after, onset/present).

   The mother, Rita, aged 47, is a head nurse. The father, Carl, aged 50, is an assembly line worker at a television plant. The older child is named Marva, aged 23, working as a teacher. The younger child is Dawn, aged 18, who has never worked. Rita's mother, Mabel, aged 70, came to live with the family about 3 months ago. Dawn has hallucinations that she sees her dead grandfather and he talks to her, telling her to kill the grandmother.

3. Circular questioning is one of the most useful skills of the systemic school, and it can be used across theoretical and technical orientations to family therapy. Select three people in your class to meet with after class, taking turns in asking five pairs of questions each, with a tentative hypothesis in mind so that the five pairs will be logically related to each other. Study the list of suggested questions in Table 14–1. Being able to use open-ended questions effectively and in a logical manner so that clients can make connections is an important skill.

4. Write down three feedforward or future questions that you might ask if you were the therapist in the following cases:
   a. Tom, a 20-year-old male, was hospitalized for a psychotic episode 6 months ago. His mother, Patricia, and father, Edward, have raised three children. Tom is their last child to leave home.
   b. Rebecca is 15 years old, 5 feet, 4 inches tall, and weighs 70 pounds. She is very intelligent and good at mathematics. Her dad, Bill, loves tennis and work. He owns his own business and has eight employees. He likes to control people. Her mom, Elizabeth, likes to cook, sew, and do embroidery work.

5. Using the following instructions, write a problem-focused positive connotation that is centered on the problem in Exercise 4 or on another problem of your choice and how each family member's behavior is connected to the problem:
   a. Reframe the symptom as a solution to a hypothetical problem;
   b. State how each person in the family is connected to the solution; and
   c. Make a restraining comment to encourage the client to continue performing the symptom.

   An example of a problem-focused positive connotation is: "It's good that Renate declines to eat, because Mom and Dad become worried and talk together. They talk more about how to help Renate. This is good because they must be ready when Renate leaves home, so Renate should continue her hard work of declining to eat for now."

6. Using the following points, write a pattern-focused positive connotation that is centered on a cognitive map or myth of the family and how each person participates:
   a. Reframe the pattern or myth in terms of a solution; and
   b. Comment on how each family member is involved.

An example of a pattern-focused positive connotation is: "It is as if this family believes that a family member is loyal and will always rescue another family member who is in trouble. Since the children are leaving home, it is as if family members have problems over and over again to be sure that the other family members will be there for them. If no one had any problems in the family, that would be a real problem" (Boscolo et al., 1987).

7. Prescribe rituals that could be effective with the following families.

   a. Harry and Sheila constantly fight over what should be done in the family. Sammy, their son, is having serious problems. What ritual would you prescribe if you were their family therapist?

   b. Irene and Mike are concerned about their anorectic daughter, Maureen. They are very worried and afraid to leave her alone for a moment. She is 16 years old now, but weighs only 85 pounds. Irene fixes her three meals and two snacks a day. Irene spends most of her day grocery shopping, cleaning, and taking care of the house.

8. Selvini Palazzoli's approach has evolved to the use of a set of invariant prescriptions. If you were seeing a family for 10 sessions, what invariant prescriptions would you probably use in each of the first 5 sessions?

PART THREE
THE PRACTICE OF MARITAL
AND FAMILY THERAPY

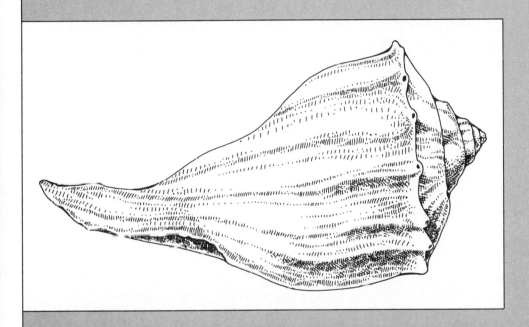

Chapter 15
The Process of Marital and Family Therapy

*The most perplexing aspect of therapy is that the relationship itself
between therapist and client is the "service" delivered.*

Wylie, 1989, p. 28.

In the previous chapters, the various theories and techniques of conducting marital
and family therapy have been elaborated. Graduate students in training often become
confused or overwhelmed by the diversity and number of approaches that have been
developed for working with couples and families. The question arises as to what
specific techniques based upon which theoretical orientations trainees will personally
adopt and actually use with clients.

In Chapter 6, an emphasis was placed on formulating a personal theory of marital
and family therapy. Even with a personal integration of diverse theories or the adoption of a single theoretical position, there still remains the question of how the actual
therapy changes from session to session until the termination of therapy. This movement and change within the therapy itself is called *the process of therapy*.

Kiesler (1973) points out that in individual therapy, regardless of theoretical orientation, in the initial stages there is an emphasis on establishing a relationship in
which the therapist accepts and supports the client as the client is. During the middle
stage of treatment, the therapist uses interventions that help the client to change
behaviors, thoughts, and feelings. In the final stage, the therapist is supportive of the
changed client and the client's new way of living. In speaking of families in therapy,
Wendorf (1984) states that families grow in an optimal way when they are "kicked"
within a supportive therapy relationship. Often, then, the initial phase of therapy,

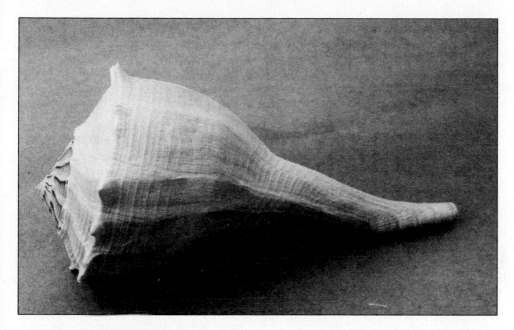

The lightning whelk represents the three-dimensional spiral of diverse marital and family therapy theories (see Chapter 6).

regardless of the theoretical orientation, focuses on the expectations for the therapeutic relationship and activities that foster its development.

Before discussing the process of therapy in depth, research on the types of skills that all family therapists should be able to exhibit and how these skills might be sequenced within the process of therapy will be discussed. Which therapeutic skills are most valuable in initial sessions, midway in therapy, and in terminating the treatment of a family? Which skills should continue to be exhibited by the therapist in order for therapy to continue and progress? These are common questions for graduate students who wish to become therapists. Such questions will be answered in this chapter.

Finally, what does it mean to be a professional marital and family therapist? What are the characteristics of a professional? What are the main professional associations affecting the field? Answers to these questions are discussed in the last part of this chapter.

Therefore, this chapter focuses on the following main topics: (1) the skills that all marital and family therapists should have; (2) the stages of marital and family therapy and how these skills are used in diverse stages; and (3) how to publicize and improve these skills through becoming a professional marital and family therapist.

SKILLS OF ALL EFFECTIVE THERAPISTS

There are two domains of therapist behavior that are necessary for effective therapeutic outcomes regardless of theoretical orientation—structuring skills and relationship skills (Alexander, Barton, Schiavo, & Parsons, 1976; Barton & Alexander, 1977, 1980, 1982; Kniskern & Gurman, 1979; Piercy, Laird, & Mohammed, 1983). Structuring skills are those directive behaviors on the part of the therapist that provide the ground rules of the therapy and the stimulus for interaction. Relationship skills are empathic behaviors on the part of the therapist that facilitate the establishment and maintenance of a therapeutic relationship. Both sets of skills are essential for effective therapy; however, if the therapist lacks empathy for a particular couple or family, they will often terminate, even if structuring skills have been present to a great degree. For example, Koch and Ingram (1985) state that therapists who hold tightly to their own goals for therapy, pushing for them, may engender a non-empathic environment in which narcissistically vulnerable couples may leave therapy because they believe they cannot meet the expectations of the therapist (the therapist's agenda) and feel misunderstood.

Piercy et al. (1983) have developed a Family Therapist Rating Scale that specifies therapist behaviors in five areas: structuring, relationship, historical, structural/process, and experiential (see Appendix A). The first two areas include generic skills essential across diverse theoretical approaches. The final three areas, usually tied to particular theoretical orientations, are comprised of the skills necessary to obtain information from the past, to link current interactional patterns in the family to the symptoms, and to create an intense affective restorative experience. A discussion of specific structuring and relationship skills follows.

Structuring Skills

Skills are easier to learn if they are taught chronologically in terms of a therapy session—what occurs first, second, and so on. Therefore, the first structuring skill that is used is to introduce oneself and to meet the family members, followed by a short introductory statement about the reason for or purpose of the session. Next, the therapist lays the ground rules for the therapy. Typically such rules cover the length of the session, the fee, how it will be paid, the frequency of the sessions, confidentiality, the name of the referral source, and any telephone calls or other contact with a member of the family. The therapist may then ask about the presenting problem and the specific needs of the family, helping them to verbalize and refine what they are seeking. It is very important to discuss expectations of the therapy next, with the therapist eliciting what the family members say that they want in terms of outcomes and the therapist clarifying what the therapist can expect to deliver successfully. Often a process of clarification and negotiation occurs.

If, during these steps, family members begin to argue, the therapist intervenes to stop negative exchanges, providing a safe and less tense environment for the therapy. During the initial session and throughout therapy, the therapist routinely asks open-ended questions (questions which cannot be answered by "yes" or "no," such as "what," "when," "how," and "who"); uses short, clear statements in communicating with the family (in outcome studies of effectiveness, the most effective therapists typically have shorter individual responses than do family members so the family does not lose the main thrust of the therapist's words); encourages family members to restate "why" questions in a more acceptable format, such as "I" statements; and changes tactics if the family neither talks nor gives the needed information. These interventions are more effective if the therapist conveys authority (Alexander & Parsons, 1982). For example, the therapist speaks without the hesitancy of anxiety, responds verbally to challenges without freezing, and sounds like an expert, assuring family members that they can work on and solve their problems. The therapist sends optimistic content messages conveying personal competence and assertiveness, completing the sentences of family members in an expert way.

The therapist then directs the actions of family members in the session. In many approaches, such as the structural and the experiential, the therapist tells the family members to interact with each other in the session, usually related to the presenting problem of the family. In this way, the therapist can actually observe the interactional patterns creating difficulty as they occur within the session. In contrast, in Bowenian-style therapy each family member is directed to speak only to the therapist. Regardless of theoretical orientation, the role of the marital and family therapist is an active one in which the therapist is directive, clearly stating the behaviors expected of the family members in the session.

Generally, there is one main theme in the session. The more experienced the family therapist, the more likely the therapist is to refocus on one topic (Pinsof, 1979). Refocusing is an important structuring tool.

Relationship Skills

The relationship skills correspond to a certain degree to the facilitative core dimensions that Rogers (1957) identified as the necessary and sufficient conditions for personality change—empathy, unconditional positive regard, respect, warmth, and genuineness. Empathy means seeing the world through the eyes of the client. The therapist listens carefully to the family members and paraphrases what they have said or reflects what the family members feel by using "feeling" words. Effective therapists use self-disclosure sparingly and appropriately to personalize the therapy and increase rapport. Confirmation of a family member's experience is essential, because often in dysfunctional families communications are not completed so family members have no confirmation of their experiences. Ivey (1987) would include the dimension of cultural empathy (being aware that differences in cultural heritage exist between the therapist and family members) and would ask about the meaning of issues in that culture and for those unique family members to understand each family member more deeply. For example, rejection of a wife by her mother-in-law might be catastrophic in a large extended Italian-American family but less of a problem in a mobile, nuclear Anglo-Saxon family.

Warmth consists of nonverbal behaviors, especially smiling and postures that express caring. A calm, soft tone of voice can convey sensitivity to the needs of family members. It is important to speak at a moderate to slow pace. Often families are excited and nervous. When the therapist speaks in a slow, deliberate manner, family members tend to imitate and slow down their interaction and verbalization, thereby reducing the tension.

Positive regard involves attending to the strengths of family members and engendering hope. Respect usually means using positive verbal responses that enhance the self-esteem of family members as well as accepting and celebrating any expression of differences. Therapists avoid blaming and refrain from criticism. They make responses aimed at enhancing the self-esteem of family members. When a family member labels another family member, the therapist translates the label into a feeling linked to a behavior—feeling/behavior integration (Barton & Alexander, 1982). For example, a family member might say, "She's a messy housekeeper," which the therapist translates into "You feel angry when she leaves papers all over your office; after all, it's your territory." Therapists take clients seriously and convey that their problems are important. Yet therapists also use humor effectively, not putting any family member down.

When therapists use these relationship skills effectively, they are able to retain families in therapy and prevent premature termination. Graduate students in counseling often learn about and practice the core facilitative dimensions in their courses in theories and techniques of counseling and psychotherapy. They need not leave these at the door of the treatment room when conducting family therapy. To the contrary, the use of concise rephrasing statements, reflections of feeling, affirmation of strengths, warmth, and empathy are recommended within marital and family therapy, especially in the initial interview, to establish rapport and build the therapeutic alliance with each family member.

In using structuring and relationship skills in marital and family therapy, models of healthy family functioning come to mind. The therapist plays the role of the parent in the family, taking charge and directing the activities of the family. However, the input of family members is also encouraged. Family members are prompted to express their feelings and thoughts, even if they differ from those of the therapist. Collaborative efforts between the therapist and the family members, similar to those in healthy families, lead to effective outcomes.

In addition to the structuring and relationship skills essential for effective marital and family therapy, the skills necessary to carry out techniques and strategies based on various theoretical approaches are also important. This text has emphasized the importance of a personal theory of healthy family functioning and therapeutic change toward health (see Chapter 3). Piercy & Sprenkle (1988) have developed a set of theory-building questions to be used by graduate students in discussing their evolving theories (Table 15–1). In addition, attempts by this author (see Chapter 6) and others to integrate diverse theories into an overall framework for treatment have been discussed (see also Feldman, 1985; Friedman, 1981; Kramer, 1980; Lebow, 1984, 1987; Liddle, 1982; Moultrup, 1981; Nelsen, 1983; Piercy & Sprenkle, 1986; Pinsof, 1983).

The behaviors that Piercy et al. (1983) have identified in the last three components (historical, structural/process, and restoration through affect) are congruent with the results of a study by Pinsof (1979), which isolated the behaviors of experienced therapists. In addition to providing support and maintaining a theme by refocusing, such therapists tend to make statements that deal with the function of the symptoms for the system ("I think your worry over Alice's bulimia may be keeping you together and reducing your conflict"). These statements point out interactional patterns happening in the session and deal with feeling interpersonally communicated and behavior in the here and now of the session. The more experience the therapists had, the greater the number of types of interventions they risked and the more active they were, making many more interventions. Therefore, using an eclectic model adapted to the realities of private practice, experienced therapists do use a number of these identified interventions during the middle phases of therapy (Piercy et al., 1983; Pinsof, 1979).

THE STAGES OF TREATMENT

Since the stages of treatment are often similar for marital therapy and family therapy, they will be considered simultaneously. Although the stages of treatment vary from one theoretical approach to another (Breunlin, 1985), the integrative, pragmatic elaboration presented can be utilized across theoretical orientations and augmented by techniques from diverse schools of therapy.

Telephone Contact

The therapeutic relationship begins with the first telephone call from a family member (Ables with Brandsma, 1977; Stierlin, Rucker-Embden, Wetzel, & Wirsching, 1980). Early on, the therapist should state how confidentiality is handled in the therapy. For example, the therapist should warn the caller that information volunteered in the private context of a telephone call will be shared with the whole family in the initial interview.

The caller should be asked about the nature of the presenting problem and the referral source. If the problem involves a child or adolescent or if a parent has been hospitalized due to a reaction to a child such as a rebellious teenager, typically an initial family therapy session is warranted to assess the need for family treatment. A choice of therapeutic modality (individual, marital, family, or group) can be made during the initial session (Sider & Clements, 1982). Usually, the therapist will also ask about any present or previous treatment. Sometimes potential clients who call are dissatisfied with their current therapists; care must be taken to encourage them to persevere with their present therapists to work through their difficulties. A long history of previous treatment is a poor prognostic sign (Coleman with Gurman, 1985).

In setting up an appointment with a new family, it is wise to ask if an emergency exists or if the client is suicidal or homicidal. The clinician assumes responsibility for the case from the point of agreement on an appointment time. The trend nationwide is for therapists to make their own initial appointments and screen potential clients before agreeing to an initial interview to manage and reduce the risk of liability. If the caller's problem is not a good match for the services provided by the therapist, the family therapist can refer the caller to other therapists or agencies for the requested services. Since a therapist can be held liable for poor services provided by a referral source when it is the only referral given, the names of at least three are usually provided to reduce any risk of successful suit.

Typically the caller will be asked if there are any questions. If asked, the therapist provides information about the fee. Often clients ask about the length of the session and how much time to allocate for the first visit. The client should be told the estimated length of the first session and the amount of time needed prior to the appointment to complete necessary paperwork and any assessment instruments.

TABLE 15–1 Family therapy theory-building questions

Influences

What models/schools of therapy have most influenced your own approach to therapy? Discuss the specific aspects of the models/schools that have influenced you.

What book has had the most impact on your approach to family therapy? Why?

Components

How does change occur in therapy and how does this relate to what you do?

What are several major theoretical tenets (assumptions) that guide your practice?

What are the major goals of your treatment approach?

How are your interventions consistent with your theoretical tenets and therapeutic goals?

How important are the following in your own evolving theory?

- Intrapsychic dynamics.
- Skill building.
- Assessment (e.g., appraisal, history taking, diagnosis).
- Administrative control/structuring skills.
- Therapist-client relationship.
- Enrichment.

How do you decide whether a behavior is "normal" or "dysfunctional"? Discuss your theory of normal and dysfunctional family functioning.

To what extent do you see therapy as education?

Discuss how one or more of these constructs or principles fit or do not fit into your evolving theory: power, resistance, homeostasis, morphogenesis, family structure, self-disclosure, self-awareness, circularity, reinforcement, transference, behavioral rehearsal, differentiation, object relations, paradox, triangles. What other constructs are important in your theory?

What relative importance do you give affect, cognitions and behavior change in your approach to family therapy? Why?

Delimitations

How do you decide what unit to see in therapy (individual, couple, family, extended family, etc.)?

Since families present multiple problems, what are your decision rules regarding what problem to attend to first?

What are the formal stages of your treatment approach?

Therapist-Client Considerations

What personal qualities do you believe are important for the therapist to demonstrate in treatment?

What personal values do you have that may affect how you work with families?

From "Family Therapy Theory-Building Questions" by F. P. Piercy and D. H. Sprenkle, 1988, *Journal of Marital and Family Therapy, 14* (3), pp. 307–309. Reprinted by permission.

TABLE 15–1 *continued*

Therapist-Client Considerations (cont.)

How do you determine and deal with the "fit" between a particular family, the treatment approach you employ, and how you employ it?

How is your approach modified when working with individuals and families with different religious, ethnic, and socioeconomic backgrounds? How does it change across life cycle stages?

What place do gender, sex role issues, and feminist theory have in your approach to therapy?

How much responsibility do you take for change and how much do you allow the family?

Interventions

A beginning therapist usually starts with a delimited range of interventions. What are *your* major interventions?

What do you attempt to do in a first session? What does this say about the theory that guides your therapy?

How does the nature of your interventions change as the stages of your therapy progress?

What role do you give in-session enactments? How important are out-of-session assignments? What guides you in the development of these assignments?

Change in Theory

How has your family therapy approach changed since entering this training program?

How could your approach to the theory and practice of family therapy be strengthened?

How do you propose to accomplish this?

Assessment and Diagnosis of the Family

To facilitate the gathering of information, demographic and other essential information is obtained on forms that are completed prior to the initial session. An intake interview protocol aids the therapist in remembering the sequence of the interview and the content areas to be addressed in the intake process (Table 15–2). The protocol is implemented over more than one session (typically as many as three sessions). In this way, the data collection does not overshadow the development of the therapeutic relationship and the implementation of some active interventions that help the family in crisis and "hook" the family into treatment. The actual form to be used in the initial session is the assessment form (Figure 5–4 in Chapter 5). The family is assessed on the diverse developmental domains over the life structures of self, career, and family to obtain triggering event(s) stages and themes of the family. The Lightning Whelk: A Co-Evolutionary Helix of the Individual Life Span provides a developmental model against which the family and its members can be evaluated in the intake process.

Also, standardized instruments can be used to assess the family. The Family Adaptability and Cohesion Evaluation Scales (FACES) instruments, especially FACES III

TABLE 15–2 Intake protocol

1. *Waiting Area.* Observe family members in the waiting area and note their behaviors or lack of interaction.

2. *Making Contact.* Introduce self to family members, ask the name and something about each family member to establish rapport with each member, and join the family.

3. *Seating.* Observe the arrangement of family members for evidence of an effective hierarchy or coalitions.

4. *Ground Rules.* State the ground rules concerning the intake process and the frame of therapy (fees, length of session, frequency of sessions, and confidentiality).

5. *Non-Initiating Spouse.* Begin to ask open-ended questions about the presenting problem of the spouse who did not initiate the therapy such as, "What brings you to treatment now?"

6. *Other Spouse.* Ask the other spouse a similar question.

7. *Assessment Form.* Alternating spouses, assess strengths and areas needing improvement in the diverse developmental domains across the life structures of family, career, and self (see assessment form, based on the concept of the lightning whelk, Figure 5–4).

8. *Assessment of Risk.* Alternating spouses, assess risk—any feelings of depression (assess vegetative signs) or homicidal tendencies, alcohol/drug use, spouse abuse, child abuse, sexual abuse, medications, medical problems, and any previous mental health treatment.

9. *Make Contact With Children.* Ask similar questions of each child, for example, "What do you think the problems are in this family?" "How have you been feeling?" and "Do you feel sad or depressed?" Ask each child about how parents relate and each parent about how each child gets along with the other parent.

10. *History of Relationships.* Ask each spouse for a short history of the marital relationship and about the family of origin. What strengths do members of the family of origin have? Do they use or abuse alcohol or drugs? How satisfied are the partners with the marriage, including sexual, affectionate, and instrumental behaviors? How realistic are their expectations of marriage?

11. *Direct Interaction.* If marital therapy, direct each spouse to talk with the other about the presenting problems while the therapist observes. If family therapy, direct the family members to talk with each other about the presenting problems.

12. *Actively Intervene.* Based on observation of the interaction and the content of answers to previous questions, intervene in an active way by using a quid pro quo, a paradoxical intervention, a behavioral contract, or another active intervention based on the family's level of development.

13. *Homework.* Give homework assignment.

14. *Summary.* Summarize what has happened, noting any progress. Become aware of feelings evoked by family and possible family theme.

(Olson, Portner, & Lavee, 1987), can be used as pretest/posttests to measure therapeutic outcome. FACES III consists of 20 items, which are repeated twice: once when directions are given asking family members to describe their family as it is now and again after directions are given to respond as to how they would like their family to become—the ideal. The scores can be recorded in graphic profiles that show discrepancies between the real and ideal—areas of potential growth—for the family.

The Family Environmental Scale (FES), by Moos and Moos (1981), is the most popular instrument for assessing families within health care settings (Campbell, 1986). There are three forms: Form R (the Real Form), Form I (the Ideal Form), and Form E (the Expectations Form). The first two can be used together to measure dissatisfaction, and the third is typically used with engaged couples. The FES measures three relationship dimensions (cohesion, expressiveness, and conflict), five personal growth dimensions (independence, achievement motivation, intellectual/cultural, recreational, and religious/moral), and two systemic maintenance dimensions (control and organization). Translations are available in several languages.

A third family assessment tool that is being used frequently is the Family Assessment Device (FAD), developed by Epstein, Baldwin, and Bishop (1983), to measure family functioning against the McMaster Model of Family Functioning. Fredman and Sherman (1987) especially recommend the 12-item General Functioning Scale as a reliable, short measure of family functioning.

Therapists can choose one instrument among FACES III, the FES, and the General Functioning Scale of the FAD to administer as a pretest/posttest measure of therapeutic outcome or only at the beginning of therapy to aid treatment planning. A number of other available instruments can also be used, such as the Family Strengths instrument by Olson, Larsen, and McCubbin (1987), the Family Crisis-Oriented Personal Evaluation Scales by McCubbin, Olson, and Larsen (1987), and the Family Inventory of Life Events and Changes by McCubbin, Patterson, and Wilson (1987)—three of the Minnesota Family Inventories. A therapist must weigh carefully the purpose of the information to decide how much time can be allotted to such paper-and-pencil assessments. An instrument should not be given if the information will not be used in treatment planning and if the results will not be shared with the family.

Tomm and Sanders (1983) developed a three-part model for assessing the structure, functioning, and development of families. In the initial interview, data are obtained, from which a list of problems is generated. Treatment plans with specific interventions are designed for the problems that have been identified. Such an assessment typically proceeds from the individual subsystem level, to the marital subsystem, to the family as a whole, and to other systems in the environment with which the family interacts.

With marital therapy, typically either the Marital Adjustment Test of Locke and Wallace (1959) or Spanier's (1976) Dyadic Adjustment Scale is given. Particularly effective is the MATE (Schutz, 1967, 1976), which measures how each partner sees the other and how each thinks the other sees the partner. This instrument often reveals that it is the spouse's beliefs about what the partner is viewed as perceiving about the spouse that creates difficulties in close relationships. New instruments by Olson,

Fournier, and Druckman (1982), called PREPARE and ENRICH, offer promise for engaged couples (PREPARE) (Flowers & Olson, 1986) and for spouses who want to improve their relationship (ENRICH).

For those with appropriate coursework and training, the use of personality inventories can be very helpful in marital therapy. There is a computerized marriage counseling printout for the 16PF that is useful. The Myers-Briggs Type Indicator provides data about the complementary personality styles that are most compatible, according to the theory of Jung. Some college campuses even have clubs based on the personality codes of this test, one way to meet a potential marital partner with a similar personality style. The Millon Clinical Multi-Axial Inventory (MCMI) provides useful data about the personality disorders or traits of marital partners and documents *DSM III-R* diagnoses for individual psychotherapy. The Minnesota Multi-Phasic Personality Inventory (MMPI) can also be useful.

After assessing whole families and married couples, typically a diagnosis is made. Liddle (1983) compared diagnosis and assessment among six schools of therapy. The most often used diagnoses, however, are those from the *Diagnostic Statistical Manual of Mental Disorders—Revised.* Simon (1989) points out that "faced with insurance companies that often don't recognize family therapy as a reimbursable form of treatment, family therapists typically resort to the subterfuge of calling what they do 'individual psychotherapy' and assigning somebody in the family—take your pick—a DSM III-R diagnosis" (p. 2). According to the *Casebook on Ethical Principles of Psychologists* (1987), such a procedure is considered unethical. DSM III-R code V-61.10 should be used to indicate marital problems. It is much better over the long term to tell it like it is than to have an irate married couple or family have to pay back an insurance company that has found out that, indeed, marital therapy was the treatment provided.

The Intake Process

A delicate balance needs to be maintained in order to hook the family into treatment. If too much session time is spent asking questions of the family members (which can resemble a "third degree" treatment to a stressed family), a family may not come back to the next session. At a number of community mental health centers, more than 50% of the families who present for treatment do not return for a second session. Family members need to feel supported and understood in the initial session. In addition, some action needs to be taken to deal with the problem. Family members resist giving information to answer questions about the history of the family and other required areas if they do not understand that it is important and relevant to the reason they are in therapy.

With the amount of information that must be obtained in the intake process to provide data for treatment planning and risk management to protect a private practitioner or agency from liability and potential litigation, it is unrealistic to expect that one intake interview will be sufficient. Too much emphasis can be placed upon data gathering to the detriment of the building of the relationship and the use of innovative, active interventions such as strategic or systemic paradoxical techniques, and a family may not return. Typically one to three sessions are necessary to complete the intake process (see intake protocol, Table 15–2, for the sequence of the intake process), and even then an ongoing process of assessment occurs during therapy. The therapist can gather high-risk information during the initial session, along with establishing rapport and making an initial, active intervention. In the next sessions, additional developmental and family of origin material can be obtained.

With the intake process extending over three sessions, the stages of any given intake session remain the same. First, introductions and informal welcoming occur. Next, open-ended questions are asked to obtain some of the necessary information. Priority is given to obtaining data related to reducing potential risk. In family therapy, the therapist may go around the group, asking each family member about what the family member thinks the presenting problems are. Finally, the family or couple is directed to interact with each other so that the therapist can observe the interaction, interrupting and intervening where necessary (see Table 15–2).

From observation, the therapist identifies problematic interactional behavior patterns being enacted in the session between spouses or family members. Based on the identified presenting problems and the behavioral transactions, the therapist directs an active intervention. Sometimes homework assignments are given so that new behaviors are practiced between sessions. The therapist summarizes the session, requests the reactions of family members, decides on the modality of proposed treatment (marital, family, or individual), and sets future appointments.

These interview stages are repeated in subsequent intake sessions as additional information is obtained. Typically, intake questions are asked of the parent who was not the initiator of the therapy in order to engage this party in treatment. Next, the other parent, if there is an intact marriage, is engaged. Finally, each child is asked a question, beginning with the oldest and ending with the youngest. By using this process of questioning, all members of the family become involved in the treatment.

In obtaining information about multilevel systems, it is important to gather information from the smallest subsystems first, building up to the marital subsystem, parent-child subsystem, and finally the family system (Tomm & Sanders, 1983). Meaning emanates from each human being and is the starting point for a systems assessment. As problem lists evolve for individuals, problematic patterns of interaction between individuals are identified, followed by the abstract sequences within the family that are creating difficulties. Sometimes more is said by what is not stated by the family than by what is.

A systems assessment checklist (see Appendix B) has been formulated to be used by the therapist after the initial session and before subsequent sessions to review what further information needs to be obtained. In this way, a multilevel systemic evaluation can be conducted, including the macrosystems, the family system, the marital subsystem, the parent-child subsystems, the sibling subsystem, and the individual subsystems of the family.

Most importantly, a family treatment plan form has been developed to aid in consolidating the information essential to treatment planning and effective health-care delivery (Figure 15–1). This form and the assessment form (see Figure 5–4) are placed in the client folder to document the assessment process undergirding decisions about diagnosis and treatment. Tentative goals and appropriate strategies or techniques for reaching them are selected. These goals can then be negotiated with the family, where appropriate.

FIGURE 15–1   Family treatment plan

Names and ages of family members _____

_____

_____

_____

Reason for referral _____   _____

Stage of family life cycle _____

Developmental description of family (Attach assessment form) _____

_____

_____

_____

_____

_____

_____

Assessment of risk: Vegetative signs (weight loss or gain, sleep pattern, crying, depressed mood, loss of interest)

_____

_____

_____

Assessment of risk of suicide, homicide, alcohol, drugs, eating disorders, abuse

Comment: _____

_____

_____

Previous therapy: _____

_____

_____

Requested release for contact or records   Yes _____ No _____

Expectations for present therapy: _____

_____

_____

DSM III diagnosis, if any _____

Medical consultation needed?   Yes _____ No _____ To whom _____

_____ For what? _____

Other referral needed?   Yes _____ No _____ To whom _____

_____ For what? _____

Relationship history: marital _____

_____

_____

_____

Families of origin _____

_____

_____

FIGURE 15−1 *continued*

Each child _____
_____
_____
_____
_____
_____
_____

(Draw genogram, when appropriate, on back of sheet)
Typical day _____
_____

Theme of the family _____
_____

Feeling tone of the family _____
Interactional patterns in session _____
_____
_____
_____
_____

Key defense mechanisms _____
Strengths of the family _____
_____
_____
_____
_____

Problems _____
_____
_____

Hypotheses _____
_____

Diagram of present and proposed family structures:

FIGURE 15—1 *continued*

Goals	Techniques/Strategies

Signature _____ Date _____

In addition, care must be taken to refer for medical consultations when warranted. For example, a depressed family member may need to be evaluated by a psychiatrist for possible prescription of an antidepressant. Or a spouse may need to be referred to a medical specialist for treatment of a physical problem causing a sexual dysfunction. In some cases, the therapist may need to refer a family member to a 28-day treatment program for alcohol or drug rehabilitation. It is also imperative to obtain permission to contact previous therapists concerning what occurred in prior therapy. The assessment of any risks due to potential suicide or abuse should be well documented. All of these factors impact the effectiveness of any treatment plan formulated by the marital and family therapist.

The Work of the Middle Stage

According to the integration of theories proposed in Chapter 6, the more active interventions, such as the paradoxical interventions of the strategic and systemic schools, are very effective in the beginning stages of family treatment. As families move into the middle stage of therapy, the pace is slower but deeper. Often feelings emerge that need to be dealt with through psychoanalytically oriented efforts to uncover early object relations formed in the family of origin.

Humanistic/experiential/existential interventions are used to consider their meaning within the context of the family. The belief system of the family may be shared as the family members trust the therapist and relax within the therapeutic context. The therapist may use cognitive behavioral approaches to change values and beliefs, leading to long-term change. All of these interventions are less spectacular than earlier systemic, strategic, or structural moves. Therefore, the therapist may become bogged down and bored in this middle stage of treatment.

McGuire (1985) recommends exhibiting self-confidence and leadership skills, maintaining the focus and frame of the therapy when family members press for a negative view and obtaining supervision from a senior colleague to obtain support and fresh ideas for the case. Holding firm can be particularly important when dealing with narcissistically vulnerable couples who continue to test the therapist throughout treatment and who need a lengthy middle phase of therapy.

One indication that the middle stage of treatment is well under way is the surfacing of ambivalent feelings on the part of family members (Nelsen, 1983). Often the therapist needs to recognize each person for attendance and participation. Open expression of direct ambivalence about treatment is a healthy sign. When family members state such feelings directly to the therapist and work toward resolution of any problems, they make important therapeutic progress, even though their complaints can be frustrating or demoralizing to an inexperienced therapist.

Other changes that may occur in the middle stage of treatment include additional work on structure and developmental issues (McGuire, 1985). For example, in the early stages of treatment, the therapist may have worked to strengthen the hierarchy in the family. Now, in the middle stages, the spouses want to work alone to increase their level of intimacy, thereby strengthening the structure further. Parents may wish to deal with individual developmental issues that are creating pressure on them by sorting them out in marital therapy. Therefore, what began as family therapy, with all members of the family present, has now evolved to marital therapy, focusing on what each spouse is experiencing internal to the self.

One way that a therapist can indicate that the middle phase of treatment is ending is to decrease the frequency of sessions. Client families appropriately interpret such a change as a sign of progress.

The Termination of Therapy

It is important to set a formal date of termination. Often client families will cancel appointments, present with additional problems, or in some other way attempt to sabotage the ending of treatment. The therapist has become a trusted member of the family and a role model upon whom they can depend. Separating from such a relationship can engender many conflicting feelings and thoughts.

Sometimes the termination mirrors the death of a parent or other loved one earlier in life. Unresolved grief toward earlier significant figures from the past may surface during this time. Termination should be discussed in a minimum of three sessions—one in which the formal date is set, one session prior to the last, and the final farewell session in which the door is left open if the family wants to return when undergoing future transitions.

During the termination stage, it is particularly important for the family members and the therapist to discuss what they liked about the therapy and what they did not. The progress made should be pointed out and reinforced by each (Heath, 1985). Often families leave treatment because the pain has been reduced, because they are dissatisfied with the treatment being provided, or because they are afraid of what will happen in the treatment if they continue. It is important that the therapist use open-ended questions, asking about each of these possibilities in turn and eliciting true feelings and thoughts. If dissatisfaction is present, a referral to another provider is given, accompanied by statements of hope and encouragement that therapy can still work for the family even though they were not completely pleased with this therapist. Reinforcing the belief in the efficacy of professional help is crucial to increasing and maintaining the health of the family.

Some legal authorities encourage therapists to send letters to premature terminators, emphasizing that, in the therapist's opinion, additional therapy is needed and including a list of at least three professionals to whom the patient(s) can go (Stromberg et al., 1988). Such a procedure protects the therapist from liability on the grounds of abandonment.

BECOMING A PROFESSIONAL MARITAL AND FAMILY THERAPIST

What does it mean to be a professional? A professional is a person who meets the educational, training, and experience criteria to belong to an association of similar practitioners. They adhere to a code of ethics that governs their conduct in the delivery of services to clients. In addition, there is a body of research or knowledge base undergirding the field. The network of colleagues is called a profession. A professional has a great deal of freedom within the constraints of obligations to society and fellow human beings. Therefore, there is an accompanying expectation of autonomous, responsible functioning. A professional takes the initiative to ensure client welfare and to consistently gain new knowledge of treatment techniques and technology. It is an honor to belong to a professional association, and members should conduct themselves in an exemplary manner that will reflect favorably on colleagues in the association.

In contrast to most jobs, where individuals are held liable for not following orders, professionals may be held legally liable for following orders rather than stating their positions and holding firm. For example, a doctoral practicum supervisee offhandedly reported that a teenage client had shared the fact of a recently attempted suicide with the comment of wanting to do it again the next time that he was allowed to return home. The supervisee had not reported the conversation, tried to talk with the client about the situation, or notified the parents. During supervision, the supervisee was held responsible for taking action in the matter by bringing it to the attention of the on-site supervisor, which the supervisee faithfully did.

During the next supervision session, the supervisee did not volunteer what had happened, so he was asked. As it turned out, the on-site supervisor decided to do nothing and told the supervisee to forget about it, and the supervisee had followed orders. The supervisee was encouraged to use an ethical decision-making process to generate alternatives. After thinking about the ethical principles, especially client welfare, he decided to write a request to his on-site supervisor that action be taken. Soon the supervisor and agency took action to observe the client, via a suicide watch with no home passes, and to develop emergency guidelines, thereby preventing a possible suicide.

A therapist can, indeed, be held legally (*Tarasoff v. Regents of University of California,* 1976) and ethically liable for taking no action. For example, if a client were to express thoughts of suicide as a part of marital and family therapy, the therapist would be held responsible if the client committed suicide and the therapist had done nothing to assess the situation. The remaining family members of the dead client would probably sue for damages and rightly so, because the professional had failed to act based on the knowledge base and ethical code of the profession. The role of a marital and family therapist is an active one, structuring interaction and taking responsibility for any actions initiated or omitted. As therapists, we are as responsible for what we fail to do as what we do.

Belonging to Professional Associations

To be a professional is to belong and to participate fully in professional associations. Membership and attendance at conventions and other events provide opportunities for learning about the field and staying current. Most professional association memberships include subscriptions to at least one newsletter and one journal, with most providing even more. Reading the literature acquaints the member with the body of research that undergirds the practice of the profession.

Most importantly, the professional association is a network of peers dedicated to the profession who can become mentors, give informal advice, and furnish leads for jobs and promotions in the field. Such role models are invaluable to the development of a professional career. In *Pathfinders,* Sheehy (1981) points out the value of polestars, those individuals who are not parents but who serve as guides because they have been through similar adult developmental passages. The quality of these relationships can sustain people through difficult times, both professionally and personally. In terms of a career over the life span, the professional association can be a buffer in hard times with professional polestars sharing alternative solutions and other job options

A professional continues to learn about the field and to stay current by attending workshops and classes.

with those whose institutions have closed or whose contracts for private services have decreased.

Although this is important for every professional, it is even more valuable for first-generation professionals and those newly involved in the labor force, such as women and the first-generation college-educated members of minority groups. In addition to formal and informal networks within the professional association, there are often women's caucuses and networks supporting minority concerns. It can be reassuring to identify with professionals of similar backgrounds who share world views and promote support and growth of other individuals.

Professional associations can be only what you make them. Some people belong for years but never make a presentation, join a committee, write a position paper, or make a friend. Others, beginning in graduate school, volunteer to serve on committees, offer to give presentations with their faculty advisors, send vita and letters of request to become journal editorial reviewers, and make friends by attending meetings and introducing themselves, learning as much as they can about the field and other professionals.

In addition, leadership in professional organizations prepares a person for positions of responsibility within organizations and institutions. Active participation in professional associations means a voice in the future direction of the field. If you have not already joined professional associations, join now while you are in graduate school when you can join for half-price and obtain the journals at a reduced price or for free, using them to help with papers and other course assignments. Now is the time to make a commitment to grow and develop with the field throughout your life.

Marital and Family Therapy: Professional Specialization or Separate Field?

As stated in Chapter 1, marital and family therapy began as a specialty within other professions (Olson, 1970). Most people practicing marriage counseling or family therapy held membership in the National Association of Social Workers, the American Psychiatric Association, the American Psychological Association, the American Association for Counseling and Development, or other professional associations in home economics, pastoral counseling, sex therapy, medicine, nursing, or sociology in addition to their membership in the American Association for Marriage and Family Therapy (AAMFT). In other words, practitioners first saw their professional identity as that of a social worker, psychiatrist, psychologist, or counselor, and then secondarily according to what they predominantly did—marital and family therapy. For example, a psychologist might identify first with the American Psychological Association as a psychologist and then with the American Association for Clinical Hypnosis because of conducting a practice that used hypnosis heavily. Today this historical trend continues, but to a lesser degree as the majority of the members of the AAMFT now list "marriage and family therapist" as their primary identification.

Such dual membership has had advantages and disadvantages. The cross-disciplinary mix of professionals focused on marital and family therapy has created an extremely stimulating environment for the fertilization of ideas and the inculcation of a broad view of the helping professions. On the other hand, people may experience tension when resources of time, energy, and finances are worn thin by participation in a number of associations. As licensing laws have been passed for marriage and family therapists in a number of states, some professionals may be viewed as disloyal by a few of those in their primary profession who identify with only one professional organization.

One result of this tension has been the development of interest networks and divisions related to marital and family therapy in other professional associations. For example, the Division of Family Psychology—Division 43—was established within the American Psychological Association in 1984. This division has its own journal and highlights the role of marital and family therapy researchers and practitioners within psychology.

Within the American Association for Counseling and Development, one of its founding divisions, the Association for Counselor Education and Supervision (ACES), formed the Marital and Family Therapy Interest Network in 1982 under the leadership of Tom Elmore, president of ACES. Interested practitioners met at the Los Angeles convention and drew up a list of goals and objectives for the network. Since courses in marriage and family counseling were the single largest source of additional new classes in counselor education and supervision, according to Wantz, Scherman, and Hollis (1982), the idea of helping counselor education programs gear up for training in marital and family therapy was proposed, and a monograph, entitled *Issues in Training Marriage and Family Therapists* (Okun & Gladding, 1983), was published.

In the monograph, Thomas (1983) compared accreditation requirements for counselor education programs (the Council of Accreditation of Counseling and Related Educational Programs—CACREP) and for marital and family therapy programs (AAMFT), suggesting that counselor education programs consider accreditation by both professional groups simultaneously. As interest in marital and family therapy continued to increase within the counseling profession, the International Association of Marriage and Family Counselors became an organizational affiliate of AACD in 1989.

In addition, another association has developed, devoted to research on families and family therapy. The American Family Therapy Association (AFTA) is composed of mainly doctoral-level researchers and practitioners. This organization does not lobby for licensure but rather functions as a scientific association focused on improving the quality and amount of scholarship on families and family therapy. Founded in 1978 with Murray Bowen as its first president, the AFTA admits to membership only teachers of family therapy with 5 years of teaching experience who have made some contribution to the field of family therapy. The AFTA is a scientific society of advanced professionals dedicated to research and dissemination of knowledge related to families and family therapy (Nichols, 1984).

At the present time in the United States, the question of whether marital and family therapy is a specialty or a profession remains. The answer is "both." The case has already been made for its early development as a specialty within other professional associations and the recent establishment of a scientific society for the study of families and family therapy (AFTA). However, since being founded in 1942, the American Association for Marriage and Family Therapy has grown in numbers and strength. AAMFT has formulated and updated a code of ethics for marital and family therapists (see Appendix C). A body of research on marriage counseling and family therapy has been refined into a knowledge base undergirding the practice of the profession. AAMFT accreditation of marital and family therapy programs was recognized by HEW in 1978. Finally, state legislatures have recognized marital and family therapists as freestanding health-care providers by passing certification and licensure laws. Thus, marital and family therapy meets the criteria for a separate profession (Ard & Ard, 1976; Haley, 1984; Huber & Baruth, 1987; Nichols, 1979; Winkle, Piercy, & Hovestadt, 1981).

A three-level model of training for the preparation of marriage and family therapists has been proposed by Fenell and Hovestadt (1986). The first level represents a graduate degree in family therapy; the second level, a specialty within another graduate degree program such as counseling or psychology; and the third level, elective courses in family therapy within a department or as continuing education. In such a model, the first level represents marital and family therapy as a separate profession; the second level, as a specialty within another professional degree; and, the third level, as a course to provide skills.

This text has been designed to be used in the latter two levels of this training model, although it could be used in a marital and family therapy degree program as well. However, typically in such a degree program there are separate courses in a number of areas. These areas are covered in this book—for example, family development, behavioral marital therapy, and object relations family therapy. This text aims to cover the material professionals should know in order to conduct family therapy, especially for students who are limited to one graduate course in the discipline. The three-level training model builds upon an earlier paper by Hovestadt, Fenell, and Piercy (1983), first delivered on a panel sponsored by the ACES Marital and Family Interest Network.

The American Association for Marriage and Family Therapy

In 1934, Lester Dearborn, a sexual hygiene counselor with the Y.M.C.A. in Boston, generated the idea of a professional association for marriage and family relations and discussed it with Dr. Emily Mudd, who headed the Marriage Council of Philadelphia. It was not until he talked with Ernest Groves, a family life educator at the University of North Carolina, that the idea began to take hold. Groves called for the formation of the association in 1942 at the annual conference on the family that he convened each year (Broderick & Schrader, 1981). Dearborn convened the first organizational meeting for the association with Dr. Robert Laidlaw, Drs. Ernest and Gladys Groves, Dr. Emily Mudd, Dr. Abraham Stone, Dr. Valerie Parker, and Dr. Robert L. Dickenson on June 20, 1942. Ernest Groves was elected as the first president of the American Association of Marriage Counselors in 1945. The association changed its name to the American Association of Marriage and Family Counselors in 1970, and again in 1979 to its present name, the American Association for Marriage and Family Therapy.

Presently there are two levels of membership in the AAMFT—associate membership and clinical membership. In addition, a separate credential as an AAMFT-approved supervisor exists and is open to non-AAMFT members.

One of the unique characteristics of the AAMFT training and membership model is the supervision. Although it is similar to the apprenticeship model practiced in training professionals in individual therapy, live supervision of marital and family therapy is used. Trainees have receivers or "bugs" in their ears so that supervisors, who watch through one-way mirrors, can give supervisees feedback during the actual therapy session with the family (Beavers, 1986).

Supervision in family therapy began in the same way that supervision of individual psychoanalytic therapy was and is carried out—that is, by the verbal sharing of what happened in the session and session notes. This sharing eventually evolved from role play, to exploration of genograms of the therapist's family, then to videotapes of the family therapy session. It further evolved from live supervision from behind a one-way mirror with a meeting after the session, to a planned break in the therapy for consultation, then to such observation with a telephone call to the trainee in the session, to communicating with the trainee who was "bugged." Later, the supervisors' notes were actually carried into the treatment room, and finally the supervisors were in the treatment room as a chorus, so that supervisors became part of the actual therapy session (Byng-Hall, de Carteret, & Whiffen, 1982).

Using an earphone or bug is the most straightforward way of impacting the therapist's interventions with the family and is characteristic of family therapy supervision. As early as 1973, Montalvo spelled out the ground rules for live supervision that make it work. Byng-Hall (1982) shares the process that he uses to introduce the use of the earphone or "bug" to his supervisory group. Liddle and Halpin (1978) reviewed the literature on supervision in family therapy training.

In addition to membership and supervisory credentials, the AAMFT accredits training programs in marital and family therapy. The *Directory of Accredited Marital and Family Therapy Training Programs* (Reid, Kipnis, & Hardy, 1988) states the demographic and curricular information about each of the 19 accredited master's, 9 accredited doctoral, and 11 post-degree programs. All of these programs must meet the curricular and other criteria for accreditation by the AAMFT.

Another significant function that the AAMFT has provided for marital and family therapy as a profession has been its intensive lobbying efforts to pass certification or licensure bills in state legislatures. Certification bills typically protect the use of a title, whereas licensure bills not only restrict the use of a title, but they also forbid the practice of marriage and family therapy unless the person has a license. Currently, 17 states have bills that regulate marital and family therapy ("MFT Regulation Growing," 1988). In some of these states, there are joint boards that govern marital and family therapy as well as other professions such as professional counseling.

One of the most important contributions of the AAMFT has been its development of a code of ethics, entitled the *AAMFT Code of Ethical Principles for Marriage and Family Therapists* (see Appendix C). As one key characteristic of a profession, the refinement of the code of ethics, which went into effect on August 1, 1988, was an important step in the evolution of marital and family therapy as a separate profession. In Chapter 16, the ethics of marital and family therapy will be considered based on this code as well as the codes of the American Association for Counseling and Development, the American Psychological Association, the National Association of Social Workers, and the American Psychiatric Association.

SUMMARY

Across all theoretical orientations, marital and family therapists must exhibit structuring skills and relationship skills to be effective therapists. Structuring skills include initial introductions, setting the ground rules for therapy, asking about the presenting problem, and clarifying/negotiating expectations for therapy. In addition, the therapist is active: intervening to stop negative interactions; asking open-ended questions; making short, clear statements to the family; encouraging "I" statements on the part of family members; changing tactics if needed; conveying authority with assertive, optimistic content messages; directing the family in behaviors expected in the session; and refocusing the family to one central theme for the session. Relationship skills include confirming a family member's experience; expanding empathy to an interest in the culture of the family; showing warmth, including slow, calm voice tone and caring nonverbal behaviors; focusing on the strengths of the family through positive regard; enhancing self-esteem through respect; and converting labels into a feeling linked to a behavior.

Depending on the theoretical orientation, additional skills are used by experienced therapists. They tend to make statements dealing with the function of symptoms for the family system, point out interactional patterns in the session, and deal with behavior and feelings interpersonally communicated in the present. The more experience the therapist has, the more active she is, especially during the middle phase of treatment.

The stages of treatment include: (1) telephone contact; (2) assessment and diagnosis of the family; (3) the intake process; (4) the work of the middle stage; and (5) the termination of therapy. Both structuring and relationship skills are used throughout the stages of treatment, but particular care should be taken to balance these skills in the initial phases of treatment. If data collection is overemphasized, the family may drop out of treatment before a relationship has been built. Typically, many more active interventions are made during the middle stage of therapy, and during the termination stage, the therapist is more supportive of the changes that have been made by the family.

Marital and family therapists increase their skills by belonging to professional associations. A code of ethics governs their conduct in the delivery of services to clients. The American Association for Marriage and Family Therapy is the main professional association for marital and family therapists, although many belong to interest divisions within other professional associations such as the Division of Family Psychology of the American Psychological Association and the International Association of Marriage and Family Counselors, a division of the American Association for Counseling and Development. The American Family Therapy Association is a scientific association that focuses on increasing research on families and family therapy.

EXERCISES

1. Your instructor will show a videotape of a family therapy session. Using the family therapist rating scale (see Appendix A), rate the behaviors exhibited by the therapist and generate a profile for this therapist.

2. Count off according to the instructions of the professor. You will be assigned to a group of six in which the first person is the family therapist, the second person is the mother, the third person is the father, the fourth person is the oldest child,

the fifth person is the youngest child, and the sixth person is an observer. Review the intake protocol (Table 15–2). Using the assessment form (Figure 5–4) and the information from the following case study, conduct an intake interview with the family until your instructor calls "time." At that point, the observer will share feedback.

Vignette

Alice and Harry Madison divorced 5 years ago but the hostility and anger between them remains. Harry is a recovered alcoholic who thinks that Alice should never drink. Harry does not have a job, and Alice is dating Sylvester, whom she would like to marry. Alice is functioning well in her responsible administrative job. Susan, their 16-year-old daughter, was picked up for soliciting by the local police and taken to the police station. At the police station, amphetamines were found in her purse. The judge ordered a family intervention because it was Susan's first offense. Both Harry and Alice say that they are willing to do anything to help their daughter. Alice found laxatives in Susan's room. Susan's weight had dropped significantly over the last 2 months. She was experiencing rapid mood swings. In particular, Susan has been preoccupied with her body image, mainly her weight, and engaging in excessive exercise activities to lose weight. Her younger brother, Michael (12 years old), feels close to his mother. He excels at everything he does, including athletics, social activities, and academics.

3. Having finished the simulated interview with the Madison family, complete a family treatment plan form on this family. Simulating a staffing conference, present your plan to the same group with whom you simulated the intake interview. Brainstorm and gather ideas about treatment goals and the possible strategies you would use in working with the family to reach the goals. You may wish to review the techniques covered in previous

chapters (see Tables 6–4 and 6–5 and Figure 6–4) to help you in selecting techniques. Also review the systems assessment checklist in Appendix B. What further information may be important to obtain from the Madison family in subsequent sessions?

4. Given the following case study, complete the family treatment plan form (see Figure 15–1) for the Jones family. Following the directions of your instructor, form a small group. Share your diagnosis and treatment plan with the group. Develop a consensus treatment plan, which will be presented to the class by the leader of your group.

Vignette

The family was referred to family therapy by the treating physician when the older child, John, was hospitalized. John was a scholar who wanted to attend an Ivy League college. When he was rejected by the college of his choice, he was found wandering on lower Broadway unshaven and unkempt, carrying on a conversation with imaginary people who he said were reprimanding him for failing and were persecuting him. Ted, the father of the family, had planned to go to college when his father died suddenly. Ted became the "man of the house" and delayed his plans for higher education in order to protect and care for his mother out of a sense of obligation. His mother, Henrietta, lives with the family. Cecile, John's mother, has always felt closer to John than to Sally, his younger sister. In reaction, Sally continually demeans John. Cecile has not been well over the years, having been hospitalized for her first psychotic episode after the birth of Sally. Ted withdrew from his family at that time, taking a job as a traveling salesman, and has limited contact with the family. Sally has become involved with a married college student and has vented her anger about her own frustrations with him toward her brother by verbal assaults about his academic ability and of his inadequacy as a male in filling his father's role.

Chapter 16
The Ethical Practice of Marital and Family Therapy

Ethics is an attitude of caring for both the short-term and long-term welfare of clients.

Michele Thomas

Presenting the marital and family therapist as a full-fledged member of the health-care team has been one of the main themes of this book. To be an effective health-care practitioner, a marital and family therapist must act responsibly in the health-care arena according to a code of ethics. Therapists who violate ethical codes may be brought before the state licensing boards that regulate the practice of health care and/or risk civil litigation for negligence or malpractice.

Ethical codes are based on key underlying principles, especially the welfare of the patients being treated. Sometimes what may appear to be helpful to a client in the short term may be damaging or even severely traumatic over the long term. Through the experience of practitioners in the field, research on therapeutic effectiveness, and legal cases over the years, what is ethically appropriate practice for health-care professionals in various situations has been established.

This chapter focuses on the main ethical considerations in setting up and maintaining a marital and family therapy practice. First, the process of ethical decision-making will be emphasized because it can be used to deal with any situation that arises in a health-care practice. Then the following specific ethical concerns will be addressed: (1) competency; (2) confidentiality; (3) informed consent; (4) duty to warn and involuntary hospitalization; (5) dealing with suicidal clients; (6) welfare of the client; (7) ethical issues peculiar to marital and family therapy, including systemic epistemology, gender and family therapy, cross-cultural issues, and the use of paradox; and (8) interfacing with the legal system. Being an effective marital and family therapy health-care provider over the long term requires understanding and implementing these ethical guidelines, both appropriately and consistently.

ETHICAL DECISION-MAKING PROCESS

Every professional in training should formulate an ethical decision-making process so that it is ready to use when an ethical dilemma occurs (Van Hoose, 1980; Van Hoose & Kottler, 1985). It is often too late to think about the steps to take when actually in the middle of a life-threatening emergency or under pressure in a family session. Therefore, the following steps are suggested as an ethical decision-making process (Table 16–1).

Each of the steps in the ethical decision-making process will now be elaborated, and specific advice is given.

Define the Situation

Ask yourself questions about the situation, such as: (1) What happened? (2) When did it occur? (3) Where did it occur? (4) How did it happen? (5) Who is involved in the situation? (6) What issues are involved? (7) How serious a situation is it? (8) What do you think about it? (9) How do you feel about it? (10) Is this a possible ethical dilemma? It is important to ask oneself these questions about many of the situations that occur in conducting marital and family therapy with families so that such self-talk becomes an automatic response. In this way, most potentially harmful situations can be dealt with effectively before actual damage is done to anyone, including the family members and the therapist. If the answer to the 10th question is "yes," then the therapist should move to the next step of the ethical decision-making process.

TABLE 16–1 Steps in the ethical decision-making process

1. Define the situation.
2. Consult ethical codes and other sources.
3. Generate a continuum of alternative actions.
4. Evaluate each alternative by the yardstick of client welfare.
5. Evaluate each alternative according to your responsibility as a professional therapist.
6. Evaluate the consequences of each alternative.
7. Make a tentative decision.
8. Obtain supervision, consultation, or informal peer advice.
9. Make and implement the ethical decision.
10. Be sure to document your ethical decision-making process concisely in the client records.

Consult Ethical Codes and Other Sources

Read the parts of the *AAMFT Code of Ethical Principles for Marriage and Family Therapists* (1988) that apply (see Appendix C) and sections of any of the other ethical codes such as those of the American Association for Counseling and Development, the American Psychological Association, the National Association of Social Workers, and the American Medical Association. Consult this text or others that have been mentioned. With an ethical dilemma, there are a number of alternative ethical solutions, not necessarily just one "right" one, so do not be surprised if you become confused by one authority suggesting one issue or method of handling a situation while another recommends another.

Generate a Continuum of Alternative Actions

Such alternatives may run the gamut from doing nothing, to some routine behavior like asking the clients questions to obtain more information, to a serious measure such as involuntary hospitalization (for a suicidal family member). Being creative in formulating alternatives can be very helpful in handling an ethical dilemma.

Evaluate Each Alternative by the Yardstick of Client Welfare

The therapist should ask how the welfare of the client will be served by each alternative. What rights does the client have in the situation? In addition, the rights of the general public to safety should be taken into consideration. This is particularly true when dealing with a homicidal client who might harm other family members or an innocent victim on the street.

In marital and family therapy, sometimes it is difficult to determine who the client actually is. From a systems perspective of family therapy, the family system as a whole is the client. However, if one member of the family becomes suicidal, should the therapist be concerned only about the family system then? In this case, the life of the individual would be of primary importance, and the family system would be only of secondary importance (Huber & Baruth, 1987). Attention should be given to the welfare of the individuals in the marital and family therapy as well as to the relationship, in a balanced manner. After all, healthy families support the differentiation of their members, which in turn strengthens the family bonds.

Evaluate Each Alternative According to Your Responsibility as a Professional Therapist

As a professional therapist, you are trusted by clients to act as a professional. They share their most carefully guarded secrets with you. In legal terms, the therapy relationship is a fiduciary one—that is, clients depend on you and place their trust in you to act in their own best interests.

An analogy for the therapist's role is that of loving parent. Clients come to view the therapist as a parental figure who cares about them. To act irresponsibly is to damage the trust clients have in the therapy process, not only with you, but also with any other future practitioners whom they may encounter. This is particularly important when sexual dilemmas arise, because to act irresponsibly here mirrors an incestuous relationship with a parent and is extremely damaging to the client.

A professional must realize that although egalitarian collaboration is often the mode in effective therapeutic outcomes, in matters of ethics the therapist is the authority figure in the therapeutic relationship and has many more responsibilities than the clients do. Just as a parent in the family may ask for a child's input and involve the child in collaborative, egalitarian decision-making processes while the parent takes responsibility for the final decision in the family, the therapist is ultimately responsible for the ethical decisions that relate to how the therapy will be conducted. The therapist and client are not equal in the eyes of the law.

Evaluate the Consequences of Each Alternative

A cost benefit analysis should be done on each alternative, weighing both short-term and long-term results. The psychological, social, and financial consequences of each alternative should be assessed (Keith-Spiegel & Koocher, 1985). Even if the probability of a specific consequence occurring is remote, it should be taken into consideration.

Often the selection of potential consequences is a value judgment on the part of the therapist. The values of the therapist impact the therapist's style and effectiveness in family therapy. Family problems are, by their very nature, value laden and sensitively influenced by the actions and statements of the therapist. This is most apparent in the gray area of ethical judgment, where there are no absolutes, only ambiguous options to which human beings attach meaning and consequences. Therefore, it is particularly important for therapists to be aware of their own values by clarifying them during training (Seymour, 1982) and continuing to grow in self-knowledge over the life span. Such a process of ongoing values clarification helps a therapist to maintain personal honesty in evaluating consequences and limits personal gain at the expense of the client.

Make a Tentative Decision

After reviewing the data from the previous steps, a tentative decision should be made by choosing the best alternative for the given situation in the particular context. Most ethical decisions are ambiguous, and it is typical for the therapist to feel ambivalent about the decision. However, if the steps in the ethical decision-making process have been followed, the therapist can be reasonably sure that the decision can be justified and is in the best interests of the profession and the clients.

Obtain Supervision, Consultation, or Informal Peer Advice

Before implementing an ethical decision, it is often wise to obtain objective feedback from professional colleagues. Such advice can be obtained in several ways. In serious matters, it is best to set up a formal session with a supervisor where the standard hourly fee is paid. The longer therapists are in the field, the more likely they are to have another professional to whom they go for supervision of difficult cases. During supervision, the therapist shares the steps of the ethical decision-making process, what alternatives were considered, and the rationale for the tentative ethical decision. In this way, the supervisor can point out factors or alternatives not considered as part of the process, faulty logic, or consequences of which the therapist may not be aware.

Typically, the confidentiality of the clients involved is maintained. Usually the therapist documents the nature and outcome of the supervision in the client case files.

Another way of obtaining objective feedback from a colleague is consultation. The clients are officially referred to another professional for evaluation of a specific question. In these situations, the therapist calls the other professional to indicate that a consultation is requested and that the clients will be calling to make an appointment. Sometimes a letter is sent to the other professional specifying the nature of the question for which consultation is sought. The protocol is to talk with the consulting professional and discuss how each likes to handle the consultation process. The most common consultations made are for evaluations by psychiatrists of the need for medication, by gynecologists related to specific types of sexual dysfunctions, or to internists for physicals where diabetes or hypoglycemia may be suspected in terms of the effects of changing mood on marital satisfaction, but consultation may also be sought related solely to ethical matters. The consulting professional typically sends a letter stating the nature and outcome of the consultation, which is placed in the client file.

The most common way of gaining objective feedback about minor ethical matters is to obtain the informal advice of peers. Sometimes the chair of a local or state ethics committee can be contacted. The details of the case are carefully disguised so that the identity of clients will be protected. The therapist verbally walks through the ethical decision-making process leading to the tentative decision and asks for input. Often the chair of the ethics committee will give informal reactions, which can be very helpful. A colleague in the professional association may be used as a sounding board, with the idea that the therapist may return the favor in a reciprocal manner. One source of informal peer feedback that is growing in popularity is the professional "cuddle group," in which a small number of colleagues meet on a regular basis to share ethical and practical concerns about their cases while protecting the confidentiality and anonymity of their clients. Such groups help to reduce burnout, which is a key problem in the highly stressful helping professions.

Regardless of the means used to obtain objective feedback about the tentative decision, it is important for the professional to request such information and document what was learned in the records of the client. One of the key questions commonly asked in disciplinary cases is, "What measures did you take to gain objective advice from professional colleagues?" By definition, it is expected that a professional will seek and value feedback from colleagues in the profession.

Make and Implement the Ethical Decision

The last step in the process is to make and implement the ethical decision, apprising all affected parties of your decision. It is important to obtain input from the groups affected. A decision may need to be reconsidered if new information is brought to light as a result of interaction with the affected parties.

As a professional, the therapist takes responsibility for the consequences of the ethical decision that has been made. The therapist may be called upon in court to justify the decision and the process by which it was made.

Document Ethical Decision-Making Process in the Client Records

Client records should contain at a minimum entries of all appointments with dates and a concise description of what occurred, any telephone contacts with the client or others related to the client, statements of progress, any therapeutic contract or informed consent statement, all testing, and copies of any correspondence to the client (Cohen, 1979). It is important to document all key decisions and the process by which the decisions were reached in the record.

For example, with a suicidal client, a risk assessment should be included with the various alternatives that were considered for treatment and to prevent suicide, with the advantages, disadvantages, and consequences of each (Soisson, VandeCreek, & Knapp, 1987). Notations should be made concerning any supervision, consultation, or peer advice that was requested and received. In cases of malpractice litigation, the records will be used to establish a standard of care, that is, whether or not the professional provided a level of care that would be expected of a similar professional in the local community (Woody, 1988).

COMPETENCY

In all of the ethical codes in the mental health professions, there is a clear statement that professionals should practice within the limits of their competency. This is a major overarching ethical principle. For example, according to the *AAMFT Code of Ethical Principles for Marriage and Family Therapists* (1988), "Marriage and family therapists do not attempt to diagnose, treat, or advise on problems outside the recognized boundaries of their competence" (p. 4).

When establishing a private practice or applying for a job, the therapist should assess carefully past education, training, and experience in order to decide on the scope of practice—what services the therapist is competent to perform. Basically, the therapist must decide what types of clients and client problems will be accepted and which ones will be referred. Such decisions lead to marketing services in a specialty or in a narrower scope, which makes it easier to advertise the practice to potential clients and to gain the professional reputation necessary for referrals from other professionals. Rather than giving a long list of broad skills, the therapist clearly knows the nature of personal competencies and communicates this to interested constituencies.

Any statement of competence should also include those services that the practitioner is not competent to perform and for which potential clients will be referred. For example, a marital and family therapist may have had no course work, training, or experience in divorce mediation. When a potential client asks for help with divorce mediation, the therapist would refer the person to two or three individuals in the community who specialize in divorce mediation. Such a procedure reduces the risk of liability and also increases business, as clients tend to see the therapist as a specialist who is not desperate for business.

The most ethical procedure is to limit one's practice to services that one is competent to give (Woody, 1988). Keep in mind that the perception of competence would also need to be shared by expert witnesses in one's behalf if a legal conflict arose. Would colleagues in the community or members of the ethics committee or the regulatory board think that the therapist was competent to perform such services, based on educational credentials, training, and experience? Such a question should be kept in mind when determining one's competence.

CONFIDENTIALITY

Three separate terms with different meanings are important in discussing client rights regarding disclosure: privacy, confidentiality, and privileged communication. Privacy is an individual right set forth in the Fourth Amendment to the Constitution of the United States to decide when and what feelings, behaviors, and thoughts should be withheld or shared with others. For example, insurance companies require that certain information, such as a diagnosis, be released. Clients should be advised of this so that they can decide if they want to use their insurance or if they want to pay for treatment directly. Therapists who write and teach should take care to protect the identity of clients in any case examples that they share or obtain the permission of the clients to use the case material (Huber & Baruth, 1987).

The therapist is obligated ethically not to share what has been learned in therapy with anyone else, according to the principle of confidentiality. In contrast, *privileged communication* is a legal term which means that information acquired during certain types of relationships is exempted from disclosure in legal proceedings in court. For privileged communication to exist in a given state, there must be a state law establishing it for a given profession. For example, in Tennessee there is a statute that protects communications shared in an attorney-client relationship and one for psychologists which states that information shared in the relationship shall be covered by the same privilege as though it were an attorney-client relationship. It is very clear that

When a therapist conducts conjoint marital and family therapy (both spouses in the treatment room), it is unclear whether or not such communication is covered by privileged communication. In fact, privileged communication will differ from state to state in this regard.

privileged communication applies to individual psychotherapy by psychologists, according to this statute, and that the client holds the privilege and could ask a psychologist to testify by waiving the privilege.

However, the situation becomes more complicated when the psychologist conducts conjoint marital and family therapy, because there is more than one person in the treatment room with the therapist. It is unclear whether or not such communication is covered by privileged communication. In one case in Tennessee and another in New York, a psychiatrist was allowed privileged communication in working with a married couple because the couple was seen as the "single" patient (Margolin, 1982), but in Virginia the court ruled against privileged communication in a similar situation (Herrington, 1979). Therefore, it is best to err on the side of not expecting that privileged communication exists for marital and family therapy, since clients should be apprised in advance of the nature of privilege and it cannot be guaranteed in most states. You will need to contact a local attorney or professional association to find out about privileged communication relative to marital or family therapy in your state (Gumper & Sprenkle, 1981).

Even if privileged communication exists in your state for individual, marital, and family therapy, there are a number of exceptions. Stromberg et al. (1988) elaborate on the following: (1) consent of the patient through a release of information form; (2) child abuse and other reporting laws; (3) Medicare and Medicaid reimbursement; (4) if the patient uses mental status as a defense in litigation; (5) the duty to warn a potential victim; (6) ongoing or future criminal activity; (7) client emergencies; (8) family conflicts, divorce, and child custody dispositions, depending upon the written understanding at the beginning of therapy; and (9) sexually transmissible diseases, especially in cases of AIDS where the patient has refused to take precautions and to notify future sexual partners of the risk of infection. Additional exceptions include: (1) malpractice litigation against the therapist (Woody, 1988); (2) when the therapist has been appointed by the court (DeKraai & Sales, 1982); (3) when hospitalization for a mental problem is indicated (DeKraai & Sales, 1982); and (4) when criminal court action is pending, such as in a fraud case against the therapist (Everstine et al., 1980).

One way of dealing with privileged communication is to state clearly in any practice policies, informed consent documents, and therapeutic contracts that the clients in marital and family therapy agree not to request court disclosures of information gained in the therapy as a condition of entering the therapeutic relationship with you. Although the agreement may not be enforceable, the process of court disclosure if pursued will often be more restrained or subdued (Gumper & Sprenkle, 1981; Thomas, 1983). When initiating a practice, it is essential to establish a relationship with an attorney who understands mental health law in order to review practice policies and to obtain preventive legal advice in such situations as when a subpoena is received (Thomas, 1983).

Regardless of whether or not privileged communication is honored for marital and family therapy in your state, confidentiality is expected. The second ethical principle of the AAMFT code states, "Marriage and family therapists have unique confidentiality problems because the 'client' in a therapeutic relationship may be more than one person. The overriding principle is that marriage and family therapists respect the confidences of their client(s)" (p. 2). A therapist who conducts marital or family therapy is ethically bound to keep confidential what has been learned in the therapy. The importance of confidentiality cannot be overemphasized, for without it, it is doubtful whether clients would enter into therapeutic relationships at all—or if they did, they might withhold information negating or neutralizing treatment.

In marital and family therapy there are three common positions on confidentiality: (1) treating each family member as an individual client and keeping the person's material confidential from other family members; (2) conducting only conjoint sessions and making clear that all information shared even in individual phone calls will be shared in the conjoint sessions; or (3) sharing information received from individuals as the therapist sees fit in the conjoint sessions (Huber & Baruth, 1987). A marital and family therapist must decide which position will be taken before answering the first phone call from a family member, because the therapist must be able to tell potential clients what will and will not be shared with others in the marital or family session.

Those who adhere to the first position will allow the caller to talk with the assumption that the material will not be shared with the spouse or other family members in the marital or family session, maintaining that such a position leads to finding out secrets, which will expedite therapy. Those who are committed to the second position will inform the caller that only conjoint sessions are held for marital and family therapy and that it is best to hold one's remarks until everyone can hear them or that the therapist will share whatever the person has said over the phone in the opening session so that everyone will know that there is no special alliance between the therapist and the caller. Such a position is easier on the memory of the therapist since there are no secrets and no alliances. The third position—the therapist choosing to share when appropriate—is perhaps the most difficult because clients do not know what to expect. They do not know whether or not the therapist will share the information or when it will be done. In addition, the therapist must make many individual judgment calls, which puts more pressure on the therapist. For example, if a spouse finds out at some point that the therapist knew about an extramarital affair and did not share it, the spouse will become angry at the therapist and may terminate treatment because the therapist is viewed as an ally of the partner, and trust may be shaken in any future therapeutic work.

There are four exceptions to confidentiality cited in the AAMFT code: (1) if each family member present in the therapy signs a waiver in writing stating to whom and under what circumstances information may be disclosed; (2) where required by the law; (3) if the marriage and family therapist is being sued in criminal or civil court or being disciplined by a state board relative to what happened in the therapy; or (4) if there is an imminent and clear danger to a client or clients in the therapy. When faced with a request for confidential information, two rules apply: "When in doubt, don't give it out!" and "If still in doubt, call your redoubtable lawyer!" (Stromberg et al., 1988, p. 389).

INFORMED CONSENT

With any mental health treatment, the limits and scope of confidentiality should be shared openly with clients before beginning treatment (Stromberg et al., 1988). This can be done through written practice policies, in which all clients read and sign a contract indicating that they have read them and agree with them (Table 16–2 and Figure 16–1).

In addition to establishing the expectation of confidentiality and possible exceptions to it, the practice policies may include an objective and realistic summary of the credentials and qualifications of the practitioner, the scope of practice, an explanation of the process of therapy including the steps in therapy if an intake procedure is used, any possible risks that might reasonably be incurred as part of therapy, and fees for various services and how they are collected. Practice policies should also include frequency of sessions, length of therapy, emergency phone numbers and how emergencies are typically handled, any rights of the client if you wish to specify them, what waivers will be required in marital or family therapy before information is released, a statement encouraging the client to ask questions about anything in the policies or about therapy throughout the process, and any other information that you think clients should know that might affect their willingness to begin therapy.

The informed consent contract has a box where the client indicates that the practice policies have been read and understood and that the client agrees to abide by them. Other background information is requested on the contract form such as name, address, place of employment, employment address, phone numbers at work and at home, names and ages of family members, name of referral source, insurance information, indication of willingness to have insurance filed, who will be responsible for payment, payment policy, fee collection policy (whether unpaid bills will be referred to a collection agency), a statement of agreement to pay, a place for the signatures of the client and witness, and the date the form was completed.

Such practice policies and contracts establish the expectations for the therapeutic relationship and the obligations of the therapist and the client in the relationship. These written documents establish the standard of care for the practitioner, which is an important risk management tool in the face of any complaints or litigation. In marital therapy each spouse should be required to read the practice policies and complete the signed contract before therapy begins. Likewise, in family therapy each parent should complete the material, giving relevant information for other members of the family.

In addition to this information, each client should also complete a medical checklist, indicating health problems, medications, last date of physical examination, names of physicians, use of alcohol and drugs, legal difficulties such as DUI, arrests, or bankruptcy, previous hospitalizations, and suicide attempts (Figure 16–2). This information is essential for making a referral for the evaluation of a physical problem which may be affecting the emotional health or interpersonal relationships of the client. Failure to refer for medical problems is one of the main sources of recent litigation against mental health providers (Woody, 1988). It does not matter if a particular mental health provider has no medical training: The practitioner is expected to know enough about symptoms to be able to refer when particular complaints could have a medical component. Woody (1988) recommends that practitioners obtain consultation or supervision from a physician or obtain additional education if they feel inadequate in recognizing physical health problems and knowing when to refer.

TABLE 16–2 Sample practice policies

Fee Policy

Charges for consultation and out-patient counseling are billed at the rate of $80 per session, which is approximately one hour in length. No additional charges are made for couple or family therapy.

New clients are asked to complete a medical review form and an information sheet for which there are no charges. Frequently new clients are requested to complete the Million Multi-Axial Personality Inventory or the Minnesota Multiphasic Personality Inventory. Each of these psychological instruments requires about 1 hour to complete and costs $35. Clients in couple therapy or family therapy may be asked to complete the MATE, ENRICH, or FACES III, for which there is a $25 charge per couple or family. Charges for other psychological tests are billed separately, depending on the instrument administered.

Typically, Dr. Jane Doe will spend one to three sessions as part of the intake process, at the end of which time a decision is made as to whether or not she will take the client(s) into ongoing therapy. If not, referral will be made to several appropriate professionals and/or agencies in the community, and upon the request of the client(s), records will be released to the professional to whom the client has been referred.

It is customary to pay professional fees at each visit. Fees are paid at the time of consultation at the end of each session. Each month you will receive a receipt from this office showing all payments made for income tax purposes.

Your health insurance may provide reimbursement for psychological services. Consult your policy for specifics. If you will bring any claim forms with you at the time of your sessions, this office will complete the Provider section of the insurance forms, which enables you to receive reimbursement for your payment. Usually the insurance company prefers that these forms be submitted monthly.

Cancellation must be made 24 hours in advance; otherwise, you will be billed for the visit. Questions regarding appointments, charges, and insurance matters are handled by the secretary at 555-1234 or by talking with Dr. Jane Doe directly.

Confidentiality

The legal code in this state establishes privileged communication. Information regarding services is controlled by the client. There are three exceptions to this rule. In the case of an emergency when there is imminent danger to the client or other persons, the psychologist may breach the requirement of confidentiality. Secondly, the law requires that child abuse be reported to the Department of Human Services. Thirdly, in the case

---

DUTY TO WARN—INVOLUNTARY HOSPITALIZATION

In deciding to take people into treatment as clients, helping professionals must take into consideration potential danger to self and others. This is particularly true in light of the high frequency of suicide, domestic violence, and spouse abuse in the United States. Wise mental health professionals are careful to screen the clients they select for treatment. Therefore, it is important to take a detailed history of each person and the relationship. For example, past suicide attempts and assaultive behavior are particularly important predictors of current danger. Also, a mental health professional should obtain any past medical records of mental health treatment.

TABLE 16–2 *continued*

of more than one client being seen in the same room, i.e., a couple or a family or a group, the code may not apply. However, Dr. Doe believes in confidentiality and strongly recommends that all participants maintain the confidentiality of any information revealed in therapy.

Professional Services

The regular working hours are from 8:00 a.m. until 5:00 p.m., Monday through Friday. The secretary is on duty during these times at 555-1234.

Emergency services are available after hours and 24 hours a day by calling 555-1234 (Medical Answering Service) and asking for Dr. Doe. The Medical Answering Service will beep her, and she will return your call immediately. You must leave the telephone number from which you are calling with the telephone answering personnel in order for Dr. Doe to return your call. On the few occasions in which Dr. Doe is out of town, the Medical Answering Service will beep her back-up professional. In addition, the telephone number of the 24-hour crisis intervention service is 888-3434. In the event of an emergency, the service can be called.

Benefits and Risks of Psychotherapy

Persons contemplating psychotherapy should realize that clients frequently make significant changes in their lives. For example, people often modify their emotions, attitudes, and behaviors. Also, clients may make changes in their marriages or significant relationships such as with parents, children, friends, relatives, and supervisors at work. Because of psychotherapy, clients may change employment, begin to feel differently about themselves, and to otherwise alter significant aspects of their lives. If you have questions about the benefits and risks of psychotherapy (or any other procedure), ask Dr. Doe for specifics. She will be glad to discuss these matters with you in simple, nontechnical terms.

Credentials

A copy of Dr. Doe's vita is available upon request. Dr. Doe is a licensed psychologist, professional counselor, and marital and family therapist.

If a therapist conducting marital and family therapy takes into treatment clients who become dangerous to themselves or others, there is a duty to warn the potential victim and to involuntarily hospitalize the client if the danger is clear and imminent to the potential victim.

The duty to warn was first established by the landmark case, *Tarasoff v. Regents of University of California* (Cal. 1976). Poddar was a foreign student from India who was studying at the University of California at Berkeley. He had fallen in love with Miss Tarasoff, who did not return his affection. Poddar was heartbroken and attended the counseling center at the university for therapy. Poddar began to make threats to kill

FIGURE 16–1 Sample information sheet

Referral source: _____ Date: _____

Client's name: _____ Date of birth: _____ Age: _____

Address: _____ S. S. #: _____

_____ Home phone: _____

Person responsible for payment: _____

Address: _____

Client's employer: _____

Address: _____ Office phone: _____

Spouse's name: _____ Home phone: _____

Spouse's employer: _____

Address: _____ Office phone: _____

Names and ages of other family members: _____

_____

_____

☐ I have received, read, and understand the practice policies (Please check if appropriate)

   A. I agree to pay for the above services at the time of consultation at the end of each session.

   B. Dr. Jane Doe does not accept insurance assignment. Your insurance is a contract between you and your insurance company. If desired, however, this office will process your claim for you. Please check the appropriate box below.

     ☐ Do not bill an insurance company for me.

     ☐ I have filled out and signed an insurance claim form. Please process my claim. I understand that I remain responsible for the entire bill regardless of whether or not the insurance company makes payment on my claim.

     ☐ I understand that a past due bill will be turned over to collections if not paid within 90 days and if no payment plan has been approved by Dr. Doe.

Insurance company: _____

Insured's I.D./Medicare number: _____

Insured's group number/name: _____

Other health insurance coverage: _____

Client's signature: _____ Witness: _____

Tarasoff. Dr. Moore, the treating psychologist, took the threats seriously and called the university security personnel to have Poddar committed involuntarily. After leaving the counseling center, the university security personnel thought that Poddar was normal and let him go. Dr. Moore's supervisor had been away when the incident occurred and when he returned was concerned about what he considered to be a breech of confidentiality. The supervisor ordered Dr. Moore to destroy the session notes and audiotape of the therapy session, which he did. Tarasoff was abroad at the time, and when she returned home a few weeks later, Poddar killed her. Her family sued all those involved and won the suit. The court concluded that mental health professionals are expected to take reasonable care to protect an identified potential victim by notifying the victim, the victim's family, and/or the local law enforcement personnel.

Later cases (Table 16–3) have expanded the duty to warn to groups of potential victims including the public where a dangerous person might drive and endanger citizens who are on the highways (*Peterson v. State,* 1983). It becomes difficult to know how to warn broad classes of potential victims. Often notifying local law enforcement agencies is expected to protect large groups of people.

Because of the vague expansion of the duty to warn, a number of states have passed duty to warn bills that make explicit what a therapist is expected to do in handling a dangerous client. Therapists should become familiar with the status of duty to warn requirements in their state.

Typically, courts have held therapists liable where the threats were specific, the client had a past history of violence, there was an identifiable victim or a target of violence, and there were conventional practices that were ignored such as taking a thorough client history or obtaining prior medical records. Liability was not imposed where it was found that the client was not dangerous when evaluated even though alcoholism or a history of violence was present. In summary, care must be taken to carefully evaluate clients in intake sessions and to work within the professional network by obtaining information from past treatment sources with the permission of the client. Woody (1988) suggests working out in advance a written plan for dealing with a dangerous client, including who would be called to effect involuntary commitment if needed.

DEALING WITH SUICIDAL CLIENTS

It is not unusual for one or both spouses to present for marital therapy with symptoms of depression, which can escalate to suicidal proportions if the possibility of divorce becomes realistic. As in any form of therapeutic modality, but particularly in marital treatment, the therapist should take care to assess depression, suicidal ideation, and intent, not only during the initial session but throughout the therapy as well. The initial session should include a short assessment of the vegetative signs of depression for each partner and be noted in the session notes.

Inquiries about vegetative signs include questions about recent weight loss or gain, lack of or increase in appetite, difficulty sleeping or oversleeping, lack of pleasure in usually enjoyable activities (anhedonia), loss of sexual desire, feeling sad or depressed, apathy or loss of interest, lack of energy, frequent crying, problems in concentrating, slowed movement or agitated pacing/walking, feelings of worthlessness, preoccupation with or talk about death, unwarranted feelings of guilt, stomach cramps or other physical signs of anxiety, and suicidal ideation (*DSM III-R,* 1987; Miller, 1986; Rosenthal, 1988).

FIGURE 16–2   Sample medical review form

Name: _____ Date: _____

Name of family physician(s): _____ Phone: _____

Other professional health providers: _____ Phone: _____

Last exam date: _____ Height: _____ Weight: _____

Have you ever been treated for or had indications of (underline applicable items):

A. High blood pressure, hypoglycemia, diabetes, anemia, or any other disorder of the blood.

B. Chest pains, shortness of breath, heart attack, rheumatic fever, heart murmur, irregular pulse, or other disorders of the heart or blood vessels.

C. Disorders of the thyroid, skin, or lymph glands.

D. Sugar, albumen, blood, or pus in the urine, or syphillis, gonorrhea, or other venereal disease.

E. Any disorder of the kidney, bladder, prostate, breast, or reproductive organs.

F. Ulcer, chronic indigestion, intestinal bleeding, hepatitis, colitis, diarrhea, or other disorders of the stomach, intestine, rectum, spleen, pancreas, liver, or gall bladder.

G. Asthma, tuberculosis, bronchitis, emphysema, or other disorders of the lung.

H. Fainting, convulsions, tension or migrane headaches, paralysis, epilepsy, memory loss or confusion, or any disorders of the brain or nervous system.

I. Arthritis, gout, back pain, or other disorders of the muscles, bones, or joints.

J. Disorders of the eyes, ears, nose, throat, or sinuses.

Have you noticed any recent changes in your: A) vision, hearing, coordination, balance, strength, speech, memory, or thinking; B) energy, sleeping, eating, elimination, menstrual cycle, or sexual activity. (Please underline changes.)

Please list all prescriptions you are now taking:

_____   _____

_____   _____

Are you allergic or sensitive to any medication, food, pollens, etc. If so, please list.

_____   _____

If the somatic vegetative signs are positive and there is suicidal ideation, the therapist should ask about the frequency of the ideas and whether or not there is a plan. If there is a plan that is capable of being carried out within a short time, the therapist should take steps to hospitalize the patient voluntarily or involuntarily, obtain any weapons or other means of lethality, and elicit a promise to call and talk to the therapist before acting on any impulses. Often the spouse can take responsibility for a suicide watch to prevent hospitalization. Court decisions have been very clear in indicating that a promise not to commit suicide is insufficient and that the therapist must take steps to protect the client from himself. Referring the client for individual

FIGURE 16-2 *continued*

Other comments:

How often do you drink alcohol? (Circle the responses that fit.)

6+ per day,   3+ drinks daily,   2–3 per day,   1 per day,

6+ per weekend,   3–6 per weekend,   1–3 per weekend,

3+ per month,   1–2 per month

What is your favorite drink? _____

Have you ever been arrested for driving under the influence (DUI)?
Yes   No

If "yes," how many times?   1, 2–3, more than 3

Do you use drugs?   Yes   No

If "yes," how often? _____

If so, what drugs do you use? _____

Have you ever been arrested?   Yes   No

If so, how many times and for what? _____
_____

Have you ever been hospitalized for mental or nervous problems?
Yes   No

If so, where and when? _____

Have you ever attempted suicide?   Yes   No

If so, where and when? _____

Have you ever declared bankruptcy?   Yes   No

If so, where and when? _____

---

treatment by giving two or three names of other practitioners and being sure that the client has followed up on the referrals is an important requirement for continued work in the marital therapy, using therapeutic direction and leverage to protect the client's welfare without abandoning the client.

Rosenthal (1988) suggests eight steps for preventing suicide: (1) ask the client if the person is actually suicidal; (2) find out about the plan; (3) get rid of the means of lethality; (4) be sure the person has the telephone number of the local crisis center suicide hotline; (5) obtain a verbal and written agreement not to commit suicide (Figure 16–3); (6) eliminate the stressor that is triggering the suicidal feelings; (7)

TABLE 16–3 Selected legal cases establishing duty to warn

Tarasoff v. Regents of University of California (1976): Landmark case that established duty to warn potential victim of dangerous client.

McIntosh v. Milano (1979): Teenage boy threatened to kill a woman and did so. The family won the suit because there was a clear duty to warn.

Thompson v. County of Alameda (1980): Upheld definition of victim from the Tarasoff case to be an identifiable victim. Male juvenile offender threatened to kill any child in the neighborhood upon release and did so, but family lost case because there was no foreseeable victim.

Lipari v. Sears, Roebuck & Co. (1980): Held psychiatrist liable when patient murdered people enjoying themselves at a night club. The duty to warn was expanded to a class or group who might be expected to be victims.

Leedy v. Hartnett (1981): Veterans Administration personnel were not found liable to warn people with whom the person lived of the patient's dangerousness.

Brady v. Hopper (1983): Did not find against Hinckley's psychiatrist for the attempt on President Reagan's life because Hinckley had not made specific threats toward designated individuals nor did he have a history of dangerous behavior.

Petersen v. State (1983): Psychiatrist held liable to warn the public when releasing a patient who used angel dust and drove recklessly when doing so. Much caution should be exercised in releasing potentially dangerous patients.

Jablonski v. United States (1983): Found against therapist for not obtaining previous medical record that would have indicated a history of dangerousness.

require that someone be with the person 24 hours a day; and (8) encourage the client to obtain professional help for the depression. The therapist conducting the marital or family therapy would establish an alignment with the client by treating the client for depression as well as marital or family therapy, which would actually sabotage the marital or family treatment; therefore, the client should be referred for treatment. A follow-up should be made to ensure that the client has entered psychotherapy for the treatment of the depression. The best therapeutic outcomes for the treatment of depression have been achieved through a combination of antidepressive medication and psychotherapy.

FIGURE 16–3 Written suicide prevention pact

I, ___[name of client]___, hereby promise to not attempt suicide nor hurt myself in any way. If I feel suicidal, I promise to call the crisis hotline (phone _____) and talk with a crisis worker.

                           Signatures

                           [client] _____

                           [therapist] _____

A therapist should have a written plan as to how to deal with suicidal threats that aims at preventing suicide attempts as well as successful suicides (Woody, 1988). Such a written plan would contain the telephone numbers of appropriate referral sources, crisis hotlines, emergency rooms, and local law enforcement officials as well as the specific steps and alternatives of the ethical decision-making process outlined earlier in this chapter, tailored to the requirements of the local community.

WELFARE OF THE CLIENT

Central to all ethical codes in the mental health field is the principle of welfare of the client. The first ethical principle in the code of ethics of the AAMFT is entitled "Responsibility to Clients" and states, "Marriage and family therapists are dedicated to advancing the welfare of families and individuals, including respecting the rights of those persons seeking their assistance, and making reasonable efforts to ensure that their services are used appropriately" (p. 1).

One question that quickly arises in marital and family therapy is "Who is the client?" Often one spouse will present for treatment of marital problems. Since the outcome literature is very clear in demonstrating the optimal therapeutic outcome for conjoint marital therapy in comparison to individual therapy for the treatment of marital problems (Gurman & Kniskern, 1981), an ethical dilemma emerges for the clinician immediately. Should the therapist take the client into individual treatment or attempt to involve the spouse? If the therapist believes strongly that both partners should be involved, what procedures should the therapist use to engage the absent spouse?

A therapist may hold firmly to withholding services unless both partners are present (O'Shea & Jessee, 1982). Wilcoxon (1986) recommends the following steps. (The wife is most often the spouse who calls, and the guidelines reflect this.) (1) see the wife, encouraging her to invite her spouse and focusing on the need for conjoint therapy for this brief session; (2) if the first step does not work, the therapist can obtain the wife's permission to contact the husband to invite him to one individual session to talk about his point of view as a beginning of conjoint work; (3) if the wife does not want to do this or the husband refuses, the wife can be given a letter for both to sign indicating their agreement to one-spouse, individual therapy, understanding its inherent risks to the marital relationship and proceeding only if the letter is received. Wilcoxon and Fenell (1983) have provided a model letter to be used in this process (Figure 16–4).

If the therapist begins marital therapy with a couple, the therapist must make clear that the decision to divorce, to stay married, or to separate is the responsibility of the couple, not the therapist (see AAMFT, 1988). Often a couple sees the therapist as an expert or omnipotent judge who can say whether or not they should part. A therapist should avoid such a position at all costs and openly discuss expectations with the couple.

Another possible key ethical dilemma is the opportunity for the development of a dual relationship, which exploits the dependency of clients and neglects their welfare. The AAMFT code specifically cites the examples of having business relationships with clients or relationships of a close, personal nature. In particular, according to the

FIGURE 16–4   Sample letter to engage a nonattending spouse

[Date]

Mr. John Jones
111 Smith Street
Anytown, USA 00000

Dear Mr. Jones,

As you may know, your wife, Jill, has requested therapy services for difficulties related to your marriage. However, she has stated that you do not wish to participate in marital therapy sessions.

As a professional marriage therapist, I have an obligation to inform each of you of the possible outcome of marital therapy services to only one spouse. The available research indicates that one-spouse marital therapy has resulted in reported increases in marital stress and dissatisfaction for both spouses in the marriage. On the other hand, many couples have reported that marital therapy which includes both spouses has been helpful in reducing marital stress and enhancing marital satisfaction.

These findings reflect general tendencies in marital research and are not absolute in nature. However, it is important for you and Jill to be informed of potential consequences which might occur through marital therapy in which only your spouse attends. Knowing this information, you may choose a course of action which best suits your intentions.

After careful consideration of this information, I ask that you and Jill discuss your options regarding future therapy services. In this way, all parties will have a clear understanding of one another's intentions regarding your relationship.

As a homework assignment for Jill, I have asked that each of you read this letter and sign in the spaces provided below to verify your understanding of the potential consequences to your relationship by continuing one-spouse marital therapy. If you are interested in joining Jill for marital therapy, in addition to your signature below, please contact my office to indicate your intentions. If not, simply sign below and have Jill return the letter at our next therapy session. I appreciate your cooperation in this matter.

Sincerely,

Therapist X

_____

We verify by our signatures below that we have discussed and understand the potential implications of continued marital therapy with only one spouse in attendance.

_____   _____
Attending Spouse   Date

_____   _____
Non-Attending Spouse   Date

From "Engaging the Non-attending Spouse in Marital Therapy Through the Use of Therapist-Initiated Written Communication" by A. Wilcoxon and D. Fenell, 1983, *Journal of Marital and Family Therapy, 9,* 199–203. Reprinted by permission.

AAMFT code, sexual intimacy is prohibited with present clients and for 2 years after the termination of therapy.

All dual relationships have in common the playing of more than one role with the client—that is, therapist and professor, therapist and friend, therapist and business associate, or therapist and lover. Pope (1988) summarizes some examples of such dual relationships: (1) a professor seeing a student in the program for therapy; (2) trading therapy for material goods; (3) trading therapy for typing or other services provided by a needy client; (4) sexual intimacy with a former patient; (5) providing therapy to a former social acquaintance; (6) providing therapy to the relative of a friend; (7) combining the roles of minister, therapist, and friend; (8) marriage to a former marital client; (9) being both a therapist and a supervisor; (10) bartering therapy for the services of a relative; and (11) being both a professor and a sexual partner.

Such dual relationships are unethical because they affect the professional judgment of the therapist. The therapist is in a more powerful position than the client and can easily misuse this power for self-interest. In such relationships, the client's transference issues are inappropriately handled, and it is difficult for the client to file a complaint if a problem occurs. Therapists may not realize the level of their influence on former patients when they ask them to participate in business deals, social activities, or personal relationships. In addition, most malpractice liability policies do not cover litigation involving suits over business dealings between clients or ex-clients, and they limit monetary liability for sexual intimacies with clients or former clients.

The AAMFT code is different from the interpretation of the ethical codes for both psychologists and psychiatrists in relation to former clients. Being sexually intimate with a present or former client, regardless of the time since termination, is grounds for disciplining a psychologist or psychiatrist (Ethics Committee of the American Psychological Association, 1988; Sell, Schoenfeld, & Gottlieb, 1986). Edelwich with Brodsky (1982) point out that a therapeutic relationship never ends because an ex-client could decide at any point to return to a previous therapist when encountering stressful transition points later in life. By establishing a personal or intimate relationship with the ex-client, the therapist makes it impossible for the client to return to therapy in the future. Also, in successful therapy the client often carries an internalized image of the therapist, and use and vividness are linked to improvement.

In addition, the psychotherapeutic relationship mirrors the parent-child relationship. Would a parent have sex with a child whom the parent has not seen for 2 years? No, a parent is always a parent, regardless of the elapsed time. Also, in terms of mere pragmatic considerations, a personal relationship based on such an unequal power distribution as that of therapist-client does not lead to the egalitarianism often needed to maintain a long-term romantic or marital relationship. Such relationships typically do not work out over the long term.

Sexual relationships with present or former clients are particularly damaging to the clients. Some damaged clients have written accounts of their involvements and the personal consequences of them (Freeman & Roy, 1976; Plaisil, 1985). Such intimate relationships are particularly damaging if the therapist is also a minister, viewed by the client as a representative of God.

Feelings of sexual attraction or personal aversion are normal but should neither be acted upon nor shared with a client (Edelwich with Brodsky, 1982; Pope & Bouhoutsos, 1986). If a therapist becomes aware of such feelings, the therapist should seek supervision on the case from another professional by paying the standard hourly fee, enter psychotherapy to talk about such feelings, or obtain informal peer support.

The therapist can be viewed as a musical instrument that the client plays. Often the feelings the therapist experiences are the result of the same transference the client typically tries to elicit from others in close relationships. Sometimes the theme is sexual, which may indicate strong sexual feelings toward a parent or a past incestuous relationship. Other times the client may provoke intense anger in the therapist, which may be what the client does with most people in close relationships. The therapist is duped into assuming that the client has the feelings only for this therapist as an individual.

After obtaining supervisory feedback, it is important to set limits and to confront any seductive behavior of the client directly, encouraging the client to explore the behavior in a therapeutic manner and talking about its meaning and goals. The theme can be expanded to look at past relationships in adulthood and to examine parental relationships in early childhood. It is appropriate to express nonsexual caring for the client verbally (Edelwich with Brodsky, 1982). If the therapist is not able to deal with the strength of the sexual feelings or anger toward a client even with supervision of the case, the client should be referred by giving the client the names of three other appropriate colleagues. Failure to refer when such action is indicated has been grounds for many recent cases of litigation (Woody, 1988).

Mental health professionals who care about increases in malpractice insurance rates are particularly concerned about the escalating incidence of sexual misconduct complaints in all of the mental health professions. For example, sexual misconduct was grounds for the largest number of complaints against social workers who were individual practitioners (Besharov, 1985). The Ethics Committee of the American Psychological Association (1988) reported that the majority of violations were due to dual relationships, of which the most frequent was sexual intimacy between the psychologist and client. Pope (1989) reviewed data from the American Psychological Association Insurance Trust and found that sexual misconduct represented 53.2% of the expenses related to malpractice cases in comparison to the next most expensive category of suicides, which was only 11.2% of the total expenses. Sell et al. (1986) found that sexual misconduct cases increased by 67% from 1982 to 1983 for ethics committees and by 141% for state boards in the field of psychology. Rates of complaints against practitioners in other mental health helping professions are similar (Woody, 1988).

One way of dealing with this growing problem is to emphasize how to handle such ethical dilemmas as part of courses in graduate training. This is one reason for the inclusion of this material in an introductory text, where students will be exposed to its contents early in their graduate training.

Some state boards for mental health professions are now requiring continuing education units which deal specifically with ethics for licensure renewal. State professional associations are sponsoring similar workshops and, in some cases, lobbying that sexual misconduct by professionals be made a criminal offense punished by fines and mandatory imprisonment.

One of the best ways an individual mental health practitioner can lessen the possibility of sexual misconduct occurring is to be sure that personal needs are being met. For example, satisfying intimate relationships help the therapist to stay on an even keel. In addition, growing as a human being through raising a family of one's own gives invaluable insight to help other people with their problems, even though a therapist must be careful not to play out current family conflicts onto client families in therapy. By learning about healthy family functioning and what is important in developing marital and family relationships, therapists have a higher probability of enjoying life and avoiding the burnout that is so characteristic of the high-stress helping fields.

ETHICAL ISSUES PARTICULAR TO MARITAL AND FAMILY THERAPY

Although many ethical issues are common to all mental health professions and to the diverse psychotherapy modalities, some issues are particular to marital and family therapy. In outlining a course in ethics, law, and professional issues for graduate students who will be practicing marital and family therapy, Piercy and Sprenkle (1983) emphasize five ethical components of particular concern to marital and family therapists: (1) systemic epistemology; (2) feminism and family therapy; (3) the use of paradox; (4) the use of ethical codes; and (5) questions of confidentiality and privileged communication. Having already dealt with the latter two issues, the first three issues will now be emphasized as crucial issues unique to marital and family therapy as a modality and as a profession.

Systems Epistemology

How do we know what we know? That is what epistemology by definition is concerned with. The field finds itself in the middle of a constructivist revolution. People's perspectives that they create themselves are their realities. Rather than the knower being separate from the known and adapting to the known as an external, the knower and the known are one (Taggart, 1982). Self-organizing human systems evolve through unstable sequences by creating new structures. Such an approach means that values are evolutionary and refer to the whole changing system, not to the rights of a single individual. Rather than clear linear values, which are absolute, values are of themselves multilevel. They are continuous (time binding) and discontinuous (space binding). Systems operate in a balance between affirmation and innovation.

The key question then becomes, "What happens to the rights and long-held values of the individual?" Does individual responsibility, in fact, exist (Dell, 1982)? How ethical is the use of systems thinking and the method of intervention based on it called family therapy? These questions have no easy answers as theoreticians in the field of family therapy grapple for explanations.

One explanation is that of co-evolution and co-responsibility. The system and the individual subsystem evolve together. Each individual differentiates from the family as the family also develops. Both the family and individual are responsible. Yet the specific ways in which this process works within the economic frame, culture, and society in which we live have not been explained and represent the challenge of the new espistemology.

Gender and Family Therapy

If systems theory focuses on social systems as causes of behavior and de-emphasizes individual rights, feminist theorists (Ault-Riche, 1986; Goldner, 1985; Hare-Mustin, 1978, 1987a, 1987b; James & McIntyre, 1983; Weiner & Boss, 1985) maintain that it can be detrimental to the growth and development of women as human beings. Because family therapy models are systemic, they ignore gender issues (treating men and women as gender-free), and there is no organized way in which to discuss the current sex roles of each partner in the couple (Margolin, Fernandez, Talovic, & Onorato, 1983). Such non-discussion leads to reinforcement of the traditional sex roles held by the couple and, in many cases, the therapist. The Task Force on Sex Bias and Sex Role Stereotyping of the American Psychological Association (APA, 1975) concluded that family therapists tended to perpetuate the following sexual stereotyping beliefs and behaviors: (1) staying in the marriage was better for the woman; (2) showing less interest in the career of the wife; (3) the problems of the child were the responsibility of the mother; (4) a double standard regarding extramarital affairs; and (5) seeing the needs of the husband as more important than those of the wife.

In addition, Bograd (1986) points out that a pure systemic model would absolve from responsibility a perpetrator of rape, incest, or physical abuse. Regardless of the specific explanation of family violence, all systems approaches assume that: (1) the abuse serves a function in the family system; (2) each partner has equal influence in maintaining the dysfunctional system; (3) there are repetitive cycles of violence (the escalation of tension, abuse, and the honeymoon of reconciliation); and (4) there are common structures in abusive families. In fact, in situations in which women are abused, they are typically economically dependent on their husbands, who hold a power position of superiority in the relationship. Such men choose to act on aggressive impulses by battering their wives. They are responsible for their actions and should be appropriately punished if they break the laws in a given jurisdiction. To state that the battered wife is responsible is to blame the victim for the crime and to blame women for the inequities of society and the economic distribution of jobs and status.

Taggart (1985) offers the proposal that in punctuating a system, the context of the system is established as what lies outside the boundaries of the system but affects the system. By including the context in any epistemological formulation, its role in the socialization of the therapist can be called into play. Therapists can be exhorted to look at the economic, social, and political biases that they bring to their therapy. Likewise, clients can be asked to examine the context in which they were raised to understand what presuppositions underlie their emotions, thoughts, and actions. The new constructivist epistemology states that human beings construct their own reality. Yet, that construction does not emanate from a vacuum but rather from cultural, ethnic, social, and economic roots. The new family therapy can do no less, as family members create their own family from the history of the past within such traditions and their experience in family therapy.

Pittman (1985) argues that at this point in the development of American society, traditionally male and female sex roles may, in fact, be pathological. He views one job of the therapist as assisting clients of both sexes to see the limitations of their current sex roles and the possibilities of future sex roles, which they create. Ganong and Coleman (1986) found that androgynous individuals were more cognizant of feelings of love and expressed affectionate, loving behaviors more to other family members than did undifferentiated, traditionally feminine or traditionally masculine individuals. Sex role predicted loving family relationships better than gender. Androgynous people had family relationships in which more loving behaviors were expressed. In comparing non-clinic and clinic couples, there were larger numbers of androgynous husbands and wives than other sex roles among non-clinic couples, whereas with clinic couples, there were very few individuals with androgynous sex roles (Baucom & Aiken, 1984).

Since sex roles change over time with many men becoming more affectionate and family oriented as they age and many women exercising assertive skills at midlife and beyond (see the sexual diamond of Sheehy, 1981, in Figure 5–1), spouses in a long-term relationship need to talk about their sex roles and how they affect various factors in the relationship such as sexual behavior, household management, and social roles. Margolin et al. (1983) recommend that during the initial session questions should be asked about who does what around the house, who pays the bills or controls the money, how the husband sees himself as a man and the wife as a woman, how people carry out their role assignments, and how the couple handles sex role issues. During behavioral marital therapy, sex role issues should be addressed directly. The couple can then decide how they would like their own sex roles to be and how that might affect their relationship.

Female family therapists often need to learn to function more directively and powerfully—to be more instrumental (achieving, competitive, and logical)—to be effective family therapists (Libow, 1986; Okun, 1983). Rather than being dependent on clients for approval, such female therapists should take more risks and confront male authority figures in appropriate ways, behaving instrumentally while retaining warm, nurturing qualities. On the other hand, male therapists may need to become more comfortable with affect and non-stereotypic behaviors—to be more expressive and traditionally "female"—in order to be effective models for male family members. Androgynous sex role behaviors for family therapists of both sexes facilitate their leadership in the family's exploration of both the instrumental and expressive dimensions of relationships.

Most importantly, gender issues should be discussed in graduate courses in marital and family therapy and throughout the training program. Sometimes departments offer courses in psychology of sex roles or gender issues in marital and family therapy. At a minimum, gender issues should be discussed as part of any ethics course in marital and family therapy. The Counseling Psychology Division (Division 17) of the American Psychological Association has formulated a set of guidelines entitled *Principles Concerning the Counseling and Therapy of Women* (1985), which may be of help in such discussions.

Cross-Cultural Issues
The culture or ethnic minority status of individuals should be considered in effective treatment. Pinderhughes (1986) points out that minority women in particular suffer

Gender issues should be discussed in graduate courses in marital and family therapy and throughout the training program.

from the effects of both sexism and racism. Will such variables also adversely impact family therapy with minority families?

How ethical is it for a therapist to treat a family from another culture or ethnic group whose values differ from those of the therapist? What precautions should be taken? These questions are not easy to answer, require reflection, and are still in the process of being considered by the mainstream of family therapy.

The concept of cultural calibration, finding out what has meaning to particular family members within their culture, is an important one. Asking questions about what is important to them can lead to information that stimulates reframing within the context of the culture. Studying ethnicity by reading *Ethnicity and Family Therapy* by McGoldrick, Pearce, and Giordano (1982) and gaining cross-cultural experience through travel and meeting people from different countries add to the ability to see the world from the perspectives of others with diverse cultural and ethnic heritages.

The Use of Paradox

Whether and when the use of paradox is ethical are concerns of many students and proponents of family therapy. Is a therapist in some way lying to clients by using reframing or paradox?

When paradoxical interventions are successful, it is because they, indeed, reflect the truth of the unique individuals who are in the dysfunctional system (Fisher, Anderson, & Jones, 1981; O'Shea & Jessee, 1982). However, if such techniques are used in a theatrical fashion in a way that impedes trust in the therapeutic relationship, are based on an inaccurate diagnosis, put down the family, are utilized to express the anger of the therapist, or are used unskillfully in a poorly timed way, paradoxical techniques can be unethical.

INTERFACING WITH THE LEGAL SYSTEM

It is important that those practicing marital and family therapy know family law. Since it varies from state to state, it is often helpful to consult with a local attorney who specializes in divorce and family litigation. Sometimes an attorney is invited to class to discuss key legal issues that affect marital and family practice.

Learning about privileged communication, child abuse, and divorce statutes is particularly important. In addition, tips on how to give courtroom testimony can be helpful, since marital and family therapists may be called to testify in court cases and custody hearings.

One area in which practitioners may experience ethical dilemmas is in doing child custody evaluations. One parent may approach the therapist asking for therapy and then request that the therapist appear in court in behalf of the parent's bid for custody of the children in the contested divorce. Of course, such an appearance is inappropriate and unethical because no child custody evaluation has been done. The practitioner has been asked initially to function as a therapist and then later to play a dual role of evaluator. A child custody evaluation typically involves observation of the child

TABLE 16–4 Ground rules for doing custody evaluations

1. No evaluation will be undertaken unless attorneys for all litigants agree to it. Before the evaluator will set up appointments, he or she must have in hand a stipulation signed by the litigants agreeing to participate in the evaluation, or an order from the court requesting the evaluation.

2. In every case, all litigants will be evaluated. The evaluator will refuse to evaluate just one party or to evaluate a child and litigant together without seeing the rest of the family. This rule applies even when one party is living out of state.

3. The children in question will be observed in interaction with each litigant. Each child will be assessed individually and will be interviewed privately, if old enough.

4. Visits will be made to the residence of each litigant at a time when all household members are present. The children in question must be at the residence at the time of the visit. If a litigant has traveled from out of state for the evaluation, provisions will be made to see that party with the children in a non-office setting.

5. Each litigant will provide the evaluator with names of teachers, physicians, babysitters, and others who have been involved with the family. The parents will sign releases allowing the evaluator to talk to these collateral sources of information.

6. The results of the evaluation will be written up in a report that will be sent to each attorney on the same day. If the evaluation was carried out under a court order, the evaluation will be filed in the appropriate court. No attorney or litigant will be told about the results of the evaluation in advance of others.

7. Each litigant will be entitled to a feedback session with the evaluator after the reports are filed, providing an opportunity to ask questions, make comments, and obtain potentially helpful information concerning the children.

From *Child Custody Evaluations: A Practical Guide* (pp. 17–18) by D. Skafte, 1985, Beverly Hills: SAGE Publications. Reprinted by permission.

with each parent separately, a private interview and assessment of the child, a visit to the home of each parent with the child present, and talks with physicians, babysitters, teachers, neighbors, and/or friends who have been involved with the family with the appropriate signed consent forms from both parents (Skafte, 1985). Ground rules should be established in the beginning with both attorneys and both parents before agreeing to conduct the evaluation (see Table 16–4). Inappropriately handling a child custody evaluation by not observing and interviewing everyone can result in a lawsuit for millions of dollars against the therapist or a possible disciplinary hearing before a state licensing board.

Another area of activity that interfaces with the law which should not be attempted unless appropriate specialized training has been obtained is divorce mediation. There are several institutes and specialists who offer one-week workshops and longer courses that lead to credentials in this area. In addition, knowledge of state laws related to divorce is absolutely essential to competent functioning in divorce mediation.

SUMMARY

The 10 steps in the ethical decision-making process are: (1) define the situation, (2) consult ethical codes, (3) generate alternatives, (4) evaluate alternatives according to client welfare, (5) evaluate alternatives according to your responsibility as a professional therapist, (6) evaluate the consequences of each alternative, (7) make a tentative decision, (8) obtain supervision, consultation, or informal peer advice, (9) make and implement the ethical decision, and (10) document this process in the client's record.

Marital and family therapists should assess their own education, training, and experience and decide on what services they are competent to perform. Limiting one's scope of practice to such services makes good business sense because it encourages marketing of specific, targeted services and reduces liability. Competency is a key ethical principle that undergirds all others.

Confidentiality is an ethical requirement of all marital and family therapists in the ethical code. However, there are special problems related to confidentiality in marital and family therapy because more than one client is in the therapy room during a session. Therefore, in many states privileged communication (a legal term where information obtained during therapy is exempted from disclosure in court) does not cover marital and family therapy. It is the responsibility of the therapist to find out about state laws and advise clients of any limits to privileged communication or confidentiality. This is one of several aspects of therapy that should be explained in the written practice policies given to clients prior to the initial session. Clients typically sign an informed consent contract signifying that they have read and agree to abide by the practice policies.

Recent court cases such as *Tarasoff v. Regents of University of California* have established the duty to warn. Marital and family therapists are responsible for assessing risk to self and others; when there is imminent danger to potential victims, the victims should be notified. In addition, their families and law enforcement officials may also need to be contacted, depending upon the nature of the risk and any duty to warn legislation in effect in a given state. Sometimes a client may need to be hospitalized involuntarily because of the risk of suicide or homicide. Marital and family therapists should have contingency plans formulated in advance for dealing with such emergencies.

One key ethical principle is the welfare of the client. The therapist should avoid any dual relationship with clients. In particular, sexual exploitation of clients violates the principle of client welfare and is very damaging to clients because it damages basic trust. Other ethical issues of particular concern to marital and family therapists are systemic epistemology, gender and family therapy, cross-cultural issues, and the use of paradox. It is important for a marital and family therapy to know about ethical dilemmas that interface with the legal system such as court testimony, how to do child custody evaluations, and specialized training for divorce mediation.

EXERCISES

1. Your instructor has invited an attorney to meet with your class. Pretend that you are a private practitioner who conducts marital and family therapy. Prepare a list of questions related to marital and family therapy to ask in front of the class.

2. Find a normal, healthy family who will consent to be audiotaped for an intake process of three sessions with you in the role of the family therapist. You should not know the family, and they should not be relatives. Play the tapes and listen to your structuring skills and relationship skills. Write down 10 areas of strength and 3 areas needing improvement in these skills and in the intake process. Also write down your observations about healthy family functioning.

3. Pretend that you are in private practice. Write a set of policies for your practice that will be given to clients and an informed consent document for clients to sign. If your instructor directs, also design a brochure that outlines the scope of your practice and your standard of care.

4. Prepare a personal contingency plan, tailored to your local community, for what you would actually do if you had a suicidal client in marital or family therapy.

5. Prepare a personal contingency plan, tailored to your local community, for what you would actually do if you had a homicidal client in marital or family therapy.

APPENDIX A
Family Therapist Rating Scale

Directions: Rate the relative effectiveness with which the family therapist engaged in the behaviors listed below. Some of these behaviors may be associated with a school of therapy other than your own. Try to be neutral and rate the relative effectiveness with which the therapist performs each behavior regardless of whether you agree or disagree with the type of intervention. In other words, try not to rate the model of therapy, just the behavior as identified by the statement on the rating scale. Use the following rating scale: Not Present (0); Ineffective (1); Neutral (2); Minimally Effective (3); Effective (4); Very Effective (5); Maximally Effective (6)

Structuring Behaviors							
1. Helps the family define their needs.	0	1	2	3	4	5	6
2. Stops chaotic interchanges.	0	1	2	3	4	5	6
3. Shifts approach when one way of gathering information is not working.	0	1	2	3	4	5	6
4. Uses short, specific and clear communications.	0	1	2	3	4	5	6
5. Asks open-ended questions.	0	1	2	3	4	5	6
6. Helps clients rephrase "why" questions into statements.	0	1	2	3	4	5	6
7. Makes a brief introductory statement about the purpose of the interview.	0	1	2	3	4	5	6
8. Lays down ground rules for therapeutic process.	0	1	2	3	4	5	6
9. Clarifies own and client's expectations of therapy.	0	1	2	3	4	5	6
10. Explicitly structures or directs interaction among family members.	0	1	2	3	4	5	6

Relationship Behaviors

1. Engenders hope.	0	1	2	3	4	5	6
2. Uses self-disclosure.	0	1	2	3	4	5	6
3. Demonstrates warmth.	0	1	2	3	4	5	6
4. "Communicates" the attitude that the client's problem is of real importance.	0	1	2	3	4	5	6
5. Tone of voice conveys sensitivity to the client's feelings.	0	1	2	3	4	5	6
6. Speaks at a comfortable pace.	0	1	2	3	4	5	6
7. Empathizes with family members.	0	1	2	3	4	5	6
8. Confirms family members' experience of an event.	0	1	2	3	4	5	6
9. Attempts to improve the self-esteem of individual family members.	0	1	2	3	4	5	6
10. Demonstrates a good sense of humor.	0	1	2	3	4	5	6

Historical Behaviors

1. Directly asks about the current relationship between a spouse and his/her parents and siblings.	0	1	2	3	4	5	6
2. Explores the couple's mate selection process.	0	1	2	3	4	5	6
3. Emphasizes cognitions.	0	1	2	3	4	5	6
4. Assembles a detailed family history.	0	1	2	3	4	5	6
5. Avoids becoming triangulated by the family.	0	1	2	3	4	5	6
6. Attempts to help clients directly deal with parents and adult siblings about previously avoided issues.	0	1	2	3	4	5	6
7. Assigns or suggests that family members visit extended family members.	0	1	2	3	4	5	6
8. Maintains an objective stance.	0	1	2	3	4	5	6
9. Makes interpretations.	0	1	2	3	4	5	6
10. Collects detailed information about the etiology of the identified problem.	0	1	2	3	4	5	6

Structural/Process Behaviors

1. Checks out pronouns to see who did what to whom.	0	1	2	3	4	5	6
2. Assigns tasks both within the session and outside it.	0	1	2	3	4	5	6
3. Concentrates on the interaction of the system rather than the intrapsychic dynamics.	0	1	2	3	4	5	6
4. Employs paradoxical intention.	0	1	2	3	4	5	6
5. Relabels family symptoms.	0	1	2	3	4	5	6
6. Reorders behavioral sequences (e.g., order of speaking, who speaks to whom).	0	1	2	3	4	5	6
7. Rearranges the physical seating of family members.	0	1	2	3	4	5	6
8. Helps the family establish appropriate boundaries.	0	1	2	3	4	5	6
9. Elicits covert family conflicts, alliances and coalitions.	0	1	2	3	4	5	6
10. Assumes the role of expert technician who observes and then intervenes.	0	1	2	3	4	5	6

Experiential Behaviors

1. Uses family sculpting.	0	1	2	3	4	5	6
2. Encourages family members to find their own solutions.	0	1	2	3	4	5	6
3. Encourages individuals to share their fantasies.	0	1	2	3	4	5	6
4. Asks for current feelings.	0	1	2	3	4	5	6
5. Lets the clients choose the subject of the session.	0	1	2	3	4	5	6
6. Attempts to focus on process rather than content.	0	1	2	3	4	5	6
7. Uses role playing.	0	1	2	3	4	5	6
8. Responds to his/her own discomfort.	0	1	2	3	4	5	6
9. Uses own affect to elicit affect in family members.	0	1	2	3	4	5	6
10. Keeps the interaction in the here and now.	0	1	2	3	4	5	6

Family Therapist Rating Scale Profile

Therapist's name _____   Comments _____

Date _____   _____

Rater _____   _____

Mean Rating	Raw Score	Structuring	Relationship	Historical	Structural/ Process	Experiential
6	60	•	•	•	•	•
	55	•	•	•	•	•
5	50	•	•	•	•	•
	45	•	•	•	•	•
4	40	•	•	•	•	•
	35	•	•	•	•	•
3	30	•	•	•	•	•
	25	•	•	•	•	•
2	20	•	•	•	•	•
	15	•	•	•	•	•
1	10	•	•	•	•	•
	5	•	•	•	•	•

Note: A profile of a family therapist's behavior may be constructed in two ways. In one approach, raw scores, the total points within each category, may be added and placed on the profile. However, it may at times be helpful to use the mean ratings of only those behaviors actually observed within each category. The above profile has been constructed to accommodate either method.

Adapted from "A Family Therapist Rating Scale" by F. P. Piercy, R. A. Laird, and Z. Mohammed, 1983, *Journal of Marital and Family Therapy, 9*(1), pp. 49–59. Reprinted by permission.

APPENDIX B
Systems Assessment Checklist

Macro-Systems

From what culture or ethnic group is this family? Are the parents from the same cultural background? How are any cultural differences handled in this family?

At what socio-economic level is the family? Have there been any financial reversals or changes in the last year?

What is the religious affiliation of each of the family members? How involved is each member in an organized religion?

What are the gender roles exhibited in this family by each member? How do these relate to the larger culture and the family of origin?

How involved in the community is this family? Does the married couple spend time with a network of couple friends? What support networks does this family have?

Family System

At what stage of the family life cycle is this family (underline one)—independent, adult, marital dyad, infant family, pre-school family, grade school family, adolescent family, launching family, mentoring dyad, retired family, or elderly family? What issues are typically associated with this stage?

What is the characteristic style of this family in a crisis? Do they cling together (centripetal or integration) or fly apart (centrifugal or differentiation)? How might this family style affect treatment and the interventions chosen?

What defense mechanisms are most often used by this family? Are they more or less mature? How can less mature defense mechanisms be dealt with in family therapy?

How is "family" defined for this family? Nuclear family? Single-parent family? Extended family? Emotional family of friends?

What does this family consider "normal" to be? What are their expectations for treatment?

What is the presenting problem(s)? Is there an identified patient in this family? What is the function(s) of the symptom(s) for this family?

What is the nature of any prior family treatment? Has written permission been obtained to request the records? If not, why not?

What is the theme of this family?

What are the strengths and resources of this family? How do they have fun?

What is a typical weekday like for this family? A routine weekend?

How and what kind of emotions are expressed in this family? Between members in the therapy session? What is the feeling experienced at the gut level by the therapist while in a session with this family? How emotionally involved are family members with each other?

What are the structure, hierarchy, rules, roles, boundaries, alignments, coalitions, allocations of power, and degree of flexibility of this family?

How do family members communicate in this family?

How do family members solve problems in this family?

How do family members manage conflict in this family?

What are the hopes and dreams of this family? How does this family view the world? What are their belief systems?

Marital Subsystem

How good is the marriage of the parents, if still intact?

What is the history of this relationship? How did it begin? Reach a commitment?

What are the expectations of each partner for the marriage? How realistic are they?

How satisfied are the partners with their current gender roles?

How satisfied are the partners with their instrumental and appetitive behaviors?

What patterns of interaction in the session are problematic for the couple?

How is the sexual relationship between the partners? How frequently do they have sexual intercourse? Are there any dysfunctions?

How well does each partner get along with in-laws?

Is there any ongoing verbal or physical abuse of the spouse? If so, what is being done to protect the spouse?

Parent-Child Subsystem(s)

What is the quality of each child's relationship with each parent? With any step-parent(s)? With any grandparents or neighbors who are bonded to the child?

Has any child been physically abused? Sexually abused? Neglected? Has ongoing child abuse been reported to the appropriate authorities if mandated by statute?

Sibling Subsystem

How do the children get along with each other? Is there significant sibling rivalry? How do children get along with any step-children?

Individual Subsystems

What is the developmental stage of each individual family member? What issues are associated with the stage? How do the issues of one or more family members conflict with the issues associated with the family's stage of the family life cycle?

How have family members developed their careers, separate selves, and families? What is each family member doing to make progress in each of these major areas of life? What is the level of self-esteem of each family member?

What are the strengths of each family member on each developmental do-main—spiritual, intellectual, behavioral, physical, sensual, sexual, interpersonal, emotional, and imaginal?

What is the health of each family member? What are the medical problems and medications of each family member? Who are the treating professionals? Should a referral be made to a physician or other health care professional for a health problem?

How frequently does each family member use alcohol and drugs? Has any family member been treated in a rehabilitation center?

Has any family member been involved with DUIs or other illegal offenses?

Has any family member received mental health treatment? If so, has permission been obtained to request the records?

What are the results of an assessment of the vegetative signs of family members? Is anyone depressed? Is any family member dangerous to self or others? If so, what steps have been taken to protect potential victims?

What is the family of origin like for each parent? Any particular strengths, problems, or themes? Has there been a death in the family in the last year? An unresolved death that has not been grieved, regardless of when it occurred?

What are the expectations and life dreams of each family member? How realistic are they? What are their attributional styles?

APPENDIX C
AAMFT Code of Ethics*

*From *AAMFT Code of Ethical Principles for Marriage and Family Therapists* by American Association for Marriage and Family Therapy, 1988. Reprinted by permission.

AAMFT Code of Ethical Principles for Marriage and Family Therapists

The Board of Directors of the American Association for Marriage and Family Therapy (AAMFT) hereby promulgates, pursuant to Article II, Section (1)(C) of the Association's Bylaws, the Revised AAMFT Code of Ethical Principles for Marriage and Family Therapists, effective August 1, 1988.

The AAMFT Code of Ethical Principles for Marriage and Family Therapists is binding on all Members of AAMFT (Clinical, Student, and Associate) and on all AAMFT Approved Supervisors.

If an AAMFT Member or an AAMFT Approved Supervisor resigns in anticipation of or during the course of an ethics investigation, the Ethics Committee will complete its investigation. Any publication of action taken by the Association will include the fact that the Member attempted to resign during the investigation.

Marriage and family therapists are encouraged to report alleged unethical behavior of colleagues to appropriate professional associations and state regulatory bodies.

1. Responsibility to Clients

Marriage and family therapists are dedicated to advancing the welfare of families and individuals, including respecting the rights of those persons seeking their assistance, and making reasonable efforts to ensure that their services are used appropriately.

1.1 Marriage and family therapists do not discriminate against or refuse professional service to anyone on the basis of race, sex, religion, or national origin.

1.2 Marriage and family therapists are cognizant of their potentially influential position with respect to clients, and they avoid exploiting the trust and dependency of such persons. Marriage and family therapists therefore make every effort to avoid dual relationships with clients that could impair their professional judgement or increase the risk of exploitation. Examples of such dual relationships include, but are not limited to, business or close personal relationships with clients. Sexual intimacy with clients is prohibited. Sexual intimacy with former clients for two years following the termination of therapy is prohibited.

1.3 Marriage and family therapists do not use their professional relationship with clients to further their own interests.

1.4 Marriage and family therapists respect the right of clients to make decisions and help them to understand the consequences of these decisions. Marriage and family therapists clearly advise a client that a decision on marital status is the responsibility of the client.

1.5 Marriage and family therapists continue therapeutic relationships only so long as it is reasonably clear that clients are benefiting from the relationship.

1.6 Marriage and family therapists assist persons in obtaining other therapeutic services if a marriage and family therapist is unable or unwilling, for appropriate reasons, to see a person who has requested professional help.

1.7 Marriage and family therapists do not abandon or neglect clients in treatment without making reasonable arrangements for the continuation of such treatment.

1.8 Marriage and family therapists obtain informed consent of clients before taping, recording, or permitting third party observation of their activities.

2. Confidentiality

Marriage and family therapists have unique confidentiality problems because the "client" in a therapeutic relationship may be more than one person. The overriding principle is that marriage and family therapists respect the confidences of their client(s).

2.1 Marriage and family therapists cannot disclose client confidences to anyone, except: (1) as mandated by law; (2) to prevent a clear and immediate danger to a person or persons; (3) where the marriage and family therapist is a defendant in a civil, criminal or disciplinary action arising from the therapy (in which case client confidences may only be disclosed in the course of that action); or (4) if there is a waiver previously obtained in writing, and then such information may only be revealed in accordance with the terms of the waiver. In circumstances where more than one person in a family is receiving therapy, each such family member who is legally competent to execute a waiver must agree to the waiver required by sub-paragraph (4). Absent such a waiver from each family member legally competent to execute a waiver, a marriage and family therapist cannot disclose information received from any family member.

2.2 Marriage and family therapists use client and/or clinical materials in teaching, writing, and public presentations only if a written waiver has been received in accordance with sub-principle 2.1(4), or when appropriate steps have been taken to protect client identity.

2.3 Marriage and family therapists store or dispose of client records in ways that maintain confidentiality.

3. Professional Competence and Integrity

Marriage and family therapists are dedicated to maintaining high standards of professional competence and integrity.

3.1 Marriage and family therapists who (a) are convicted of felonies, (b) are convicted of misdemeanors (related to their qualifications or functions), (c) engage in conduct which could lead to conviction of felonies, or misdemeanors related to their qualifications or functions, (d) are expelled from other professional organizations, (e) have their licenses or certificates suspended or revoked, (f) are no longer competent to practice marriage and family therapy because they are impaired due to physical or mental causes or the abuse of alcohol or other substances, or (g) fail to cooperate with the Association at any stage of an investigation of an ethical complaint of his/her conduct by the AAMFT Ethics Committee or Judicial Council, are subject to termination of membership or other appropriate action.

3.2 Marriage and family therapists seek appropriate professional assistance for their own personal problems or conflicts that are likely to impair their work performance and their clinical judgement.

3.3 Marriage and family therapists, as teachers, are dedicated to maintaining high standards of scholarship and presenting information that is accurate.

3.4 Marriage and family therapists seek to remain abreast of new developments in family therapy knowledge and practice through both educational activities and clinical experiences.

3.5 Marriage and family therapists do not engage in sexual or other harassment or exploitation of clients, students, trainees, employees, colleagues, research subjects, or actual or potential witnesses or complainants in ethical proceedings.

3.6 Marriage and family therapists do not attempt to diagnose, treat, or advise on problems outside the recognized boundaries of their competence.

3.7 Marriage and family therapists attempt to prevent the distortion or misuse of their clinical and research findings.

3.8 Marriage and family therapists are aware that, because of their ability to influence and alter the lives of others, they must exercise special care when making public their professional recommendations and opinions through testimony or other public statements.

4. Responsibility to Students, Employees, and Supervisees

Marriage and family therapists do not exploit the trust and dependency of students, employees, and supervisees.

4.1 Marriage and family therapists are cognizant of their potentially influential position with respect to students, employees, and supervisees, and they avoid exploiting the trust and dependency of such persons. Marriage and family therapists, therefore, make every effort to avoid dual relationships that could impair their professional judgement or increase the risk of exploitation. Examples of such dual relationships include, but are not limited to, provision of therapy to students, employees, or supervisees, and business or close personal relationships with students, employees, or supervisees. Sexual intimacy with students or supervisees is prohibited.

4.2 Marriage and family therapists do not permit students, employees, or supervisees to perform or to hold themselves out as competent to perform professional services beyond their training, level of experience, and competence.

5. Responsibility to the Profession

Marriage and family therapists respect the rights and responsibilities of professional colleagues; carry out research in an ethical manner; and participate in activities which advance the goals of the profession.

5.1 Marriage and family therapists remain accountable to the standards of the profession when acting as members or employees of organizations.

5.2 Marriage and family therapists assign publication credit to those who have contributed to a publication in proportion to their contributions and in accordance with customary professional publication practices.

5.3 Marriage and family therapists who are the authors of books or other materials that are published or distributed should cite appropriately persons to whom credit for original ideas is due.

5.4 Marriage and family therapists who are the authors of books or other materials published or distributed by an organization take reasonable precautions to ensure that the organization promotes and advertises the materials accurately and factually.

5.5 Marriage and family therapists, as researchers, must be adequately informed of and abide by relevant laws and regulations regarding the conduct of research with human participants.

5.6 Marriage and family therapists recognize a responsibility to participate in activities that contribute to a better community and society, including devoting a portion of their professional activity to services for which there is little or no financial return.

5.7 Marriage and family therapists are concerned with developing laws and regulations pertaining to marriage and family therapy that serve the public interest, and with altering such laws and regulations that are not in the public interest.

5.8 Marriage and family therapists encourage public participation in the designing and delivery of services and in the regulation of practitioners.

6. Financial Arrangements

Marriage and family therapists make financial arrangements with clients and third party payors that conform to accepted professional practices and that are reasonably understandable.

6.1 Marriage and family therapists do not offer or accept payment for referrals.

6.2 Marriage and family therapists do not charge excessive fees for services.

6.3 Marriage and family therapists disclose their fee structure to clients at the onset of treatment.

6.4 Marriage and family therapists are careful to represent facts truthfully to clients and third party payors regarding services rendered.

7. Advertising

Marriage and family therapists engage in appropriate informational activities, including those that enable laypersons to choose marriage and family services on an informed basis.

7.1 Marriage and family therapists accurately represent their competence, education, training, and experience relevant to their practice of marriage and family therapy.

7.2 Marriage and family therapists claim as evidence of educational qualifications in conjunction with their AAMFT membership only those degrees (a) from regionally-accredited institutions or (b) from institutions recognized by states which license or certify marriage and family therapists, but only if such regulation is accepted by AAMFT.

7.3 Marriage and family therapists assure that advertisements and publications, whether in directories, announcement cards, newspapers, or on radio or television, are formulated to convey information that is necessary for the public to make an appropriate selection. Information could include: (1) office information, such as name, address, telephone number, credit card acceptability, fee structure, languages spoken and office hours; (2) appropriate degrees, state license and/or certification, and AAMFT Clinical Member status; and (3) description of practice.

7.4 Marriage and family therapists do not use a name which could mislead the public concerning the identity, responsibility, source, and status of those practicing under that name and do not hold themselves out as being partners or associates of a firm if they are not.

7.5 Marriage and family therapists do not use any professional identification (such as a professional card, office sign, letterhead, or telephone or association directory listing) if it includes a statement or claim that is false, fraudulent, misleading, or deceptive. A statement is false, fraudulent, misleading, or deceptive if it (a) contains a material misrepresentation of fact; (b) fails to state any material fact necessary to make the statement, in light of all circumstances, not misleading; or (c) is intended to or is likely to create an unjustified expectation.

7.6 Marriage and family therapists correct, wherever possible, false, misleading, or inaccurate information and representations made by others concerning the marriage and family therapist's qualifications, services, or products.

7.7 Marriage and family therapists make certain that the qualifications of persons in their employ are represented in a manner that is not false, misleading, or deceptive.

7.8 Marriage and family therapists may represent themselves as specializing within a limited area of marriage and family therapy, but may not hold themselves out as specialists without being able to provide evidence of training, education, and supervised experience in settings which meet recognized professional standards.

7.9 Only marriage and family therapist Clinical Members, Approved Supervisors, and Fellows —**not** Associate Members, Student Members, or organizations—may identify these AAMFT designations in public information or advertising materials.

7.10 Marriage and family therapists may not use the initials AAMFT following their name in the manner of an academic degree.

7.11 Marriage and family therapists may not use the AAMFT name, logo, and the abbreviated initials AAMFT. The Association (which is the sole owner of its name, logo, and the abbreviated initials AAMFT) and its committees and regional divisions, operating as such, may use the name, logo, and the abbreviated initials AAMFT. A regional division of AAMFT may use the AAMFT insignia to list its individual Clinical Members as a group (e.g., in the Yellow Pages); when all Clinical Members practicing within a directory district have been invited to list themselves in the directory, any one or more members may do so.

7.12 Marriage and family therapists use their membership in AAMFT only in connection with their clinical and professional activities.

Violations of this Code should be brought in writing to the attention of the AAMFT Committee on Ethics and Professional Practices at the central office of AAMFT, 1717 K Street, N.W., Suite 407, Washington, DC 20006.

Effective August 1, 1988

References

Chapter One

Anderson, C. M., & Reiss, D. J., (1982). Approaches to psychoeducational family therapy. *International Journal of Family Psychiatry, 3*(4), 501–517.

Anderson, C. M., Reiss, D. J., & Hogarty, G. E. (1986). *Schizophrenia and the family: A practitioner's guide to psychoeducation and management.* New York: Guilford Press.

Anderson, D. (1987). *Chronic illness: Commonalities of coping and caring.* Speech presented at the Rutgers Univ. Summer School of Alcohol Studies, New Brunswick, NJ.

Anderson, R. A. (1988). *Wellness medicine.* Lynnwood, WA: American Health Press.

Ashby, W. R. (1956). *An introduction to cybernetics.* London: Methuen.

Barton, C., & Alexander, J. F. (1981). Functional family therapy. In A. S. Gurman & D. P. Kniskern (Eds.), *Handbook of family therapy* (pp. 403–443). New York: Brunner/Mazel.

Bateson, G. (1972). *Toward an ecology of mind.* New York: Ballantine Books.

Bateson, G., Jackson, D. D., Haley, J., & Weakland, J. (1956). Toward a theory of schizophrenia. *Behavioral Science, 1,* 251–264.

Berkman, L. F., & Syme, S. L. (1979). Social networks, host resistance and mortality: A nine-year follow-up study of Alameda County residents. *American Journal of Epidemiology, 109,* 186–204.

Bernal, G., Konjevich, C., & Deegan, E. (1987). Families with depression, school, marital, family and situational problems. A research note. *American Journal of Family Therapy, 15*(1), 44–51.

Birchler, G. R. (1979). Communication skills in married couples. In A. S. Bellack & M. Hersen (Eds.), *Research and practice in social skills training* (pp. 273–315). New York: Plenum Press.

Blackburn, H., Watkins, L. O., Agras, W. S., Carleton, R. A., & Falkner, B. (1987). Task Force 5: Primary prevention of coronary heart disease. *Circulation, 76* (supp. I), I-164–167.

Blumenthal, J. A., & Levinson, R. M. (1987). Behavioral approaches to secondary prevention of coronary heart disease. *Circulation, 76* (supp. I), I-130–137.

Bowen, M. (1978). *Family therapy in clinical practice.* New York: Jason Aronson.

Broderick, C. B., & Schrader, S. S. (1981). The history of professional marriage and family therapy. In A. S. Gurman & D. P. Kniskern (Eds.), *Handbook of family therapy* (pp. 5–35). New York: Brunner/Mazel.

Bruhn, J. G., & Wolf, S. (1979). *The Roseto story: An anatomy of health.* Norman, OK: Univ. of Oklahoma Press.

Campbell, T. L. (1986). Family's impact on health: A critical review. *Family Systems Medicine, 4,* 135–200.

Caplan, G. (1982). The family as a support system. In H. I. McCubbin, A. E. Cauble, & J. M. Patterson (Eds.), *Family stress, coping and social support* (pp. 200–220). Springfield, IL: Charles C. Thomas, Publisher.

Cobb, S. (1982). Social support and health through the life course. In H. I. McCubbin, A. E. Cauble, & J. M. Patterson (Eds.), *Family stress, coping and social support* (pp. 189–199). Springfield, IL: Charles C. Thomas, Publisher.

Cookerly, J. R. (1980, October). Does marital therapy do any good? *Journal of Marital and Family Therapy,* 393–397.

Coyne, J. C. (1984) Strategic therapy with depressed married persons: Initial agenda, themes and interventions. *Journal of Marital and Family Therapy, 10*(1), 53–62.

Coyne, J. C. (1987). Depression, biology, marriage and marital therapy. *Journal of Marital and Family Therapy, 13*(4), 393–407.

de Shazer (1985). *Keys to solutions in brief therapy.* New York: W. W. Norton & Co.

Doherty, W. J., Lester, M. E., & Leigh, G. K. (1986). Marriage encounter weekends: Couples who win and couples who lose. *Journal of Marital and Family Therapy, 12*(1), 49–61.

Emmelkamp, P. M. G., Van Linden Van Den Heuvell, C., Sanderman, R., & Scholing, A. (1988). Cognitive marital therapy: The process of change. *Journal of Family Psychology, 1,* 385–389.

Engel, G. (1977). The need for a new medical model: A challenge for biomedicine. *Science, 196,* 129–136.

Falloon, I. R., Boyd, J. L., McGill, C. W., Williamson, M., Razani, J., Moss, H. B., Gilderman, A. M., & Simpson, G. M. (1985). Family management in the prevention of morbidity of schizophrenia: Clinical outcome of a two-year longitudinal study. *Archives of General Psychiatry, 42*(9), 887–896.

Freymann, J. (1987). *Swinging with the shifting paradigm.* Speech presented at the annual meeting of the Society of Teachers of Family Medicine, New Orleans, LA.

Giblin, P. (1986). Research and assessment in marriage and family enrichment: A meta-analysis study. *Journal of Psychotherapy and the Family, 2*(1), 79–96.

Glick, I. D., Clarkin, J. F., Spencer, J. H., Haas, G. L., Lewis, A. B., Reyser, J., De Mane, N., Good-Ellis, M., Harris, E., & Lestelle, V. (1985). A controlled evaluation of inpatient family intervention: I. Preliminary results of the six-month follow-up. *Archives of General Psychiatry, 42*(9), 882–886.

Gordon, D. A., Arbuthnot, J., Gustafson, K. E., & Mc-Green, P. (1988). Home-based behavioral-systems family therapy with disadvantaged juvenile delinquents. *American Journal of Family Therapy, 16*(3), 243–255.

Gordon, S. B., & Davidson, N. (1981). Behavioral parent training. In A. S. Gurman & D. P. Kniskern (Eds.), *Handbook of family therapy* (pp. 517–555). New York: Brunner/Mazel.

Gottman, J. M. (1982). Emotional responsiveness in marital conversations. *Journal of Communication, 32*(3), 108–120.

Grossman, R. (1985). *The other medicines.* Garden City, NY: Doubleday & Co.

Guerin, P. J., Jr. (1976). Family therapy: The first twenty-five years. In P. J. Guerin, Jr. (Ed.), *Family therapy: Theory and practice* (pp. 2–22). New York: Gardner Press.

Gurman, A. S., & Kniskern, D. P. (1978). Research on marital and family therapy: Progress, perspective and prospect. In S. Garfield & A. Bergin (Eds.), *Handbook of psychotherapy and behavior change* (2nd ed.) (pp. 817–901). New York: John Wiley & Sons.

Gurman, A. S., & Kniskern, D. P. (1981). Family therapy outcome research: Knowns and unknowns. In A. S. Gurman & D. P. Kniskern (Eds.), *Handbook of family therapy* (pp. 742–775). New York: Brunner/Mazel.

Gurman, A. S., Kniskern, D. P., & Pinsof, W. M. (1986). Research on the process and outcome of marital and family therapy (3rd ed.). In S. L. Garfield & A. E. Bergin (Eds.), *Handbook of psychotherapy and behavior change* (pp. 565–622). New York: John Wiley & Sons.

Haas, G., Glick, I. D., Clarkin, J. F., & Spencer, J. H. (1988). Inpatient family intervention: A randomized clinical trial: II. Results at hospital discharge. *Archives of General Psychiatry, 45*(3), 217–224.

Hahlweg, K., & Markman, H. J. (1988). Effectiveness of behavioral marital therapy: Empirical status of behavioral techniques in preventing and alleviating marital distress. *Journal of Consulting and Clinical Psychology, 56*(3), 440–447.

Hahlweg, K., Revenstorf, D., & Schindler, L. (1984). Effects of behavioral marital therapy on couples' communication and problem-solving skills. *Journal of Consulting and Clinical Psychology, 52*(4), 553–66.

Haley, J. (1980). *Leaving home: The therapy of disturbed adolescents.* New York: McGraw-Hill Book Co.

Hartley, L. H., Foreyt, J. P., Alderman, M. H., Chesney, M. A., Friedman, M., Hendrix, G. H., Herd, J. A., Levenson, R. M., Ruberman, W., & Thoresen, C. E. (1987). Task Force 6: Secondary prevention of coronary artery disease. *Circulation, 76* (supp. I), I-168–172.

Hazelrigg, M. D., Cooper, H. M., & Borduin, C. M. (1987). Evaluating the effectiveness of family therapies: An integrative review and analysis. *Psychological Bulletin, 101*(3), 428–442.

House, J., Robbins, C., & Metzner, H. (1982). The association of social relationships and activities with mortality: Prospective evidence from the Tecumseh Community Health Study. *American Journal of Epidemiology, 116,* 125.

Jacobson, N. S. (1978). A review of the research on the effectiveness of marital therapy. In T. J. Paolino & B. S. McCrady (Eds.), *Marriage and marital therapy* (pp. 395–444). New York: Brunner/Mazel.

Jacobson, N. S. (1979). Behavioral treatments for marital discord: A critical appraisal. In M. Hersen, R. M. Eisler, & P. M. Miller (Eds.), *Progress in behavior modification,* Vol. 8 (pp. 169–205). New York: Academic Press.

Jacobson, N. S. (1989). The maintenance of treatment gains following social learning-based marital therapy. *Behavior Therapy, 20*(3), 325–336.

Jacobson, N. S., Follette, W. C., Revenstorf, D., Baucom, D. H., Hahlweg, K., & Margolin, G. (1984). Variability in outcome and clinical significance of behavioral marital therapy: A reanalysis of outcome data. *Journal of Consulting and Clinical Psychology, 52*(4), 497–504.

Jacobson, N. S., Schmaling, K. B., & Holtzworth-Munroe, A. (1987). Component analysis of behavioral marital therapy: 2-year follow-up and prediction of relapse. *Journal of Marital and Family Therapy, 13*(2), 187–95.

Johnson, S. M., & Greenberg, L. S. (1985). Differential effects of experiential and problem-solving interventions in resolving marital conflict. *Journal of Consulting and Clinical Psychology, 53*(2), 175–184.

Johnson, S. M., & Greenberg, L. S. (1988). Relating process to outcome in marital therapy. *Journal of Marital and Family Therapy, 14*(2), 175–83.

Kaslow, F. W. (1977). *Supervision, consultation, and staff training in the helping professions.* San Francisco: Jossey-Bass.

Kaslow, F. W. (1982). History of family therapy in the United States: A kaleidoscopic overview. In F. W. Kaslow (Ed.), *The international book of family therapy* (pp. 5–40). New York: Brunner/Mazel.

Kaslow, F. W. (1987). Trends in family psychology. *Journal of Family Psychology, 1,* 77–90.

Kleinman, A. (1980). *Patients and healers in the context of culture.* Berkeley, CA: Univ. of California Press.

Kolevzon, M. S., & Green, R. G. (1985). *Family therapy models: Convergence and divergence.* New York: Springer Publishing Co.

Kosten, T. R., Jalali, B., Hogan, I., & Kleber, H. D. (1983). Family denial as a prognostic factor in opiate addict treatment outcome. *Journal of Nervous and Mental Disease, 171*(10), 611–616.

Kushi, M. (1981). *The macrobiotic approach to cancer.* Wayne, NJ: Avery Publishing.

Leigh, H., & Reiser, M. F. (1985). *The patient: Biological, psychological and social dimensions of medical practice.* (2nd ed.). New York: Plenum Press.

Lewis, J. M., Beavers, R. W., Gossett, J. T., & Phillips, V. A. (1976). *No single thread: Psychological health in family systems.* New York: Brunner/Mazel.

Lewis, J. M., & Looney, J. G. (1983). *The long struggle: Well-functioning working-class black families.* New York: Brunner/Mazel.

Libman, E., Fichten, C. S., & Brenden, W. (1985). The role of therapeutic format on the treatment of sexual dysfunction: A review. *Clinical Psychology Review, 5*(2), 103–117.

Liddle, H. A. (1987). Family psychology: The journal, the field. *Journal of Family Psychology, 1,* 5–22.

Matthews-Simonton, S., Simonton, O. C., & Creighton, J. L. (1978). *Getting well again: A step-by-step, self-help guide to overcoming cancer for patients and their families.* New York: Bantam Books.

McHugh, S., & Vallis, M. (1986). Illness behaviour: Operationalization of the biopsychosocial model. In S. McHugh & M. Vallis (Eds.), *Illness behavior: A multi-disciplinary model* (pp. 1–30). New York: Plenum Press.

Meeks, L., & Heit, P. (1988). *The Merrill Wellness Series: AIDS—What you should know.* Columbus, OH: Merrill.

Miller, W. L. (1988). Models of health, illness, and health care. In R. B. Taylor (Ed.), *Family medicine: Principles and practice* (pp. 35–42). New York: Springer-Verlag.

Minuchin, S., Baker, L., Rosman, B. L., Liebman, R., Milman, L., & Todd, T. C. (1975). A conceptual model of psychosomatic illness in children: Family organization and family therapy. *Archives of General Psychiatry, 32,* 1031–1038.

Minuchin, S., Montalvo, B., Guerney, B., Rosman, B., & Schumer, F. (1967). *Families of the slums*. New York: Basic Books.

Minuchin, S., Rosman, B., & Baker, L. (1978). *Psychosomatic families*. Cambridge, MA: Harvard Univ. Press.

Morokoff, P. J., & LoPiccolo, J. (1986). A comparative evaluation of minimal therapist contact and 15-session treatment for female orgasmic dysfunction. *Journal of Consulting and Clinical Psychology, 54*(3), 294–300.

Mosby's Medical & Nursing Dictionary (2nd ed.). (1986). St. Louis, MO: C. V. Mosby Co.

Nichols, M. P. (1987). *The self in the system: Expanding the limits of family therapy*. New York: Brunner/Mazel.

O'Farrell, T. J. (1989). Marital and family therapy in alcoholism treatment. *Journal of Substance Abuse Treatment, 6*(1), 23–29.

Olson, D. H. (1970). Marital and family therapy: Integrative reviews and critique. *Journal of Marriage and the Family, 32*, 501–538.

Olson, D. H., Russell, C. S., & Sprenkle, D. H. (1980, November). Marital and family therapy: A decade review. *Journal of Marriage and the Family, 42*, 973–989.

Olson, D. H., Sprenkle, D. H., & Russell, C. S. (1979). Circumplex model of marital and family systems: I. Cohesion and adaptability dimensions, family types and clinical applications. *Family Process, 18*, 3–28.

Ostrow, G. (Ed.) (1987). *Biobehavioral control of AIDS*. New York: Irvington.

Patterson, G. R. (1971). *Families: Application of social learning to family life*. Champaign, IL: Research Press.

Patterson, G. R. (1974). Interventions for boys with conduct problems: Multiple settings, treatment and criteria. *Journal of Consulting and Clinical Psychology, 42*, 471–481.

Patterson, G. R. (1989). A developmental perspective on antisocial behavior. *American Psychologist, 44*(2), 329–335.

Patterson, G. R., Chamberlain, P., & Reid, J. B. (1982). A comparative evaluation of a parent-training program. *Behavior Therapy, 13*(5), 638–650.

Patterson, G. R., Weiss, R. L., & Hops, H. (1976). Training of marital skills. In H. Leitenberg (Ed.), *Handbook of behavior modification and behavior therapy*. Englewood Cliffs, NJ: Prentice-Hall.

Rabin, D. (1981, September). The single-case design in family therapy evaluation research. *Family Process, 20*, 351–366.

Reiss, D. (1981). *The family's construction of reality*. Cambridge, MA: Harvard Univ. Press.

Rolland, J. S. (1984). Toward a psychosocial typology of chronic and life-threatening illness. *Family Systems Medicine, 2*, 245–262.

Rolland, J. S. (1987). Family illness paradigms: Evolution and significance. *Family Systems Medicine, 5*, 482–503.

Rolland, J. S. (1988). Chronic illness and the family life cycle. In B. Carter & M. McGoldrick (Eds.), *The changing family life cycle: A framework for family therapy* (2nd ed.) (pp. 433–456). New York: Gardner Press.

Ross, E. R., Baker, S. B., & Guerney, G. (1985). Effectiveness of relationship enhancement therapy versus therapist's preferred therapy. *American Journal of Family Therapy, 13*(1), 11–21.

Russell, C. S., Olson, D. H., & Sprenkle, D. H. (1983). From family symptom to family system: Review of family therapy research. *American Journal of Family Therapy, 11*(3), 3–14.

Russell, G. F., Szmukler, G. I., Dare, C., & Esler, I. (1987). An evaluation of family therapy in anorexia nervosa and bulimia nervosa. *Archives of General Psychiatry, 44*(12), 1047–1056.

Ryan, R. S., & Travis, J. W. (1981). *The wellness workbook*. Berkeley, CA: Ten Speed Press.

Sachs, R. G., et al. (1985) Marital and family therapy in the treatment of multiple personality disorder. *Journal of Marital and Family Therapy, 14*(3), 249–259.

Satir, V. (1964). *Conjoint family therapy: A guide to theory and technique*. Palo Alto, CA: Science and Behavior Books.

Scharff, D. E., & Scharff, J. S. (1987). *Object relations family therapy*. New York: Jason Aronson.

Schmidt, D. D. (1983). When is it helpful to convene the family? *The Journal of Family Practice, 16*, 967–973.

Schover, L. R., & LoPiccolo, J. (1982). Treatment effectiveness for dysfunctions of sexual desire. *Journal of Sex and Marital Therapy, 8*(3), 179–197.

Schroeder, P. (1989). *The great American family*. New York: Random House.

Schumm, W. R., Burgaighis, M. A., & Jurich, A. P. (1985). Using repeated measure designs in program evaluation of family therapy. *Journal of Marital and Family Therapy, 11*(1), 87–95.

Selvini Palazzoli, M., Boscolo, L., Cecchin, G., & Prata, G. (1978). *Paradox and counterparadox*. New York: Jason Aronson.

Selvini Palazzoli, M., Cirillo, S., Selvini, M., & Sorrentino, A. M. (1989). *Family games: General models of psychotic processes in the family* (Trans. V. Kleiber). New York: W. W. Norton & Co.

Shapiro, D. A., & Shapiro, D. (1983). Comparative therapy outcome research: Methodological implications of meta-analysis. *Journal of Counseling and Clinical Psychology, 51*(1), 42–53.

Siegel, B. S. (1986). *Love, medicine and miracles*. New York: Harper & Row.

Siegel, B. S. (1989). *Peace, love & healing: Body mind communication and the path to self-healing: An exploration*. New York: Harper & Row.

Sprenkle, D. H., & Storm, C. L. (1983). Divorce therapy outcome research: A substantive and methodological review. *Journal of Marital and Family Therapy, 9*(3), 239–258.

Stanton, M. D., Todd, T. C., Steier, F., Van Deusen, J. M., Marder, L. R., Rosoff, F. J., Seaman, S. F., & Skibinski, I. (1979). *Family characteristics and family therapy of heroine addicts: Final report 1974–1978*. Report prepared for the Psychosocial Branch, Division of Research, National Institute on Drug Abuse, HEW.

Stierlin, H., & Weber, G. (1989). *Unlocking the family door: A systemic approach to the understanding and treatment of anorexia nervosa*. New York: Brunner/Mazel.

Szykula, S. A., Morris, S. B., Sudweeks, C., & Sayger, T. V. (1987). Child-focused behavior and strategic therapies: Outcome comparisons. *Psychotherapy, 24*(35), 546–551.

Teichman, Y., & Eliahu, D. (1986). A combination of structural family therapy and behavior techniques in treating a patient with two tics. *Journal of Clinical Child Psychology, 15*(4), 311–316.

Todd, T. C. (1984). A contingency analysis of family treatment and drug abuse. *National Institute on Drug Abuse Research Monograph Series, 46,* 104–114.

Wampler, K. S. (1982, November). Bringing the review of literature into the age of quantification: Meta-analysis as a strategy for integrating research findings in family studies. *Journal of Marriage and the Family,* 1009–1023.

Watzlawick, P. (1955). The army ant analogy. In T. C. Schneider & G. Piel (Eds.), *Twentieth century bestiary* (pp. 65–66). New York: Simon & Schuster.

Weakland, J., Fisch R., Watzlawick, P., & Bodin, A. (1974). Brief therapy: Focused problem resolution. *Family Process, 13,* 141–168.

Wiener, N. (1948). *Cybernetics, or control and communication in the animal and the machine*. Cambridge, MA: Massachusetts Institute of Technology Press.

Woody, J. D. (1985). The family in health crisis. In J. R. Springer & R. H. Woody (Eds.), *Health promotion in family therapy* (pp. 71–82). Rockville, MD: Aspen Systems Corp.

Woody, R. H. (1985). Shaping public policy for family health. In J. R. Springer & R. H. Woody (Eds.), *Health promotion in family therapy,* (pp. 1–12). Rockville, MD: Aspen Systems Corp.

Woody, R. H. (1989). *Protecting your mental health practice: How to minimize legal and financial risk*. San Francisco: Jossey-Bass.

Woody, R. H., & Springer, J. R. (1985). A holistic health model for family therapy. In J. R. Springer & R. H. Woody (Eds.), *Health promotion in family therapy* (pp. 36–45). Rockville, MD: Aspen Systems Corp.

Wynne, L. C. (1988). Search and research: Inquiry in the field of family therapy. In L. C. Wynne (Ed.), *The state of the art in family therapy research: Controversies and recommendations*. New York: Family Process Press.

Zarski, J. J., Hall, D. E., & DePompei, R. (1987). Closed head injury patients: A family therapy approach to the rehabilitation process. *American Journal of Family Therapy, 15*(1), 62–68.

Zimmerman, C. C., & Cervantes, L. F. (1960). *Successful American families*. New York: Pageant Press.

Zimpfer, D. G. (1988). Marriage enrichment programs: A review. *Journal of Psychotherapy and the Family, 2*(1), 79–96.

Chapter Two

Abramson, L. Y., & Alloy, L. B. (1981). Depression, non-depression, and cognitive illusions: Reply to Schwartz. *Journal of Experimental Psychology: General, 110,* 436–447.

Alloy, L. B., & Abramson, L. Y. (1979). Judgment of contingency in depressed and nondepressed students: Sadder but wiser? *Journal of Experimental Psychology: General, 108,* 441–485.

Bateson, G. (1972). *Steps to an ecology of mind.* New York: Ballantine Books.

Becvar, R. J., & Becvar, D. S. (1982). *Systems theory and family therapy: A primer.* Lanham, MD: Univ. Press of America.

Berne, E. (1964). *Games people play.* New York: Grove Press.

Bertalanffy, L. von (1949). *Problems of life: An evaluation of modern biological thought.* New York: John Wiley & Sons.

Bertalanffy, L. von (1968). *General systems theory: Foundations, development, applications* (rev. ed.). New York: George Braziller.

Bertalanffy, L. von (1981). *A systems view of man* (P. A. Laviolette, Ed.). Boulder, CO: Westview Press.

Bowen, M. (1978) *Family therapy in clinical practice.* New York: Jason Aronson.

Bradt, J. O., & Moynihan, C. J. (1971). Opening the safe: A study of child-focused families. In J. O. Bradt & C. J. Moynihan (Eds.), *Systems therapy—selected papers: Theory, techniques, research* (pp. 1–24). Washington, DC: Systems Therapy.

Casas, C. C. (1979). *Relationship patterns of strong families in Latin America.* Unpublished master's thesis, Univ. of Nebraska–Lincoln, Lincoln, NE.

Constantine, L. L. (1986). *Family paradigm: The practice and theory in family therapy.* New York: Guilford Press.

Doub, G. T., & Scott, V. M. (1987). *Family wellness workbook: Survival skills in healthy families.* San Jose, CA: Family Wellness Associates.

Dulfano, C. (1982). *Families, alcoholism & recovery: Ten stories.* Center City, MN: Hazelden Educational Materials.

Gray, S. W., & Ruttle, K. (1980). The family-oriented home visiting program: A longitudinal study. *Genetic Psychology Monograms, 102,* 229–316.

Greenspan, S. I., & Weider, S. (1984). Dimensions and levels of the therapeutic process. *Psychotherapy, 21,* 5–23.

Gutman, H. G. (1976). *The Black family in slavery and freedom: 1750–1925.* New York: Pantheon Books.

Haley, A. (1976). *Roots.* Garden City, NY: Doubleday & Co.

Huberty, D. J., & Huberty, C. E. (1986). Sabotaging siblings: An overlooked aspect of family therapy with drug dependent adolescents. *Journal of Psychoactive Drugs, 18*(1), 31–41.

Jung, C. G. (1959). *The archetypes and the collective unconscious.* In V. S. Lazlo (Ed.), *The basic writings of C. G. Jung.* New York: Modern Library.

Keeney, B. P. (1983). *Aesthetics of change.* New York: Guilford Press.

Minuchin, G. (1974). *Families and family therapy.* Cambridge, MA: Harvard Univ. Press.

Nichols, W. C., & Everett, C. A. (1986). *Systemic family therapy: An integrative approach.* New York: Guilford Press.

Okun, B. F., & Rappaport, L. J. (1980). *Working with families: An introduction to family therapy.* North Scituate, MA: Duxbury Press.

Oster, G. D., & Gould, P. (1987). *Using drawings in assessment and therapy: A guide for mental health professionals.* New York: Brunner/Mazel.

Patterson, G. R., & Stouthamer-Loeber, M. (1984). The correlation of family management practices and delinquency. *Child Development, 55*(4), 1299–1307.

Phares, E. L. (1976). *Locus of control in personality.* Morristown, NJ: General Learning Press.

Pressman, B. (1987). The place of family-of-origin therapy in the treatment of wife abuse. In A. J. Hovestadt & M. Fine (Eds.), *Family of origin therapy* (pp. 45–56). Rockville, MD: Aspen Publishers.

Root, M. P. P., Fallon, P., & Friedrich, W. N. (1986). *Bulimia: A systems approach to treatment.* New York: W. W. Norton & Co.

Rotter, J. B. (1966). Generalized expectancies for internal versus external control of reinforcement. *Psychological Monographs, 80* (Whole No. 609).

Satir, V. M. (1972). *Peoplemaking.* Palo Alto, CA: Science and Behavior Books.

Scheinfeld, D. R. (1983). Family relationships and school achievement among boys of lower-income urban Black families. *American Journal of Orthopsychiatry, 53*(1), 127–143.

Schultz, S. J. (1984). *Family systems therapy: An integration*. New York: Jason Aronson.

Thomas, M. B., & Dansby, P. G. (1984). *Prevention/intervention with healthy black families*. Ann Arbor, MI: Univ. of Michigan, Center for Counseling and Personnel Services. (ERIC Document Reproduction Service No. ED 251 773).

Thomas, M. B., & Dansby, P. G. (1985). Black clients: Family structures, therapeutic issues and strengths. *Psychotherapy, 22*(2), 398–407.

Treadway, D. (1985). Who's on first? Mapping the terrain for family systems therapy. *Focus on the Chemically Dependent Family,* 14–15, 34–35.

U. S. Bureau of the Census. (1982). *Household and family characteristics: March 1982* (Current Population Reports Series, No. 308).

Weber, M. (1977). *Attitudes of black and white children concerning running away from home*. Unpublished master's thesis, Tennessee State Univ., Nashville, TN.

Winfield, F. E. (1985). *Commuter marriage: Living together, apart*. New York: Columbia Univ. Press.

Wolf, A. M. (1983). A personal view of Black inner-city foster families. *American Journal of Orthopsychiatry, 53,* 144–151.

Chapter Three

Abbott, D. A., & Meredith, W. H. (1986). *Minority families: Strengths of four ethnic groups*. Lincoln, NE: Department of Human Development and the Family, Univ. of Nebraska–Lincoln.

Achord, B., Berry, M., Harding, G., Kerber, K., Scott, S., & Schwab, L. (1986). *Building family strengths: A manual for families*. Lincoln, NE: The Center for Family Strengths, Univ. of Nebraska-Lincoln.

Albert, L., & Einstein, E. (1986). *Strengthening your stepfamily*. Circle Pines, MN: American Guidance Services.

Beavers, W. R. (1977). *Psychotherapy and growth: A family systems perspective*. New York: Brunner/Mazel.

Beavers, W. R. (1982). Healthy, midrange, and severely dysfunctional families. In F. Walsh (Ed.), *Normal family processes* (pp. 45–66). New York: Guilford Press.

Beavers, W.R. (1985). *Successful marriage: A family systems approach to couples therapy*. New York: W. W. Norton & Co.

Beavers, W. R., & Hampson, R. B. (1990). *Successful families: Assessment and intervention*. New York: W. W. Norton & Co.

Brigman, K. M. L. (1984). Religion and family strengths: An approach to wellness. *Wellness Perspectives, 1*(2), 3–9.

Carnes, P. (1987). *Understanding us*. Littleton, CO: Interpersonal Communication Programs.

Casas, C. C. (1979). *Relationship patterns of strong families in Latin America*. Unpublished master's thesis, Univ. of Nebraska–Lincoln, Lincoln, NE.

Dinkmeyer, D., & Carlson, J. (1984). *Time for a better marriage*. Circle Pines, MN: American Guidance Service.

Epstein, N. B., Bishop, D. S., & Baldwin, L. M. (1982). McMaster model of family functioning: A view of the normal family. In E. Walsh (Ed.), *Normal family processes* (pp. 115–141). New York: Guilford Press.

Fields, N. S. (1986). *The well-seasoned marriage*. New York: Gardner Press.

Gabler, J., & Otto, H. A. (1963). The family resource development program: The production of criteria for assessing family strengths. *Family Process, 2*(2), 329–339.

Guerney, B. G., Jr. (1977). *Relationship Enhancement*. San Francisco: Jossey-Bass.

Guerney, B. G., Jr. (1986a). *Relationship enhancement manual*. State College, PA: Ideals.

Guerney, B. G., Jr. (1986b). *Relationship enhancement: Marital/family therapists manual*. State College, PA: Ideals.

Hicks, M. W., & Platt, M. (1970). Marital happiness and stability: A review of the research of the 60's. *Journal of Marriage and the Family, 32,* 553–579.

Holmes, O. W. (1889). *The Holmes birthday book*. Boston: Houghton Mifflin Co.

Hoopes, M. H., Fisher, B. L., & Barlow, S. H. (1984). *Structured family facilitation programs*. Rockville, MD: Aspen Publishers.

King, J. (1980). *The strengths of Black families*. Unpublished doctoral dissertation, Univ. of Nebraska–Lincoln, Lincoln, NE.

Knaub, P. K. (1985, Summer). Professional women perceive family strengths. *Journal of Home Economics, 52*–55.

Knaub, P. K., Hanna, S. L., & Stinnett, N. (1984). Strengths of remarried families. *Journal of Divorce, 7*(3), 41–55.

L'Abate, L., & Weinstein, S. E. (1987). *Structured enrichment programs for couples and families.* New York: Brunner/Mazel.

L'Abate, L., & Young, L. (1987). *Casebook: Structured enrichment programs for couples and families.* New York: Brunner/Mazel.

Lauer, J. C., & Lauer, R. H. (1986). *'Til death do us part: A study and guide to long-term marriage.* New York: Harrington Park Press.

Lewis, J. M., Beavers, W. R., Gossett, J. T., & Phillips, V. A. (1976). *No single thread: Psychological health in family systems.* New York: Brunner/Mazel.

Lewis, J. M., & Looney, J. G. (1983). *The long struggle: Well-functioning working class black families.* New York: Brunner/Mazel.

Lingren, H. G., Kimmons, L., Lee, P., Rowe, G., Rottmann, L., Schwab, L., & Williams, R., (Eds.). (1987). *Family strengths 8–9: Pathways to well-being.* Lincoln, NE: Center for Family Strengths.

Lynn, W. D. (1983). *Leisure activities in high strength, middle-strength and low-strength families.* Unpublished doctoral dissertation, Univ. of Nebraska–Lincoln., Lincoln, NE.

Mace, D. (1982). *Close companions: The marriage enrichment handbook.* New York: Continuum Publishing.

Mace, D. (1983). *Prevention in family services.* Beverly Hills, CA: SAGE Publications.

Mace, D., & Mace, V. (1977). *How to have a happy marriage.* Nashville, TN: Abingdon Press.

Mackinnon, R. F., Mackinnon, C. E., & Franken, M. L. (1984). Family strengths in long-term marriages. *Lifestyles: A Journal of Changing Patterns, 7*(2), 115–126.

Mathews, V. C., & Milhanovich, C. S. (1963). New orientations on marital maladjustment. *Marriage and Family Living, 25,* 300–304.

Miller, S., Nunnally, E., & Wackman, D. B. (1977). *Couple communication instructor's manual.* Littleton, CO: Interpersonal Communication Programs.

Miller, S., Nunnally, E. W., & Wackman, D. B. (1979). *Couple communication: Talking together.* Littleton, CO: Interpersonal Communication Programs.

Miller, S., Wackman, D. B., Nunnally, E. W., & Miller, P. A. (1988). *Connecting with self and others.* Littleton, CO: Interpersonal Communication Programs.

Miller, S., Wackman, D., Nunnally, E., & Saline, C. (1981). *Straight talk: A new way to get closer to others by saying what you really mean.* New York: Signet.

Oliveri, M. E., & Reiss, D. (1982). Family styles of construing the social environment: A perspective on variation among nonclinical families. In F. Walsh (Ed.), *Normal family processes* (pp. 94–114). New York: Guilford Press.

Olson, D. H., McCubbin, H. I., Barnes, H., Larsen, A., Muxen, M., & Wilson, M., (1983). *Families: What makes them work.* New York: SAGE Publications.

Olson, D. H., Russell, C. S., & Sprenkle, D. H. (1980). Marital and family therapy: A decade review. *Journal of Marriage and the Family, 42,* 973–993.

Olson, D. H., Russell, C. S., & Sprenkle, D. H. (1983). Circumplex model of marital and family systems: Theoretical update *Family Process, 22,* 69–83.

Olson, D. H., Sprenkle, D., & Russell, C. (1979). Circumplex Model of marital and family systems: I. Cohesion and adaptability dimensions, family type and clinical applications. *Family Process, 18,* 3–28.

Otto, H. A. (1951). *Otto pre-marital counseling schedules.* Palo Alto, CA: Consulting Psychologists Press.

Otto, H. A. (1962). What is a strong family? *Marriage and Family Living, 24*(1), 77–81.

Otto, H. A. (1963). Criteria for assessing family strength. *Family Process, 2*(2), 329–338.

Otto, H. A. (1964). The personal and family strength research: Some implications for the therapist. *Mental Hygiene, 48*(3), 439–450.

Otto, H. A. (1967). How can a family deliberately build strengths? *International Journal of Religious Education, 43*(9), 6–7, 40–41.

Otto, H. A. (1975). *The use of family strength concepts and methods in family life education.* Beverly Hills, CA: Holistic Press.

Otto, H. A. (Ed.). (1976). *Marriage and family enrichment: New perspectives and programs.* Nashville, TN: Parthenon Press.

Porter, R. W. (1981). *Family strengths of Russian emigrants.* Unpublished master's thesis, Univ. of Nebraska–Lincoln, Lincoln, NE.

Rampey, T. S. (1983). *Religiosity, purpose in life, and other factors related to family success: A national study.* Unpublished doctoral dissertation, Univ. of Nebraska–Lincoln, Lincoln, NE.

Rowe, G., DeFrain, J., Lingren, H., MacDonald, R., Stinnett, N., Van Zandt, S., & Williams, R. (Eds.). (1984). *Family strengths 5: Continuity and diversity.* Lincoln, NE: Univ. of Nebraska Press.

Sanders, G. F. (1979). *Family strengths: A national study.* Unpublished master's thesis, Univ. of Nebraska–Lincoln, Lincoln, NE.

Smith, R. C. (1983). *The family life of executives: A descriptive study.* Unpublished master's thesis, Univ. of Nebraska–Lincoln, Lincoln, NE.

Stierlin, H. (1974). *Separating parents and adolescents.* New York: Quadrangle.

Stierlin, H., Levi, L. D., & Savard, R. J. (1973). Centrifugal versus centripetal separation in adolescence: Two patterns and some of their implications. In S. Feinstein and P. Giovacchini (Eds.), *Annals of the American society for adolescent psychiatry, vol. II: Developmental and clinical studies* (pp. 211–239). New York: Basic Books.

Stinnett, N., Chesser, B., & DeFrain, J. (Eds.). (1979). *Building family strengths: Blueprints for action.* Lincoln, NE: Univ. of Nebraska Press.

Stinnett, N., Chesser, B., DeFrain, J., & Knaub, P. (Eds.). (1980). *Family strengths: Positive models for family life.* Lincoln, NE: Univ. of Nebraska Press.

Stinnett, N., & DeFrain, J. (1985). *Secrets of strong families.* New York: Berkley Publishing Group.

Stinnett, N., DeFrain, J., King, K., Knaub, P., & Rowe, G. (Eds.). (1981). *Family strengths 3: Roots of well-being.* Lincoln, NE: Univ. of Nebraska Press.

Stinnett, N., DeFrain, J., King, K., Lingren, H., Rowe, G., Van Zandt, S. V., & Williams, R. (Eds.). (1982). *Family strengths 4: Positive support systems.* Lincoln, NE: Univ. of Nebraska Press.

Stinnett, N., Knorr, B., DeFrain, J., & Rowe, G. (1984). How strong families cope with crises. *Family Perspective, 15,* 159–166.

Stinnett, N., & Sauer, K. H. (1977, Fall). Relationship characteristics of strong families. *Family Perspectives, 3*–11.

Stoll, B. (1984). *Family strengths in Austria, Germany, and Switzerland.* Unpublished master's thesis, Univ. of Nebraska–Lincoln, Lincoln, NE.

Strand, K. B. (1979). *Parent-child relationships among strong families.* Unpublished master's thesis, Univ. of Nebraska–Lincoln, Lincoln, NE.

Streit, F. (1987a). *Perception kit T-201.* Highland Park, NJ: Peoplescience.

Streit, F. (1987b). *Perception of love kit T-203.* Highland Park, NJ: Peoplescience.

Streit, F. (1987c). *Through my child's eyes.* Highland Park, NJ: Peoplescience.

Streit, F. (1987d). *Representational systems kit T-204.* Highland Park, NJ: Peoplescience.

Streit, F. (1987e). *Expectations and standards kit T-202.* Highland Park, NJ: Peoplescience.

Streit, F. (1987f). *Building well families: EPAC SP: expectations, perceptions, assessment, change.* Highland Park, NJ: Peoplescience.

Van Zandt, S. V., Lingren, H., Rowe, G., Zeece, P., Kimmons, L., Lee, P., Shell, D., & Stinnett, N. (Eds.). (1986). *Family strengths 7: Vital connections.* Lincoln, NE: Univ. of Nebraska Press.

Weber, V. P. (1984). *The strengths of Black families in Soweto, Johannesburg, South Africa.* Unpublished master's thesis, Univ. of Nebraska–Lincoln, Lincoln, NE.

Williams, R., Lingren, H., Rowe, G., Van Zandt, S. V., Lee, P., & Stinnett, N. (Eds.). (1985). *Family strengths 6: Enhancement of interaction.* Lincoln, NE: Univ. of Nebraska Press.

Wills, T. A., Weiss, R. L., & Patterson, G. R. (1974). A behavioral analysis of the determinants of marital satisfaction. *Journal of Counsulting and Clinical Psychology, 42*(6), 802–811.

Zimmerman, C. C., & Cervantes, L. F. (1960). *Successful American families.* New York: Pagent Press.

Chapter Four

Ables, B. S., with Brandsma, J. M. (1977). *Therapy for couples.* San Francisco: Jossey-Bass.

Boyd-Franklin, N. (1989). *Black families in therapy: A multi-systems approach.* New York: Guilford Press.

Breunlin, D. C. (1988). Oscillation theory and family development. In C. Falicov (Ed.), *Family tran-*

sitions: Continuity and change over the life cycle (pp. 133–158). New York: Guilford Press.

Carter, E. (1978). The transgenerational scripts and nuclear family stress: Theory and clinical implications. In R. R. Sager (Ed.), *Georgetown family symposium* (Vol. 3, 1975–76). Washington, DC: Georgetown Univ.

Carter, E., & McGoldrick, M. (1980). *The family life cycle: An overview of family therapy*. New York: Gardner Press.

Carter, E., & McGoldrick, M. (1988). *The changing family life cycle: A framework for family therapy* (2nd ed.). New York: Gardner Press.

Combrinck-Graham, L. (1985). A developmental model for family systems. *Family Process, 24*(2), 139–150.

Duvall, E. M., & Hill, R. (1948). *When you marry*. Lexington, MA: D. C. Heath Co.

Duvall, E. M., & Miller, B. C. (1985). *Marriage and family development* (6th ed.). New York: Harper & Row.

Falicov, C. J. (1988). Family sociology and family therapy contributions to the family development framework: A comparative analysis and thoughts on future trends. In C. J. Falicov (Ed.), *Family transitions: Continuity and change over the life cycle* (pp. 3–54). New York: Guilford Press.

Fulmer, R. (1988). Lower-income and professional families: A comparison of structure and life cycle process. In E. Carter & M. McGoldrick (Eds.), *The changing family life cycle: A framework for family therapy* (2nd ed.). New York: Gardner Press.

Gutman, H. (1976). *The black family in slavery and freedom: 1750–1925*. New York: Vintage.

Hill, R. (1986). Life cycle stages for types of single-parent families: Of family development theory. *Family Relations, 35,* 19–29.

Hines, P. M. (1988). The family cycle of poor black families. In E. Carter & M. McGoldrick (Eds.), *The changing family life cycle: A framework for family therapy*. New York: Gardner Press.

Hines, P. M., & Boyd-Franklin, N. (1982). Black families. In M. McGoldrick, J. K. Pearce, & J. Giordano (Eds.), *Ethnicity and family therapy* (pp. 84–107). New York: Guilford Press.

Labouvie-Vief, G., Hakim-Larson, J., & Hobart, C. J. (1987). Age, ego level, and the life-span development of coping and defense processes. *Psychology and Aging, 2*(3), 286–293.

Lappin, J. (1983). On becoming a culturally conscious family therapist. In J. Hansen (Ed.), *Culture in family therapy* (pp. 122–136). Rockville, MD: Aspen Publishers.

Lederer, W. J. (1984). *Creating a good relationship*. New York: W. W. Norton & Co.

Lederer, W., & Jackson, D. D. (1968). *Mirages of marriage*. New York: W. W. Norton & Co.

McAdoo, H. P. (1988). Transgenerational patterns of upward mobility in African-American families. In H. P. McAdoo, *Black families* (2nd ed.), (pp. 248–268). Newbury Park, CA: SAGE Publications.

McGoldrick, M. (1982). Ethnicity and family therapy: An overview. In M. McGoldrick, J. K. Pearce, & J. Giordano (Eds.), *Ethnicity and family therapy* (pp. 3–30). New York: Guilford Press.

McGoldrick, M. (1988). Ethnicity and the family life cycle. In B. Carter & M. McGoldrick (Eds.), *The changing family life cycle: A framework for family therapy* (2nd ed.), (pp. 69–90). New York: Gardner Press.

Montalvo, B., & Gutierrez, M. (1983). A perspective for the use of the cultural dimension in family therapy. In J. Hansen (Ed.), *Culture in family therapy* (pp. 15–32). Rockville, MD: Aspen Publishers.

Montalvo, B., & Gutierrez, M. (1988). The emphasis on cultural identity: A developmental-ecological constraint. In C. J. Falicov (Ed.), *Family transitions: Continuity and change over the life cycle* (pp. 182–210). New York: Guilford Press.

Olson, D. H. (1988). Family types, family stress, and family satisfaction: A family developmental perspective. In C. Falicov (Ed.), *Family transitions: Continuity and change over the life cycle* (pp. 55–80). New York: Guilford Press.

Olson, D. H., McCubbin, H. I., Barnes, H., Larsen, A., Muxen, M., & Wilson, M. (1983). *Families: What makes them work*. New York: SAGE Publications.

Olson, D. H., Sprenkle, D. H., & Russell, C. S. (1979). Circumplex Model of marital and family systems: I. Cohesion and adaptability dimensions, family types, and clinical applications. *Family Process, 18,* 3–28.

Olson, D. H. L. (Ed.). (1976). *Treating relationships*. Lake Mills, IA: Graphic Pub. Co.

Patterson, G. R. (1986). Performance models for antisocial boys. *American Psychologist, 41*(4), 432–444.

Pinderhughes, E. (1982). Afro-American families and the victim system. In M. McGoldrick, J. K. Pearce, & J. Giordano (Eds.), *Ethnicity and family therapy* (pp. 108–122). New York: Guilford Press.

Rolland, J. S. (1988). Chronic illness and the family life cycle. In B. Carter & M. McGoldrick (Eds.), *The changing family life cycle: A framework for family therapy* (2nd ed.) (pp. 433–456). New York: Gardner Press.

Singer, M. T., & Wynne, L. C. (1965). Thought disorder and family relations of schizophrenics: IV. Results and implications. *Archives of General Psychiatry, 12,* 201–212.

Stierlin, H. (1974). *Separating parents and adolescents: A perspective on running away, schizophrenia, and waywardness.* New York: Quadrangle.

Stierlin, H. (1981). *Separating parents and adolescents.* (2nd enlarged edition). New York: Jason Aronson.

Stierlin, H., & Weber, G. (1989). *Unlocking the family door: A systemic approach to the understanding and treatment of anorexia nervosa.* New York: Brunner/Mazel.

Usher, C. H. (1989). Recognizing cultural bias in counseling theory and practice: The case of Rogers. *Journal of Multicultural Counseling and Development, 17,* 62–71.

Vaillant, G. E. (1977). *Adaptation to life.* Boston: Little, Brown & Co.

Wilson, L., & Green, J. W. (1983). An experiential approach to cultural awareness in child welfare. *Child Welfare, 42*(4), 303–311.

Wynne, L. C. (1988). An epigenetic model of family processes. In C. J. Falicov (Ed.), *Family transitions: Continuity and change over the life cycle* (pp. 81–106). New York: Guilford Press.

Chapter Five

Baltes, P. B. (1987). Theoretical propositions of life-span developmental psychology: On the dynamics between growth and decline. *Developmental Psychology, 23*(5), 611–626.

Baltes, P. B., Reese, H. W., & Lipsitt, L. P. (1980). Life-span developmental psychology. *Annual Review of Psychology, 31,* 65–110.

Bardwick, J. M. (1986). *The plateauing trap: How to avoid it in your career . . . and your life.* New York: American Management Assoc.

Belenky, M. F., Clinchy, B. M., Goldberger, N. R., & Tarule, J. M. (1986). *Women's way of knowing.* New York: Basic Books.

Brazelton, T. B., & Yogman, M. W. (1986). Introduction: Reciprocity, attachment, and effectance: Anlage in early infancy. In T. B. Brazelton (Ed.), *Affective development in infancy* (pp. 1–9). Norwood, NJ: Ablex Publishing Co.

Brim, O. G. (1976). Theories of the male midlife crisis. *The Counseling Psychologist, 6*(1), 2–9.

Cutler, W. B. (1988). *Hysterectomy: Before and after.* New York: Harper & Row.

Erikson, E. (1963). *Childhood and society* (2nd ed.). New York: W. W. Norton & Co.

Erikson, E. (1968). *Identity, youth and crisis.* New York: W. W. Norton & Co.

Erikson, E. (Ed.). (1978). *Adulthood.* New York: W. W. Norton & Co.

Freud, S. (1915–17). A general introduction to psycho-analysis (J. Riviere, Trans.). In M. J. Adler (Ed.), *The major works of Sigmund Freud* (pp. 449–638). Chicago: Encyclopaedia Britannica.

Friedan, B. (1989, April–May). Not for women only: America's foremost feminist talks about men, women, aging, and the new traditionalism. *Modern Maturity,* 66–71.

Gilligan, C. (1982). *In a different voice.* Cambridge, MA: Harvard Univ. Press.

Ginzberg, E., et al. (1951). *Occupational choice.* New York: Columbia Univ. Press.

Goldner, V. (1988). Generation and gender: Normative and covert hierarchies. *Family Process, 17,* 17–31.

Gould, R. (1978). *Transformations.* New York: Simon & Schuster.

Gutmann, D. L. (1967). Aging among the highland Maya: A comparative study. *Journal of Personality and Social Psychology, 7,* 28–35.

Gutmann, D. L. (1985). The parental imperative revisited: Towards a developmental psychology of adulthood and later life. *Contributions to Human Development, 14,* 31–60.

Hagestad, G. O. (1986). Dimensions of time and the family. *American Behavioral Scientists, 29*(6), 679–694.

Hansen, S. (1988). *Integrative life planning (ILP): Work, family, and community.* Workshop presented at the First National Conference of the Assoc. for Counselor Education and Supervision, St. Louis, MO.

Hargrove, J. T., & Abraham, G. E. (1982). The incidence of premenstrual tension in a gynecologic clinic. *The Journal of Reproductive Medicine, 27*(12), 721–724.

Havighurst, R. J. (1972). *Developmental tasks and education* (3rd ed.). New York: David McKay Co.

Heidt, H. (1984). *The relationship between self-disclosure, trust, and marital adjustment*. Unpublished doctoral dissertation, George Peabody College of Education of Vanderbilt Univ., Nashville, TN.

Holland, J. L. (1973). *Making vocational choices: A theory of careers*. Englewood Cliffs, NJ: Prentice-Hall.

Hopson, B. (1981). Response to the papers by Schlossberg, Brammer and Abrego. *The Counseling Psychologist, 9*(2), 36–39.

Hughes, L. (1969). *Don't you turn back*. New York: Alfred A. Knopf.

Ivey, A. E. (1986). *Developmental therapy*. San Francisco: Jossey-Bass.

Josselson, R. (1987). *Finding herself*. San Francisco: Jossey-Bass.

Jung, C. (1933). *Modern man in search of a soul*. New York: Harcourt Brace.

Kegan, R. (1982). *The evolving self: Problem and process in human development*. Cambridge, MA: Harvard Univ. Press.

Kohlberg, L. (1976). *Collected papers on moral development and moral education*. Cambridge, MA: Center for Moral Education.

Lederer, W. J. (1984). *Creating a good relationship*. New York: W. W. Norton & Co.

Levinson, D. (1978). *The seasons of a man's life*. New York: Alfred A. Knopf.

Loevinger, J. (1976). *Ego development: Conceptions and theories*. San Francisco: Jossey-Bass.

Lowenthal, M. F., Thurnher, M., & Chiriboga, D. (Eds.). (1975). *Four stages of life: A comparative study of men and women facing transitions*. San Francisco: Jossey-Bass.

Marcia, J. E. (1966). Development and validation of ego identity status. *Journal of Youth and Adolescence, 5,* 145–160.

McKinlay, S. M., McKinlay, J. B., & Avis, N. E. (1989). The Massachusetts women's health study: A longitudinal study of the health of middle-aged women and the epidemiology of the menopause. *Psychology of Women Newsletter of Division 35, American Psychological Association, 16*(2), 1–4.

Neugarten, B. L. (Ed.). (1964). *Personality in middle and late life*. New York: Atherton.

Neugarten, B. L. (Ed.). (1968). *Middle age and aging*. Chicago: Univ. of Chicago Press.

Neugarten, B. L. (1976). Adaptation and the life cycle. *The Counseling Psychologist, 6*(1), 16–21.

Neugarten, B. L. (1979). Time, age, and the life cycle. *American Journal of Psychiatry, 136,* 887–898.

Neugarten, B., & Neugarten, D. A. (1987). The changing meanings of age. *Psychology Today, 21*(5), 29–33.

Okun, B. F. (1984). *Working with adults: Individual, family and career development*. Monterey, CA: Brooks/Cole Publishing.

Piaget, J. (1952). *The origins of intelligence in children*. New York: International Universities Press.

Reinke, B. J. (1985). Psychosocial changes as a function of chronological age. *Human Development, 28,* 266–269.

Reinke, B. J., Ellicott, A. M., Harris, R. L., & Hancock, E. (1985). Timing of psychosocial changes in women's lives. *Human Development, 28,* 259–280.

Roe, A. (1956). *The psychology of occupations*. New York: John Wiley & Sons.

Rosenfeld, A., & Stark, E. (1987). The prime of our lives. *Psychology Today, 21*(5), 62–72.

Rossi, A. (1980). Life-span theories and women's lives. *Signs, 6,* 1–24.

Sadker, M., & Sadker, D. (1986). Sexism in the classroom: From grade school to graduate school *Phi-Delta-Kappan, 67,* 512–515.

Schlossberg, N. (1984). *Counseling adults in transition*. New York: Springer Publishing Co.

Sheehy, G. (1974). *Passages: Predictable crises in adult life*. New York: E. P. Dutton.

Sheehy, G. (1981). *Pathfinders*. New York: William Morrow & Co.

Smith, A., Cardillo, J. E., & Choate, R. O. (1984). Age-based transition periods and the outcome of mental health treatment. *Evaluation and Program Planning, 7,* 237–244.

Strickland, B. (1989). Sex-related differences in health and illness. *Psychology of Women Quarterly, 12*(4), 381–400.

Super, D. (1957). *The psychology of careers*. New York: Harper.

Super, D., Stavishesky, R., Matlin, N., & Jordan, J. P. (1963). *Career development: Self-concept theory*. New York: College Entrance Examination Board.

Thomas, M. B. (1976). *Career guidance, counseling, and placement: A developmental perspective in Tennessee*. Nashville, TN: Tennessee Department of Education.

Thomas, M. B., Meador, L., Najem, L., Layman, J., Fite, C., & Baker, C. T., Jr. (1974). *A competency-based manual for Area VI: Vocational and career development for the minimum competency requirements for secondary school counselors of the state of Tennessee* (4 vols.). Nashville, TN: Tennessee Department of Education.

Vaillant, G. E. (1977). *Adaptation to life*. Boston: Little, Brown & Co.

Chapter Six

Aradi, N. S., & Kaslow, F. W. (1987). Theory integration in family therapy: Definition, rationale, content and process. *Psychotherapy, 24,* 595–608.

Beavers, W. R. (1977). *Psychotherapy and growth: A family systems perspective*. New York: Brunner/Mazel.

Capra, F. (1982). *The turning point: Science, society and the rising culture*. New York: Simon & Schuster.

Capra, F. (1975). *The Tao of physics*. Boulder, CO: Shambhala.

de Shazer, S. (1985). *Keys to solution in brief therapy*. New York: W. W. Norton & Co.

Dell, P. F. (1987). Maturana's constitutive ontology of the observer. *Psychotherapy, 234,* 462–465.

Doherty, W. J., Coangelo, N., Green, A. M., & Hoffman, G. S. (1985). Emphases of the major family therapy models: A family FIRO analysis. *Journal of Marital and Family Therapy, 11,* 299–303.

Freed, A. O. (1982, October). Building theory for family practice. *Social Casework: The Journal of Contemporary Social Work*, pp. 472–481.

Friesen, J. D. (1985). *Structural-strategic marriage and family therapy*. New York: Gardner Press.

Haley, J. (1969). The power tactics of Jesus Christ and other essays. New York: Grossman Publishers.

Haley, J. (1973). *Uncommon therapy: The psychiatric techniques of Milton H. Erickson, M. D.: A case-book of an innovative psychiatrist's work in short-term therapy*. New York: W. W. Norton & Co.

Haley, J. (1980, October). How to be a marriage therapist without knowing practically anything. *Journal of Marital and Family Therapy*, pp. 385–391.

Kaslow, F, Cooper, B., & Linsenberg, M. (1979). Family therapist authenticity as a key factor in outcome. *International Journal of Family Therapy, 2,* 184–199.

Keeney, B. P. (1983). *Aesthetics of change*. New York: Guilford Press.

Keeney, B. P. (1987). The construction of therapeutic realities. *Psychotherapy, 24,* 469–476.

Kegan, R. (1982). *The evolving self: Problem and process in human development*. Cambridge, MA: Harvard Univ. Press.

L'Abate, L. (1981). Toward a systematic classification of counseling and therapy theories, methods, processes and goals: The E-R-A model. *The Personnel and Guidance Journal, 59,* 263–265.

L'Abate, L. (1983). Styles in intimate relationships: The A-R-C model. *The Personnel and Guidance Journal, 61,* 277–283.

L'Abate, L. (Ed.). (1985). *Handbook of family psychology and therapy*. Homewood, IL: Dorsey Press.

L'Abate, L. (1986). *Systematic family therapy*. New York: Brunner/Mazel.

L'Abate, L., Ganahl, G., & Hansen, J. C. (1986). *Methods in family therapy*. Englewood Cliffs, NJ: Prentice-Hall.

L'Abate, L., & McHenry, S. (1983). *Handbook of marital interactions*. New York: Grune & Stratton.

L'Abate, L., & Weinstein, S. E. (1987). Structured enrichment programs for couples and families. New York: Brunner/Mazel.

Lebow, J. L. (1987). Integrative family therapy: An overview of major issues. *Psychotherapy, 24,* 587–594.

Liddle, H. A. (1982). On the problems of eclecticism: A call for epistemologic clarification and human-scale theories. *Family Process, 21,* 243–250.

Minuchin, S. (1974). *Families and family therapy*. Cambridge, MA: Harvard Univ. Press.

Minuchin, S., & Fishman, H. D. (1981). *Family therapy techniques*. Cambridge, MA: Harvard Univ. Press.

Napier, A. Y. (1976, January). Beginning struggles with families. *Journal of Marriage and Family Counseling,* pp. 3–12.

Napier, A. Y., & Whitaker, C. (1973). Problems of the beginning family therapist. *Seminars in Psychiatry, 5,* 229–242.

Schultz, S. J. (1984). *Family systems therapy: An integration.* New York: Jason Aronson.

Singer, M. T. (1977). The Rorschach as a transaction. In M. A. Rickers-Ovsianking (Ed.), *Rorschach Psychology.* Melbourne, FL: Robert E. Krieger.

Sluzki, C. E. (1983). Process, structure and world views: Toward an integrated view of system models in family therapy. *Family Process, 22,* 469–476.

Stanton, M. D. (1981, October). An integrated structural/strategic approach to family therapy. *Journal of Marital and Family Therapy,* pp. 427–439.

Stone, J. F. (1986). *T'ai chi chih.* San Leandro, CA: Satori Resources.

Vaillant, G. E. (1977). *Adaptation to life.* Boston: Little, Brown & Co.

Watts, A, with the collaboration of Huang, A. C. (1975). *Tao: The watercourse way.* New York: Pantheon Books

Watzlawick, P., Weakland, J. H., & Fisch, R. (1974). *Change: Principles of problem formation and problem resolution.* New York: W. W. Norton & Co.

Whitaker, C. (1976). The hindrance of theory in clinical work. In P. J. Guerin (Ed.), *Family therapy: Theory and practice* (pp. 154–164). New York: Gardner Press.

Wynne, L. C. (1977). Schizophrenics and their families: Research on parental communication. In J. M. Tanner (Ed.), *Developments in psychiatric research.* London: Hoddler & Stroughton.

Chapter Seven

Andreas, S. (1989). The true genius of Virginia Satir. *Family Therapy Networker, 13*(1), 50–56, 78–80.

Avanta Network presents the Eighth Annual International Training Institute (1987). 139 Forest Ave., Palo Alto, CA 94301.

Corrales, R. (1989). Drawing out the best. *Family Therapy Networker, 13*(1), 44–49.

Duhl, B. S. (1976). *The vulnerability contract: A tool for turning alienation into connection, with couples, families and groups.* Paper presented at the First International Family Encounter, Mexico City, Mexico.

Duhl, B. S. (1983). *From the inside out and other metaphors: Creative and integrative approaches to training in systems therapy.* New York: Brunner/Mazel.

Duhl, B. S. (1987, October). *Metaphor in family therapy.* Workshop presented at the annual convention of the American Assoc. for Marriage and Family Therapy, Chicago, IL.

Duhl, B. (1989). Remembering Virginia. *Family Therapy Networker, 13*(1), 28–31.

Duhl, B. S., & Duhl, F. J. (1981). Integrative family therapy. In A. S. Gurman & D. P. Kniskern (Eds.), *Handbook of family therapy* (pp. 483–516). New York: Brunner/Mazel.

Duhl, F. (1989). Remembering Virginia. *Family Therapy Networker, 13*(1), 30–33.

Duhl, F. J., Kantor, D., & Duhl, B. S. (1973). Learning, space, and action in family therapy: A primer of sculpture. In D. A. Bloch (Ed.), *Techniques of family psychotherapy. A primer* (pp. 47–64). New York: Grune & Stratton.

Johnson, S. M., & Greenberg, L. S. (1985). Differential effects of experiential and problem-solving interventions in resolving marital conflict. *Journal of Consulting and Clinical Psychology, 53*(2), 175–184.

Johnson, S. M., & Greenberg, L. S. (1988). Relating process to outcome in marital therapy. *Journal of Marital and Family Therapy, 14*(2), 175–183.

Kantor, D., & Lehr, W. (1975). *Inside the family.* San Francisco: Jossey-Bass.

Kolevzon, M. S., & Green, R. G. (1985). *Family therapy models: Convergence and divergence.* New York: Springer Publishing Co.

Napier, A. Y., with Whitaker, C. A. (1978). *The family crucible.* New York: Harper & Row.

Neill, J. R., & Kniskern, D. P. (Eds.). (1982). *From psyche to system: The evolving therapy of Carl Whitaker.* New York: Guilford Press.

Nerin, W. (1989). You can go home again. *Family Therapy Networker, 13*(1), 54–55.

Satir, V. (1964). *Conjoint family therapy.* Palo Alto, CA: Science and Behavior Books.

Satir, V. (1965). The family as a treatment unit. *Confina Psyciatrics, 8,* 37–42.

Satir, V. (1967). *Conjoint family therapy*. Palo Alto, CA: Science and Behavior Books.

Satir, V. (1970). *Self esteem*. Millbrae, CA: Celestial Arts.

Satir, V. (1972a). *Peoplemaking*. Palo Alto, CA: Science and Behavior Books.

Satir, V. (1972b). Family systems and approaches to family therapy. In G. D. Erickson & T. P. Hogan (Eds.), *Family therapy: An introduction to theory and technique* (pp. 211–225). Monterey, CA: Brooks/Cole Publishing Co.

Satir, V. (1976). *Making contact*. Millbrae, CA: Celestial Arts.

Satir, V. (1983). *Conjoint family therapy* (3rd ed.). Palo Alto, CA: Science and Behavior Books. (Original work published 1967)

Satir, V. (1986). A partial portrait of a family therapist in process. In H. C. Fishman & B. L. Rosman (Eds.), *Evolving models for family change: A volume in honor of Salvador Minuchin* (pp. 278–293). New York: Guilford Press.

Satir, V., & Baldwin, M. (1983). *Satir step by step: A guide to creating change in families*. Palo Alto, CA: Science and Behavior Books.

Simon, R. (1989). Reaching out to life: An interview with Virginia Satir. *Family Therapy Networker, 13*(1), 36–43.

Whitaker, C. A. (1976). A family is a four dimensional relationship. In P. J. Guerin, Jr. (Ed.), *Family therapy: Theory and practice* (pp. 182–192). New York: Gardner Press.

Whitaker, C. A., & Bumberry, W. M. (1988). *Dancing with the family: A symbolic-experiential approach*. New York: Brunner/Mazel.

Whitaker, C. A., & Keith, D. V. (1981). Symbolic-experiential family therapy. In A. S. Gurman & D. P. Kniskern (Eds.), *Handbook of family therapy* (pp. 187–225). New York: Brunner/Mazel.

Whitaker, C. A., & Malone, T. P. (1953). *The roots of psychotherapy*. New York: Blakiston.

Chapter Eight

Ables, B. S., with Brandsma, J. M. (1977). *Therapy for couples: A clinician's guide for effective treatment*. San Francisco: Jossey-Bass.

Ackerman, N. (1956). Interlocking pathology in family relations. In S. Rado & G. Daniels (Eds.), *Changing concepts of psychoanalytic medicine* (pp. 135–150). New York: Grune & Stratton.

Ackerman, N. (1958). *The psychodynamics of family life: Diagnosis and treatment of family relationships*. New York: Basic Books.

Ackerman, N. (1966). *Treating the troubled family*. New York: Basic Books.

Ackerman, N. (1967). Prejudice and scapegoating in the family. In G. H. Zuk & I. Boszormenyi-Nagy (Eds.), *Family therapy and disturbed families* (pp. 105–121). Palo Alto, CA: Science and Behavior Books.

Ackerman, N. (Ed.). (1970). *Family process*. New York: Basic Books.

Ackerman, N. W. (1982). The psychoanalytic approach to the family. In D. Bloch & R. Simon (Eds.), *The strength of family therapy: Selected papers of Nathan W. Ackerman* (pp. 250–259). New York: Brunner/Mazel.

Allen, D. M. (1988). *Unifying individual and family therapies*. San Francisco: Jossey-Bass.

Bales, R. F. (1950). *Interaction process analysis: A method for the study of small groups*. Cambridge, MA: Addison-Wesley.

Bales, R. F. (1955). *Family, socialization and interaction process*. Glencoe, IL: Free Press.

Beavers, W. R. (1985). *Successful marriage: A family systems approach to couples therapy*. New York: W. W. Norton & Co.

Bell, J. (1961). Family group therapy. *Public Health Monograph, 64*. Washington, DC: U. S. Government Printing Office.

Bell, J. (1972). Preface. In N. W. Ackerman, *The psychodynamics of family life*. New York: Basic Books. (Original work published 1958)

Bell, J. (1975). *Family therapy*. New York: Jason Aronson.

Benjamin, L. S. (1974). Structural analysis of social behavior, *Psychological Review, 81,* 392–425.

Benjamin, L. S. (1979). Structural analysis of differentiation failure. *Psychiatry, 42,* 1–23.

Bion, W. R. (1961). *Experience in groups, and other papers*. New York: Basic Books.

Blanck, G., & Blanck, R. (1974). *Ego psychology: Theory and practice*. New York: Brunner/Mazel.

Bloch, D., & Simon, R. (Eds.). (1982). *The strength of family therapy: Selected papers of Nathan W. Ackerman*. New York: Brunner/Mazel.

Bowen, M. (1978). *Family therapy in clinical practice*. New York: Jason Aronson.

Dicks, H. V. (1967). *Marital tensions*. Boston: Rutledge and Kegan Paul.

Dinkmeyer, D. C., & Carlson, J. (1984). *Time for a better marriage*. Circle Pines, MN: American Guidance Service.

Dinkmeyer, D. C., Dinkmeyer, D. C., Jr., & Sperry, L. (1987). *Adlerian counseling and psychotherapy* (2nd ed.). Columbus, OH: Merrill.

Dinkmeyer, D. C., & McKay, G. (1982). *Systematic training for effective parenting (STEP)*. Circle Pines, MN: American Guidance Service.

Dinkmeyer, D., & McKay, G. (1983). *STEP/Teen*. Circle Pines, MN: American Guidance Service.

Dreikurs, R. (1971). *Maintaining sanity in the classroom: Illustrated teaching techniques*. New York: Harper & Row.

Fairbairn, W. R. D. (1952). *Psychoanalytic studies of the personality*. London: Tavistock.

Foulkes, S. H. (1948). *Introduction to group-analytic psychotherapy*. London: Heinemann.

Foulkes, S. H. (1964). *Therapeutic group analysis*. London: Allen & Unwin.

Foulkes, S. H., & Anthony, E. (1957). *Group psychotherapy: The psychoanalytic approach*. Harmondsworth, England: Penguin Books.

Foulkes, S. H., & Anthony, E. J. (1965). *Group psychotherapy: The psychoanalytic approach*. New York: Penguin Books.

Framo, J. L. (1982). *Explorations in family and marital therapy: Selected papers of James L. Framo*. New York: Springer Publishing Co.

Freud, S. (1900). *The interpretation of dreams* (A. A. Brill, Trans.). London: Allen & Unwin.

Freud, S. (1920). *Beyond the pleasure principle* (C. J. M. Hubback, Trans.). London: Hogarth Press.

Freud, S. (1923). *The ego and the id*. J. Riviere (Trans.). London: Hogarth Press.

Freud, S. (1926). *Inhibitions, symptoms and anxiety*. A. Strachey (Trans.). London: Hogarth Press.

Greist, J. H., Mathison, K. S., Klein, M. H., Benjamin, L. S., Erdman, H. P., & Evans, F. J. (1984). *Hospital Psychiatry, 35*(11), 1089–90, 1093.

Grunwald, B. B., & McAbee, H. V. (1985). *Guiding the family: Practical counseling techniques*. Muncie, IN: Accelerated Development.

Guerin, Jr., P. J., Fay, L. F., Burden, S. L., & Kaulto, J. G. (1987). *The evaluation and treatment of marital conflict: A four-stage approach*. New York: Basic Books.

Guntrip, H. (1968). *Schizoid phenomena, object relations, and the self*. New York: International Universities Press.

Humphrey, L., & Benjamin, L. (1986). Using structural analysis of social behavior to assess critical but elusive family processes: A new solution to an old problem. *American Psychologist, 41*(9), 979–989.

Kernberg, O. F. (1975). *Borderline conditions and pathological narcissism*. New York: Jason Aronson.

Kirschner, D. A., & Kirschner, S. (1986). *Comprehensive family therapy: An integration of systemic and psychodynamic treatment models*. New York: Brunner/Mazel.

Klein, M. (1948). *Contributions to psychoanalysis, 1921–1945*. London: Hogarth Press and the Institute of Psychoanalysis.

Kohut, H. (1977). *The restoration of the self*. New York: International Universities Press.

Lewin, K. (1951). *Field theory in social science*. New York: McGraw-Hill Book Co.

Loevinger, J. (1976). *Ego development*. San Francisco: Jossey-Bass.

Mahler, M. (1968). *On human symbiosis and the vicissitudes of individuation*. New York: International Universities Press.

Mahler, M. (1975). *The psychological birth of the human infant*. New York: Basic Books.

Martin, P. A. (1976). *A marital therapy manual*. New York: Brunner/Mazel.

Masterson, J. F. (1985). *The real self: Structure, function, development, psychopathology, treatment, creativity: A developmental self and object relations approach*. New York: Brunner/Mazel.

Masterson, J. F. (1988). *The search for the real self: Unmasking the personality disorders of our age*. New York: Free Press.

Midelfort, C. F. (1957). *The family in psychotherapy*. New York: The Blakeston Division, McGraw-Hill Book Co.

Miller, A. (1981). *The drama of the gifted child: The search for the true self* (R. Ward, Trans.). New York: Basic Books.

Miller, A. (1984). *Thou shalt not be aware: Society's betrayal of the child* (H. Hannum & H. Hannum, Trans.). New York: Meridian.

Mosak, H. H., & Shulman, B. H. (1988). *Life style inventory*. Muncie, IN: Accelerated Development.

Nichols, M. P. (1987). *The self in the system: Expanding the limits of family therapy*. New York: Brunner/Mazel.

Nichols, W. C. (1988). *Marital therapy: An integrative approach*. New York: Guilford Press.

Paul, N. L., & Paul, B. B. (1975). *A marital puzzle: Transgenerational analysis in marriage counseling*. New York: W. W. Norton & Co.

Perry, H. S., & Gaevel, M. L. (Eds.). (1954). *The psychiatric interview*. New York: W. W. Norton & Co.

Sager, C. J. (1976). *Marriage contracts and couple therapy: Hidden forces in intimate relationships*. New York: Brunner/Mazel.

Sager, C. J. (1981). Couples therapy and marriage contracts. In A. S. Gurman & D. P. Kniskern (Eds.), *Handbook of family therapy* (pp. 85–132). New York: Brunner/Mazel.

Sager, C. J., & Hunt, B. (1979). *Intimate partners: Hidden patterns in love relationships*. New York: McGraw-Hill Book Co.

Scharff, D. E., & Scharff, J. S. (1987). *Object relations family therapy*. Northvale, NJ: Jason Aronson.

Schulman, B. H., & Mosak, H. H. (1988). *Manual for life style assessment*. Muncie, IN: Accelerated Development.

Schutz, W. F. (1960). *FIRO: A three dimensional theory of interpersonal behavior*. New York: Rinehart.

Schutz, W. F. (1967). *MATE: A FIRO awareness scale*. Palo Alto, CA: Consulting Psychologists Press.

Schutz, W. F. (1976). *MATE: A FIRO awareness scale* (rev. ed.). Palo Alto, CA: Consulting Psychologists Press.

Sherman, R., & Dinkmeyer, D. (1987). *Systems of family therapy: An Adlerian integration*. New York: Brunner/Mazel.

Simon, F. B., Stierlin, H., & Wynne, L. C. (1985). *The language of family therapy: A systemic vocabulary sourcebook*. New York: Family Process Press.

Skynner, A. C. R. (1976). *Systems of family and marital psychotherapy*. New York: Brunner/Mazel.

Slipp, S. (1984). *Object relations: A dynamic bridge between individual and family treatment*. New York: Jason Aronson.

Stierlin, H. (1974). *Separating parents and adolescents*. New York: The New York Times Book Co.

Stierlin, H., Rucker-Embden, I., Wetzel, N., & Wirsching, M. (1980). *The first interview with the family*. New York: Brunner/Mazel.

Strean, H. S. (1985). *Resolving marital conflicts: A psychodynamic perspective*. New York: John Wiley & Sons.

Strupp, H. H., & Binder, J. L. (1984). *Psychotherapy in a new key*. New York: Basic Books.

Sullivan, H. S. (1953). *The interpersonal theory of psychiatry*. New York: W. W. Norton & Co.

Sullivan, H. S. (1954). *The psychiatric interview* (II. S. Perry & M. L. Gawel, Eds.). New York: W. W. Norton & Co.

Vaillant, G. (1977). *Adaptation to life*. Boston: Little, Brown & Co.

Wile, D. B. (1981). *Couples therapy: A nontraditional approach*. New York: John Wiley & Sons.

Winnicott, D. W. (1965). *The maturational process and the facilitating environment*. New York: International Universities Press.

Chapter Nine

Boszormenyi-Nagy, I. (1965a). A theory of relationships: Experience and transaction. In I. Boszormenyi-Nagi & J. L. Framo (Eds.), *Intensive family therapy: Theoretical and practical aspects* (pp. 33–86). New York: Harper & Row.

Boszormenyi-Nagy, I. (1965b). Intensive family therapy as process. In I. Boszormenyi-Nagy & J. L. Framo (Eds.), *Intensive family therapy: Theoretical and practical aspects* (pp. 87–142). New York: Harper & Row.

Boszormenyi-Nagy, I. (1967). Relational modes and meaning. In G. Zuk & I. Boszormenyi-Nagy (Eds.), *Family therapy and disturbed families* (pp. 58–73). Palo Alto, CA: Science and Behavior Books.

Boszormenyi-Nagy, I. (1981). Contextual therapy: Therapeutic leverages in mobilizing trust. In R. J. Green & J. L. Framo (Eds.), *Family therapy: Major contributions* (pp. 395–415). New York: International Universities Press.

Boszormenyi-Nagy, I., with Krasner, B. R. (1986). *Between give and take: A clinical guide to contextual therapy*. New York: Brunner/Mazel.

Boszormenyi-Nagy, I. (1987). *Foundations of contextual therapy: Collected papers of Ivan Boszormenyi-Nagy, M. D.* New York: Brunner/Mazel.

Boszormenyi-Nagy, I., & Spark, G. (1973). *Invisible loyalties*. Hagerstown, MD: Harper & Row.

Boszormenyi-Nagy, I., & Ulrich, D. (1981). Contextual family therapy. In A. S. Gurman & D. F.

Kniskern (Eds.), *Handbook of Family Therapy*. New York: Brunner/Mazel.

Bowen, M. (1978). *Family therapy in clinical practice*. New York: Jason Aronson.

Bowen, M. (1980). Preface. In E. A. Carter & M. McGoldrick (Eds.), *The family life cycle: A framework for family therapy* (p. xiii). New York: Gardner Press.

Buber, M. (1958). *I and thou*. New York: Charles Scribner's Sons.

Framo, J. L. (1976). Family of origin as a therapeutic resource for adults in marital and family therapy: You can and should go home again. *Family Process, 15,* 193–210.

Framo, J. L. (1981). The integration of marital therapy with sessions with family of origin. In A. S. Gurman & D. P. Kniskern (Eds.), *Handbook of family therapy*. New York: Brunner/Mazel.

Framo, J. L. (1982). *Explorations in family and marital therapy: Selected papers of James L. Framo*. New York: Springer Publishing Co.

Haley, A. (1976). *Roots*. Garden City, NY: Doubleday & Co.

Hof, L., & Berman, E. (1986). The sexual genogram. *Journal of Marital and Family Therapy, 12*(1), 39–47.

Kellerman, J., & Kellerman, G. (Nov.–Dec. 1985). The family triangle. Alcsm. & Addict. *Recovery,* Natl. Mag., p. 13.

Kerr, M. E. (1981). Family systems theory and therapy. In A. S. Gurman & D. P. Kniskern (Eds.). *Handbook of family therapy* (pp. 226–264). New York: Brunner/Mazel.

Kerr, M. E., & Bowen, M. (1988). *Family evaluation: An approach based on Bowen theory*. New York: W. W. Norton & Co.

McClure, B. A., & Milardo, R. M. (1986). *The marriage and family workbook*. Belmont, CA: Wadsworth Publishing Co.

McGoldrick, M., & Gerson, R. (1985). *Genograms in family assessment*. New York: W. W. Norton & Co.

Novotny, P. C. (1987). Bowen family systems theory and psychoanalysis—Echo or metamorphosis? *Bulletin of the Menninger Clinic, 51,* pp 323–337.

Schroeder, E. (1987a). *Diagrams of triangles*. Material presented at the Summer School of Alcohol Studies, Rutgers Univ.

Schroeder, E. (1987b). *Research on birth order*. Material presented at the Summer School of Alcohol Studies, Rutgers Univ.

Simon, F. B., Stierlin, H., & Wynne, L. C. (1985). *The language of family therapy: A systemic vocabulary and source book*. New York: Family Process Press.

Steirlin, H. (1974). *Separating parents and adolescents*. New York: The New York Times Book Co.

Toman, W. (1961). *Family constellation*. New York: Springer Publishing Co.

Toman, W. (1988). *Family therapy & sibling position* (W. Toman, Trans.). New York: Jason Aronson.

Van Heusden, A., & Van Den Eerenbeemt, E. M. (1987). *Balance in motion: Ivan Boszormenyi-Nagy and his vision of individual and family therapy*. New York: Brunner/Mazel.

White, B. M. (1986). *In search of kith and kin: The history of a southern black family*. Baltimore, MD. Gateway Press.

Chapter Ten

Achord, B., Berry, M., Harding, G, Kerber, K., Scott, S., & Schwab, L. O. (1986). *A manual to assist families in building family strengths*. Lincoln, NE: Univ. of Nebraska–Lincoln.

Alexander, J. F. (1973). Defensive and supportive communication in normal and deviant families. *Journal of Consulting and Clinical Psychology, 40,* 223–231.

Alexander, J. F. (1988). Phases of family therapy process: A framework for clinicians and researchers. In L. C. Wynne (Ed.), *The state of the art in family therapy research: Controversies and recommendations* (pp. 175–188). New York: Family Process Press.

Alexander, J. F., & Barton, C. (1976). Behavioral systems therapy for families. In D. H. Olson (Ed.), *Treating relationships*. Lake Mills, IA: Graphic Pub. Co.

Alexander, J. F., & Barton, C. (1980). Intervention with delinquents and their families: Clinical, methodological, and conceptual issues. In J. P. Vincent (Ed.), *Advances in family intervention, assessment, and theory*. Greenwich, CT: JAI Press.

Alexander, J. F., & Parsons, B. V. (1973). Short-term behavioral intervention with delinquent families: Impact on family process and recidivism. *Journal of Abnormal Psychology, 81,* 219, 225.

Alexander, J., & Parsons, B. V. (1982). *Functional family therapy*. Monterey, CA: Brooks/Cole Publishing.

American Psychiatric Association. (1987). *Diagnostic and statistical manual of mental disorders III—revised*. Washington, DC: Author.

Arias, I., & O'Leary, D. (1988). Cognitive-behavioral treatment of physical aggression in marriage. In N. Epstein, S. E. Schlesinger, & W. Dryden (Eds.), *Cognitive-behavioral therapy with families* (pp. 118–150). New York: Brunner/Mazel.

Arrindell, W. A., Emmelkamp, P. M. G., & Best, S. (1983). The Maudley Marital Questionnaire (M.M.Q.): A further step toward its validation. *Personality and Individual Differences, 4,* 457–464.

Bandura, A. (1977). *Social learning theory*. Englewood Cliffs, NJ: Prentice-Hall.

Barlow, D., O'Brien, G., & Last, C. (1984). Couples treatment of agoraphobia. *Behavior Therapy, 5,* 41–58.

Barton, C., & Alexander, J. F. (1977a). Therapists' skills as determinants of effective systems-behavioral family therapy. *International Journal of Family Therapy, 11,* 1–15.

Barton, C., & Alexander, J. F. (1977b). Treatment of families with a delinquent member. In G. Harris (Ed.), *The group treatment of human problems: A social learning approach*. New York: Grune & Stratton.

Barton, C., & Alexander, J. F. (1981). Functional family therapy. In A. S. Gurman & D. P. Kniskern (Eds.), *Handbook of family therapy* (pp. 403–443). New York: Brunner/Mazel.

Barton, C., & Alexander, J. F. (1982). Appendix A: Coding system for therapist skills. In J. F. Alexander & B. V. Parsons, *Functional family therapy* (pp. 247–263). Monterey, CA: Brooks/Cole Publishing.

Baucom, D. H., & Lester, G. W. (1986). The usefulness of cognitive restructuring as an adjunct to behavioral marital therapy. *Behavior Therapy, 17,* 385–403.

Beck, A. T. (1988). *Love is never enough*. New York: Harper & Row.

Beck, A. T., Rusch, A. J., Shaw, B. F., & Emery, G. (1979). *Cognitive therapy of depression*. New York: Guilford Press.

Bedrosian, R. C. (1988). Treating depression and suicidal wishes within the family context. In N. Ep-stein, S. E. Schlesinger, & W. Dryden (Eds.), *Cognitive-behavioral therapy with families* (pp. 292–324). New York: Brunner/Mazel.

Bornstein, P. H., & Bornstein, M. T. (1986). *Marital therapy: A behavioral-communications approach*. New York: Pergamon Press.

Dalton, P. (1983). Family treatment of an obsessive-compulsive child: A case report. *Family Process, 22,* 99–108.

DiGiuseppe, R. (1988). A cognitive-behavioral approach to the treatment of conduct disorder children and adolescents (pp. 183–214). In N. Epstein, S. E. Schlesinger, & W. Dryden (Eds.), *Cognitive-behavioral therapy with families*. New York: Brunner/Mazel.

Dinkmeyer, D., & Losoncy, L. E. (1980). *The encouragement book*. Englewood Cliffs, NJ: Prentice-Hall.

Eidelson, R. J., & Epstein, N. (1982). Cognition and relationship maladjustment: Development of a measure of dysfunctional relationship beliefs. *Journal of Consulting and Clinical Psychology, 50,* 715–720.

Emmelkamp, P. M. G., Krol, B., Sanderman, R., & Ruphan, M. (1987). The assessment of relationship beliefs in a marital context. *Personality and Individual Differences, 8,* 775–780.

Emmelkamp, P. M. G., Van Linden Van Den Heuvell, C., Ruphan, M., Sanderman, R., Scholing, A., & Stroink, F. (1988). Cognitive and behavioral interventions with distressed couples. *Journal of Family Psychology, 1,* 365–377.

Emmelkamp, P. M. G., Van Linden Van Den Heuvell, C., Sanderman, R., & Scholing, A. (1988). Cognitive marital therapy: The process of change. *Journal of Family Psychology, 1,* 385–389.

Epstein, N., & Baucom, D. H. (1988). Outcome research on cognitive-behavioral marital therapy: Conceptual and methodological issues. *Journal of Family Psychology, 1,* 378–384.

Epstein, N., Pretzer, J. L., & Fleming, B. (1982). The role of cognitive appraisal in self-reports of marital communication. *Behavior Therapy, 18,* 51–69.

Epstein, N., Schlesinger, S. E., & Dryden, W. (1988). Concepts and methods of cognitive-behavioral family treatment. In N. Epstein, S. E. Schlesinger, & W. Dryden (Eds.), *Cognitive-behavioral therapy with families* (pp. 5–48). New York: Brunner/Mazel.

Gordon, S. B., & Davidson, N. (1981). Behavioral parent training. In A. S. Gurman & D. P. Kniskern (Eds.), *Handbook of family therapy* (pp. 517–555). New York: Brunner/Mazel.

Hahlweg, K., & Markman, H. J. (1988). Effectiveness of behavioral marital therapy: Empirical status of behavioral techniques in preventing and alleviating marital distress. *Journal of Consulting and Clinical Psychology, 56*(3), 440–447.

Hahlweg, K., Revenstorf, D., & Schindler, L. (1984). Effects of behavioral marital therapy on couples' communication and problem-solving skills. *Journal of Consulting and Clinical Psychology, 52*(4), 553–566.

Hahlweg, K., Schindler, L., Revenstorf, D., & Brengelmann, J. C. (1984). The Munich marital therapy study. In K. Hahlweg & N. S. Jacobson (Eds.), *Marital interaction: Analysis and modification* (pp. 3–26). New York: Guilford Press.

Heiman, J. R., LoPiccolo, L., & LoPiccolo, J. (1981). The treatment of sexual dysfunction. In A. S. Gurman & D. P. Kniskern (Eds.), *Handbook of family therapy* (pp. 592–630). New York: Brunner/Mazel.

Hof, L. (1987). Evaluating the marital relationship of clients with sexual complaints. In G. R. Weeks & L. Hof (Eds.), *Integrating sex and marital therapy: A clinical guide* (pp. 5–22). New York: Brunner/Mazel.

Hollon, S. D., & Garber, J. (1980). A cognitive-expectancy theory of therapy for helplessness and depression. In J. Garber & M. E. P. Seligman (Eds.), *Human helplessness: Theory and applications* (pp. 173–196). New York: Academic Press.

Holtzworth-Munroe, A., & Jacobson, N. S. (1987, August). *The role of causal attributions in marital distress and marital therapy*. Paper presented at the meeting of the American Psychological Assoc. New York, NY.

Huber, C. H., & Milstein, B. (1985). Cognitive restructuring and collaborative set in couples work. *American Journal of Family Therapy, 13*(2), 17–27.

Jacob, T., & Tennenbaum, D. L. (1988). *Family assessment: Rationale, methods and future directions*. New York: Plenum Press.

Jacobson, N. S. (1977). Problem solving and contingency contraction in the treatment of marital discord. *Journal of Consulting and Clinical Psychology, 45,* 92–100.

Jacobson, N. S. (1978a). Specific and nonspecific factors in the effectiveness of a behavioral approach to the treatment of marital discord. *Journal of Consulting and Clinical Psychology, 46,* 442–452.

Jacobson, N. S. (1978b). Increasing positive behavior in severely distressed marital relationships: The effects of problem-solving training. *Behavior Therapy, 10,* 311–326.

Jacobson, N. S. (1978c). A review of the research on the effectiveness of marital therapy. In T. J. Paolino, Jr. & B. S. McCrady (Eds.), *Marriage and marital therapy: Psychoanalytic, behavioral and systems theory perspectives* (pp. 395–444). New York: Brunner/Mazel.

Jacobson, N. S. (1981). Behavioral marital therapy. In A. S. Gurman & D. P. Kniskern (Eds.), *Handbook of family therapy* (pp. 556–591). New York: Brunner/Mazel.

Jacobson, N. S. (1984). The modification of cognitive processes in behavioral marital therapy: Integrating cognitive and behavioral intervention strategies. In K. Hahlweg & N. S. Jacobson (Eds.), *Marital interaction: Analysis and modification* (pp. 285–308). New York: Guilford Press.

Jacobson, N. S. (1989). The maintenance of treatment gains following social learning-based marital therapy. *Behavior Therapy, 20*(3), 325–336.

Jacobson, N. S., Follette, W. C., & Elwood, R. W. (1984). Outcome research on behavioral marital therapy: A methodological and conceptual reappraisal. In K. Hahlweg & N. S. Jacobson (Eds.), *Marital interaction: Analysis and modification* (pp. 113–132). New York: Guilford Press.

Jacobson, N. S., Follette, W. C., Revenstorf, D., Baucom, D. H., Hahlweg, K., & Margolin, G. (1984). Variability in outcome and clinical significance of behavioral marital therapy: A reanalysis of outcome data. *Journal of Consulting and Clinical Psychology, 52*(4), 497–504.

Jacobson, N. S., & Margolin, G. (1979). *Marital therapy: Strategies based on social learning and behavior exchange principles*. New York: Brunner/Mazel.

Jacobson, N. S., Schmaling, K. B., & Holtzworth-Munroe, A. (1987). Component analysis of behavioral marital therapy: 2-year follow-up and prediction of relapse. *Journal of Marital and Family Therapy, 23*(2), 187–95.

Kaplan, H. S. (1974). *The new sex therapy*. New York: Brunner/Mazel.

Kaplan, H. S. (1979). *Disorders of sexual desire*. New York: Simon & Schuster.

Kaplan, H. S. (1987). *The illustrated manual of sex therapy* (2nd ed.). New York: Brunner/Mazel.

King, M. L., Jr. (1972). I have a dream. In R. Barksdale & Kinnamon (Eds.), *Black writers of America* (pp. 871–873). New York: Academic Press.

Lederer, W. J., & Jackson, D. D. (1968). *The mirages of marriage*. New York: W. W. Norton & Co.

Leslie, L. A. (1988). Cognitive-behavioral and systems models of family therapy: How compatible are they? In N. Epstein, S. E. Schlesinger, & W. Dryden (Eds.), *Cognitive-behavioral therapy with families* (pp. 49–86). New York: Brunner/Mazel.

Leslie, L. A., & Epstein, N. (1988). Cognitive-behavioral treatment of remarried families. In N. Epstein, S. E. Schlesinger, & W. Dryden (Eds.), *Cognitive-behavioral therapy with families* (pp. 151–183). New York: Brunner/Mazel.

Liberman, R. P. (1970). Behavioral approaches to family and couple therapy. *American Journal of Orthopsychiatry, 40,* 106–118.

Liberman, R. P. (1975). Behavioral principles in family and couple therapy. In A. S. Gurman & D. G. Rice (Eds.), *Couples in conflict: New directions in marital therapy* (pp. 209–255). New York: Jason Aronson.

Libman, E., Fichten, C. S., & Brenden, W. (1985). The role of therapeutic format on the treatment of sexual dysfunction: A review. *Clinical Psychology Review, 5*(2), 103–117.

Losoncy, L. E. (1977). *Turning people on*. Englewood Cliffs, NJ: Prentice-Hall.

Losoncy, L. E. (1980). *You can do it*! Englewood Cliffs, NJ: Prentice-Hall.

Masters, W. H., & Johnson, V. E. (1966). *Human sexual response*. Boston: Little, Brown & Co.

Masters, W. H., & Johnson, V. E. (1970). *Human sexual inadequacy*. Boston: Little, Brown & Co.

Mays, B. E. (1969). *Disturbed about man*. Richmond, VA: John Knox Press.

Morokoff, P. J., & LoPiccolo, J. (1986). A comparative evaluation of minimal therapist contact and 15-session treatment for female orgasmic dysfunction. *Journal of Consulting and Clinical Psychology, 54*(3), 294–300.

Morton, T. L., Twentyman, C. T., & Azar, S. T. (1988). Cognitive-behavioral assessment and treatment of child abuse. In N. Epstein, S. E. Schlesinger, & W. Dryden (Eds.), *Cognitive-behavioral therapy with families* (pp. 87–117). New York: Brunner/Mazel.

Nichols, M. (1984). *Family therapy: Concepts and methods*. New York: Gardner Press.

O'Dell, S. (1974). Training parents in behavior modification: A review. *Psychological Bulletin, 81,* 418–433.

Patterson, G. R. (1968). *Direct intervention in families of deviant children*. Eugene, OR: Oregon Research Institute.

Patterson, G. R. (1975a). *Professional guide for families and living with children*. Champaign, IL: Research Press.

Patterson, G. R. (1975b). *Families* (Rev. ed.). Champaign, IL: Research Press.

Patterson, G. R. (1982). *Coercive family process*. Eugene, OR: Castalia Press.

Patterson, G. R., Chamberlin, P., & Reid, J. B. (1982). A comparative evaluation of a parent training program. *Behavior Therapy, 13,* 638–650.

Patterson, G. R., & Forgatch, M. (1987, 1989). *Living with adolescents part I and II*. Eugene, OR: Castalia Press.

Patterson, G. R., & Gullion, M. E. (1968). *Living with children: New methods for parents and teachers* (Rev. ed.). Champaign, IL: Research Press.

Qualls, S. H. (1988). Problems in families of older adults. In N. Epstein, S. E. Schlesinger, & W. Dryden (Eds.), *Cognitive-behavioral therapy with families* (pp. 215–253). New York: Brunner/Mazel.

Raps, C. S., Reinhard, K. E., & Seligman, M. E. P. (1980). Reversal of cognitive and affective deficits associated with depression and learned helplessness by mood elevation in patients. *Journal of Abnormal Psychology, 89*(3), 342–349.

Revenstorf, D. (1984). The role of attribution of marital distress in therapy. In K. Hahlweg & N. S. Jacobson (Eds.). *Marital Interaction: Analysis and modification* (pp. 325–336). New York: Guilford Press.

Rios, J. D., & Gutierrez, J. M. (1986). Parent training with non-traditional families: An unresolved issue. *Child & Family Behavior Therapy, 7*(4), 33–45.

Schlesinger, S. E. (1988). Cognitive-behavioral approaches to family treatment of addictions. In N. Epstein, S. E. Schlesinger, & W. Dryden (Eds.), *Cognitive-behavioral therapy with families* (pp. 254–291). New York: Brunner/Mazel.

Schover, L. R., & LoPiccolo, J. (1982). Treatment effectiveness for dysfunctions of sexual desire. *Journal of Sex and Marital Therapy, 8*(3), 179–197.

Seligman, M. E. P. (1975). *Helplessness: On depression, development, and death.* San Francisco: W. H. Freeman.

Seligman, M. E. P., Castellon, C., Cacciola, J., Schulman, P., Luborsky, L., Ollove, M., & Lowning, R. (1988). Explanatory style change during cognitive therapy for unipolar depression. *Journal of Abnormal Psychology, 97*(1), 13–18.

Stuart, R. (1969). Operant interpersonal treatment for marital discord. *Journal of Consulting and Clinical Psychology, 33,* 675–682.

Stuart, R. (1973). *Premarital counseling inventory.* Champaign, IL: Research Press.

Stuart, R. (1975). Behavioral remedies for marital ills: A guide to the use of operant-interpersonal techniques. In A. S. Gurman & D. G. Rice (Eds.), *Couples in conflict: New directions in marital therapy* (pp. 241–257). New York: Jason Aronson.

Stuart, R. (1980a). *Helping couples change: A social learning approach to marital therapy.* New York: Guilford Press.

Stuart, R. (1980b). *Helping couples change: Clinical demonstrations and client guides for marital therapy.* New York: BMA Audio Cassette Publications.

Stuart, R. (1980c). *Practitioner's manual to accompany helping couples change: Clinical demonstrations and client guides for marital therapy.* New York: BMA Audio Cassette Publications.

Thibaut, J. W., & Kelley, H. H. (1959). *The social psychology of groups.* New York: John Wiley & Sons.

Thomas, M. B. (1970). *An annotated bibliography of behavioral counseling and theory for use in school counselor training.* Department of Educational Psychology and Guidance: The Univ. of Mississippi.

Thomas, M. B. (1986). The use of expectancy theory and the theory of learned helplessness in building upon strengths of ethnic minorities: The Black experience in the United States. *International Journal for the Advancement of Counseling, 9,* 371–379.

Thomas, M. B., & Dansby, P. G. (1985). Black clients: Family structures, therapeutic issues, and strengths. *Psychotherapy, 22,* 398–407.

Thomas, M. B., Moore, H. B., & Sams, C. (1980, September). Counselor renewal workshop in sex equality. *Counselor Education and Supervision,* 56–61.

Ulrici, D. K. (1983). The effects of behavioral and family interventions on juvenile recidivism. *Family Therapy, 10*(1), 25–36.

Walen, S. R., & Perlmutter, R. (1988). Cognitive behavioral treatment of adult sexual dysfunctions from a family perspective. In N. Epstein, S. E. Schlesinger, & W. Dryden (Eds.), *Cognitive behavioral therapy with families* (pp. 325–360). New York: Brunner/Mazel.

Washington, J. M. (Ed.). (1986). *A testament of hope: The essential writings of Martin Luther King, Jr.* San Francisco: Harper & Row.

Weiss, R. L. (1978). The conceptualization of marriage from a behavioral perspective. In T. J. Paolino & B. S. McCrady (Eds.), *Marriage and marital therapy: Psychoanalytic, behavioral and systems theory perspectives* (pp. 165–239). New York: Brunner/Mazel.

Weiss, R. L. (1984). Cognitive and strategic interventions in behavioral marital therapy. In K. Hahlweg & N. S. Jacobson (Eds.), *Marital interaction: Analysis and modification* (pp. 337–385). New York: Guilford Press.

Weiss, R. L., & Perry, B. A. (1979). *Assessment and treatment of marital dysfunction.* Eugene, OR: Oregon Marital Studies Program.

Wendorf, R. J. (1984). Family therapy with an enuretic, encopretic child. *Family Systems Medicine, 2*(1), 46–52.

Zimmerman, J. L., & Elliott, C. H. (1984). The relationship of stress to angioneurotic edema: Implications for improved management. *Child & Family Behavior Therapy, 6*(1), 57–62.

Chapter Eleven

Andolfi, M. (1979). *Family therapy: An interactional approach* (H. R. Cassin, Trans.). New York: Plenum Press.

Andolfi, M. (1980, January) Prescribing the family's own dysfunctional rules as therapeutic strategy. *Journal of Marital and Family Therapy,* pp. 29–36.

Aponte, H. J. (1986). "If I don't get simple, I cry." *Family Process, 25,* 531–548.

Aponte, H. J., & Van Deusen, J. M. (1981). Structural family therapy. In A. S. Gurman & D. P. Kniskern (Eds.), *Handbook of family therapy*. New York: Brunner/Mazel.

Auerswald, E. (1968). Interdisciplinary versus ecological approach. *Family Process, 7,* 204.

Barrows, S. E. (1981). Family therapy in Europe: An interview with Maurizio Andolfi. *The American Journal of Family Therapy, 9*(4), 70–75.

Berger, H., Honig, P., & Liebman, R. (1977). Recurrent abdominal pain: Gaining control of the symptom. *American Journal of Disorders of Childhood, 131,* 1340–1344.

Boyd-Franklin, N. (1987). The contribution of family therapy models to the treatment of black families. *Psychotherapy, 24*(3S), 621–629.

Brown, N., & Samis, M. (1987). The application of structural family therapy in developing the binuclear family. *Mediation Quarterly,* No. 14/15, 51–69.

Carlson, C. I. (1987). Resolving school problems with structural family therapy. *School Psychology Review, 16,* 457–468.

Cohen, M. M. (1982) In the presence of your absence: The treatment of older families with a cancer patient. *Psychotherapy: Theory, Research and Practice, 29,* 453–460.

Davis, P., Stern, D., & Van Deusen, J. (1977). Enmeshment-disengagement in the alcoholic family. In F. Seixas (Ed.), *Alcoholism: Clinical and experimental research*. New York: Grune & Stratton.

Falicov, C. J. (1982). Mexican families. In M. McGoldrick, J. K. Pearce, & J. Giordano (Eds.), *Ethnicity and family therapy* (pp. 134–163). New York: Guilford Press.

Fulmer, R. H. (1983). A structural approach to unresolved mourning in single parent family systems. *Journal of Marital and Family Therapy, 9,* 259–269.

Fulmer, R. H., Cohen, S., & Monaco, G. (1985). Using psychological assessment in structural family therapy. *Journal of Learning Disabilities, 18,* 145–150.

Jalali, B. (1982). Iranian families. In M. McGoldrick, J. K. Pearce, & J. Giordano (Eds.), *Ethnicity and family therapy* (pp. 289–309). New York: Guilford Press.

Jung, M. (1984). Structural family therapy: Its application to Chinese families. *Family Process, 23,* 365–374.

Ko, H. Y. (1986). Minuchin's structural therapy for Vietnamese Chinese families: A systems perspective. *Contemporary Family Therapy, 8*(1), 20–32.

Liebman, R., Honig, P., & Berger, H. (1976). An integrated treatment program for psychogenic pain. *Family Process, 15,* 397–405.

McGill, D., & Pearce, J. K. (1982). British families. In M. McGoldrick, J. K. Pearce, & J. Giordanao (Eds.), *Ethnicity and family therapy* (pp. 457–482). New York: Guilford Press.

Minuchin, S. (1974). *Families & family therapy*. Cambridge, MA: Harvard Univ. Press.

Minuchin, S. (1984). *Family kaleidoscope*. Cambridge, MA: Harvard Univ. Press.

Minuchin, S., Baker, L., Rosman, B., Liebman, R., Milman, L., & Todd, T. (1975). A conceptual model of psychosomatic illness in children. *Archives of General Psychiatry, 32,* 1031–1038.

Minuchin, S., & Fishman, H. C. (1981). *Family therapy techniques*. Cambridge, MA: Harvard Univ. Press.

Minuchin, S., Montalvo, B., Guerney, B., Rosman, B., & Schumer, F. (1967). *Families of the slums*. New York: Basic Books.

Minuchin, S., Rosman, B., & Baker, L. (1978). *Psychosomatic families*. Cambridge: Harvard Univ. Press.

Moitoza, E. (1982). Portuguese families. In M. McGoldrick, J. K. Pearce, & J. Giordano (Eds.), *Ethnicity and family therapy*. New York: Guilford Press.

O'Sullivan, S., Berger, M., & Foster, M. (1984). The utility of structural family therapy nomenclature: Between-clinician agreement in the conjoint family assessment interview. *Journal of Marital and Family Therapy, 10,* 179–184.

Rosenberg, J. B., & Lindblad, M. B. (1978). Behavior therapy in a family context: Elective mutism. *Family Process, 17,* 77–82.

Rosman, B., Minuchin, S., & Liebman, R. (1975). Family lunch session: An introduction to family therapy in anorexia nervosa. *American Journal of Orthopsychiatry, 45,* 846–853.

Ross, J. L., Phipps, E. J., & Milligan, W. L. (1985). Irritable bowel syndrome in an adolescent adjusting to divorce: A case report. *Family Systems Medicine, 3,* 334–339.

Russell, C. S., Atilano, R. B., Anderson, S. A., Jurich, A. P., & Bergen, L. P. (1984). Intervention strategies: Predicting family therapy outcome. *Journal of Marital and Family Therapy, 10*(3), 241–251.

Sargent, J. (1983a). The family and childhood psychosomatic disorders. *General Hospital Psychiatry, 5,* 41–48.

Sargent, J. (1983b). The sick child: Family complications. *Developmental and Behavioral Pediatrics, 4,* 50–56.

Stanton, M. D. (1981, October). An integrated structural/strategic approach to family therapy. *Journal of Marital and Family Therapy,* pp. 427–439.

Stanton, M. D., Todd, T., Steier, F., Van Deusen, J., Marder, L., Rosoff, R., Seaman, S., & Skibinski, E. (1979). *Family characteristics and family therapy of heroin addicts: Final report, 1974–1978.* Philadelphia: Philadelphia Child Guidance Clinic.

Umbarger, C. C. (1983). *Structural family therapy.* New York: Grune & Stratton.

Welts, E. P. (1982). Greek families. In M. McGoldrick, J. K. Pearce, & J. Giordano (Eds.), *Ethnicity and family therapy* (pp. 269–288). New York: Guilford Press.

Zeigler-Driscoll, G. (1977). Family research study at Eagleville Hospital and Rehabilitation Center. *Family Process, 16,* 175–190.

Zeigler-Driscoll, G. (1979). The similarities in families of drug dependents and alcoholics. In E. Kaufman & P. Kaufman (Eds.), *The family therapy of drug and alcohol abuse.* New York: Gardner Press.

Chapter Twelve

Bateson, G., (1972). *Steps to an ecology of mind.* New York: Ballantine Books.

Bodin, A. M. (1981). The interactional view: Family therapy approaches of the Mental Research Institute. In A. S. Gurman & D. P. Kniskern (Eds.), *Handbook of family therapy* (pp. 267–309). New York: Brunner/Mazel.

Broderick, C. B., & Schrader, S. S. (1981). The history of professional marriage and family therapy. In A. S. Gurman & D. P. Kniskern (Eds.), *Handbook of family therapy* (pp. 58–65). New York: Brunner/Mazel.

Constantine, L. L. (1986). *Family paradigms: The practice of theory in family therapy.* New York: Guilford Press.

Coyne, J. C. (1985). Toward a theory of frames and reframing: The social nature of frames. *Journal of Marital and Family Therapy, 11,* 337–344.

de Shazer, S. (1982). *Patterns of brief family therapy: An ecosystemic approach.* New York: Guilford Press.

de Shazer, S. (1985) *Keys to solution in brief therapy.* New York: W. W. Norton & Co.

de Shazer, S. (1988). *Clues: Investigating solutions in brief therapy.* New York: W. W. Norton & Co.

Fisch, R., Weakland, J. H., & Segal, L. (1982). *The tactics of change: Doing therapy briefly.* San Francisco: Jossey-Bass.

Friedman, S., & Pettus, S. (1985). Brief strategic interventions with families of adolescents. *Family Therapy, 12,* 197–210.

Golden, L. (1983). Brief family interventions in a school setting. *Elementary School Guidance and Counseling, 17,* 288–293.

Jackson, D. D. (1960). *The etiology of schizophrenia.* New York: Basic Books.

Jackson, D. D. (1964). *Myths of madness.* New York: Macmillan Co.

Jackson, D. D. (1968a). Foreword to Mental Research Institute volumes. In D. D. Jackson (Ed.), *Communication, family, and marriage: Human communication volume 1* (pp. v–vi). Palo Alto, CA: Science and Behavior Books.

Jackson, D. D. (Ed.). (1968b). *Communication, family, and marriage: Human communication volume 1.* Palo Alto, CA. Science and Behavior Books.

Jackson, D. D. (Ed.). (1968c). *Therapy, communication, & change: Human communication volume 2.* Palo Alto, CA: Science and Behavior Books.

Jackson, D. D. (1977a). The study of the family. In P. Watzlawick & J. H. Weakland (Eds.), *The interactional view: Studies at the Mental Research Institute, Palo Alto, 1965–1974* (pp. 2–20). New York: W. W. Norton & Co.

Jackson, D. D. (1977b). Family rules: Marital quid pro quo. In P. Watzlawick & J. H. Weakland (Eds.), *The interactional view: Studies at the Mental Research Institute, Palo Alto, 1965–1974* (pp. 21–30). New York: W. W. Norton & Co.

Jackson, D. D., & Satir, V. M. (1968). A review of psychiatric developments in family diagnosis and family therapy. In D. D. Jackson (Ed.), *Therapy, communication, & change: Human communication volume 2*. Palo Alto, CA: Science and Behavior Books.

Keeney, B. (1979). Ecosystemic epistemology: An alternative paradigm for diagnosis. *Family Process, 18,* 117–129.

L'Abate, L., Ganahl, G., & Hansen, J. C. (1986). *Methods of family therapy.* Englewood Cliffs, NJ: Prentice-Hall.

Lederer, W. J., & Jackson, D. D. (1968). *The mirages of marriage.* New York: W. W. Norton & Co.

Morawetz, A., & Walker, G. (1984). *Brief therapy with single-parent families.* New York: Brunner/Mazel.

Peckman, L. (1984). Unpublished manuscript.

Watzlawick, P. (1976). *How real is real?* New York: Random House.

Watzlawick, P. (1978). *The language of change: Elements of therapeutic communication.* New York: Basic Books.

Watzlawick, P. (1983). *The situation is hopeless but not serious.* New York: W. W. Norton & Co.

Watzlawick, P. (Ed.). (1984). *The invented reality: How do we know what we believe we know? Contributions to constructivism.* New York: W. W. Norton & Co.

Watzlawick, P. (1988). *Ultra-solutions: How to fail most successfully.* New York: W. W. Norton & Co.

Watzlawick, P., Beavin, J. H., & Jackson, D. D. (1967). *Pragmatics of human communication: A study of international patterns, pathologies, and paradoxes.* New York: W. W. Norton & Co.

Watzlawick, P., & Weakland, J. H. (Eds.). (1977). *The interactional view: Studies at the Mental Research Institute, Palo Alto, 1965–1974.* New York: W. W. Norton & Co.

Watzlawick, P., Weakland, J. H., & Fisch, R. (1974). *Change: Principles of problem formation and problem resolution.* New York: W. W. Norton & Co.

Weakland, J., Fisch, R., Watzlawick, P., & Bodin, A. (1974). Brief therapy: Focused problem resolution. *Family Process, 13,* 141–168.

Chapter Thirteen

American Psychological Association (1983). *Publication manual of the American Psychological Association* (3rd ed.). Washington, DC: Author.

Andolfi, M. (1986). How to engage families with a rigid organization in therapy: An attempt to integrate strategic and structural interventions. In H. C. Fishman & B. L. Rosman (Eds.), *Evolving models for family change: A volume in honor of Salvador Minuchin* (pp. 111–121). New York: Guilford Press.

Bateson, G., Jackson, D. D., Haley, J., & Weakland, J. (1956). Toward a theory of schizophrenia. *Behavioral Science, 1,* 251–264.

Bodin, A. (1981). The interactional view: Family therapy approaches of the Mental Research Institute. In A. S. Gurman and D. P. Kniskern (Eds.), *Handbook of family therapy.* New York: Brunner/Mazel.

Bograd, M. (1982). Battered women, cultural myths and clinical interventions: A feminist analysis. In the New England Association for Women in Psychology (Eds.), *Current feminist issues in psychotherapy* (pp. 69–77). New York: Haworth Press.

Bograd, M. (1984). Family systems approaches to wife battering: A feminist critique. *American Journal of Orthopsychiatry, 54,* 558–568.

Braverman, L. (1986). Beyond families: Strategic family therapy and the female client. *Family Therapy, 13,* 143–152.

Dell, P. F. (1986a). In defense of "lineal causality." *Family Process, 25,* 513–521.

Dell, P. F. (1986b). Toward a foundation for addressing violence. *Family Process, 25,* 527–529.

Fraser, J. S. (1986). Integrating system-based therapies: Similarities, differences, and some critical questions. In D. E. Efron (Ed.), *Journeys: Expansion of the strategic-systemic therapies.* New York: Brunner/Mazel.

Friesen, J. D. (1985). *Structural-strategic marriage and family therapy*. New York: Gardner Press.

Haley, J. (1963). *Strategies of psychotherapy*. New York: Grune & Stratton.

Haley, J. (Ed.). (1967). *Advanced techniques of hypnosis and therapy: Selected papers of Milton H. Erickson*. New York: Grune & Stratton.

Haley, J. (Ed.). (1969). *The power tactics of Jesus Christ and other essays*. New York: Grossman Publishers.

Haley, J. (1973). *Uncommon therapy: The psychiatric techniques of Milton H. Erickson, M. D.* New York: Ballantine Books.

Haley, J. (1976). *Problem-solving therapy: New strategies for effective family therapy*. San Francisco, CA: Jossey-Bass.

Haley, J. (1980). *Leaving home: The therapy of disturbed young people*. New York: McGraw-Hill Book Co.

Haley, J. (1984). *Ordeal therapy: Unusual ways of changing behavior*. San Francisco: Jossey-Bass.

Haley, J. (1987). *Problem-solving therapy for effective family therapy* (2nd ed.). San Francisco: Jossey-Bass.

Harbin, H. T. (1985). Cure by ordeal: Treatment of an obsessive compulsive neurotic. *International Journal of Family Therapy, 7,* 155–163.

Hoffman, L. (1981). *Foundations of family therapy: A conceptual framework for systems change*. New York: Basic Books.

Imber-Black, E. (1986). Maybe "lineal causality" needs another defense lawyer: A feminist response to Dell. *Family Process, 25,* 523–525.

L'Abate, L., Ganahl, G., & Hansen, J. C. (1986). *Methods of family therapy*. Englewood Cliffs, NJ: Prentice-Hall.

MacKinnon, L. (1983). Contrasting strategic and Milan therapies. *Family Process, 22,* 425–440.

Madanes, C. (1980). Protection, paradox and pretending. *Family Process, 19,* 73–85.

Madanes, C. (1981). *Strategic family therapy*. San Francisco: Jossey-Bass.

Madanes, C. (1984). *Behind the one-way mirror: Advances in the practice of strategic therapy*. San Francisco: Jossey-Bass.

O'Connor, J. J. (1983). Why can't I get hives: Brief strategic therapy with an obsessional child. *Family Process, 22,* 201–209.

O'Connor, J. J. (1984). The resurrection of a magical reality: Treatment of functional migraine in a child. *Family Process, 23,* 501–509.

Scott, J. F. (1982, April). Structural and strategic family therapy: A basis for marriage, or grounds for divorce? *Journal of Marital and Family Therapy,* pp. 13–22.

Stanton, M. D. (1981, October). An integrated structural/strategic approach to family therapy. *Journal of Marital and Family Therapy,* pp. 427–439.

Stanton, M. D. (1981). Strategic approaches to family therapy. In A. S. Gurman & D. P. Kniskern (Eds.), *Handbook of family therapy* (pp. 361–402). New York: Brunner/Mazel.

Stone, G., & Peeks, B. (1986). The use of strategic family therapy in the school setting: A case study. *Journal of Counseling and Development, 65,* 200–203.

Weiner, J. P., & Boss, P. (1985). Exploring gender bias against women: Ethics for marriage and family therapy. *Counseling and Values, 30,* 9–23.

Chapter Fourteen

Andersen, T., Danielsen, H., Sonnesyn, H., & Sonnesyn, M. (1985). Circular questioning and shifting relationships: An attempt to describe the process of change in a family, and evaluate the therapy's influence on the changes. *Australian-and-New Zealand-Journal of Family Therapy, 6* (3), 145–150.

Anderson, S. A., & Bagarozzi, D. A. (1983). The use of family myths as an aid to strategic therapy. *Journal of Family Therapy, 5,* 145–154.

Ashby, W. R. (1954). *Design for a brain*. New York: John Wiley & Sons.

Barrows, S. E. (1982). Interview with Mara Selvini Palazzoli and Giuliana Prata. *The American Journal of Family Therapy, 10*(3), 60–69.

Bateson, G. (1972). *Steps to an ecology of mind*. New York: Ballantine Books.

Bateson, G. (1979). *Mind and nature: A necessary unity*. New York: E. P. Dutton.

Bennun, I. S. (1986). Evaluating family therapy: A comparison of the Milan and problem solving approaches. *Journal of Family Therapy, 8*(3), 225–242.

Boscolo, L., & Cecchin, G. (1982). Training in systemic therapy at the Milan Centre. In R. Whiffen

& J. Byng-Hall (Eds.) *Family therapy supervision: Recent developments in practice* (pp. 153–165). London: Academic Press.

Boscolo, L., Cecchin, G., Hoffman, L., & Penn, P. (1987). *Milan systemic family therapy: Conversations in theory and practice*. New York: Basic Books.

Burbatti, G. L., & Formenti, L. (1988). *The Milan approach to family therapy* (E. Cosmo, Trans.). Northvale, NJ: Jason Aronson.

Campbell, D., Reder, P., Draper, R., & Pollard, D. (1983). *An occasional paper*. London, England: The Tavistock Clinic

Di Blasio, P., Fischer, J., & Prata, G. (1986). The telephone chart: A cornerstone of the first interview with the family. *Journal of Strategic and Systemic Therapies, 5*(1&2), 31–43.

Fleuridas, C., Nelson, T. S., & Rosenthal, D. M. (1986). The evolution of circular questions: Training family therapists. *Journal of Marital and Family Therapy, 23,* 113–127.

Fraser, J. S. (1986). Integrating system-based therapies: Similarities, differences, and some critical questions. In D. E. Efron (Ed.), *Journeys: Expansion of the strategic-systemic therapies*. New York: Brunner/Mazel.

Giacomo, D. (1986). Systemic practice. *Family Process, 25,* 483–512.

Haley, J. (1963). *Strategies of psychotherapy*. New York: Grune & Stratton.

Hoffman, L. (1981). *Foundations of family therapy*. New York: Basic Books.

Hoffman, L. (1983). A co-evolutionary framework for systemic family therapy. In J. Hansen & B. Kenney (Eds.), *Diagnosis and assessment in family therapy* (pp. 37–61). Rockville, MD: Aspen Systems Corp.

Hoffman, L. (1988). The family life cycle and discontinuous change. In B. Carter & M. McGoldrick (Eds.), *The changing family life cycle: A framework for family therapy* (2nd ed.). New York: Gardner Press.

Keeney, B. P., & Ross, J. M. (1985). *Mind in therapy: Constructing systemic family therapies*. New York: Basic Books.

Liddle, H. A. (1983). Diagnosis and assessment in family therapy: A comparative analysis of six schools of thought. In J. Hansen & B. Keeney (Eds.), *Diagnosis and assessment in family therapy* (pp. 1–33). Rockville, MD: Aspen Systems Corp.

MacKinnon, L. (1983). Contrasting strategic and Milan therapies. *Family Process, 22,* 425–440.

Penn, P. (1982). Circular questioning. *Family Process, 21*(3), 267–280.

Penn, P. (1985). Feed-forward: Future questions, future maps. *Family Process, 24*(3), 299–310.

Selvini Palazzoli, M. (1975). *Paradox and counterparadox*. Unpublished manuscript.

Selvini Palazzoli, M. (1978). *Self-starvation: From individual to family therapy in the treatment of anorexia nervosa*. New York: Jason Aronson.

Selvini Palazzoli, M. (1980). Why a long interval between sessions? The therapeutic control of the family therapist suprasystem. In M. Andolfi & I. Zwerling (Eds.), *Dimensions of family therapy* (pp. 161–169). New York: Guilford Press.

Selvini Palazzoli, M. (1983). The emergence of a comprehensive systems approach. *Journal of Family therapy, 5,* 165–177.

Selvini Palazzoli, M. (1985). The problem of the sibling as the referring person. *Journal of Marital and Family Therapy, 11*(1), 21–34.

Selvini Palazzoli, M. (1987). The emergence of a comprehensive systems approach: Supervisor and team problems in a district psychiatric center. In H. Stierlin, F. B. Simon, & G. Schmidt (Eds.), *Familiar realities: The Heidelberg Conference* (pp. 109–120). New York: Brunner/Mazel.

Selvini Palazzoli, M. (Ed.). (1988). *The work of Mara Selvini Palazzoli*. New York: Jason Aronson.

Selvini Palazzoli, M., Boscolo, L., Cecchin, G. F., & Prata, G. (1974). The treatment of children through brief therapy of their parents. *Family Process, 13*(4), 419–442.

Selvini Palazzoli, M., Boscolo, L., Cecchin, G., & Prata, G. (1978a). *Paradox and counterparadox: A new model in the therapy of the family in schizophrenic transaction*. New York: Jason Aronson.

Selvini Palazzoli, M., Boscolo, L., Cecchin, G. & Prata, G. (1978b). A ritualized prescription in family therapy: Odd days and even days. *Journal of Marital and Family Counseling, 4,* 3–9.

Selvini Palazzoli, M., Boscolo, L., Cecchin, G., & Prata, G. (1979). First session of a systematic family therapy. Unpublished manuscript.

Selvini Palazzoli, M., Boscolo, L., Cecchin, G., & Prata, G. (1980a). Hypothesizing—circularity—neutrality: Three guidelines on the conductor of the session. *Family Process, 19*(1), 3–23.

Selvini Palazzoli, M., Boscolo, L., Cecchin, G., & Prata, G. (1980b). The problem of the referring person. *Journal of Marital and Family Therapy, 6,* 3–9.

Selvini Palazzoli, M., Cirillo, S., Selvini, M., & Sorrentino, A. M. (1989). *Family games: General models of psychiatric processes in the family* (V. Kleiber, Trans.). New York: W. W. Norton & Co.

Selvini Palazzoli, M., & Viaro, M. (1988). The anorectic process in the family: A six-stage model as a guide for the individual therapy, *Family Process, 27*(2), 129–148.

Simon, R. (1987, September–October). Palazzoli and the family game. *The Family Therapy Networker,* 17–25.

Stanton, M. D. (1981). Strategic approaches to family therapy. In A. S. Gurman & D. P. Kniskern (Eds.), *Handbook of family therapy* (pp. 362–402). New York: Brunner/Mazel.

Stierlin, H., Simon, F. B., & Schmidt, G. (1987). *Familiar realities: The Heidelberg Conference.* New York: Brunner/Mazel.

Stierlin, H., & Weber, G. (1989). *Unlocking the family door: A systemic approach to the understanding and treatment of anorexia nervosa.* New York: Brunner/Mazel.

Taylor, V. L., & McClain, E. R. (1987). Continuing the effectiveness of effective systemic therapy. *Family therapy, 14,* 61–65.

Tomm, K. (1984a). One perspective on the Milan systemic approach: Part I. Overview of development, theory and practice. *Journal of Marital and Family Therapy, 10,* 113–125.

Tomm, K. (1984b). One perspective on the Milan systemic approach: Part II. Description of session format, interviewing style and interventions. *Journal of Marital and Family Therapy, 10,* 253–271.

Tomm, K. (1985). Circular questioning: A multifaceted clinical tool. In D. Campbell & R. Draper (Eds.), *Application of systemic family therapy: The Milan method* (pp. 33–45). New York: Grune & Stratton.

Viaro, L. & Leonardo, P. (1983). Getting and giving information. Analysis of a family interview strategy. *Family Process, 22*(10), 17–42.

Viaro, L., & Leonardo, P. (1986). The evolution of an interview technique: A comparison between former and present strategy. *Journal of Strategic and Systemic Therapies, 5*(1&2), 14–30.

Watzlawick, P., Beavin, J., & Jackson, D. (1967). *Pragmatics of human communication: Study of interactional patterns, pathologies and paradoxes.* New York: W. W. Norton & Co.

Weeks, G. R., & L'Abate, L. (1982). *Paradoxical psychotherapy: Theory and Practice with individuals, couples and families.* New York: Brunner/Mazel.

Chapter Fifteen

Ables, B. S., with Brandsma, J. M. (1977). *Therapy for couples.* San Francisco: Jossey-Bass.

Alexander, J. F., Barton, C., Schiavo, R. S., & Parsons, B. V. (1976). Behavioral intervention with families of delinquents: Therapist characteristics and outcome. *Journal of Consulting and Clinical Psychology, 44*(4), 656–664.

Alexander, J., & Parsons, B. V. (1982). *Functional family therapy.* Monterey, CA: Brooks/Cole Publishing.

American Psychiatric Association (1980). *Diagnostic and statistical manual of mental disorders* (3rd ed.). Washington, DC: Author.

American Psychological Association (1987). *Casebook on ethical standards of psychologists.* Washington, DC: Author.

Ard, B. N., & Ard, C. (Eds.). (1976). *Handbook of marriage counseling* (2nd ed.). Palo Alto, CA: Science and Behavior Books.

Barton, C., & Alexander, J. F. (1977). Treatment of families with a delinquent member. In G. Harris (Ed.), *The group treatment of human problems: A source learning approach.* New York: Grune & Stratton.

Barton, C., & Alexander, J. F. (1980). Systems-behavioral intervention with delinquent families. In J. Vincent (Ed.), *Advances in family intervention, assessment, and theory.* Greenwich, CT: JAI Press.

Barton, C., & Alexander, J. F. (1982). Appendix A: Coding system for therapist skills. In J. F. Alexander & B. V. Parsons, *Functional family therapy.* Monterey, CA: Brooks/Cole Publishing.

Beavers, W. R. (1986). Family therapy supervision: An introduction and consumer's guide. *Journal of Psychotherapy & the Family, 1*(4), 15–24.

Breunlin, D. C. (1985). Expanding the concept of stages in family therapy. In J. C. Hansen & D. C. Breunlin (Eds.), *Stages: Patterns of change over time* (pp. 1–15). Rockville, MD: Aspen Systems Corp.

Broderick, C. B., & Schrader, S. S. (1981). The history of professional marriage and family therapy. In A. S. Gurman & D. P. Kniskern (Eds.), *Handbook of family therapy*. New York: Brunner/Mazel.

Byng-Hall, J. (1982). The use of the earphone in supervision. In R. Whiffen & J. Byng-Hall (Eds.), *Family therapy supervision: Recent developments in practice* (pp. 47–56). London: Academic Press.

Byng-Hall, J., de Carteret, J., & Whiffen, R. (1982). Evolution of supervision: An overview. In R. Whiffen & J. Byng-Hall (Eds.), *Family therapy supervision: Recent developments in practice* (pp. 3–16). London: Academic Press.

Campbell, T. L. (1986). *Family's impact on health: A critical review. Family Systems Medicine, 4,* 135–200.

Coleman, S. B., with Gurman, A. S. (1985). An analysis of family therapy failures. In S. B. Coleman (Ed.), *Failures in family therapy* (pp. 333–389). New York: Guilford Press.

Epstein, N. B., Baldwin, L. M., & Bishop, D. S. (1983). The McMaster family assessment device. *Journal of Marital and Family Therapy, 9,* 171–180.

Feldman, L. B. (1985). Integrative multi-level therapy: A comprehensive interpersonal and intrapsychic approach. *Journal of Marital and Family Therapy, 11*(4), 357–372.

Fenell, D. L., & Hovestadt, A. J. (1986). Family therapy as a profession or professional specialty: Implications for training. *Journal of Psychotherapy & the Family, 1*(4), 25–40.

Flowers, B., & Olson, D. (1986). Predicting success with PREPARE: A predictive study. *Journal of Marital and Family Therapy, 12*(4), 403–413.

Fredman, N., & Sherman, R. (1987). *Handbook of measurements for marriage & family therapy.* New York: Brunner/Mazel.

Friedman, P. H. (1981). Integrative family therapy. *Family Therapy, 8,* 171–178.

Haley, J. (1984). Marriage or family therapy. *The American Journal of Family Therapy, 12*(2), 3–14.

Heath, A. W. (1985). Ending family therapy: Some new directions. In J. C. Hansen & D. C. Breunlin (Eds.), *Stages: Patterns of change over time* (pp. 33–40). Rockville, MD: Aspen Systems Corp.

Hovestadt, A. J., Fenell, D. L., & Piercy, F. P. (1983). Integrating marriage and family therapy within counselor education: A three-level model. In B. F. Okun & S. T. Gladding (Eds.), *Issues in training marriage and family therapists* (pp. 29–42). Ann Arbor, MI: ERIC Counseling and Personnel Services Clearinghouse.

Huber, C. H., & Baruth, L. G. (1987). *Ethical, legal, and professional issues in the practice of marriage and family therapy.* Columbus, OH: Merrill.

Ivey, A. E. (1987). *Developmental therapy.* San Francisco: Jossey-Bass.

Kiesler, D. (1973). *The process of psychotherapy: Empirical foundations and systems of analysis.* Chicago: Aldine Publishing Co.

Kniskern, D. P., & Gurman, A. S. (1979). Research on training in marriage and family therapy: Status, issues and directions. *Journal of Marital and Family Therapy, 5,* 83–94.

Koch, A., & Ingram, T. (1985). The treatment of borderline personality disorder within a distressed relationship. *Journal of Marital and Family Therapy, 11*(4), 373–380.

Kramer, C. H. (1980). *Becoming a family therapist: Developing an integerated approach to working with families.* New York: Human Sciences Press.

Lebow, J. L. (1984). On the value of integrating approaches to family therapy. *Journal of Marital and Family Therapy, 10,* 127–138.

Lebow, J. L. (1987). Developing a personal integration in family therapy: Principles for model construction and practice. *Journal of Marital and Family Therapy, 13*(1), 1–14.

Liddle, H. A. (1982). Family therapy training: Current issues, future trends. *International Journal of Family Therapy,* 81–97.

Liddle, H. A. (1983). Diagnosis and assessment in family therapy: A comparative analysis of six schools of thought. In J. C. Hansen & B. P. Keeney (Eds.), *Diagnosis and assessment in family therapy* (pp. 3–33). Rockville, MD: Aspen Systems Corp.

Liddle, H., & Halpin, R. (1978). Family therapy training and supervision: A comparative review.

Journal of Marriage and Family Counseling, 4, 77–98.

Locke, H. J., & Wallace, K. M. (1959). Short marital adjustment tests: Their reliability and validity. *Marriage and the Family, 2,* 251–255.

McCubbin, H., Olson, D., & Larsen, A. (1987). Family crisis-oriented personal evaluation scales. In N. Fredman & R. Sherman (Eds.), *Handbook of measurements for marriage and family therapy* (pp. 199–203). New York: Brunner/Mazel.

McCubbin, H., Patterson, J. M., & Wilson, L. R. (1987). FILE: Family inventory of life events and changes. In N. Fredman & R. Sherman (Eds.), *Handbook of measurements for marriage and family therapy* (pp. 194–197). New York: Brunner/Mazel.

McGuire, D. (1985). The middle phase: The evolving process of change. In J. C. Hansen & D. C. Breunlin (Eds.), *Stages: Patterns of change over time* (pp. 26–32). Rockville, MD. Aspen Systems Corp.

MFT regulation growing in USA. (1988, July–August). *Family Therapy News,* p. 19.

Moos, R. H., & Moos, B. S. (1981). *Family Environment Scale manual.* Palo Alto, CA. Consulting Psychologists Press.

Moultrup, D. (1981). Towards an integrated model of family therapy. *Clinical Social Work Journal, 9,* 111–125.

Nelsen, J. C. (1983). *Family treatment: An integrative approach.* Englewood Cliffs, NJ: Prentice-Hall.

Nichols, M. P. (1984). *Family therapy: Concepts and methods.* New York: Gardner Press.

Nichols, W. C. (1979). Introduction to Part I. Education and training in marital and family therapy. *Journal of Marital and Family Therapy, 5*(3), 3–5.

Okun, B. F., & Gladding, S. T. (Eds.). (1983). *Issues in training marriage and family therapists.* Ann Arbor, MI: ERIC Counseling and Personnel Services Clearinghouse.

Olson, D. H. (1970). Marital and family therapy: Integrative review and critique. *Journal of Marriage and the Family, 32,* 501–538.

Olson, D. H., Fournier, D. G., & Druckman, J. M. (1982). *PREPARE-ENRICH counselor's manual.* Minneapolis: PREPARE-ENRICH, Inc.

Olson, D. H., Larsen, A. S., & McCubbin, H. I. (1987). Family strengths. In N. Fredman & R. Sherman

(Eds.), *Handbook of measurements for marriage and family therapy* (pp. 191–193). New York: Brunner/Mazel.

Olson, D. H., Portner, J., & Lavee, Y. (1987). Family adaptability and cohesion evaluation scales III. In N. Fredman & R. Sherman (Eds.), *Handbook of measurements for marriage and family therapy* (pp. 180–185). New York: Brunner/Mazel.

Piercy, F. P., Laird, R. A., & Mohammed, Z. (1983). A family therapist rating scale. *Journal of Marital and Family Therapy, 9*(1), 49–59.

Piercy, F. P., & Sprenkle, D. H. (1986). Family therapy theory building: An integrative training approach. *Journal of Psychotherapy and the Family, 1*(4), 5–14.

Piercy, F. P., & Sprenkle, D. H. (1988). Family therapy theory-building questions. *Journal of Marital and Family Therapy, 14*(3), 307–309.

Pinsof, W. B. (1979). The family therapist behavior scale (FTBS): Development and evaluation of a coding system. *Family Process, 18,* 451–461.

Pinsof, W. B. (1983). Integrative problem centered therapy: Toward the synthesis of family and individual psychotherapies. *Journal of Marital and Family Therapy, 9,* 19–35.

Reid, M. E., Kipnis, J. B., & Hardy, K. V. (Eds.). (1988). *Directory of accredited marital and family therapy training programs.* Washington, DC: American Assoc. for Marriage and Family Therapy, Commission on Accreditation for Marriage and Family Therapy Education.

Rogers, C. R. (1957). The necessary and sufficient conditions of therapeutic personality change. *Journal of Consulting Psychology, 21,* 95–103.

Schutz, W. F. (1967). *MATE: A FIRO awareness scale.* Palo Alto, CA: Consulting Psychologists Press.

Schutz, W. F. (1976). *MATE: A FIRO awareness scale* (rev. ed.). Palo Alto, CA: Consulting Psychologists Press.

Sheehy, G. (1981). *Pathfinders.* New York: William Morrow & Co.

Sider, R. C., & Clements, C. (1982). Family or individual therapy: The ethics of modality choice. *American Journal of Psychiatry, 139,* 1455–1459.

Simon, R. (1989, March–April). From the editor. *Family Therapy Networker,* p. 2.

Spanier, G. B. (1976). Measuring dyadic adjustment: New scales for assessing the quality of marriage and similar dyads. *Journal of Marriage and the Family, 38,* 15–28.

Stierlin, H., Rucker-Embden, I., Wetzel, N., & Wirsching, M. (1980). *The first interview with the family* (S. Tooze, Trans.). New York: Brunner/Mazel. (Original work published 1977)

Stromberg, C. D., Haggarty, D. J., Leibenluft, R. F., McMillian, M. H., Mishkin, B., Rubin, B. L., & Trilling, H. R. (1988). *The psychologist's legal handbook.* Washington, DC: The Council for the National Register of Health Service Providers in Psychology.

Tarasoff v. *Regents of University of California, 529* P.2d. 553 (Cal. 1974), 551 P.2d 334 (Cal. 1976).

Thomas, M. B. (1983). A comparison of CACREP and AAMFT requirements for accreditation. In B. F. Okun & S. T. Gladding (Eds.), *Issues in training marriage and family therapists* (pp. 17–28). Ann Arbor, MI: ERIC Counseling and Personnel Services Clearinghouse.

Tomm, K., & Sanders, G. L. (1983). Family assessment in a problem oriented record. In J. C. Hansen & B. P. Keeney (Eds.), *Diagnosis and Assessment in Family Therapy* (p. 111). Rockville, MD: Aspen Systems Corp.

Wantz, R. A., Scherman, H., & Hollis, J. (1982). Trends in counselor preparation: Courses, program emphases, philosophical orientation and experimental components. *Counselor Education and Supervision, 21,* 258–268.

Wendorf, D. (1984). A model for training practicing professionals in family therapy. *Journal of Marital and Family Therapy, 10*(1), 31–41.

Winkle, C. W., Piercy, F. P., & Hovestadt, A. J. (1981). A curriculum for graduate-level marriage and family education. *Journal of Marital and Family Therapy, 7,* 201–210.

Wylie, M. S. (1989, March–April). Looking for fence posts. *Family Therapy Networker,* pp. 22–33.

Chapter Sixteen

American Association for Marriage and Family Therapy (1988). *AAMFT code of ethical principles for marriage and family therapists.* Washington, DC: Author.

American Psychological Association (1975). *Report of the Task Force on Sex Bias and Sex Role Stereotyping.* Washington, DC: Author.

Ault-Riche, M. (1986). A feminist critique of five schools of family therapy. In J. C. Hansen & M.

Ault-Riche (Eds.), *Women and family therapy* (pp. 1–15). Rockville, MD: Aspen.

Baucom, D. H., & Aiken, P. A. (1984). Sex role identity, marital satisfaction, and response to behavioral marital therapy. *Journal of Consulting and Clinical Psychology, 52*(3), 438–444.

Besharov, D. J. (1985). *The vulnerable social worker· Liability for serving children and families.* Silver Spring, MD: National Assoc. of Social Workers.

Bograd, M. (1986). A feminist examination of family systems models of violence against women in the family. In J. C. Hansen & M. Ault-Riche (Eds.), *Women and family therapy* (pp. 34–50). Rockville, MD: Aspen.

Brady v. Hopper, 570 F. Supp. 1333 (D. Colo. 1983).

Cohen, R. J. (1979). *Malpractice: A guide for mental health professionals.* New York: Free Press.

Counseling Psychology Division of the American Psychological Association (1985). *Principles concerning the counseling and therapy of women.* Washington, DC: American Psychological Assoc.

DeKraai, M. B., & Sales, B. D. (1982). Privileged communications of psychologists. *Professional Psychology, 13,* 372–388.

Dell, P. (1982). Beyond homeostasis: Toward a concept of coherence. *Family Process, 21,* 21–41.

Diagnostic and statistical manual of mental disorders (3rd ed. rev.). (1987). Washington, DC: American Psychiatric Assoc.

Edelwich, J., with Brodsky, A. (1982). *Sexual dilemmas for the helping professional.* New York: Brunner/Mazel.

Ethics Committee of the American Psychological Assoc. (1988). Trends in ethics cases, common pitfalls, and published resources. *American Psychologist, 43*(7), 564–572.

Everstine, L., Everstine, D. S., Heymann, G. M., True, R. H., Frey, D. H., Johnson, H. G., & Seiden, R. H. (1980). Privacy and confidentiality in psychotherapy. *American Psychologist, 35,* 828–840.

Fisher, L., Anderson, A., & Jones, J. E. (1981). Types of paradoxical interventions and indications/contraindications for use in clinical practice. *Family Process, 20,* 25–35.

Freeman, L., & Roy, J. (1976). *Betrayal.* New York: Stein and Day.

Ganong, L. H., & Coleman, M. (1986). Sex, sex roles, and familial love. *Journal of Genetic Psychology, 148*(1), 45–52.

Goldner, V. (1985). Feminism and family therapy. *Family Process, 24,* 31–47.

Gumper, L. L., & Sprenkle, D. H. (1981). Privileged communication in therapy: Special problems for the family and couples therapist. *Family Process, 20,* 11–23.

Gurman, A. S., & Kniskern, D. P. (1981). Family therapy outcome research: Knowns and unknowns. In A. S. Gurman & D. P. Kniskern (Eds.), *Handbook of family therapy* (pp. 742–776). New York: Brunner/Mazel.

Hare-Mustin, R. T. (1978). A feminist approach to family therapy. *Family Process, 17,* 181–194.

Hare-Mustin, R. T. (1987a). The problem of gender in family therapy theory. *Family Process, 26*(1), 15–27.

Hare-Mustin, R. T. (1987b). Rejoinder: Theory and transformation. *Family Process, 26*(1), 32–33.

Herrington, B. S. (1979). Privilege denied in joint therapy. *Psychiatric News, 14*(1), 1–9.

Huber, C. H., & Baruth, L. G. (1987). *Ethical, legal, and professional issues in the practice of marriage and family therapy.* Columbus, OH: Merrill.

Jablonski v. United States, 712 F. 2d 391 (9th Cir. 1983).

James, K., & McIntyre, D. (1983). The reproduction of families: The social role of family therapy? *Journal of Marital and Family Therapy, 9*(2), 119–129.

Keith-Spiegel, P., & Koocher, G. P. (1985). *Ethics in psychology: Professional standards and cases.* New York: Random House.

Leedy v. Hartnett, 510 F. Supp. 1125 (M. D. Pa. 1981).

Libow, J. A. (1986). Training family therapists as feminists. In J. C. Hansen & M. Ault-Riche (Eds.), *Women and family therapy* (pp. 16–24). Rockville, MD: Aspen.

Lipari v. Sears, Roebuck & Co., 497 F. Supp. (D. Neb. 1980).

Margolin, G. (1982). Ethical and legal considerations in marital and family therapy. *American Psychologist, 37,* 788–801.

Margolin, G., Fernandez, V., Talovic, S., & Onorato, R. (1983). Sex role considerations and behavioral marital therapy: Equal does not mean identical. *Journal of Marital and Family Therapy, 9*(2), 131–145.

McGoldrick, M., Pearce, J. K., & Giordano, J. (Eds.) (1982). *Ethnicity and family therapy.* New York: Guilford Press.

McIntosh v. Milano, 403 P. 2d 500 (N. J. Super. 1979).

Miller, B. C. (1986). *Family research methods.* Beverly Hills, CA: SAGE Publications.

Okun, B. F. (1983). Gender issues of family systems therapists. In B. F. Okun & S. T. Gladding (Eds.), *Issues in training marriage and family therapists* (pp. 43–58). Ann Arbor, MI: ERIC Counseling and Personnel Services Clearinghouse.

O'Shea, M., & Jessee, E. (1982). Ethical, value, and professional conflicts in systems therapy. In J. C. Hansen & L. L'Abate (Eds.), *Values, ethics, legalities and the family therapist* (pp. 1–21). Rockville, Maryland: Aspen Systems Corp.

Petersen v. State, 671 P. 2d 230 (Wash. 1983).

Piercy, F. P., & Sprenkle, D. H. (1983). Ethical, legal and professional issues in family therapy: A graduate level course. *Journal of Marital and Family Therapy, 9,* 393–401.

Pinderhughes, E. B. (1986). Minority women: A nodal position in the functioning of the social system. In J. C. Hansen & M. Ault Riche (Eds.), *Women and family therapy* (pp. 51–63). Rockville, MD: Aspen Systems Corp.

Pittman, F. (1985). Gender myths. *The Family Therapy Networker, 9*(6), 24–33.

Plaisil, E. (1985). *Therapist.* New York: St. Martin's/Marek.

Pope, K. S. (1988). Dual relationships: A source of ethical, legal, and clinical problems. *The Independent Practitioner, 8*(1), 17–25.

Pope, K. S. (1989, January). Malpractice suits, licensing, disciplinary actions and ethics cases: Frequencies, causes and costs. *The Independent Practitioner,* 22–28.

Pope, K. S., & Bouhoutsos, J. C. (1986). *Sexual intimacy beween therapists and patients.* New York: Praeger Pubs.

Rosenthal, H. (1988). *Not with my life I don't: Preventing your suicide and that of others.* Muncie, IN: Accelerated Development.

Sell, J. M., Schoenfeld, L., & Gottlieb, M. C. (1986). Ethical considerations of social/romantic relationships with present and former clients. *Professional Psychology: Research and Practice, 17*(6), 504–508.

Seymour, W. R. (1982). Counselor/therapist values and therapeutic style. In J. C. Hansen & L. L'Abate (Eds.), *Values, ethics, legalities and the family therapist* (pp. 41–60). Rockville, MD: Aspen Systems Corp.

Sheehy, G. (1981). *Pathfinders*. New York: William Morrow & Co.

Skafte, D. (1985). *Child custody evaluations: A practical guide* (pp. 17–18). Beverly Hills, CA: SAGE Publications.

Soisson, E. L., VandeCreek, L., & Knapp, S. (1987). Thorough record keeping: A good defense in a litigious era. *Professional Psychology: Research and Practice, 18*(5), 498–502.

Stromberg, C. D., Haggarty, D. J., Leibenluft, R. F., McMillian, M. H., Mishkin, B., Rubin, B. L., & Trilling, H. R. (1988). *The psychologist's legal handbook*. Washington, DC: The Council for the National Register of Health Service Providers in Psychology.

Taggart, M. (1982). Linear versus systemic values: Implications for family therapy. In J. C. Hansen & L. L'Abate (Eds.), *Values, ethics, legalities and the family therapist* (pp. 23–29). Rockville, MD: Aspen Systems Corp.

Taggart, M. (1985). The feminist critique in epistemological perspective: Questions of context in family therapy. *Journal of Marital and Family Therapy, 2*(2), 113–126.

Tarasoff v. Regents of University of California, 529 P. 2d 553 (Cal. 1974), 551 P.2d 334 (Cal. 1976).

Thomas, M. B. (1983). A comparison of CACREP and AAMFT requirements for accreditation. In B. F. Okun & S. T. Gladding (Eds.), *Issues in training marriage and family therapists* (pp. 17–28). Ann Arbor, MI: ERIC Counseling and Personnel Services Clearinghouse.

Thompson v. County of Alameda, 514 P.2d 728 (Cal. 1980).

Van Hoose, W. H. (1980). Ethics and counseling. *Counseling and Human Development, 13*(1), 1–12.

Van Hoose, W. H., & Kottler, J. A. (1985). *Ethical and legal issues in counseling and psychotherapy* (2nd ed.). San Francisco: Jossey-Bass.

Weiner, J. P., & Boss, P. (1985). Exploring gender bias against women: Ethics for marriage and family therapy. *Counseling and Values, 30*(1), 9–23.

Wilcoxon, A. (1986). Engaging non-attending family members in marital and family counseling: Ethical issues. *Journal of Counseling and Development, 64,* 323–324.

Wilcoxon, A., & Fenell, D. (1983). Engaging the non-attending spouse in marital therapy through the use of therapist-initiated written communication. *Journal of Marital and Family Therapy, 9,* 199–203.

Woody, R. H. (1988). *Protecting your mental health practice: How to minimize legal and financial risk*. San Francisco: Jossey-Bass.

Name Index

Since the reference list is organized by chapters and can be found after the appendices, page numbers have not been listed from the reference lists in this index. The reader can conveniently look up the full citation by referring to the reference organized by chapters at the end of the book.

Subject Index

Author Profile

Michele Burhard Thomas is professor of psychology at Tennessee State University in Nashville. She received her B.A. degree summa cum laude from Ohio Dominican College, her M.E. and Ph.D. degrees from the University of Mississippi, and has done post-doctoral work at Austin Peay State, Vanderbilt, and Rutgers Universities. She has served as Acting Head of the Department of Psychology and as Associate Coordinator of the Counseling Curriculum, and she teaches graduate courses in marital and family therapy.

Dr. Thomas is also a licensed counseling psychologist in private practice in Nashville, specializing in work with individuals, couples, and families in transition. She has authored or co-authored a number of grant proposals including a Center for Bio-Behavioral Research on Health, numerous manuals, and research articles for journals such as *Psychotherapy* and *The International Journal for the Advancement of Counselling*. She has chaired more than 70 master's theses and 12 doctoral dissertations.

Dr. Thomas was selected by the Center for Family Strengths of the University of Nebraska-Lincoln to be a National Trainer in the Building Family Strengths Program funded by the United States Department of Health and Human Services. In this role she conducted a number of interdisciplinary workshops for professionals from 10 states, establishing a training network in the Southeast. She was asked by the military to train facilitators to work with families of the Navy and Marines. She has delivered workshops and presented papers in the South, across the United States, and abroad in Utrecht, Holland and Venice, Italy. She has taught in Vienna, Austria and Kobe, Japan.

Active in professional affairs, Dr. Thomas was appointed by the Governor to serve as a member of the Tennessee Board of Examiners in Psychology for a 5-year term. She chaired this licensing board from 1987 to 1989. She is a past president of the Tennessee and Southern Associations for Counselor Education and Supervision and former Executive Director of the Tennessee Personnel and Guidance Association. Most recently she was awarded the 1991 Distinguished Contributions to the Profession Award by the Tennessee Association for Marriage and Family Therapy. She is a clinical member of the American Association for Marriage and Family Therapy, a certified marital and family therapist, a National Board Certified Counselor, a certified professional counselor, a member of the American Psychological Association and its divisions 17, 29, 35, 42, and 43, and a member of the American Association for Counseling and Development and a number of its interest divisions.

In addition to her professional activities, Dr. Thomas writes with much personal experience and authority based on 28 years of marriage and parenting three daughters. Her husband and daughters have participated in conducting workshops with her at various times.